ALLELUIA!

A GOSPEL DIARY

ALLELUIA!

A GOSPEL DIARY

BY

JANIS WALKER

PALLIUM PRESS

Scripture references, unless otherwise identified, are from The New American Bible.

Excerpts from The New American Bible with Revised New Testament and Psalms Copyright ©1991, 1986, 1970 by the Confraternity of Christian Doctrine, Washington, D.C. Used with permission. All rights reserved. No part of The New American Bible maybe reproduced in any form without permission in writing from the copyright owner.

Excerpts from The New Jerusalem Bible, copyright © 1985 by Darton, Longman & Todd, Ltd. and Doubleday, a division of Random House, Inc. Reprinted by Permission.

Scripture quotations from The Message, Copyright © by Eugene H. Peterson 1993, 1994, 1995, 1996, 2000, 2001, 2002. Used by permission of NavPress Publishing Group.

Scripture quotations marked GNT are from the Good News Translation in Today's English Version -- Second Edition Copyright © 1992 by American Bible Society. Used by permission.

Scripture quotations marked N.R.S.V. are from The New Revised Standard Version Bible, copyright 1989, Division of Christian Education of the National Council of Churches of Christ in the United States of America.

Scripture quotations marked K.J.V. are from the The King James Version of the Bible.

Every effort has been made to insure accuracy of text and quotations, and any errors or omissions brought to our attention will be corrected in future editions.

FIRST PRINTING 2010

Pallium Press
P.O. Box 60910
Palo Alto, CA 94306-0910
We regret that Pallium Press cannot accept or return unsolicited manuscripts.

Check for new titles by Janis Walker at www.palliumpress.com

Pallium Press books are available at www.Amazon.com, www.BarnesandNoble.com, or at your favorite local independent bookstore.

cover photo: Terry Walker
cover design: Janis Walker

Copyright © 2006, 2010 by Janis Walker

Printed in the United States of America.

Library of Congress Control Number: 2010928105

ISBN 978-0-9826883-0-4

In loving memory of Albino Luciani

" … unless a grain of wheat falls into the earth and dies, it remains only a single grain; but if it dies it yields a rich harvest.

(John 12, 24 <u>The New Jerusalem Bible</u>).

Acknowledgements

Thanks be to God and to my husband, Terry, my son, Christopher, and to all who have encouraged me over the years. This book would not have become a reality without my husband's loving patience and technical expertise.

Special thanks to Mary Elizabeth Sperry and Robert Saley at the Confraternity of Christian Doctrine in Washington, D.C., for their wise counsel and meticulous proofreading of the quotations taken from <u>The New American Bible</u>.

A.M.D.G.

The Feast of St. Agnes
January 21, 2009

On July 7, 1998, at a noon Mass, I felt led to begin writing personal reflections on the Gospel of the day. These reflections are based on The New American Bible, the translation of the Bible on which the Mass Lectionary is based. There are also references to other translations.

Early each morning, coffee in hand, I read through Mass readings for the day, with Francis, my marmalade Gospel-cat, by my side. Then I wrote, in longhand, a short reflection on the Gospel. When we traveled, I continued writing.

The first two years (almost) of reflections were written by hand in notebooks. Faced with several fat notebooks, I began to enter the reflections into the computer.

A learning experience! I learned, for the second "set" of the reflections, to type in the reflection the very same morning it was written.

Please read the Gospel passage slowly and prayerfully before reading the reflection. These are simply my personal reflections and prayers.

Tuesday, July 7, 1998
Matthew 9, 32-38
The Healing of a Mute Person; The Compassion of Jesus

The various reactions to this healing are fascinating. The crowds were astonished. They had never seen anything like this.

The Pharisees were miffed, jealous, and mightily frustrated. Their spin on Jesus was that he was tapping into demonic power. They were perversely determined to close their minds and their hearts to the reality of Jesus' miracle-working power. They chose to attribute Jesus' ministry to the power of demons.

Jesus did not allow their derision to derail his ministry. "Jesus went around to all the towns and villages, teaching in their synagogues, proclaiming the gospel of the kingdom, and curing every disease and illness" (v. 35). His motivation was compassion. "At the sight of the crowds, his heart was moved with pity for them because they were troubled and abandoned, like sheep without a shepherd" (v. 36).

Jesus could have waved his hand and instantly healed everyone. Instead, he chose to work through his disciples. In fact, "he said to his disciples, 'The harvest is abundant but the laborers are few; so ask the master of the harvest to send out laborers for his harvest.' "

1

In our own lives, are we going to listen to the crowds and be "amazed" at the mighty deeds of Jesus? Are we going to listen to the Pharisees (both the Pharisees 'out there' and the Pharisee within each of us), sneer, and try to explain away the miracles of Jesus? Or are we going to pray to the Lord of the harvest to send us out into his harvest?

Lord Jesus, I pray, as Isaiah prayed, "Here am I ... send me (Isaiah 6, 8)!" May your purpose be accomplished in my life today . Alleluia!

Wednesday, July 8, 1998
Matthew 10, 1-7
The Mission of the Twelve; The Commissioning of the Twelve

The Twelve. Among these we find Peter, James, and John.

Peter, the impetuous, would deny Jesus. James and John were so hot-tempered that they were called "sons of thunder." Jesus knew how to channel all that energy for purposes of the Gospel.

The commission to go to the "lost sheep of the house of Israel" reminds me of yesterday's gospel in which Jesus told his disciples, "The harvest is abundant, but the laborers are few; so ask the master of the harvest to send out laborers for his harvest (Matthew 9, 37, 38)." The harvest is the Lord's! He uses us -- the frail and the fragile, the rough and the hot-tempered -- to gather in his priceless harvest of souls.

Lord Jesus, help us not to focus so much on our shortcomings. You know all about them and you chose us anyway. Help us instead to focus on you, the Lord of the harvest. Thank you for giving us your love and your power as we walk among the harvest fields today. Alleluia!

Thursday, July 9, 1998
St. Augustine Zhao Rong and Companions
Matthew 10, 7-15
Commissioning of the Twelve

"Cure the sick, raise the dead, cleanse lepers, drive out demons." What is sick within me that needs healing? What is dead within me that needs new life? What is leprous and diseased within me that needs cleansing? What is demonic within me that needs to be driven out?

Come, Lord Jesus, cleanse me and deliver me from anything that grieves or displeases you. Heal me and raise me to new life. Let me be used to free, cleanse, heal and raise others to new life, as you instructed your disciples. Alleluia!

2

Friday, July 10, 1998
Matthew 10, 16-23
Coming Persecutions

Jesus told his followers to be as shrewd and wise as serpents and as simple and harmless as doves. This is a powerful combination. We are to be aware of the possible motives and malice of others, but not to worry about them.

Sheep can be wide-eyed and naive. However, those big eyes see a lot! They can see right to the heart of a matter.

Once, a young girl with Down's syndrome was aware that her mother was very upset. Suddenly, the girl saw a beautiful butterfly and exclaimed, "Look, Mother, a butterfly!" The worried mother instantly had a new focus -- one of beauty and resurrection.

Lord Jesus, please help me today to focus on you, not on the trials of this life. Help me to exercise a combination of the shrewdness of a serpent and the innocence of a dove. Alleluia!

Saturday, July 11, 1998 St. Benedict
Matthew 10, 24-33
Coming Persecutions; Courage under Persecution

Jesus says three times in this passage, "Do not be afraid." The disciple is not above the Teacher. If the Teacher has been persecuted, the disciple can expect some form of persecution. Still, we are not too afraid.

"Therefore do not be afraid of them. Nothing is concealed that will not be revealed, nor secret that will not be known."

"And do not be afraid of those who kill the body but cannot kill the soul ..." Our Father in heaven knows when even a little sparrow falls to the ground.

Once again, we are told not be afraid. "So do not be afraid; you are worth more than many sparrows (v. 31)."

Our heavenly Father knows all and is in complete control of our lives.

My way of the Cross and your way of the Cross is to walk in the footsteps that Jesus has left for us.

3

On the beach, I may notice someone's footprints and try to walk in them. If they have a long stride, I may not be able to walk in them. Jesus knows my stride and has left specific footprints for me. I'm the only one who can walk in these particular footprints. Only you can walk in the footprints Jesus has for you. These footprints lead us to the arms of our loving Father. Alleluia!

Sunday, July 12, 1998 Fifteenth Sunday Ordinary Time, Year C
Luke 10, 25-37
The Greatest Commandment; The Good Shepherd

The cautious, cagey legal scholar, wishing to preen and to polish his image, asked Jesus "... who is my neighbor?" Jesus, in calm control of the conversation, confronted the scholar with the unwelcome news that a despised outsider, a Samaritan, was the one who had actually fulfilled the law of love by acting in love.

Do I wish to justify myself and to guard my image or do I choose to risk my reputation in order to love as Jesus loved?

Lord Jesus, help me to be merciful to everyone who crosses my path today. Help me to extend mercy to myself also. Alleluia!

Monday, July 13, 1998 St. Henry
Matthew 10, 34-11, 1
Jesus: A Cause of Division; The Conditions of Discipleship

Where is the sword of Christ falling in my life? It is not peaceful or easy to be a true disciple.

Lord Jesus, show me how to welcome you and follow you today. Alleluia!

Tuesday, July 14, 1998 Blessed Kateri Tekakwitha
Matthew 11, 20-24
Reproaches to Unrepentant Towns

"Woe" is the word Jesus spoke to Chorazin and Bethsaida. This was not an expression of hatred, but rather an expression of grief. These cities had every opportunity to repent, but had stubbornly refused to do so.

For a period of time, Jesus had spoken "peace" to these cities and had performed miracles of love in their midst. This window of opportunity was now closing.

Lord Jesus, where have I seen you in action in my life and still I have not repented? Where have I poured myself out in love to others and they have not responded? Lord, have mercy. Christ, have mercy. Lord, have mercy. Alleluia!

Wednesday, July 15, 1998, St. Bonaventure
Matthew 11, 25-27
The Praise of the Father

"I give praise to you, Father, Lord of heaven and earth, for although you have hidden these things from the wise and learned you have revealed them to the childlike." The childlike are open and candid. The childlike are humble. The childlike want Jesus more than they want their own agenda.

Am I open to receive Jesus and to follow in his steps of preaching, teaching, healing, and suffering? Do I think I already know it all and have nothing left to learn?

The basis of the Pharisees' arrogance was their assumption that they already knew it all, that they were the religious insiders, the powerful, and the elite. They did not want this threatening young upstart carpenter upsetting their apple cart.

Do I upset any apple carts by my childlike trust in Jesus? Alleluia!

Thursday, July 16, 1998, Our Lady of Mt. Carmel
Matthew 11, 28-30
The Gentle Mastery of Christ

"Come to me, all you who labor and are burdened, and I will give you rest. Take my yoke upon you and learn from me, for I am meek and humble of heart; and you will find rest for yourselves. For my yoke is easy, and my burden light."

Jesus extends three invitations --to come to him, to take his yoke, and to learn from him. The promise Jesus offers is REST.

Sometimes we are our own ruthless, relentless taskmasters. Sometimes we carry burdens Jesus never intended for us to carry.

Eugene Peterson, in The Message, expresses the familiar words of this Gospel in a fresh way. "Are you tired? Worn out? Burned out on religion? Come to me. Get away with me and you'll recover your life. I'll show you how to take a real rest. Walk with me and work with me -- watch how I do it. Learn the unforced rhythms of grace. I won't lay anything heavy or ill-fitting on you. Keep company with me and you'll learn to live freely and lightly." Alleluia!

Friday, July 17, 1998
Matthew 12, 1-8
Picking Grain on the Sabbath

There are still those who insist on putting their own rules above the needs of those for whom Christ died. Theirs is a spirit of compulsive religiosity, not a spirit of servanthood.

Jesus ministered directly to people. He saw their needs and addressed those needs first and foremost. He was not deterred by the squawks of protest from these self-righteous leaders.

If I see myself as an "insider" in the Church, how do I treat others? Do I jealously maintain what I consider the privileges of power and disregard the feelings and the hearts of others? Or do I tie a towel round my waist and wash the feet of God's children?

If I see myself as an "outsider," do I gossip, complain, and play the victim when I see leaders who do not appear to be following Christ? Do I pray for them? Do I continue to place my ultimate trust in Jesus, the Head of the Church? Alleluia!

Saturday, July 18, 1998 St. Camillus de Lellis
Matthew 12, 14-21
The Chosen Servant

Jesus had just healed the man with the withered hand and he did this on a Sabbath! This was too much for the Pharisees who "... went out and took counsel against him to put him to death." Jesus left that particular place, but was not deterred from his work of healing.

Jesus knew when to remain in a particular place or in a particular situation. He also knew when to leave and to exercise his ministry elsewhere.

He had a particular concern for the "bruised reeds," who had been wounded.

"A bruised reed he will not break,
    a smoldering wick he will not quench
    until he brings justice to victory

(Matthew 12, 20; Isaiah 42, 3, 4)."

6

Lord Jesus, I don't know how or when you will bring "justice to victory," but I trust in you and in your word. Alleluia!

Sunday, July 19, 1998 Sixteenth Sunday in Ordinary Time
Luke 10, 38-42
Martha and Mary

Martha, a real type A, was the one who welcomed Jesus! Poor dear, she often gets bad press, as though her role wasn't also important. Probably she was just super-responsible. "If I don't do it, it won't get done, or it won't get done right!" may have been her attitude when Jesus arrived. She was fixated on serving the Lord in a certain way.

Sometimes, in our own prayers, we come with our own agenda. We mean well, but perhaps Jesus would like us, first of all, simply to bask in his presence. Perhaps he will speak to us and direct our prayers. Perhaps we will simply be together in comfortable silence.

Lord Jesus, I come before you in silence and in trust. Thank you for directing my thoughts and my actions this day. Alleluia!

Monday, July 20, 1998 St. Appollinarius
Matthew 12, 38-42
The Demand for a Sign

The "sign" of Jonah was his presence for three days and three nights inside a whale. The "sign" of the Son of Man was to be three days and three nights in the tomb.

How are you a "sign?" Have you died in some way? Has God delivered you and raised you to new life?

Are you still in the "tomb?" Sometimes I have felt that major chunks of my life could be described as "Holy Saturday." In some way, I am "dead" and still in the tomb, awaiting my resurrection.

If you, too, are currently in some sort of "tomb" situation, take courage. Look and eagerly expect Jesus to come at the right time and raise you to a new life, a new vision, a new purpose. Wait in joyful expectation!

Don't waste the time in the tomb, however. In the tomb, it's cool and quiet, as well as dark. There is plenty of time to see the Lord's light in our darkness. The prophet Isaiah spoke of the "treasures of darkness."

"I will go before you
    and level the mountains;
Bronze doors I will shatter,
    and iron bars I will snap.
I will give you treasures out of the
    darkness,
    and riches that have been hidden
    away,
That you may know that I am the LORD, the God of Israel,
    who calls you by your name (Isaiah 45, 2, 3)."

Trust and wait. There will be a resurrection day for you and for me.

"... I believe I shall enjoy the LORD'S
    goodness
    in the land of the living.
Wait for the LORD, take courage;
    be stouthearted, wait for the
    LORD (Psalm 27, 13-14)!" Alleluia!

Tuesday, July 21, 1998 St. Lawrence of Brindisi
Matthew 12, 46-50
The True Family of Jesus

Jesus did not allow his ministry to be interrupted by what appeared to be a legitimate claim on his attention by members of his earthly family. Instead, he re-directed his listeners' focus to the true meaning of the family of God -- those who do the will of the heavenly Father.

Do I allow myself to be distracted from following the Lord by those who demand of me what is not mine to give? Do I allow myself to be pressured, for example, to serve on a committee to which I feel no personal calling? Do I avoid the call of God by passively allowing others to direct my life? This is not an excuse to shirk responsibility. It is, however, a call to focus first of all on the Lord.

Lord Jesus, you only did what your heavenly Father told you to do. Please help me today to do likewise. Alleluia!

Wednesday, July 22, 1998 St. Mary Magdalene
John 20, 1-2, 11-18
The Empty Tomb, The Appearance to Mary of Magdala

Mary of Magdalene came to Jesus in the darkness. All seemed lost. Jesus was dead and buried. Still, she came to be near him.

8

All she saw was that the stone had been removed from the entrance to the tomb. She ran to tell Peter and John! She still did not know where Jesus was, but she ran with what knowledge she did have. She has been called the first preacher of the resurrection.

Peter and John came to the tomb, but returned home puzzled. "But Mary stayed outside the tomb weeping." Although it was probably daylight by now, Mary was experiencing an interior darkness, because she still did not know where Jesus was. She stayed as close to him as she could, by the tomb, and wept.

Her world must have whirled before her eyes, when she realized that this stranger, the "gardener," was really Jesus! She was commissioned to tell the apostles. She has been called the "apostle to the apostles."

Are we open to seeing Jesus in a new way? When we are able to recognize him in a new way, he can send us out on a new mission. Alleluia!

Thursday, July 23, 1998 St. Bridget of Sweden
Matthew 13, 10-17
The Purpose of the Parables

A message is received according to the predisposition of the hearer. If the hearer has a crooked heart, even the purest message will seem twisted and distorted.

"A clean heart create for me, God;
　　renew in me a steadfast spirit (Psalm 51, 12)."

I long to receive God's words in simplicity and humility.

Lord Jesus, purify my heart to receive your word to me today as you intended it to be received. Alleluia!

Friday, July 24, 1998 St. Sharbel Makhluf
Matthew 13, 18-23
The Explanation of the Parable of the Sower

As in yesterday's Gospel, we see that the message is received according to the predisposition of the hearer, i.e. the "soil" in the heart of the hearer.

In Marsha Norman's Broadway musical, "The Secret Garden," (based on Frances Hodgson Burnett's novel) the young boy Dickon, who worked in the garden, told Mary, an orphaned child, " The strongest roses will fair thrive on bein' neglected if the soil is rich enough." So it is with us.

Lord Jesus, help us to nourish the soil of our hearts with adoration, thanksgiving, confession, repentance, praise, and trust. Let us freely forgive others in order that we may be forgiven. Let us receive Your word into our hearts and bear luscious fruit for Your kingdom where You live and reign forever and ever. Alleluia!

Saturday, July 25, 1998 St. James
Matthew 20, 20-28
Request of James and John

This is really an upfront mother, asking Jesus to promote her boys to the big time! Jesus basically responded, "Are you crazy? Do you have any idea what you're asking?"

Then the other disciples became quite indignant. Jesus told them to cool it and reminded them again that his kingdom is not of this world. If you turn everything upside down, then it will be right. The great one is the one who serves. The great one is secure enough to serve. The great one's identity is not in question and therefore does not need to be cosseted, protected, and defended.

Things can change so fast in this world. Today at Mass, I was last in line to receive Holy Communion. Then, all of a sudden, the Eucharistic minister walked to the back of the church and I was first in line.

Lord Jesus, help me to fix my eyes on you. Let me look into your eyes and see my own identity. Help me not to crave earthly rewards, but to live as you call me to live in this world. Alleluia!

Sunday, July 26, 1998 Seventeenth Sunday in Ordinary Time
Luke 11, 1-13
The Lord's Prayer; Further Teaching on Prayer;
The Answer to Prayer

Today I reread this familiar passage in <u>The Message</u> by Eugene Peterson.

"Father,
    Reveal who you are.
    Set the world right.
    Keep us alive with three square meals.
    Keep us forgiven with you and forgiving others.
    Keep us safe from ourselves and the Devil."

As for as persistence in prayer, "Don't bargain with God. Be direct. ask for what you need." "And don't you think the Father who conceived you in love will give the Holy Spirit when you ask Him?"

Lord Jesus, thank you for teaching us how to pray. Alleluia!

Monday, July 27, 1998
Matthew 13, 31-35
The Parable of the Mustard Seed; The Parable of the Yeast;
The Purpose of the Parables

The kingdom of heaven is like _____. If God alone ruled in my life, what would my life look like? How would his kingdom be expressed in my life and in your life?

How does God take something tiny, yet vital within us, like a mustard seed, to shelter others? How does God take something powerful within us, like yeast, and create "bread" to nourish a multitude?

God does this by our willingness, first of all, to die to our ideas of how God should use us. The mustard seed has to "die," to go into the ground, to disappear into obscurity for a season until it can rise to new life. The yeast has to be kneaded and incorporated into an another element, flour, in order to serve its powerful purpose.

Lord Jesus, help me to trust you with my inescapable death and with my certain resurrection. Thank you that you are working in unseen, yet powerful, ways in my life today to bring about my resurrection. Alleluia!

Tuesday, July 28, 1998
Matthew 13, 34-43
Use of Parables; Explanation of Parables

Follow Jesus and Jesus will explain the "parable" in your own life. After dismissing the crowds, Jesus went into the house and the disciples asked him to explain the parable. Go to Jesus and ask him to explain whatever it is that you need to understand for the living of this day.

Tempting as it is, it is not our job to go out and collect and burn the "weeds." We live and bloom for the Lord. He will deal with the "weeds" within and the "weeds" without. Alleluia!

Wednesday, July 29, 1998 St. Martha
John 11, 19-27
The Raising of Lazarus

Martha, impelled by her earthy, active faith, ran out to meet Jesus! Her sister Mary, the contemplative, remained at home. Martha wasted no time informing Jesus that if only he had been there Lazarus would not have died. Martha also manifested a tough, persistent faith, in the midst of the worst circumstances, when she said to Jesus, "[But] even now I know that whatever you ask of God, God will give you."

Martha's faith was future-oriented. She believed that Lazarus would rise in the resurrection.

Aha! This was just where Jesus wanted her. She had told Jesus about her faith in the future. Now he could tell her that he, Jesus, IS the resurrection and the life.

Notice how gently Jesus led Martha to this understanding. She responded, "I have come to believe that you are the Messiah, the Son of God, the one who is coming into the world."

As with Martha, Jesus gently takes us where we are in our understanding of him and leads us on to the next step. Do not despise and look down on where you are right now. Jesus is faithful and will take you all the way until He has you at last in his arms in the heavenly kingdom. Alleluia!

Thursday, July 30, 1998 St. Peter Chrysologus
Matthew 1, 47-53
More Parables

These parables speak of joyful, wholehearted abandonment. The person finding the treasure buried in a field gladly sells all to purchase that field. The merchant finding the costly pearl sells all to acquire it.

Lord Jesus, YOU are the treasure! Help me to be joyful in giving my entire being into your wise and loving care. Alleluia!

Friday, July 31, 1998 St. Ignatius of Loyola
Matthew 13, 54-58
Rejection at Nazareth

Jesus said, "A prophet is not without honor except in his native place and in his own house." The people in the synagogue had seen Jesus doing mighty works and yet had not responded in faith.

Rev. Jim Nisbet, reflecting on the book of Acts at a Catholic Bible Institute in the summer of 1994, noted that we find our place in the Church through a process called rejection. This is obviously a painful process.

We're not alone in this process, however. Jesus, the stone rejected, became the cornerstone (1 Peter 2, 7).

Lord Jesus, help us not to be dismayed when we go all out for you and then we are rejected. You are head of the Church and will place us where you choose. Thank you, Lord, for the freedom to live for your glory and for your smile. Alleluia!

> Saturday, August 1, 1999 St. Alphonse Liguori
> (written on a flight to New York)
> Matthew 14, 1-12
> Herod's Opinion of Jesus; Death of John the Baptist

Herod believed that Jesus was John the Baptist risen from the dead. Herod must have been strangely aware of the power of John the Baptist, even after John's death.

Herod, a tragically weak figure, initially bowed to the pressure of his wife, Herodius, to have John thrown into prison. Next, he bowed to her pressure to have John beheaded. Succumbing to the pressure of this driven woman and to the pressure of the opinion of the guests at his birthday party, he violated what little conscience he had in order to save face.

How tragic. How tragic when those in position of great responsibility and great power are so insecure that they bow to ungodly pressure, that they play politics with the lives of others. It is a very deep betrayal.

Mark's Gospel tells us that "Herod feared John, knowing him to be a righteous and holy man ... (Mark 6, 20)." Both Matthew and Mark record that Herod was "distressed" at Herodius' demand that John be beheaded, but not distressed enough to stop the execution. Always playing politics, even at the expense of innocent life.

Do I "play politics" with the lives and reputations of others? Do I truly want God's approval or would I rather have the approval of those I am pathetically trying to please? Do I want to grovel before others or stand before God? Alleluia!

Sunday, August 2, 1998 Eighteenth Sunday in Ordinary Time
Luke 12, 13-21
Saying Against Greed; Parable of the Rich Fool

Where is my focus? Is my focus on the Lord or on "things?"

Lord Jesus, teach me to be wise in my use of all resources entrusted to me. Alleluia!

Monday, August 3, 1998
Matthew 14, 13-21
Return of the Twelve and the Feeding of the Five Thousand

Jesus had just heard of the death of John the Baptist. His response was to withdraw to a place of silence and solitude, a "desert place."

The crowds, however, continued to seek him. Despite his own grief, he was touched with pity for the people and reached out to heal them. Now that it was evening, he expected his disciples to feed the crowds out of their own resources!

Jesus was teaching and preparing the disciples for the time when they would do the works which he had done. Jesus said that "... whoever believes in me will do the works that I do, and will do greater ones than these, because I am going to the Father (John 14, 12)."

What were the works that Jesus had done? We think first of his teaching, preaching, and healing.

However, as one of our seminary professors reminded us, the ministry of Jesus was not only a ministry of preaching, teaching, and healing, but also one of suffering. This "miracle" of the feeding of the five thousand was a mere preview of what the disciples were to do. They would be engaged in ministries of teaching, preaching, healing, and, inevitably, suffering.

Where is Jesus leading you to learn from him so that you can go out and do the work to which he has called you? Do you know what your work is? He reveals his will to those who ask. You may not, and probably will not, be given a full description. What he will give you is the next step of faith.

Lord Jesus, help me to take this next step, whether it's drying the dishes or ministering to a multitude. It is my obedience to your will that honors you. It is my trust in you that touches your heart. Alleluia!

Tuesday, August 4, 1998 St. John Vianney
Matthew 14, 22-36
The Walking on the Water; The Healings at Gennesaret

Jesus made the disciples get into the boat! Sometimes we say, "Oh dear, I'm in this difficult situation. It must be my fault." Not necessarily.

In today's Gospel, Jesus was clearly in charge, as he always is. After making the disciples get into the boat to precede him to the other side of the lake, he dismissed the crowds and sought a place of solitude in order to pray.

The lake became very stormy and the disciples were terrified. Jesus did not go to them right away. He did not immediately play rescuer. Instead, he chose another time, the "fourth watch" of the night, between 3:00 and 4:00 a.m. It was then that he approached them.

The Gospel records that the wind was against the boat. That was why it was being tossed about! So what? That's obvious.

Again, we have to remember that Jesus was completely in charge. His authority extended to the wind and the waves!

Jesus did not "choose" to be tempted by Satan in the desert. This temptation was a furious onslaught we find difficult to comprehend.

The Gospels of Matthew and Luke both state that it was the Holy Spirit who led him to the desert. Mark's Gospel uses even stronger language. Immediately after Jesus' baptism, it was the Holy Spirit who "drove" him, even thrust him, out into the wilderness.

Jesus sometimes leads us and sometimes drives us into turbulent situations. Our only resource is to cry out to him, as Peter did, "Lord, save me!"

Peter had the guts to venture out of the boat in the first place. He began to falter only when he focused on the turbulent wind and the waves instead of on Jesus, the One who controlled the wind and the waves.

When you are called out of your boat of safety and the waves are crashing all around you, remember to call out to Jesus. At the right time, He will take your hand and lead you to safety. Alleluia!

Wednesday, August 5, 1998
The Dedication of the Basilica of St. Mary Major in Rome
Matthew 15, 21-28
The Canaanite Woman's Faith

Jesus was sent first of all to the "children," his own Jewish people. However, he ministered to a Gentile woman when she persisted in asking for help for her child.

Jesus, moved by her persistence and humility, granted her request. Her daughter was healed at that very time!

In addition, very significantly, Jesus commended this courageous woman from Canaan. Although others had labeled her as an outsider, Jesus praised her! He praised her for her radical faith. "O woman, great is your faith! Let it be done for you as you wish."

"Dogs" and "swine" were Jewish terms of contempt for Gentile outsiders. Perhaps others have labeled us as inferior, lesser, or deficient. We need to write these words off!

We ask God to erase the effect these words have had in our lives. To God, we are precious, of infinite value.

Lord Jesus, help us to persist in trusting you and hear you say to us, "Great is your faith!" Alleluia!

Thursday, August 6, 1998 Transfiguration of the Lord
Luke 9, 28-36
The Transfiguration of Jesus

Sometimes I feel like saying, "Peter, please be quiet!" Impetuous Peter just seems to have a gift for not knowing when to remain silent. Open mouth, insert foot. That's Peter all over,

One day when I was very discouraged about my same tendency to speak out bluntly, the Lord said tenderly to me, "You're like Peter." Peter, Peter, Peter. Always Peter.

Another time, again when I was discouraged over my hot temper, the Holy Spirit flashed into my mind (Mark 9, 2). A little apprehensive, I looked up the passage." Jesus took Peter, James, and John and led them up a high mountain apart by themselves. And he was transfigured before them."

16

Jesus knowingly chose Peter, James, and John to share this moment as he had knowingly chosen them as disciples and would later send them out as apostles. Jesus knew all about Peter's volatile personality.

Then there were James and John, the hotheads. Jesus called them "sons of thunder (Mark 3, 17)." John, the mystic, the contemplative, also had a temper. Still, Jesus knowingly chose him.

When we glimpse bits of our "dark side," we can take comfort that the Lord sees all and chooses us anyway for a particular vocation. The Transfiguration is about the identity of Jesus. It is also about our own identity. Go up to the mountain with Jesus. Be silent. Let the Heavenly Father tell you, "This is my chosen Son; listen to him." And then let Jesus tell you, "I love you. I chose you. I will fulfill my purpose for your life." Alleluia!

Friday, August 7, 1998 St. Sixtus and Companions,St. Cajetan
Matthew 16, 24-28
The Conditions of Discipleship

"Whoever wishes to come after me must deny himself, take up his cross, and follow me." To make the transition from serving myself to serving Christ does not happen all at once.

The parallel passage in Luke's Gospel refers to the daily taking up of the cross. "If anyone wishes to come after me, he must deny himself and take up his cross daily and follow me (Luke 9, 23)."

It has been said that your "cross" simply means the will of God for your life. This is not something awful or something to be dreaded. It is your glory and your joy to live your life for your crucified and risen Lord. When your "crucifixion" to your old life is complete, you will be raised to a new life which will last for ever and ever. Alleluia!

Saturday, August 8, 1998 St. Dominic
Matthew 17, 14-20
The Healing of a Boy with a Demon

This healing follows immediately after the glory of the Transfiguration of Jesus. Glory on the mountain and then back down to the "valley " and to a manifestation of evil!

Jesus, however, is triumphant over the power of all evil. He, of course, cast the evil spirit out of the boy.

Notice the sequence. Notice the timing. We have all known moments "on the mountain" followed by "demons" in the valley.

We are not to be frightened or superstitious, but to be alert! This is still "the world," not heaven. We continue to pray, "Thy will be done on earth as it is in heaven."

In the meantime, as St. Peter tells us, "Be sober and vigilant. Your opponent the devil is prowling around like a roaring lion looking for [someone] to devour. Resist him, steadfast in faith, knowing that your fellow believers throughout the world undergo the same sufferings. The God of all grace who called you to his eternal glory through Christ [Jesus] will himself restore, confirm, strengthen and establish you after you have suffered a little. To him be dominion forever. Amen (1 Peter 5, 8-11)."

Jesus assured his followers, "Nothing will be impossible for you." Nothing.

Lord Jesus, thank you for these words to encourage us. Thank you for your victory in our lives. Alleluia!

Sunday, August 9, 1998 Nineteenth Sunday in Ordinary Time
Luke 12, 37-48
Vigilant and Faithful Servants

We are to hold lightly the things of this world. They are all passing away so quickly! Our task is not to "succeed" according to this world's standard, but to do the will of the Lord. Alleluia!

Monday, August 10, 1998 St. Lawrence
John 12, 24-26
The Coming of Jesus' Hour

The grain of wheat falls into the ground, or is pushed into the ground, and dies to its previous identity. It has disappeared, vanished, and is no more. Dead and buried.

Not so! During this time of obscurity and seeming disappearance and death, the God of the harvest is nurturing and preparing the little grain to come forth and fulfill its destiny.

When it comes forth into the sunshine, it will be gathered and, alas for the grain of wheat, it will be crushed. What could seem more cruel? First, it is buried and then it sees the light of day. All of this only to be crushed? What kind of cosmic joke is this?

18

The good Gardener of our souls knows what He is about. It is only when we have been buried and crushed that we can become bread to feed the starving. As Christ's Body on earth, the Church, we pray to be seen as those who have yielded to God's process.

"The bread that we break, is it not a participation in the body of Christ? Because the loaf of bread is one, we, though many, are one body, for we all partake of the one loaf (I Corinthians 10, 16b-17)." Alleluia!

Tuesday, August 11, 1998 St. Clare
Matthew 18, 1-5, 10, 12-14
The Greatest in the Kingdom; The Parable of the Lost Sheep

A small child is usually happy, believing the best, and trusting. A happy little child is not ambitious for self-promotion and is not anxious about ego or image." A healthy child focuses on the present and does not brood about the past. Most of the time, fusses on the playground are soon forgotten.

Of course, there are difficulties even in the life of the happiest child. The child then reaches for the hand of a loving parent, fully expecting to be protected.

As we know, tragically, there are abusive parents unworthy of the trust of their children God, however, is worthy of all trust.

When we put our hand into the hand of our loving God, we are trusting the Almighty One with our lives. We are becoming like little children.

We do not have to be anxious about promoting ourselves. We do not have to worry about our image. We are free to focus on the present moment and trust God to heal the past.

If we try to live this way, we will be living in a very different way from most people around us. We will be a sign of contradiction. According to Jesus, we will be called "greatest in the kingdom of heaven." Alleluia!

Wednesday, August 12, 1998
Matthew 18, 15-20
A Brother Who Sins

This is one of the most ignored passages in the Bible. It's not that it's difficult to understand. It's just that we just don't want to do it!

19

Instead of going directly to the person who has offended us, we run to the phone and complain bitterly to our friends. Or we try to write angry letters justifying our side of the situation.

Even if we do try, in our fumbling and uncertain way, to do what Jesus says to do, there is no guarantee that things will turn out the way we would like. We may go to the other person and the person may try stonewalling or smooth talk. Even if we take one or two others with us, the charade may continue.

We may, as Jesus says, "tell the church." Sometimes the members of the congregation are outraged, but have no political clout to see that justice is done.

Those in positions of leadership may be too timid and cowardly to do the right thing. How pathetic when that is the case.

If we have tried to follow the instructions of Jesus, our part in the matter is now over. We may now be at peace. The Lord will deal with those who have sinned against us. That's not our job.

As St. Paul says, "If possible, on your part, live at peace with all. Beloved, do not look for revenge but leave room for the wrath, for it is written, 'Vengeance is mine, I will repay, says the Lord (Romans 12, 18-19).'" A still higher authority, the Lord Jesus, says, "... love your enemies, and pray for those who persecute you... (Matthew 5, 44)." Alleluia!

Thursday, August 13, 1998 Sts. Pontian and Hippolytus
Matthew 18, 21- 19, 1
The Parable of the Unforgiving Servant

Peter again! It's often Peter who asks the very question no one else has the courage to ask. This time, Peter asks about someone who keeps on sinning against him.

Jesus avoids the trap of getting caught up in the relatively little picture Peter is portraying. Jesus shifts Peter's attention and our attention to the big picture.

The "big picture" is our relationship to God. When we have even an inkling of how much God has forgiven us, not just for the times when we've obviously blown it, but for our own bent or predisposition to sin, we easily forgive others. Only the self-righteous who are always pointing the finger cannot and will not forgive. Somehow they have not understood their own need for forgiveness.

Jesus said, "You should have had mercy on your fellow-servant, just as I had mercy on you." How does Jesus have mercy on us? He has mercy on us when we don't deserve mercy, when we knowingly and repeatedly sin.

Jesus also says we have to forgive from our hearts. How is this possible when our hearts have been broken and wounded by the sins of others? We forgive by receiving a heart transplant. God has to plant a new heart of forgiveness within us.

Lord Jesus, please take from me my damaged heart and give me instead a brand new heart, which beats in tune with your heart. Help me to love as you love and to forgive as you forgive. I place my trust in your mercy. Alleluia!

Friday, August 14, 1998 St. Maximilian Kolbe
Mathew 19, 3-12
Marriage and Divorce

This passage begins with geography and ends with vocation. Jesus had left Galilee and had crossed the Jordan to Judea. Crowds followed him and he reached out to cure them.

Judea was also home turf for the zealous Pharisees. The Pharisees came to Jesus to "test" him (i.e. to try to trip him up with test questions about marriage).

Jesus quoted from the book of Genesis. "Have you not read that from the beginning the Creator 'made them male and female' and said, 'For this reason a man shall leave his father and mother and be joined to his wife, and the two shall become one flesh?' So they are no longer two, but one flesh. Therefore, what God has joined together, no human being must separate."

The Pharisees were searching for a loophole. They referred to Moses who allowed divorce. Jesus again referred the matter back to God. Moses allowed divorce because of the hardness of people's hearts, but that was not God's idea.

Jesus also referred to celibacy. He said that some people "...have renounced marriage for the sake of the kingdom of heaven." Jesus, in dealing with the Pharisees, always cut to the heart of the matter and interpreted God's true purpose.

Lord Jesus, show us how to live today "for the sake of God's reign." Thank you for the example of Maximilian Kolbe, the priest who offered his life for the life of a married man in the World War II concentration camp. Alleluia!

Saturday, August 15, 1998
Assumption of the Blessed Virgin Mary
Luke 1, 39-56
Mary Visits Elizabeth; The Canticle of Mary

Mary, in the midst of her questions, accepted her vocation. She referred to herself as the Lord's handmaiden and rejoiced in the Lord's greatness. All ages would call her "blessed." This greatly honored, yet very human and humble, teenage girl rejoiced and gave all the glory to God.

God continues to have mercy on his little ones, the "anawim," as they were called. Little ones, whatever their age, understand their need for God.

Lord Jesus, thank you for the example of your mother, Mary. She believed and trusted that her "impossible" vocation would be fulfilled. Help us to remember her humility and courage when we become discouraged in our discipleship. Alleluia!

Sunday, August 16, 1998 Twentieth Sunday in Ordinary Time
Luke 12, 49-53
Jesus: A Cause of Division

Jesus asks, "Do you think I have come to establish peace on the earth? No, I tell you, but rather division." His message cuts through families, churches, and businesses. His message cuts through our hearts.

If we follow Jesus with all our heart, we will be a threat to those who pick and choose what to believe. We will be a threat to those who compromise. We may even be a threat to ourselves. Once the Holy Spirit blazes within us, watch out! Alleluia!

Monday, August 17, 1998
Matthew 19, 16-22
The Rich Young Man

What do I still lack to make my commitment to Jesus total and complete? When I've kept the obvious commandments, perhaps because I've never been tempted to do otherwise, what do I still lack?

Jesus makes it clear that it is not a matter of "being good." Only One is good.

It is a matter of discovering what it is within myself that needs to be dealt with before I can enter into "life."

For the young man, it was his wealth. He could not let go of the temporal in order to receive the eternal.

Lord Jesus, help me to let go of anything that would keep me from following you with total abandon. You see into my heart, you love me, and you are waiting to give me new life. Alleluia!

Tuesday, August 18, 1998 St. Jane Frances de Chantal
Matthew 19, 23-30
The Rich Young Man

Jesus says that in the "new age," when He comes again in glory, "many who are first will be last, and the last will be first." We have to be careful when we look down upon any one as "lesser" or as "not counting." We may be in for a surprise!

"Create in me a clean heart, O God; and renew a right spirit within me (Psalm 51, 10, K.J.V.)." Lord Jesus, please heal me of the misconceptions I have about you. Help me to see you more clearly and follow you with all my heart today. Alleluia!

Wednesday, August 19, 1998 St. John Eudes
Matthew 20, 1-16
Workers in the Vineyard

But it's not FAIR! Whether we're five or one hundred and five, we sometimes feel this way whether or not we say it aloud. Why, Jesus, why?

The verse immediately before this passage was Matthew 19, 30, "But many who are first will be last, and the last will be first." Jesus had been telling Peter what it's going to be like in the future among those who followed Jesus on earth. There are going to be some surprises!

The parable of the workers in the vineyards ends with the same idea. The last will be first and the first will be last.

It really does come out fair! The workers who worked all day had the knowledge that, not only would they be rewarded (paid) at the end of the day, but also they had the satisfaction of having used their talents and gifts in the service of the Lord. The ones who began work late in the game missed out on the joy of a longer time in the Lord's service.

"Shall not the Judge of all the earth do right (Genesis 18, 25c K.J.V.)?" Lord Jesus, help me to focus on you, do what you have called me to do, and leave the results with you. Alleluia!

Thursday, August 20, 1998 St. Bernard
Matthew 22, 1-14
The Parable of the Wedding Feast

This parable is addressed to the Pharisees, as were the preceding two parables, the parable of the two sons and the parable of the tenants in the vineyard.

God has prepared a great feast for us! Will we be like the Pharisees and find excuses not to attend or will we be among those who realize our need of God and rush to the banquet?

In the Gospel account, those who accepted the invitation were the poor, the crippled, the blind, and the lame. In other words, the ones who came to the feast were the ones who acknowledged their need.

You and I must acknowledge our need of the Savior before we can come to the feast. "Many are invited, but few are chosen." If you need the Lord, and if you acknowledge your need, you are among the chosen. Come to the feast! Alleluia!

Friday, August 21, 1998 St. Pius X
Matthew 22, 34-40
The Greatest Commandment

The Pharisees were at it again! They were not merely asking Jesus questions in order to learn, but in order to test him and to trap him.

One particular Pharisee, a scholar of the law, asked Jesus, "What commandment in the law is the greatest?" Jesus quoted Deuteronomy 6, 5, "... you shall love the LORD, your God, with all your heart, and with all your soul, and with all your strength." He then quoted Leviticus 19, 18, "You shall love your neighbor as yourself."

The Pharisees already knew these laws, so why did they ask Jesus? They had become entangled in petty rules and regulations of their own making and had, in some sense, lost their vision of the one true God.

In Matthew 15, 7-9 (N.R.S.V.), Jesus assessed the Pharisees. "You hypocrites, Isaiah prophesied rightly about you when he said:

'This people honors me with their lips,
    but their hearts are far from me;
in vain do they worship me,
    teaching human precepts as doctrines.' "

Lord Jesus, today it's "back to basics." Help us to love you, love ourselves and love others. Alleluia!

Saturday, August 22, 1998 The Queenship of Mary
Matthew 23, 1-12
Denunciation of the Scribes and Pharisees

Jesus was speaking both to the crowd and to his disciples in this passage. This where we get the injunction to practice what we preach.

Jesus told the disciples to comply with all that the scribes and Pharisees told them to do, but not to follow their example. The Pharisees were ego-driven, power hungry, and image-conscious. They always wanted to be seen by others. We each have an "inner Pharisee," so we can't become too smug or self-righteous.

Jesus, however, told his flock not to buy into that mind-set. The truly great ones are those who are the servants of the others. Everyone who attempts self-exaltation will be humbled, but humbling oneself leads to exaltation. Our part is to remain humble. It's God's part to do the exalting. Alleluia!

Sunday, August 23, 1998
Twenty-First Sunday in Ordinary Time
Luke 13, 22-30
The Narrow Door; Salvation and Rejection

As Jesus passed through the towns and villages approaching Jerusalem, he continued to teach in his own unique way. His answers were not really answers in the traditional sense. Instead, they were challenges or invitations tailored to the questioner.

Jesus said, "For behold, some are last who will be first, and some are first will be last" in the kingdom of God. The one who recognizes a need of God is the humble one who has entered the narrow gate. A person who is pumped up with self-righteous pride may be told by the Lord Jesus to depart. Alleluia!

Monday, August 24, 1998 St. Batholomew (Nathanael)
John 1, 45-51
The First Disciples

Philip had relayed to Nathanael the most astonishing news! "We have found the one about whom Moses wrote in the Law, and also the prophets, Jesus, son of Joseph, from Nazareth." Nathanael, in essence, exploded, "Are you out of your mind? Nazareth, that dump? Get a life."

Actually, Nathanael is the very one who does "get a life." He is confounded when Jesus says to him, "Before Philip called you, I saw you under the fig tree."

Nathanael really freaks out now. Quickly reversing his original suspicions, he jumps in all the way and answers Jesus, "Rabbi, you are the Son of God; you are the King of Israel."

Jesus stays with this conversation and tracks Nathanael very carefully. " He asks Nathanael, in my own paraphrase, "Hey, Nat, dude, you're impressed because I saw you under a fig tree? That's nothing. There's more to come. Just wait." That's my sense of Jesus' answer.

Nathan was a straight-shooter. He called 'em as he saw 'em. Jesus really liked that quality and carefully took his new follower on to the next step. "Amen, amen, I say to you, you will see the sky opened and the angels of God ascending and descending on the Son of Man."

Wherever you are with Jesus today, rejoice! He is right there with you. Be honest with Jesus. As with Nathanael, Jesus will take you on to the next step. You will see the glory of the Son of Man. Alleluia!

Tuesday, August 25, 1998 St. Louis, St. Joseph Calasanz
Matthew 23, 23-26
Denunciation of the Scribes and Pharisees

"Woe to you ... you hypocrites. You cleanse the outside of cup and dish, but inside they are full of plunder and self-indulgence. Blind Pharisee, cleanse first the inside of the cup, so that the outside also may be clean."

Once upon time there was a certain denominational church that produced a really good show on Sunday morning. There was even a master of ceremonies. The choir sang very well. The acolytes were carefully vested and carefully trained where to step, where to stand, etc. They were discouraged from wearing sneakers. Oh, yes, there was even a nice little opening prayer before the processional.

So, what's wrong with that? What was missing? Actually, it was more a question of who was missing. Where was Jesus in this performance?

Sure, the people used his name. They read aloud from the Bible. But where was the love of Christ? People were hurt in that place. They were betrayed. They were told to go elsewhere. The ones who believed the Bible were called "fundamentalists". A former member started taking antacids on Thursday in dreaded anticipation of Sunday.

Hypocrites! Would Jesus want his flock to be treated in this way? Repent, believe the Good News of salvation, live in love with God and with your brothers and sisters. Then, and only then, if you want to spiff up the externals on Sunday morning, go for it! Alleluia!

Wednesday, August 26, 1998
Matthew 23, 27-32
Denunciation of the Scribes and Pharisees

More "woes" to the scribes and Pharisees! Like whitewashed tombs, they appear beautiful on the outside, but there is death on the inside. The Pharisees appear righteous on the outside, but are full of hypocrisy and evil on the inside.

Outside. Inside. Inside. Outside.

While acknowledging the reality of our "inner child," we need also to remember our "inner Pharisee." The "inner Pharisee" lives on lies, serves the surface, and is terrified of looking within.

Jesus comes crashing in on this scene with radical statements such as "... you will know the truth, and the truth will set you free (John 8, 32)." Truth?

Pharisees don't really want to know the truth about themselves. They might have to change! They might have to be vulnerable. They might have to admit that they need a Savior, God forbid. It's a lot easier to hide behind scholarship, rules, and regulations.

The Pharisees continue to this day. They are "out there" and they are within each one of us.

As George Santayana wrote, "Those who cannot remember the past are condemned to repeat it." The Pharisees were an example of this. They built tombs for the prophets and then said, " 'If we had lived in the

27

days of our ancestors, we would not have joined them in shedding the prophets' blood (Matthew 23, 30).' "

Yeah, sure. Jesus tells them that God has continued to send them prophets that they continue to persecute and kill.

How is it in our own day? How is it within our very selves? How is within me? How is it within you?

Lord Jesus, help me to experience your tender love and forgiveness. Help me to be the same on the inside that I appear to be on the outside. Alleluia!

Thursday, August 27, 1998 St. Monica
Matthew 24, 42-51
The Unknown Day and Hour;
The Faithful or the Unfaithful Servant

Be prepared! Stay awake! You do not know when the Son of Man will come.

Sometimes we feel frightened by these words. Perhaps we feel threatened and uncertain. We don't know what's going to happen and we're not in control.

The key word to this passage, it seems to me, is the word "faithful." What has the Lord called you to do? What has the Lord called me to do? Are we trying to fulfill this call?

Sometimes we can only do so much. Others may or may not support us in our vocation. But, insofar as it lies in our power, are we trying to live our vocation?

We don't know how much time we have before the Son of Man will return. How exciting this is! All we need to do is to be faithful to his call to us. Then, we're ready!

The Son of Man is coming! That's a fact. It's not negotiable. It's only a matter of time. What concerns me personally is that I am faithful in living my vocation.

The Gospel says that the unfaithful ones will be assigned a place with the hypocrites. From Matthew's Gospel, we know Jesus' opinion of the hypocrites. I don't think we want to be in the place where the hypocrites are assigned, a place of weeping and teeth gnashing.

28

Lord Jesus, show me ways in which I am a hypocrite, ways in which the inside of my life does not match up with the outside. Show me the specific task you are calling me to fulfill today. Thank you for the grace to be faithful. Alleluia!

Friday, August 28, 1998 St. Augustine
Matthew 25, 1-13
The Parable of the Ten Virgins

The wise brought flasks of oil with their lamps. They were ready! When the bridegroom arrived, all they had to do was to trim their lamps.

People who offer hospitality are usually prepared. They prepare diligently, perhaps cooking and freezing casseroles. Then, if unexpected guests appear, all the host has to do is to smile, greet the guests, and pop the casserole in the oven.

An alternative is to keep frozen lasagna on hand! The idea is that the work has already been done. The host can concentrate on welcoming the guests.

What do I need to do today to be prepared for Jesus? Maybe it is not preparing a casserole. Maybe it is praying for the grace to forgive someone who has injured me. Maybe it is writing a letter or making a phone call. Maybe it is offering myself the gift of meeting Jesus in the sacrament of reconciliation. It is keeping on with my ordinary, daily work.

Thank you, Lord Jesus, for showing me what to do today to stay ready for you. Thank you for freeing me from boredom, despair, and fear. Thank you for your love and your presence. Alleluia!

Saturday, August 29, 1998 Martyrdom of John the Baptist
Mark 6, 17-29
The Death of John the Baptist

King Herod ordered the execution. The executioner went to the prison and beheaded John the Baptist. Herodius, however, was the power behind the throne in this tragedy.

John had spoken the simple truth to Herod, "It is not lawful for you to have your brother's wife." Herodius, driven by the energy of her grudge, sought to remove this teller of truth.

Herod was a tragically weak king. He was so much at the beck and call of Herodius that he was willing to violate his conscience in order to save face.

When Herod seemed trapped by Herodius' scheme, he was too cowardly to save John's life. He was "deeply distressed," but not principled enough to do the right thing.

How tragic when some in positions of public responsibility play politics. They've been given a once in a lifetime opportunity to serve God and to serve others. Instead they wimp out and serve their own egos.

Lord Jesus, show me today those I am called to serve. Help me to focus on you and seek to do your will. Help me not to be swayed by whoever may be a potential "Herodius" in my life. Alleluia!

Sunday, August 30, 1998
Twenty-Second Sunday in Ordinary Time
Luke 14, 1, 7-14
Conduct of Invited Guests and Hosts

We will be paid at the time of the resurrection of the righteous. Do we really believe that? Do we rejoice at the idea of rewards?

All who attempt self-promotion will be humbled, but those who humble themselves will be exalted. Do we believe that?

These are the Lord's own promises. God is the One who will repay us. God is the One who will exalt us if we have humbled ourselves.

Our part is simply to be real enough to acknowledge our need of the Lord. Perhaps, that is what it means to be humble.

Our part is also to serve those who cannot repay us. When we serve "the least of these," we serve the Lord (Matthew 25, 40 K.J.V.). Alleluia!

Monday, August 31, 1998
Luke 4, 16-30
The Rejection at Nazareth

Did you notice the word "all" in this passage? In his hometown synagogue of Nazareth, Jesus read the passage from Isaiah and announced, " 'Today this scripture passage is fulfilled in your hearing.'

And all spoke highly of him and were amazed at the gracious words that came from his mouth." ALL!

However, a few minutes later, after Jesus said, "no prophet is accepted in his own native place" this same group of people, all of them, were "filled with fury." ALL.

"They rose up, drove him out of the town, and led him to the brow of the hill on which their town had been built, to hurl him down headlong." Sounds like rejection, doesn't it?

ALL the people. As we follow Jesus in this life, we too will be in situations where, at one time, it seems that all the people speak well of us. Then the same group of people may turn and tell us, in effect, to go jump off a cliff.

Oh, they may not be quite that honest. They may sit in their committee rooms and write polished letters laden with malice. Their message is still the same: "We don't want you. Go away."

If we are following Jesus, this should not unduly disturb us. Remember the passage about the disciple not being above the teacher? "No disciple is superior to the teacher; but when fully trained, every disciple will be like his teacher (Luke 6, 40)." Whatever was done to Jesus will be done, in some way, to us, if we are truly following Jesus and not just playing it safe.

Like Jesus, we are simply to "[pass] through the midst of them" and go on our way. If we focus on the behavior of others, we will be sidetracked from the mission Jesus has for us. Instead, we focus on Jesus. As a colleague from my chaplaincy days advised, "Hit and move on."

Lord Jesus, where would you have me follow you today? Which words would you have me speak? Thank you for your presence in my life and for your power in my life. Thank you that you will accomplish your purpose for my life. Alleluia!

Tuesday, September 1, 1998
Luke 4, 31-37
The Cure of a Demoniac

"In the synagogue there was a man with the spirit of an unclean demon ..." IN the synagogue! You've probably noticed by now that the Evil One comes to church and torments God's people.

Jesus' response was to rebuke, not the afflicted person, but rather the demon, commanding it to come out of the person. Jesus did this by total trust that this was the will of his Father in heaven. Jesus' part consisted of speaking the word of command with power and authority.

We are to continue this work today. When Jesus sent out his twelve disciples, he gave them the power and authority to drive out evil spirits We are to continue this work. Jesus told his disciples, "As the Father sent me, so I send you (John 20, 21)."

We have courage now to pray for God to heal us and to use us as vessels of God's healing power. Now is the time to step out in trust! Lord Jesus, today show me the word to speak to set another free. Alleluia!

Wednesday, September 2, 1998
Luke 4, 38-44
Cure of Simon's Mother-in-law; Other Healings;
Jesus Leaves Capernaum

A lot has happened since the beginning of this chapter. Jesus was severely tested in the wilderness. Later, he read aloud the text from Isaiah in the synagogue of Nazareth, his hometown.

The people in the synagogue became enraged and tried to throw Jesus off the cliff. It was also in the synagogue in Nazareth that Jesus liberated a person who had the spirit of a demon.

We now see Jesus curing Simon Peter's mother-in-law. Peter was such a complex character that his relationship with his wife and family must have been very interesting.

We also see Jesus curing every single sick person brought to him. Crowds began to follow him, but Jesus moved on to the other places to which God the Father had called him to preach,

In a way, this chapter is an overview of the ministry of Jesus. We see small pieces of the entire picture. God the Father is leading and guiding his Son step by step. Just as surely, our heavenly Father is guiding you and me.

Lord Jesus, you see my life as a whole. You know how each piece will fit together. Help me to trust in you, to rest in you, and to trust in your timing in my life. Alleluia!

Thursday, September 3, 1998 St. Gregory the Great
Luke 5, 1-11
The Call of Simon the Fisherman

Jesus saw the boats beside the lake and then got into Simon Peter's boat. It was from this boat that Jesus spoke to all the people who had gathered.

Jesus wants to get into your "boat" also. He wants to get into your very life and to speak from your life to others. He will ask you to "put out into deep water." Like Peter, you may say, "I already tried that and it didn't work."

Continue on, as Peter did. Try it again, this time with Jesus with you in a new way. In Peter's case, there was such a huge catch of fish that the nets began to break! Jesus rewarded Peter's trust in this amazing way.

Your "deep water" may be an area of your life so painful you can't bear to enter it again. Don't be afraid, because Jesus will not only be with you, but he will also bring forth an abundant "catch" from your trust. The "catch" from your trust will nourish many.

Lord Jesus, please come into my "boat" today. Go with me to the deep places where I am so afraid. I put my trust in you. Bring forth an abundant "catch" for your glory. Alleluia!

Friday, September 4, 1998
Luke 5, 33-39
The Question about Fasting

"New wine must be poured into fresh wineskins." Recently, after an Eight Day silent, directed retreat, I returned to my everyday life. Although very happy to see my family and friends, I was not yet ready to be back in the "the world." It wasn't just all the traffic and the crowds and the noise. It wasn't just the terrible news spewing from the media. It was EVERYTHING!

"New wine must be poured into fresh wineskins." Somehow, I need to learn to incorporate the fresh wine of this retreat into my life.

"Create in me a clean heart, O God; and renew in me a right spirit (Psalm 51, 10, K.J.V.)." Transform me by the renewal of my mind (cf. Romans 12, 2a). Alleluia!

Saturday, September 5, 1998
Luke 6, 1- 5
Debate about the Sabbath

Jesus countered the Pharisees' hostile questions with questions of his own. "Have you not read what David did when he and those [who were] with him were hungry? [How] he went in to the house of God, took the bread of offering, which only the priests could lawfully eat, ate of it, and shared it with his companions?"

If we look back into this fascinating account (1 Samuel 21, 1-7), we find that the priest, Ahimelech, authorized David and his hungry men to eat the holy bread. The priest personally gave David this consecrated bread!

In the Gospels, we read over and over that Jesus did nothing on his own authority, but only what the Father in heaven instructed him to do. Obviously, there was an "OK" from on high for the followers of Jesus to harvest and eat grains of wheat on the Sabbath.

The Pharisees elevated rules and regulations above human need. However, it is Jesus who is Lord! He alone is Lord of the Sabbath, Lord of the Church, and Lord of our lives. Alleluia!

Sunday, September 6, 1998
Twenty-Third Sunday in Ordinary Time
Luke 14, 25-33
Sayings on Discipleship

Great crowds were following Jesus and he continued to teach them. They had seen signs and wonders. Now Jesus was inviting them to look beyond the signs and wonders to see HIM, the One who would be despised, rejected and killed.

Will you follow THIS Jesus? Or do you just want the signs and wonders?

If you really want Jesus, it's all over. Follow him. Do not look back. If you follow him and he is first in your life, you'll not only have signs and wonders, you'll have JESUS himself. You, also, will become a sign. A sign of contradiction.

Lord Jesus, I choose you. So fill me with your life that I will be a sign, and even a wonder, to those in my life who need you. Alleluia!

Monday, September 7, 1998
Luke 6, 6-11
Debates about the Sabbath

The scribes and Pharisees were watching Jesus like a hawk to
see whether he would be a rule-keeper or a Sabbath-breaker. Jesus, as
always, put the needs of the people first.

The Pharisees were glaring at Jesus with deep hostility. In contrast.
Jesus was gazing with eyes of mercy. His intent was to heal, not to destroy.
Mark's account of this healing tells us that Jesus looked at the Pharisees
"with anger" and was "grieved at their hardness of heart (Mark 3, 5)."

Nevertheless, Jesus was not to be deterred from fulfilling his
ministry. He proceeded to heal the man with the withered hand, even
though it was on the Sabbath.

Whatever opposition we encounter, we must continue to do what
we are called to do. Others suffer when we cease our ministry and cower
in fear before those who oppose us.

Lord Jesus, show me how to reach out to others today. Help me to
do your will and to rest in your love. Alleluia!

Tuesday, September 8, 1998 The Birth of the Virgin Mary
Matthew 1, 1-16; 18-23
The Genealogy of Jesus; The Birth of Jesus

This is the day the Church celebrates the birth of the Virgin Mary,
mother of Jesus. Today's Gospel, however, records the genealogy of Jesus
by tracing the family line of Joseph.

The Gospel also focuses on the character of Joseph, his stalwart
righteousness, his tender concern for Mary, and his trusting obedience
to God's message spoken by the angel.

What about Mary? Isn't this the day we celebrate Mary's birthday?
Wasn't it Mary on whose cooperation the whole salvation enterprise
hinged?

Yes. God, in his infinite love and wisdom, specifically chose a
Jewish teenage girl, Mary of Nazareth, to be the mother of his only Son.
However, Mary was prepared for her unique vocation, not only by her
own fiat, but also by the unrecorded fiat of Joseph.

Lord Jesus, thank you for the "yes" of both your mother Mary and of Joseph. Take our own "yes" to you and let us be part of the fulfillment of another's vocation. Alleluia!

Wednesday, September 9, 1998 St. Peter Claver
Luke 6, 20-26
Sermon on the Plain

The poor, the hungry, the grieving, the ones who are hated and excluded and slandered all have one thing in common. They all recognize their need of God's intervention in their lives.

They are told to rejoice! Their reward will be great in heaven.

But what about right here and right now on earth? Jesus tells us that the rich, the comfortable, the well-fed, the ones who laugh and are highly esteemed have already received their reward, here on earth.

What about the prophets? Jesus reminds us that the true prophets were despised and that the false prophets were honored.

We must choose. Do we want it all now or are we willing to live for Jesus in this world and wait for his reward?

I remember a lovely, handmade card in a hospital gift shop. The card depicted nuns in long, flowing habits, taking turns swinging. One nun stood off by herself waiting. The card read, "Be patient. Your turn will come."

Lord Jesus, I want to live for you today. Help me to be patient and to wait for your timing in all my concerns. Alleluia!

Thursday, September 10, 1998
Luke 6, 27-38
Love of Enemies; Judging Others

Jesus instructs us, "... love your enemies, do good to those who hate you, bless those who curse you, pray for those who mistreat you." Only by allowing God's love to control us can we begin to live this Gospel.

This is a Gospel of action, not a Gospel of feeling. Jesus never said that we had to "feel" love.

We are instructed, however, to act with radical love. This is possible only when we are secure enough in God to know that God is in charge. God sees and God knows all that has happened.

When we "love," we yearn for God's best for the other person. We "do good" for the other person, as the Holy Spirit inspires us. We "bless" by finding something positive to say about the one who has "cursed" us. We pray for the healing of the one who has mistreated us.

To the one who "strikes" at us or "takes" from us, we give and ask for nothing back. This is especially difficult if our reputation has been taken from us by lies and slander. Only God can set the record straight. This may take time, but God is faithful and just and will bring about total restoration.

"Do to others as you would have them do to you." We make allowances for ourselves all the time. "I was tired." " I had a bad day." "The kids drove me crazy." Perhaps we could try to make allowances for others also.

The great invitation is to enter into God's mercy. "Be merciful, just as [also] your Father is merciful." It is only then that we can "stop judging" and "stop condemning." It is then that we can savor the promises of God. "Forgive and you will be forgiven. Give and gifts will be given to you; a good measure, packed together, shaken down, and overflowing, will be poured into your lap. For the measure with which you measure will in turn be measured out to you." Alleluia!

Friday, September 11, 1998
Luke 6, 33-42
Judging Others

"A disciple is not above the teacher, but everyone who is fully qualified will be like the teacher (Luke 6, 40 N.R.S.V.)." To be fully qualified and carefully trained requires continuing self-knowledge.

If we are open to the Lord, we will become increasingly aware, not only of sins in our lives, but of sin itself, of our sinful nature. Not just the laundry list of dreary everyday sins, but the powerful drive deep within us to put ourselves first and to justify ourselves.

At a recent Greek festival at a church, I cautioned my husband not to get carried away by the books and computer accessories in the bazaar. We wandered around the festival enjoying the music, exhibits, and the delicious Greek food.

Then I headed for the room where the icons were sold and I went wild! All sales benefited the church, not the artists. Besides, I would give a lot of those icons away for gifts.

So, armed with a noble purpose, I gathered up icon after icon! When I left , I had spent $100! My husband had spent only a quarter for a used paperback.

Well, you're probably laughing by now and I don't blame you. Don't we all do this sort of thing, though?

Lord Jesus, please reveal to us today the huge beams in our own eyes. Forgive us and remove these beams, so we can see clearly and compassionately to remove gently the tiny splinter in another's eye.

Alleluia!

Saturday, September 12, 1998
Luke 6, 43-49
A Tree Known by Its Fruit; The Two Foundations

The tree that bears good fruit. The house built on a firm foundation. What do they have in common?

There is a saying that what you see is what you get. This is not necessarily true.

In the case of the fruit-bearing tree and the house capable of withstanding floods, you are getting a lot more than you see.

What you cannot see is the root structure of the tree. The roots go down deep and draw up nourishment for the tree. The builder of the house also dug deeply and made sure the foundation was built on solid rock.

What is sustaining my life today? Am I believing and living a lie? On what foundation am I building my life?

Lord Jesus, help me to nourish the roots of my inner life in you and build a strong foundation for my outer life. I trust in You. Alleluia!

Sunday, September 13, 1998
Twenty-Fourth Sunday in Ordinary Time
Luke 15, 1-32
Parables of the Lost Sheep, The Lost Coin, and the Lost Son

"The tax collectors and sinners were all drawing near to listen to him, but the Pharisees and scribes began to complain ..." Therefore, it was to the Pharisees and the scribes that Jesus addressed these parables.

There appears to be only two responses to the parables. The first response is to rejoice because there is completion and resolution.

The lost sheep has been rescued and is safely back in the arms of the shepherd. The lost coin has been found and the woman calls in her friends and neighbors to celebrate.

Finally, the beloved lost son has been received safe and sound back home. The father pulls out all the stops in order to express his joy!

Joy! The first two parables refer to the joy in heaven and among the holy angels when even one of God's lost children repents and is "found."

The other response, that of the Pharisees who thought they have no need to repent, is to complain. The elder brother is an excellent example of the whining spirit of the self-righteous Pharisees. The elder brother is downright furious.

The theologian, Helmut Thielcke, wrote of this parable in his book, The Waiting Father. Both the father in the parable and the Father in heaven rejoice over the return of the lost child.

Lord Jesus, please change my heart today. Help me to repent and to know that you welcome me back into relationship with you and others. When I am self-righteous and indignant with others, help me to see them with your eyes of compassion. Where there has not yet been repentance or change of heart in those for whom I pray, help me to wait with you in loving confidence. You are still hearing my prayers. You are still acting in the lives of those for whom I pray. Search out, bring home, and heal all your lost lambs just as you are healing me. Alleluia!

Monday, September 14, 1998 Triumph of the Holy Cross
John 3, 13-17
Nicodemus

The Israelites, safely out of Egypt, were getting sick and tired of tromping around in the wilderness. They even "... complained against God and Moses (Numbers 21, 5)."

God didn't like that, so he sent serpents to bite them. Then, lo and behold, they realized that it was not a good idea to complain. Moses prayed for them and then, at God's instruction, he made a bronze serpent and mounted it upon a pole. When someone who had been bitten by one these fierce serpents looked at the bronze serpent, that person would be healed. The afflicted person could choose whether or not to look upon the bronze serpent.

The choice continues today. The Son of Man was lifted high on the Cross. If we choose to believe in him, we have eternal life, true life with and in God. It is our choice.

God's purpose in providing the bronze serpent was to heal the person who had repented. God's purpose in his Son's death on the Cross was to provide salvation, healing in the deepest sense.

God's purpose and desire is ever to heal and restore. Ours is the choice to look to Jesus, ask for forgiveness, receive forgiveness, and be healed. Alleluia!

Tuesday, September 15, 1998 Our Lady of Sorrows
Luke 2, 33-35
The Presentation in the Temple

Years ago, I saw a Sunday church bulletin which had on the cover a simple, yet striking line drawing of a heart with a sword plunged through it. That's the way I used to visualize this passage about Mary. Simeon told her, "... you yourself a sword will pierce ..."

Mary's entire being -- body, soul, and spirit -- would be affected by her Son's vocation. "This child is destined for the fall and rise of many in Israel, and to be a sign that will be contradicted."

Simeon goes on to give the reason why Jesus will be a sign of contradiction and why Mary's heart will be pierced. Jesus is to be sign of contradiction because, through his life, "the thoughts of many hearts may be revealed."

Mary's life, at least from the moment of the Annunciation, was one of constant challenge. How would she fulfill her unique vocation?

"Behold, I am the handmaid of the Lord.
     May it be done to me according to your word (Luke 1, 38)."

Mary did nor fully understand at that moment what her life would involve and the suffering that would ensue. Still, she said yes.

"My soul proclaims the greatness of the Lord;
     my spirit rejoices in God my Savior (Luke 1, 46)."

This is only way Mary survived her vocation. She said "yes" to God and rejoiced in God!

40

This is the only way we can survive the uncertainties in our own lives, by saying our own "Yes" to God. Alleluia!

Wednesday, September 16, 1998 St. Cornelius, St. Cyprian
Luke 7, 31-35
Jesus' Testimony to John

The Pharisees were hell-bent in their determination to reject the holy messengers sent from God. They rejected not only the messengers, but also the message.

They rejected John, an ascetic, who preached the need for repentance. John came to prepare the way for Jesus.

The Pharisees then rejected Jesus, who enjoyed the things of this world. He went to parties. He enjoyed life! He ate and drank.

Jesus not only reached out to sinners, but he also truly loved them and they knew it. He was their friend and they trusted him.

The Pharisees, on the other hand, hated his guts. He upset their apple cart. He upset their stupid legalism which had nothing to do with God and everything to do with sustaining their power trip. They could not keep on pumping up their egos with Jesus around. He saw right through them.

So, who won? Who lost? The Pharisees "rejected the plan of God for themselves (Luke 7, 30)." They lost.

The sinners who repented, believed John, were baptized, believed Jesus, and put their trust in him were the winners! Jesus took them from where they were and transformed them because they were willing to embrace the truth.

The Pharisees lost. They stuck their fingers in their ears and hardened their hearts to shut out the truth. How tragic that the ones charged to uphold God's truth could not accept Truth incarnate.

Jesus always wins! Those who trust in Jesus win. That is why "wisdom is vindicated by all her children."

Lord Jesus, sometimes hearing the truth hurts. I have to hear things about myself I would rather not hear. Help me not to put my fingers in my ears. Help me not to close my heart. Help me to trust you enough to listen to the truth, do what you say to do, and then to enjoy the freedom to live for you. Alleluia!

Thursday, September 17, 1998 St. Robert Bellarmine
Luke 7, 36-50
The Pardon of the Sinful Woman

"Things are not what they seem." "Look underneath the surface." "Read between the lines." These sayings certainly apply in today's Gospel.

Jesus, as usual, cut right through the surface -- the surface behavior, the surface social etiquette, the surface labeling of human beings. Jesus cut right through to the hearts of the people involved in the Gospel.

Simon, a Pharisee, was Jesus' host. He invited Jesus for dinner, but what were his motives? Hospitality? A chance to learn more about Jesus? Simon neglected the important custom of washing the tired, dusty feet of his guest. A household slave usually performed this task.

The "sinful" woman, on the other hand, welcomed Jesus in deep humility, because of her gratitude. She brought with her an alabaster flask filled with a costly fragrant ointment.

She also brought something even more costly. She brought herself and her reputation as a sinner. She brought her very heart of love. She went all out to show her love and gratitude.

With reverence, she stood behind Jesus. She then fell to his feet and wept, bathing his feet with her tears, wiping his feet with her long hair, and anointing his feet with the costly, fragrant ointment.

Simon was about to blow a fuse! Can't you just see the veins throbbing in his temple? Spluttering with righteous indignation, he said, not aloud, but in his heart, "If this man were a prophet, he would know who and what sort of woman this is who is touching him, that she is a sinner."

Jesus answered him, because Jesus could see into his heart. He gently told Simon about his neglect of hospitality, the washing of a guest's feet.

Simon had not even offered water for washing Jesus' feet. The woman, on the other hand, had offered the very essence of hospitality, her very self.

She washed Jesus' feet, not with water, but with her own tears. The fragrance of her costly ointment wafted throughout the air as a silent testimony to her love.

It is very wounding to offer ourselves and to be rejected. People may not understand. They may see insincerity, if they are insincere themselves. Jesus, however, joyfully accepts us.

Lord Jesus, look into my heart today. Where have I been self-righteous and judgmental like Simon the Pharisee? Please forgive me and cleanse me. Help me to see people and situations today as you see them. Alleluia!

Friday, September 18, 1999
Luke 8, 1-3
Galilean Women Follow Jesus

One day I dropped off some papers at the home of Mary, my son's nursery school teacher years ago. In her window was a tiny sign, something to the effect that "Feminism is the radical notion that women are human beings!" This sign adorns the home of a devoted wife, mother, grandmother, church member, teacher, writer and translator. Not exactly a dangerous, threatening person.

In Jesus' day as in our day, there were women who longed to express their gratitude for how the Lord had transformed their lives. Mary of Magdalene had been set free in an especially dramatic way. Joanna and others perhaps risked misunderstanding and condemnation for their devotion to the Lord.

Setting aside the labels of "traditionalist" or "feminist," how do we believe that Jesus is calling us to serve him today? Are we willing to serve him even if others do not understand or approve the nature of our vocation?

Lord Jesus, you are Head of the Church. Please enable each of us, male or female, to serve you and your Church as you have called us to serve. Show us the heart of the vocation to which we are called and help us to be faithful to you. Alleluia!

Saturday, September 19, 1998 St. Januarius
Luke 8, 4-15
The Parable of the Sower

"But as far as the seed that fell on rich soil, they are the ones who, when they have heard the word, embrace it with a generous and good heart, and bear fruit through perseverance." Perseverance.

Over the years, the "seed" of God's word has sometimes fallen on the path of my life without taking root. It seemed that the life of God's word to me had been "trampled."

There have been times that the rocky ground of difficult circumstances has seemed to prevail. The seed "withered for lack of moisture."

Also, there have been thorns in my heart. These thorns appeared to choke the possibility of growth.

Still, God is greater . God is greater than my circumstances. God is greater than my failures. God is greater than my sins.

The essential quality of the good soil, I believe, is trust. Trust is what enables me to persevere. To persevere requires, not heroic deeds, but rather a continuing, tranquil belief in the sovereignty and the goodness of God.

The richly descriptive Psalm 92, a song for the Sabbath, lifts our spirits. It refers to being planted in the Lord's house, growing like a cedar, flourishing like a palm tree in the courts of God, and bearing fruit in old age. Strong, fresh and green!

Lord Jesus, help me to hear your word to me today, to embrace your word with trust, and to bear fruit. With you, it is never too late. Alleluia!

Sunday, September 20, 1998
Twenty-Fifth Sunday in Ordinary Time
Luke 16, 1-13
The Parable of the Dishonest Steward

"The person who trustworthy in very small matters is also trustworthy in great ones; and the person who is dishonest in very small matters is also dishonest in great ones." That's today's Gospel in a nutshell.

Lord Jesus, in this dark world, help us to shine brightly for you. Help us to be faithful in the small and faithful in all. Alleluia!

Monday, September 21, 1998 St. Matthew
Matthew 9, 9-13
The Call of Matthew

Jesus said to Matthew, "Follow me." For Matthew, following Jesus meant walking away from the predictable business world he knew, and being plunged immediately into the controversies surrounding Jesus, this far-out radical rabbi.

After all, Jesus loved sinners and showed mercy and compassion to them. He showed this mercy to Matthew, a despised tax collector. The Pharisees were outraged!

Lord Jesus, in the midst of those who argue about you, help me to live for you. Thank you for the mercy you have shown to me, a sinner. Help me to extend this mercy to others. Alleluia!

Tuesday, September 22, 1998
Luke 8, 19-21
Jesus and His Family

Growing up, I always wanted an older brother. This was an ache, a missing part of my life. I loved my younger brother very much, but still secretly yearned for a big brother.

In today's Gospel, Jesus says, "My mother and my brothers are those who hear the word of God and act on it." A new criterion has been set for being in the family of Jesus.

Lord Jesus, I already love you as my Savior. Help me today to understand in a deeper way that you are truly my Brother and I am your little sister. Thank you for holding my hand and leading me home at last to our Father in heaven. Alleluia!

Wednesday, September 23, 1998
Luke 9, 1-6
The Mission of the Twelve

In today's Good News (Gospel), Jesus tells his followers, ",,, as for those who do not welcome you, when you leave that town, shake the dust from your feet in testimony against them." This advice is from One who has been there and done that.

Jesus advises shaking off the dust and detaching emotionally from situations in which his followers experience rejection. It isn't enough to detach geographically. It's imperative to "leave" emotionally as well.

45

Remember, Jesus was rejected. The Son of God was rejected by the religious leaders. Later, he was tortured, murdered, and buried.

We cannot follow in his footsteps without experiencing some form of suffering and rejection because of our faith. It is crucial to learn how to shake off the dust.

For Jesus, suffering was not the last word. Resurrection was the last word! Jesus rose from the dead and so will we!

Lord Jesus, forgive me for brooding over times in the past when I have followed you and experienced rejection. I shake off the dust from the past and joyfully continue to follow you. Alleluia

Thursday, September 24, 1998
Luke 9, 7-9
Herod's Opinion of Jesus

Recall the background of today's Gospel about King Herod. His wife, Herodius, was one of the powers behind the throne. She was bound and determined to get John the Baptist!

Herod, her pathetically weak, irresolute husband, knew that John was a righteous man. Still, Herod buckled under pressure and had John beheaded.

What happened next? Herod was then confronted, not with John the Baptist risen from the dead, but with Jesus the Christ!

The Gospel tells us that Herod was interested in seeing Jesus. Herod was curious to see Jesus perform a "sign." Jesus refused to play Herod's game,

Herod was said to be "greatly perplexed." If we truly live for Jesus, those around us are certainly going to be "greatly perplexed." Our calling is to follow Jesus and not to be concerned with the Herods or the Herodiuses who would seek to derail us from our vocation.

Lord Jesus, you are the only true King. Let us look into your eyes of love today and continue to follow you. Alleluia!

Friday, September 25, 1998
Luke 9, 18-22
Peter's Confession about Jesus

"The Son of Man must suffer greatly and be rejected by the elders, the chief priests, and the scribes, and be killed and on the third day be raised." Suffer greatly. Be rejected by the religious leaders. Be killed. Be raised. What an assignment!

Everyone who follows Jesus will, in some way, pass through these events. Everyone knows this. No one wants these things to happen.

I remember once saying to a group of chaplain interns, "You want to follow Jesus? You're going to be crucified!" There was silence.

Jesus was not rejected by the "little" people, those who had been discounted by the "important" ones. Jesus was rejected by the big cheeses in the Sanhedrin and the power elite of the Temple.

Jesus saw right through them, right into their malicious hearts, right through their ridiculous sham. He was a threat to their continuation in power. Of course, they killed him!

What about us? The cross and the crown are interwoven in our lives today. There is a particular cross to carry. There is a crown that awaits us. Alleluia!

Saturday, September 26, 1998 Sts. Cosmos and Damian
Luke 9, 43-45
The Second Prediction of the Passion

The disciples were overwhelmed and amazed at what they were witnessing. They had seen the Transfiguration of Jesus. The had witnessed the healing of the boy with a demon. Jesus could do anything! Hooray for Jesus!

Jesus wasted no time in bringing his followers back to earth. "Pay attention," he told them. He was to be "handed over" to suffering and death.

The disciples simply could not grasp this. Indeed, "its meaning was hidden from them so that they should not understand it, and they were afraid to ask him about this saying."

The disciples were not ready to grasp the meaning of all this. They could not understand the first prediction of the passion and they could not understand this prediction either.

As we'll see later, they still could not understand, when, for the third time, Jesus predicted his suffering, death, and resurrection. It was too much to comprehend.

Still, the plan of God was not stopped. This should give us hope when there is so much we do not understand.

Lord Jesus, please help us to receive the grace to understand what we need to understand for the living of this day. Alleluia!

Sunday, September 27, 1998
Twenty-Sixth Sunday in Ordinary Time
Luke 16, 19-31
The Parable of the Rich Man and Lazarus

Jesus said to the disciples that they would always have the poor with them, but that they would not always have him with them. This was said in response to the outrage over the woman who had anointed his feet with costly ointment (John 12, 8, Matthew 26, 11, Mark 14, 7).

The rich man, in today's Gospel. did not reach out to Lazarus in any way. His attitude was one of indifference.

It is not a matter of how much of the world's riches we have. It is a matter of the attitude of our heart. Do we have a generous heart?

Jesus wants us to be generous in our use of time, money, and concern. "Lazarus" may be a member of our family who is starving for understanding.

Lord Jesus, please forgive our indifference as well as our selfishness. Open our eyes, our minds, and our hearts to see and to respond, as you direct, to the needs of those around us. Alleluia!

Monday, September 28, 1998
St. Wenceslaus, St. Lawrence Ruiz and Companions
Luke 9, 46-50
The Greatest in the Kingdom; Another Exorcist

"Jesus realized the intentions of their hearts ..." "The least among all of you is the one who is the greatest." "Whoever is not against you is for you."

Jesus is again looking deeply within the human heart. Jesus alone knows the true intentions of our hearts.

We may think we know our intentions, but who are we to judge ourselves or others? We may observe actions, but we lack the knowledge to judge or to evaluate the motives behind the actions. Only Jesus is qualified to evaluate our motives and the motives of others.

Children were not greatly esteemed in times past. They could be mistreated and no one intervened. They were disposable. They were considered property.

Jesus said, in effect, "If you treat any other human being as of no account, as someone you look down on, as someone you "dispose of," you reject Me. If you welcome or accept such a pure soul, whether a child or an adult, you welcome and accept Me."

Lord Jesus, help us to see that we "count" and that all others "count." When others have mistreated us and told us to go away, you have held out you arms and welcomed us. Help us to welcome with our eyes, our voices, our hearts, and our arms the "little ones" of whatever age or stature you send across our path today. Alleluia!

Tuesday, September 29, 1998
Sts Michael, Gabriel, Raphael, and the Archangels
John 1, 47-51
The First Disciples

Nathanael! It was Nathanael who had asked, rather dubiously, "Can anything good come from Nazareth?"

The excited Philip had just told Nathanael, "We have found the one about whom Moses wrote in the Law, and also the prophets, Jesus, son of Joseph, from Nazareth."

Instead of accepting this amazing statement at face value, Nathanael was very cautious. He inquired, "Can anything good come from Nazareth?" Philip invited his friend, "Come and see."

Jesus saw into Nathanael's heart, as he sees this day into our own hearts. He did not condemn Nathanael, as later he did not condemn Thomas, for his doubts.

Instead, Jesus led Nathanael closer to himself. When Jesus saw Nathanael, he did not say, "Here comes that skeptic." Rather, he remarked, "Here is a true Israelite. There is no duplicity in him."

Nathanael persisted in asking questions. "How do you know me?" he asked Jesus. Later, Nathanael proceeded from his questioning to a bold proclamation of faith. "Rabbi, you are the Son of God; you are the King of Israel."

Jesus again took Nathanael to the next step. "You will see the sky opened and the angels of God ascending and descending on the Son of Man." In one short conversation, Jesus had led Nathanael from asking an honest question to receiving the promise of seeing, not merely a dusty rabbi from Nazareth, but the Son of Man.

Lord Jesus, help me to be honest with you today. I bring to You my doubts, my fears, and my weariness. Thank you for gently leading me step by step from where I am at this moment to the time I behold you in all your glory, with the angels. Alleluia!

Wednesday, September 30, 1998 St. Jerome
Luke 9, 57-62
The Would-Be Follower of Jesus

One of the "would-be" followers asked permission first to bury his father. Another asked first to go to say farewell to his family. As serious as these family obligations appeared, Jesus redirected the priorities of these aspiring disciples.

Jesus Christ, the Son of God and Son of Man, gives us an invitation to follow him. Nothing takes precedence over following Jesus.

Following Jesus means to obey Jesus and to trust that whatever he asks of us is for our ultimate good. Jesus may indeed tell us to attend to family matters. He may tell us to leave other matters alone.

The best place for us to be is in the center of God's will. If we are following Jesus, He will work out all the details of our lives and attend to all our relationships. Jesus alone is Lord.

Lord Jesus, help me today to follow where you lead. You are Lord. Alleluia!

Thursday, October 1, 1998 St. Therese of the Child Jesus
Luke 10, 1-12
Mission of the Seventy-Two

The "72" were sent ahead to the places Jesus intended to visit. The manner in which they were received would tell Jesus a lot about "the natives." A litmus test, of sorts. Would his followers be welcomed or rejected?

Jesus told his disciples in advance that they were being sent out as lambs among wolves. They did not carry designer briefcases. They did not engage in power lunches. They themselves were the message!

If we follow Jesus, do we expect it's going to be easy? As the old saying goes, do we focus on the Lord of the work or upon the work of the Lord?

If we put ministry first, we may be devoured by wolves. Not everyone will welcome us. Not everyone will wish us peace.

A story is told of St. Francis traveling incognito. He was treated with contempt by the very ones who would have made quite a show of welcoming him had they known his true identity.

If we focus on the Lord of the work, we can be serene in the midst of the times when we are not welcome. We can shake the dust off our feet when necessary and continue on to the Lord's next assignment. Alleluia!

Friday, October 2, 1998 The Guardian Angels
Matthew 18, 1-5, 10
The Greatest in the Kingdom

Jesus is teaching us to think with kingdom minds, to see with kingdom eyes, and to love with kingdom hearts. In God's kingdom, things are different.

On earth, some might consider humility as weakness, as a deficiency. Not so in the kingdom. Not so with Jesus.

Jesus doesn't advise being stupid, naive or immature. Rather, he redefines true greatness.

Jesus tells us that the one who is humble and childlike is greatest in heaven's kingdom. What exactly does that mean?

What did the child in today's Gospel actually do? The child merely came to Jesus when Jesus called! The child responded to Jesus with simple, trusting obedience.

Lord Jesus, help me to come to you today in simplicity and trust. You put a child in the midst of your disciples to teach them about greatness. In the midst of the circumstances of my life today, in the midst of the people surrounding me today, help me to look to you and to be a reflection of you. Alleluia!

Saturday, October 3, 1998
Luke 10, 17-24
Reproaches to Unrepentant Towns; Return of the Seventy-Two

Several years ago, Peggy Noonan wrote a book called <u>What I Saw During The Revolution</u>, about her work as a speechwriter in the White House. In today's Gospel, "the seventy-two" return to Jesus to report what they saw, in what, for them, must have seemed like a revolution! They had been sent forth by Jesus, followed his instructions, and returned rejoicing.

Jesus rejoiced with them! The disciples now knew the power of the name of Jesus. Even the demons were subject to the name of Jesus. What the disciples knew in their own hearts, they were experiencing in actual practice in the world.

Jesus shared their exhilaration and reassured them that nothing of eternal consequence would harm them. "Nevertheless, do not rejoice because the spirits are subject to you, but rejoice because your names are written in heaven."

This is also the cause of our own rejoicing, as we grow in the exercise of our faith. As with the seventy-two, we will see the power of the name of Jesus.

Nevertheless, this is not the true cause of our rejoicing. Although we rejoice in the ministry that the Lord has given us, we rejoice first of all in our relationship with the crucified and risen Lord Jesus. Because of Jesus, our names are written in heaven. Because of Jesus, we will live forever and ever.

Lord Jesus, I rejoice in you! I rejoice in your love for me and in your saving power in my life and in the lives of those for whom I pray. No revolution on this earth can compare to the revolution of your entry into the human heart. Alleluia!

Sunday, October 4, 1998
Twenty-Seventh Sunday in Ordinary Time
Luke 17, 5-10
Saying of Faith; Attitude of a Servant

Once upon a time, in a certain city, in the midst of a valley, there was a beautiful, old-fashioned tearoom. The women of the city, although they dwelt in the midst of a land of high technology, desired a haven of civility. Here they could clink china teacups instead of claw over corporate catastrophes.

In time, there really was such a tearoom. The tea was steeped and so were the prices. Never mind. The genteel atmosphere of the tearoom in the midst of the brutally competitive valley was what mattered.

The young women who waited table in this establishment were dressed as servants of a bygone era. They were truly courteous and solicitous as they poured the tea

Unfortunately, it is possible to dress as a servant while maintaining an attitude of superiority. When one is in a high position of accountability, it is crucial to maintain the attitude of a servant.

At the Last Supper, Jesus' vestment, his sign of office, was a towel tied round his waist . He poured water into a basin and humbly washed the dirty, smelly feet of his disciples. His vestment was in keeping with his attitude and his actions.

Lord Jesus, in whatever way I serve, help me to keep before me the image of you, the King of kings and Lord of lords, as you knelt as a servant at the feet of your disciples and washed their feet. Alleluia!

Monday, October 5, 1998
Luke 10, 25-37
The Greatest Commandment; Parable of Good Samaritan

Testing. Testing. One, two, three.

The scholar of the law was testing Jesus. As the Rev. Dr. Paul Clasper has said, those who presume to judge Jesus only judge themselves. This was borne out by the subsequent statement that the scholar did indeed wish to justify himself

The scholar asked Jesus two questions. First, "What must I do to inherit eternal life?" Jesus turned the tables on this legal expert by asking him, "What is written in the law?" The scholar was bound to answer, "You shall love the Lord your God with all your heart, with all your being, with all your strength, and with all your mind and your neighbor as yourself." In sum, love God and love your neighbor.

Still determined to ensnare Jesus, the scholar pushed the point by asking a second question, "Who is my neighbor?" Again, Jesus nailed him by telling the parable of the Good Samaritan and asking the scholar to identify the one who was neighbor to the victim.

The scholar had to answer, "The one who treated him with mercy." Jesus dismissed his interrogator with the command, "Go and do likewise." In other words, "Love God. Love others. Show mercy."

Lord Jesus, sometimes I try to "test" you when I am afraid. Sometimes, I seem to need endless reassurance. Forgive this lack of trust. Thank you for your love and your mercy. Alleluia!

Tuesday, October 6, 1998 St. Bruno
Luke 10, 38-42
Martha and Mary

Jesus told Martha, as she bustled about, "There is need of only one thing." The "one thing" was illustrated by her sister, Mary, who "sat beside the Lord at his feet listening to him speak." This Gospel is important for me today as I am rushing about, having just returned from a trip to Texas to visit my mother. While I was away, my husband and son re-tiled the kitchen. A beautiful surprise!

The jet lag is minimal, but it still takes a while to "return." Stacks of mail. Phone calls to return. Manuscripts waiting. A healing institute about to begin.

Where to start?

Lord Jesus, please show me the one thing necessary for today. Alleluia!

Wednesday, October 7, 1998 Our Lady of the Rosary
Luke 11, 1-4
The Lord's Prayer

"Forgive us our sins as we ourselves forgive everyone in debt to us." Our Father in heaven forgives us to the extent that we forgive those who have wronged us.

What if I think I haven't forgiven because I don't feel a certain way? Truly, forgiveness is an act of the will. If and when the feelings catch up with our obedience is not our concern.

Lord Jesus, I choose to forgive all those who have wronged me. I release them to you. Thank you for setting me free to follow you today. Alleluia!

Thursday, October 8, 1998
Luke 11, 5-13
Further Teachings on Prayer

Persist! Keep on asking. Keep on seeking. Keep on knocking.

Sometimes it seems that we keep asking with our minds and voices when we've given up in our hearts. Sometimes the answer takes so long that we're tempted to think that God has forgotten us.

All I know is that God changes us in the waiting. Whatever God has promised is going to happen! The longer it takes, the greater the answer will be. Hooray and hallelujah!

Years ago, I had several minor surgeries. The hospital had a beautiful chapel and also a very attractive gift shop. I became well acquainted with both during visits to the surgeons. In the gift shop, there were original cards drawn by a talented and whimsical artist. These cards really made an impression on me. One card depicted nuns in long, flowing habits, on a playground by the swings. One nun stood off to the side watching another swinging happily. The message on this card was, "Wait. Your turn will come."

Your turn will come. My turn will come. You are waiting. I am waiting. We're really waiting for Jesus!

The answer Jesus brings is secondary to the fact that he himself is the answer to our deepest longing. Jesus will answer. He will not be late.

Lord Jesus, please still my heart as I wait for you. I ask for the grace to trust you in a deeper way. Thank you for your perfect timing. You not only will appear on the scene and glory will fill my soul, but you are already here! Sustain me with a steady sense of your presence and power as I wait for the full unfolding of your plans and purposes for me. I love you and thank you and praise you and trust you. Alleluia!

Friday, October 9, 1998 St. Denis and Companions,
St. John Leonardi
Luke 11, 15-26
Jesus and Beelzebub

Those who had closed their minds and hearts to Jesus refused to believe. Period! Then they had the nerve to ask for a sign.

Jesus, the Son of God, was amongst them, not only performing signs and wonders, but also being a sign and wonder. Jesus was aware of their thoughts and refused to play their game.

What do we do when we encounter those who close their minds and hearts to us? We pray for them, but we do not attempt to curry favor with them. We continue to look to Jesus and to do the work he has called us to do.

Lord Jesus, help me to keep my eyes fixed on you today. It is your approval I seek. Alleluia!

Saturday, October 10, 1998
Luke 11, 27-28
True Blessedness

How often we restrict our understanding of God and our understanding of ourselves. Jesus is constantly seeking to enlarge our understanding.

A woman in the crowd called out to Jesus, "Blessed is the womb that carried you and the breasts at which you nursed." Jesus, however, redirected her attention to God. "Rather, blessed are those who hear the word of God and observe it."

Lord Jesus, thank you for your blessing upon us as we listen to the word of God to us today and act upon it. Alleluia!

Sunday, October 11, 1998
Twenty-eighth Sunday in Ordinary Time
Luke 17, 11-19
The Cleansing of Ten Lepers

Jesus was continuing his journey to Jerusalem where he would suffer at the hands of the religious leaders and be crucified. It was on his journey to Jerusalem that this incident with the ten lepers occurred. Jesus healed all ten of the lepers.

However, only one of the ten verbalized his gratitude to Jesus. This was a Samaritan, the one considered an outsider.

As soon as he realized that he had been healed, he went back to Jesus. He praised God in a loud voice, fell prostrate at the feet of the Lord Jesus and thanked him.

Jesus, remember, is both human and divine. In his humanity, he would naturally wonder why the other nine did not even bother to express gratitude.

What about our own journey? As we move towards a particular goal or destination, what about our ministry along the way?

The lepers encountered Jesus for a very brief time, yet their entire lives were changed forever. They were new people set free to live a new life!

What about the people we meet today on our journey? Let us not wait until we get "there" to be used to heal God's suffering children. Jesus is with us here and now to minister to others through our lives. Often, we are used of God when we are least aware of it. Alleluia!

Monday, October 12, 1998
Luke 11, 29-32
The Demand for a Sign

We live in a time when an astonishing number of people claim to see visions or to hear God's voice in special ways. We have to have compassion for those who are called to discern the veracity of these claims.

We are living in a world of immense suffering. Jesus is the great sign of God's love in our struggling world.

You and I are called to manifest God's love and care in this world. We are called to be signs of hope and light.

Lord Jesus, today, let us gaze upon you as the greatest of all signs. Shine through us as we love others in word and in deed. Alleluia!

Tuesday, October 13, 1998
Luke 11, 37-41
Denunciation of the Pharisees and Scholars of the Law

Jesus really fried the Pharisees! No political schmoozing here! He went for the jugular.

Jesus did not condemn the Pharisees for any overt sin. He condemned them for their pretense. He condemned them for not being real.

The Pharisees were carefully showing off their fancy china, so to speak, while serving filth and evil. Jesus ignored the brand name of the china and looked instead at the contents.

"Oh you Pharisees! Although you cleanse the outside of the cup and the dish, inside you are filled with plunder and evil." Jesus was calling for the contents to match the exterior. It was the hypocrisy he condemned.

Lord Jesus, you invite me to be real and to trust you to transform me. "Create in me a clean heart, O God; and renew a right spirit within me (Psalm 51, 10, K.J.V.)." Alleluia!

Wednesday, October 14, 1998 St. Callistus
Luke 11, 42-46
Denunciation of the Pharisees and Scholars of the Law

"Woe also to you scholars of the law! You impose on people burdens hard to carry, but you yourselves do not lift one finger to touch them." Pharisees still exist in various forms and under a number of guises. There is also an "inner Pharisee" within each of us.

In Bread For The Journey, Rev. Henri Nouwen wrote, "The political, economic, social, and even religious powers surrounding us all want to keep us in bondage so that we will obey their commands and be dependent on their rewards." While we are called to honor and to respect all, true freedom lies in following Jesus into the light. Alleluia!

Thursday, October 15, 1998 St. Teresa of Avila
Luke 11, 47-54
Denunciation of the Pharisees and Scholars of the Law

God sent prophets and apostles, some of whom were persecuted and killed. Whether in the time of the Hebrew scriptures, the time of the New Testament, or in our own time, apostles and prophets do not always fare very well. They may make us feel uncomfortable if we are living a comprised life. Their holy presence convicts us.

True prophets speak forth the word of God. They may not have long white beards or voices of thunder.

True prophets may wear hard hats and speak with a Brooklyn twang. They may wear flowered frocks and speak with a Southern drawl. It doesn't matter. God uses them as vessels through whom he delivers a particular message at a particular time to a particular group of people.

It is the same with apostles. They have been commissioned and sent out on God's business. If they act as Jesus acted, if they love as Jesus loved, they will suffer and die as Jesus did. Maybe not on an actual cross, but they will indeed suffer.

In whatever way God may ask us to speak forth his message or to be sent forth on his business, we have to be aware that we may not be well-received. We can backtrack and curry favor with the powerful, or we can quietly go forward and live and speak for the Lord.

"If we have died with him,
  we shall also live with him;
If we persevere
  we shall also reign with him.
But if we deny him
  he will deny us.
If we are unfaithful
  he remains faithful,
  for he cannot deny himself (2 Timothy 2, 11-13)."

Lord Jesus, help us this day to live for you, speak for you, and be about your business. Alleluia!

Friday, October 16, 1998 St. Hedwig, St. Margaret
Mary Alacoque, St. Marguerite d'Youville
Luke 12, 1-7
The Leaven of the Pharisees; Courage under Persecution

"There is nothing concealed that will not be revealed." This statement by Jesus is both comforting and challenging!

When we seek understanding and discernment in difficult situations, we are able to go only so far with our educated guesses. We are dependent upon the Holy Spirit's gifts of knowledge and wisdom.

When we think we are hiding something from others, we are in for a rude awakening. I remember once my five year old son looking at me and saying, "Your little kid knows when you're unhappy." So much for trying to hide feelings!

Lord Jesus, help me to welcome your light coming into my life. Your light brings life, healing, resurrection and restoration. Reveal today your presence in me. Reveal through me your love for others. Alleluia!

Saturday, October 17, 1998 St. Ignatius of Antioch
Luke 12, 8-12
Courage under Persecution; Sayings about the holy Spirit

'When they take you before synagogues and before rulers and authorities, do not worry about how or what your defense will be or about what you are to say. For the holy Spirit will teach you at that moment what you should say." Jesus was reassuring his followers by telling them not to worry. The Holy Spirit would be right there to give them their instructions.

We want to be prepared and to be in control. We are not. The Holy Spirit lives within us and will provide the words to say.

Does this mean that our hearers will "like" us or "like" what we say? Only God knows. This is not our concern. Our duty is to speak the words the Holy Spirit gives us to say.

I used to think that the Holy Spirit would only give me words of love and peace to speak to others. Generally, that is true.

However, there are also times when the words we are to speak are to be simple, blunt words of truth. If our hearers don't want to hear the truth, they are not going to welcome us or our message

Shooting the messenger is easy for the powerful who are without principle. Our part is simply to deliver the message and leave the results with God, who is judge of all.

Lord Jesus, as I pray so often, please give me your eyes with which to view a particular situation, your heart of love and compassion, and your words of truth to speak in love. Alleluia!

Sunday, October 18, 1998
Twenty-ninth Sunday in Ordinary Time
Luke 18, 1-8
Parable of the Persistent Widow

"Hang in there, girl. Go get 'em!" From our comfortable sidelines, we cheer on the brave woman in today's Gospel. She just won't give up!

Some time ago, there was a very famous criminal trial in which the truth screamed out. The exhausted prosecuting attorney persisted in telling the truth and seeking justice. Nevertheless, the verdict came back "not guilty."

This travesty of justice was in spite of overwhelming evidence to the contrary. Many were outraged. What could be done? A subsequent trial, with a different judge and jury, acknowledged the truth.

In today's Gospel, God is telling us that he will secure the rights of his people who have been treated unjustly. The deeper question is, "When the Son of Man comes, will he find faith on earth?"

If the answer seems slow in coming, will we persevere and keep on trusting? We are waiting for our King. He will settle all scores, gather us into his arms and take us to our true home in heaven. Alleluia!

Monday, October 19, 1998 North American Martyrs
Luke 12, 13-21
Saying against Greed; Parable of the Rich Fool

To be rich in "what matters to God" is all that really matters. This is what I really want. This alone will bring peace.

Even though it's autumn, our house needs spring cleaning! There is too much clutter. Boxes of books and papers need to be sorted. Unused clothing needs to be given away.

Even when all the external clutter is gone (and it's not gone yet), there is also clutter in my soul and spirit that needs to be swept away. There are cobwebs of fear and anxiety. There is an old layer of the dust of despair. I try to sweep it away, but it returns.

Do you ever feel that way? Or do you ever stop the busyness long enough to feel at all?

That's one of the scary things about learning to be quiet in God's presence. Stuff that's been stuffed comes to the surface.

That's very healthy, though! Knowing our need, we may confidently ask the Holy Spirit to accomplish within us what needs to be done.

Lord Jesus, please send your Holy Spirit to accomplish a thorough house cleaning of my soul and spirit. "Create in me a clean heart, O God; and renew a right spirit within me (Psalm 51, 10, K.J.V.)." I want to be rich in what matters to you. Alleluia!

Tuesday, October 20, 1998 St. Paul of the Cross
Luke 12, 35-38
Vigilant and Faithful Servants

Jesus tells his followers to "be like servants who await their master's return from a wedding, ready to open immediately when he comes and knocks." A person returning from a wedding is usually full of joy! A wedding is a time of rejoicing, not only for the newlywed couple, but also for family and friends.

Jesus will come, rejoicing, for you and for me! He will come to us, call our name, and take us home.

Lord Jesus, help us today to be ready for you. Ready to hear your voice and ready to receive you. Ready to recognize you in others. Ready to greet you when you come again in glory. Alleluia!

Wednesday, October 21, 1998
Luke 12, 39-48
Vigilant and Faithful Servants

Faithfulness to the known will of God is what is required. Not necessarily to do great things, but to put our trust in a great God!

What does the Lord want me to do today? If he wants me to pray for a certain person, that person will continually be on my mind and in my heart. Perhaps I am being asked to release that person to God in a new way.

To hear God's voice, it is essential to make time for silence, to be alone with the Love of my life. He loves you and he loves me and he is waiting eagerly for us to spend time with him. It may not be a long time, but it needs to be time totally given to hearing God's voice.

Lord Jesus, thank you for your presence. I want to learn to love you and to trust you more fully. Today, please show me how to order my priorities. Make it clear to me step by step what you would have me do. Help me to go about this day in peace and serenity, knowing that there is time to do what you have called me to do. I relax into your will and your plan for this day. Alleluia!

Thursday, October 22, 1998
Luke 12, 49-53
Jesus: A Cause of Division

So it's come to this. The Prince of Peace tells us that he has not come to earth to establish peace, but rather division. What on earth is going on?

What is going on earth is that it's going to get worse before it gets better! When I have a clean-up project, such as an area of the house, I usually begin by getting rid of things I no longer want or need. Then I look at what's left and try to reorganize it

For awhile, everything looks like a mess because it really is a mess! The mess is not my goal, but it is a necessary step in creating order out of chaos.

Jesus does not set out to create division. That is not his ultimate goal. However, there are some people who don't want either Jesus or his message. He is a threat to them. Bad news.

On the other hand, there are others who embrace Jesus and his message. Good news. You can imagine the chaos within a family when some are actively following Jesus and others are violently rejecting Jesus.

The message is always received according to the predisposition of the hearer. Do you remember the parable of the sower and the seed? There were several different kinds of soil. The "seed" (the word of God) was the same. The type of soil was the determining factor in how the seed was received.

We are, of course, imperfect human beings. Nevertheless, if we truly set out to follow Jesus, we will be a cause of division.

Remember the aged Simeon in the Temple of Jerusalem. At the presentation of the infant Jesus, Simeon said to Mary, "This child is destined for the fall and rise of many in Israel, and to be a sign that will be contradicted (and you yourself a sword will pierce) so that the thoughts of many hearts may be revealed (Luke 2, 34-35)."

Jesus and Mary know all about this business of being a sign of contradiction. They've been through it!

The more you bear the family resemblance, the more you will remind people of your big Brother, Jesus. The more you remind people of Jesus, the more you will be despised by and rejected by those who despise and reject Jesus.

Lord Jesus, help me today to focus on you and to love those around me. At the same time, help me not to be dependent on their approval. This life is not a contest of popularity, but rather a challenge to fidelity. I look to you, Lord Jesus, for your smile of approval. Alleluia!

Friday, October 23, 1998 St. John of Capistrano
Luke 12, 54-59
Signs of the Times; Settlement with an Opponent

I puzzled over this Gospel. Signs of the times.

Signs. A sign can announce something exciting! A sign can also warn us of danger.

I recall a newspaper photo used in a friend's homily. The photo was of a one-way sign pointing to a road which ended with a dead-end sign.

Very descriptive of how our lives sometimes seem! We may feel stuck, trapped, cornered, and afraid. How do we find a way through this difficulty?

Jesus has told us that he is the Way. The Way to the Father, yes, but also the Way to live our lives. He will not only show us the way, but he himself is the Way.

Lord Jesus, when we feel stuck, thank you for showing us the next step. Lead us to a deeper understanding of your love for us. Thank you for your plan to lead us to a place of renewal and refreshing. Alleluia!

Saturday, October 24, 1998 St. Anthony Mary Claret
Luke 13, 1-9
A Call to Repentance: The Parable of the Barren Fig Tree

There is an unstated common element that runs through the account of the slaughter of the Galileans, the reference to those killed by the tower, and the parable of the fig tree. What is this common element?

There seems to be a certain time of grace, a time to ponder and to repent. This time is a gift, but it does not last forever.

Pilate's successors may not take our blood, a tower may not fall on us, and we may not be cut down like the fig tree. However, for each of us, there will come a time of accountability.

My prayer is, "Lord, help me to do this day what You want me to do. Not necessarily what seems the most urgent, but what you ask me to do."

Increasingly, as I am called to write and to pray, there are distractions. The floor needs mopping. The bills need to be paid, phone calls need to be returned. On and on.

When I was running away from one of my first writing projects, the Lord reminded me of my negligence. The phone rang. It was someone from church, someone I really did not know that well. She asked me, "Are you working on your book?" Swallow. Gulp. Then other people "out of the blue" asked the same question.

Lord Jesus, I'm sorry for not being faithful to your call in this area of my life. Whether it's my writing or any other area of my life, help me to respond in trust and joyful obedience. Alleluia!

Sunday, October 25, 1998
Thirtieth Sunday in Ordinary Time
Luke 18, 9-14
The Parable of the Pharisee and the Tax Collector

This parable is addressed to those who were convinced of their own righteousness and looked down on others. It is significant that the Pharisee spoke the prayer "to himself."

The tax collector, on the other hand, stood far off and did not even presume to look up to heaven. Instead, he prayed, "O God, be merciful to me a sinner." He prayed out of a deep awareness of his need for God's mercy and forgiveness.

The Lord does not want us to be afraid of him, but he does want us to acknowledge our sinfulness and to cast ourselves on his mercy. He hears our prayer, forgives us, and raises us to a new position of trust in him and respect for ourselves.

Jesus said that humbling oneself leads to exaltation. In other words, God will engineer a promotion! On the other hand, exalting oneself leads to being brought low.

Lord Jesus, thank you for showering us with the mercy we need each day. Alleluia!

Monday, October 26, 1998
Luke 13, 10-17
Cure of a Crippled Woman on the Sabbath

The time had come! God's time. The time for this woman to be set free!

Wait, wait, wait, and pray, pray, pray if you are about to give up. God does hear you and God will answer in the very best way for you, and also at the very best time for you.

For the crippled woman, the time was on a Sabbath. The place was in the synagogue.

Jesus took the initiative. Jesus called to her and laid his hands on her. Glory! A new day. A new life. Surely she did not complain because Jesus healed her on a Sabbath. She stood up and praised God! Wouldn't you?

The synagogue leaders' reaction, however, told more about them than about Jesus. Instead of rejoicing with the woman, their first reaction was indignation because Jesus did not keep the "rules."

A word of caution. Beware the "inner Pharisee!" We each have one. We might have such thoughts as, "It's strange that God chose that particular person for that particular purpose." It is God's call and frankly none of our business.

Lord Jesus, thank you for healing this poor, crippled woman . Thank you for renewing hope within me that you see me today, you call to me today, and in your time and in your place, you will gloriously answer the cry of my heart to be set free. Alleluia!

Tuesday, October 27, 1998
Luke 13, 18-21
The Parable of the Mustard Seed; The Parable of the Yeast

Both parables in today's Gospel illustrate the tremendous power in obscurity. A period of obscurity is essential before results can be manifest. There needs to be a time and space for silence, when nothing seems to be happening, before the glory of God's plan can be unveiled.

The mustard seed, tiny enough to start with, was buried alive! Gone, into the ground, and seemingly forgotten. However, "when it was fully grown, it became a large bush and 'the birds of the sky dwelt in its branches.' "

God alone knows when we are "fully grown" and when the results of our secret prayers and longings will be made manifest. For the mustard seed, it was quite a change from being buried in the ground to being raised to display vigorous green leaves and strong branches to support the beautiful song birds flying to its shelter. God also has lovely surprises waiting for us when we are "fully grown."

Likewise, the yeast is "buried" in the dough. Its holding power permeates the dough and explodes with power. The fragrance of bread baking would not happen without the yeast. The hidden yeast is essential for the nourishing loaf of bread.

Our prayers may be all that some people have to nourish their souls. The stranger on the autumn leaf-strewn street for whom we feel led to pray. The unhappy driver pushing through traffic. The tense, anxious person waiting in the dentist's office. Our presence and our prayers can be used by God to transform their lives.

Lord Jesus, help me to understand today that nothing is small, nothing is hidden, nothing is insignificant with you. Take my life, my yearning, my prayers and provide shelter for another's soul and nourishment for another's spirit. One day you may show me the results. For now, let me be content to remain, like the mustard seed and the yeast, hidden in perplexity and obscurity. Alleluia!

Wednesday, October 28, 1998 Sts. Simon and Jude
Luke 6, 12-16
The Mission of the Twelve

Jesus chose Twelve. He chose Peter first.

Peter, Peter, Peter. Peter is always listed first. Is Peter the "Teacher's pet?" Is Peter better than the other disciples?

I don't think so. Jesus saw in Peter someone who was full of life. Full of eagerness. Full of faults. Full of righteous indignation, sometimes inappropriately expressed!

It was Peter, shortly before the crucifixion of Jesus, who cut off the ear of Malchus, the servant of the high priest (John 18, 10, 26). However, it was also Peter who was the first to say to Jesus, "You are the Messiah, the Son of the living God (Matthew 16, 16)."

If Jesus could work in the life of this rough Galilean fisherman, this emotional, hasty, impetuous hothead, he could work in the life of anyone. Jesus chose Peter.

JESUS chose Peter. Jesus CHOSE Peter, Jesus chose PETER!

Jesus chooses you. Jesus chooses me. Believe me, Jesus is up to the challenge of his choice.

Jesus has a particular message he wants to speak through your life. Jesus has a particular message he wants to speak through my life.

Jesus wants to shine forth in our lives! Jesus wants to love and to heal others through our lives.

All glory and praise to you, Lord Jesus Christ. Let your purpose for our lives come closer to fulfillment today. Shine through us. Alleluia!

Thursday, October 29, 1998
Luke 13, 31-35
Herod's Desire to Kill Jesus; Lament over Jerusalem

Jesus' opinion of the Pharisees was pretty clear as was his opinion of the king. He called King Herod "that fox."

Not politically correct! No schmoozing here. No flattering of those who consider themselves in control.

Jesus calls it as he sees it. He knows who is truly in charge -- his heavenly Father. He knows what awaits him in Jerusalem. He will suffer and be killed at the hands of the religious leaders.

He has set his face like flint towards Jerusalem (Isaiah 50, 7, Luke 9, 51) and will not turn back. He will not be deterred from accomplishing his mission, in spite of his grief over Jerusalem.

Jerusalem. "Jerusalem, Jerusalem, you who kill the prophets and stone those sent to you, how many times I yearned to gather your children together as a hen gathers her brood under her wings, but you were unwilling!"

Lord Jesus, we put our trust in you and thank you for showing us what the "next step" is on our journey to you. Help us set our face like flint to fulfill your purpose in our lives. Help us not to be deterred by opposition from without or by grief from within. Thank you that you will finish the work you have begun in us. Alleluia!

Friday, October 30, 1998
Luke 14, 1-6
Healing of the Man with Dropsy on the Sabbath

The people at this Sabbath meal were watching Jesus very closely! After all, Jesus had this irritating habit of expressing his compassion by healing all sorts of odd people at all sorts of odd times.

Would he do something they considered unlawful today? After all, there was a man suffering from dropsy right in front of him.

Jesus responded to this unspoken question by asking a question of his own, another of his irritating habits. "Is it lawful to cure on the sabbath or not?"

There was no answer. The silence spoke volumes.

Jesus, of course, healed the suffering person and then squared off with the Pharisees. He asked them if they would rescue their own son or even their ox on a Sabbath. Again, no answer.

According to St. Ambrose, "not only for every idle word, but for every idle silence must man render an account." The Pharisees had again chosen their careful keeping of rules over compassion in action.

Lord Jesus, today, let me be an instrument of your healing. Help me to be courageous in my compassion and leave the consequences with you. Alleluia!

Saturday, October 31, 1998
Luke 14, 1, 7-11
Healing of the Man with Dropsy on the Sabbath;
Conduct of Invited Guests and Hosts

Jesus said that humbling oneself leads to being exalted and that exalting oneself leads to being humbled. In Eugene Peterson's The Message, this verse reads, "If you're content to simply be yourself, you will become more than yourself."

I believe this is the key -- to be myself and to trust in the Lord to place me where I am meant to be. This is not a matter of striving to be humble. It is a matter of focusing on the Lord and then being free to serve others.

It means not being obsessed with what I think others are thinking about me. That's between them and God.

People who are truly great in God's eyes are wonderfully natural and very easy to be with. They are truly concerned for others. They are not preoccupied with their own concerns.

Lord Jesus, today, I am aware of only some of my sins, faults, and failures. You are aware of all of them! You still love me and invite me to come to you, to be forgiven, and to be transformed. Help me today to rest in you and trust in you as I go about my day (the open air market, Mass, writing, baking, lap swimming, etc.), and to know that I am loved as I am. Alleluia!

Sunday, November 1, 1998 All Saints
Matthew 5, 1-12
The Sermon on the Mount: The Beatitudes

The long view. The big picture. Heaven.

In the beatitudes, Jesus gives us the reason for our rejoicing. If we are insulted and suffer persecution for our faith in Jesus, we are to rejoice. "Rejoice and be glad, for your reward will be great in heaven. Thus they persecuted the prophets who were before you."

I used to visualize the prophets as those fiery spiritual giants who probably had long beards and went around thundering against the "establishment." Maybe and maybe not.

The gift of prophecy goes far beyond saying, "Thus saith the Lord." St. Paul exhorts us, "Pursue love, but strive eagerly for the spiritual gifts, above all that you may prophesy (1 Corinthians 14, 1)." I believe that's because the person who prophesies "builds up the church (1 Corinthians 14, 4)."

Are you a prophet? Am I?

To be a prophet is to pay a price. Prophets can be rough around the edges. They speak forth God's words, but they do so within the framework of their own wounded and frayed humanity.

70

Lord Jesus, are you speaking to me today through one of your prophets? Please help me to hear your voice. Are you trying to speak your words through me today? Help me to rejoice and be glad. Alleluia!

Monday, November 2, 1998 All Souls
Luke 23, 33, 39-43
The Crucifixion

"Jesus, I want to be with you." This cry comes from the heart of the penitent thief when he says, "Jesus, remember me when you come into your kingdom." All this poor man knows is that wherever Jesus is going, he wants to be there, too. He trusts in Jesus. He knows that Jesus' kingdom is not of this world.

When this cry arises from my heart, "Jesus, I want to be with you," it does not mean necessarily that I want to leave this earth. It means that I long for the kingdom life of Jesus to be active in my life here on earth.

"Jesus, I want to be with you." The Lord responds, "You are already with me and I am with you. Be patient with yourself and rest in my love. Go out into the world today rejoicing." Alleluia!

Tuesday, November 3, 1998 St. Martin de Porres
Luke 14, 15-24
The Parable of the Great Feast

Jesus continues to teach about social etiquette. He instructs the host to invite "the poor, the crippled, the lame, the blind ... " Although they would not be able to reciprocate, the generous host would be repaid at the resurrection.

In today's Gospel, Jesus zeroes in on the response of those invited to the festive dinner. Those who considered the invitation of negligible value made excuses and sent their regrets. They had absolutely no understanding of the significance of the invitation. The ones who probably never expected to receive invitations were the very ones welcomed into the banquet hall with open arms.

This parable is often said to illustrate Israel's rejection of Jesus as Messiah. When rejected by his own people, Jesus then extended the invitation to the poor, the "insignificant," and even to the Gentiles, who were considered the "outsiders."

This could be called a parable of the insiders and the outsiders. If we consider ourselves insiders, Jesus wants us to reach out to the poor and needy. If we realize that we are the poor and needy, we may rejoice because our invitation is in the mail! Alleluia!

Wednesday, November 4, 1998 St. Charles Borromeo
Luke 14, 25-33
Sayings on Discipleship

Jesus is speaking, not to the inner core of his committed disciples, but to the great crowds following him. He is being ruthlessly honest about what it really means to be his disciple.

"Whoever does not carry his own cross and come after me cannot be my disciple." CANNOT. It is not our neighbor's cross we have to carry. It is our own cross.

What is our cross? Someone jokingly said that this refers to one's mother-in-law. Another said, more seriously, that it refers to God's will for one's life.

What is my cross? I believe that my cross is whatever suffering comes into my life as a result of my commitment to follow Jesus. I can squawk and cry and scream and phone my friends to pray away my cross. Or I can be still and receive the Lord's strength to carry my cross. Alleluia!

Thursday, November 5, 1998
Luke 15, 1-10
The Parable of the Lost Sheep; The Parable of the Lost Coin

The sinners and the tax collectors were trying to be near Jesus and to listen to him. They knew that he was their friend and that he would help them.

The Pharisees were fussing about Jesus hanging out with the ones they considered "low life." Therefore, it was to the Pharisees that Jesus addressed these parables.

For me, these are parables of completion. The owner of the sheep and the owner of the coin may not have really needed to find what they had lost. The sheep was only one in ten. The coin was only one in ten. Still, there was a deep yearning to seek and to find the lost.

Recently, I misplaced a small crucifix. It did not have great monetary value, but it did have great personal significance. Eventually I found it and great was the rejoicing!

Jesus was trying to tell the Pharisees that no one is expendable in the eyes of the heavenly Father. God the Father keeps yearning over the lost one. Like the owner of the sheep and the owner of the coin, God rejoices when the lost one is found. Indeed the angels rejoice when one sinner repents.

Lord Jesus, we are aware of our sinfulness before you and our need to repent. Let us also remember that, when we repent, there is rejoicing in heaven over us. Alleluia!

Friday, November 6, 1998
Luke 16, 1-8
The Parable of the Dishonest Steward; Application of the Parable

Jesus closed this parable with the observation that " … the children of this world are more prudent in dealing with their own generation than are the children of light." The crafty steward was commended for acting prudently in a crisis situation. He was not commended, however, for his original squandering of his employer's resources.

Jesus cautioned his followers, "... I am sending you like sheep in the midst of wolves; so be shrewd as serpents and simple as doves (Matthew 10, 16)." Jesus wants us to be careful managers of all our resources.

In our relationship to this world, Jesus instructs us to be gentle and amiable, yet cautious and discerning. This is a balancing act for which the Holy Spirit will gladly give us the wisdom.

Lord Jesus, with you all things are possible. Thank you that you will enable us to serve you wisely. Alleluia!

Saturday, November 7, 1998
Luke 16, 9-15
Application of the Parable; A Saying Against the Pharisees

Jesus said, "For where your treasure is, there also will your heart be (Luke 12, 34)." If we are lovingly tethered to the Lord, we will have his wisdom in the use of the things of this world. We will be able to enjoy the good things of this world without being enslaved by them. The Lord is our real and lasting treasure!

There is an puzzling injunction in today's Gospel to "make friends for yourselves with dishonest wealth, so that when it fails, you will be welcomed into eternal dwellings." What does that mean? This is one of those puzzling sayings that I continue to ponder.

Jesus also reminded us that if we are trustworthy in small matters, we will also be trustworthy in great matters. On the other hand, if we are dishonest in small matters, we will also be dishonest in great matters. "No servant can serve two masters. He will either hate one and love the other, or be devoted to one and despise the other. You cannot serve God and mammon." The term "mammon" is more than a reference to material wealth. It refers to that in which we place our trust.

If, instead of being tethered to the Lord, we are tied to the things of this world by a rough, coarse rope, we will get spiritual "splinters." This is because we are constantly clenching and clutching what can never satisfy.

"The Pharisees, who loved money, heard all these things and sneered at him. And he said to them, 'You justify yourselves in the sight of others, but God know your hearts; for what is of human esteem is an abomination in the sight of God.' "

Lord Jesus, I don't yet understand all of this parable. Sometimes, I think I don't really trust you. Forgive me for the underlying fear and pride. Thank you for your mercy and your compassion as you gently guide me to a deeper level of trust. Alleluia!

Sunday, November 8, 1998
Thirty-second Sunday in Ordinary Time
Luke 20, 27-38
The Question about the Resurrection

Jesus speaks of the present age and the age to come. In this present time, people marry and remarry. In the age to come, there is no marriage.

Sometimes the curtain is briefly drawn, as it were, and we have glimpses into the eternal. Perhaps it happens on a retreat. Perhaps it is looking into the eyes of someone we love. The love and the power of God break through and we are living in the eternal.

Truly, "... he is not God of the dead, but of the living, for to him all are alive." I find this very reassuring when I become gloomy and filled with anxious thoughts.

In the hallway at home, there is a dimmer switch we leave on at night. There is just the tiniest bit of light always there. In the morning, I turn off this light. The new day has come. The dim light is no longer needed.

In God's time, the New Day will dawn for each of us and we will no longer need this earthlight. Let us rejoice and trust and live this day to the fullest. Alleluia!

Monday, November 9, 1998
Dedication of St. John Lateran Basilica in Rome
John 2, 13-22
Cleansing of the Temple

"Stop making my Father's house a marketplace." Jesus was furious about what was taking place, in the name of God, in the temple. He drove out the moneychangers and ordered them to stop their travesty.

Today, in ways subtle and sometimes not so subtle, God's "temple" is being profaned. There are always those who care little for God. They have somehow arrived at positions of leadership and authority and care only about defending their power. They care little or nothing about loving God and serving God's people.

We are not responsible for removing them. God is. We are to respect their office and to pray for them. We are not to imitate them.

In Jesus' day, the "anawim," the "little people" prayed and stayed faithful to God. Perhaps Jesus had them in mind as he drove out the corrupt money changers.

Jesus' final triumph was that he himself was the true temple! "Destroy this temple and in three days I will raise it up." It is to Jesus that we look. No one can prevent us from going to Jesus. It is Jesus, our crucified and risen Lord, whom we worship. Alleluia!

Tuesday, November 10, 1998 St. Leo the Great
Luke 17, 7-10
Attitude of a Servant

It's fun to go out for dinner (or breakfast, morning coffee, lunch, or afternoon tea). It doesn't have to be expensive. It's just refreshing to go "elsewhere" and to have attentive servers bring ice water and fresh bread to the table. Then there's the fun of studying the menu and making the big decision. There might be a bit of negotiating, such as, "If you get the lasagna, I'll get the scampi."

Those who greet us at the door, escort us to our table, take our order, and prepare our food are all paid to do these things. It's their job! Their attitude is also part of their job. It just wouldn't do to walk into your favorite restaurant and be yelled at and told, "Get lost. I don't 'feel' like serving you today." No, we expect to be treated politely.

The servants in today's Gospel are expected to serve their employers first and to take their own meals later. Although we are the sons and daughters of the living God, we are also God's servants.

> "Yes, like the eyes of a servant
>   on the hand of his master,
> Like the eyes of a maid
>   on the hand of her mistress,
> So our eyes are on the LORD our God,
>   till we are shown favor (Psalm 123, 2)."

Our attitude is ever to be attentive to what God would have us say and do. Jesus is speaking to his faithful, committed disciples in this Gospel.

Lord Jesus, I need an attitude check today. I've been so preoccupied with my own needs and those of others that I have not looked to YOU as the absolute sovereign. Please forgive me, adjust my attitude, and help me to be completely attentive and obedient to you. Alleluia!

Wednesday, November 11, 1998 St. Martin of Tours
Luke 17, 11-17
The Cleansing of Ten Lepers

Jesus speaks a word of command to the lepers and they are all healed! He doesn't say, "Oh, I'm so sorry for you and I'm going to heal you."

No, what he says is, "Go show yourselves to the priests." It was as they obeyed and were going to the priests that they were actually healed or cleansed. They didn't hang around looking at their skin to decide whether or not they were healed. They ran with the word of Jesus!

It's the same with us. Jesus does things in his own way. He is always ahead of us. He asks us to be a step ahead of our feelings and our circumstances. We are to praise him now, before he solves our current dilemma, before we are healed, and before we can see anything happening.

Lord Jesus, I need you so much today! I cry out to you for cleansing. Cleanse me of my weariness, my doubts, and my fears. Thank you for all you are doing in my life, whether or not I can see anything at all. I put all my trust in you. When the answer is made fully visible, please remind me to fall at your feet and to give you all the glory. Alleluia!

Thursday, November 12, 1998 St. Josaphat
Luke 17, 20-25
The Coming of the Kingdom of God;
The Day of the Son of Man

"The kingdom of God is among you." It is not just "out there" somewhere. The kingdom of God means that God is truly sovereign in our lives.

The "day" of the Son of Man, however, will come suddenly. To be prepared, we must already be living with God as our sovereign. God must be absolutely first in our lives.

In his first coming, Jesus, the Son of Man and Son of God, lived, loved, and suffered as a servant. He was rejected by his own people and was crucified by those who should have comprehended his identity and worshipped him.

When Jesus returns, it's going to be a different story! He will return as our triumphant, victorious KING!

Lord Jesus, as we wait and work, we gaze upon you. You are coming in glory! Our present trials will be over. We will be with you for ever and ever. Please send your Holy Spirit to energize us, forgive us, heal us, and set us free to be and to do all you have called us to be and to do. Alleluia!

Friday, November 13, 1998 St. Frances Cabrini
Luke 17, 26-37
The Day of the Son of Man

Business as usual. People were "…eating, drinking, buying, selling, planting, building; on the day when Lot left Sodom, fire and brimstone rained from the sky to destroy them all. So it will be on the day the Son of Man is revealed."

Jesus tells us over and over, "Be ready." We're not to dwell in a crisis mentality, but we are to be ready.

The key to being ready is found in Jesus' words, "Whoever seeks to preserve his life will lose it, but whoever loses it will save it." Our lives must be constantly surrendered to the Lord.

77

This mindset has to be "practiced" every day. Whether one is a child practicing scales on the piano or a famous concert pianist, it is still necessary to practice daily.

We are not to lose heart. Jesus is coming!

Lord Jesus, today, I release any imaginary control I may think I have over my life. You've been in control all along. Only occasionally have I been trusting enough to realize it. Today, I want to trust you in a new way. Alleluia!

Saturday, November 14, 1998
Luke 18, 1-8
Parable of the Persistent Widow

Sometimes this is referred to as the parable of the unjust judge. Fixating on the unjust judge may stir up feelings of anger, fear and futility.

Reflecting instead on the trust of this persistent woman instills courage and trust in us. She is gutsy and she refuses to give up!

What about you? Is there an "unjust judge" in your life who has seemingly deprived you of what the Lord says is yours?

Go directly to the Supreme Court of Heaven. God has already won your case! The earthly judge may try to get rid of you by ridicule or abuse. God, however, will lift you up, embrace you, heal you, and restore you.

What is your part? Don't give up! Trust aggressively in the Lord and in his power on your behalf. His plans for you will succeed. Psalm 27, 14 says,

"Wait for the LORD, take courage;
   be stouthearted, wait for the
LORD!" Alleluia!

Sunday, November 15, 1998
Thirty-third Sunday in Ordinary Time
Luke 21, 5-19
The Destruction of the Temple Foretold;
The Signs of the End; The Coming Persecution

Consider the "nots" in this Gospel. Jesus offers us a very healthy way to think.

The magnificent temple in Jerusalem? Of all its costly stones, not one will escape destruction.

False teachers? Jesus says that we are not to be deceived, even if they come in his name. We are not to follow them.

Wars and insurrections? We are not to be terrified. Jesus also refers to "powerful earthquakes, famines, and plagues from place to place; and awesome sights and mighty signs" from the sky.

Persecution? Jesus says not to prepare a defense statement beforehand. Jesus himself will give wisdom that cannot be refuted.

Betrayal by those near and dear? Jesus says that "not a hair of your head will be destroyed."

Jesus says, "By your perseverance you will secure your lives." Alleluia!

Monday, November 16, 1998 St. Margaret of Scotland
Luke 18, 35-43
The Healing of the Blind Beggar

I can't see anything, but, Jesus, I know you are near. I'm shouting out to you for help!

In a situation where I can't see a way out, a solution, a resolution, all I can do is to cry out to Jesus. Help!

The crowd was impatient with the blind beggar and told him to hush. He ignored them and kept on crying out to Jesus. Like the persistent widow in Luke 18, he refused to give up.

Jesus, I feel poor like the beggar. What can I bring you except my rags, my sins?

Jesus, I feel blind and hollow. I can't see a way out. Just as you compassionately singled out the blind beggar and helped him, please hear my own cries to you. With the blind beggar, I pray, "Lord, please let me see." Let me see this situation as you see it, and then, Lord, help me to follow you and give you glory. Alleluia!

Tuesday, November 17, 1998 St. Elizabeth of Hungary
Luke 19, 1-10
Zacchaeus the Tax Collector

Zacchaeus was very real and transparent. He let it all hang out.

Look at what he did. Being realistic and recognizing the limitations of his height, he was enterprising enough to run ahead of the crowd and quickly climb a sycamore tree.

Better viewing up there! Clearly he was more concerned with seeing Jesus than he was with safeguarding his own dignity.

When Jesus spoke to him, he "came down quickly and received him with joy." When others criticized Jesus' action, Zacchaeus boldly stood his ground and proclaimed, "Behold, half of my possessions, Lord, I shall give to the poor, and if I have extorted anything from anyone I shall repay it four times over."

In essence, he confessed his sins and made superabundant restitution. He really went whole hog over his Jesus-encounter!

Jesus announced, "Today salvation has come to this house because this man too is a descendant of Abraham. For the Son of Man has come to seek and to save what was lost."

Lord Jesus, help me to be real before you just as Zacchaeus was real. Help me to seek you today more than ever. Help me to confess whatever stands in the way of our relationship. I need you, Lord. Come to my house today. Alleluia!

Thursday, November 18, 1998
Dedication of Churches of Sts. Peter and Paul
Luke 19, 11-28
The Parable of the Ten Gold Coins

God has a perfect time for every person and every event in this universe. I need to stop wasting time and energy by worrying.

Lord Jesus, forgive me for fretting about everything from famines to fallen national leaders. Forgive me for being a poor steward of the resources you have entrusted to me. I have squandered time, money, and talents. Today, Lord, I come before you to thank you for all you have given to me. Show me how to live this day. Let your love and power shine through me. Alleluia!

Thursday, November 19, 1998
Luke 19, 41-44
The Lament over Jerusalem

Jesus wept at the tomb of his friend, Lazarus. He also wept over Jerusalem. Jerusalem did not recognize the time of God's visitation.

At the tomb of Lazarus, Jesus called, "Lazarus, come out (John 11, 43)!" Lazarus emerged from the tomb. Jesus then instructed the mourners themselves to untie him and let him go free from his tomb and from his grave wrappings.

At the tomb of Lazarus, Jesus had been surrounded by his friends, Mary and Martha, who were stunned and desolate at their brother's death. Nevertheless, gutsy Martha boldly stated her belief that Lazarus would rise " ' ... in the resurrection on the last day (John 11, 24).' "

As Jesus wept over Jerusalem, he was surrounded, not by friends, but by the hostile religious leaders (the chief priests, elders, and experts in the Jewish traditions) who were so closed in mind and heart that they could not see the answer, in flesh, to their prayers for the Messiah. He was in their midst and they did not recognize him!

How many times does Jesus weep because I do not recognize him in the answer to my prayer? Perhaps I did not like the answer. Perhaps the answer was not what I expected. How many times was disaster averted because the Lord removed me from danger which I was too blind to see?

Lord Jesus, open my eyes to see YOU as the answer. Let me be open today to your visitation in my life. Alleluia!

Friday, November 20 , 1998
Luke 19, 45-48
The Cleansing of the Temple

The tears of the Lord Jesus Christ preceded his anger. Before Jesus drove the merchants out of the temple, he wept over Jerusalem. He saw the suffering which lay ahead because Jerusalem did not recognize the time of the Lord's visitation.

The account of the cleansing of the temple, recorded in all four Gospels, is sometimes said to portray Jesus' anger and righteous indignation. "It is written, 'My house shall be a house of prayer, but you have made it a den of thieves.' "

You and I are now the "temple" of God. St. Paul said, "Do you not know that you are the temple of God, and that the Spirit of God dwells in you? If anyone destroys God's temple, God will destroy that person, for the temple of God, which you are, is holy (I Corinthians 3, 16-17)."

Jesus was furious that the temple in Jerusalem was being misused. It was meant to be a house of prayer, but it was being diverted from its purpose.

What is it within the temple of my life that is diverting me from being "a house of prayer?" Am I too busy with the work of the Lord that I neglect spending time in silent adoration of the Lord of the work?

Lord Jesus, please let my life today reflect the fact that I am your temple and that your Spirit dwells within me. Alleluia!

Saturday, November 21, 1998
Presentation of the Blessed Virgin Mary
Luke 20, 27-40
Paying Taxes to the Emperor; The Question of the Resurrection

Glory! A verse about glory came to mind as I read today's Gospel. "All of us, gazing with unveiled face on the glory of the Lord, are being transformed into the same image from glory to glory, as from the Lord, who is the Spirit (2 Corinthians 3, 18)." Transformation is taking place while we are still in this earthly life.

The "earthly" is not bad, but it's just temporary. It's a prelude to a world beyond our wildest imaginations. We have so much ahead of us!

Remembering that Jesus struggled, we refuse to lose heart in our own struggles Jesus struggled not only with blatant unbelievers, but, more tragically, with the established religious leaders who were determined to discredit him. He saw through them and answered them with wisdom given by his heavenly Father.

This same wisdom is available to us today through the power of the Holy Spirit. Take heart! The battle is not ours, really, but the Lord's. The Lord has already won!

As we struggle with foes within and foes without, we do so with the sure knowledge that we are victorious. In Jesus, we have the victory. Praise his name!

Lord Jesus, please comfort us when we feel defeated by the powers of this passing world. Raise our eyes to heaven to see your smile and your welcoming embrace. Alleluia!

Sunday, November 22, 1998 Christ the King
Luke 23, 35- 43
The Crucifixion

Christ the King. Power? A purple robe? A crown? An earthly kingdom?

No. Instead, our King hangs on a cross. Powerless. Naked. Blood streaming from his crown of thorns. Blood issuing from his poor, scourged body.

A kingdom? Terrifying though it is, Jesus has come into his kingdom. "Thy kingdom come, thy will be done on earth as it is in heaven." The kingdom exists when and where the will of God is being carried out. Jesus, by the willing sacrifice of himself on the cross, is carrying out God's will for our salvation.

No. there was no other way.

Jesus, my King, I stand at the foot of your cross and worship you. May your kingdom come and your will be done in my life today. Alleluia!

Monday, November 23, 1998
Sts. Clement I, Columban and Bl. Miguel Pro
Luke 21, 1-4
The Poor Widow's Contribution

The "poor widow" may be a CEO. The "poor widow" may be a teenage cheerleader. The "poor widow" may be pursuing postdoctoral research at the university hospital and medical school. Whatever the "outer" vocation, the "poor widow" is anyone who acknowledges total dependence upon God and is willing to give all, in loving trust and abandonment to God. Alleluia!

Tuesday, November 24, 1998
St. Andrew Dung-Lac and Companions
Luke 21, 5-11
The Destruction of the Temple Foretold; The Signs of the End

If this Gospel sounds familiar, it is! This was the Gospel of the Sunday before last. We are approaching Advent through the back door.

Before the coming of Jesus as an infant, we are reading blood curdling, scary predictions of destruction and natural disasters.

At the pool where I used to lap swim, I would occasionally see Eva, a remarkably beautiful, holy woman who was fascinated by prophecies of the end times. Three days of darkness was the prediction of one writer. Even more frightening was the prediction that we would all see the darkness of our own hearts. Eva wasn't being morbid when she spoke of these predictions. She was a joyful person who brought laughter and hope into the lives of all around her. She truly concentrated on loving and serving the Lord and every person who crossed her path. We found out later that she gave $2 bills to beggars.

Eva is with the Lord now. She died quite suddenly, but she was quite prepared. Her memorial Mass was crowded, joyful, and triumphant. Eva had quietly and quickly slipped from this life to the next.

Father, thank you for Eva. She loved you and spoke of you, whether she was at Mass, at the swimming pool, or at the market. Help me today to trust you for the future. Eva did not have to experience the three days darkness or any of those other predictions. Maybe I won't either. Or, if I do, you will be there with me. Help me not to focus on predictions of this or that, but to focus on you. Alleluia!

Wednesday, November 25, 1998 St. Catherine of Alexandria
Luke 21, 12-19
The Coming Persecution

Fear not. When I read passages like this one, I have two choices. I can give way to fears of torture, concentration camps and terrible suffering. Or, I can look back in my life and remember situations, dark and fearsome though they were, and praise God for his deliverance.

Jesus told his followers that persecution, whether in the synagogue or in a prison, would lead to their giving testimony. He specifically said not to prepare a defense statement.

Years ago, I was in a situation in a conference room where a kangaroo court was being played out. The testimony I gave was blunt and was not well-received. At the time it seemed a death experience. I had unwisely placed my trust in those who were pursuing their own agendas.

Some time later, in a healing service, the Lord showed me this experience in a new way. He showed me that he had been there all along and had led me out of that conference room through a door filled with light. When I looked back, not a wise idea, considering the fate of Lot's wife, (Genesis 19, 26), I "saw" the people still at the table, but surrounded with prison bars. Glancing back one last time, all was darkness in that room. The Lord had led me out the door into the light.

I am now walking in that light. The Lord truly delivered me from a situation of darkness into his marvelous light.

Fear not. He will tell you what to say. He will lead you to a new life. Alleluia!

Thursday, November 26, 1998 Thanksgiving Day (U.S.A.)
Mark 5, 18-20
The Healing of the Gerasene Demoniac

Strange reading for Thanksgiving Day. Alternate lectionary selections were tempting! Staring down this text and then letting the text stare me down is beginning to yield a fruitful harvest,

This little passage is the conclusion of the healing or the deliverance of the Gerasene demoniac. This poor man had an unclean spirit and roamed around tombs crying and hurting himself. "Legion" was the name which indicated the presence of numerous demons within him.

Jesus simply commanded the unclean spirit to come out of the man. Naturally the man wanted to stay with Jesus! Who wouldn't? Jesus had set him free from the tormenting spirits.

Jesus, however, had another plan. Jesus told him to go back home to his family and to tell them of the merciful Lord's great favor. As the man proclaimed all that Jesus had done for him, the people were just amazed.

We may feel that we don't have anything quite so dramatic to proclaim. However, when others can see how Jesus has intervened on our behalf, sometimes after many years of waiting, patient or otherwise, they too will be just amazed. Imagine that!

Lord Jesus, today, let others see you at work in my life. I give you thanks for all you have done for me, all you are doing for me today, and all that you plan to do in the future. Be glorified in my life. Alleluia!

Friday, November 27, 1998
Luke 21, 20-33
The Demand for a Sign

Jonah was a sign to the people of Ninevah. Jesus, the Son of Man, was a sign to his own generation. You and I are called to be a sign to everyone around us, a sign of God's presence and power.

Signs are also related to judgment and to repentance. The people of Ninevah repented at Jonah's message and were spared from destruction.

When Jesus came to earth, some believed him and received him. Others refused to believe him and to receive him. As Simeon had foretold, Jesus was "a sign that will be contradicted (Luke 2, 34)."

We often see only our sins and failures. However, if we are truly following the Lord, the light of the Holy Spirit is shining through us and we are, even now, signs of God's presence and power.

Lord Jesus, let me be a sign to point others to you. Let there be something about my life to show that you are active and present. Alleluia!

Saturday, November 28, 1998
Luke 21, 34-36
Exhortation to be Vigilant

On this last day of the Church year, it happens that this is the last page in my loose leaf notebook! One of God's "coincidences."

One day we will be living on the last page of our lives. With my notebook, I didn't realize how close I was getting to the last page. How close am I to the last page of my earthly life? I don't know.

However, I do know that I want to live differently this Advent. Jesus said not to let our hearts become drowsy. He said to be vigilant, to pray for strength, and to stand before him.

We are waiting, yes, but Jesus is waiting too. He is waiting with us and waiting for us. Waiting for his perfect plan for our lives to be realized.

Recently, during a time of quiet prayer, I knew that Jesus was beside me, his arm around me, waiting with me. I remembered a line from the hymn, "I Heard the Voice of Jesus Say." I remembered the invitation to rest.

Before we can be alert, vigilant, pray, and stand, we would be wise to take a moment to rest our entire being upon Jesus. He is already here waiting for us and waiting with us. He will lead us through this Advent . He will lead us into his kingdom. Alleluia!

Sunday, November 29, 1998 First Sunday of Advent - Year A
Matthew 24, 31-44
The Unknown Day and Hour

Be prepared! Stay awake. Only the Father knows the exact day and hour when Jesus the Son will return. Today's Gospel tells us that just as things looked rather ho-hum right up until the flood in Noah's day, it would be just like that when the Son of Man came back.

On the day before Thanksgiving, I wasn't thinking of this Gospel injunction to be prepared, but I'm certainly thinking of it now. For me, being prepared means to keep short accounts in all my relationships.

The day before Thanksgiving, I was driving along a busy expressway. Normally, I really do try, in this extremely competitive area, to drive courteously. I blew that resolve that day!

The car ahead of me was in the right lane. Signaling left, it stopped. I blew my resolve along with the horn. The driver started gesturing wildly, so I pulled over to see what was going on. The driver was an older woman who angrily asked if I had noticed her emergency lights. I apologized and offered to phone for help. She carried a cell phone and had already done so. We parted in friendship rather than in anger. Lord, forgive me.

Keeping relationships in order is mandatory. St. Paul said, "If possible, on your part, live at peace with all (Romans 12, 18)."

Lord Jesus, when you return, help me to be as caught up as possible in all my relationships. Forgive me and help me to forgive others, leaving the outcome to you. Alleluia!

Monday, November 30, 1998 St. Andrew
Matthew 4, 18-22
The Call of the First Disciples

Andrew and Peter were casting a net into the Sea of Galilee when Jesus called them. They were not on a silent retreat seeking God's will for their lives.

Good, honest, simple, and shrewd, they were out there in the busy world doing what they had to do to earn a living. Jesus found them and called them to a new life with himself.

Where are you right now? Are you restlessly wishing you could be somewhere else? Are you happy in your daily round or are you wishing for an elusive, unknown "something else?"

Stay where you are. Stay faithful to your present task. The Lord will either change your understanding of your work or will change your work. Be faithful at your present task, but look to Jesus for your hope and expectation. Jesus will never disappoint you.

Our King and Savior has drawn near to us. Let us worship and adore him. Alleluia!

Tuesday, December 1, 1998 Advent Weekday
Luke 10, 21-24
Praise of the Father; Privileges of Discipleship

The childlike do not scoff. They are grateful for what they have been given and incorporate the new gift into their lives at once.

The seemingly wise and the learned, on the other hand, sometimes form a committee to analyze and discuss the relative merits of what Jesus called "these things." They decide to study the issue and issue a statement.

Is it any wonder Jesus chose to reveal the treasures of the kingdom of God to the little ones, the humble ones of this world? They were simple enough to take him at his word and to obey him.

Jesus warned us not to cast our "pearls" before "swine." "Do not give what is holy to dogs, or throw your pearls before swine, lest they trample them underfoot, and turn and tear you to pieces (Matthew 7, 6)." Those who have closed their hearts to Jesus are not capable of receiving his treasures.

Lord Jesus, thank you for your treasures. Today, please help me to understand in a deeper way who the Father really is. Heal me of any misconceptions and fears hidden deep within my heart. Let there be a new release of hope, trust, and joy in my life today. Alleluia

Wednesday, December 2, 1998 Advent Weekday
Matthew 15, 29-37
The Healing of Many People; The Feeding of the Four Thousand

"Great crowds came to him, having with them the lame, the blind, the deformed, the mute, and many others." In their diseased conditions, they came to Jesus. Jesus transformed them into people who were whole.

The lame, the blind, the deformed, and the mute. I used to think of them as merely poor, unfortunate people. It was too bad they had all those problems.

After years of foot problems, I can now identify with "the lame." What if I came to Jesus in my big, sturdy, clunky shoes and left dancing in delicate pink ballerina slippers?

The blind? Even with glasses or contact lens, I still can't see as Jesus sees. Sometimes I misplace my best glasses and then use the old glasses to go around the house searching for the good ones. I need new vision to see as Jesus sees.

The deformed? How am I crippled? I may have crippled emotions as well as a crippled body. Jesus can heal me.

The hungry? Am I starving to know Jesus in a deeper way? Jesus used whatever was available (such as loaves and fishes) to feed a multitude. He didn't grab a cell phone and ring up the nearest deli for pita and gefilte. Jesus still takes whatever we have, blesses it, breaks it, and uses it to feed others.

Lord Jesus, I need you today. Please heal me, fill me with your Holy Spirit, and then use me to heal and feed others. I trust in you. Alleluia!

Thursday, December 3, 1998 St. Francis Xavier
Matthew 7, 21, 24-27
The True Disciple; The Two Foundations

Jesus said, "Everyone who listens to these words of mine and acts on them will be like a wise man who built his house on rock." The term "these words" refers to the instructions in righteousness, or right living, found in Matthew 5-7.

In Matthew 7, we see Jesus telling us not to judge others and to be cautious and discreet in sharing our spiritual treasures. He told us to persevere in prayer, follow the "Golden Rule," and beware of false prophets.

We are not simply to say, "Lord, Lord" and listen passively to the words of Jesus. We are to put his words into action.

Lord Jesus, please show me how to put "these words" into practice in my life today. Alleluia!

Friday, December 4, 1998 St. John of Damascus
Matthew 9, 27-31
The Healing of Two Blind Men

"Let it be done for you according to your faith." Or, as The Message says, "Become what you believe."

Let's look at the sequence of events. The blind men followed Jesus, called him by the messianic title, "Son of David," and then asked him for pity or compassion.

Jesus asked if they really believed that he could heal them. After they answered, "Yes, Lord," Jesus touched their eyes and said, "Let it be done for you according to your faith." It was then that their eyes were opened.

The two men participated with Jesus in their healing. He did not anesthetize them and then perform surgery.

As an Anglican bishop, Richard Hare, once said, "Realize your baptism." Perhaps this was another way of saying, "Become what you believe,"

Lord Jesus, by baptism I have a secure place in your family, I don't have to prove myself. I don't have to defend myself. You are watching out for me. Please show me the step of trust I need to take today truly to comprehend this truth. Help me to become what I believe. Open my heart today in a new way to see you. Alleluia!

Saturday, December 5, 1998 Advent Weekday
Matthew 9, 35 - 10:1, 6-8
The Compassion of Jesus; The Mission of the Twelve;
The Commissioning of the Twelve

Jesus saw the crowds and "his heart was moved with pity for them because they were troubled and abandoned, like sheep without a shepherd." He cured every disease and illness, without exception. Jesus "healed their bruised and hurt lives (Matthew 9, 25, The Message)."

Jesus then gave his disciples the power and authority to do just the same things he did. They were to "tenderly care for the hurt and bruised lives (Matthew 10, 1, The Message)."

His disciples were not to run off to a distant mission field, but were to concentrate on the "lost sheep of the house of Israel" or, as Eugene Peterson puts it, "the lost, confused people right here in the neighborhood (Matthew 10, 6, The Message)."

The troubled and the abandoned are right here in our midst. Perhaps you and I are feeling troubled and abandoned ourselves. Perhaps our lives have been bruised and hurt. How can we reach out to others when we need help ourselves?

Lord Jesus, your disciples spent time with you. They saw your motivation, your heart of compassion before they saw your power. Please bring your healing touch to my own life. Help me to know deep within my spirit that you have never abandoned me. Send me out this morning to the kitchen to make breakfast for my family, to the Farmer's Market in busy downtown, to the neighborhood, and to the healing institute this afternoon with your compassion in my heart and your healing touch in my hands. Alleluia!

Sunday, December 6, 1998 Second Sunday of Advent
Matthew 3, 1-12
The Preaching of John the Baptist

John the Baptist, preaching in the desert, crying out, "… 'Repent, for the kingdom of heaven is at hand!' " wearing rough camel hair clothes and eating locusts and wild honey, is quite a fascinating character. Fearlessly, he challenged the Pharisees and Sadducees, calling them a bunch of snakes.

Who IS John the Baptist? Who IS this loose cannon, this politically incorrect lone ranger in the desert?

His very birth was a miracle. The first chapter of the Gospel of Luke tells us how John was born to aged parents.

Zechariah, his father, was a priest. Elizabeth, his mother, was also from a priestly family. The angel Gabriel instructed Zechariah, stunned by the news that he and Elizabeth would have a baby, to name the child John, which meant "Yahweh has shown favor."

If John's birth seemed impossible, his ministry seemed even more impossible. As his father, Zechariah, prophesied,

"And you, child, will be called
    prophet of the Most High,
        prepare his ways,
    to give his people knowledge of salvation
    through the forgiveness of their sins … (Luke 1, 76-77)."

During this Advent, you and I may be feeling tired, frazzled, and weary of the daily grind. Today, let us ask to see ourselves as the Lord sees us. The Lord God has called us into existence. We are living in this very time and in this very place for a very particular purpose.

Lord Jesus, please energize us today and let our lives be a sign that You are active and present in this world. Fill us afresh with your Holy Spirit and with your holy fire. Let our lives proclaim that You are coming soon. Alleluia!

Monday, December 7, 1998 St. Ambrose
Luke 5, 17-26
The Healing of a Paralytic

I believe that this healing was a "set-up." It was a "set-up" by God the Father!

There were Pharisees and teachers of the law present, not only from the local village, but also from every single village of Galilee and Judea as well as from Jerusalem. That meant that religious leaders from all over the country were present for this event.

I believe that God the Father had specifically arranged this event in order to demonstrate that his Son, Jesus was truly human and truly divine. After all, who but God could forgive sins?

As for Jesus, he had stated over and over in his earthly ministry that he could do nothing on his own, but only what his Father had instructed him to do (John 8, 28). Even as Jesus was teaching the people that particular day, "the power of the Lord was with him for healing."

Where did Jesus direct his attention? He had been teaching when this "interruption" occurred.

The creative and persistent friends of the paralyzed man lowered him down through the roof right in front of Jesus. Did Jesus say, "Beat it! Can't you see I'm busy teaching?"

92

No, of course not. Jesus directed his attention to the man before him and addressed the man's deepest need. He told the paralytic, "... your sins are forgiven."

Well, the Pharisees really blew up over that! They did not say anything aloud, but they were still enraged that Jesus would actually have the nerve to say such a thing as "Your sins are forgiven." Who in the world did he think he was, anyway? God?

Jesus saw everything. He always does. He saw the deepest need of the paralytic, the trust of the paralytic's friends, and also the incredulity and the hostility of the religious leaders. He knew exactly how to address everyone involved.

He asked the Pharisees, "What are you thinking in your hearts? Which is easier to say, 'Your sins are forgiven,' or to say, 'Rise and walk? But that you may know that the Son of Man has authority on earth to forgive sins' -- he said to the man who was paralyzed, 'I say to you, rise, pick up your stretcher, and go home.' "

What a glorious "set-up!" Representatives of the entire religious community had just seen God in action. This is what is like when God shows up on the scene.

The friends of the paralytic had been rewarded for their plucky persistence. The paralytic had had his deepest need met. His sins had been forgiven! And, yes, he walked again.

Lord Jesus, how great you are! Your timing is perfect. You saw the trust of the friends of the paralytic. You saw deeply into the heart of the paralytic and gave him total healing. Today, help me to trust you in a deeper way and to expect your healing. Alleluia!

Tuesday, December 8, 1998 The Immaculate Conception
Luke 1, 26-38
Annunciation of the Birth of Jesus

The annunciation passage begins with God sending the angel Gabriel to deliver an "impossible" message to a young, unassuming teenage girl named Mary. The passage ends with the reassurance from God's messenger, Gabriel, that "nothing will be impossible for God."

Whatever God is announcing to me today, I pray to receive it with trust and say, with Mary, "May it be done to me according to your word."

The "in between" part which is so crucial is my "yes" to God. No matter how impossible God's promise may seem to me, I say "yes" with heart and mind and voice. God will make it happen.

Lord Jesus, you are drawing near. Let us adore you and honor you with our trust. Alleluia!

Wednesday, December 9, 1998 Advent Weekday
Matthew 11, 28-30
The Gentle Mastery of Christ

Jesus has a question for us today. "Are you tired? Worn out? Burned out on religion? Come to me. Get away with me and you'll recover your life. I'll show you how to take a real rest. Walk with me and work with me -- watch how I do it. Learn the unforced rhythms of grace. I won't lay anything heavy or ill-fitting on you. Keep company with me and you'll learn to live freely and lightly (Matthew 11, 28-30, The Message)."

Lord Jesus, I am so tired today. I've tried so hard for so long. Take from me any burden that is not from you. Refresh and renew me in your love. Alleluia!

Thursday, December 10, 1998 Advent Weekday
Matthew 11, 11-15
Jesus' Testimony to John

Flannery O' Connor's novel, The Violent Bear It Away, offers fascinating insights about prophets. In today's Gospel, we are confronted with the puzzling verse which inspired the title of this novel.

"From the days of John the Baptist until now, the kingdom of heaven suffers violence, and the violent are taking it by force." What does this mean? What is Jesus saying?

It is necessary to balance Scripture with Scripture. The violent may be trying to take the kingdom by force, or, as The Message says, "people have tried to force themselves into God's kingdom."

With energy and with violence, some may strive to seize the kingdom and crowd into it. Do they succeed?

What did Jesus say about the way to enter the kingdom? He gave us a very concrete answer.

Jesus took a child into the midst of the disciples and said, "Truly I tell you, unless you change and become like children, you will never enter the kingdom of heaven. Whoever becomes humbles like this child is the greatest in the kingdom of heaven (Matthew 18, 3-4, N.R.S.V.)."

Jesus turned everything upside down! He told us that no one is greater than John the Baptist. Still, the least in the kingdom is greater than John the Baptist,

Lord Jesus, my eyes are weary looking upon this earthly kingdom. Help me today to see you in a new way and see the kingdom of heaven in a new way. May your kingdom come and may your perfect will be done on this earth as it is being done right now in heaven. Alleluia!

Friday, December 11, 1998 St. Damasus I
Matthew 11, 16-21
Jesus' Testimony to John

Jesus reminded us that "…wisdom is vindicated by her works." He spent his time on earth doing the will of his heavenly Father. Although he was exasperated with those who were perversely determined to misinterpret his actions, he persevered doing his Father's will.

The books of Ezra and Nehemiah describe the return of the Jewish exiles to Jerusalem to rebuild the Temple and the walls. There was great opposition and many attempts to intimidate those called to the task of rebuilding. Under the wise leadership of Ezra and Nehemiah, however, the work continued.

Jesus was determined to continue his work which would be completed with his passion, death, resurrection, ascension, and return in glory. He restored our relationship with our Father in heaven and is currently rebuilding our lives. He still refuses to be stopped by those who mock and misinterpret his ministry and mission.

Lord Jesus, today, please strengthen my hands and my heart to do the work you have given me to do. Let your purpose for my life be fulfilled. Alleluia!

Saturday, December 12, 1998 Our Lady of Guadalupe
Luke 2, 15-19
The Visit of the Shepherds

"Mary kept all these things, reflecting on them in her heart." Looking over the last nine months of her life, Mary could count so many wonders.

The angel Gabriel had appeared to her, announcing the birth of Jesus. She tried to explain these wonders to her parents and to Joseph. She traveled to visit Elizabeth. She traveled with Joseph to Bethlehem. This young girl, so devoted to the Lord, so strong in her trust, and yet so tender and vulnerable, gave birth in very humble surroundings.

Now, out of the blue, came excited shepherds, gesturing wildly, telling of an angelic visitation. "Mary kept all these things, reflecting on them in her heart."

Lord Jesus, I understand so little. When life swirls around me with bewildering sorrows and unanticipated joys, help me to focus on you. Help me to reflect on "all these things" in my heart and to place "all these things" in your heart for safekeeping. Alleluia!

Sunday, December 13, 1998 Third Sunday of Advent
Matthew 11, 2-11
The Messengers from John the Baptist;
Jesus' Testimony to John

Jesus referred to John the Baptist, saying, "This is the one about whom it is written:

Behold, I am sending my messenger ahead of you;
    he will prepare your way before you ..."

John set out on his wilderness mission to prepare the way of the Lord.

Sometimes I think of John in a jungle setting, wielding a machete, clearing a path! That's what he did, spiritually.

John set out, knowing his mission, and yet needing reassurance. Does that sound familiar? He sent some of his followers to ask Jesus, "Are you the one who is to come, or should we look for another?" Jesus did not rebuke him, but instead, reassured him.

When we set out on our mission to live for Jesus, we will need to turn to him again and again for reassurance. Not reassurance about who Jesus is, but reassurance about who we are.

Even if we're the very least in the kingdom of heaven, Jesus calls us greater than John the Baptist (Matthew 11, 11). Being in the kingdom is what is of the greatest importance.

Lord Jesus, I certainly don't feel greater than John the Baptist. I'm not stomping around the desert preaching repentance. John's preaching prepared the way for you. Let the way I live today help to prepare the way for your return in glory. Alleluia!

Monday, December 14, 1998 St. John of the Cross
Matthew 21, 23-24
The Authority of Jesus Questioned

One thing was certain. The priests and elders were not going to stop Jesus. When they questioned him and undermined his authority, he adroitly turned the tables by asking them a question, a straightforward, yet shrewd, question.

Jesus is always in charge. He was in charge then and he is in charge now.

Lord Jesus, when I feel trapped, help me to look to you. You are in the driver's seat of my life. I am not trapped by circumstances. You are in control today and every day. Alleluia!

Tuesday, December 15, 1998 Advent Weekday
Matthew 21, 28-32
The Parable of the Two Sons

Eugene Peterson, in The Message, gives this familiar parable a new jolt. Jesus, speaking to the chief priests and elders of the people, stated bluntly, "I tell you that crooks and whores are going to precede you into God's kingdom. John came to you showing you the right road. You turned up your noses at him, but the crooks and whores believed him. Even when you saw their changed lives, you didn't care enough to change and believe him (Matthew 21, 31, 32)."

Whew! Jesus, you sure aren't being politically correct. This is definitely not the way to curry favor.

Jesus, you see, does not need to curry favor with anyone. He loves all and will die for all. He does not, however, violate anyone's personal liberty. He does not use force.

The first son in the parable initially refused his father's command to go and work in the vineyard, but later reconsidered and went there after all. The second son said he would go and work, but did not follow through with his actions.

97

Lord Jesus, how patient you were with those who refused to believe in you. How patient you are with me. I believe in you, but I become frightened sometimes and find it difficult to trust even you. Please lead me out of this excursion into the kingdom of fear and remind me that my true home is in your kingdom where you live and reign. Alleluia!

Wednesday, December 16, 1998 Advent Weekday
Luke 7, 18-23
The Messengers from John the Baptist

This Gospel sounds familiar because Sunday's Gospel was the parallel passage from Matthew's Gospel. John the Baptist, languishing in Herod's prison, decided to check out Jesus a bit more closely.

Even John did not want to waste his sufferings. Why bother unless this Jesus was the real McCoy, or the real Messiah?

Jesus obliged by giving John's followers an on-site demonstration of his ministry. He healed many people and said, "Go and tell John what you have seen and heard: the blind regain their sight, the lame walk, lepers are cleansed, the deaf hear, the dead are raised, the poor have the good news proclaimed to them. And blessed is the one who takes no offense at me."

People did take offense at Jesus when he walked on this earth. He was humbly born amongst smelly farm animals. His mother had a questionable reputation. As a twelve year old, he sat in the temple in Jerusalem and calmly referred to the temple as his Father's house.

He was a controversial and radical rabbi who hung out with rough characters. He irritated and alienated the power elite in Jerusalem. He was a gentle man whose very words brought life and healing. He was God in human flesh.

Lord Jesus, when you're around, "the blind regain their sight, the lame walk, lepers are cleansed, the deaf hear, the dead are raised, the poor have the good news proclaimed to them." Help me not to take offense at your ways and your timing in my life. Alleluia!

Thursday, December 17, 1998 Late Advent Weekday
Matthew 1, 1-17
The Genealogy of Jesus

This is the family tree of Jesus on the side of Joseph, his foster father. The people listed in this genealogy are the human instruments used by God to form Joseph for his unique vocation. Joseph was the one to whom the infant Jesus and the child Jesus first looked to as his "abba," his father.

It's fascinating to notice all the "characters" in this family tree! No one was unimportant. Every single one was loved by God and was important in God's plan to bring a Redeemer to his people.

When we look at ourselves and our family tree, we may think "if only." If only this person was not in our family. If only I didn't have this particular temperament. If only this. If only that.

Lord Jesus, for whatever reason, you specifically chose all my ancestors. You also specifically called my life into being in this very place and at this very time for your own purposes. Help me to lay aside the "if only's." Thank you for my life and for all my relatives. Thank you for their role in forming me to fulfill your purpose for my life. Alleluia!

Friday, December 18, 1998 Late Advent Weekday
Matthew 1, 18-24
The Birth of Jesus

God the Father orchestrated the birth of his Son, Jesus, but still sought the cooperation of human beings. Wonder of wonders!

When we go into a church and see the beautiful statues of Mary and Joseph or when we admires a peaceful nativity scene, we are obviously not seeing the real people. The real flesh and blood people struggled and were beset with many questions.

Mary asked, "How can this be (Luke 1, 34)?" Joseph's painful inner struggles are not recorded. We are told, however, that he was righteous and unwilling to allow Mary, his betrothed, to be humiliated and possibly stoned to death.

I wonder if, in the midst of Joseph's anguish and grief, he fell asleep. It was while Joseph was asleep that the angel of the Lord appeared to him with the solution to the dilemma. As Joseph awoke and obeyed, he fulfilled his role in the drama of the birth of Jesus.

Lord Jesus, when I feel confused and overwhelmed by bewildering circumstances, please come to me, calm my fears, and reveal to me your solution. I place all my trust in you. Alleluia!

Saturday, December 19, 1998 Late Advent Weekday
Luke 1, 5-25
Annunciation of the Birth of John

"So has the Lord done for me at a time when he has seen fit to take away my disgrace before others." Elizabeth proclaimed this message as she entered a five month period of seclusion to prepare for the birth of John the Baptist.

Eight years ago today, on my birthday, my husband and I visited the lovely mission town, San Juan Bautista (Spanish for St. John the Baptist). As we headed home and approached a church, I had a very strong sense of being led by God to stop to pray there. Mass had just begun. The Gospel was the same as today's Gospel, the announcement of the birth of John the Baptist.

As I listened to the last words of the Gospel, "So has the Lord done for me at a time when he has seen fit to take away my disgrace before others," I rejoiced. For many years I had been waiting and trusting for the Lord's intervention in a particular situation in my own life.

In prophecy, there is often a little preview before the ultimate fulfillment. The Lord gives a little glimpse of the fulfillment of the prophecy promised so long ago. Sometimes there is a prolonged period of waiting, both in restful green pastures and also in the dry, seemingly barren wilderness.

Timing is everything! The Lord acts in a certain way in a certain time as he sees fit. He intervened for Elizabeth at the right time. He will intervene for you and for me at the right time. Lord Jesus, help us to wait and to trust. Alleluia!

Sunday, December 20, 1998 Fourth Sunday of Advent
Matthew 1, 18 - 24
The Birth of Jesus

The angel of the Lord reassured Joseph, "... Joseph, do not be afraid ..." At the Annunciation of the birth of Jesus, it was Mary who heard the words from the angel Gabriel, "Do not be afraid, Mary ..."

Fear can paralyze us. When God tells us to not to fear, but to stand firm and carry on, we still may falter and hesitate.

The key, I believe, is to trust in the Lord and in the Lord's word to us. Then, we are to step out in trust and do what the Lord has said to do.

Mary's trust and obedience lay in her willingness for the Holy Spirit to plant the Savior of the world within her heart and her womb. Joseph's trust and obedience lay in his action of taking Mary into his home, regardless of his own doubts and regardless of public opinion.

Lord Jesus, I believe your word to me will be fulfilled. Help me to rest in you and to take whatever step of trust you call me to take. Alleluia!

Monday, December 21, 1998 St. Peter Canisus
Luke 1, 39-45
Mary Visits Elizabeth

"Blessed are you who believed that what was spoken to you by the Lord would be fulfilled." Elizabeth spoke these words to Mary. The Lord is speaking these words to you and to me today.

What is that the Lord has spoken to you that has not been fulfilled? The Lord asks us to wait, not in a state of dull, listless passivity, but with a bright, joyful anticipation and a purposeful participation in the present moment. We cannot just live for "then." The Lord is with us right now.

Of course, we rejoice when a particular answer to prayer comes, but most of all we rejoice in the Lord's presence and provision in the present moment. Joy and fulfillment are found in the Lord himself and in our relationship with him.

Lord Jesus, help me not to become so fixated on particular answers to particular prayers. Instead, help me to sing your praises today, to enjoy my relationship with you, and to trust in you in a deeper way. Alleluia!

Tuesday, December 22, 1998 Late Advent Weekday
Luke 1, 46 -56
The Canticle of Mary

The Song of Mary. The Magnificat. The outpouring of praise from a young Jewish girl to her mighty God.

"My soul proclaims the greatness of the Lord;
    my spirit rejoices in God my savior."

Mary begins by focusing and concentrating the energy of her soul -- her mind, her will, and her emotions -- on the greatness of the Lord. She does not refer to her own uncertainties or concerns at this time. This is the time to praise God!

Mary's spirit rejoices in God her savior. She is not in this situation alone. The mighty God who has visited her in such an extraordinary way will accomplish what seems humanly impossible.

Lord Jesus, help me to concentrate on you and to rejoice in you. You are my savior and you will take care of all that concerns me. Alleluia!

Wednesday, December 23, 1998 St. John of Kanty
Luke 1, 57-66
The Birth of John

This morning I turned to The Message for fresh insight into this familiar passage. "When Elizabeth was full-term in her pregnancy, she bore a son (Luke 1, 57, The Message)."

Full-term. Sometimes I think it's too late for something to take place in my life. I may think I'm not just full-term, but overdue!

God sees in a different way. In God's eyes, I'm still not full-term, much less overdue. The life within still needs nurturing and maturing.

Elizabeth's relatives and neighbors were going to call the newborn baby Zechariah after his father. "But his mother intervened: 'No. He is to be called John (Luke 1, 60, The Message)." Zechariah, still speechless after nine months, confirmed his wife's announcement by writing on a tablet that "John" was indeed the child's name.

From before the time of John's conception, his identity had been determined by God. The angel Gabriel told the stunned, elderly father-to-be, Zechariah, "Do not be afraid, Zechariah, because your prayer has been heard. Your wife Elizabeth will bear you a son, and you shall name him John. And you will have joy and gladness, and many will rejoice at his birth, for he will be great in the sight of [the] Lord (Luke 1, 13-15a)." The angel went on to describe John's future ministry.

Lord Jesus, John the Baptist knew your identity when you were both still in the wombs of your mothers. You know my identity. You know me through and through. You know all about my past, present and future. Sometimes, in my life, it seemed that no one intervened for me. I felt that I was wandering in a desert of futility. Still, you were there, speaking your word to me and giving me my identity. Today, late in Advent, I look to you in trust that you are still intimately involved in my waiting. Alleluia!

Thursday, December 24, 1998 Vigil of Christmas
Matthew 1, 1-25
The Genealogy of Jesus; The Birth of John

The time had come for Isaiah's ancient prophecy to be fulfilled.

"Behold, the virgin shall be with child and bear a son,
    and they shall name him Emmanuel,
    which means 'God is with us.' "

This long genealogy, with its mixed cast of characters, shows us how long and involved was the human preparation to bring forth Joseph. Joseph was carefully chosen by God to be the foster father of Jesus. It was Joseph that Jesus would first call "father" or "abba" ("daddy").

Prophecy. Waiting. Fulfillment. Help us to wait for you, Lord Jesus. Your word to us will come to pass at the right time.

"For as the rain and snow come down from heaven,
    and do not return there unti they have watered the earth,
    making it bring forth and sprout,
    giving seed to the sower and bread to the eater,
    so shall my word be that goes out from my mouth;
it shall not return to me empty,
    but it shall accomplish that which I purpose,
    and succeed in the thing for which I sent it."
                              Isaiah 55, 10-11, N.R.S.V.
Alleluia!

Friday, December 25, 1998 The Birth of the Lord
John 1, 1-18
Prologue

Don't wait for recognition before you do your ministry. God sent you into this world just as surely as surely as he sent John the Baptist into this world and just as surely as he sent his only Son Jesus into this world.

John the Baptist did the work he was called to do to prepare the way of the Lord. Some believed and were baptized. Others opposed him and put him in prison and chopped off his head. That's called rejection. He still accomplished the task God gave him to do.

Jesus? He came to his very own people, but they did not all accept him. Some of them, the chief priests, authorized his agonizing torture and then his murder on a cross. Rejection. Nevertheless, Jesus accomplished the work God gave him to do.

103

What are you supposed to do? Accept Jesus, trust Jesus, and confidently count on the Holy Spirit to reveal your own mission in this life.

Will you have your head chopped off or be nailed to a cross? Probably not. All that matters is that you accomplish the task God is giving YOU to do.

"But to those who did accept him he gave power to become children of God, to those who believe in his name ..." You and I believe in his name. God is our Father. We have the same Father in heaven as Jesus, our Lord and our Brother.

Starting this Christmas Day, let us emerge from the womb of darkness, safe though it seems, into the brightness of God's plan for our lives. Let us be open to this light, this glory, this grace, and this truth. Let us adore Christ our Lord. Alleluia!

Saturday, December 26, 1998 St. Stephen
Matthew 10, 17-22
Coming Persecutions

Basking in the afterglow of Christmas, we're suddenly confronted with harsh realities. We must choose, and choose very soon, where to look, where to fix our gaze.

Stephen, whose martyrdom we remember today, fixed his eyes on heaven. He had been seized and brought before the Sanhedrin. False witnesses rose up against him. Does this sound familiar?

Stephen, "... filled with the holy Spirit, looked up intently to heaven and saw the glory of God and Jesus standing at the right hand of God, and he said, 'Behold, I see the heavens opened and the Son of Man standing at the right hand of God (Acts 7, 55-56)' " His infuriated hearers stoned him to death. Rejection.

What a way to begin the octave of Christmas! We can't say that "that was then and this is now." Jesus is speaking urgently to us in today's Gospel warning us that there is a price for discipleship.

"Don't be naive. Some people will impugn your motives, others will smear your reputation -- just because you believe in me. When people realize it is the living God you are presenting and not some idol that makes them feel good, they are going to turn on you, even people in your own family. There is a great irony here: proclaiming so much love, experiencing so much hate! But don't quit. Don't cave in. It is all well worth it in the end. It is not success you are after in such times, but survival. Be survivors (Matthew 10, 17-22 in <u>The Message</u>)!"

To survive spiritually, it is essential to focus on God, not on the bewildering circumstances swirling around us. Jesus knew this. Dying on the cross he cried out, "Father, into your hands I commend my spirit (Luke 23, 46)."

Stephen knew this. As he died, he called out, "Lord Jesus, receive my spirit."

Lord Jesus, I'm not being stoned by a mob today nor am I being nailed to a cross. However, I still shrink from the hard realities of following you. Today, help me to put into practice your admonition not to worry about what to say. Thank you that the Holy Spirit will speak through me. I rest in you. Alleluia!

Sunday, December 27, 1998 The Holy Family
Matthew 2, 13-14; 19-23
The Flight to Egypt; The Return from Egypt

Ancient prophecy was fulfilled because Joseph, for three recorded times, heard the voice of God in his dreams and immediately obeyed. The first time was after Joseph was agonizing over the news of Mary's pregnancy.

Joseph was compassionate, yet righteous. While struggling with his decision, the angel of the Lord spoke to him in a dream. "Joseph, son of David, do not be afraid to take Mary your wife into your home. For it is through the holy Spirit that this child has been conceived in her. She will bear a son and you are to name him Jesus, because he will save his people from their sins." This was the fulfillment of Isaiah's prophecy that a virgin would bear a child to be named Emmanuel (Isaiah 7, 14).

In today's Gospel, the flight into Egypt was a fulfillment of the prophecy of Hosea 11, 1, "Out of Egypt I called my son." The return from Egypt and the move to Nazareth were was also designated by Matthew as a fulfillment of prophecy.

God permitted the survival of Jesus to be dependent upon Joseph, specifically upon Joseph's ability to discern the meaning of his dreams. Long before the current interest in personality types, God had designed Joseph's personality to be receptive to dreams.

Lord Jesus, you have designed my personality as a vehicle to be used to fulfill your destiny for me. Help me to respond with joy and sensitivity to your leadings in my life today. Alleluia!

Monday, December 28, 1998 Holy Innocents
Matthew 2, 13-18
The Flight into Egypt

Today's Gospel illustrates free will at its best and at its worst. Joseph was instructed to flee to Egypt in order to save the life of the newborn Christ. Joseph obeyed God and the Child's life was saved.

Herod, on the other hand, could see only a threat to his own temporal sovereignty. Because of his jealousy and rage, he ordered the brutal murder of innocent children.

Lord Jesus, in your eternal sovereignty, redeem the lives of all who suffer any form of injustice. Receive them into the arms of your mercy. Alleluia!

Tuesday, December 29, 1998 St. Thomas Becket
Luke 2, 22-35
The Presentation in the Temple

Simeon was a man who knew how to wait and how to depend upon the Holy Spirit. The Holy Spirit was directing him. The Holy Spirit revealed to him that he would not die until he had seen the Christ. The Holy Spirit led him to be in the temple at the precise time Mary and Joseph brought the infant Jesus. Simeon took the child into his arms and referred to Jesus as

"a light for revelation to the Gentiles
    and glory for your people Israel."

Simeon blessed Mary and Joseph and then spoke prophetically to Mary. "Behold, this child is destined for the fall and rise of many in Israel, and to be a sign that will be contradicted (and you yourself a sword will pierce) so that the thoughts of many hearts may be revealed."

All of this concentrated prophetic wisdom from Simeon, an elderly man yielded to the Holy Spirit! The Holy Spirit had prepared him all his life for these few moments in the temple in Jerusalem.

Holy Spirit, when my life seems to be going nowhere, please help me to remember that you are truly in charge, that you are truly directing my thoughts, my hands, my heart, and my steps. Help me to be sensitive to you as you lead me closer and closer to the fulfillment of your purpose for my life. Alleluia!

Wednesday, December 30, 1998
Luke 2, 36-40
The Presentation in the Temple

For Anna and for all who live a life of praise and prayer, it's not over! There is only the next step, in a life surrendered to God.

For Anna, the next step was the one in which she stepped into the physical presence of the Son of God. The infant Jesus was now before her very eyes. God the Father had lovingly arranged for Anna, his faithful prophet, to see for herself his answer to the human dilemma.

If Anna had been less attuned to the voice of God, she could have missed this moment, Her life, however, had been wholly given to listening to God.

A true prophet always listens to God first and then speaks only as God directs. Anna, after seeing the infant Jesus, "spoke about the child to all who were awaiting the redemption of Jerusalem."

Lord Jesus, help me not to become weary in waiting for you. Help me to continue to praise you and to be ready for you. Alleluia!

Thursday, December 31, 1998 St. Sylvester I
John 1, 1-18
Prologue

The beautiful prologue to the Gospel of John was the Gospel for Christmas Day. Standing, as it were, on tiptoe, inhaling the fresh air of the Gospel, I feel ready to greet the new year.

It's early morning, not quite dawn. I'm in my usual spot in the living room, the corner of the flowered chintz sofa, with a steaming cup of coffee, my Bible, breviary, and notebook. I have a cold and feel dreadful.

Today's Gospel speaks of "the beginning," of "life" and "light." Jesus was already there "in the beginning." Jesus brings life and light. His light shines in the darkness and cannot be extinguished.

Lord Jesus, I cannot think of anything right now except how awful I feel with this cold! Please take my hand and lead me to a new beginning in this new year. Let your life flow into me and heal me. Let your light shine through me into the world around me. I love you and I trust you. Alleluia!

Friday, January 1, 1999 Solemnity of Mary
Luke 2, 16-21
The Vision of the Shepherds;
The Circumcision and Naming of Jesus

"When eight days were completed for his circumcision, he was named Jesus, the name given him by the angel before he was conceived in the womb." At the Annunciation, the angel Gabriel had told Mary, "Behold, you will conceive in your womb and bear a son, and you shall name him Jesus (Luke 1, 31)."

Joseph also had been told that Mary would bear a son and that Joseph was to name him Jesus (Matthew 1, 21) because Jesus would save his people from their sins. That was his mission!

Nevertheless, the formal or official naming took place at a certain time. In this case, it was only eight days.

What about you? Perhaps the formal naming of your mission has not occurred in a way that you expected. Nevertheless, your mission is still there, still safe and secure in the heart of God.

Timing is everything. When your "eight days" are complete, you will be formally named. Nevertheless, live NOW in the light you have. Your mission began in the womb. You are now living it, regardless of what the world around you thinks or says.

Lord Jesus, sometimes I really wonder about your timing! Thank you for your total sovereignty. You know and understand everything, whereas I know and understand so little. I am not yet ready. Please show me how to live and how to follow you today. I love you, I trust you, and I trust your timing in my life. Alleluia!

Saturday, January 2, 1999 Sts. Basil and Gregory
John 1, 19-28
John the Baptist's Testimony to Himself

Priests and Levites were sent from Jerusalem to ask John who he was. John told them that his was the voice crying out in the wilderness to prepare the way for Jesus the Messiah.

Before John revealed his own identity, he proclaimed Jesus! "This is he of whom I said, 'The one who is coming after me ranks ahead of me because he existed before me (John 1, 15).' "

We must look to Jesus first, not to ourselves. Like John the Baptist, we must first of all proclaim who Jesus is. Only then will we begin to understand our own identity.

Lord Jesus, today, I look to you and acknowledge you as King of my life. Help me to testify to you faithfully and to understand and to accept my own identity. Alleluia!

Sunday, January 3, 1999 Epiphany of the Lord
Matthew 2, 1-12
The Visit of the Magi

The bold, yet cautious, behavior of the magi reminds me of what Jesus would later tell his followers. "Behold, I am sending you like sheep in the midst of wolves; so be shrewd as serpents and simple as doves (Matthew 10, 16)."

That's exactly what the magi did! The Holy Spirit guided them straight through Herod's manipulations and machinations to the infant Messiah in Bethlehem.

It was there that they completed their mission. They saw the Child for themselves. They saw Mary, his mother. They worshipped. They gave their treasures. Then they departed by another way.

Lord Jesus, thank you for guiding me today. Lead me through the mazes of this life to you. I worship you today and give you the treasure of my heart. Alleluia!

Monday, January 4, 1999 St. Elizabeth Ann Seton
Matthew 4, 12-17; 23-25
The Beginning of the Galilee Ministry:
Ministering to a Great Multitude

"He left Nazareth and went to Capernaum by the sea ..." Jesus was at a turning point in the beginning of his ministry.

He had just been baptized by John and had undergone a period of severe temptation in the desert. John the Baptist, the one who had prepared his way, had been removed from the scene. What next?

It was time for a change. Leaving Nazareth, his hometown, and his family, he went to live in Capernaum by the sea. After a sabbatical by the sea, Jesus went forth on his mission and began to preach, saying, "Repent, for the kingdom of heaven is at hand."

This time by the sea was crucial for Jesus. It was a time and a place to pray, to reflect, and to receive more fully the solace brought to him by the angels who had ministered to him after his ordeal in the desert.

The sea has always been a place where I have found restoration and renewal. Even an hour by the sea brings healing to my spirit.

Lord Jesus, thank you that you heal in so many different ways. Right now, I need to be "by the sea," in some way. Refresh and renew me so that I may continue on to the next step. Alleluia!

Tuesday, January 5, 1999 St. John Neumann
Mark 6, 34-44
The Feeding of the Five Thousand

Jesus was deeply concerned about the temporal as well as the spiritual needs of the crowd who had come to hear his teaching. His disciples informed him that it was getting very late and the place was deserted. As if he didn't already know!

In other words, they were saying, "No use looking for help here." They thought the only way for the people to find food was to go buy it somewhere in the surrounding countryside.

Jesus had a completely different solution." Give them some food yourselves." We know the rest of the story. Jesus took what they had, two fish and five loaves of bread, blessed it, broke it, and gave it to the hungry crowd. There were twelve baskets of leftovers!

Sometimes I feel that my life is a "deserted place" and that the hour is "very late." How can I be expected to feed anyone else when I am exhausted and depleted myself? I need to give what I have and trust that it is enough.

Lord Jesus, I give you my life as it is today to be blessed, broken and given to others. Alleluia!

Wednesday, January 6, 1999 Blessed Andre Bessette
Mark 6, 45-52
The Walking on the water

You would think that after just witnessing the miracle of the feeding of the five thousand, the disciples would be predisposed to trust Jesus in a big way. Were they?

No. Instead, they were terrified! They had not really understood the feeding of the multitude and their hearts were strangely hardened. Puzzling.

It seems amazing to us, sitting back reading about this event two thousand years later. Why in the world couldn't they trust Jesus?

Why in the world can't I trust Jesus? I've seen him work in so many ways and yet I have so far to go in this journey of trust.

In this passage, the geography alone is very telling. The boat the disciples were in was out on the Sea of Galilee and Jesus was on the shore. He could see exactly what was happening in that boat.

They thought they were alone, but all along Jesus had his eye on them. He knew exactly when to intervene. He came at the right time and said, "Take courage, it is I, do not be afraid!" Then he got into the boat with them. The wind subsided.

Lord Jesus, please come soon and stop the storm in my life. Thank you that you are in control. Thank you for your perfect timing. Alleluia!

Thursday, January 7, 1999 St. Raymond of Penyafort
Luke 4, 14-22
The Beginning of the Galilean Ministry;
The Rejection at Nazareth

So far, so good. It's difficult to read this passage and to stop, knowing full well what is to follow. Still, today's Gospel is essential in showing us how to take life as it comes, our eyes fixed on God.

Jesus just does what he's accustomed to doing. He goes to the synagogue in his hometown on the Sabbath. Same old routine, right? Not this time.

After reading the passage from Isaiah 61, Jesus rolled up the scroll and announced, "Today this scripture passage is fulfilled in your hearing." Not, "will be" fulfilled, but "is" fulfilled. Things are about to change, but at this particular moment, "all spoke highly of him and were amazed at the gracious words that came from his mouth."

The tide began to turn with the innocent little question, "Isn't this the son of Joseph?" Today's Gospel, however, stops here.

Loving Father, you knew what was in store for your Son. You know what is in store for me. Help me today to go forward and to follow you with the light that I have. Keep me close to you whether I am praised or condemned. I trust you. Alleluia!

Friday, January 8, 1999
Luke 5, 12-16
The Cleansing of a Leper

Who's pulling my strings? Am I pulling my own strings? Am I living my life doing what I want to do? Are other people pulling my strings with their demands? Who is directing my life?

In today's Gospel, Jesus demonstrates for us that it was God the Father directing and controlling his life. "I cannot do anything on my own; I judge as I hear, and my judgment is just, because I do not seek my own will but the will of the one who sent me (John 5, 30)."

Although great crowds were swarming around him, Jesus was listening to a different drummer. He reached out to cleanse a leper and to instruct him to go to the priest to fulfill the Mosaic requirement. Then, Jesus went away to pray in isolated places.

It was from this solitude that Jesus discerned the will of the Father. How many times do I rush out playing "room parent to the universe," assuming false responsibility, instead of asking, "Father, what is on your heart for me today?"

Lord Jesus, thank you for giving me this example of solitude and prayer. Thank you for speaking to me. Alleluia!

Saturday, January 9, 1999
John 3, 22-30
Final Witness of John the Baptist

The timing was becoming tighter and tighter. John the Baptist had not yet been imprisoned. He was still free to exercise his ministry of preparing the way of the Lord.

John was very clear about his vocation. He knew who he was and who he was not. He was not the Messiah. He was not the Bridegroom. He was the "best man."

John had prepared the people of Israel for the Messiah. It was now drawing near to the time when he would step aside. "So this joy of mine has been made complete. He must increase; I must decrease."

Lord Jesus, help me to be more sensitive than ever to your timing in my life. Today I am free to be a witness to You. Help me to live today fully. Heal me in the depths of my being so that I may be a purer vessel of your love. Alleluia!

Sunday, January 10, 1999 The Baptism of the Lord
Matthew 3, 13-17
The Baptism of Jesus

God, the Almighty, chooses to work through human beings! God the Father could have sent the Holy Spirit upon Jesus without having Jesus baptized at all.

Not only was Jesus baptized, but he was baptized by John the Baptist. Not only was he baptized by John the Baptist, but Jesus also made the journey from Galilee to go to John. True humility.

It was after humbling himself to be baptized and to be identified with those he came to save, that Jesus received the applause of his Abba. The heavens were opened, the Spirit of God descended "like a dove" and God spoke directly. "This is my Beloved Son, with whom I am well pleased."

Often, it is after we submit to earthly processes, the earthly "chain of command," that God rains down his blessing. This may take awhile! However, God's plan for us cannot ultimately be thwarted by human beings. They do not have the final word.

Jesus, clearly superior to John the Baptist, still submitted to baptism. John himself had said, "I am baptizing you with water, for repentance, but the one coming after me is mightier than I. I am not worthy to carry his sandals. He will baptize you with the holy Spirit and fire (Matthew 3, 11)."

Lord Jesus, today I yield afresh to your agenda for my life. Help me to be open to your voice speaking through others and to remember that you alone have the final word. Alleluia!

113

Monday, January 11, 1999
Mark 1, 14-20
The Beginning of the Galilee Ministry;
The Call of the First Disciples

Bad news. Good news.

Something which seemed very bad had just happened. John the Baptist had been arrested. He would never be released. He would eventually be beheaded by Herod's henchmen.

The Gospel begins with the announcement that John had been arrested and that Jesus had come to Galilee to preach the Good News of the kingdom of God. "After John had been arrested, Jesus came to Galilee proclaiming the gospel of God: 'This is the time of fulfillment. The kingdom of God is at hand. Repent, and believe in the Gospel.' "

Jesus, being fully human, could have gone into a depression and asked, "Why did John have to go to prison? Why, God, why?"

Instead, Jesus did what he himself was called to do. John the Baptist had been faithful to fulfill his mission of preparing the way for Jesus. It was time now for Jesus to begin his own public ministry. Good news.

Today, I need to repent, literally to "rethink" how I have responded to "bad news." Maybe it wasn't so bad, after all. Maybe it was God's way to take me to a new "place."

Lord Jesus, I am sorry for wasting time and tears. Help me to do today what you are calling me to do. Alleluia!

Tuesday, January 12, 1999
Mark 1, 21-28
The Cure of a Demoniac

"In their synagogue was a man with an unclean spirit ..." Surely the people of Capernaum knew this man and had observed his behavior for some time. Now this radical, Jesus, comes along and really upsets the apple cart!

The people were already startled at the way Jesus taught. He taught not as a member of the insiders' club, but rather as one who intimately knew the God of whom he spoke.

114

This astonished them. Their own leaders stressed keeping numerous rules and regulations as a way to please God. Jesus had other ideas.

The heads of those in the synagogue were already swimming, but there was more to come! Jesus did not rebuke the poor tormented man. Rather, Jesus rebuked the unholy, unclean spirit tormenting the man.

Jesus set the man free before their eyes! Jesus had taken the existing situation, spoken the word of authority, and created a startling new dynamic within the synagogue.

Lord Jesus, you know what torments the "synagogue" of my life. Come and speak your word to me today. Heal me and free me. Alleluia!

Wednesday, January 13, 1999 St. Hilary
Mark 1, 29-31
The Cure of Simon's Mother-in-Law;
Other Healings; Jesus Leaves Capernaum

Simon (Peter), Andrew, James and John had just witnessed Jesus in action in the synagogue, teaching powerfully and freeing the man with an unclean spirit. This gave them even stronger trust in Jesus.

Now there was a need closer to home. The mother of Peter's wife was ill with a fever.

Having just witnessed Jesus' power to heal, the disciples told him about her. Jesus went to her, took her by the hand, and helped her up. The fever then left her and she responded in thanksgiving by serving those around her.

Lord Jesus, you help all who come to you. I need for you to come to my home today. You know the needs, spoken and unspoken, hidden and obvious, in our lives. Take each member of our family by your hand and lead us through this day. Alleluia!

Thursday, January 14, 1999
Mark 1, 40-45
The Cleansing of a Leper

Have you ever felt like a leper? Have you ever been in a situation in which you knew you were unwelcome? You were aware that your presence was merely being tolerated. You were considered an outsider and you were treated as a nuisance.

In today's Gospel, we see Jesus reassuring the poor leper that it was indeed his will to cleanse and to heal. The leper, cleansed of his disease, ignored the part of Jesus' injunction to keep quiet. Instead, in his exuberance, he told all about it.

As a result of all the publicity, Jesus was restricted in traveling about freely. Although he sought seclusion, the people still found him.

Sometimes, we are secluded for reasons we may not understand at the time. When we are on the outside and seem to be in a deserted place, we need not fret. Jesus is still with us. We are not alone. In deserted places, we enjoy a freedom unknown to many whose lives are programmed by others. There is an interior work which the Holy Spirit is accomplishing in us as we live in deserted places.

Lord Jesus, you welcomed the leper and cleansed him. Forgive me for moping about when I seem to be on the outside looking in. In truth, I am in the best of all places, hidden away with You, the Lover of my soul. Recreate me in this time in the desert. Heal the wounds I have suffered in your service. Let this time with you bring healing, restoration, and renewal. Alleluia!

Friday, January 15, 1999
Mark 2, 1-12
The Healing of a Paralytic

What's going on under your own roof? Today's Gospel begins by quietly telling us that Jesus, who had taken some time away, had returned to Capernaum and was "at home."

Where did this healing take place? At whose home?

Could it have been the home of Simon (Peter) and Andrew where Jesus had stayed before? The same home where he had healed Peter's mother-in-law? We don't know.

Regardless of whose home this was, it was a "visited" home. It was a home where Jesus entered, ate, slept, preached and healed. A place where both seekers and scoffers were welcome. Friends of a paralytic man were determined to get him to Jesus. They broke through the roof and let him down on a mat!

Jesus honored the adventurous creativity of the paralytic's friends by forgiving and healing the paralytic. Jesus probed the minds and hearts of the scribes who could not understand how Jesus, a mere mortal, as they thought, could have the authority to forgive sins.

The Gospel passage ends with the statement that "they were all astounded and glorified God, saying, 'We have never seen anything like this.' " Quite.

Lord Jesus, I invite you to come and be welcome in our home. You gave us this home and it is yours. Enter it in a new way today. Bless, heal, confront and comfort as You see fit. Let your love and your truth be spoken in this home. Alleluia!

Saturday. January 16, 1999
Mark 2, 13-17
The Call of Levi

Jesus saw into the hungry, hurting heart of Levi, the tax collector. Jesus knew that Levi was ready to leave his old life and to enter a new life.

In the midst of the crowd swirling around, Jesus not only saw, but also actively sought out Levi. He looked at Levi and said, "Follow me."

To the caustic, critical Pharisees, who questioned the association of Jesus with tax collectors and sinners, Jesus responded, "Those who are well do not need a physician, but the sick do. I did not come to call the righteous but sinners."

A new chapter had opened in Levi's life! This chapter would be filled with wonder and awe as Levi watched Jesus in action.

In his old life, Levi had experienced hostility because he was a tax collector. In his new life he would also experience hostility and misunderstanding because of his vocation as a disciple.

Lord Jesus, I need you today as my Physician. Come and heal the wounds of my heart. Help me to leave my old mindset behind, arise and follow you into this exciting new chapter of my life. Alleluia!

Sunday, January 17, 1999 Second Sunday in Ordinary Time
John 1, 29-34
John the Baptist's Testimony to Jesus

John the Baptist's testimony to Jesus came the day after his testimony to himself. John knew his own role, which was to prepare the way for Jesus. As Jesus walked toward him, John proclaimed, "Behold, the Lamb of God, who takes away the sin of the world."

Jesus, the Lamb of God, takes AWAY the sin of the world. Jesus takes AWAY my sins.

117

How can I live another minute under the burden of my sin? Not just my numerous sins, but also my entire sinful nature? I cannot come into the shining presence of the pure Agnus Dei, the Lamb of God, without being confronted with my sinful nature.

Jesus died so that I do not have to live another moment under this burden. He is waiting to remind me that when he died on the Cross he paid the price for my sins. I am free!

Lord Jesus, pure, spotless Lamb, thank you for forgiving my sins and for taking them AWAY. Thank you for a fresh start today. Thank you for the beautiful sacrament of reconciliation. Thank you for those who speak to me your words of forgiveness. Thank you for my freedom to forgive. Alleluia!

Monday, January 18, 1999
Mark 2, 23-28
The Question about Fasting

New wine for new wineskins! Every November, the French wine makers proudly release their nouveau Beaujolais, a lovely fresh new wine. There are celebrations and festivities in France to mark this occasion. American wine makers also offer Beaujolais just in time for Thanksgiving.

New wine is just that -- new! It is unpretentious and full of flavor. It has not been stored away for years to collect dust and distinction.

At crucial times in our lives we need the infusion of fresh "new wine" into our spirits. Without this, we languish. We are alive, but we are without joy.

Lord Jesus, I feel today the need of freshness, joy and newness in my life. Blow away the dust of despair. Fill my entire being with a new joy, a new life, and a new purpose. Alleluia!

Tuesday, January 19, 1999
Mark 2, 23-28
The Disciples and the Sabbath

The Pharisees were, in reality, serving themselves. Their human-made rules served to inflate their pride and to bolster their power. They managed to take something God meant for good -- the Sabbath-- and to twist it into yet another burden for God's people.

Jesus turns us back to God's original intent for the Sabbath, a time of rest and renewal. Jesus himself is Lord of the Sabbath!

Lord Jesus, sometimes I'm plagued by my "inner Pharisee" who imposes burdens you never intended me to carry. Today, as I work with my mind and my hands, please let my tired heart rest in you. Alleluia!

Wednesday, January 20, 1999 Sts. Fabian and Sebastian
Mark 3, 1-6
A Man with a Withered Hand

Notice the place. The synagogue! When Jesus entered the synagogue and saw the man with the diseased hand, he responded as he always responded. He responded in compassion.

Notice the time. We don't know how long the man had had this affliction. Possibly, it was a birth defect . Anyway, or "anyhoo," as Elizabeth, my 93 year old Scottish neighbor would say, this was his day to be healed! Jesus was here and Jesus healed him.

The hard-hearted Pharisees just could not comprehend this supposed "breaking" of the Sabbath. Their hearts were so hardened that they preferred to see the poor man continue to suffer rather than to be healed on the Sabbath. Jesus looked at the Pharisees with grief and anger.

Today's Gospel reminded me of an ecumenical conference I attended, just prior to a busy summer of hospital ministry. During one of the lectures, a woman, probably in her twenties, began to weep quietly. The speaker noticed her distress and gently spoke with her. She poured out a story of abuse by clergy.

The speaker later described his own emotions at hearing her story. He described his reaction as a mixture of rage, grief and forgiveness. The young woman began to be set free that day, just as the man in the synagogue was healed and set free by Jesus.

Lord Jesus, you are the same yesterday, today, and forever. You still look with anger and grief at those in positions of authority who hurt your little ones. Thank you for healing us, restoring us, and commissioning us be instruments of your forgiveness and healing. Alleluia!

Thursday, January 21, 1999 St. Agnes
Mark 3, 7-12
The Mercy of Jesus

In the ministry of Jesus, there is a pattern. There is a time of active ministry, a time for withdrawing for solitude, and then another time of active ministry.

Even when Jesus sought solitude, the people pursued him. The crowds sought him for what he could do for them. They knew he could heal them, feed them, and set them free from evil spirits.

Why do we seek Jesus? For himself or for what he can do for us?

When Jesus called his apostles, he called them first and foremost to be with him (Mark 3, 14). This is why he calls and continues to call you and me. He wants our hunger and thirst to be assuaged by his presence.

Jesus said, "... whoever believes in me will do the works that I do, and will do greater ones than these because I am going to the Father (John 14, 12)."

Do we really believe this? If we do, our lives will begin to change.

We must then withdraw for solitude to the sea or to some other place, perhaps to a quiet garden, to nourish our relationship with him. Praying before the Blessed Sacrament is an especially concentrated way to be renewed and refilled with the Holy Spirit. Jesus knows what we're going through right now. He is merciful and calls us anew to be with him. Alleluia!

Friday, January 22, 1999 St. Vincent
Mark 3, 13-19
The Mission of the Twelve

Are you a human "being" or a human "doing?" With Jesus, it's not either/or but rather both/and. He called his apostles first of all to "be" with him and only later to "do," that is, to preach and to drive out demons.

Lord Jesus, every time I reverse this order of being and doing I become exhausted. I cannot do the works you call me to do unless I have first spent time alone with you. Today, Lord, I offer this day -- Mass, the Prayer Walk, the trip to the market, lap swimming, preparing dinner -- all to you. Thank you for this early morning time alone with you. Restore and renew me so that I may be a sign of your love. Alleluia!

120

Saturday, January 23, 1999
Mark 3, 20-21
The Blasphemy of the Scribes

This is a tragic passage. It begins with the brief statement, "He came home."

Jesus came home. He came home after an exhausting times of active ministry. Alas, there was no peace and quiet even at home. Again the crowds pressed in, making it impossible even to have a meal.

To make things worse, Jesus' relatives appeared on the scene to try to take him away. They thought he was crazy!

Then the hostile scribes, who had come from Jerusalem to scrutinize him, proceeded to offer their own unsolicited assessment. "He is possessed by Beelzebul." and "By the prince of demons he drives out demons." Thanks, guys.

Where is there a place of serenity in the midst of this mayhem? The Gospel passage doesn't say.

Who is Jesus to believe? His family? They think he's crazy. The hostile religious leaders? They're out for his scalp.

Jesus was clear about his identity. At his baptism, his Father in heaven had proclaimed, "You are my beloved Son; with you I am well pleased (Mark 1, 11)."

Lord Jesus, thank you for my identity as a child of God. "Beloved, we are God's children now; what we shall be has not yet been revealed (I John 3, 2a)." Holy Spirit, thank you for reminding us of our true identity as we live this day. Alleluia!

Sunday, January 24, 1999 Third Sunday in Ordinary Time
Matthew 4, 12-23
The Beginning of the Galilean Ministry;
The Call of the First Disciples

"Repent, for the kingdom of heaven is at hand." Jesus calls us to repentance over and over. He calls us to a new way of thinking.

This morning I asked Jesus how to think in a new way about a situation in the past. I had tried to forgive and to pray about the situation, apparently without success. The unhappy memories would not subside, much less go away.

Jesus came to my aid! A friend prayed about the situation and perceived a huge "boulder."

Exactly! This had indeed become an obstacle. Now, what do I do about it? "Let the Lord take care of it," was the advice of the friend who prayed for me. Simple, yes. Easy, no.

This morning, after reading the Gospel, I believe the Holy Spirit added these words to me: "Turn your back on this situation. Don't put energy there. Don't 'go' there. Stop brooding about it. Don't discuss it."

The Lord had already removed me from the situation and had brought me into a bright, glorious new place. However, because I had been so weighed down with the past, I was carrying a "boulder," and could not see the promise of the future.

Lord Jesus, I repent. I leave the past with you. Forgive me for brooding. I reach out to the new life you have given me today. Alleluia!

Monday, January 25, 1999 The Conversion of St. Paul
Mark 16, 15-18
The Commissioning of the Eleven

The crucified and risen Jesus is giving his last instructions to his disciples before returning home to heaven, home to his "abba," Father. His mission on earth has been gloriously completed. Alleluia!

Your mission on this earth will one day be over and so will mine. We may or may not have the opportunity to give a farewell discourse to our nearest and dearest.

Today, Lord Jesus, as the storms of life swirl around us, keep us focused on you. Keep us occupied doing what you told us to do -- proclaiming the Gospel to all. Shape and mold us to proclaim your Good News to each person you bring across our path today. Thank you for your resurrection power flowing through us to accomplish your purpose for our lives. Alleluia!

Tuesday, January 26, 1999 Sts. Timothy and Titus
Mark 3, 31-35
Jesus and His Family

Some of Jesus' relatives had just attempted to take him away, saying, "He is out of his mind." A real vote of confidence there! Jesus, not to be deterred, continued his teaching in the home of his host.

In today's Gospel, Mary, the mother of Jesus, arrived, along with the brothers and sisters of Jesus. The crowd listening to Jesus informed him that his relatives had arrived and were asking for him.

Jesus gave a new meaning to the word "family." Looking at his followers, he said, "Here are my mother and my brothers. [For] whoever does the will of God is my brother and sister and mother."

My most important relationship is my relationship with God. Obvious? Yes, but in the wear and tear of daily life, I may try to play God in the lives of those near and dear.

When I do that, I do others a disservice and I do myself a disservice. Where should I be and what should I do? The best place for me to be is in the center of God's will. Everything else will fall into place. Alleluia!

Wednesday, January 27, 1999 St. Angela Merici
Mark 4, 1-20
The Parable of the Sower; The Purpose of the Parables

According to Shakespeare, "If it be now, 'tis not to come; if it be not to come, yet it will come: the readiness is all (<u>Hamlet</u> v. ii)." These words came to mind as I read today's Gospel. The farmer must be faithful to prepare the fields for the harvest, The sun shines, the rains fall, and the seeds sprout. The seedlings are carefully tended until maturity.

The Lord knows when to bring forth the fruit. His timing is perfect in our lives.

Lord Jesus, help me to prepare now and to be ready, Alleluia!

Thursday, January 28, 1999 St. Thomas Aquinas
Mark 4, 21-25
Parable of the Lamp

The lamp's purpose is to reveal and to expose. If the lamp is hidden away, it cannot fulfill its purpose. If people don't like what the light from the lamp reveals, they may take the lamp and smash it and throw it away. However, they can never throw away the light from the lamp and what the lamp revealed when it was among them.

"For there is nothing hidden except to be made visible; nothing is secret except to come to light. Anyone who has ears to hear ought to hear." Alleluia!

Friday, January 29, 1999
Mark 4, 26-34
Seed Grows of Itself; The Mustard Seed

Scatter seed and then go to sleep. Scattering the seed or sowing the seed is the easy part. "Sleep," for me, is the hard part

When I "scatter" or "sow" a seed in prayer, the next step is to "sleep," to relinquish the "seed," or the prayer to God. God is in control. My part is to trust.

Instead of trusting that God is really at work, I tend to walk up and down the "prayer garden," staring at the bare ground where the seed has been planted. Nothing is there, so I begin to agonize. Did I really plant the seed? Maybe I should dig around and make sure the seed is still there. Maybe this, maybe that.

Lord Jesus, whether I scatter a prayer to you in an informal way or whether I sow a prayer in agony, help me to "sleep," to rest secure that you are now tending the tiny "seed" of prayer. You are in charge. You are watching over the little seed, sending sunshine and soft rain, or maybe even fierce storms. You are watching over my prayer! Forgive me for being so anxious. Help me to wait patiently for the blossoms and the fruit. Alleluia!

Saturday, January 30, 1999
Mark 4, 35-41
The Calming of the Storm at Sea

"You can't mess around with the weather in Chicago!" I still smile when I remember that earnest expression of incredulity.

In the mid-1970's, I was in a wonderful ecumenical prayer group in California. We met once a week, studied Scripture, and prayed for others and for ourselves. Then, one of our members moved to Chicago for graduate study in theology. A dramatic change of climate!

Another member of the prayer group was married to an agnostic physicist. When we prayed for our friend in Chicago and for the storms to subside, the physicist, hearing about our prayers and exclaimed "You can't mess around with the weather in Chicago."

In today's Gospel, Jesus was at the helm of the situation, even though he was sleeping, I was reminded of a painting of a little bird safely asleep in its nest while a fierce storm raged all around.

Jesus was asleep in the boat, in the midst of the storm, knowing that his Father in heaven was in control. For the sake of the terrified disciples, however, he spoke to the wind and the sea. All was calm.

The physicist, now a deeply committed Christian, came to Jesus with humble, childlike faith. Jesus wants us too to trust that he is in control of the winds and the waves of our lives. He is in the boat with us and we won't sink. Alleluia!

Sunday, January 31, 1999 Fourth Sunday in Ordinary Time
Matthew 5, 1-12
The Sermon on the Mount; The Beatitudes

Jesus addressed these words, not to the curiosity-seeking crowds, but to his own, committed disciples, those who had accepted the call to follow him in a radical way. I call this a course in "Kingdom Thinking 101."

Eugene Peterson, in The Message, gives these words a fresh, "hold-your-breath-as-you-read" interpretation. Here are a few examples.

"You're blessed when you're at the end of your rope. With less of you, there is more of God and his rule (Matthew 5, 3)."

"You're blessed when you feel you've lost what is most dear to you. Only then can you be embraced by the One most dear to you (Matthew 5, 4)."

"You're blessed when your commitment to God provokes persecution. The persecution drives you even deeper into God's kingdom (Matthew 5, 10)."

"Not only that -- count yourselves blessed every time people put you down or throw you out or speak lies about you to discredit me. What it means is that the truth is too close for comfort and they are uncomfortable. You can be glad when that happens -- give a cheer, even! -- for though they don't like it, I do! And all heaven applauds (Matthew 5, 11, 12)."

Lord Jesus, help us today to "inhale" your startling words to us and then to breathe them out victoriously with our lives. Alleluia!

Monday, February 1, 1999
Mark 5, 1-20
The Healing of the Gerasene Demoniac

"The man had been dwelling among the tombs, and no one could restrain him any longer ..." The people around this poor man had done all they could, but their best efforts were not enough. He lived amongst the tombs, crying out and injuring himself. The situation seemed hopeless and impossible.

How often do we rage against circumstances we regard as impossible? We work, pray, seek professional help, consider legal action, ask others to intercede or intervene, and do all in our power to solve the dilemma.

In today's Gospel, Jesus stepped into a mind-boggling situation. He spoke directly to the unclean spirit. "Unclean spirit, come out of the man!"

The entire situation was transformed! The possessed man was delivered, healed, transformed, and set free to live a new life.

What is it in your life you just can't fix? Ask God to reveal what your part is in this situation. After you have done your part, release the situation into the God's hands. Ask God to step in and do what you cannot do, namely the impossible.

Lord Jesus, no situation is impossible for you. You speak and the winds and waves obey you. You speak and people are healed. I don't know anything else I can do in this troubling situation. I kneel before you and ask for you to bring your solution. Thank you for your answer whenever and however it arrives. Alleluia!

Tuesday, February 2, 1999 Presentation of the Lord
Luke 2, 22-40
The Presentation in the Temple; The Return to Nazareth

Doing the known will of God without full understanding! That is what we see in Mary and Joseph and in Simeon and Anna. There were elements of the known and the unknown for each of them.

The known will of God was the law of Moses. The Law stated when a couple was to come to the Temple to present their newborn.

The Law stated the nature of the offering. Finances dictated that Mary and Joseph would bring a pair of turtledoves or pigeons, rather than a year-old lamb.

The known will of God came to Simeon through the Holy Spirit. Simeon knew how to listen to the voice of the Holy Spirit. The Holy Spirit told Simeon exactly when to come to the Temple in Jerusalem,

Anna also knew how to listen to the voice of the Holy Spirit. "And coming forward at that very time, she gave thanks to God and spoke about the child to all who were awaiting the redemption of Jerusalem."

Endeavoring to fulfill the known will of God is all we can do. We may limited understanding as we step out to obey the Lord.

This is what Mary did when she and Joseph came to the Temple to present the infant Jesus. The young Mary must have wondered at Simeon's strange words.

The aged Simeon declared, "Behold, this child is destined for the fall and rise of many in Israel, and to be a sign that will be contradicted (and you yourself a sword will pierce) so that the thoughts of many hearts may be revealed (Luke 2, 34-35)." Only later would Mary understand those prophetic words.

So with us today. We can only do what is in our power to fulfill what we believe to be the God's call on our lives. The difficult, the unknown, and the mysterious components we try to accept without distress. All will be made clear in God's time.

Lord Jesus, I present myself to you today, to do your will as I understand it. I leave all that I do not understand with you. Alleluia!

Wednesday, February 3, 1999 St. Blase
Mark 6, 1-6
The Rejection at Nazareth

Gospel? Good news?

Is it really good news that Jesus was rejected in the synagogue of his own hometown, Nazareth? Jesus was not surprised. As he said, "A prophet is not without honor except in his native place and among his own kin and in his own house."

By their harsh judgment, the people of Nazareth chose to lock Jesus into their own expectations. Son of God though he was, "... he was not able to perform any mighty deed there, apart from curing a few sick people by laying his hands on them."

That's no small feat, but Jesus could have done so much more if the hometown folks had opened their hearts to him. Jesus was "amazed at their lack of faith."

This still happens today. A very large, dynamic church once had as its pastor a man who was rejected in his hometown. A successful author and speaker experienced jealous jabs from those who were amazed that someone with merely a high school education could actually write books and minister around the world! Fancy that!

Perhaps the good news here is that the rejection at Nazareth did not stop Jesus from living the life the Father in heaven had called him to live. He was accepted and honored in other places and by other people, the Gentiles.

Having experienced rejection in his hometown synagogue prepared Jesus to teach his disciples about rejection. "Whatever place does not welcome you or listen to you, leave there and shake the dust off your feet in testimony against them (Mark 6, 11)."

Lord Jesus, when I am not well-received, help me to continue on the path you have ordained for me. Thank you that you persevered in doing the will of your Father and that you call me also to persevere. Alleluia!

Thursday, February 4, 1999
Mark 6, 7-13
The Mission of the Twelve

Jesus, sending out his followers on their mission, instructed them, "Wherever you enter a house, stay there until you leave from there." That seems obvious, but is it?

I believe Jesus is telling his followers that they are to remain in an assigned place until his assignment, or mission, for them in that place is complete. When the time comes to leave, Jesus will make it clear. "Whatever place does not welcome you or listen to you, leave there and shake the dust off your feet in testimony against them."

It is not up to us to determine the length of time we spend in a certain place while on assignment from the Lord. We proclaim Jesus and leave the results with Jesus . Alleluia!

Friday, February 5, 1999 St. Agatha
Mark 6, 14-29
Herod's Opinion of Jesus;
The Death of John the Baptist

"The fear of the LORD is the beginning of knowledge…. (Proverbs 1, 7)." If I can understand this, the rest of my life will fall into place. If you can understand this, the rest of your life will fall into place.

The fear of the Lord does not mean a servile, cringing trepidation or timidity. Rather, it is a bold, radical reverence for the living God!

The best place for me to be is in the center of God's will. The best place for you to be is in the center of God's will.

In the center of God's will is the sweet stillness and knowledge of his presence and protection. Even in the midst of struggle and uncertainty, we are safe in his arms. He will never forsake us.

Poor Herod must not have understood the fear of the Lord, because he was tormented by earthly fears. What would Herodius think? What would Herodius' daughter think? What would the dinner guests think?

Herod, what will GOD think if you knock off John the Baptist? "Herod feared John, knowing him to be a righteous and holy man …." Still, Herod's focus was on public opinion and not on God.

Fear God, stand in awe of God, and you won't have to fear anyone else. You will be courteous to all, but afraid of none. You will look to your God and be radiant. Alleluia!

Saturday, February 6, 1999 St. Paul Miki and Companions
Mark 6, 30-31
The Return of the Twelve

You've heard the one about " … no peace for the wicked …(Isaiah 48, 22)?" This one's about "no rest for the righteous!"

The twelve apostles returned triumphant, exhilarated, and perhaps exhausted. Jesus could see all of this.

He knew they needed to have a rest, a time away. He told them, "Come away by yourselves to a deserted place and rest a while."

In ministry, it is essential to love yourself and to care for yourself. Sometimes, the time away is very short.

The apostles only had time for a boat ride. "People saw them leaving and many came to know about it. They hastened there on foot from all the towns and arrived at the place before them."

I wish I could say that the amount of time wasn't important. The old "quantity vs. quality" myth. Maybe I'm cranky and greedy, but I want BOTH! Still, to be realistic, sometimes we have to enjoy whatever time is available.

While studying in the seminary and raising a family, I learned to take "little retreats." I remember a particular "hour with the Lord" in the beautiful gardens of the seminary. There would also be times when, instead of walking through the hallways to class, I would cross through the Marian courtyard for a bit of air.

During these years, I learned to study in different places, such as Children's Library. Even with children buzzing around, I could still tackle a medical ethics case study or ponder my thesis research.

One of my seminary classes involved a practicum in hospital ministry. I needed some way to ease the transition from being with terminally ill patients on the cancer ward and then going home to care for my family. Sometimes I would stop by the gift shop to enjoy the flowers or to browse through the colorful cards. Just a little break.

Still later, in a summer chaplaincy assignment, I did the same. Little breaks. One afternoon, the canteen was out of coffee and I was about to fall asleep. Walking outside for some fresh air, I was delighted to spot the "coffee man" with his cart. A cup of fresh, hot coffee was just the thing that long afternoon.

Lord Jesus, today as I serve you, help me also to love myself and to care for myself. Take me to "a deserted place" and help me to "rest a while." Alleluia!

Sunday, February 7, 1999 Fifth Sunday in Ordinary Time
Matthew 5, 13-16
The Similes of Salt and Light

Jesus said, "You are the salt of the earth" and "You are the light of the world." It is not a matter of whether or not we feel like "salt" or "light." Jesus said that we ARE salt and light.

During difficult, stressful times I may not "feel" very salty or shiny. I may feel very blah and dim. Never mind. I was reminded of Isaiah 42, 3, that the Lord will not extinguish a dimly burning wick.

Lord Jesus, thank you for the joy of being nourished in your presence, in Word and Sacrament, in solitude, song, or silence. Let me remember that, whether I feel like it or not, I am "salt" and "light." Alleluia!

Monday, February 8, 1999 St. Jerome Emiliani
Mark 6, 53-56
The Healings at Gennesaret

Villages. Towns. Countryside. Marketplaces.

Wherever Jesus went, people sought him. They ran to find him! No cell phones in those days. No cars. No big auditoriums to rent for healing services.

We don't need all the fancy extras to serve God and the people of God. Whether we feel like it or not, we are Jesus' Body, the Church, here on this earth. As we simply live our lives and move about the villages, the towns, the countryside, and the marketplaces, we carry the healing presence of Jesus Christ. Alleluia!

Tuesday, February 9, 1999
Mark 7, 1-13
The Tradition of the Elders

Jesus tackled the Pharisees, calling them hypocrites and referring to Isaiah 29, 13, "Well did Isaiah prophesy about you hypocrites, as it is written:

'This people honors me with their lips,
    but their hearts are far from me;
 In vain do they worship me;
    teaching as doctrines human precepts.'
You disregard God's commandment but cling to human tradition."

As The Message has it, "Isaiah was right about frauds like you, hit the bulls-eye in fact:

'These people make a big show of saying the right thing,
    but their heart isn't in it.
 They just use me as a cover
    for teaching whatever suits their fancy,

> Ditching God's command
>   and taking up the latest fads.' "

Lord Jesus, help me to worship you "in Spirit and truth (John 4, 23)." Reveal to me any ways in which I have put human tradition above true worship. Alleluia!

Wednesday, February 10, 1999 St. Scholastica
Mark 7, 14-23
The Tradition of the Elders

This Gospel reminds me of the proverb, "With closest custody, guard your heart, for in it are the sources of life (Proverbs 4, 23)." As Today's English Version (GNT) has it, "Be careful how you think; your life is shaped by your thoughts."

Jesus is saying that what we hold and cherish in our hearts is what defines us and also affects others. "A clean heart create for me, God; renew in me a steadfast spirit (Psalm 51, 12)." Alleluia!

Thursday, February 11, 1999 Our Lady of Lourdes
Mark 7, 24-30
The Syrophoenician Woman's Faith

This event is also recorded in Matthew's Gospel, in which Jesus tells the woman, "I was sent only to the lost sheep of the house of Israel (Matthew 15, 24)." At that time the Gentiles were considered "dogs" or "low life."

Jesus came to do the will of his Father in heaven. Notice what he actually says in today's Gospel. Jesus does not immediately refuse the woman's request, but he does say, "Let the children be fed first." This is because Jesus was sent first of all to minister to his own Jewish people.

Nevertheless, Jesus stepped outside the safety of the "rules" and ministered directly to the Greek woman and her daughter. She readily acknowledged the prior claim of the Jews, yet was bold enough to remind Jesus that "... even the dogs under the table eat the children's scraps."

In essence she was saying that she would even take the "leftovers" in order to find help for her child. An amazing combination of humility, persistence, and audacity!

Jesus was clearly moved. He replied, "For saying this, you may go. The demon has gone out of your daughter." Her courage and her willingness even to accept the humiliating label, "dog," had moved Jesus to grant her appeal.

Have you ever been unkindly labeled? Go directly to Jesus. He sees your need, he reads your heart, he loves you and he will heal you. Alleluia!

Friday, February 12, 1999
Mark 7, 31-37
The Healing of a Deaf Man

"*Ephphatha!*" "Be opened!"

Lord Jesus, speak to whatever it is within me that blocks or hinders my ability to hear your voice. Speak "*Ephphatha!*"

Lord Jesus, speak to whatever it is within me that blocks or hinders my ability to speak your words. Speak "*Ephphatha!*"

Lord Jesus, thank you for opening me to hear your voice. Thank you for opening me to speak your words. Alleluia!

Saturday, February 13, 1999
Mark 8, 1-10
The Feeding of the Four Thousand

"Where can anyone get enough bread to satisfy them here in this deserted place?" The disciples did not know how even Jesus could do anything in this isolated place.

How can we blame the disciples when we fall prey to this same mindset? Sometimes, we may feel our lives are a "deserted place." We wander around listlessly, wondering if even the Lord knows where we are.

Not only is Jesus active and present in our deserted places, but he is also actively planning to break through in a life-giving way. He is planning not only to feed us, but also to feed others through us. He is truly the Lord of the breakthrough.

Lord Jesus, today I ask you to break through my "deserted place." Thank you for feeding me and then allowing me to participate in the miracle of feeding a multitude. Alleluia!

Sunday, February 14, 1999 Sixth Sunday in Ordinary Time
Matthew 5, 17-37
Teaching About the Law; Teaching About Anger;
Teaching About Divorce; Teaching About Oaths

Jesus said, "I have come not to abolish but to fulfill." Have you ever watched small children playing with building blocks or construction toys? For awhile they watch as someone else, an adult or an older child, carefully and painstakingly creates a unique structure. Then, unexpectedly, shouting with glee, one of the children smashes the whole structure!.

Tearing down seems such fun. It is easier to tear down than to build. It's only as they mature that children find joy in creating and building rather than in the brief thrill of destruction.

Jesus did not intend to destroy the teachings of the law or the prophets, but rather to show us the deeper meaning of these teachings. He did not kick over or smash these laws, but instead shone the light of the Holy Spirit on them to illuminate their true meaning.

We may not smash a work of art or kill another with a gun, but behind the closed doors of a committee room, we may quietly destroy another person's reputation. We have committed murder.

Lord Jesus, may your design for my life be fulfilled. Alleluia!

Monday, February 15, 1999
Mark 8, 11-13
The Demand for a Sign

Just walk away! Jesus did it and sometimes we have to do it, too. One feels deeply for Jesus in his humanity in this passage. He had had it with the Pharisees and "sighed from the depths of his spirit." His answer to them was terse. Then he left and "went off to the other shore."

We are not put on this earth to convince everyone about the call of God on our lives. Even Jesus could not do that. The Pharisees were bound and determined to trip him up and to discredit him.

Some things we must leave in the hands of God. As my grandmother used to say, "It will all come out in the wash."

Truth will triumph. The truth about ourselves and the truth about others. We have to live our lives as God calls us to live our lives and then wait. We may have to wait a long, long time. The result will be worth the wait. "Though the mills of God grind slowly, yet they grind exceedingly small (Friedrich von Logan, Poetic Aphorisms)." Alleluia!

Tuesday, February 16, 1999
Mark 8, 14-21
The Leaven of the Pharisees

Those meathead disciples! Jesus had just warned them, "Watch out, guard against the leaven the Pharisees and the leaven of Herod." They erroneously concluded that Jesus was talking about the fact that they had forgotten to bring bread.

Poor Jesus! How did he ever put up with those characters? How does he ever put up with us?

Jesus had just multiplied bread before their eyes. Then those dratted Pharisees came to pester him. To top it off, his own disciples were acting like blockheads. Jesus quizzed them, " 'Do you not yet understand or comprehend? Are your hearts hardened? Do you have eyes and not see, ears and not hear? And do you not remember, when I broke the five loaves for the five thousand, how many wicker baskets full of fragments you picked up?' They answered him, 'Twelve.' When I broke the seven loaves for the four thousand, how many full baskets of fragments did you pick up?' They answered [him], 'Seven.' He said to them, 'Do you still not understand?' "

Lord Jesus, we are just like your first disciples. We are so slow to understand. Illumine our hearts and minds. Help us to guard against the influence of the inner and outer Pharisees and Herods in our lives." Alleluia!

Wednesday, February 17, 1999 Ash Wednesday
Matthew 6, 1-6, 16-18
Teaching about Almsgiving; Teaching about Prayer;
Teaching about Fasting

Unto the Lord. Unto the Lord. Unto the Lord.

Our giving, praying, and fasting is to be done unto the Lord and not for the recognition of others. God knows.

When you give alms ... When you pray ... When you fast ...

"When," not "if." Jesus takes it for granted that we will give, pray, and fast.

Lord Jesus, simplify me this Lent.

Thursday, February 18, 1999 Lenten Weekday
Luke 9, 22-25
The Conditions of Discipleship

The Lord is saying, "Give me your heart. The rest will follow." Deny yourself, take up your personal cross, and follow Jesus.

How do I deny myself, my wishes, my longings and my desires? By opening my heart to the Lord and giving him all the pieces of my heart.

Resolutions on my part to "do this" or to "give up that" may not last. That's because they are done on my own initiative and are fueled by my own efforts.

Instead, I need to acknowledge that the Lord is in charge of my heart. I am at peace to follow his initiative.

How do I take up my cross daily? What precisely is my cross? Again, I yield my heart to the Lord and receive his wise, loving assignment for me today.

Truly following Jesus will be the result of this simple exercise. He now has my heart and my will. He will lead me today and every day until the day he leads me Home.

Friday, February 19, 1999 Lenten Weekday
Matthew 9, 14-15
The Question about Fasting

Mardi Gras! Whether it's in New Orleans or in our hometown, it's a time of celebration before Lent. Whether or not there are pancakes or parades, it's still a time of celebration.

The disciples of Jesus celebrated the presence of the Son of God in their midst. There were times of difficulty, times of testing and trial, but still it was a time of celebration. Jesus was with them, so why should they fast?

Jesus, at the Last Supper, told his disciples, "I shall not drink this fruit of the vine until the day I drink it with you new in the kingdom of my Father (Matthew 26, 29)." Jesus was moving towards his destiny in Jerusalem.

So it is with us. Jesus is with us always, through his Holy Spirit. Still, especially during Lent, we long to draw even closer to the Lord to prepare for our celebration in heaven.

Lord Jesus, show me how to fast.

Saturday, February 20, 1999 Lenten Weekday
Luke 5, 27-32
The Call of Levi

We've heard the saying, "You can give without loving, but you cannot love without giving." This saying is illustrated in a vivid way in today's Gospel.

Jesus touched Levi's heart in such a profound way that Levi left everything behind and followed Jesus. Then he hosted a great banquet for Jesus. Friends from his former life attended this celebration.

Levi left the old life of taking and began a new life of giving. There was a great exuberance as Levi began to know the joy of abandonment to Jesus.

"Leave your past in ashes." Those were the words spoken at today's Ash Wednesday Day of Recollection. "Leave your past in ashes." That's what Levi did. That's what Jesus is calling us to do this Lent.

Lord Jesus, I choose today to leave my past in ashes. Forgive me for all my selfishness and all my "taking." Help me now to follow you and give you "a great banquet" by loving and giving to others in a new way this Lent.

Sunday, February 21, 1999 First Sunday of Lent
Matthew 4, 1-11
The Temptations of Jesus

"It is written ..." "It is written ..." "Again it is written ..." "Then the devil left him and, behold, angels came and ministered to him."

What in the world?! What was all that about?

Jesus, newly baptized, was firmly led by the Holy Spirit into the wilderness, into the desert. This was a prolonged time in which he was severely tempted by the devil.

Jesus was truly human. In his humanity, he experienced every temptation that we experience. He had to know, for himself and for us, how to respond to every form of temptation. Jesus, in essence, went through the "experiments" ahead of us, so we would know what to do.

When my son was a teaching assistant in a college physics lab, he conscientiously performed, ahead of time, each of the experiments the students would be required to perform. When their questions arose, he knew from personal experience how to offer expert advice.

Jesus countered each temptation with the appropriate "It is written" from scripture. He had a profound knowledge and understanding of the scriptures and knew exactly which scripture was necessary for countering each sly suggestion from the devil.

Jesus surrendered, not to the temporary satisfaction of his earthly desires, but to the loving will of his Father in heaven. Jesus said, "… Get away, Satan! It is written:

'The Lord, your God, shall you worship,
   and him alone shall you serve.' "

Lord Jesus, help us to recognize the tactics of the enemy of our soul, especially when they are cleverly disguised. Help us to say our own "it is written …" Thank you for sending angels to minister to us.

Monday, February 22, 1999 Chair of St. Peter, Apostle
Matthew 16, 13-19
Peter's Confession about Jesus

Peter. It's Peter again! What's that fisherman up to this time?

Jesus saw something in Peter that caused him to give to Peter the keys to the kingdom of heaven.

We need to pay attention, not only to Peter, but also to the way Jesus treated Peter.

After all, it was to Peter that the heavenly Father revealed the identity of Jesus. To Jesus' question, "Who do people say that the Son of Man is?" Peter responded, "You are the Messiah, the Son of the Living God."

Peter, for all his flaws and failings, was chosen from among all the apostles for the terrifying privilege of holding the keys of the kingdom. Jesus knew what he was doing.

Jesus had submitted his humanity initially to Mary, his virgin mother. Mary was the chosen one to lead and to guide and to care for the infant Jesus.

Jesus was carried in Mary's heart, in her womb, and in her arms. Mary loved and cared for Jesus as infant, child, and teenager. Yes, Jesus knew what it was like to be a teenager!

Jesus now submits his Church, his Body on this earth, to Peter. Peter is the chosen one to lead and guide and care for the Church. Peter is the Vicar of Christ on earth. The Pope.

Do you see? Do you understand?

Even heaven bends to the teaching of "Peter." Whatever "Peter" prohibits on earth is prohibited in heaven. Whatever "Peter" permits on earth is permitted in heaven. "A yes on earth is a yes in heaven. A no on earth is a no in heaven (Matthew 16, 19, The Message)."

Lord Jesus, you are the Head of the Church. In your sovereignty, you have given particular authority to "Peter." We adore you, O Lord, we praise you, we thank you, and we trust you. We pray today for "Peter," for the one occupying the chair of Peter. May your chosen one continue in the faithful execution of this holy office.

Tuesday, February 23, 1999 Lenten Weekday
Matthew 6, 7-15
Teaching about Prayer; The Lord's Prayer

In the Lord's Prayer, we are asking our Father in heaven to forgive us in just the same way we forgive others. Do we really mean what we pray?

"If you forgive others their transgressions, your heavenly Father will forgive you. But if you do not forgive others, neither will your Father forgive your transgressions (Matthew 6, 14-15)."

When I am outraged by another's behavior, I tend to focus more on what that particular person did to me than on my own need for the Father's forgiveness. This is not a matter of bargaining with God and thinking, "Oh well, I have to forgive so that I will be forgiven." No, it goes much deeper than that.

It is a process to forgive those who have wronged us. It takes time and often wise counsel. The words, "I forgive you" can be spoken in an instant. Sometimes, there is indeed an instant release, a lifting of the heavy burden. Sometimes, it takes longer.

What is this burden? The burden is our perception of the other person's sin against us as well as the actual sin.

When we refuse to make the act of the will to forgive, we "carry" the other person around with us all the time. A huge burden.

The hurtful situation may be obsessing us and controlling our lives. We may even be defining ourselves as victims.

Jesus says "ENOUGH!" There is a way out of this toxic wasteland of grief and rage.

A friend, Hilda, condenses forgiveness prayer to four words: "Bless them. Heal me." Short and powerful.

I am releasing the ones who offended, wounded, or betrayed me. I am releasing them from all responsibility. I am radically trusting God to put the matter right.

Heavenly Father, help me today to experience your forgiveness in a deeper way. I choose to forgive and to release all who have sinned against me. Thank you, Jesus, for dying on the Cross for my sins. Holy Spirit, heal me and help me to view myself and others in a new way, a healthier way.

Wednesday, February 24, 1999 Lenten Weekday
Luke 11, 29-32
The Demand for a Sign

"This generation is an evil generation; it seeks a sign, but no sign will be given it, except the sign of Jonah." Four times in this passage, Jesus used the expression, "this generation."

Jesus warned that at the judgment, condemnation would arise from the Ninevites. They were the wicked inhabitants of the city of Nineveh. Israel considered Nineveh a big-time enemy.

Jonah, flawed and reluctant prophet though he was, finally obeyed God and preached to the Ninevites. Surprise! They repented.

Condemnation of Jesus' generation would also come from the "queen of the south" (the Queen of Sheba). She traveled "from the ends of the earth to hear the wisdom of Solomon."

Jesus emphasized, "there is something greater than Solomon here." The "something greater" was actually "Someone" greater.

Jesus, the Son of God, was here before them. Jesus himself was the message. Jesus was the "something greater."

Even with their limited understanding, the people of Nineveh repented at the preaching of Jonah, a mere mortal. Even the powerful Queen of Sheba marveled at the wisdom of Solomon, a mere mortal.

Lord Jesus, YOU are the Sign! You died, rose again, and will return in dazzling glory to earth. Until then, Lord, let us, your followers, repent, receive your forgiveness, and shine as signs to our generation.

Thursday, February 25, 1999 Lenten Weekday
Matthew 7, 7-12
The Answer to Prayer; The Golden Rule

Jesus tells us to be straightforward with God. He tells us to ask, seek, and knock.

We ask, of course, from our limited human perspective. Our Father loves us, sees into the recesses of our hearts, and gives us what is truly good for us. He does not trick us or shortchange us.

In turn, we are to treat others as we would like to be treated. We make allowances for ourselves all the time. Therefore, we should make allowances for others and offer them our concern and understanding.

Lord Jesus, today I am weary and do not even know what to ask, much less what to seek and still less on what doors to knock. Help me simply to rest in you and be gentle with myself and with others.

Friday, February 26, 1999 Lenten Weekday
Matthew 5, 20-26
Teaching about the Law; Teaching about Anger

Words have the power to kill. Words can kill dreams, relationships, and reputations.

Yes, God can heal. Yes, God can restore, but sometimes it is a very long, slow process.

The old saying, "Sticks and stones may break my bones, but words can never hurt me" is simply not true. Words wound and kill.

Lord Jesus, forgive me for the thoughts I've entertained and for the words I've spoken that have hurt others. Please bring healing where I have brought harm. I need your healing, also, from the harm done to me by the words of others. Uproot the words that have taken root in my heart. Plant your sweet words of love in place of the bitter words. Let my own words today be words of love and life and healing.

Saturday, February 27, 1999 Lenten Weekday
Matthew 5, 43-48
Love of Enemies

What the Lord is after is the transformation of our inner selves. As followers of Christ, we are in the process of being conformed to the image of Christ (Romans 8, 29). The state we are to be in is the state of receiving and giving unconditional love.

Like the rain, which falls on the just and the unjust alike, God's love flowing through us waters and refreshes all around us. Some will receive our love. Some will not. Some will actively resist us. This does not affect the state of our being (a vessel filled with love) nor the ground of our loving (the love of God).

Lord Jesus, we are so far from this ideal. Instead of loving and praying for our enemies, we file lawsuits to protect our "rights." Please help us to see our enemies, those who wish us harm, with your eyes. Help us to love them with your love.

Sunday, February 28, 1999 Second Sunday of Lent
Matthew 17, 1-9
The Transfiguration of Jesus

The Transfiguration of Jesus occurred between the first and the second predictions of his Passion or suffering. This was a carefully chosen time.

God the Father was drawing back the curtain and speaking words confirming Jesus' identity. "This is my beloved Son, with whom I am well pleased ..."

These were also the words spoken by God the Father at the baptism of Jesus. "This is my beloved Son, with whom I am well pleased (Matthew 3, 17)."

At the Transfiguration, the Father in heaven also spoke to Peter, James and John, "Listen to him." Listen to Jesus! Peter finally stopped his nervous, excited jabbering and fell prostrate on the ground along with James and John.

Lord Jesus, at certain moments in our lives, you take us "up a high mountain" and reveal your glory, your love, and your power in our lives. You know we need these moments in our school of discipleship. We need to experience afresh who you are and who we are. Whether we are in the pits or on the pinnacle today, help us to listen to you.

Monday, March 1, 1999 Lenten Weekday
Luke 6, 36-39
Love of Enemies; Judging Others

Commands jump out of this passage. Some commands tell us what to do.

"Be merciful, just as [also] your Father is merciful."
"Forgive and you will be forgiven."
"Give and gifts will be given to you; a good measure, packed together, shaken down, and overflowing, will be poured into your lap."

Other commands caution us what to stop doing.

"Stop judging and you will not be judged."
"Stop condemning and you will not be condemned."

As you notice, there are promises attached to the commands. The commands are tied together with a ribbon in verse 38. "For the measure with which you measure will in return be measured out to you."

Lord Jesus, today I seek your mercy, your forgiveness, and your gifts. Help me to offer gifts of mercy and forgiveness to others. I don't want to be judged or condemned. Help me to stop judging and condemning other, even in the silence of my heart.

Tuesday, March 2, 1999 Lenten Weekday
Matthew 23, 1-12
Denunciation of the Scribes and the Pharisees

Jesus is teaching us about leadership and about recognition. We are wise to look to Jesus alone for recognition.

The scribes and the Pharisees, poor dears, had it all wrong. They insisted on getting their recognition right here, right now. They preached, but did not put their own preaching into practice. They burdened God's people with demands that God never intended.

Lord Jesus, draw me closer to you this Lent. I feel very weary and heavily burdened. You said, "Come to me, all you who labor and are burdened, and I will give you rest. Take my yoke upon you and learn from me, for I am meek and humble of heart; and you will find rest for yourselves. For my yoke is easy, and my burden light (Matthew 11, 28, 29)."

Wednesday, March 3, 1999 Lenten Weekday
Matthew 20, 17-28
The Third Prediction of the Passion;
The Request of James and John

After the first prediction of the Passion, Peter tried to deny that such a terrible thing could ever happen to Jesus. Jesus spoke sternly to Peter and rebuked him, saying, "Get behind me, Satan! You are an obstacle to me. You are thinking not as God does, but as human beings do (Matthew 16, 23)."

After the second prediction of the Passion, the disciples were "overwhelmed with grief (Matthew 17, 23)." However, after the third prediction of the Passion, James and John decided to try to cash in on the future glory and even used their mamma to plead their case!

After the first prediction, Jesus told all the disciples. "Whoever wishes to come after me must deny himself, take up his cross, and follow me (Matthew 16, 24)." This is foundational. Following Jesus is to be our priority.

In today's Gospel, Jesus continued his teaching on discipleship. Rather than savoring and relishing earthly power, the disciples were to use their authority as a means to serve. "Whoever wishes to be first among you shall be your servant; and whoever wishes to be great among you shall be your slave. Just so, the Son of Man did not come to be served but to serve and to give his life as a ransom for many."

Lord Jesus, help me to follow you as you direct. Thank you for giving me discernment.

Thursday, March 4, 1999 St. Casimir
Luke 16, 19-31
The Parable of the Rich Man and Lazarus

"There was a rich man who dressed in purple garments and fine linen and dined sumptuously each day. And lying at his door was a poor man named Lazarus, covered with sores, who would gladly have eaten his fill of the scraps that fell from the rich man's table."

So begins today's Gospel. This is Good News?

If the Gospel motivates me to live more simply and to give to the poor, that is very good news. Still, there might be a poor person who needs my love as well as my material gifts. This is a poor person from whom I never escape.

I may be the poor person if I have not discovered the imperishable riches Jesus offers me. Perhaps there are gifts of the Holy Spirit I have not yet understood or appropriated. I am rich, yet I may be living like a pauper.

Lord Jesus, today, help me to reach out in gentleness and generosity to all the "poor," to realize my own wealth in you, and joyfully to share with others.

Friday, March 5, 1999 Lenten Weekday
Matthew 21, 33-43, 45-46
The Parable of the Tenants

The landowner took such care in the planning, planting, protection, and provision of his vineyard. There was a hedge planted around it, a wine press dug in it, and even a tower above it. How tragic it was that the tenants were unworthy of his trust.

Heavenly Father, you have planned my life and planted me in this particular part of your vineyard. You are protecting me and providing for me. Help me to recognize the prophets you send into my life today. Help me to recognize and honor your Son.

Saturday, March 6, 1999 Lenten Weekday
Luke 15, 1-3; 11-32
The Parable of the Lost Sheep; The Parable of the Lost Son

The sick are drawn magnetically to strength, wholeness, and health. Today's Gospel tells us that "the tax collectors and sinners were all drawing near to listen to him (Jesus) ..." They knew he would help them and heal them.

Lord Jesus, I draw near to you today. I'm in Texas, my mother is sick in the hospital, and I feel so frightened. Speak the word I need to make me whole. Help me to speak the word to offer balm to Mother and to others I encounter in the hospital today.

Sunday, March 7, 1999 Third Sunday of Lent
John 4, 5-42
The Samaritan Woman

"He had to pass through Samaria." Jesus was on his way from Judea to Galilee. There was a divine detour through Samaria. This detour resulted in the liberation of the woman at the well.

Lord Jesus, here in Texas, I feel like I'm on a detour. In the midst of it all, help me to be an instrument of liberation in someone's life today.

Monday, March 8, 1999 St. John of God
Luke 4, 24-30
The Rejection at Nazareth

"No prophet is accepted in his own native place." Jesus reminded the people in the synagogue of the powerful ministries of the prophet Elijah to an outsider, a widow from Sidon, and of the prophet Elisha to another outsider, a leper from Syria named Naaman. Elijah and Elisha were God's instruments to reach and to touch and to heal those who were considered outsiders.

Jesus emphasized that there were many widows in Israel and many lepers in Israel at that time. "It was to none of these that Elijah was sent, but only to a widow in Zarephath in the land of Sidon. Again, there were many lepers in Israel during the time of Elisha the prophet; yet not one of them was cleansed, but only Naaman the Syrian."

This was too much for the people in the synagogue! What Jesus had said was absolutely true, but they did not want to be reminded of it.

"When the people in the synagogue heard this, they were all filled with fury. They rose up, drove him out of town, and led him to the brow of the hill on which their town had been built, to hurl him down headlong. But he passed through the midst of them and went away."

Lord Jesus, help me to hear your word to me spoken through any "prophet" you choose to send to me. Help me not to take offense at the messenger, but, in humility, to recognize and to receive your message.

Tuesday, March 9, 1999 St. Frances of Rome
Matthew 18, 21-35
The Parable of the Unforgiving Servant

In this parable, the servant pleaded with his master, "Be patient with me, and I will pay you back ..." The master, in effect, drew a line through the bill and then tore it up and threw it away. The debt was cancelled and destroyed. The servant was now free! The debt was gone.

Amazingly, this man's fellow servant then pleaded with him in the same words. "Be patient with me, and I will pay you back." The forgiven servant inexplicably refused to pass on the forgiveness which he himself had received.

When we truly know that we are forgiven, there is a tremendous release, elation, and a sense of freedom. This is one of blessings of the sacrament of reconciliation. We long to reach out to others in love and forgiveness, because we have just been given a new lease on life

Lord Jesus, thank you, thank you for forgiving me. I release all who have sinned against me and pray for them to experience joy and freedom.

Wednesday, March 10, 1999 Lenten Weekday
Matthew 5, 17-19
Teaching about the Law

A tiny bud needs time to grow. It takes time to grow and to unfold into a beautiful blossom. It would be unthinkable to pluck it from the vine before its time or to destroy it.

Jesus said, "I have come not to abolish but to fulfill." The bud of the Law was brought to ripeness and fulfillment in the teachings of Jesus. The Law blossomed into Love.

The Pharisees asked Jesus, "Which commandment is the greatest?" Jesus said, "Love the Lord, your God, with all your heart, with all your soul, and with all your mind. This is the greatest and the first commandment. The second is like it: You shall love your neighbor as yourself. The whole law and the prophets depend on these two commandments (Matthew 22, 36-39)."

Thursday, March 11, 1999 Lenten Weekday
Luke 11, 14-23
Jesus and Beelzebul

"When a strong man fully armed guards his palace, his possessions are safe. But when one stronger than he attacks and overcomes him, he takes away the armor on which he relied ..." We may arm ourselves with our education, reputation or sophistication.

Every bit of "armor" not of God can leave us stripped and exposed. Only the armor of God (Ephesians 6, 13-17) will ultimately protect us. "Put on the Lord Jesus Christ ... (Romans 13, 14)."

Friday, March 12, 1999 Lenten Weekday
Mark 12, 28-35
The Greatest Commandment

This is another of those familiar passages in which Eugene Peterson's The Message offers fresh insight. Jesus told Israel that "... the Lord your God is one; so love the Lord God with all your passion and prayer and intelligence and energy.' And here is the second: 'Love others as well as you love yourself.' "

Saturday, March 13, 1999 Lenten Weekday
Luke 18, 9-14
The Parable of the Pharisee and the Tax Collector

Have you ever heard people say any of the following? "I pray every single day." "I fast on Wednesdays and Fridays." "I give more than a tithe to God's work."

" I." "I." "I." Jesus is addressing this parable in today's Gospel "to those who were convinced of their own righteousness and despised everyone else."

Jesus expects me to pray, to fast, and to give. That's taken for granted for everyone one who follows him.

What Jesus is seeking is my heart. What is my attitude? What are my motives? Do I see my profound need of a Savior or do I make a performance of praying, giving, and fasting?

As The Message expresses it, "If you walk around with your nose in the air, you're going to end up flat on your face, but if you're content to be simply yourself, you will become more than yourself."

Lord Jesus, since I don't want a flat nose, I'm happy to be myself with you and with others. Help me to be as gentle and forgiving with myself and with others as you are with me.

Sunday, March 14, 1999 Fourth Sunday of Lent
John 9, 1-41
The Man Born Blind

When you carry the light of Christ, watch out! The more you are filled with the light of Christ, the more division you will cause and the more you will be a threat to those around you who do not seek the reign of God.

The blind man received his sight as a gift from God. His healing made a profound impact on Jesus' disciples, the man's neighbors, the Pharisees, and, of course, his own parents.

The disciples wondered if the man was born blind because of sin in his own life or because of sin in his parents' lives. Jesus quickly corrected that notion. "Neither he nor his parents sinned; it is so that the works of God might be made visible through him."

The neighbors found it difficult to reconcile this "new man" with the little blind boy they had known for so long. The were very curious.

" 'Isn't this the one who used to sit and beg?' Some said, 'It is,' but others said, 'No, but he looks just like him.' " The neighbors were truly bewildered.

This healing really caused a division among the Pharisees! Some thought Jesus could not be from God because he broke the Sabbath. Others asked, "How can a sinful man do such signs?"

The man's parents were no doubt happy for their son, but they were also frightened for their own skin. They were afraid that the religious leaders might exclude them from the synagogue.

Indeed, the religious leaders did expel the man who had received his sight. What did the man have left?

He had physical sight, a wonderful gift! Of far greater significance, he now enjoyed a relationship with Jesus, which involved spiritual sight and insight. He openly acknowledged his belief in Jesus. " 'I do believe, Lord,' and he worshiped him."

Jesus said, "I came into this world for judgment, so that those who do not see might see, and those who do see might become blind." The shoe fit, but the Pharisees refused to wear it. Jesus told them, "... your sin remains."

149

Do not be afraid when Jesus heals you, makes you see, and fills you with light. Others may ridicule you or reject you, but Jesus loves you and has called you to a new relationship with him. Go forward into his light and do not look back.

Monday, March 15, 1999 Lenten Weekday
John 4, 43-54
Return to Galilee; Second Sign at Cana

The royal official believed the words spoken by Jesus. Jesus had told him, "You may go; your son will live." The official then returned home. At that moment, he had no evidence that what Jesus had said would come true.

The official simply had bare-bones trust that the answer would be fleshed out in his son. Not only was his son healed, but the official and his entire family now believed in and trusted Jesus!

In this case the answer to the promise of Jesus came very quickly. If Jesus has spoken, the answer will come. It will come in minutes, hours, days, weeks, months, or long, long years. The answer will be apparent for all to see!

Lord Jesus, today I affirm my belief in the word you have spoken. I will act on that word, even though the word has yet to be fulfilled. Let my trust bring joy to you.

Tuesday, March 16, 1999 Lenten Weekday
John 5, 1-3, 5-16
Cure on a Sabbath

The time had come! For thirty-eight years, this man had been ill. "When Jesus saw him lying there and knew that he had been ill for a long time, he said to him, 'Do you want to be well?' The sick man answered him, 'Sir, I have no one to put me into the pool when the water is stirred up; while I am on my way, someone else gets down there before me.' "

Jesus quickly changed everything! He completely redirected the man's mindset and expectations.

"Rise, take up your mat, and walk." Instead of making a way for the sick man to enter the pool, Jesus spoke a word of command. "Immediately, the man became well, took up his mat, and walked."

Do you wait and wait and wait for Jesus to answer your prayer? Do you think Jesus will answer your prayer in one particular way? Surprise!

Be open to Jesus and be open to a very innovative answer to your prayer. Jesus knows your heart. He knows the deepest longing of your heart. Be prepared for Jesus, at a time known only to him, to surprise you with a wonderful answer!

Wednesday, March 17, 1999 St. Patrick
John 5, 17-30
Cure on a Sabbath; The Work of the Son

Jesus and the Father. The Father and Jesus. They act in perfect accord and give life in perfect accord. They are to be equally honored.

Twice in today's Gospel, Jesus reiterates that he does not work on his own and that he cannot work on his own. He only does what he sees his Father doing.

When Jesus makes a judgment, it is just, because he is not seeking his own will, but rather the will of his Father. Indeed, Jesus stated, "The Father and I are one (John 10, 30)."

Before we can go forth in Jesus' name, we must grasp this vital relationship between Jesus and his Father. It was after his death and resurrection that Jesus said to his disciples, "As the Father has sent me, so send I you (John 20, 21)."

Lord Jesus, today I choose to die to my own agenda. Raise me to a new life with you and send me forth to bring your life to those around me.

Thursday, March 18, 1999 St. Cyril of Jerusalem
John 5, 31-47
Witnesses to Jesus; Unbelief of Jesus' Hearers

The leaders of the religious establishment kept their eyes so much on other people that they could not lift their eyes to God's level. John the Baptist was in their midst as "a burning and shining lamp," but Jesus was in their midst as God's own Son.

Although these leaders searched the Scriptures, they did not accept Jesus, who was sent in fulfillment of these same Scriptures. As Jesus observed, they did not have God's love within them.

Lord Jesus, how can I condemn others for not recognizing you when often I don't recognize you either? Please fill me with your love and light. Let me see you anew today, and like John the Baptist, become "a burning and shining lamp" to reveal you to others.

Friday, March 19, 1999 St. Joseph
Matthew 1, 16, 18-21, 24
The Genealogy of Jesus; The Birth of Jesus

Just as surely as Mary was chosen to be the mother of Jesus, so Joseph was chosen to be the foster father, the earthly shepherd, of Jesus, the Lamb of God.

Saturday, March 20, 1999 Lenten Weekday
John 7, 40-53
Discussion about the Origins of the Messiah

Another discussion and another division. Wherever Jesus went and whatever he said and did, the hearts of his hearers were exposed. Division happened.

In last Sunday's Gospel, the Pharisees disputed among themselves. In today's Gospel, there was still more division.

First, the crowd was divided on whether the Messiah would come from Galilee or Bethlehem in Judea. Then, the Temple guards who had been sent to arrest Jesus went back to the chief priests and Pharisees who demanded why the arrest had not been made.

The Pharisees viciously attacked the motives and the integrity of anyone audacious enough to believe in Jesus. When the Temple guards who had refused to arrest Jesus began instead to extol him, the Pharisees interrogated them, demanding, "Have you also been deceived?" The Pharisees dismissed "the crowd," by accusing it of not knowing the law and therefore being "accursed."

Into this melee stepped Nicodemus, the Pharisee who had once had a private conversation with Jesus (John 3, 1-20). Nicodemus asked his fellow Pharisees, "Does our law condemn a person before it first hears him and finds out what he is doing?"

This question was too much for the chief priests and Pharisees. They turned on Nicodemus, one of their own, and demanded, "You are not from Galilee also, are you? Look and see that no prophet arises from Galilee."

Today, can we expect to be treated any differently if we reflect the light of Christ? People may backbite, but that's not our concern. We keep our eyes on Jesus and walk in the path he has illumined for us.

Sunday, March 21, 1999 Fifth Sunday of Lent
John 11, 1- 45
The Raising of Lazarus

"This illness is not to end in death, but is for the glory of God, that the Son of God may be glorified through it. This was Jesus' first comment, his personal prognosis, about the illness of Lazarus.

His last comments, or commands, were, "Lazarus, come out!" spoken to Lazarus directly and then, "Untie him and let him go," spoken to the bystanders.

In between the beginning and the conclusion of the Lazarus episode, Jesus, fully aware of the pain and misunderstanding his absence would cause, chose to wait two days before going to Bethany. He had something better in store for Mary, Martha, and his disciples than merely healing Lazarus from his illness. He intended to show his power over death itself!

Even so, Jesus was "perturbed and deeply troubled …." He wept. Jesus loved his friends, Lazarus, Martha, and Mary. He had enjoyed their hospitality on numerous occasions. This was a time of deep grief and he tasted that grief to the full.

Lord Jesus, today, help me to trust you with a very painful situation. Knowing that you intend life and resurrection, help me to continue to trust that your victory will be manifest in your time.

Monday, March 22, 1999 Lenten Weekday
John 8, 1-11
A Woman Caught in Adultery

This woman escaped with her life! I was reminded of Psalm 124, 6-7:

> "Blessed be the LORD, who did not leave us
>   to be torn by their fangs.
> We escaped with our lives
>   like a bird from the fowler's snare;
>   the snare was broken and we escaped."

We have all escaped with our lives because of Jesus. He did not escape with his life. He freely gave his life for us. Jesus, the sinless one, was condemned and did not escape. He paid the full price, not for his sins, because he had none, but for our sins.

The Pharisees in today's Gospel did not escape either. Their sins were lovingly, but inexorably, exposed by Jesus. How they hated and feared him.

Lord Jesus, thank you for setting us free from our sins, free from our past. Like the bird escaping the snare, we fly away today, in freedom and peace to love and serve you.

Tuesday, March 23, 1999 St. Turibius de Mongrovejo
John 8, 21-30
Jesus, the Father's Ambassador

Jesus perfectly reflected the Father in heaven. There was no distortion. Jesus came and showed us what the Father was really like.

Jesus was fully human. He walked this earth as one of us.

Jesus was fully divine. He walked this earth saying and doing everything at the Father's direction.

Now it's our turn! Jesus wants us so filled with the Holy Spirit that we will be a true reflection of himself.

The people of our world are looking and looking for Jesus. Sometimes they look in the wrong places, but they are still looking. They are still searching.

Lord Jesus, today I look to you. Help me to trust you in a deeper way. Let your light shine through me today. Let me reflect in a deeper way your love and your truth.

Wednesday, March 24, 1999 Lenten Weekday
John 8, 31-42
Jesus and Abraham

Jesus' word had "no room" among the people in today's Gospel because they were so stubbornly fixated and insistent upon their sense of personal identity. They were very proud to be descendants of Abraham. Rightly so!

The problem was that they stopped there. They did not truly grasp what Abraham actually did.

Even Jesus did not get through to them! He attempted to point out that if they really were Abraham's children, they would be doing what Abraham did.

154

What was it that Abraham actually did? Abraham took a great leap of faith and trusted and believed God!

God told Abraham, who was then called Abram, "Go forth from the land of your kinsfolk and from your father's house to a land that I will show you (Genesis 12, 1)." Abraham was not exactly a spring chick. He was seventy-five years old when he started this adventure with God!

Abraham "went as the LORD directed him (Genesis 12, 4)." He began and continued his journey into the unknown.

Abraham trusted God, without full understanding of how God's promises to him would be fulfilled. Hello?

In today's Gospel, we read that Jesus told Abraham's descendants the truth. Instead of believing Jesus, Abraham's descendants tried to kill him!

Jesus told them that their real father was the devil. This was not well received.

Lord Jesus, I need to remember Abraham, who "... believed, hoping against hope ... (Romans 4, 18)." Thank you for reminding me that it is God alone who "... gives life to the dead and calls into being what does not exist (Romans 4, 17)." Holy Spirit, I invite you and implore you to strengthen me today to continue to believe.

Thursday, March 25, 1999 The Annunciation of Our Lord
Luke 1, 26-38
Announcement of the Birth of Jesus

God. Angel. Mary. Jesus. HOW CAN THIS BE? The Holy Spirit. "Yes."

This is the way it was for Mary. This is the way it is for you and me.

God communicates with us and asks us to do something impossible. We are troubled. We ponder.

If we are wise, we do not ask "Why?" Instead, we ask "How?"

The answer is always the same. The Holy Spirit. Our part is to say "yes," for " ,,, nothing will be impossible for God." Yes. With Mary, we say, "Behold, I am the handmaiden of the Lord. May it be done to me according to your word."

Friday, March 26, 1999 Lenten Weekday
John 10, 31-42
Feast of the Dedication

Even after the religious leaders tried to kill Jesus, he continued to state the truth about his identity and his work. He was the Son of God. He was performing his Father's work. Again, there was an attempt to arrest him.

Jesus left that place. He "went back across the Jordan to the place where John first baptized, and there he remained."

The mission of Jesus, of course, had originated from heaven. This mission also involved the consent of a young woman, carefully selected by God, Mary of Nazareth.

In another sense, however, the mission of Jesus was launched by the ministry of John the Baptist. John had faithfully fulfilled his part to prepare the way for the Messiah.

Jesus returned to the place of John's testimony. John the Baptist had proclaimed that, although " ... the law was given through Moses, grace and truth came through Jesus Christ (John 1, 17)."

John had called Jesus the Lamb of God and the one who would baptize with the Holy Spirit. John had stated the truth about Jesus' identity and mission. John's mission of preparation was over. Jesus was here!

So Jesus "went back across the Jordan to the place where John first baptized, and there he remained. Many came to him and said, ' John performed no sign, but everything John said about this man was true.' And many there believed in him (John 10, 40-42)."

In our own discipleship, there will come a time to leave a certain place. It may be difficult to leave, but our work in that place is over. We were assigned there for a season and the season is over.

Jesus told his disciples to depart and to shake the dust from their feet when they were not well-received (Matthew 10, 14). He also told his followers to be as cautious as serpents and as innocent as doves, because he was sending them out as lambs among the wolves (Matthew 10, 16, 17).

Lord Jesus, you alone know when we are to remain in a difficult situation and when we are to depart. You may also lead us to revisit a particular place where we began to be aware of your call in our lives. Thank you for your Holy Spirit who gives us the strength and courage to do your will wherever you place us.

Saturday, March 27, 1999 Lenten Weekday
John 11, 45-57
Session of the Sanhedrin; The Last Passover

The love and power of God versus vested interests. Why in the world were the Pharisees so afraid? What could they possibly lose?

These important leaders answered these questions themselves. "If we leave him [Jesus] alone, all will believe in him, and the Romans will come and take away both our land and our nation." The (GNT) version is: "If we let him go on in this way, everyone will believe in him, and the Roman authorities will take action and destroy our Temple and our nation."

What was so bad about everyone believing in Jesus? What was so bad was that the Pharisees would no longer rule. Jesus would rule. It was a matter of power.

"The Romans will destroy our Temple." The temple in Jerusalem was the Washington D.C. of their nation. Their power base would be destroyed if Jesus ruled. Again, a question of power.

We condemn the Pharisees, but what about us? Do we really want Jesus in total control of our lives?

As we enter Holy Week, let us pray to be purified. Let us pray to be prepared to acclaim Jesus as Lord, to walk with Jesus to the Cross, to die to our own agenda of how to live the Christian life, and to rise to new life with Jesus.

Sunday, March 28, 1999 Palm Sunday of the Lord's Passion
Matthew 26, 14-27, 66
The Betrayal by Judas; Preparations for the Passover;
The Betrayer; The Lord's Supper; Peter's Denial Foretold;
The Agony in the Garden; The Betrayal and Arrest of Jesus;
Jesus before the Sanhedrin; Peter's Denial of Jesus;
Jesus before Pilate; The Death of Judas;
Jesus Questioned by Pilate;
The Sentence of Death; Mockery by the Soldiers;
The Way of the Cross; The Crucifixion; The Death of Jesus;
The Burial of Jesus; The Guard at the Tomb

The will of the Father reigned supreme throughout the life, death, and resurrection of his obedient Son, Jesus. As true man and true God, Jesus suffered in a way not one of us will ever have to suffer.

Jesus, in the midst of his own agony, concentrated on caring for his disciples. He proceeded to celebrate the Passover, knowing that his betrayer shared the same meal. He instituted the Lord's Supper to sustain us until he returned in glory.

Jesus knew that the events to come would shake the faith of all his disciples. He knew that Judas would betray him. He knew that Peter would deny him.

In the Garden of Gethsemane, Jesus agonized in prayer and accepted the Father's will. When Jesus was arrested, all his disciples deserted him. He was truly abandoned and bereft of all human comfort.

The mockery of the "trial" of the Sanhedrin was played out, with all its unsubstantiated false accusations. Jesus remained silent and in control, not only of himself, but of the whole pathetic situation.

Peter, frightened out of his wits, caved in and denied that he even knew Jesus. Pilate, frightened, but too weak and cowardly to act on his conscience, questioned Jesus. Because Jesus knew this was a kangaroo court, he chose to remain silent.

Jesus, abandoned by all human support, hung on the Cross, apparently abandoned by his own Father. "My God, my God, why have you forsaken me?" We leave the Gospel with the image of the stone sealing the tomb.

Lord Jesus, we know what happened. We know that you did not stay in the tomb. Still, 2000 years later, we want to comfort you and to be with you. Guide us this week as we walk our own way of the Cross.

Monday, March 29, 1999 Monday of Holy Week
John 12, 1-11
The Anointing at Bethany

There were several players in this drama. Jesus was visiting his friends, Mary, Martha, and Lazarus in Bethany. Martha, of course, was busy serving. The newly raised Lazarus was near Jesus. Judas was posturing about giving money to the poor.

The curious crowd showed up to gawk at Jesus and Lazarus. The chief priests, who were freaked out because Jesus had raised Lazarus from the dead, were plotting to kill Lazarus as well as Jesus. They knew they had to eliminate any and all threats to their power.

It was Mary's anointing of Jesus that is the focus of today's Gospel. Mary's extravagant love and devotion were poured out along with the fragrant oil.

She gave without concern about the cost. Without full understanding of the events to follow, she was expressing, in advance, her belief in Jesus' resurrection.

Jesus had wept with Mary when her brother Lazarus lay in his tomb. Mary was now sharing in advance what she could share of the sorrow of Jesus as he awaited his torture and death.

Lord Jesus, Mary's love and faith are a rebuke to my own indifference and apathy. This Holy Week, let me somehow pour out my own life to you. Let me comfort you and anoint you with my love and trust.

Tuesday, March 30, 1999 Tuesday of Holy Week
John 13, 21-33, 36-38
Announcement of Judas' Betrayal; The New Commandment;
Peter's Denial Predicted

The bread of betrayal. Supper. It was during this supper that Jesus arose and began to wash the feet of his disciples.

Jesus, who knew Judas would betray him, was "deeply troubled." There is seldom a pain so deep as betrayal by one with whom we have shared bread.

Glory, however was shining forth in the midst of the knowledge of Judas' betrayal and Peter's denial. "Now is the Son of Man glorified, and God is glorified in him."

Then Peter was at it again, blustering about his devotion to Jesus. Jesus asked, "Will you lay down your life for me? Amen, amen, I say to you, the cock will not crow before you deny me three times."

Lord Jesus, I have betrayed you and denied you, in ways known and unknown. Thank you for forgiving me as I have released to you those who have betrayed and denied me. Let your glory shine through my life.

Wednesday, March 31, 1999 Wednesday of Holy Week
Matthew 26, 14-25
The Betrayal by Judas; Preparation for the Passover;
The Betrayer

In Matthew's Gospel today, as in John's Gospel yesterday, we are confronted with the subject of betrayal. This is a subject at which we peer with timidity and from which we rapidly retreat. The hurt is too deep. Somehow, it never seems to get quite healed.

Judas. There were many factors and many players in this terrible drama, but there is still no way of avoiding Judas.

Who was "Judas" in your life? Who did you trust, who did you laugh with, share a meal with, pray with, weep with, and with whom did you share your heart? Who was this person who then turned on you and betrayed you?

Lord Jesus, we go in prayer to be with you in the Upper Room where the Passover was celebrated. You loved Judas and chose him to be one of your disciples, one of your inner circle of followers. He not only forfeited your trust, but he also took the initiative in betraying you. He collected his thirty pieces of silver and waited his time.

The Father's plan, however, could not be thwarted. In fact, it was facilitated by this terrible betrayal. You continued on with the next step in the Father's will and plan for our salvation. You made arrangements to celebrate the Passover. Your appointed time was drawing near.

Lord Jesus, let this be the last Passover in which we mourn over anyone who was a "Judas" in our lives. We release this "Judas" to you once and for all. Free us to celebrate Passover with you and, over the next few days, to die to the past, to rise with you, and to continue the next step in our journey with you and to you.

Thursday, April 1, 1999 Maundy Thursday
John 13, 1-15
The Washing of the Disciples' Feet

The "Book of Glory" in John's Gospel begins with the washing of the disciples' feet. "Glory" to wash the dirty feet of twelve people? "Glory" to know that you are doing the job of a slave? "Glory" to wash the feet of the person who is going to betray you?

The "vestment" Jesus wore was a simple towel tied round his waist. This was "glory" for the Son of God?

Jesus could serve in this way because he knew who he was. He was "fully aware that the Father had put everything into his power and that he had come from God and was returning to God."

Do we know who we are? Do we really believe and enter into our baptismal identity? If we are truly secure in our identity we can freely serve all who are in our lives, even those who betray us. No one can take away our identity as God's beloved children.

Lord Jesus, you knew who you were, what you were doing, and where you were going. Today, please send your Holy Spirit to illumine me in a deeper way about my identity as a Christian. Help me to know in a deeper way that I am eternally secure, that I am going home to the arms of my Father in heaven. Jesus, help me to realize afresh that you are my Brother holding my hand all the way through my journey through this world. Show me today whose feet I need to wash.

Friday, April 2, 1999 Good Friday
John 18, 1-19, 42
Jesus Arrested; Peter's First Denial;
The Inquiry before Annas; Peter Denies Jesus Again;
The Trial before Pilate; The Crucifixion of Jesus;
The Blood and Water; The Burial of Jesus

The Garden of Eden. The Garden of Gethsemane. The garden with a new tomb.

Today, it has all come full circle. The sin that originated in the Garden of Eden where Adam and Eve said "no" to God led to the Garden of Gethsemane where Jesus said "yes" to God. At the garden with the new tomb, we wait for resurrection.

Saturday, April 3, 1999 Holy Saturday, Easter Vigil
Matthew 28, 1-10
The Resurrection of Jesus

This is a Gospel of tumultuous emotions. After the giant earthquake, a dazzling angel came from heaven and rolled back the stone in front of the new tomb in the garden.

The guards at the tomb were understandably terrified! The angel reassured Mary Magdalene and the other Mary, "Do not be afraid! I know that you are seeking Jesus the crucified. He is not here, for he has been raised just as he said. Come and see the place where he lay."

The angel then instructed the women to proclaim the message to the disciples that Jesus, raised from the dead, was going before them to Galilee. They would see him there.

The women were "fearful yet overjoyed." They literally ran to announce this message. As they obeyed, Jesus himself met them on the way. Jesus also told them, "Do not be afraid. Go tell my brothers to go to Galilee, and there they will see me."

It has been said that the more healed we are the more we feel all our emotions. Sometimes, life has a way of numbing us, anesthetizing us, to joy as well as to sorrow.

Jesus can change all that! Jesus can help us to experience joy in a deeper way than we could ever imagine when we were in the midst of our pain. Jesus can bring balance and stability to all tumultuous emotions.

Father, today of all days, please send the Holy Spirit to transform our listless, lifeless spirits to share in the awe, the amazement, and the joy of the resurrection of our Lord Jesus. As we go into the "Galilees" of our everyday life, thank you, Jesus, that you are already there waiting for us.

Sunday, April 4, 1999 Easter Sunday
John 20, 1-9
The Empty Tomb

Mary of Magdala proceeded in the darkness before dawn to the tomb of her beloved Lord. She raced to tell Peter and John that the stone in front of the tomb had been removed. Peter and John also ran to the tomb.

Have you ever awakened after having surgery, still groggy from the anesthesia? You cautiously open your eyes and blink. Maybe you move a bit and wonder, "Where am I?"

You've been through an ordeal and although you've survived and are awake, you're not yet "all there." You're not yet fully awake. The pain may have abated, but the relief that the ordeal is over has not yet penetrated.

Although Peter and John observed the empty tomb and burial cloths, they did not yet fully comprehend the resurrection of Jesus. Jesus had told them repeatedly that he would suffer at the hands of the religious leaders. He would be crucified. He would be raised on the third day.

How could that be? Where were the disciples in their grasp of this hard saying? Where was Jesus?

Jesus was gloriously alive and it was the third day! Although the dazed disciples ran physically, they had not yet "arrived" in their understanding of this wonder.

The disciples were like the Jewish exiles who had returned to their land, but could not yet take it all in.

> "When the LORD restored the fortunes of Zion,
>   then we thought we were dreaming.
> Our mouths were filled with laughter;
>   our tongues sang for joy (Psalm 126, 1, 2a)."

The first disciples "arrived," in time, to the understanding that Jesus was alive. They "arrived" and we too will "arrive." Alleluia!

Monday, April 5, 1999 St. Vincent Ferrer
Matthew 28, 8-15
The Resurrection of Jesus; The Report of the Guard

The women were " …fearful yet overjoyed …" Again, as in the Gospel on Holy Saturday, we learn of the powerful sentiments of the women who came to the empty tomb and then ran to tell the disciples.

We also note the chief priests stubbornly continuing to deny Jesus. They denied him in life, they denied him in death, and then they denied him in his resurrection. They chose to refuse the gift of God in sending his only Son into this world.

In contrast, the women in today's Gospel ran joyfully with the message of the Resurrection. Jesus greeted them in the midst of their fear and their joy.

The priests and the elders, on the other hand, huddled fearfully in their conference room to continue in their darkness. All they could think to do was to bribe the soldiers to say that the body of Jesus had been stolen.

Lord Jesus, on this Easter Monday, we offer to you our conflicting emotions. Like the women in the Gospel, we know what it is to be simultaneously overjoyed and fearful. Thank you for meeting us on our way and speaking to us the same words of comfort. "Do not be afraid." Alleluia!

Tuesday, April 6, 1999 Easter Tuesday
John 20, 11-18
The Appearance of Mary of Magdala

The disciples Peter and John had checked out the empty tomb and returned home. They left without fully understanding what they had seen.

Mary of Magdala did not fully understand either, but she remained at the tomb, weeping. She could not and would not leave. She was rooted to the spot.

Jesus came to her as she wept. "Woman, why are you weeping? Whom are you looking for?" Then came the wild joy as Mary realized that she was not speaking to the gardener, but to JESUS!

Jesus was speaking her name as only he could speak her name. "Mary!" He was right here with her. He was alive!

Jesus directed Mary's joy into a mission. "Go to my brothers and tell them, 'I am going to my Father and your Father, to my God and your God.'" Mary, the first to announce the resurrection, told the disciples first of all, "I have seen the Lord" and then she gave them Jesus' message.

Lord Jesus, sometimes it is still hard to grasp the fact of your resurrection. You are alive, you are here, and you are with me! In the midst of my weeping, speak my name and give me my mission for this day. Alleluia!

Wednesday, April 7, 1999 St. John Baptist de la Salle
Luke 24, 13-35
The Appearance on the Road to Emmaus

The apostles of Jesus were still dazed and confounded. Mary Magdalene, Joanna, and Mary, the mother of James, and others, had just returned from the empty tomb.

They recounted their experience to the apostles who did not believe them. Peter, however, ran to the tomb, saw the burial cloths, but left "amazed (Luke 24, 12)."

Even those who knew and loved Jesus were having a hard time recognizing him. In yesterday's Gospel, Mary of Magdala initially thought she was speaking to a gardener. Surprise! She recognized Jesus when he spoke her name, "Mary!"

In today's Gospel, the two followers of Jesus initially believed him to be a "visitor to Jerusalem," who was somehow unaware of the events of the last few days. Cleopas asked, "Are you the only visitor to Jerusalem who does not know of the things that have taken place there in these days?"

Jesus did not immediately reveal his identity. He met the two where they were in their understanding. He asked, "What sort of things?" They answered, "The things that happened to Jesus the Nazarene, who was a prophet mighty in deed and word before God and all the people, how our chief priests and rulers handed him over to a sentence of death and crucified him."

Since they had referred to Jesus as a prophet, Jesus began at that point in their understanding. "Then beginning with Moses and all the prophets, he interpreted to them what referred to him in all the scriptures."

It was in the breaking of the bread, however, that "their eyes were opened and they recognized him." With jubilation, they returned to Jerusalem to hear from the others, "The Lord has been raised and has appeared to Simon!"

Lord Jesus, thank you for opening my eyes and my heart to recognize you. Alleluia!

Thursday, April 8, 1999 Easter Thursday
Luke 24, 35-48
The Appearance to the Disciples in Jerusalem

Over the last few days we've watched as Mary of Magdala thought Jesus was a gardener. We've marveled as the disciples on the road to Emmaus thought that he was a tourist visiting Jerusalem!

In today's Gospel, the disciples in Jerusalem have just heard the report of the two who recognized Jesus in the breaking of the bread. In the midst of their testimony, Jesus himself appeared. This time he was mistaken for a ghost!

The disciples were still "startled and terrified." Scared silly.

The disciples were not scared to death, but scared of Life. Jesus was alive and he was right here!

Notice the moment when Jesus drew near. He drew near when his followers were giving testimony about having seen him in Emmaus when he broke the bread.

After convincing his followers in Jerusalem that he was truly risen, Jesus taught them, as he had already taught the two on the way to Emmaus. Patiently, he explained how he had fulfilled what was written about him in the law of Moses, the prophets, and the psalms.

The next time you think you aren't "counting for Jesus," remember that Jesus is indeed with you. When you speak of him to others, Jesus himself appears in the person of the Holy Spirit and you are truly a witness. Alleluia!

Friday. April 9, 1999 Easter Friday
John 21, 1-14
The Appearance to the Seven Disciples

In today's Gospel, Jesus is again teaching his disciples to recognize him in a new way. On the road to Emmaus, he was mistaken for a stranger, someone who was merely visiting Jerusalem. His true identity was revealed in the breaking of the bread.

In yesterday's Gospel, Jesus was recognized as his followers testified about him. Jesus himself appeared in their midst.

In today's Gospel, he is recognized first by "the disciple whom Jesus loved" and then by the others. He was initially recognized, not by appearance, but by his presence and his power. He entered into an unpromising situation and transformed it.

The discouraged disciples had fished all night and caught nothing. At dawn Jesus was waiting for them on the shore, but he was not immediately recognized.

It was as the disciples obeyed his instruction, "Cast the net over the right side of the boat and you will find something," that the amazing catch occurred. To some, the miracle may have seemed to be the huge catch of fish. Of far greater significance was that the disciples recognized the Lord.

Lord Jesus, today, please come into a particularly trying situation in which I've prayed and prayed and have not caught any "fish." What I long for is to experience your presence, even more than your power, in this situation. Thank you for being present with me. I trust in you and wait for your instructions on how to cast my net today. Alleluia!

Saturday, April 10, 1999 Easter Saturday
Mark 16, 9-15
The Appearance to Mary Magdalene;
The Appearance to the Disciples;
The Commissioning of the Eleven

"Go into the whole world and proclaim the gospel to every creature." Jesus is sending his disciples on mission.

He had now appeared a number of times to his followers. The ones who had seen him believed. The ones who had not yet seen him for themselves did not believe.

Jesus appeared in different ways to different people. Mark's Gospel records that he appeared "in another form" to the two walking to Emmaus.

"[But] later, as the eleven were at table, he appeared to them and rebuked them for their unbelief and hardness of heart because they had not believed those who saw him after he had been raised." The message Jesus gave to the eleven, irrespective of the state of their belief, was, "Go into the whole world and proclaim the gospel to every creature."

We have seen Jesus! We have heard Jesus! We have seen him in other Christians. We have heard him in the proclamation of the Gospel. We have been baptized into his death and resurrection. We have received him in Holy Communion.

"Go into the whole world and proclaim the gospel to every creature." Alleluia!

Sunday, April 11, 1999 Second Sunday of Easter
Divine Mercy Sunday
John 20, 19-31
Appearance to the Disciples; Thomas; Conclusion

The disciples were hiding behind locked doors because they were gripped with fear. After all, look what happened to Jesus!

He had been tortured and crucified. They were his followers. What would happen to them?

Jesus himself had said, "No disciple is above his teacher, no slave above his master. It is enough for the disciple that he become like his teacher …. (Matthew 10, 24-25a)."

167

I remember a cartoon of an elderly gentleman barricaded behind his door. The door had many locks to protect the fearful old man. Surprise! Some brave soul decided to slip a Valentine underneath his door. "Love" came in the door in an unexpected way.

In today's Gospel, Jesus walked into the room in spite of the locked door. He stood in the midst of his followers and said, "Peace be with you." The fearful followers began to rejoice!

Jesus again bestowed his gift of peace and gave the gift of the Holy Spirit. "Receive the holy Spirit. Whose sins you forgive are forgiven them, and whose sins you retain are retained."

How amazed the disciples must have been! Perhaps they remembered the time the paralyzed man was let down through the roof by his friends. Jesus, seeing the faith of the man's friends, had said, "Courage, child, your sins are forgiven (Matthew 9, 2)."

Jesus spoke the words of forgiveness to the paralytic before saying, "Rise, pick up your stretcher, and go home (Matthew 9, 6)." The scribes and the Pharisees were outraged. "Who is this who speaks blasphemies? Who but God alone can forgive sins? (Luke 5, 21)."

Jesus is now telling his disciples that they themselves will forgive sins. "Whose sins you forgive are forgiven them, and whose sins you retain are retained."

A week later, the disciples were again hiding behind locked doors. Jesus again walked into their midst and said, "Peace be with you."

Thomas now expressed his personal belief. "My Lord and my God." Jesus told Thomas, "Have you come to believe because you have seen me? Blessed are those who have not seen and have believed."

Not everything Jesus did was recorded. Enough was recorded, however, for us to believe. "But these are written that you may [come to] believe that Jesus is the Messiah, the Son of God, and that through this belief, you may have life in his name." Alleluia!

Monday, April 12, 1999
John 3, 1-8
Nicodemus

"Born from above." "Born again." Jesus uses the term, "born from above." Nicodemus uses the term, "born again."

Jesus is saying that we need a new immersion into the reality of God. It is necessary not only to read between the lines but also to read above the lines.

In a foreign film, we "hear" the words of the actors, but unless we know their language, we rely on the subtitles to tell us what is being spoken. This is a case of reading "under" the lines! We need a translation in order to understand what is happening.

Jesus came as God's "translation." Everything Jesus thought, said, and did came directly from "on high," directly from God. When we give ourselves to Jesus and allow him to transform us, we understand more and more the work of the Holy Spirit.

Come, Holy Spirit. Move among us, breathe on us, and fill us with the sure knowledge of your reality and of your love for us. Alleluia!

Tuesday, April 13, 1999 St. Martin I
John 3, 7-15
Nicodemus

This conversation with Jesus was not easy for Nicodemus. His understanding was being stretched to the breaking point. Still, he remained with Jesus to ask Jesus his questions. He asked, "How can a person once grown old be born again?"

Jesus told him, "What is born of flesh is flesh and what is born of spirit is spirit." Nicodemus again asked, "How can this happen?" At least Nicodemus, scholarly Pharisee though he was, was honest enough to admit his spiritual ignorance.

Maybe we're also asking the Lord "how." The answer to the Virgin Mary's "how" was "the Holy Spirit."

The answer to Nicodemus' "how" was "the Holy Spirit." It is essential to be born of the Spirit to understand the things of the Spirit.

To our own question of "how," Jesus answers, "the Holy Spirit." The Holy Spirit is the explanation.

Lord Jesus, to every puzzling "how" in our lives, please speak your peace and send your Holy Spirit to illumine us. Alleluia!

Wednesday, April 14, 1999
John 3, 16-21
Nicodemus

Light brought the verdict. "And this is this the verdict, that the light came into the world, but people preferred darkness to light, because their works were evil." That's the bad news.

However, there is good news! The good news, the Gospel, is that "whoever lives the truth comes to the light, so that his works may be clearly seen as done in God."

Jesus was simply living the truth as Son of God, Son of Man, and Light of the World. Simeon had prophesied about this when Mary and Joseph brought the infant Jesus to the Temple. "Behold, this child is destined for the fall and rise of many in Israel and to be a sign that will be contradicted ... so that the thoughts of many hearts may be revealed (Luke 2, 34, 35)."

There is a piercing version of John 3, 19-21 in Eugene Peterson's The Message . "This is the crisis we're in: God-light streamed into the world, but men and women everywhere ran for the darkness. They went for the darkness because they were not really interested in pleasing God. Everyone who makes a practice of doing evil, addicted to denial and illusion, hates God-light and won't come near it, fearing a painful exposure. But anyone working and living in truth and reality welcomes God-light so the work can be seen for the God-work it is."

Lord Jesus, let your light stream into my life today. Let all I think, say, and do reflect your light. Alleluia!

Thursday, April 15, 1999
John 3, 31-36
The One from Heaven

"The Father loves the Son and has given everything over to him." The Son has come to earth from the heavenly kingdom. He has been there and knows what it is like.

Travel agencies and universities sometimes offer programs featuring native speakers. The speakers lecture about their countries and show slides. People pay money and stand in line for these travel lectures.

Jesus paid the price, so we don't have to pay. We don't even have to stand in line to see the show. Jesus IS the "show." Jesus is "the message." Jesus is the Father's first and last word. Alleluia!

Friday, April 16, 1999
John 6, 1-15
Multiplication of the Loaves

Although Jesus knew what he was going to do in this dilemma, he withheld the information. He knew how he was going to feed the multitude.

Still, he asked Philip, "Where can we buy enough food for them to eat?" He was testing Philip to see how Philip would respond to the dilemma. Philip could see only one solution -- money!

Andrew mentioned the little boy with the five barley loaves and two fish. So far, so good. Andrew then focused on the seemingly insufficient amount of food and asked, "What good are these for so many?"

Jesus took what he was given by the boy and the "miracle" occurred. Now came the real test. How would the people respond? "When the people saw the sign he had done, they said, 'This is truly the Prophet, the one who is to come into the world.' "

Jesus knew what they had in mind -- to make him Bread King. He withdrew to be alone. The people had missed the point.

Jesus had said, "I do not accept human praise, moreover, I know that you do not have the love of God in you. How can you accept praise from one another and do not seek the praise that comes from the only God (John 5, 41, 42, 44)?"

Jesus had performed a great sign. Signs point to something and this sign pointed to God.

The people involved focused only on themselves. Philip focused on his doubt when there appeared to be no solution. The people who were fed focused on their satisfaction when the crisis was solved. Jesus withdrew.

Lord Jesus, help me to stay focused on you, not on signs and wonders. Help me to look beyond the problem and even beyond the solution, to you. Alleluia!

Saturday, April 17, 1999
John 6, 16-21
Walking on the Water

"It is I. Do not be afraid." Jesus is Lord! He does things in his own loving way and in his own sweet time.

The disciples were not trapped in a situation of their own making. They had not blundered into this boat at this time. This was a divine set-up. A date with destiny! The Gospels of Matthew and Mark, in recording this adventure on the waves, stated that Jesus "made" his disciples get into the boat. It was a dark and stormy night and the disciples were scared out of their wits!

The next time there is a dark and stormy night in your life, don't be so quick to wring your hands and lament, "What did I do wrong?" Instead, ask, "Jesus, where are you in this storm?" He will answer you. "It is I. Do not be afraid." He will be with you in the storm and he will take you safely to "shore." Alleluia!

Sunday, April 18, 1999 Third Sunday of Easter
Luke 24, 13-35
The Appearance on the Road to Emmaus

Jesus, my Good Shepherd, is leading me. Sometimes to soft green pastures. Sometimes to serene waters. Sometimes along a road which leads to a new understanding. A new understanding of who he really is and who I really am.

In the Academy Award winning film, "Chariots of Fire," there is an amusing scene in which several puzzled officials of the 1924 Olympic Games in Paris are discussing a point of order. They are frantically trying to decide how to save face because of the runner Eric's quiet decision not to participate on Sunday. To do so would have been a violation of Eric's conscience. One of the officials announces that this is a matter for "the committee" to decide. Another member indignantly snorts, "... We ARE the committee!"

Jesus KNEW who he was. He was the risen Christ, the Son of God and Son of Man.

Jesus was walking, in his resurrection body, along the road to Emmaus with two of his followers. He knew who they were, but they did not yet know who he was. They did not really know who they were either.

Nevertheless, Jesus led them. Although he was comfortable with them in their present understanding, still he was leading them to a deeper understanding of his identity.

"Then beginning with Moses and all the prophets, he interpreted to them what referred to him in all the scriptures." Even so, they did not yet recognize that it was Jesus who was their teacher along this road.

Jesus led them a step further. "And it happened that, while he was with them at table, he took bread, said the blessing, broke it, and gave it to them. With that their eyes were opened and they recognized him ..." They knew it was Jesus who had been walking along the road with them.

He had patiently led them to this new understanding. Their burning hearts also told them who they were and what their next assignment was. They ran to Jerusalem with their message, "The Lord has truly been raised ..."

Today, you still may not know who you are or where you are on your journey to Jesus. Not to worry. Jesus knows who you are and also where you are. Jesus is patiently leading you even in this moment. You WILL arrive! Alleluia!

Monday, April 19, 1999
John 6, 22-29
The Bread of Life Discourse

Jesus knew exactly what was going on. He knew why all these people were pursuing him. They wanted free bread, but they did not want to receive him as the true Bread of Life.

Earlier in John's Gospel (John 2, 24-25) we saw Jesus in Jerusalem for the Passover. During that time, many people believed in him because of the signs and wonders he was performing. "But Jesus would not trust himself to them because he knew them all, and did not need anyone to testify about human nature. He himself understood it well."

This is exactly why he confronts the crowds in today's Gospel with the blunt truth. "Amen, amen, I say to you , you are looking for me not because you saw signs but because you ate the loaves and were filled. Do not work for food that perishes but for food that endures for eternal life, which the Son of Man will give you."

Today, you may not be sure what "the works of God" mean in your life. Jesus tells you the answer. "This is the work of God, that you believe in the one he sent." Believe in Jesus. Trust in Jesus. This inner work of trust in your heart precedes any outer work. Your "work" will flow naturally from your relationship with Jesus. He has promised to send you the Holy Spirit to teach you. Alleluia!

Tuesday, April 20, 1999
John 6, 30-35
The Bread of Life Discourse

The nerve of these people asking Jesus, "What sign can you do that we may see and believe in you? What can you do?"

Do they think they're interviewing Jesus for a job? They really don't seem to give a hoot about his identity. All they seem to care about is what Jesus can do for them.

What about us? Do we humble ourselves and worship Jesus for who he is or do we just want to use him for our own purposes?

Wednesday, April 21, 1999 St. Anselm
John 6, 35-40
The Bread of Life Discourse

Over and over in John's Gospel, Jesus says that he did not come from heaven to do his own will, but rather the will of his Father. "This is the work of God, that you believe in the one he sent (John 6, 29)."

Jesus assures us, " ... I will not reject anyone who comes to me... (John 6, 37b)." The Father's will is eternal life for everyone who trusts in Jesus.

We need not run from the will of God. The will of God is simply the specific purpose of God for our life. God's will is not to frighten us, but to fulfill us! Jesus, the Bread of Life, satisfies our every longing. He knows every need we have in our earthly pilgrimage and is leading us home to our loving Father. Alleluia!

Thursday, April 22, 1999
John 6, 44-51
The Bread of Life Discourse

Total self-giving is what Jesus is about. He did not give a few classes about God ("GOD 101") and then return to heaven. He WAS God.

Jesus gave himself completely to the will of his Father. Over and over he made it clear in word and deed that he came from heaven to accomplish and to fulfill the will, or the purpose, of his Father.

The Bread of Life. The Living Bread. It is the will of the Father that "everyone who sees and believes in him (Jesus) may have eternal life.

When Paul wrote to Timothy, he stated that God … wills everyone to be saved and to come to knowledge of the truth (1 Timothy 2, 4)." Paul continued,

> "For there is one God.
> There is also one mediator between God and the human race,
> Christ Jesus, himself human,
>   who gave himself as ransom for all (1 Timothy 2, 5-6)."

Lord Jesus, you gave yourself over completely to the will of the Father. You are the Bread of Life. You are the Living Bread. Today, I give myself anew to the will of the Father in my life. Holy Spirit, please plant within me the firm assurance that the purpose for my life will indeed be fulfilled. Help me to cooperate with joy and trust. Alleluia!

Friday, April 23, 1999 St. George
John 6, 52-59
The Bread of Life Discourse

This challenging discourse has been about life, real life. Jesus is the Bread of Life. Jesus is the Living Bread from heaven. Those who eat this Bread will have life.

Moses spoke God's words to the Israelites. "I have set before you life and death … Choose life, then, that you and your descendants may live, by loving the LORD, your God, heeding his voice and holding fast to him (Deuteronomy 30, 19-20a)."

Those who heard Jesus speak about eating his flesh and drinking his blood "quarreled among themselves" and asked each other what Jesus meant. When we are baffled and confused, we need to stay with Jesus and ask him to bring clarity. This is a matter of eternal life.

If we are rushed into an emergency room, we do not question how the physician will save us. We trust in the physician, because we have no other choice. It is even more true when we speak to the Physician of our souls. We trust in him to give us life, whether or not we understand his words or his methods. Alleluia!

Saturday, April 24, 1999 St. Fidelis of Sigmaringen
John 6, 60-69
The Words of Eternal Life

Some of the saddest words in Scripture are in this passage. After Jesus referred to himself as the "Bread of Life," many of his disciples objected. "This saying is hard; who can accept it?"

Jesus, keenly aware of their response, pressed the point. " 'Does this shock you? What if you were to see the Son of Man ascending to where he was before? It is the spirit that give life, while the flesh is of no avail. The words I have spoken to you are spirit and life. But there are some of you who do not believe.' Jesus knew from the beginning the ones who would not believe and the one who would betray him. And he said, 'For this reason I have told you that no one can come to me unless it is granted him by my Father.' "

Here is the tragic part. "As a result of this, many [of] his disciples returned to their former way of life and no longer accompanied him." Not just a few, but "many."

Jesus asked the Twelve if they wanted to leave also. It was Peter who replied. Peter answered, "Master, to whom shall we go? You have the words of eternal life. We have come to believe and are convinced that you are the Holy One of God."

Jesus has the words of eternal life.

"The LORD GOD has given me
    a well-trained tongue,
That I might know how to speak to the weary
    a word that will rouse them (Isaiah 50, 4)."

Jesus has the word to energize us for the living of this day.

Lord Jesus, thank you for your words of life. Help us not to turn away from you when we are confused, but to cling to you more than ever. Alleluia!

Sunday, April 25, 1999 Fourth Sunday of Easter
John 10, 1-10
The Good Shepherd

Jesus, the Good Shepherd, "calls his own sheep by name and leads them out. When he has driven out all his own, he walks ahead of them ..."

We always think of the Good Shepherd calling gently to his sheep and his lambs. Sometimes, however, he has to shout and to drive them out! That may sound severe, but the Good Shepherd knows the terrain and knows where he wants to pasture his flock.

Have you ever felt "driven out"? Perhaps you agonized over why it happened and searched for answers. Perhaps the Good Shepherd was gently, but firmly, leading you out, removing you from a toxic place for your own protection. Follow him very carefully. He knows where he is leading you. He is walking ahead of you into a new place of joy, peace, and fulfillment. Alleluia!

Monday, April 26, 1999
John 10, 11-18
The Good Shepherd

Jesus, the Good Shepherd, lays down his life for the sheep. The hired hand is not a true shepherd. Self-preservation is the driving force of the hireling. The hireling is a coward and runs away at the sight of a wolf. The hireling "works for pay and has no concern for the sheep."

What about the wolves? Jesus, the Good Shepherd, does not run away from wolves. He knows, however, that his followers will be faced with wolves." "Go on your way; behold, I am sending you like lambs among wolves (Luke 10, 3)." He instructs his followers to "be shrewd as serpents and simple as doves (Matthew 10, 16)."

How do you recognize hirelings or wolves? They may look like shepherds. Observe their actions as well as their words. Are they like Jesus? Wolves and hirelings always put self first -- self-image, self-protection, and self-promotion. They do not truly care for the flock, but are so skilled in duplicity that they may project the illusion of being shepherds.

Jesus warned his followers, "Beware of false prophets, who come to you in sheep's clothing, but underneath are ravenous wolves. By their fruits you will know them (Matthew 7, 15, 16a)."

Jesus, on the other hand, is the Good Shepherd, who lays down his life for the sheep. He has concern for "the other sheep that do not belong to this fold." He promises us that one day there will be "one flock and one shepherd."

Lord Jesus, only you can give us the grace of being as innocent as doves and as shrewd as serpents. Help us this day to concentrate on

177

following you as the Good Shepherd. Thank you for reaching out in mercy and compassion to all your sheep. Alleluia!

Tuesday, April 27, 1999
John 10, 22-30
Feast of the Dedication

Today's Gospel refers to Hanukkah, the beautiful festival of lights, which takes place over an eight-day period in the winter. This festival commemorates the reconsecration of the Temple in 164 B.C. after its desecration by Antiochus IV Epiphanes.

Jesus, the Light of the world, was walking in the temple area during this particular Hanukkah. He was the answer to centuries of prayers for the Messiah.

Here he was in the midst of his own people, and yet so few recognized him. His presence and his ministry caused division.

This division continues today. We still fail to see Jesus in our midst. We fail to see Jesus in his followers.

Jesus said to his followers, "You are the light of the world," and "your light must shine before others, that they may see your good deeds and glorify your heavenly Father (Matthew 5, 14, 16)."

Jesus said, "My sheep hear my voice; I know them, and they follow me. I give them eternal life, and they shall never perish. No one can take them out of my hand." We are safe and secure in the care of Jesus.

Lord Jesus, thank you for being our Good Shepherd, leading us today in the paths you have chosen for us. Let your light shine through us. Alleluia!

Wednesday, April 28, 1999 St. Peter Chanel
John 12, 44-50
Recapitulation

Again and again throughout John's Gospel, Jesus tells us that he is on earth to be about his Father's business. "Whoever believes in me believes not only in me but also in the one who sent me. I came into the world as light, so that everyone who believes in me might not remain in darkness."

Jesus, in loving, intelligent obedience, says whatever his Father in heaven wishes him to say. He is so completely in tune with his Father that he and his Father are one.

Jesus did not fret about being rejected by others. "Whoever rejects me and does not accept my words has something to judge him: the word that I spoke, it will condemn him on that last day, because I did not speak on my own, but the Father who sent me commanded me what to say and speak."

Lord Jesus, help me to be so in tune with you that I speak your words and leave the results in your hands. Alleluia!

Thursday, April 29, 1999 St. Catherine of Siena
John 13, 16-20
The Washing of the Disciples' Feet

"The one who ate my food has raised his heel against me." Jesus quoted this verse from Psalm 41, 10 in reference to Judas.

"Even the friend who had my trust,
    who shared my table, has scorned me."

Painful though it is to have a false friend and to be betrayed, it is often part of the package of discipleship. Jesus said that "… no slave is greater than the master nor any messenger greater than the one who sent him."

He said this after washing the feet of all the disciples, including Judas. Then he said, "If you understand this, blessed are you if you do it."

Lord Jesus, help us to understand your words and to look to you as our model in serving others. Alleluia!

Friday, April 30, 1999 St. Pius V
John 14, 1-6
Last Supper Discourse

"Do not let your hearts be troubled." As I write this, I am feeling unwell, the carpet cleaners are arriving any minute, my mother is still in the hospital in Texas, and there is uncertainty about a ministry situation. Plus a few other concerns!

Jesus tells us, "Do not let your hearts be troubled." He has it all under control. He is Lord.

179

Jesus is the Way, the Truth, and the Life. He is the way to the Father in heaven and the way through all my uncertainties. He is Truth in a world that lies. He is Life in a culture of death.

Lord Jesus, I trust you. Alleluia!

Saturday, May 1, 1999 St. Joseph the Worker
Matthew 13, 54-58
The Rejection at Nazareth

Have you noticed that when you're with some people you feel joyful and alive? You feel that whatever you say is witty! You're in an atmosphere of affirmation. Anything is possible.

When you're with other people, you feel that you can do no right. They are critical and hostile. It seems that whatever you say or do is misinterpreted. Being in their presence is toxic. You feel dead around them.

Jesus was obviously not in an atmosphere of affirmation. The people in Nazareth scorned him because they thought they knew all about him. How wrong they were! They " … took offense at him."

As a result, " … he did not work many mighty deeds there because of their lack of faith." The Message puts it even mores strongly. "He didn't do any miracles there because of their hostile indifference."

Lord Jesus, we love you and appreciate you! Let us give you "space" today to do mighty works in us and through us. Alleluia!

Sunday, May 2, 1999 Fifth Sunday of Easter
John 14, 1-12
Last Supper Discourse

Once, at a local Black and White ball, I was fascinated by one particular couple. The young man appeared almost to be standing still, while the young woman who was his partner whirled around and around. They were beautiful to watch.

In today's Gospel, Jesus whirls his disciples swiftly, yet gently, into a new dance. This is a dance of trust. "Do not let your hearts be troubled." " … I am going to prepare a place for you … I will come back again and take you to myself, so that where I am you may also be." "I am the way and the truth and the life." "The words that I speak to you I do not speak on my own. The Father who dwells in me is doing his work."

As the disciples paused to catch their breath in this new dance, Jesus whirled them once again. "Amen, amen, I say to you, whoever believes in me will do the works that I do and will do greater ones than these, because I am going to the Father."

Lord Jesus, you are truly Lord! You have whirled us into a new understanding of who you are, whirled us out into the world to do your works and even greater works. You will then open your arms and whirl us at last to be home with you forever. Alleluia!

Monday, May 3, 1999 Sts Philip and James
John 14, 6-14
Last Supper Discourse

The Father. The Father. The Father.

Jesus said to Thomas, "No one comes to the Father except through me." "If you know me, then you will also know my Father."

When Philip said to Jesus, "Master, show us the Father, and that will be enough for us," Jesus gently challenged him. "Have I been with you for so long a time and you still do not know me, Philip? Whoever has seen me has seen the Father." "The Father who dwells in me is doing his works."

The reason Jesus tells us that we will do even greater works than he did is because he is going to the Father. The reason that whatever we ask in the name of Jesus will be granted is so that the Father may be glorified in his Son.

Lord Jesus, thank you for the Holy Spirit who illumines our minds and hearts about the Father in heaven. If we have been wounded by earthly fathers or by other authority figures, please heal us and help us to trust our heavenly Father. Alleluia!

Tuesday, May 4, 1999
John 14, 27-31
Last Supper Discourse

Peace. Shalom. "Do not let your hearts be troubled or afraid."

Jesus gives us his peace. The peace of Christ is not necessarily a passive peace in which all is calm around us.

A friend once gave me an little icon of Jesus and his disciples on the Sea of Galilee. The waves are turbulent and are crashing all around the boat. Jesus is sleeping peacefully in the midst of it all, because he is in charge of the situation. The disciples are safe because Jesus is with them.

All may be crashing about you today. Jesus speaks "peace" to you. He is with you in the storm and is in control. Peace. Shalom. Alleluia!

Wednesday, May 5, 1999
John 15, 1-8
The Vine and the Branches

It is up to the Father to take away the branches that are not growing. Sometimes we'd like to break them off ourselves, but that is not the Father's way.

It hurts to be pruned. It feels like something precious is being taken from us. It is! It's called our self-will, our stubbornness, and our pride. These get in the way of our fruit-bearing for the Lord.

Blossom or burn! That is the choice. A branch is treated in one of two ways. Either it is pruned in order to bear more fruit or it is broken off and burned.

"Anyone who does not remain in me will be thrown out like a branch and wither; people will gather them and throw them into a fire and they will be burned." That's the final destiny of deadwood.

The destiny of the pruned branch is quite different, however. Jesus says, "If you remain in me and my words remain in you, ask for whatever you want and it will be done for you. By this is my Father glorified, that you bear much fruit and become my disciples."

Lord Jesus, let our lives blossom and bear much fruit for you. Let our joy be to know you and to know that you are being glorified in our lives. Alleluia!

Thursday, May 6, 1999
John 15, 9-11
The Vine and the Branches

Jesus tells us, "Remain in my love. If you keep my commandments, you will remain in my love, just as I have kept my Father's commandments and remain in his love."

Jesus draws a boundary, a line of protective love, around our lives. It is within this boundary that we, as branches, are able to survive, thrive, blossom, and bear fruit.

Although nothing can separate us from the love of God (Romans 8, 38-39), we may still choose whether or not to remain united to Jesus, the true Vine. Our love for Jesus is shown by our obedience to his commandments. "If you love me, you will keep my commandments (John 14, 15)."

Jesus tells us, "Remain in me as I remain in you. Just as a branch cannot bear fruit on its own unless it remains on the vine, so neither can you unless you remain in me."

Lord Jesus, sometimes I feel as if I'm withering on the vine. Help me to be aware of your life flowing through me today and let my life blossom afresh for you. Alleluia!

Friday, May 7, 1999
John 15, 12-17
The Vine and the Branches

Jesus said, "I have called you friends, because I have told you everything I have heard from the Father." This is one of the joys of true friendship. Friends tell each other everything, because they trust each other.

There may be limits to earthly friendships. Friends may disagree and remain friends, or they may disagree and discontinue the relationship. There may be misunderstandings.

Jesus is the only friend who always remains true to us and who always understands us completely. Jesus wants us to run first to him with all our cares.

Instead, sometimes we run to tell an earthly friend and to ask that friend to pray for us. It requires spiritual maturity and self-discipline to go first to Jesus and to seek the counsel of Jesus and the Church. Jesus waits for us in the sacraments.

The greatest love is to lay down one's life for one's friends. Jesus has done this for us. He now commands us to love one another as he has loved us.

Lord Jesus, thank you for being our best Friend. Thank you for choosing us to bear fruit for you. We bring to you all the cares and concerns of this day and give them all to you. Thank you for walking beside us every moment of this day. Alleluia!

183

Saturday, May 8, 1999
John 15, 18-21
The World's Hatred

Traveling in Yugoslavia in October, 1988, I was once stopped by a suspicious airport security guard. He looked at my small blue carry-on bag (from the travel agent), looked at me, and asked if I was from a particular country. Surprised, I answered, "No." He had assumed that because the bag had the name of a particular country that I was from that country. Not so unreasonable.

Jesus says that we are going to be so closely identified with him that people will treat us just as they treated him. We wear the Jesus label!

We will be loved by those who love him. We will be hated by those who hate him. We will be persecuted by those who persecuted him. Those who kept his words will keep ours.

Lord Jesus, help us to live so closely in union with you that loving and glorifying you is our vision and our goal, no matter how we are treated on this earth. Help us to remember that our carry-on bag is stamped with "HEAVEN" as our final destination. Alleluia!

Sunday, May 9, 1999 Sixth Sunday of Easter
John 14, 15-21
The Advocate

The Holy Spirit is the Spirit of truth. The Holy Spirit reveals the truth in any given situation. When we are perplexed, we may pray, "Holy Spirit, reveal the truth in this situation."

When we allow the Holy Spirit freedom in our lives, we will be truth-bearers as well as light-bearers. We will live, speak, and act the truth.

We are not alone. Jesus loves us and reveals himself to us, The Holy Spirit is very wise and gentle in showing us areas of our lives where we are not yet filled with light and truth.

Lord Jesus, thank you that your loving Father has sent us the Holy Spirit. Alleluia!

Monday, May 10, 1999
John 15, 26 - 16, 4
The World's Hatred

The Holy Spirit is the Spirit of truth. Jesus said, "I am the way and the truth and the life. No one comes to the Father except through me (John 14, 6)." The Advocate, the Holy Spirit, testifies to Jesus. We are also to testify to Jesus.

Truth. Pontius Pilate asked Jesus, "What is truth?" Truth was standing before his eyes, yet Pilate refused to see.

Lord Jesus, even when some around us may speak lies and live lies, let us speak the truth and live the truth. Alleluia!

Tuesday, May 11, 1999
John 16, 5-11
Jesus' Departure; Coming of the Advocate

Jesus prayed for his Father to send us the Holy Spirit, the Advocate. The Advocate is the one to "convict the world in regard to sin and righteousness and condemnation ..."

Sometimes we try to play Holy Spirit or Advocate in the lives of others. We cannot do this. We may pray for others, but only the Holy Spirit can touch their minds, wills, and emotions. Only the Holy Spirit can bring the victory!

Holy Spirit, promised Advocate, please enter the "impossible" situations in our lives today and bring Easter victory. Alleluia!

Wednesday, May 12, 1999 Sts. Nereus and Achillus Pancras
John 16, 12-15
Jesus' Departure; Coming of the Advocate

The Holy Spirit is the Spirit of truth. Jesus says that "when he comes, the Spirit of truth, he will guide you to all truth."

When we face a puzzling situation, a situation in which different people are telling different stories, when the truth seems elusive, we are wise to pause and to ask the Holy Spirit to guide us to recognize the truth. The Holy Spirit will guide us gently.

We will be given the knowledge we need to have about the situation. This knowledge may not be given all at once. It may be given gradually. Although we may be in a hurry, God is not in a hurry.

Lord Jesus, I have exhausted myself trying to figure things out with my limited understanding. Thank you that the Holy Spirit is already living within me to illumine my understanding. Help me to receive the truth and to speak the truth in gentleness and love. Alleluia!

Thursday, May 13, 1999 The Ascension of the Lord
John 16, 16-21
Jesus' Departure; Coming of the Advocate

Seven times the expression "a little while" is used in this Gospel. Again and again we see that our idea of time is not God's idea of time. Peter tells us, "... with the Lord one day is like a thousand years and a thousand years like one day (2 Peter 3, 8)."

Jesus said, "... you will weep and mourn, while the world rejoices; you will grieve, but your grief will become joy." Our ideas of grief are not God's ideas of grief.

We may see grief as lasting forever, but that is not so. Our grief will be turned to everlasting joy. Alleluia!

Friday, May 14, 1999 St. Matthius
John 15, 9-17
The Vine and the Branches

Jesus is the vine and we are the branches. Our ability to bear fruit is dependent on remaining in Jesus through our trust and our obedience.

Our joy is dependent on our obedience. Jesus said, "I have told you this so that my joy may be in you and your joy may be complete. This is my commandment: love one another as I love you. No one has greater love than this, to lay down one's life for one's friends."

We lay down our lives for our friends when we surrender our own agenda for God's agenda. This does not mean blindly doing everything a friend asks us to do. It means doing what God tells us do in that particular situation.

Lord Jesus, please show me what it means for me today to lay down my life for others. Alleluia!

Saturday, May 15, 1999
John 16, 23-28
Jesus' Departure; Coming of the Advocate

Jesus said, "I came from the Father and have come into the world. Now I am leaving the world and going back to the Father."

There was a beginning of Jesus' earthly ministry, the completion of his mission, and his triumphant return to his Father. We are waiting for his coming again in glory!

Jesus is now educating his followers about their Father in heaven. "For the Father himself loves you ... " "Whatever you ask the Father in my name he will give you."

The Father in heaven is actively, yet patiently, waiting for us. He waits with outstretched arms. He wants us ask him at this moment for whatever we need for our joy to be complete.

Father, I ask you, in Jesus' name, to help me to release a difficult situation into your strong, loving hands. I ask you for the joy of the Holy Spirit. Alleluia!

Sunday, May 16, 1999 Seventh Sunday of Easter
John 17, 1-11
The Prayer of Jesus

Jesus prayed for his followers, for the Twelve, and for you and me. Jesus knew that, although he would no longer be in the world, his followers would still be in the world.

Jesus prayed, "Holy Father, keep them in your name that you have given me, so that they may be one just as we are." In The Message, this passage reads, "Holy Father, guard them as they pursue this life that you conferred as a gift through me, so they can be one heart and one mind as we are one heart and one mind."

We do not proceed alone on this mission. Yes, we have an intimate, personal relationship with God. Jesus, however, specifically prayed that his followers would be one just as he and the Father are one. We are not on a solo journey.

Why do some people at church refuse to exchange the Peace? I wonder. How can they follow Jesus with this aloof attitude towards the brothers and sisters of Jesus?

When a choir is not friendly to someone of a different race who wants to join them in singing praise to God, I wonder. How can this attitude be called following Jesus?

When a committee meets behind closed doors to attempt to destroy the reputation of another follower of Jesus, I wonder. How can this be called following Jesus?

Lord Jesus, we dress up in various ways and call ourselves Christians. Look deeply into our hearts and purify our hearts so that we may truly be one with our sisters and brothers. Alleluia!

Monday, May 17, 1999
John 16, 29-33
Jesus' Departure; Coming of the Advocate

"I have told you this so that you might have peace in me. In the world you will have trouble, but take courage, I have conquered the world."

Jesus does not merely say the word "Peace" in a casual, "feel good" way. This peace is to be found in him, in Jesus himself. It is his

own personal peace. It is the deep peace which is a result of the branch's loving, trusting union with the vine.

"Take courage." On our first trip to England, we kept noticing signs saying, "TAKE COURAGE." I thought that perhaps they were signs left from World War II to bolster the spirits of the suffering English people. Instead, I found out that they were advertisements for a popular drink. The kind of courage Jesus wants us to take is the courage we have which is a result of our security born from our union with him.

Jesus has conquered the world. It is a "done deal."

Jesus has conquered the world and we are in Jesus. We are riding on the shoulders of Jesus, our big Brother! As St. Paul wrote to the Romans, "... in all these things we conquer overwhelmingly through him who loved us (Romans 8, 37)."

With joy, we receive this free gift of peace in Jesus. He has already paid the price for us to have it. We take courage in Jesus. Jesus has already won. Alleluia!

Tuesday, May 18, 1999 St. John I
John 17, 1-11
The Prayer of Jesus

Glory! Chapters 13-20 of John's Gospel are called "The Book of Glory." This prayer of Jesus is packed with the words "glory," "glorify, " and "glorified."

Indeed, the "glory" begins much earlier in John's Gospel, in the beautiful Prologue.

"And the Word became flesh
    and made his dwelling among us,
    and we saw his glory,
    the glory of the Father's only Son,
    full of grace and truth (John 1, 14)."

God the Father revealed his nature through Jesus. Philip once asked Jesus, "Master, show us the Father, that will be enough for us (John 14, 8)."

Jesus responded, "Have I been with you for so long a time and you still do not know me, Philip? Whoever has seen me has the seen the Father (John 14, 9)."

God the Father has been glorified and honored through his Son's work on earth. Now it is time for the Father to glorify his Son. "Now glorify me, Father, with you, with the glory that I had with you before the world began."

Jesus has also been glorified in all his disciples. "I pray for them. I do not pray for the world but for the ones you have given me, because they are yours, and everything of mine is yours and everything of yours is mine, and I have been glorified in them."

Lord Jesus, we are dazzled by these flashes of your glory! Shine through us today, that we may honor and glorify you. Alleluia!

Wednesday, May 19, 1999
John 17, 11-19
The Prayer of Jesus

We do not belong to this world, any more than Jesus belonged to this world. Jesus prayed for us to be consecrated to the truth which would set us free.

This world lives on lies. We are to live and to thrive on God's truth.

We may try to have it both ways. Enough of Jesus to go to heaven and enough of this world to relish the power and possessions it has to offer.

Jesus said the world would hate us because we do not belong to the world. This world is not our real home. Jesus prays for our protection from evil.

Jesus has gone ahead to prepare a place for us. He is "the way and the truth and the life (John 14, 6)." Our assignment is to walk joyfully in his way, to speak and to live his truth, and to discover eternal life here and now on earth. Alleluia!

Thursday, May 20, 1999 St. Bernadine of Siena
John 17, 20-26
The Prayer of Jesus

In this part of the prayer, Jesus is praying for us. We are the ones who have believed through the word of the apostles.

Jesus prays that we may all be one in order that the world may believe that God the Father sent Jesus and that he loves us just as he loved Jesus.

What a prayer! This prayer implies both privilege and responsibility. An assignment is involved.

Jesus says that he has given us the glory that the Father gave to him. The purpose is for unity in the Church, the Body of Christ. The intertwined love of God the Father, the Lord Jesus, and the followers of Jesus is to be a powerful witness to the world.

Sometimes we are weary of the struggle in this world and want to go to be with Jesus in heaven. The feeling is mutual. Jesus prayed, "Father, they are your gift to me. I wish that where I am they also may be with me ..."

Lord Jesus, help us to live the answer to your prayer. Shine through us today. Glory! Alleluia!

Friday, May 21, 1999
John 21, 15-19
Jesus and Peter

"Feed my lambs." "Tend my sheep." "Feed my sheep." Jesus is giving Peter a description of Peter's vocation in the Church.

Note the pronoun, "my." The lambs and the sheep belong to JESUS. "My lambs." "My sheep." "My sheep."

Peter's call is a call to serve. An archaic meaning of "tend" is "to attend as a servant."

Peter may not have understood very much of this at first. Later, he did understand. He referred to Jesus as "the shepherd and guardian of your souls (1 Peter 2, 25)."

To those with a pastoral office, Peter wrote, "Tend the flock of God ... Do not lord it over those assigned to you, but be examples to the flock. An when the chief Shepherd is revealed, you will receive the unfading crown of joy (1 Peter 5, 2-4)."

When we feel overwhelmed with the responsibility of caring for those entrusted to us, we need to remember that they do not belong to us. They belong to Jesus, the Shepherd.

We are to care for them, nourish them, and serve them. That is our responsibility. They are not here to fuel our ego trips. We are here to serve them with humility. Jesus will hold us accountable.

Lord Jesus, you are the Good Shepherd. Help us to follow you today where you lead us. Help us to release those you have entrusted to our care into your Shepherd's heart and hands. Alleluia!

Saturday, May 22, 1999
John 21, 20-25
The Beloved Disciple

We all ask, "What about so and so?" Jesus says to Peter and to us, "What concern of it is yours? You follow me."

Over the marshes at the nearby baylands, there is a long, narrow walkway with a protective fence. There is protection, yet freedom to walk straight to the end and to enjoy the view.

191

Our path to the Lord is like that. There is both protection and freedom. It is our personal path. No one else can walk this path for us.

We can jump over the fence and land in the marsh or stay on our path. On this path we are free to anticipate the new Jerusalem where the Lamb of God, Jesus, our Risen Lord, is waiting for us.

Lord Jesus, sometimes we become very discouraged and even distressed. We look around at others and wonder, "What about them?" You gently invite us to return our attention to you. You gently lead us back to the path you have already prepared for us to walk, the path that leads to you." Alleluia!

Sunday, May 23, 1999 Pentecost Sunday
John 20, 19-23
Appearance to the Disciples

The disciples are afraid! Jesus goes to meet them right there in their place of fear.

First, he gives them the gift of his peace. Then he shows them his hands and side, reassuring them of the fact that he is indeed their crucified and risen Lord!

Only then does Jesus say again, "Peace be with you. As the Father has sent me, so I send you." Jesus then breathed on them and said, "Receive the holy Spirit. Whose sins you forgive are forgiven them, and whose sins you retain are retained."

If we are to follow Jesus, we are required to follow this example. If we are to set others free, we must go to them where they are, not where we would like them to be.

Are they afraid? We pray to understand why they are afraid. Why we are so afraid, ourselves?

As a child, I had a pet wire-haired fox terrier named Nippy. He would occasionally get little stickers, called goatheads, in his paws. He would come to me and hold up his little paw, confident that I would remove the thorn so he could again run free.

Are there "goatheads" in our "paws?" Although the Lord longs to send us out to do his work of setting the captives free, he also longs to set US free.

Lord Jesus, please come into the place where I am so afraid and I don't even know why. You know the reasons and the history of my fears. Speak your word of peace to me, set me free from all my fears, and then send me out to speak peace and freedom to others. Alleluia!

Monday, May 24, 1999
Mark 10, 17-27
The Rich Man

A rich man, self-satisfied, yet seeking reassurance about his claim to eternal life, ran up to Jesus and knelt down before him. His heart seemed to be in the right place. Jesus referred to the commandments and the rich man assured Jesus that he had kept them, all of them, since his youth.

Jesus looked intently at him. The Gospel even says that Jesus loved him.

Jesus, however, knew what this man needed to hear. "You are lacking in one thing. Go, sell what you have, and give to [the] poor and you will have treasure in heaven; then come, follow me."

Everything changed! The enthusiasm quickly drained away and the man sadly went away. He allowed his attachment to his possessions to keep him from being a committed follower of Jesus. Jesus may be looking at you and me today and saying, "You are lacking in one thing."

Lord Jesus, search our hearts and tell us if there is anything that would stand in the way of our wholehearted discipleship. Help us to offer this "one thing" to you. You will more than make up to us whatever our "sacrifice" involves. Alleluia!

Tuesday, May 25, 1999 Venerable Bede, St. Gregory VII,
St. Mary Magdalene de Pazzi
Mark 10, 28-31
The Rich Man

Peter was quick to point out to Jesus that, unlike that rich man who had declined to give away his riches and follow Jesus, he, good old Pete, and the other disciples had given up everything!

Wow! Gee whiz! How lucky can Jesus be!

Jesus reassured Peter that these sacrifices would indeed be rewarded both now and in the life to come. However, in between the

193

promises of temporal and eternal rewards, came the little phrase "with persecutions."

Persecution is part of the price of discipleship. It's a package deal!

This is a lot to take in, to understand, and to absorb. Yes, there are rewards. Yes, there are persecutions. Yes, there is eternal life. Then Jesus concluded with the startling announcement, "Many who are first will be last, and (the) the last will be first."

Do you remember how yesterday's Gospel ended? "All things are possible for God." This mind set, centered on the sovereignty of God, is essential in order to receive today's Good News.

Lord Jesus, please send your Holy Spirit to us today to illumine this passage. We offer you ourselves to you in loving trust and obedience. Alleluia!

Wednesday, May 26, 1999 St. Philip Neri
Mark 10, 32-45
The Third Prediction of the Passion;
Ambition of James and John

After the stretching of Lent, the glory of Easter, the rapture of the Ascension, and the fulfillment of Pentecost, we are plunged back into Gospels dealing with the earthly ministry of Jesus. Jesus warns his disciples of what lies ahead.

"Behold, we are going up to Jerusalem, and the Son of Man will be handed over to the chief priests and the scribes, and they will condemn him to death and hand him over to the Gentiles who will mock him, spit upon him, scourge him, and put him to death, but after three days he will rise."

And we thought it was all over! Easter and Pentecost. Alleluia and all that!

James and John had the audacity to speak of their personal ambition at a time like this. Not a cry of anguish over the suffering awaiting Jesus, but a cry of self-interest in its most rampant form.

I believe that this Gospel was chosen for today, the feast of St. Philip Neri, to show us the road that we, the modern followers of Jesus, still have ahead of us. We're on the way, glory to God, but we're not there yet. St. Philip Neri, the gentle "Apostle of Rome," lived out this mandate to serve. "For the Son of Man did not come to be served but to serve and to give his life as a ransom for many." Alleluia!

Thursday, May 27, 1999 St. Augustine of Canterbury
Mark 10, 46-52
The Blind Bartimaeus

Jesus and his disciples came to Jericho and left Jericho. It was as they were leaving Jericho that the blind man, Bartimaeus, received his sight.

Sometimes we think, "The conference is over. I'm packing my suitcase and leaving town. It's all over." That can be the very moment when "the main event" occurs for us.

Several years ago I attended a conference in San Diego. The speakers had been terrific, the music ministry had been heavenly, and the January weather had been bright and beautiful. Still, I wondered, "Why did I attend?" Something was missing. I felt incomplete.

While waiting in the lobby for my husband to bring the car around to drive to the airport, a total stranger walked over to me. She had also attended the conference and was going back to cold Chicago.

As we were chatting, she felt led to pray for me. As she prayed very quietly, almost inaudibly, she told me what the Lord was showing her. Her "vision" or "prayer-picture" would have made no sense to anyone else. It was for me and I knew exactly what the Lord was telling me. I received the gift of a new sight and a new insight into a long situation of waiting, waiting, waiting. I was energized and went on my way rejoicing.

Lord Jesus, help us to know that your timing is perfect. Like Bartimaeus, we may feel stuck and without either sight or insight. Thank you for coming at the right moment and opening our eyes. Alleluia!

Friday, May 28, 1999
Mark 11, 11-26
The Entry into Jerusalem; Jesus Curses a Fig Tree;
Cleansing of the Temple; The Withered Fig Tree

This is a very jarring passage. There are issues of time and issues of faithfulness.

Time. The Gospel begins with Jesus entering Jerusalem and going to the Temple area. Since it was late, he and the disciples left and went to Bethany.

After leaving Bethany, Jesus, truly human as well as truly God, experienced hunger. The fig tree had leaves, but no figs. "It was not the time for figs."

Meanwhile, back at the Temple, issues of faithfulness or lack of faithfulness, were being played out. The merchant mentality was not in keeping with the spirit of this sacred place.

Jesus practiced scriptural confrontation. "Is it not written:
  'My house shall be called a house of prayer for all peoples?'
  But you have made it a den of thieves."

The chief priests and scribes were simultaneously furious and terrified, an unhealthy combination!

The next morning, Jesus and his disciples observed the withered state of the fig tree. Jesus seized that moment to teach on prayer.

"Therefore, I tell you all that you ask for in prayer, believe that you will receive it and it shall be yours." Jesus stated the need to forgive, so that our Father in heaven would be released to forgive us.

The fig tree and the religious leaders had a lot in common. Their timing was off! Just as the fig tree withered, so the hearts of the priests had withered.

Jesus said, "A tree is known by its fruit (Matthew 12, 33)." He also said, on another occasion, "Every plant that my heavenly Father has not planted will be uprooted (Matthew 15, 13)."

Lord Jesus, may we not only bloom where we are planted, but may we also bear fruit in your time. May we be faithful to recognize you, faithful to forgive others, and faithful to dare to pray the prayers you give us to pray. Alleluia!

Saturday, May 29, 1999
Mark 11, 27-33
The Authority of Jesus Questioned

Jesus was walking in the temple area, the province of the religious elite, the chief priests, scribes, and elders. His very presence was an affront to the leaders.

The first time we know that Jesus was in this area was the time when Mary and Joseph had carried him as an infant to Jerusalem to present him to the Lord. At that time, the aged Simeon had disclosed to

Mary, "Behold this child is destined for the fall and rise of many in Israel, and to be a sign that will be contradicted (and you yourself a sword will pierce) so that the thoughts of many hearts may be revealed (Luke 2, 34-35)."

Jesus overturned the tables in the temple in more ways than one. He overturned the tables of the money changers. He overturned the arrogance of the chief priests, the scribes, and the elders. Their hostile question, "By what authority are you doing these things?" was countered by Jesus in no uncertain terms.

Jesus turned the tables by asking them a question, "Was John's baptism of heavenly or of human origin? Answer me."

The leaders weasled out of this question to save face while Jesus remained serenely in control. The authority given to him by his heavenly Father was once more demonstrated.

Jesus has given us the authority to do the same works he did on earth and even greater works (John 14, 12)! This privilege carries a price. Since Jesus himself encountered opposition, we have to realistic enough to expect the same. "No disciple is above his teacher ... (Matthew 10, 24)." The good news is that Jesus will show us how to live out the vocation to which he has called us. Alleluia!

Sunday, May 30, 1999 Most Holy Trinity
John 3, 16-18
Nicodemus

Jesus was speaking to Nicodemus, a Pharisee, who came unobtrusively in the evening to question him. Jesus was speaking to Nicodemus, the strict keeper of rules, of the God of love, the God who is above all human rules. The Pharisees had become so fixated on the rules of their own making that they seemed to have lost sight of the God of love and compassion.

How often do I live my life like Nicodemus? How often do I believe I "must" do this or "must" do that before God will love me?

"God did not send his Son into the world to condemn the world, but that the world might be saved through him." Heavenly Father, thank you for sending Jesus to be my Savior. Help me to live this day in the light of your love, in the light of Jesus, and in the liberty of the Holy Spirit. Alleluia!

Monday, May 31, 1999 The Visitation
Luke 1, 39-56
Mary Visits Elizabeth

Elderly Elizabeth joyfully cried out to young Mary, "Blessed are you who believed that what was spoken to you by the Lord would be fulfilled." Elizabeth knew how to rejoice with Mary.

Elizabeth had waited a long, long time to bear a son. When she became pregnant, she went into seclusion, saying, "Now at last the Lord has helped me (Luke 1, 25a , (GNT))."

Joy and fulfillment came for Elizabeth at a time when she had given up all hope of childbearing. Indeed, it was no longer humanly possible.

God, on the other hands, had not forgotten Elizabeth. Indeed, God delighted in stepping into the picture at this time and granting her heart's desire. It was not too late after all!

With Mary, God also entered the picture in a miraculous way. Mary's puzzled, but sweet, willing acceptance, would cause her to be called "blessed among women."

Rejoice in the Lord if you are still waiting for the Lord's promise to you to be fulfilled. What the Lord has spoken to you will indeed be fulfilled. God is a God of surprises and will amaze and delight you with his timing. Alleluia!

Tuesday, June 1, 1999 St. Justin
Mark 12, 13-17
Paying Taxes to the Emperor

What do I owe you? Jesus knew the meaning of this question.

Jesus knew all about the hypocrisy of the Pharisees and precisely how to deal with them. They had hoped to catch him in a trap of their own contrivance, but they were in for a surprise!

Jesus knew how to practice what he preached. In dealing with the Pharisees, he was as "shrewd as a serpent and as simple as a dove (Matthew 10, 16)."

Jesus turned the tables by asking the Pharisees a question of his own. Referring to a Roman coin, he asked, "Whose image and inscription is this?" They answered, "Caesar's."

Jesus told them simply, "Repay to Caesar what belongs to Caesar and to God what belongs to God." His questioners were floored!

What do I owe you? What do I owe God? What do I owe myself? St. Paul answered this question by saying, "Owe nothing to anyone, except to love one another; for the one who loves another has fulfilled the law (Romans 13, 8)." Alleluia!

Wednesday, June 2, 1999 Sts Marcillinus and Peter
Mark 12, 18-27
The Question about the Resurrection

A play (on word)s and a movie! The Sadducees did not believe in resurrection. That is why they were "sad, you see!"

The old movie, "Seven Brides for Seven Brothers" did not quite describe the situation in today's Gospel. This Gospel refers to seven brothers and only one bride.

The Sadducees were the priestly party and were considered very powerful. Like the Pharisees, they tried to trap Jesus. Jesus, aware of this tactic, asked, "Are you not misled because you do not know the scriptures or the power of God?"

Jesus also confronted their refusal to believe in resurrection. "As for the dead being raised, have you not read in the book of Moses, in the passage about the bush, how God told him, 'I am the God of Abraham, [the] God of Isaac, and [the] God of Jacob?' He is not the God of the dead but of the living. You are greatly misled."

The Sadducees were considered powerful. How sad that Jesus told them that they did not really know the power of GOD! Willful refusal to believe the Scriptures and lack of belief in God's power had led them into error.

Lord Jesus, today, help us today to believe the Scriptures and to experience your power in our lives. Alleluia!

Thursday, June 3, 1999 St. Charles Lwanga and Companions
Mark 12, 28-34
The Greatest Commandment

This was an amazing exchange since the scribes were supposed to be the legal experts! This particular scribe posed his question, "Which is the first of all the commandments?" after the Sadducees had attempted, unsuccessfully, to trap Jesus with a question about the resurrection.

The greatest commandment remains, "Hear, O Israel! The Lord our God is Lord alone! You shall love the Lord your God with all your heart, with all your soul, with all your mind, and with all your strength."

Eugene Peterson, in The Message, gives the following spin on these familiar words. "Love the Lord God with all your passion and prayer and intelligence and energy."

The second commandment, to love your neighbor as yourself, then falls into place. Jesus said that there are no commandments more important than these two. They are more important than any self-imposed sacrifice or devotions.

Lord Jesus, take me a step further today in loving you with all that is within me. Alleluia!

Friday, June 4, 1999
Mark 12, 35-37
The Question about David's Son

Jesus, speaking to those gathered in the temple area, addressed a particular question about his identity. He asked, "How do the scribes claim that the Messiah is the son of David? David himself, inspired by the holy Spirit, said:

"The Lord said to my lord,
'Sit at my right hand
    until I place your enemies under your feet.' "

David himself calls him 'lord'; so how is he his son?" [The] great crowd heard this with delight."

Lord Jesus, although we acknowledge you as Lord, we still try to run our own lives. Show us how to live the next hour consciously under your sovereignty. Thank you that our freedom is realized under your gentle dominion. Alleluia!

Saturday, June 5, 1999 St. Boniface
Mark 12, 38-44
Denunciation of the Scribes; The Poor Widow's Contribution

When I read this passage, I thought of how two different people faced retirement. A bishop in one of the Protestant churches found it very difficult to retire, without exercising the position and the privileges to which he had grown accustomed.

200

In contrast, Cardinal Joseph Bernadin wrote a very moving book, The Gift of Peace, shortly before his death. He wrote openly and honestly both of the anguish and the joy of his last years and how he learned to relinquish his public ministry.

Clearly, the scribes in today's Gospel relished their status symbols, including their long robes, their places of honor, and the signs of respect

which they received as their due. There was nothing intrinsically wrong with enjoying these good things.

What Jesus condemned was the hypocrisy and duplicity of these leaders. It was reprehensible that they would pray their impressive prayers while feeding upon the very people they were called to serve. Shepherds are meant to feed the sheep, not to devour them.

The poor widow, on the other hand, quietly and unobtrusively, gave her all. She flaunted no designer clothes and no signs of prestige. She was rich, however, in God's eyes. She gave all, knowing that God would provide for her.

Lord Jesus, help me today to realize that my true riches and honor are with you. Out of these riches, help me to give to others. Alleluia!

Sunday, June 6, 1999 The Body and Blood of Christ
John 6, 51-58
The Bread of Life Discourse

Jesus was speaking to the crowds that had insisted on following him across the sea to Capernaum after he had multiplied the loaves and the fish. He had previously warned them about their motives.

Jesus had told them, "Amen, amen, I say to you, you are looking for me not because you saw signs but because you ate the loaves and were filled. Do not work for food that perishes but for the food that endures for eternal life, which the Son of Man will give you
(John 6, 26-27a)."

Then the crowds asked, "What can we do to accomplish the works of God (John 6, 28)?" Jesus promptly answered, "This is the work of God, that you believe in the one he sent (John 6, 29)."

Believe! Jesus then led them to connect their understanding of the manna God had long ago provided in the desert to their understanding of himself. Jesus himself was the "bread of life," the "bread from heaven," and the "living bread."

It was then that the quarreling started. It started then and it has continued to our day among those who call themselves the followers of Christ. There was a sharp break. "As a result of this, many [of] his disciples returned to their former way of life and no longer accompanied him (John 6, 66)."

Lord Jesus, the quarreling is still happening today. All across the world your followers are divided. Dear Lord, have mercy on us. Let the sacrament you instituted as a sign of our unity be restored to your original intent for all your followers. Alleluia!

Monday, June 7, 1999
Matthew 5, 1-12
The Sermon on the Mount; The Beatitudes

God is at work for our happiness in every single one the conditions listed in the Beatitudes. Over and over we notice the words "blessed" or "fortunate" or "happy."

We are called to cooperate with God in the working out of our own happiness. We can choose to acknowledge our poverty of spirit. We can choose to have an attitude of meekness, gentleness, and humility. We can choose to be generous in offering mercy to those who have harmed us. We can yearn for purity of heart. We can actively work to be peacemakers.

Difficult circumstances may be thrust upon us. We may mourn. We may suffer insults or even persecution because we follow Jesus.

Jesus says, "Rejoice and be glad, for your reward will be great in heaven. Thus they persecuted the prophets who were before you."

Lord Jesus, thank you for flooding us with your amazing joy regardless of our circumstances. Thank you for promising us supreme blessedness on this earth and your reward in heaven. Alleluia!

Tuesday, June 8, 1999
Matthew 5, 13-16
The Similes of Salt and Light

Live your life! You may not think your life is having much of an impact, but it is! If you are following Jesus and asking guidance of the Holy Spirit, your life is having a tremendous impact on the world around you.

Lord Jesus, sometimes we become so weary and discouraged. We don't feel like salt or light. However, you are greater than our passing feelings. You said, "You are the salt of the earth… You are the light of the world." Please send your Holy Spirit to us today in a powerful way to enable us to live out your job description of us. Alleluia!

Wednesday, June 9, 1999 St. Ephrem
Matthew 5, 17-19
Teaching about the Law

Jesus said, "I have not come to abolish but to fulfill." Or, as The Message has it, "I'm not here to abolish, but to complete." In the Good News Bible (GNT), the rendition is, "I have not come to do away with them (the law and the prophets), but to make their teachings come true."

Jesus works within the "given" of the present, all the while knowing that there will be a glorious fulfillment for each of us, when we wake up and realize, "Oh, that's what it was all about."

Lord Jesus, help me to do my work and to trust you today with the "given" of my present circumstances. Thank you for your love and light and liberty. Thank you that there will be a time of fulfillment when all your promises have become a glorious reality. Alleluia!

Thursday, June 10, 1999
Matthew 5, 20-26
Teaching about the Law; Teaching about Anger

Jesus is concerned not only with our outer actions, but also with the inner attitudes of our hearts. We may silently seethe with anger and then openly destroy with our rage.

Our righteousness has to exceed that of the scribes and Pharisees. They followed the letter of the law, but refused to show tenderness and compassion in the face of human need.

Lord Jesus, change my heart. Help me today to extend mercy to myself and to others. Alleluia!

Friday, June 11, 1999 Sacred Heart of Jesus
Matthew 11, 25-30
The Praise of the Father; The Gentle Mastery of Christ

Jesus invites to come to him, to take his yoke, and to learn from him. His yoke is easy and his burden is light. He is the wise teacher who daily offers us exercises in the workbook of our life in which we can come to him and ask him for direction.

Lord Jesus, I know now that I have been carrying burdens that you did not give me to carry. Through my own fault, I am exhausted and need rest and renewal. Help me to come to you in childlike trust. Please remove the burdens that you never intended me to carry. Please readjust the remaining burdens so that they will truly be only your assigned burdens that I am carrying. Thank you for this new freedom. Alleluia!

Saturday, June 12, 1999 Immaculate Heart of Mary
Luke 2, 41-51
The Boy Jesus in the Temple

Jesus understood that God was his true Father. He also understood that he was required to be obedient to Mary and Joseph. A tall order for a twelve year old!

When Jesus told Mary and Joseph that he must be in his Father's house, they did not understand. So back to Nazareth they traveled! In the routine of daily life in Nazareth, Jesus "advanced [in] wisdom and age and favor before God and man."

Jesus, even as a twelve year old, is our model for relationships. We have the daily challenge of living with the knowledge that God is our Father and living in love with those around us even when they may not understand our relationship with God. We too will advance, not only in age, but also in wisdom before God and before others.

Heavenly Father, thank you for giving us the example of your Son's obedience to Mary and Joseph. Thank you for the example of Mary, who "kept all these things in her heart." Help us to trust you in the midst of our uncertainties. Alleluia!

Sunday, June 13, 1999 Eleventh Sunday in Ordinary Time
Matthew 9, 36-10:8
The Compassion of Jesus; The Mission of the Twelve;
The Commissioning of the Twelve

Jesus has the heart of a shepherd because he IS the Good Shepherd. "At the sight of the crowds, his heart was moved with pity for them because they were troubled and abandoned, like sheep without a shepherd.

After giving his disciples the "authority over unclean spirits to drive them out and to cure every disease and every illness," he sent them out to the "lost sheep of the house of Israel." "Cure the sick, raise the dead, cleanse lepers, drive out demons." Quite a field education for the twelve!

Lord Jesus, open our eyes to the harvest field of the "troubled and abandoned" ones around us. Touch our hearts with compassion and show us the field work you have for us today. Alleluia!

Monday, June 14, 1999
Matthew 5, 38-42
Teaching about Retaliation

Jesus said, "… offer no resistance to one who is evil." This goes against everything within us!

Sometimes it takes a long time to see that that the one who wronged us is not really "getting away" with anything. God is a God of justice as well as a God of mercy.

The one who wronged us is not God. Only God is God. God alone has the final word.

This is not blind innocence. It is the highest, clearest form of vision. Alleluia!

Tuesday, June 15, 1999
Matthew 5, 43-48
Love of Enemies

Jesus says. "Love your enemies, and pray for those who persecute you …" Yesterday at Mass I was led to pray for an "enemy," someone who had brought great harm to my life. Earlier that same morning I had discovered a letter from this person and had torn it up in great fury. I had tried and tried and prayed and prayed, but this hurt was taking forever to heal. With the help of others, I had forgiven with my will. However, the sense of outrage lingered.

In The Message, the familiar words of Jesus are offered with fresh insight. "I'm telling you to love your enemies. Let them bring out the best in you, not the worst. When someone gives you a hard time, respond with the energies of prayer, for then you are working out of your true selves, your God-created selves. This is what God does."

Enemies can come in handy! God can use them to help us arrive at God's own destination for us. As a young man, Pope John Paul II was once refused by a particular bishop and a particular religious order because God had other plans for his life, namely to bring him to the papacy!

In <u>Abandonment to Divine Providence</u>, Jean-Pierre de Caussade stated that "God uses our enemies and makes them his own instruments and employs them in such a way that no plans of our enemies directed against his chosen souls can possibly succeed."

Thank you, Lord Jesus, for our enemies. You love them and you enable us to love them. You even use them for our good, to transport us to a new place. Alleluia!

Wednesday, June 16, 1999
Matthew 6, 1-6, 16-18
Teaching about Almsgiving; Teaching about Prayer;
Teaching about Fasting

Do you want a receipt or a reward? Is your relationship with a cashier or with a caring, loving Father?

The scribes and Pharisees received what is translated "receipt" for their observable almsgiving, prayer, and fasting. This receipt was an acknowledgement that they had "paid their dues."

Jesus tells us to give, pray, and fast in another way, a secret way. Our loving Father in heaven wants to reward us in a way that will delight and console us.

Giving. When you give to others, "do not let your left hand know what your right is doing, so that your almsgiving may be in secret." This is lots of fun.

Praying. When you pray, "go into your inner room, close the door, and pray to your Father in secret." He understands you completely.

Fasting. When you fast, "do not look gloomy," but rather "anoint your head and wash your face ..." Look spiffy or pretty, not sad and pathetic.

When you give, pray, and fast in these ways, "your Father who sees in secret will repay you." This is really true.

Do we believe this? Lord Jesus, show us how to give, pray, and fast in secret. Alleluia!

Thursday, June 17, 1999
Matthew 6, 7-15
Teaching about Prayer; The Lord's Prayer

Today's Gospel begins with straightforward instruction about prayer. There are words of caution and words of comfort. The Gospel concludes with the condition required to receive that comfort. Jesus reassures us, "Your Father knows what you need before you ask him."

Jesus teaches us how to pray. He gives us a pattern or an outline for praying, and makes certain that we understand the requirement or the prerequisite of forgiveness.

Forgiveness is *sine qua non*. It is essential.

"If you forgive others their transgressions, your heavenly Father will forgive you. But if you do not forgive others, neither will your Father forgive your transgressions." Simple as that. Difficult as that.

In The Message, we are told, "In prayer, there is a connection between what God says and what you do. You can't get forgiveness from God, for instance, without forgiving others. If you refuse to do your part, you cut yourself off from God's part."

Heavenly Father, thank you for the teaching Jesus gave us about prayer. Thank you for sending the Holy Spirit to empower us to forgive. Thank you for your sovereignty in my life. Trusting you, I forgive and release to you those who have injured me. What they did is no longer my concern. It's between you and them. Thank you for forgiving me. Thank you for this new freedom which is being worked out in my life. Alleluia!

Friday, June 18, 1999
Matthew 6, 19-23
Treasure in Heaven; The Light of the Body

Today it occurred to me that I have been hoarding! I haven't been hoarding a treasure, but rather a bit of rubbish. The rubbish is an old resentment.

Over and over I've struggled and prayed over this matter, but the feelings never seem to go away entirely. The feelings of outrage and betrayal have lingered in my heart.

Heavenly Father, please give me a heart transplant. This is just what you promised to the house of Israel through your priest and prophet, Ezekiel. "I will give them a new heart and put a new spirit within them;

I will remove the stony heart from their bodies, and replace it with a natural heart, so that they will live according to my statutes and observe and carry out my ordinances; thus they shall be my people and I will be their God (Ezekiel 11, 19, 20)."

"Create in me a clean heart, O God and renew a right spirit within me" (Psalm 51, 10 K.J.V.)

YOU are my treasure. I do not need to hoard anything. YOU are the light of my life.

Jesus tells us over and over, "Do not worry." We are not to worry about what we need today and we are not to worry about tomorrow, either. Our Father is watching out for us and he knows what we need. Alleluia!

Saturday, June 19, 1999 St. Romuald
Matthew 6, 24-34
God's Money; Dependence on God

Often I feel like the writer in a particular passage in Isaiah. It appears that I have exhausted myself for nothing.

"Though I thought I had toiled in vain,
    and for nothing, uselessly spent my strength,
yet my reward is with the LORD,
    my recompense is with my God (Isaiah 49, 4)."

This is precisely what happens when we think it's all up to us! We exhaust ourselves.

Your life is in God's hands, not in yours. My life is in God's hands, not in mine.

As The Message says, "Steep your life in God-reality, God-initiative, God-provisions. You'll find that all your everyday human concerns will be met. Give your entire attention to what God is doing right now ..."

Right now, I'm by the window enjoying the early morning sunshine and birdsong. Blueberry muffins are ready for breakfast.

There is still reading for my class this afternoon, but there will be enough time. There is always enough time for what God wants me to do.

Today, Lord Jesus, we rest in you. Thank you for taking us by the hand and leading us through the day. Let us seek only your sovereignty in our lives. Let us leave the results in your hands and refuse to worry. Alleluia!

Sunday, June 20, 1999 Twelfth Sunday in Ordinary Time
Matthew 10, 26-33
Courage under Persecution

In today's Gospel, Jesus tells us over and over, "Do not be afraid." In yesterday's Gospel, he told us over and over, "Do not worry."

We are not to worry about the suffering which comes as a result of our trust in God. "Therefore do not be afraid of them. Nothing is concealed that will not be revealed, nor secret that will not be known."

"And do not be afraid of those who kill the body but cannot kill the soul ..." Jesus tells us of the Father's tender knowledge of the little sparrows. "Do not be afraid; you are worth more than many sparrows."

Sometimes we are afraid because we feel alone in our suffering. Sometimes we wonder if God really knows we are suffering. We wonder if God knows or cares what is going on around us.

The fact is that God knows a lot more about what is going on than we know! "Nothing is concealed that will not be revealed, nor secret that will not be known."

Heavenly Father, you do know and you care. Please help us to rest in you and in your care. At the right time you will intervene and bring our suffering to an end. Somehow you will make it all work out for our good and your glory. Alleluia!

Monday, June 21, 1999 St. Aloysius Gonzaga
Matthew 7, 1-5
Judging Others

"Stop judging, that you may not be judged." It's not so much that we shouldn't judge, but that we cannot judge. That is not our role.

We would not walk into a court room and order the presiding judge to step down so that we could be the judge. That is simply not our prerogative.

Sometimes it seems so obvious that we are right and that others are wrong. Maybe and maybe not.

Only God knows. Only God can judge. Only God sees the entire picture. Only God can see deeply into the human heart. Only God can judge. We can observe and discern to some extent, but we cannot judge.

Lord Jesus, sometimes I don't like what I see in myself and in others. Still, I am not the judge. Help me to be as compassionate with others as I want you to be with me. Alleluia!

Tuesday, June 22, 1999 Sts. John Fisher and Thomas More,
St. Paulinus of Nola
Matthew 7, 6, 12-13
Pearls Before Swine: The Golden Rule; The Narrow Gate

"Do not give what is holy to dogs, or throw your pearls before swine, lest they trample them underfoot and tear you to pieces." It's fascinating to read these astonishing words on the day we remember the martyrdom of John Fisher, a bishop, and Thomas More, a lawyer. They were both murdered at the command of King Henry VIII of England.

The narrow gate leads to life. Jesus said, "How narrow the gate and constricted the road that leads to life. And those who find it are few." It is this gate that we must enter and this road we must walk in order to enter true life.

What is the gate? Rather, who is the gate?

Jesus! Jesus himself is the gate. He is the Good Shepherd who said, "I am the gate for the sheep (John 10, 7)." "I am the gate. Whoever enters through me will be saved, and will come in and out and find pasture. A thief comes only to steal and slaughter and destroy; I came so that they might have life and have it more abundantly (John 10, 9-10)."

What is this constricted road we must walk to enter true life? Rather, who is the road?

Jesus! Jesus said, "I am the way and the truth and the life. No one comes to the Father except through me (John 14, 6)."

Where did Jesus walk? The narrow road he walked led to the Cross. If we follow Jesus, we too will walk the way of the Cross, the way of suffering which leads to eternal joy and life. Alleluia!

Wednesday, June 23, 1999
Luke 1, 5-17
Announcement of the Birth of John

"In the days of Herod, King of Judea, there was a priest ..." Even in times when the wicked reign, there are still God's priests, servants, and chosen ones.

Both the priest, Zechariah, and his wife, Elizabeth, who was of priestly heritage, were "righteous in the eyes of God ..." Even so, they were childless in an time when childlessness implied lack of favor with God. They had prayed for a child, but they were too old now. It was too late.

Not so! At the right time, God's time, God entered the picture in a wonderful way.

God sent the angel, Gabriel, to announce that their prayer had indeed been heard. Elizabeth would bear a son destined for greatness in the Lord's sight. Even in her womb, the infant John would be filled with the Holy Spirit. John's mission would be to "prepare a people fit for the Lord."

It has been said that the longer a prayer takes to be answered, the greater the answer will be. God had not forgotten Elizabeth and Zechariah. Over the long years of faithfulness and waiting, they were being prepared to be the parents of this unique servant of God, the man we call John the Baptist. The long years of waiting were not in vain.

Lord Jesus, help me to continue to trust in your love, your faithfulness, and your perfect timing in my life. Alleluia!

Thursday, June 24, 1999 Birth of John the Baptist
Luke 1, 57-66
The Birth of John

God's timing is perfect! For Elizabeth, it was finally time for her child to be born. For Zechariah, there were still eight more days of being unable to speak.

Then, the child was born! God's word had been fulfilled. On the eighth day after the birth, at the baby's circumcision, Zechariah's silent retreat ended.

As soon as Zechariah wrote the words, "John is his name," he was able to speak again. "Immediately his mouth was opened, his tongue freed, and he spoke blessing God."

God may seem to move very, very slowly in our lives. Sometimes, if we're honest, we wonder if God even hears our prayers.

The account of the birth of John the Baptist should encourage us to continue to trust God. Remember, the angel Gabriel had assured Zechariah, "Your prayer has been heard. Your wife Elizabeth will bear you a son, and you shall name him John (Luke 1, 13)."

Elizabeth rejoiced, "So has the Lord done for me at a time when he has seen fit to take away my disgrace before others." Or, as another translation has it, " 'Now at last the Lord has helped me,' she said, 'He has taken away my public disgrace' (Luke 1, 25, Good News Bible (GNT))."

Thank you, Heavenly Father, for hearing our prayers. Thank you for answering all our prayers in the right way at the right time -- your time. Alleluia!

Friday, June 25, 1999
Matthew 8, 1-4
The Cleansing of a Leper

Read Leviticus 14, 1-32 to find out what Jesus told the leper to do after his cleansing. Yes, it is true that Jesus healed him instantaneously.

Even so, Jesus worked within the framework of the Jewish law, which required a purification ritual. It would be at least another eight days before the man would be officially declared "clean."

God may heal us in an instant. Or, we may be led through a long process of healing. God has something larger in mind than simply our own healing, important though it is. Our healing will be used to bless many others. Alleluia!

Saturday, June 26, 1999
Matthew 8, 5-17
The Healing of a Centurion's Servant;
The Cure of Peter's Mother-in-Law

No one in Israel had yet demonstrated the faith of this Gentile military officer. Even Jesus was amazed!

This military officer understood the relationship between authority and the spoken word. He himself was under authority and other soldiers and servants were under his authority.

The officer recognized ultimate authority in Jesus. Jesus was willing to go in person and heal the officer's servant, but the officer knew that this was unnecessary. If Jesus merely spoke the word, the servant would be healed. Jesus spoke the word and the servant was indeed healed.

After healing Peter's mother-in-law, Jesus then liberated those who were demon-possessed. He "drove out the spirits by a word and cured all the sick." Again, the power of the word of Jesus!

Lord Jesus, today please speak the word to set me free to know you, love you, trust you, and serve you in a deeper way. Alleluia!

Sunday, June 27, 1999 Thirteenth Sunday in Ordinary Time
Matthew 10, 37-42
The Conditions of Discipleship; Rewards

Jesus is our point of reference. Earthly relationships are not to be our point of reference.

Self-fulfillment is not to be our goal. JESUS is the goal! JESUS is the prize.

When we go out into the world with this mind-set, the way we are received is the way Jesus would be received. Recently, I observed this first hand.

I was having coffee with a friend at a little sidewalk cafe. Helen has a heart which burns with a passion to bring people to Jesus. She has a beautiful smile and a gentle voice. As people walked by, she would smile and ask if they knew Jesus

A young nanny with two little ones in a stroller stopped and was very open to my friend's words about Jesus. An older woman was rushing off to the dentist's office. She asked if Jesus could help her not to be afraid about having a root canal. A third person when asked if she had ever asked Jesus into her heart, answered angrily, "I never have and I never will!" I believe that how people treated Helen that morning was how they would have treated Jesus.

Lord Jesus, help me to follow you and not turn back. You are my goal. Alleluia!

Monday, June 28, 1999 St. Irenaeus
Matthew 8, 18-22
The Would-be Followers of Jesus

The scribe called Jesus "Teacher." He was well-intentioned, but very naive about what it would mean for him to follow Jesus.

Jesus told him plainly that "the Son of Man has nowhere to rest his head." Someone else called Jesus "Lord," but wanted to attend to family matters first. Jesus told him, "Follow me, and let the dead bury their dead."

Today, what is it that stands in my way and prevents me from following Jesus with all my heart? Holy Spirit, I ask you to reveal the blockage in my heart. Forgive me and help me to be a wholehearted disciple. Alleluia!

Tuesday, June 29, 1999 Sts. Peter and Paul
Matthew 16, 13-19
Peter's Confession about Jesus

Jesus asked his disciples, " 'Who do people say that the Son of Man is?' They replied, 'Some say John the Baptist, others Elijah, still others Jeremiah or one of the prophets.' He said to them, 'But who do you say that I am?' Simon Peter said in reply, 'You are the Messiah, the Son of the living God.' Jesus said to him in reply, 'You are Peter, and upon this rock I will build my church, and the gates of the netherworld shall not prevail against it. I will give you the keys of the kingdom of heaven. Whatever you bind on earth shall be bound in heaven; and whatever you loose on earth shall be loosed in heaven.' "

The heavenly Father revealed to Peter who Jesus really was. The same heavenly Father will reveal to you who Jesus really is. Jesus then told Peter both his identity and his vocation. "You are Peter, and upon this rock I will build my church ..."

Heavenly Father, today please reveal to me in a deeper way who Jesus truly is. Lord Jesus, please send your Holy Spirit to tell me who I really am. Alleluia!

Wednesday, June 30, 1999 First Martyrs of the Church of Rome
Matthew 8, 28-34
The Healing of the Gadarene Demoniacs

The time had come for the two men who had been liberated by
Jesus to rejoin the world of the living. They had lived among the dead,
literally in burial caves, long enough.

Jesus was here! According to the Good News Bible (GNT), the
two men actually screamed at Jesus.

The Message says that they asked Jesus, "What business do you
have giving us a hard time? You're the Son of God! You weren't supposed
to show up here yet!"

Jesus paid no attention to their cries. He had something better for
them than living forsaken among the tombs. He sent the terrible entities
out of them and they were free!

The people in the town, instead of rejoicing that the men were free
from their torment, begged Jesus to leave. They were reeling from the
report of the swineherds who were understandably freaked out over the
fate of their pigs.

Dear Jesus, what a Gospel! You certainly do things in your own
way and in your own time. Today, please help me to be open to your
action in my life and in the lives of those for whom I pray. Alleluia!

Thursday, July 1, 1999
Matthew 9, 1-8
The Healing of a Paralytic

Jesus healed the paralytic in Capernaum, the seaside town where
he went to live after leaving his hometown, Nazareth. In today's Gospel,
we see yet another illustration of Jesus' own adage, "A prophet is not
without honor except in his native place and in his own house (Matthew
13, 57)."

In both Capernaum and Nazareth, there were those who were
offended by Jesus. There were those who were amazed by Jesus. There
were those who were healed by Jesus.

The offended ones thought that Jesus was blaspheming when he
declared to the paralytic, "Courage, child, your sins are forgiven." The
amazed crowd was "struck with awe and glorified God who had given

215

such authority to human beings." The paralytic person was forgiven, healed, and empowered to begin to live a new life.

Lord Jesus, I bring to you the paralysis of my fear and my lack of trust. Help me not to be offended at the way you choose to act in my life. Let me continually rejoice in you and glorify you. Say to me, "Courage, child, your sins are forgiven" and let me walk into a new life. Alleluia!

Friday, July 2, 1999
Matthew 9, 9-13
The Call of Matthew

Jesus had just healed the paralytic! The scribes thought that Jesus was blaspheming when he told the paralytic, "Courage, child, your sins are forgiven."

In today's Gospel, the Pharisees criticize Jesus for eating with tax collectors and sinners. Jesus tells them, "Those who are well do not need a physician, but the sick do."

Those who are sick and do not know it are the ones who most need a physician. The out and out sinners knew that they were sick and needed healing, while the Pharisees did not appear to recognize their own sickness of soul and spirit.

The sinners were grateful and were healed. The Pharisees kept both their snooty attitudes and their sickness.

Lord Jesus, I need you as my physician today. Thank you for all in my life who are instruments of your healing. Alleluia!

Saturday, July 3, 1999 St. Thomas
John 20, 24-29
Thomas

Don't envy Thomas! Jesus said. "Even better blessings are in store for those who believe without seeing (John 20, 29, The Message)."

Jesus did not condemn Thomas. Instead, Jesus walked through a locked door and said, "Peace be with you" to all the disciples.

He then spoke personally to Thomas. He knew the struggle Thomas was having and knew what it would take for Thomas to believe.

Jesus is walking up to you today. He is singling you out for his loving attention.

216

Jesus knows your struggles. He knows why it is so hard for you to believe in his love for you. He is with you at this moment showering you with his love. Whether you feel his love or not does not alter the reality of his love.

"My Lord and my God." Thank you for understanding me even when I do not understand myself. Thank you for loving me even when I do not love myself. Thank you for walking through the locked doors of my heart and speaking peace. Alleluia!

Sunday, July 4, 1999 Fourteenth Sunday in Ordinary Time
Matthew 11, 25-30
The Praise of the Father; The Gentle Mastery of Christ

Our heavenly Father has handed all things over to Jesus. This gives us great peace.

Last night I was unable to sleep because I was foolishly fretting over something too difficult for me to understand. This morning, after reading this Gospel, I reminded myself that the whole matter had already been handed over to Jesus. He is in charge!

This same wise, gentle Jesus invites us to come to him with all of our burdens. He will give us rest. With trust in his love and wisdom, we welcome his yoke and pray to discern his viewpoint of the situations which concern us. St. Peter reminds us, "Cast all your worries upon him because he cares for you (1 Peter 5, 7)."

Lord Jesus, thank you that you are at work dealing with the issues which concern us. Thank you for your peace and for your rest. Alleluia!

Monday, July 5, 1999 St. Anthony Zaccaria
Matthew 9, 18-26
The Official's Daughter and the Woman with a Hemorrhage

One thing after another! Perhaps Jesus did not even get a coffee break (or a pomegranate juice break) that day!

He had just finished teaching about fasting when a synagogue official rushed in with a desperate plea! In spite of his colleagues' persecution of Jesus, this official perceived that Jesus was truly an instrument of God's power. He knew that Jesus could help his child. "My daughter has just died. But come, lay your hand on her, and she will live."

On the way to the home where the dead child lay, a woman, who had been ill for twelve years, followed Jesus, and merely touched the tassel of his cloak. Jesus, aware of her, turned around to say, "Courage, daughter, your faith has saved you."

At last, this suffering woman was healed! Jesus did not brush her aside, even for the emergency with the child. He did not put her on "call waiting" She had already waited twelve years!

At the synagogue official's home, Jesus was derided for saying that the child was not dead, but only sleeping. Jesus, undeterred, took the child's hand, spoke to her, and she arose!

Whether he was greeted with grief, timidity, or ridicule, Jesus calmly proceeded about his Father's business. His presence and his touch brought life and health.

Lord Jesus, today, I'm feeling overwhelmed with "one thing after another." Thank you that you have already given me what I need to follow you! Thank you for sending me out refreshed and renewed. Alleluia!

Tuesday, July 6, 1999 St. Maria Goretti
Matthew 9, 32-38
The Healing of a Mute Person; The Compassion of Jesus

As Jesus went about his ministry of teaching, preaching, and healing, "his heart was moved with pity" for the people. He saw them as "troubled and abandoned, like sheep without a shepherd." The leaders who should have been loving shepherds were too busy trying to impugn Jesus' motives and miracles.

Are you feeling troubled or abandoned today? Jesus is your loving Shepherd. During this summer, ask Jesus to lead you to a place of peace, renewal, and restoration. Alleluia!

Wednesday, July 7, 1999
Matthew 10, 1-7
The Mission of the Twelve; The Commissioning of the Twelve

Jesus "summoned his twelve disciples." The word "summoning" has an urgency about it! This was not a casual invitation, such as "y'all come on over."

Jesus was the Divine Convener. He summoned his disciples for a specific reason. They were to announce, "The kingdom of heaven is at hand."

Jesus gave them the authority to drive out unclean spirits, to heal and "to tenderly care for the bruised and hurt lives (Matthew 10, 1, The Message)." They were to stay in Israel. "Go to the lost, confused people right here in the neighborhood (Matthew 10, 6, The Message)."

Today, Jesus is summoning us! He is calling to us to come to him, to listen attentively to him, and to accept his mission for us.

Lord Jesus, although we may not feel ready for your assignment for us today, we love you and place all our trust in you. Thank you that you will reveal moment by moment your plan for us. Thank you for trusting us. Alleluia!

Thursday, July 8, 1999
Matthew 10, 7-15
The Commissioning of the Twelve

Jesus instructed the twelve to go to their own people, the Jews, "the lost sheep of the house of Israel." Later, of course, they would go out into the whole world, but not right now. This was the time for ministry to their own people.

"The kingdom of heaven is at hand." This was what Jesus instructed them to announce. They were to "cure the sick, raise the dead, cleanse lepers, drive out demons." They were to speak peace, "shalom," to the house where they stayed. If the house was not worthy, the peace would return to the disciples. If they were not well-received, they were to leave the house or the town.

The Lord instructs us to illustrate his kingdom concretely -- to heal the sick, raise the dead, and drive out demons. We are to do what the Lord says and leave the results with him. Within our own family, our church, and our community are those who need to know the love and power of God expressed through us.

Lord Jesus, teach us how to declare your peace to those close to us. In your name, let us bring healing, life, cleansing, and freedom to the lost lambs silently crying out for you. Alleluia!

Friday, July 9, 1999
Matthew 10, 16-23
Coming Persecutions

Jesus says to "be shrewd as serpents and simple as doves." That's quite a combination. The serpent is keenly aware of its surroundings and circumstances. The gentle dove is a sign of peace.

219

Jesus cautions his disciples to "beware," but not to be worried. The Father in heaven is always in charge and will provide the words to say in any given situation. The disciples' assignment is to "cure the sick, raise the dead, cleanse lepers, drive out demons (Matthew 10, 8)."

This is an assignment for those truly seeking to grow in the Christian faith, not for those who need constant ego boosts. Not only hostility and misunderstanding, but also persecution and death are in store for the committed followers of Jesus.

Lord Jesus, help us not to be overwhelmed at these words. You are always faithful to your followers. You are leading us through this earthly pilgrimage to our Father in heaven. Help us to be faithful in bearing witness to you today. Alleluia!

Saturday, July 10, 1999
Matthew 10, 24-33
Coming Persecutions; Courage under Persecution

Looking up to a revered teacher, such as a college professor, has powerful consequences in the life of the student. The student may constantly quote the teacher, begin to sound like the teacher, and even take on the mannerisms of the teacher.

This can be very irritating and annoying to family, friends, and colleagues. It's also unhealthy for the student's own sense of personal worth.

If Jesus is the teacher, however, it's a whole different matter. If we look up to Jesus and seem to lose our identity in his, that's very healthy! Why?

We are beginning to "find" our true selves. Looking to Jesus and living for Jesus will reveal our authentic identity.

The consequences of so resembling Jesus, who is our Teacher, our Brother, and our Lord, can be costly. If Jesus, truly God and truly human, was persecuted and nailed to a Cross, what will happen to those who are like him?

Will they escape? Jesus said, "You will be hated by all because of my name, but whoever endures to the end will be saved (Matthew 10, 22)."

220

We need to rethink our discipleship. We are contrary critters and want it both ways. We want to be God-pleasers and people-pleasers at the same time!

There must be a daily decision to put Jesus first and to trust Jesus with our lives. He is in charge of all that concerns us. Jesus tells us three times in today's Gospel, "Do not be afraid." He reminds us that "... whoever endures to the end will be saved." Alleluia!

Sunday, July 11, 1999 Fifteenth Sunday in Ordinary Time
Matthew 13, 1-23
The Parable of the Sower; The Purpose of the Parables;
The Privilege of Discipleship
The Explanation of the Parable of the Sower

"Jesus-by-the-sea" or "Jesus 101?" The crowds could listen to Jesus till the cows came home, but if they weren't committed to him, they would not understand the parables.

The curious crowd wanted to audit the course for free, see the famous teacher and his miracles, but they did not want to pay the tuition, attend all the classes, do all the homework, the field education, and take the final exam. They only wanted the patina of the presence of God, the fun, the fireworks, and the glory.

The disciples, on the other hand, had signed up, paid the full tuition, and fulfilled all the course requirements including field education. They were learning to walk the walk as well as to talk the talk! They were hearing the word, understanding it, and bearing much fruit. They were actively participating in the presence of God amongst them.

How is it with you? Do you want to audit "Jesus-by-the-sea" or do you want to enroll in the practicum of "Jesus 101?"

Lord Jesus, speak to us today and expand our capacity to respond to you with our whole being. Alleluia!

Monday, July 12, 1999
Matthew 10, 34-11, 1
Jesus: A Cause of Division; The Conditions of Discipleship

If you follow Jesus, gentle, quiet, and unassuming though you may be, your life and your witness will cause division. The disciple is not above the teacher. You may think you're quietly going about your Father's business, but those who do not love Jesus, as well as those who do, notice you.

221

For God's sake, literally don't try to be a people-pleaser. That will destroy you! It will tear you apart to try to please people and to please God at the same time. It won't work and you'll be a wreck.

Concentrate on pleasing God. That is what is best for you and ultimately what is best for those around you. The very best place for you to be is in the center of God's will.

You yourself are really not the cause of division. JESUS is! Don't focus on yourself and think you're a victim. You're not. Jesus was the victim, the sacrificial Lamb of God. You may, however, be a martyr. The word martyr means "witness." Jesus said, "Whoever receives you receives me and whoever receives me receives the one who sent me." Alleluia!

Tuesday, July 13, 1999 St. Henry
Matthew 11, 20-24
Reproaches to the Unrepentant Towns

The New Jerusalem Bible calls this Gospel, "Lament over the lake-towns." These are the towns by the beautiful Sea of Galilee, where Jesus performed most of his miracles or "mighty deeds." Jesus reproached these towns because they had not repented.

Jesus was truly human as well as truly divine. He was intensely frustrated over the stubborn, resistant, hardened hearts of the people in these towns.

Have you poured yourself into a job, a ministry, or a relationship, only to be met with indifference, contempt, or rejection? You gave yourself. You spent yourself in their service and they ridiculed and rejected you.

Lord Jesus, help us to continue to follow you, no matter what the response of others. Help us to be sensitive to your Holy Spirit and to repent. Thank you for forgiving us and setting us free to continue to follow you. Alleluia!

Wednesday, July 14, 1999 St. Camillus de Lellis
Matthew 11, 25-27
The Praise of the Father

Joy springs up in strange places! Jesus, the Son of God and Son of Man, had just been lamenting the stubborn unbelief of those who should have embraced his teaching.

Then, Jesus rejoices! Why in the world does he rejoice?

Jesus rejoices and praises his Father for the trust of the "childlike." The childlike have no hidden agendas, no schemes to discredit others, and no crafty syllogistics.

The childlike, even those with doctorates in sacred theology, are those who look first of all to Jesus. They are humble enough to recognize their need of a Savior. They respond with trust and gratitude. They are pure in heart. They see God.

Father, thank you for handing everything over to your Son. Let us to be childlike today in acknowledging our needs and expressing our joy. Let us trust you and express our joy in you when what we think is the "answer" hasn't yet arrived. Alleluia!

Thursday, July 15, 1999 St. Bonaventure
Matthew 11, 28-30
The Gentle Mastery of Christ

On the campus of Santa Clara University, there is a statue of Christ with the words, "Come to me and learn of me" written in Latin. Nearby is the beautiful Mission Church, with its wisteria arbor and rose gardens. A very peaceful place.

It is easy to "come to Jesus" and to learn from him when we are exhausted and depleted. Where else can we go but to Jesus?

In times of peace and joy, we still need to come to Jesus and to learn from him. Life is not all struggle.

If we have been through many trials, we may develop a "foxhole" mentality, always braced for the next crisis. Instead, Jesus invites us into his peace. He promises us rest.

Lord Jesus, I have unwisely carried too many burdens. I need your rest today. I need to learn from you today. Your yoke is easy and your burden is light. Alleluia!

Friday, July 16, 1999 Our Lady of Mount Carmel
Matthew 12, 1-8
Picking Grain on the Sabbath

"Something greater than the temple is here." Jesus told the Pharisees that he, the Son of Man, was Lord of the Sabbath.

The Pharisees had become so fixated on rules that they could not see God. They sincerely thought that they were worshipping God by keeping all these rules. They were sincerely wrong. They had forgotten all about mercy and compassion.

Jesus said, "I desire mercy, not sacrifice." He said his hungry disciples were "innocent" even though they had violated the Sabbath by "working" when they picked wheat grains to eat.

"Something greater than the temple is here." Jesus is here! Whatever Jesus says goes.

Lord Jesus, thank you that you are greater than any rules or regulations. You are Lord of the Sabbath and Lord of my life. Alleluia!

Saturday, July 17, 1999
Matthew 12, 14-21
The Man with a Withered Hand; The Chosen Servant

The Gospel begins with the Pharisees leaving the synagogue to plot the death of Jesus. Realizing their intentions, "[Jesus] withdrew from that place." Wouldn't you?

In the synagogue, Jesus had just healed a man with a withered hand. It was the Sabbath and the Pharisees were infuriated.

It was time to leave. Jesus knew this. The Pharisees did not stop the healing ministry of Jesus. They just assisted in the relocation of the earthly ministry of Jesus, the Son of God!

Later, of course, the same religious elite would persecute the apostles. The apostles, undeterred, continued their ministry of spreading the Gospel.

It's not worth your time to contest those who misunderstand and misjudge you. Let your light shine! Continue the work God has given you to do within the parameters that have been measured out to you at this particular time. It is up to Jesus to bring forth justice. It is in Jesus that we hope. Alleluia!

Sunday, July 18, 1999 Sixteenth Sunday in Ordinary Time
Matthew 13, 24-43
The Parable of the Weeds among the Wheat;
The Parable of the Mustard Seed; The Parable of the Yeast;
The Use of Parables;
The Explanation of the Parable of the Weeds

In the parable of the weeds among the wheat, there is a sense of bewilderment. A man, in good faith, sowed his seed in his field.

Not just any enemy, but "his" enemy came at a time when everyone was asleep, and deliberately sowed weeds. This was an act of deliberate malice. Yet, the man who had sowed the good seed said to wait until the time of harvest and then let the harvesters separate the good and the bad.

In her book, <u>Without a Doubt</u>, attorney Marcia Clarke wrote, "I had to believe that suffering is part of something bigger. Justice, like the will of God, doesn't always manifest itself on the spur of the moment. It doesn't always come when you think it should. You just gotta wait it out." (p. 479 in the chapter, "Soul Survivor")

In the parable of the mustard seed, we are reminded of the importance of the tiny and the seemingly insignificant. In the kingdom of heaven, no one can be called insignificant. It was the tiny mustard seed which grew to become a large bush where "the birds of the sky came to dwell in its branches."

In the parable of the yeast, we might consider the "yeast" of intercessory prayer. Our prayers are powerful and can change entire situations. As we pray, God is at work changing us, also.

Jesus told us about the end of the age, the harvesting angels and the different fates of the evildoers and the righteous. Until that time, we continue to work, wait, and pray that all may turn to God. God is very patient, " ... not wishing that any should perish but that all should come to repentance (2 Peter 3, 9)." Alleluia!

Monday, July 19, 1999
Matthew 12, 38-42
The Demand for a Sign

Jesus said, "There is something greater than Jonah here" and "there is something greater than Solomon here." What did he mean?

225

Jonah, the prophet in spite of himself, was used of God to save a huge city, Ninevah. Then there was King Solomon, who had prayed for and received great wisdom from God.

This king was considered a marvel. Even the queen of the south traveled "from the ends of the earth to hear the wisdom of Solomon."

Here is Jesus, Son of God and Son of Man, in the midst of the scribes and Pharisees, the scripture scholars, the experts in the law. What do they do? Kneel in adoration before Jesus? No, they ask for a sign.

Do you ever ask for a sign? Do I?

Of course we do. We may camouflage the indelicate word "sign" by calling it "reassurance" or "confirmation." Same thing. We look at our difficult circumstances, become frightened, and start to reach out for help, any kind of help.

Peter looked at the waves on the stormy Sea of Galilee and started to sink. Jesus called Peter and Jesus calls you and me to keep our eyes on him! Jesus is still in charge of the "waves."

Lord Jesus, thank you that YOU are the sign. Help us to look above our troubling, but temporary, circumstances us to you. You are great and you are in charge. Alleluia!

Tuesday, July 20, 1999
Matthew 12, 46-50
The True Family of Jesus

Blood is thicker than blood. The blood of Jesus is stronger than the blood of our earthly family tree.

We are actually in Jesus' family tree! His Father is our Father. His sisters and brothers are our sisters and brothers.

We are to honor our earthly parents and to care for our earthly relatives. However, our true and eternal family is the family of God.

Father, help me to remember that you are my true Father and that Jesus is my Brother. Free me to reach out to others, in the power of the Holy Spirit, knowing that I always have the security of your love to embrace me and to heal me. Alleluia!

Wednesday, July 21, 1999 St. Lawrence of Brindisi
Matthew 13, 1-9
The Parable of the Sower

Jesus was speaking to the large crowds. Although there were the curiosity seekers and the sick hoping for healing, there were also those who were truly capable of mature, committed discipleship. The different groups were all mixed up together, like weeds amongst the wheat.

Therefore, Jesus wisely taught them in such a way that the idle and curious would be puzzled, while the committed would continue to follow him for himself. With a bit of reflection, they would be able to see themselves in the parable. Were their hearts shallow, rock hard, choked with "thorns," or deeply prepared?

Lord Jesus, it's easy to see the times when I have been shallow in my commitment to you, stubborn and hard-hearted in my response to you, and entwined with the frustrating and thorny cares of this world. I know this is true, but I also know that you are greater than my heart. I trust you to change my heart and to prepare my heart to receive your word today. Let my life bring forth a rich harvest. Alleluia!

Thursday, July 22, 1999 St. Mary Magdalene
John 20, 1-2; 11-18
The Empty Tomb; The Appearance to Mary Magdalene

Even the joy of the resurrection had elements of confusion. Shortly before dawn, Mary Magdalene, weeping and exhausted from the agony of watching the crucifixion, was bewildered by the absence of Jesus' body from the tomb.

We know, from Mark's Gospel that Mary Magdalene was one of the women who had brought spices with which to anoint the body of Jesus (Mark 16, 1). What had happened? The body of the crucified Jesus was nowhere to be seen!

The risen Jesus was speaking to Mary, but she did not yet recognize him. Tragedy had been turned into triumph!

Mary's confusion and grief were instantly changed when she realized that Jesus was alive and was with her. She boldly proclaimed, "I have seen the Lord."

What are you confused about today? What are you weeping about today? Jesus is alive! Your tragedy will be turned to triumph! You may not recognize him, but Jesus is here with you in the Person of the Holy Spirit. Go and tell your world, "I have seen the Lord." Alleluia!

Friday, July 23, 1999 St. Bridget
Matthew 13, 18-23
The Explanation of the Parable of the Sower

Jesus said that, "the seed sown on the path is the one who hears the word of the kingdom without understanding it, and the evil one comes and steals away what was sown in his heart." To hear without understanding is perilous. There is the danger of never having the seed sprout, blossom, and bear fruit.

Lord Jesus, let even the tiniest seed you sow in my life be received with understanding. Help me to cooperate with you in order to bear fruit.

The seed sown on rocky ground has trouble getting rooted. The soil has not been adequately prepared.

Lord Jesus, plow the ground of my being and break up the rocky soil in my heart. Let your word enter and take deep root.

The seed sown among the thorns is crowded out and choked by the cares of this world. Setting priorities and making correct choices are essential for this seed to grow

Lord Jesus, prune out the weeds and thorns in my heart. Let me put you first and trust you with all my worries. You know what to do with these concerns better than I do.

The seed sown on the rich, plowed, and prepared soil is "the one who hears and understands" and then bears fruit. The preparation may have been painful, but this fruit is going to be very, very sweet.

Lord Jesus, help me today to have a heart prepared by prayer to receive your word in my life, act on it, and bear fruit. Alleluia!

Saturday, July 24, 1999
Matthew 13, 24-30
The Parable of the Weeds Among the Wheat

"The kingdom of heaven is like this (Matthew 13, 24, Good News Bible (GNT))." God has a unique way of doing things. That's why Jesus is telling these teaching stories, these parables with a punch.

The parables illustrate that God's ways are not necessarily our ways. We'd like to yank out the weeds! Whether we consider the "weeds" to be our own bad habits or whether we consider the "weeds" to be irritating people or frustrating situations, we'd like to yank them out pronto, no two ways about it.

Alas, for the hotheads amongst us, that's not usually God's way! When we think of our "enemies" (those who do not wish us well), we'd like to rip off their heads, but Jesus says to pray for them and to bless them.

"You have heard that it was said, 'You shall love your neighbor and hate your enemy.' But I say to you, love your enemies, and pray for those who persecute you ... (Matthew 5, 43-44)."

God's way is to wait. We need to learn to wait and let God sort it out.

Even the weeds have a purpose in illustrating how God's kingdom is run. God is at work conforming us into the image of Christ (Romans 8, 29).

Lord Jesus, I'd like to grab all the weeds in my life and burn them up! That's not your way, though, so help me to wait. Help me to trust that you know all about the weeds and the wheat in my life. You alone know when harvest time is here and when it's time to remove the weeds. Help me to "chill," as teenagers say, and to trust you. Alleluia!

Sunday, July 25, 1999 Seventeenth Sunday Ordinary Time
Matthew 13, 44 - 52
More Parables; Treasures New and Old

This scribe, who became a disciple of Jesus, had the best of both worlds He knew the Jewish roots of the Christian tradition in a profound way.

St. Paul, apostle to the Gentiles, cautioned the Christians in Rome to remember their "place," to remember that they were "grafted in." "You Gentiles are like the branch of a wild olive tree that is broken off and then, contrary to nature, is joined to a cultivated olive tree. The Jews are like this cultivated olive tree, and it will be much easier for God to join these broken-off branches to their own tree again (Romans 11, 24 <u>Good News Bible</u>, (GNT))." "You are just a branch; you don't support the roots -- the roots support you (Romans 11, 18c <u>Good News Bible</u> (GNT))."

Christians need to understand and to respect their Jewish roots. Only then can they truly value the treasures of the kingdom of heaven and share these treasures. Hallelujah!

Monday, July 26, 1999 Sts. Joachim and Ann
Matthew 13, 31-35
The Parable of the Mustard Seed; The Parable of the Yeast;
The Use of Parables

The kingdom of heaven may not be recognized at first. The mustard seed seems so tiny and insignificant. Only God knows its destiny. It will grow to be a large bush where birds will find shelter.

The identity of the yeast appears to be lost in the dough. Yet, without the yeast, the bread will not rise and fill the house with its fragrance.

Jesus chose to speak in parables. That was his teaching method.

How often today do people remember only the stories in homilies! A wise homilist knows how to offer the truth wrapped in a narrative package.

Lord Jesus, thank you that you are always speaking truth to me. Help me to hear your message to me through the seemingly small and insignificant events of the day. Help me to recognize your voice through unconventional messengers. Alleluia!

Tuesday, July 27, 1999
Matthew 13, 35-43
The Use of Parables;
The Explanation of the Parable of the Weeds

Right now, I want to pull a human "weed" out of my life, actually out of someone else's life. I am suspect that this "weed" is up to no good and is pulling the wool over the eyes of a trusting elderly lady.

The Lord says to me, "NO!" Stop!

It is not my job to pull this " weed" out of the situation. Instead, I need to go and weed my own garden.

"The Son of Man will send his angels, and they will collect out of his kingdom all who cause others to sin and all evildoers. They will throw them into the fiery furnace, where there will be wailing and grinding of teeth. Then the righteous will shine like the sun in the kingdom of their Father. Whoever has ears ought to hear."

Lord Jesus, you said, "Seek first the kingdom [of God] and his righteousness, and all these things will be given to you besides. Do not worry about tomorrow; tomorrow will take care of itself (Matthew 6, 33, 34c)." Today, help me to seek first your sovereignty in my own life and to leave all the "weeds" to you. Alleluia!

Wednesday, July 28, 1999
Matthew 13, 44-46
More Parables

Finding and risking. Jesus said that the kingdom of heaven is like finding a treasure and then risking everything to acquire it.

You and I risked nothing, yet we gained everything when we entered the kingdom. The riches of the kingdom are already ours!

The next step is to offer our earthly lives in God's service because our heavenly lives have already been secured by Jesus. In the midst of tragedies and traffic jams, it may not seem so, but it is so.

Lord Jesus, help me to live my life today knowing that all the riches of the kingdom are at my disposal. Alleluia!

Thursday, July 29, 1999 St. Martha
John 11, 19-27
The Raising of Lazarus

"Yes, Lord, I have come to believe that you are the Messiah, the Son of God ..." Martha was honest when she said that she had "come to believe."

It took time. It took getting to know Jesus. It did not happen all at once.

The Lord is so patient with us. Martha, Mary, and Lazarus had all come to know Jesus. He came to see them. He spent time in their home. He was their friend.

Lord Jesus, I want to come to know you better. I want to spend time with you. Please help today to trust you a little more and to know that you are my Friend, as well as the Messiah, the Son of God. Alleluia!

231

Friday, July 30, 1999 St. Peter Chrysologus
Matthew 13, 54-58
The Rejection at Nazareth

This week-end, our family came to Temple, Texas, to celebrate the eightieth birthday of my father-in-law. Temple is quite different from the area of California where we have lived since 1972. Our son, Christopher, at age ten, wrote an essay, hilariously contrasting the "natives" of Temple and the "natives" of our city.

Jesus was in his hometown synagogue of Nazareth. He was among the "natives," his friends and neighbors. Instead of rejoicing at the way God was obviously working in his life, they "took offense." They were jealous. "Where did this man get all this?"

Jesus got "all this" where you and I can get "all this." Jesus got "all this" from his heavenly Father.

There is no need to feel jealous or threatened when we see God working in the lives of others. There's plenty of "all this" to go around. Let us believe this so that we will see "mighty deeds" today. Alleluia!

Saturday, July 31, 1999 St. Ignatius of Loyola
Matthew 14, 1-12
The Death of John the Baptist

Herod was driven by fear. Because of his fear of public opinion, he put John the Baptist in prison. Because of his fear of what his dinner guests would think, he ordered John to be executed.

Herod was one of the most tragic figure in Scripture. How many Herods are there in our world today? How many times are we ourselves guided by fear rather than faith?

There is a healthy form of fear. "The fear [reverence] of the LORD is beginning of wisdom (Proverbs 1, 7)." Lord Jesus, when I am afraid , help me to put my trust and confidence in you. Help me to be guided by faith, not driven by fear. Alleluia!

Sunday, August 1, 1999 Eighteenth Sunday Ordinary Time
Matthew 14, 13-21
The Return of the Twelve and the Feeding of the Five Thousand

Jesus, having just heard of the death of John the Baptist, withdrew to be alone. Even in his grief, he was pursued by crowds.

Instead of insisting on his own need for solitude, Jesus was more concerned for the people who needed him. In compassion, he reached out to them and healed them.

Jesus then took what his disciples perceived as "lack" and transformed it into abundance. Jesus taught his followers that the solution was already at hand. He took what was available (five loaves of bread and two fish), blessed and broke the bread, and gave the food to his disciples who in turn gave it to the people.

Lord Jesus, I would like some space today myself. Even so, please take whatever resources of time and energy are available in my life and use them to heal and feed others. Thank you for replenishing me as I continue to trust in you. Alleluia!

Monday, August 2, 1999 St. Eusebius of Verelli
Matthew 14, 22-36
The Walking on the Water: The Healings at Gennesaret

After the time of testing came the time of rewards. Jesus took Peter and his other disciples through another exercise, another "learning station." This time they learned to focus on their Lord and not on their stormy circumstances.

Peter alone had the pluck to get out of the boat and to take Jesus at his word! "Lord, if it is you, command me to come to you on the water."

After the storm, those who had remained safely in the boat said, "Truly, you are the Son of God." Yeah.

After "making the crossing," they arrived at Gennesaret where many people were healed. The disciples received at least two rewards.

Inwardly, their trust in Jesus was greatly strengthened. Outwardly, they saw the power of Jesus to heal. Merely touching the tassel on his cloak brought healing.

Lord Jesus, help me to focus on you and not on the storm. Give me the pluck of Peter to get out of the boat and walk on water. Alleluia!

233

Tuesday, August 3, 1999
Matthew 15, 1-2; 10-14
The Tradition of the Elders

Jesus told his disciples how to deal with the Pharisees and scribes. "Every plant that my heavenly Father has not planted will be uprooted. Let them alone; they are blind guides ..."

Leave them alone. Don't even try to reason with them. They are not open to reason. They are not open to truth. They are not open to God.

Jesus himself called them hypocrites and asked them, "Why do you break the commandment of God for the sake of your tradition (Matthew 15, 3)?" Their so-called worship of God was "in vain" because they were "teaching as doctrines human precepts (Matthew 15, 8)."

I wasted a lot of time earlier in my life wondering about certain "Pharisees." How could people call themselves Christians and treat others so terribly? Jesus told me to "let them alone."

Thank you, Lord Jesus, that your plans for our lives can never be uprooted. Your love for us and your power is greater than all opposition. Alleluia!

Wednesday, August 4, 1999 St. John Vianney
Matthew 15, 21-28
The Canaanite Woman's Faith

"O woman, great is your faith." Sometimes we find great faith where we least expect it.

Sometimes those we least expect to speak for God are the very ones who speak the strong words we need to hear. We need to listen for the message, regardless of the identity of the messenger.

Jesus listened with his heart and heard the strong determined faith of an "outsider," a Canaanite woman. Her determination to ignore obstacles and to go directly to Jesus touched Jesus very much.

Her willingness to persist even in the face of apparent insult and rejection moved him to intervention on her behalf. This gutsy woman even accepted being called a "dog" and turned that into a reason why Jesus should help her!

"O woman, great is your faith! Let it be done for you as you wish."

Lord Jesus, you listened with your heart and heard the faith of someone considered an "outsider." Thank you for listening to me today and hearing the cry of my heart, even if that cry is not very articulate. Let me listen with my heart today and receive your message even if I am puzzled by the "messenger." Alleluia!

Thursday, August 5, 1999 The Dedication of St. Mary's in Rome
Matthew 16, 12-23
Peter's Confession about Jesus

God indeed chooses the weak and makes them strong! Many are confounded by God's unlikely choices.

Jesus said to Peter. "... you are Peter, and upon this rock I will build my church, and the gates of the netherworld shall not prevail against it. I will give you the keys of the kingdom of heaven. Whatever you bind on earth shall be bound in heaven; and whatever you loose on earth shall be loosed in heaven."

Was Peter perfect? After all, it was Jesus Christ himself who chose Peter for this unique task. It was to Peter that Jesus entrusted the keys to the kingdom.

We know that Peter was not perfect. Within minutes of Jesus' declaration about Peter's role, Peter blew it. Jesus was telling his disciples that he would go to Jerusalem, "... suffer greatly from the elders, chief priests, and the scribes, and be killed and on the third day be raised."

Peter refused to accept this. "God forbid, Lord! No such thing shall ever happen to you."

Jesus responded in no uncertain terms, "Get behind me, Satan! You are an obstacle to me. You are thinking not as God does, but as human beings do."

Peter was not perfect. Still, Jesus chose him. You and I are not perfect. Still, Jesus chooses us and strengthens us to fulfill our vocation. Alleluia!

Friday, August 6, 1999 Transfiguration of the Lord
Matthew 17, 1-5
The Transfiguration of Jesus

Peter, please practice silence! Do you always have to put your foot in your mouth?

Sometimes I really wonder why in the world Jesus chose Peter. In yesterday's Gospel, Peter boldly confessed Jesus as the Messiah, the Son of the living God. Jesus promised to give to Peter the keys of the kingdom.

According to today's Gospel, Jesus was transfigured before Peter, James and John. "His face shone like the sun and his clothes became white as light."

Peter rose to the occasion by generously offering to capture the moment, not with an instant photo, but by making three tents, one each for Jesus, Moses, and Elijah. Good grief, Peter, get a grip!

Our heavenly Father is very merciful and very patient with all of us. On this particular occasion, he spoke from a cloud. "This is my beloved Son, with whom I am well-pleased; listen to him."

The thoroughly terrified disciples fell prostrate. Jesus came to them, touched them, and said, "Rise, and do not be afraid."

Lord Jesus, you are so patient with us. We are often like Peter. We say idiotic things when we are frightened. Thank you for speaking to us and gently telling us, "Rise, and do not be afraid." Alleluia!

Saturday, August 7, 1999 Sts Sixtus II, Cajetan
Matthew 17, 14-20
The Healing of a Boy with a Demon

Jesus spoke directly to the demon, not to the boy himself. The poor boy already had been labeled a "lunatic."

Jesus expelled the demon, thus healing and freeing the boy. Although that may sound obvious, I believe it is important to make this distinction. Jesus was in no way condemning the boy himself.

The disciples had tried and failed to effect a cure for the boy. Then they watched Jesus succeed where they had failed.

Jesus, totally human as well as totally divine, was exasperated. Still, he did not give up on his followers. Instead, he encouraged them. "Amen, I say to you, if you have faith the size of a mustard seed, you will say to this mountain, "Move from here to there,' and it will move. Nothing will be impossible for you."

Lord Jesus, sometimes I feel stuck in "lunatic" situations. You said, "Nothing will be impossible for you." Help me how to step out in faith, speak to one of these "mountains" and see it move. Alleluia!

Sunday, August 8, 1999 Nineteenth Sunday in Ordinary Time
Matthew 14, 22-33
The Walking on the Water

Peter, with his frightened, yet brave heart, began to walk on the water and then to sink. "Jesus immediately stretched out his hand and caught him, and said to him, 'O you of little faith, why did you doubt?' "

I used to think Jesus was reproaching Peter with these words. Now I tend to think that Jesus had a twinkle in his eye and was smiling at Peter.

Jesus was proud of Peter for confronting his fear by getting out of the boat and trying. The other disciples were scared stiff and stayed in the boat. It was risky to leave the relative safety of the boat for the unknown.

Once Jesus was in the boat, the other disciples "did him homage, saying, 'Truly you are the Son of God.' " Their fears were relieved, but they missed the adventure of launching out on the waves for themselves.

Lord Jesus, help me to hear your voice telling me to confront my fears, trust you. and to "walk on the water." Alleluia!

Monday, August 9, 1999
Matthew 12, 22-27
Jesus and Beezebul

Jesus, knowing exactly what the Pharisees were thinking, answered their unspoken criticism. They refused to rejoice when Jesus set the blind, mute demoniac free.

The Pharisees could only recycle their rejection of Jesus. "This man drives out demons only by the power of Beelezebul, the prince of demons."

237

What a crazy thing to say! The person who had been termed a demoniac was set free, while the Pharisees persisted in their obstinate rejection of Jesus, Son of God and Son of Man.

Lord Jesus, sometimes we are like the demoniac who was blind and mute. We need you to set us free. Other times we are like the stubborn Pharisees who refused to believe in you and to trust you. Within our very selves we may be divided. We need you to set us free. Open our eyes to see you. Open our mouth to speak your praises. Open our minds and hearts to know that you alone are the One who can heal us. Alleluia!

Tuesday, August 10, 1999 St. Lawrence
John 12, 24-26
The Coming of Jesus' Hour

Refusing to "die" condemns us and keeps us in bondage. It is when the grain of wheat falls into the ground and "dies" that it produces an abundant harvest.

What do we need to do to "die" today? Maybe it's as simple and as terrible as acknowledging that we are in bondage to ourselves and to having our own way. To be free, we need to "die" to our own agenda.

Lord Jesus, thank you for the freedom to follow where you lead today. Thank you for a new freshness and a new fruitfulness. Alleluia!

Wednesday, August 11, 1999 St. Clare
Matthew 18, 15-20
A Brother Who Sins

Jesus is present in this situation of attempted conflict resolution. "For where two or three are gathered together in my name, there am I in the midst of them."

We usually think of this promise in a nice, civilized way. When we are gathered together in peace, the Lord is present. That's true, but the Lord is also present when we are gathered together in conflict. The Lord is still present.

Lord Jesus, thank you for your presence as we obey you and go to the one who has sinned against us. We are not responsible for the other person's reaction, but we are responsible for obeying you in this matter of conflict resolution. Thank you that it may be messy and it may take time, but you and you alone have the last word, the word that brings peace and justice. Alleluia!

Thursday, August 12, 1999
Matthew 18, 21-19, 1
The Parable of the Unforgiving Servant; Marriage and Divorce

No pay back. Often, people who feel obliged for past favors try to find a way to reciprocate.

If you took me out for lunch for my birthday, maybe I'll take you out for lunch on your birthday. If you helped to put me through college, I'll help you with your medical expenses. Whatever the scenario, it's now "pay back" time.

NO! It's not "pay back" time. No "pay back" for favors received and no "pay back" for injuries sustained.

God is in charge of our lives. We freely give, expecting nothing in return. We freely forgive, whether or not or forgiveness is received.

"Pay back" means focusing on ourselves, on others, and on temporal matters. Giving and forgiving means focusing on God and on the eternal.

Father, we can never pay you back for the gift of your only Son. Today, we simply offer ourselves to you, body, soul, and spirit to be used according to your loving will. We lose nothing by forgiving. We gain everything. We look to you alone to defend us. Alleluia!

Friday, August 13, 1999 Sts. Pontian and Hippolytus
Matthew 19, 3-12
Marriage and Divorce

"So they are no longer two, but one flesh." The Pharisees were at it again trying to trap Jesus.

Jesus wisely took the Pharisees back to the book of Genesis and restated God's view of marriage. "Have you not read that from the beginning the Creator 'made them male and female' and said, 'For this reason a man shall leave his father and mother and be joined to his wife, and the two become one flesh?' So they are no longer two, but one flesh. Therefore what God has joined together, no human being must separate.'"

The Pharisees, by persisting in their questions, exhibited the same hardness of heart that rationalized Moses' decision to allow some divorces. Jesus, however, refused to be detoured by this tactic.

239

Jesus took another approach. To the Pharisees, he quoted the book of Genesis. To his own disciples, on the other hand, he elaborated on states of life other than marriage.

Lord Jesus, thank you for those called to celibacy and for those called to marriage. Give us today the understanding we need to seek first your sovereignty in our lives. Alleluia!

Saturday, August 14, 1999 Assumption Vigil
Matthew 19, 13-15
Blessing of the Children

"Let the children come to me." Jesus has just taught about God's purposes for marriage. He now blesses children, the fruit of marriage. "Let the children come to me, and do not prevent them; for the kingdom of heaven belongs to such as these."

Lord Jesus, please lay your hands on us and on our children. Pray for us. Bless us. Alleluia!

Sunday, August 15, 1999 The Assumption of the Virgin Mary
Luke 1, 39-56
Mary Visits Elizabeth

"Blessed are you who believed that what was spoken to you by the Lord would be fulfilled." The elderly Elizabeth, bearing John the Baptist in her womb, spoke these words to the young Mary, bearing the Christ child.

Has the Lord spoken a "word" to you which has not yet been fulfilled? Wait God's time and trust God's provision.

God zeroed in on Mary. Here was a young woman who dared to believe the impossible! Here was someone who understood the character of God in a way few ever understand.

Mary proclaimed that it is God who disperses "the arrogant of mind and heart." It is God who lifts up the lowly to new heights. It is God who speaks and the "impossible" is accomplished.

Mary, in her state of puzzled wonder, set off in haste to visit Elizabeth. She would soon hear Elizabeth's words of reassurance, encouragement, and vocational confirmation.

Lord Jesus, thank you for the example of your mother. She always leads us to you. She "magnifies" you and not herself.

Mary, "most blessed are you among women, and blessed is the fruit of your womb." Mary, pray for us to believe that what was spoken of to us by the Lord will indeed be fulfilled. Alleluia!

Monday, August 16, 1999 St. Stephen of Hungary
Matthew 19, 16-22
The Rich Young Man

Jesus is saying, "Whatever you're holding onto or clinging to in order to preserve your identity, " 'LET IT GO!' " Some of us hide behind our jobs, our religious vocations, our upscale addresses, the designer labels in our clothes (mine are a combination of faded Laura Ashleys and Lands' End long torso swimsuits), our degrees, etc., etc. and so on.

None of these things are wrong in and of themselves. God indeed may have called us to our particular way of life. What concerns Jesus is our "attachment."

Heavenly Father, please lead me today to a deeper trust in you. Holy Spirit, please counsel me in my following of Jesus. Jesus, you are Lord. Alleluia!

Tuesday, August 17, 1999
Matthew 19, 23-30
The Rich Young Man

If you think you've arrived, you'll never get "there." The rich may think they've "arrived." They seem to have it all in the here and now. Do they?

Jesus says it will be "hard for one who is rich to enter the kingdom of heaven." The disciples were so surprised at this that they questioned Jesus about it. "Who then can be saved?" Jesus answered, "For human beings this is impossible, but for God all things are possible."

Jesus surprises us with the statement that, "many who are first will be last, and the last will be first." What does he mean?

Entering the kingdom of heaven and living in this kingdom requires us to give up our own ideas of "how" and "why." We simply follow the Lord and trust in him both "here" and "there."

It is then that we have "arrived." It is then that God's will is being done in our lives. Alleluia!

Wednesday, August 18, 1999 St. Jane Frances de Chantal
Matthew 20, 1-16
The Workers in the Vineyard

Here we go again with Jesus upsetting the apple cart! In yesterday's Gospel about the young man who was wealthy, Jesus said, "Many who are first will be last and the last will be first (Matthew 19, 30)."

In today's Gospel, our human sense of "fairness" is thoroughly outraged. The workers who had toiled since dawn received the very same wages as the Johnny-come-latelys who showed up at the last minute, or at least at the last hour. It's not FAIR!

Say it again, Jesus. "Thus, the last will be first, and the first will be last.

Perhaps we need a new way of seeing, a new way of understanding. Perhaps we need to stop trying to be God's little sheriffs. Perhaps we should stop spouting off about our ideas of what is fair and equitable. After all, each group received what was promised!

The first group grumbled, "These last ones worked only one hour, and you made them equal to us, who bore the day's burden and the heat." What really irked this group was that the latecomers were made "equal" to them.

However, the first group did not have to worry and wonder what they would do that day to provide for their families. The latecomers were still in the marketplace because no one had yet hired them.

The gracious landowner assured them that there was a place for them also in the vineyard. He turned no one away.

Lord Jesus, thank you for thoroughly upsetting our apple cart of ideas about what is fair. Give us the grace to be generous as you are generous, to love as you love, and to work joyfully in your vineyard today. Alleluia!

Thursday, August 19, 1999 St. John Eudes
Matthew 22, 1-4
The Parable of the Wedding Feast

"Many are invited, but few are chosen." In the Gospel of Matthew, we have already heard that "many who are first will be last, and the last will be first (Matthew 19, 30)."

Some years ago, there was to have been a great society wedding, meticulously planned. At the last minute, the wedding was cancelled. The one who had been "stood up" at the altar decided to throw open the doors of the lavish reception to anyone, street people and all. What a party!

Jesus is again telling of the grief and outrage of his Father who had invited Israel, his chosen people, into a covenant relationship. Israel's refusal resulted in the feast being thrown open to all. Luke's Gospel specifically refers to inviting the "poor and crippled, the blind and the lame (Luke 14, 21)."

The writer to the Hebrews repeats the exhortation of Psalm 95, 7:

"Oh, that today you would hear his voice:
   'Harden not your hearts ... (Hebrews 4, 7).' "

The Father in heaven is calling us today! He is inviting us to a feast for his Son. We don't have to be concerned about what to wear. His Son has already provided our wedding garment, "a robe of salvation (Isaiah 61, 10)." What a celebration! Alleluia!

Friday, August 20, 1999 St. Bernard
Matthew 22, 34-40
The Greatest Commandment

The idea of a Pharisee "testing" Jesus is even more ludicrous than that of a toddler, pacifier in mouth and clutching a security blanket, "testing" Einstein about physics . At least the toddler would be pure and innocent in seeking information.

The Pharisees were anything but guileless. Coldly calculating, they were furious with Jesus and were determined to trap him.

When asked by the Pharisees which command was the most important, Jesus answered them steadily. "You shall love the Lord, your God, with all your heart, with all your soul, and with all your mind. This is the greatest and the first commandment. The second is like it: you shall love your neighbor as yourself. The whole law and the prophets depend on these two commandments."

The Message offers these verses with fresh insight. "Love the Lord your God with all your passion and prayer and intelligence: This is the most important, the first on any list. But there is a second to set alongside it: 'Love others as well as you love yourself. These two commandments are pegs; everything in God's Law and the Prophets hangs from them."

Lord Jesus, today we come to you, not to test you, but to follow you. Send your Holy Spirit to lead us into a deeper knowledge and love of you. Help us to trust you even when we feel weak and afraid. Your strength and your love are so much greater than our feelings. Sometimes we have trouble loving our neighbors because we cannot love ourselves. Help us to know deep down in our hearts that you love us dearly and that we may rest in you and trust you. From our place of security in you, free us to act in love to those around us. Alleluia!

Saturday, August 21, 1999 St. Pius X
Matthew 23, 1-12
Denunciation of the Scribes and Pharisees

"Practice what you preach!" It is in Matthew's Gospel that we locate the source of that familiar bit of advice.

The Pharisees were religious practitioners who were caught up in the externals of their job description. We don't see the Pharisees weeping over Jerusalem, kneeling to wash the feet of smelly, rough fishermen, or joyfully blessing little children. The Pharisees' good deeds were performed to be seen.

Even so, Jesus did not say to ignore the Pharisees or to treat them with contempt. On the contrary, he said, "Therefore do and observe all things whatsoever they tell you, but do not follow their example. For they preach but they do not practice."

A simple exercise is to look up the words "practice" and "preach" in the dictionary. To "practice" means to "carry out."

To "preach." on the other hand, may refer not only to public proclamation, but also "to exhort in an officious or tiresome manner," according to Webster's 7th New Collegiate Dictionary. Among all the words in between "practice" and "preach," I spotted the word "pray" or "to address God with adoration, confession, supplication, or thanksgiving." Could this be the key?

Lord Jesus, before we "preach," let us first "pray" and "practice." Alleluia!

Sunday, August 22, 1999 Twenty-First Sunday in Ordinary Time
Matthew 16, 13-20
Peter's Confession about Jesus

Peter's answer to Jesus' question, "Who do people say the Son of Man is?" was "You are the Messiah, the Son of the living God." Jesus then addressed Peter. "And so I say to you, you are Peter, and upon this rock I will build my church, and the gates of the netherworld shall not prevail against it. I will give you the keys of the kingdom. Whatever you bind on earth shall be bound in heaven; and whatever you loose on earth shall be loosed in heaven."

Some try to maneuver around this and say, "Well, the Greek word for Peter was "petros," whereas Jesus said that he would build his church on the "petra," the so-called rock of Peter's confession.

However, Jesus did not speak Greek. Jesus spoke Aramaic and the Aramaic for "rock" is Kepa. As The New American Bible notes, "You are the Rock (Kepa) and upon this rock (kepa) I will build my church."

Peter, in his first letter to the Christian community in Asia Minor, referred to Jesus as "a living stone." The Greek word for stone in this verse is "lithos," a stumbling stone or a millstone. "Come to him, a living stone, rejected by human beings but chosen and precious in the sight of God, and, like living stones, let yourselves be built into a spiritual house to be a holy priesthood to offer spiritual sacrifices acceptable to God through Jesus Christ. For it says in Scripture:

'Behold, I am laying a stone in Zion,
    a cornerstone, chosen and precious,
    and whoever believes in it shall not be put to shame
                                        (1 Peter 2, 4-6).'

Jesus is the cornerstone of our faith. Jesus builds his church on Peter the Rock. Peter, in turn, reminds us that we are the living stones in this temple, the Church. The apostle Paul referred to the Church as " … the pillar and foundation of truth." (1 Timothy 3, 15)

Lord Jesus, Peter witnessed to you as the Messiah, the Son of the living God. Strengthen us, the "living stones" in your Church to bear witness to you today. Alleluia!

Monday, August 23, 1999 St. Rose of Lima
Matthew 23, 13-22
Denunciation of the Scribes and Pharisees

Well, this isn't a very upbeat way to start the work week! Yesterday we started the "real" week with Peter's confession or solemn profession of faith. It appears that today's Gospel is a real downer.

Jesus goes after the religious head honchos and really tells them off! He calls them "hypocrites" over and over. He also calls them "blind guides," "blind fools," and "blind ones."

What a contrast to what Jesus called Peter, the fisherman. "Blessed are you, Simon son of Jonah. For flesh and blood has not revealed this to you, but my heavenly Father. And so I say to you, you are Peter, and upon this rock I will build my church, and the gates of the netherworld shall not prevail against it (Matthew 16, 17-18)."

How did Peter, clod though he was sometimes, "get" it?" How did this klutzy fisherman receive the understanding that Jesus was indeed the Messiah, the Son of the living God? He was a simple working guy, while the scribes and the Pharisees were the highly educated religious elite.

Jesus told Peter right off the bat that "flesh and blood" did not reveal this discernment of identity. The heavenly Father revealed to Peter who Jesus really was.

So why didn't the heavenly Father reveal to the scribes and Pharisees who Jesus was? He did, but they chose to close their minds and hearts to the truth.

Lord Jesus, we acknowledge you as the Son of the living God. Say to us what you said to Peter, "Blessed are you." Alleluia!

Tuesday, August 24, 1999 St. Bartholomew
John 1, 45-51
The First Disciples

You and Jesus go way back! Long before you were aware of God's presence in your life, God was carefully at work drawing you, through the power of the Holy Spirit, into a deep relationship with your Redeemer.

Sometimes people say, "I was saved on such and such a date." "I" this and "I" that.

246

They may have "accepted" their salvation on a particular date, but Jesus paid the price for their salvation long before then. Jesus paid the price two thousand years ago on Calvary.

Jesus said to Nathanael, "Before Philip called you, I saw you under the fig tree." Nathanael was flustered. "Rabbi, you are the Son of God; you are the King of Israel."

Jesus responded, " 'Do you believe because I told you that I saw you under the fig tree? You will see greater things than this!' And he said to him, 'Amen, amen, I say to you, you will see the sky opened and the angels of God ascending and descending on the Son of Man.' "

Jesus is always ahead of us. Yes, he is with us always, but he is also ahead of us beckoning us onward.

Lord Jesus, all authority on heaven and earth is yours! You are Lord and you are leading us through this day. Show us "greater things." Open our eyes, minds, and hearts to see the answer to this prayer. Alleluia!

Wednesday, August 25, 1999 Sts. Louis and Calasanz
Matthew 23, 27-32
Denunciation of the Scribes and Pharisees

Jesus persisted in calling the scribes and Pharisees "hypocrites" for their outer show of righteousness which masked their inner malice. It is illuminating to read this passage in The Message.

Jesus said to them, " 'You're hopeless, you religion scholars and Pharisees! Frauds! You're like manicured grave plots, grass clipped and the flowers bright, but six feet down it's all rotting bones and worm-eaten flesh. People look at you and think you're saints, but beneath the skin you're total frauds.

'You're hopeless, you religion scholars and Pharisees! Frauds! You build granite tombs for your prophets and marble monuments for your saints. And you say that if you had lived in the days of your ancestors, no blood would have been on your hands. You protest too much! You're cut from the same cloth as those murderers, and daily add to their death count (Matthew 23, 27-32, The Message).' "

Dear Lord, forgive us when we are not the same inside as the image we try so hard to project. Help us to receive your mercy and forgiveness for our own "inner Pharisee." When we encounter contemporary "scribes and Pharisees," give us the grace to treat them with courtesy, wisdom, and compassion. Alleluia!

247

Thursday, August 26, 1999
Matthew 24, 42-51
The Unknown Day and Hour;
The Faithful or the Unfaithful Servant

"Who, then, is the faithful and prudent servant, whom the master has put in charge of his household to distribute to them their food at the proper time? Blessed is that servant whom his master on arrival finds doing so."

In the household of God there are tasks of love and service we are all called upon to perform. This is the living out of our baptismal covenant.

In some families, before dinner, each child is given a task to perform. One may pour the water or fold the napkins. Another may set out the plates. Another may arrange the flowers and light the candles. Dinner doesn't just "happen" until each child has completed a particular task.

The Lord Jesus will return for his Bride, the Church. You and I need to be doing what we know we are called to do, not out of fear, but out of love for our Bridegroom.

Lord Jesus, sometimes I feel so overwhelmed by it all. Perhaps I'm not doing enough or I'm trying to do too much. Perhaps I'm not trusting you. Let me see clearly the task you have laid out for me today. Thank you for the grace to complete that task. Alleluia!

Friday, August 27, 1999 St. Monica
Matthew 25, 1-13
The Parable of the Ten Virgins

Sometimes we focus so much on the negative that we become "paralyzed." When this happens, we cannot see the answer to our prayer even when it comes. We did not think of preparing for joy, because we had had fallen into doubt and despair. It's not to late to change!

At Mass, in the Our Father, we pray, "Thy kingdom come; thy will be done on earth as it is in heaven." The priest then prays the Libere nos:

"Deliver us, Lord, from every evil,
   and grant us peace in our day.
In your mercy keep us free from sin
   and protect us from all anxiety
   as we wait in joyful hope
   for the coming of our Savior, Jesus Christ."

We are to wait in "joyful hope." To focus on Jesus is to be joyful! To focus on our problems is to be miserable and to be unprepared.

Lord Jesus, we wait for you in joy. Thank you for showing us today how we are to prepare for you. Show us how to fill our lamps with the oil of joy. Alleluia!

Saturday, August 28, 1999 St. Augustine of Hippo
Matthew 25, 14-30
The Parable of the Talents

Fidelity to present tasks leads to even greater responsibility. The master in the parable rewards the initiative and enterprise of the servants who had the courage to do something with what they were given.

What about the servant who literally "buried" the "talent," or gold coin? The master had this servant thrown into outer darkness.

In The Message, the wording is very strong. "The master was furious. 'That's a terrible way to live! It's criminal to live cautiously like that! If you knew I was after the best, why did you do less than the least? The least you could have done would have been to invest the sum with the bankers, where at least I would have gotten a little interest. Take the thousand and give it to the one who risked the most. And get rid of this 'play it safe' who won't go out on a limb. Throw him into utter darkness.' "

We delude ourselves if we think it doesn't matter what we do with what we're given. There will be an accounting.

Lord Jesus, help me not to be frightened by this passage of Scripture. On the contrary, help me to be faithful and disciplined to complete the task you have given me to do. Help me to be bold to go out on a limb for you today. Alleluia!

Sunday, August 29, 1999
Twenty-Second Sunday in Ordinary Time
Matthew 16, 21-27
The First Prediction of the Passion

"From that time on ..." From what time?

From the time following Simon Peter's confession about Jesus. At that time, Peter had said, "You are the Messiah, the Son of the living God (Matthew 16, 16)."

Jesus then told Peter, "... you are Peter, and upon this rock I will build my church, and the gates of the netherworld shall not prevail against it. I will give you the keys of the kingdom of heaven. Whatever you bind on earth shall be bound in heaven, and whatever you loose on earth shall be loosed in heaven (Matthew 16, 18-19)."

Jesus is now drawing the disciples' attention to the fact that he will go to Jerusalem, "suffer greatly from the elders, chief priests, and the scribes, and be killed and on the third day be raised." When Peter objected, Jesus rebuked Peter, "Get behind me, Satan! You are an obstacle to me. You are thinking not as God does, but as human beings do."

This did not change Peter's identity, vocation, or destiny. It did point out that Jesus requires us to learn to think as God thinks! This involves taking up our "cross," accepting and embracing God's plan for our lives, and following Jesus.

No cross of suffering, no crown of glory. "For the Son of Man will come with the angels in his Father's glory, and then he will repay everyone according to his conduct."

Lord Jesus, help me today to learn to think as you think. Help me to be willing to "lose" my life your sake. Alleluia!

Monday, August 30, 1999
Luke 4, 16-30
The Rejection at Nazareth

"Depressed because the New Yorker turned down the 27th poem you submitted? Feel blue because your boss didn't like your suggestion in the suggestion box? Got the blahs because everywhere you turn you feel rejected? Then join the ranks of Beethoven, Rembrandt, James Joyce, George Washington, and the Muppets." These words are on the cover of John White's amazing book, Rejection.

We could add, join the ranks of the prophets of the Hebrew scriptures, Jesus Christ, and the apostles. When Jesus preached in his hometown synagogue and said, in essence, "Well, folks, here I am, the fulfillment of Isaiah 61, 1-2, " the congregation was "amazed" and "all spoke highly of him." They were perplexed, however, since all they knew of Jesus was that he was presumed to be the son of Joseph, the village carpenter.

The tide turned when Jesus pointed out the prophetic nature of his ministry. "Amen, I say to you, no prophet is accepted in his own native place."

Jesus reminded the people that the great prophet Elijah was not sent to his own people, but rather to Zarephath in Sidon, to a particular widow. Another great prophet, Elisha, was not sent to the lepers in Israel, but to Naaman, a leper in Syria.

When Jesus preached "glad tidings," healing, and freedom from oppression, he was accepted. When the prophetic nature of his ministry was manifest, the people turned on him.

They became "filled with fury." They did not want to hear that God blessed and healed "outsiders." THEY were God's chosen people, after all! They drove Jesus out of town and tried to push him off a hill.

Rejection! Jesus kept his cool and "passed through the midst of them and went away."

Lord Jesus, it's so easy to play to the audience and to say what is pleasing and politically correct. Help me today to follow you, to trust you, and to look to you alone for approval. Alleluia!

Tuesday, August 31, 1999
Luke 4, 31-37
The Cure of a Demoniac

As in yesterday's Gospel, the people in the synagogue in today's Gospel were also "astonished" at the teaching of Jesus. Jesus was different. They were riveted to his words because "he spoke with authority."

In yesterday's Gospel, Jesus was teaching in his hometown synagogue of Nazareth. The people, initially favorable, turned on him and tried to push him off a hill. Not very good for one's self-esteem!

Today, we see Jesus in the synagogue of Capernaum. Right there in the synagogue was a man "with the spirit of an unclean demon." The demon recognized Jesus. Jesus rebuked the demon and commanded the demon to come out of the man.

The people were surprised twice during that synagogue service. First, they were astonished at the teaching of Jesus "because he spoke with authority." Second, they were "amazed" when Jesus commanded the evil spirit to come out of the man.

"What is there about his word? For with authority and power he commands the unclean spirits, and they come out."

Are we surprised, astonished, and amazed at the word of Jesus? All authority on heaven and earth has been given to Jesus (Matthew 28, 18). JESUS is Head of the Church (Colossians 1, 18).

Lord Jesus, we never cease to marvel at the power of your word. Let us never cease to expect your word to accomplish miracles. Speak your word to us today. Alleluia!

Wednesday, September 1, 1999
Luke 4, 38-44
The Cure of Simon's Mother-in-Law;
Other Healings; Jesus Leaves Capernaum

Jesus is leaving Capernaum and we are also leaving. We are leaving this turbulent fourth chapter of Luke's Gospel which tells of the beginning of Jesus' ministry in the Galilee.

We have seen Jesus, filled with the Holy Spirit, undergo severe testing. After forty days of fasting in the wilderness, Jesus was subjected to a whole spectrum of temptations from the devil. He countered each temptation as he confronted the devil with the written Word of God.

Powerfully anointed by the Holy Spirit, Jesus preached in the synagogues of Nazareth and Capernaum. He cast a demon out of a man in the synagogue, healed Simon Peter's mother-in-law, and also healed many others.

Now, it was time to leave. This time the fickle crowd, instead of trying to push Jesus off a cliff, implored him to stay.

Jesus knew it was time to leave. "To the other towns also I must proclaim the good news of the kingdom of God, because for this purpose I have been sent."

Jesus stayed in tune with the Father's strategy for his earthly ministry. There was much that lay ahead -- the calling of his disciples, training them, sending them out, debating the chief priests and scribes, suffering, the triumph of the Cross, and the resurrection. This particular phase of his life, however, was over.

Lord Jesus, please show me where to go and what to do today. You alone know where I am in my journey with you and to you. On this fresh, first day of September, please infuse freshness into my life and lead me to my next assignment. Alleluia!

Tuesday, September 2, 1999
Luke 5, 1-11
The Call of Simon the Fisherman

The excited crowd by the lake was pressing in on Jesus! He stepped into Simon Peter's boat and asked Peter to take him out a bit from the shore.

After teaching the crowds, Jesus turned to Peter, who was tired and discouraged. "Put out into deep water and lower your nets for a catch." Peter had worked hard all night, but had caught nothing.

Things were different now. Jesus was right here beside him! Peter obeyed Jesus and the results were overwhelming. So many fish were caught that the nets began to tear.

Lord Jesus, I'm feeling rather discouraged too. Come into the boat of my life and take me out into the deep. It's scary out there in the deep, but you are with me. Help me cast my net as you direct this day. The results are in your hands. Alleluia!

Friday, September 3, 1999 St. Gregory the Great
Luke 5, 33-39
The Question about Fasting

According to Ecclesiastes 3, 1, "There is an appointed time for everything ..." Today's Gospel tells us that the time of Jesus' earthly ministry was not to be a time of fasting.

You wouldn't want to go to a wedding where everyone was looking sad and depressed, would you? A wedding should be a time of rejoicing!

Jesus gives us new wine, new joy, and new hope. Even if our circumstances today are not as joyful as we would like, let us rejoice in Jesus! He will lead us through these temporary circumstances to a place of joy and hope. His love for us is strong and steady. We are secure in him. Alleluia!

Saturday, September 4, 1999
Luke 6, 1-5
Debates about the Sabbath

Jesus is Lord! Jesus is Lord of the Sabbath. Jesus is Lord, period.

Wherever Jesus went, whatever he did, the Pharisees seemed to appear on the scene, harassing him and attempting to ensnare him with every sort of stratagem. How clever they seemed.

Jesus, however, could not be trapped. He knew exactly how to turn the tables by meeting the Pharisees on their own turf, the Law!

The Pharisees were squawking about picking grain on the Sabbath. Big deal. Jesus countered by reminding them that David and his hungry followers had gobbled up the holy bread from the house of God.

Jesus always put human need above human-made rules and regulations. It was the priest who had given David and his followers permission to eat the bread of offering in the house of God. Now it is Jesus, the Son of God, Son of Man, and our Great High Priest, who gave his disciple permission to pick grain even on the Sabbath.

Jesus, our Great High Priest, thank you for giving yourself to us as the Bread of Life. You alone satisfy our hungry hearts. Alleluia!

Sunday, September 5, 1999
Twenty-third Sunday in Ordinary Time
Matthew 18, 15-20
A Brother Who Sins

"Treat him as you would a Gentile or a tax collector." That's how Jesus says to treat a fellow-believer who will not listen to you, to the other one or two you take with you, or even to the wider church.

How would you treat a "Gentile" or a "tax collector"? You would treat such a person with courtesy.

However, you would be wise not to expect reconciliation at this time. You would intercede. You would practice forgiveness with the same discipline that a concert pianist humbly practices scales. You certainly would not try to antagonize.

You would love yourself enough to take care of yourself. You would put the matter in God's hands and go about your life.

Lord Jesus, these are difficult words. You loved the Gentiles and the tax-collectors. Teach us to love with your wisdom. Alleluia!

Monday, September 6, 1999
Luke 6, 6-11
Debates about the Sabbath

Another showdown on the Sabbath! It's not exactly a shoot-out at the OK corral, but it's getting there.

In the synagogue, the Pharisees were watching Jesus like a hawk. They did not appear to be concerned about the human suffering involved.

There was a man in their very midst with a withered hand. Their only interest in this man was whether or not Jesus would cure him on the Sabbath.

To them, he was a pawn. To Jesus, he was a person. The compassionate Jesus restored the man's hand.

The man who had been cured by Jesus left the synagogue with a restored hand and a restored life. The Pharisees left with their hearts withered by rage.

Lord Jesus, you reached out, acting in compassion at all times. You healed on the Sabbath, because you were lord of the Sabbath. Reach out today, Lord, and heal whatever has become withered within our hearts, restoring joy and hope. You are Lord of our hearts. Alleluia!

Tuesday, September 7, 1999
Luke 6, 12-19
The Mission of the Twelve; Ministering to a Great Multitude

Jesus spent the "night" in prayer. When the "day" arrived, he had made his decision. Jesus had been observing and evaluating discipleship candidates for some time. That night of prayer, however, was a crucial time.

Whether or not we make annual retreats, we still need daily time alone with God. This time is for basking in God's presence, praising him, and seeking his direction in our lives. Not only will we benefit, but those around us will benefit.

255

Jesus chose Twelve that day. As soon as they returned to "the world," they were confronted by a large crowd seeking Jesus. "Everyone in the crowd sought to touch him because power came forth from him and healed them all."

We may not realize that we are surrounded by multitudes needing healing, but we are! As baptized followers of Jesus, we are to be bright, shining lights of peace and healing to the needy ones around us.

Lord Jesus, during this quiet time alone with you, please refresh and renew us in your love. Alleluia!

Wednesday, September 8, 1999 Birth of the Virgin Mary
Matthew 1, 1-16
The Genealogy of Jesus

This is the family tree of Joseph, spouse of Mary, the mother of Jesus. So why does the genealogy on Joseph's side get written down in such painstaking detail? Why not Mary's genealogy?

I don't know. In any case, on this day when the Church celebrates the birth of the Virgin Mary, the scriptural highlight is on Joseph.

Joseph was to be the "righteous man" (Matthew 1, 19) who came to believe that the conception of Jesus was of divine origin. Joseph came to know that God chose particular people for particular vocations.

It was from Joseph that Jesus learned the love of a human father. As a tiny infant, toddler, young boy, Jesus was dependent on Joseph's strong, loving , and wise care.

Whatever the Lord is calling us to be and to do, he is going to use our genealogy, our family tree. The people in our family tree have been part of our formation, like it or not.

Lord Jesus, we may not be comfortable with some of the people in our family tree. We may not even be comfortable with ourselves. Give us the grace to accept who we are, who our ancestors were, and to be thankful. Alleluia!

Thursday, September 9, 1999
Luke 6, 27-38
Love of Enemies

The Most High God is "kind to the ungrateful and the wicked." God is our model and as God's children, we are to live with the same generosity.

Be kind to the ungrateful? Maybe. Be kind to the wicked? Very difficult.

Jesus is not advocating stupidity or gullibility in these verses. Rather, he is setting forth a series of behaviors that will identify us as God's children.

Scripture must always be balanced with scripture. It was Jesus, after all, who told his disciples, "Behold, I am sending you like sheep in the midst of wolves; so be shrewd as serpents and simple as doves (Matthew 10, 16)."

It is a particular behavior based on a particular mind-set that Jesus is teaching us. If we truly know our identity as God's children, we will reflect that relationship and we will astound the world.

Instead of seeking revenge, we will bless those who wish to injure us. We will even pray for their happiness!

We will keep our eyes on the prize. Jesus is the prize!

Not only are we promised rewards, great rewards, but we are also entering into a most exhilarating way of living. There is power and freedom and strength waiting for us as we embrace this mind-set and step into this way of living.

Lord Jesus, thank you for the opportunity today to practice at least one of these ways of loving and living. Thank you for the power of the Holy Spirit within us to be kind and merciful as our Heavenly Father is kind and merciful. Alleluia!

Friday, September 10, 1999
Luke 6, 39-42
Judging Others

In the middle of last night, I awoke remembering some people I've judged harshly. My discernment regarding their conduct was probably correct, but my thoughts and words about them were very critical and unloving.

Forgive me, Lord. Observation is one thing. Condemnation, even silent condemnation, is another.

Lord Jesus, help me to turn my discernment into compassionate intercession. You have been so patient with me and forgiven me over and over. Help me to remove this "beam" from my eye. Alleluia!

Saturday, September 11, 1999
Luke 6, 43-49
A Tree Known by Its Fruit; The Two Foundations

Have you every watched anyone sew? Sewing by hand involves holding the material in one hand and stitching in and out with a threaded needle with the other hand. A sewing machine also involves holding the material and stitching.

With both methods of sewing, a sharp needle is used both to pierce and to stitch the fabric. Merely taking a bit of thread and holding it on the fabric will not work. The sharp needle is essential.

Jesus wants us not merely to come to him and to listen to his words, but also to act on his words. His words, like the threaded needle, need to pierce the fabric of our lives. Yes, this hurts!

We have to willing to hear the Lord's words and then to act on his words. "A good person out of the store of goodness in his heart produces good, but an evil person out of a store of evil produces evil; for from the fullness of the heart the mouth speaks." And then the Lord adds, "Why do you call me, 'Lord, Lord,' but do not do what I command?"

Lord Jesus, we truly want our lives to bear good fruit for you. We also want to withstand the storms of this life. Today, let your words pierce deeply within us and produce the trust and the action you desire. Alleluia!

Sunday, September 12, 1999
Twenty-fourth Sunday in Ordinary Time
Matthew 18, 21-35
The Parable of the Unforgiving Servant

We need a heart transplant in order to live this Gospel! A new heart, the heart of the merciful God who forgives us.

It is only as we see our profound need of forgiveness that we can even begin to forgive and to release others, no matter how outraged we may be at their conduct

This is a Gospel of impossibilities transformed into miracles. It was impossible for the servant to pay back his enormous debt.

Knowing this, he threw himself on the mercy of his master. "Be patient with me, and I will pay you back in full." Knowing that this was impossible, the compassionate master cancelled the debt. A miracle!

Instead of fleshing out this miracle in humble gratitude, the servant seized a fellow servant who owed him a trifle and tried to choke him! The fellow servant begged for mercy and also cried out, "Be patient with me, and I will pay you back in full." The first servant, the one whose enormous debt had been graciously cancelled, inexplicably refused.

Lord Jesus, I really need your help. I'd still like to seize and choke a few people, maybe rip out their gizzards! (I know, people don't have gizzards, but it just sounds like a deliciously mean thing to do!) These are my feelings, but you are greater than my feelings. I throw myself on your mercy. Please take away my heart of hatred and give me a tender heart of compassion even if my forgiveness is never asked. Open my heart to comprehend the immensity of your love and compassion for me. You know all my sins, and yet you have forgiven me and cancelled the debt I owe you. I am free! Today, let me live in this joy and freedom and offer forgiveness and release to others. Alleluia!

Monday, September 13, 1999 St. John Chrysostom
Luke 7, 1-10
The Healing of a Centurion's Slave

Jesus said. "I tell you, not even in Israel have I found such faith." He was astonished at the trust and confident expectation of the centurion.

Are you ever been surprised at the acute spiritual perception of someone who does not move in your particular spiritual circles? Someone who does not go to your church or attend your prayer group. Maybe someone who does not even read the Bible very much. "How can this be?" we, the self-righteous, ask.

God loves to send us certain people as wake-up calls! They are sent into our lives to alert us, to wake us up to our own need to trust the Lord. They are used by God to show us a real need in our lives. They show us that we do not have all the answers.

259

Lord Jesus, thank you for every person you will send into my life today. Help me to be especially alert to receive your message through unlikely messengers. Alleluia!

Tuesday, September 14, 1999 Triumph of the Holy Cross
John 3, 13-17
Nicodemus

Jesus was speaking to Nicodemus, a Pharisee who came to see him at night. Nicodemus, bound by literal interpretation, could not grasp the concept of being "born from above" and being "born of the Spirit." Jesus asked him, "If I tell you about earthly things and you do not believe, how will you believe if I tell you about heavenly things?"

The famous John 3, 16 passage is in the midst of today's Gospel. "For God so loved the world that he gave his only Son, so that everyone who believes in him might not perish but might have eternal life."

This verse is often quoted to unbelievers in an attempt to bring them to Jesus for salvation. We need to remember the context of this verse.

Jesus was speaking these words to a scholarly religious leader! Corrie ten Boom, author of The Hiding Place, used to say that just because a mouse gets into the cookie jar doesn't mean that the mouse is a cookie! Rising in the ranks of the ecclesiastical establishment does not necessarily imply a deep, personal love relationship with Jesus.

The ground is level at the foot of the Cross. We all need to come in humility to Jesus. Our Heavenly Father sent Jesus not to condemn us, but to rescue us, to save us, to heal us, and to make us whole.

Lord Jesus, by your Cross and Resurrection, you have set us free. You are the Savior of the world and you are my Savior. Today, let me experience the healing and the wholeness you came to bring. Alleluia!

Wednesday, September 15, 1999 Our Lady of Sorrows
John 19, 25-27
The Crucifixion of Jesus

This is a very short Gospel, almost too intense to bear. No wonder today we remember Mary as Our Lady of Sorrows.

The sword prophesied by Simeon at the presentation of the infant Jesus in the temple is piercing Mary's heart (Luke 2, 35). To be present at the cross was all Mary could do. It was all the others keeping vigil could do. Be there. Wait. Weep.

Jesus, you are now the risen Lord! You will come again in glory. Today help me to be sensitive to those who are standing by crosses of various kinds in their lives. Help me to be there with them. Thank you for the strengthening presence of the Holy Spirit. Alleluia!

Thursday, September 16, 1999 Sts Cornelius and Cyprian
Luke 7, 36-50
The Pardon of the Sinful Woman

"A Pharisee invited him to dine with him, and he entered the Pharisees' house and reclined at table." The opening sentence alone in today's Gospel is almost enough to take our breath away!

The Pharisees were not very friendly to Jesus, you recall. This invitation was merely another opportunity for the Pharisees to watch Jesus like a hawk and to find something to criticize.

Never mind. Jesus was invited and, regardless of Simon the Pharisee's motives, he accepted the invitation. Once inside the door, Jesus began his amazing work of reconciliation.

The woman, painfully aware of her need for forgiveness, poured out her costly, fragrant ointment from the exquisite alabaster flask on the feet of Jesus. She wept, anointed the feet of Jesus, and kissed his feet. She bathed his feet with her tears.

She, the famished one, received the gift of forgiveness. Simon the Pharisee, the sated, self-righteous one, was also offered a gift that day. He was offered the gift of seeing himself through the eyes of the Son of Man.

The woman was told, "Your faith has saved you; go in peace." We are not told whether or not Simon received the gift of truth spoken by Jesus.

Lord Jesus, today I invite you to enter my life in a deeper way. I need both the gift of forgiveness and the gift of seeing myself as you see me. Help me not to run from the truth. It is the truth that will set me free. Thank you for your gentleness and compassion as you set me free. Alleluia!

Friday, September 17, 1999 St. Robert Bellarmine
Luke 8, 1-3
Galilean Women Follow Jesus

Did you ever wonder about Joanna? She was one of the women mentioned in today's Gospel. Her husband was Chuza, the steward or business manager for King Herod, the ruler of Galilee.

Joanna, a follower of Jesus, was also a supporter of his ministry out of her own resources. It must have been very difficult juggling act spiritually, emotionally, and financially. Her spouse's employer, King Herod, was a weak, ego-driven tyrant who beheaded John the Baptist to save face in front of his dinner guests.

Joanna experienced being in a very tight place. She was a committed follower of Jesus and yet her husband was paid to serve a petty, pathetic despot.

Do you ever feel you're squeezed into a very difficult position? Do you wonder, "Where do I fit in?" Once, I asked that question of my friend Cynthia, another chaplain intern in our summer Clinical Pastoral Education program. Cynthia answered, "You fit in with Jesus."

Lord Jesus, there are so many matters in my life over which I have no control. I feel stressed, resentful, fearful, and exhausted. Show me what it means to accept living in a tight place. Thank you that I fit in with you. Alleluia!

Saturday, September 18, 1999
Luke 8, 4-15
The Parable of the Sower; The Purpose of the Parables;
The Parable of the Sower Explained

It's a tough being a seed. Here's what can happen. If the seed is on the path, it can be trampled and gobbled up by birds. Have you ever been trampled?

The seed on the rocky ground withered for lack of moisture. Have you ever felt depleted, listless, and lifeless?

The seed that fell among thorns was choked. Have you ever been hedged in by the "thorns" of life and felt stifled?

Fortunately, there is one more possible fate for the seed. The seed that fell on good soil flourished and produced fruit!

Jesus said that the seed in this parable is the word of God. Merely hearing the word of God is not enough.

Remember the seed on the path? The devil "takes away the word from their hearts that they may not believe and be saved."

The seed that falls on the rocky ground is joyfully received, but it does not take root. Without being strongly rooted, it is unable to withstand trials.

The seed that falls among the thorns doesn't stand a chance. Its very life is choked out by various "anxieties," "riches," and the "pleasures of life."

Let's look at the seed that fell on the good soil and produced fruit. This happens for the ones who, "when they have heard the word, embrace it with a generous and good heart, and bear fruit through perseverance."

God has planted a particular "seed," a word, within your heart. Guard this word. Don't let it be taken away. It's yours! Guard the seed and don't let it be choked by earthly concerns. Do what Jesus said and "embrace" his word to you "with a generous and good heart, and bear fruit through perseverance."

Lord Jesus, thank you for the word you have already spoken to us. Thank you that your word will triumph! Thank you for the words spoken through the prophet:

> "For just as from the heavens
>   the rain and snow come down
> And do not return there
>   till they have watered the earth,
>   making it fertile and fruitful,
> Giving seed to him who sows
>   and bread to him who eats,
> So shall my word be
>   that goes forth from my mouth;
> It shall not return to me void,
>   but shall do my will,
>   achieving the end for which I sent
>   it."
>   Isaiah 55, 10-11

Alleluia!

Sunday, September 19, 1999
Twenty-fifth Sunday in Ordinary Time
Matthew 20, 1-16
The Workers in the Vineyard

Consider a group lunch scenario. You ordered a small salad while others ordered big entrees such as beef teriyaki or the giant enchilada. The bill cometh. The person in charge of the group whisks out a pocket calculator and equally divides the bill. You feel stuck. You don't want to make a fuss in front of all these people and you don't want to look cheap. So you resentfully pay, not only your own share, but way over and above your share. It's not fair!

Or say you're on a group lab project and nerves start getting frayed. The others give up and leave you to do their work. You are committed to the project, so you stick it out and pull an all-nighter. The project head praises everyone, but you're the one who did more than your share. It's not fair!

The workers who had worked all day in the vineyard were griping because they felt they should receive a bonus. Why should the one who showed up at the end of the work day get the same pay they did? After all, they were the good guys, the ones who had sweated and toiled all day. Right?

Wrong! The owner of the vineyard was the one who paid the salaries. He was the one who rose before dawn to go to the marketplace and hire the workers. He was checking all day long on the situation and was happy to hire others. He asked, "Am I not free to do as I wish with my own money? Are you envious because I am generous?"

Father, we're still like the second-graders on the school playground. We still cling to our selfish ideas of what is fair and what is right. You alone are God. You paid the price of seeing your only Son, the sinless One, suffer and die on the Cross so that we, the sinners, could go free. You are gracious and generous to all. Today, soften our hard hearts and let us live in a manner worthy of your children. As we work in your "vineyard," let us not concentrate on our grievances, our "whine list," but rather on our relationship to the Vine. Alleluia!

Monday, September 20, 1999
Luke 8, 16-18
The Parable of the Lamp

Use it or lose it! We already carry within us the Light of Christ.

In the Easter Vigil processional, we chant the Exultet.
"The Light of Christ." "Thanks be to God."

You are in a processional this day! As you proceed through your day, you not only carry the Light of Christ, but you actually are the Light of Christ! Jesus told his followers, "You are the light of the world (Matthew 5, 14)."

You may feel that your light is burning dimly, or barely flickering. You may need some time away to rest and to nurture the light. Even so, you still carry the light. Sometimes your very presence in a situation sheds light previously concealed.

Lord Jesus, illumine our hearts and minds with your light and your love. Whether in silence or in speech, let us be bearers of your light to those around us today. Alleluia!

Tuesday, September 21, 1999 St. Matthew
Matthew 9, 9-13
The Call of Matthew

Did Jesus know what he was getting into when he called the tax-collector Matthew? Right away, Matthew took Jesus home with him for a meal.

Guess who also came to dinner? Matthew's friends! "Many tax collectors and sinners came and sat with Jesus and his disciples." This was cool with Jesus, but not so cool with the Pharisee watch birds and guard dogs.

Does Jesus know what he is getting into when he calls you and me? Along with the "good" part of us, Jesus also gets the "outcast" part of us. The part of our inner selves we ourselves reject, the part of ourselves the accusing "inner Pharisee" mocks, ridicules, and despises.

Jesus knows. He loves us so much more than we love ourselves. He loves us every single minute. He is here today as our gentle Friend and wise Physician. He is here to welcome, touch, calm, and heal the poor outcast we carry within us.

Lord Jesus, we bring all the fragments of our lives to you today. Thank you for your mercy and your compassion. Thank you for the twinkle in your eye as you tell us to let go of our frantic attempts at self-improvement. You know what you're doing. Alleluia!

Wednesday, September 22, 1999
Luke 9, 1-6
The Mission of the Twelve

In our walk with God, challenges are the norm. Today's Gospel reassures us that Jesus has given his followers power and authority "over all demons, and to cure diseases ... to proclaim the kingdom of God ... and to heal [the sick]."

Jesus told his followers to "take nothing for the journey ... As for those who do not welcome you, when you leave that town, shake the dust from your feet in testimony against them."

Jesus is with us on this journey and he is enough. Our reception of the sacraments, our theology degrees, our training, our study of the Bible, and our years in spiritual direction are all valid and can be used by the Lord.

Still, it is our own personal, lived-out relationship with the Lord that is often the key to reaching others. It is the life of Jesus being lived out in our lives that brings healing to those around us.

One of the assignments the Lord gave his followers was to heal the sick. So, yesterday, in a burst of Holy Spirit boldness, I invited a checker at the grocery store to a healing service. She has to stand for hours and this is very tiring for her back and feet. Will she be there? I don't know, but I do know that Jesus will be there. Jesus can meet her at this service or in a thousand other ways.

Lord Jesus, you are enough for this journey. You are enough for any challenge. Alleluia!

Thursday, September 23, 1999
Luke 9, 7-9
Herod's Opinion of Jesus

Herod was "greatly perplexed." Herod, you recall, was the petty tyrant, ego-driven and insecure, who was responsible for the death of John the Baptist.

Egged on by his "wife," Herodius, he was a pathetic slave of public opinion. Lacking the courage of his convictions, he easily buckled under pressure.

There are Herods all around us. They are often curiosity seekers. It is tragic when they are in power, because they serve only themselves. They are very threatened and jealously guard their power.

What was Jesus' opinion of Herod? Jesus referred to Herod as "that fox (Luke 13, 32)." Hmmm.

Lord Jesus, it is your opinion that matters. Help us today to live for you and not to be dismayed or deterred by the Herods around us. Alleluia!

Friday, September 24, 1999
Luke 9, 18-22
Peter's Confession about Jesus;
The First Prediction of the Passion

Identity. Vocation. Suffering. Death. Resurrection. They are all intertwined.

We need to be firm in our identity. Who we are, the beloved of the Father, is independent of our vocation.

Some people try to live OUT their vocation without first having truly lived IN their identity. When their vocation is in jeopardy, they may feel stripped of their identity.

Jesus knew who he was. Yes, he was the beloved Son of God. Yes, he was the Son of Man. Yes, he was the Messiah.

Knowing his identity made it possible for him to endure the suffering of his vocation. "The Son of Man must suffer greatly and be rejected by the elders, the chief priests, and the scribes, and be killed and on the third day be raised."

We are God's children. Our identity is secure.

We are called to follow Jesus. That is our vocation, which flows from our baptism. We will suffer. We will die. We will be raised to new life. This will happen over and over in our vocation, until at last we see our God face to face.

Lord Jesus, remind me today of who you are and who I am. Let your joy flood my entire being as I focus on the eternal while treading in the temporal. Alleluia!

Saturday, September 25, 1999
Luke 9, 43-45
The Second Prediction of the Passion

Jesus was again preparing his disciples for his future suffering and death. He chose a moment when the crowds were "astonished" and "amazed" at his powerful deeds.

Jesus knew it was crucial for his disciples to understand that his life did not involve merely performing an endless series of exciting deeds, called "miracles" by some, but also involved being "handed over." The powerful one, the doer of mighty deeds, was to be given into the hands of those who hated him.

The disciples weren't ready to hear this. How could Jesus not be in charge? How could Jesus be "handed over?"

What the disciples could not foresee was the glorious Resurrection! They could not yet understand the glory that was to come. They were too bound up with their fears and uncertainties.

Lord Jesus, when I am in the midst of situations involving suffering and death, help me to focus on resurrection. You have already won the victory! Today, help me to live in the power of your resurrection victory. Alleluia!

Sunday, September 26, 1999
Twenty-sixth Sunday in Ordinary Time
Matthew 21, 28-32
The Parable of the Two Sons

Jesus was teaching in the temple and the chief priests and other leaders were busy questioning his authority. Jesus turned the table by asking them a question.

Jesus asked them whether the baptism of John was of heavenly or earthly origin. What a question! Since they staunchly refused to answer, Jesus countered with the parable of the two sons.

To the chief priests and elders, Jesus said, "Yes, and I tell you that crooks and whores are going to precede you into God's kingdom. John came to you showing you the right road. You turned up your noses at him, but the crooks and whores believed him. Even when you saw their changed lives, you didn't care enough to change and believe him (Matthew 21, 31-32 , The Message)."

Sometimes we can hear the same message from two different people. We seem programmed to reject anything one person says, but then we accept the very same message from another person. A mystery?!

Lord Jesus, help me to hear your word to me today and believe you. Alleluia!

Monday, September 27, 1999 St. Vincent de Paul
Luke 9, 46-50
The Greatest in the Kingdom; Another Exorcist

To an argument about "greatness," Jesus responded, first with action and then with words. The disciples had been busy arguing amongst themselves about which of them was the greatest.

Jesus "realized the intention of their hearts" and answered in an unexpected way. He placed a child by his side and only then spoke to his disciples.

Jesus told them that whoever received or welcomed a child in his name received Jesus himself. Receiving Jesus was equated to receiving the Father.

Merely tolerating the existence of another is not the same as welcoming or "receiving" that person. The word "welcome" implies "gladness" or "delight."

What about greatness? "You become great by accepting, not asserting. Your spirit, not your size, makes the difference (Luke 9, 48b, The Message)." This flies in the face of our competitive culture, doesn't it?

I don't think the disciple, John, quite understood this. He piped up about someone who didn't "follow our company" (i.e. an outsider) who was casting out devils in Jesus' name.

Jesus answered, "Do not prevent him, for whoever is not against you is for you." With Jesus, there are no "outsiders."

Lord Jesus, it's the same today. We, your followers, are sometimes as pushy and as competitive as those out there in "the world." We, your followers, are sometimes suspicious of "outsiders" who are following you according to their understanding. Have mercy on us, Lord. Today, let us live before you in humility and simplicity. Alleluia!

Tuesday, September 28, 1999 St. Wenceslaus
Luke 9, 51-56
Departure for Jerusalem; Samaritan Inhospitality

Change of plan. Plan B? Maybe even Plan C. Even Jesus had to make adjustments along the way.

Jerusalem was his destination. Jerusalem was where his destiny would be fulfilled.

Jesus knew it was time to go there. Today's Gospel tells us that "he resolutely determined to journey to Jerusalem." The inhabitants of a particular Samaritan village refused to welcome him because he was traveling to Jerusalem.

James and John, the hot-tempered "sons of thunder" were mad at the villagers and were ready to "call down fire from heaven to consume them." Jesus rebuked them for this display of misguided zeal. He was sent to save and to heal, not to destroy.

Jesus refused to be deterred from reaching Jerusalem. He simply took another path to his destination and to his destiny. He could not be stopped, because he was on his Father's mission.

God has called you to a particular destiny to be fulfilled in a particular destination at a particular time. When you are not welcomed along your journey, the Holy Spirit will continue to guide you. Nothing can prevent God's will being done in your life if you continue to follow him in trust and obedience. Alleluia!

Wednesday, September 29, 1999
Michael, Gabriel, and Raphael, Archangels
John 1, 47-51
The First Disciples

Jesus told Nathanael, "Amen, amen, I say to you, you will see the sky opened and the angels of God ascending and descending on the Son of Man." Nathanael was the skeptic who had earlier inquired of his friend Philip, "Can anything good come from Nazareth (John 1, 46)?"

Jesus knew about Nathanael long before Nathanael had any notion of even meeting Jesus, much less following him. Nathanael was astonished when Jesus said to him, "Before Philip called you, I saw you under the fig tree."

From figs to angels! Lord Jesus, thank you for lifting us today from the earthly to the heavenly. Alleluia!

Thursday, September 30, 1999 St. Jerome
Luke 10, 1-12
The Mission of the Seventy-two

Jesus sent the Twelve on a mission. Jesus sent the Seventy-Two on a mission. Jesus has sent you and me on a mission. We are also "lambs among the wolves" and we must follow our Lord's instructions very carefully.

Travel light. No room for carrying old fears or hurts or resentments. This is a new day.

Jesus knows about our yesterdays and he is healing us. He needs us out on the mission field today.

We are to speak "peace" everywhere we go. Our gift of peace will either be received or it will return to us. Not a bad deal.

If we are welcome in a particular place, we are to "cure the sick in it and say to them, 'The kingdom of God is at hand for you.' "

If we are not received, we are to leave and say, " 'The dust of your town that clings to our feet, even that we shake off against you.' Yet know this: the kingdom of God is at hand."

This same passage in The Message is even more blunt. "The only thing we got from you is the dirt on our feet and we're giving it back. Do you have any idea that God's kingdom was right here on your doorstep?"

Jesus tells his followers that Sodom's fate is better than the fate of the place where his followers are rejected. Something to consider!

Lord Jesus, help us to live our mission today, traveling light, speaking peace, and bringing your kingdom. Alleluia!

Friday, October 1, 1999 St. Therese of the Child Jesus
Luke 10, 13-16
Reproaches to the Unrepentant Towns

Jesus made it clear to his followers, "Whoever listens to you listens to me. Whoever rejects you rejects me. And whoever rejects me rejects the one who sent me."

Jesus then spoke strong words of reproach and censure to the towns of Chorazin, Bethsaida, and Capernaum.

Jesus, who was fully human, must have grieved especially over Capernaum, a seaside village in the Galilee. It was in the Capernaum synagogue that he freed the demoniac (Luke 4, 31-37).

This man, the demoniac, had an unwelcome companion in his mind. As a friend of mine would say, he had "company." Jesus got rid of the bad company in the man's mind and released him into a whole new realm of freedom. The onlookers in the synagogue were amazed at the authority and the power they saw in Jesus.

It was also in Capernaum that Jesus healed Peter's mother-in-law. Presumably Peter was grateful for this!

Later, at sunset that same day in Capernaum, "all who had people sick with various diseases brought them to him [Jesus]. He laid his hands on each of them and cured them. And demons came out of many, shouting, 'You are the Son of God (Luke 4, 40-41).' "

The next day at dawn, Jesus went to "a deserted place (Luke 4, 42)." Even there the crowds from Capernaum followed him and tried to prevent him from leaving. He told them, "To the other towns also I must proclaim the good news of the kingdom of God, because for this purpose I have been sent (Luke 4, 43)."

Does your heart ache over a particular place where you gave your "all" for God and where you were still rejected? Jesus shares your pain. Jesus assures you that the ones who listened to you were in actuality listening to him. The ones who rejected you were in reality rejecting him.

Lord Jesus, you knew what it was like to experience deep disappointment during your ministry, especially over Capernaum. Thank you for your reassuring words when we are in perplexity or pain in our own ministry. Send your Holy Spirit to give us wisdom and understanding. Is there something in our ministry that you would like us to address or to change? How do want to change us? Where do you want us to serve you? You did not allow your pain to deter you from proceeding ahead with the ministry your Father had assigned to you. Strengthen us to continue to be faithful in the ministry you have given to us. Alleluia!

Saturday, October 2, 1999 The Guardian Angels
Matthew 18, 1-5, 10
The Greatest in the Kingdom

Who's watching out for me? Whether we're nine or one hundred and nine, we wonder about that sometimes. When we're tired or bewildered or in pain, we may wonder if God knows or cares.

Today's Gospel gently reassures us that God's ideas of greatness are not the ideas we see in the world. We see so much competition, so much self-promotion, and so much vaunting of self.

No. God's way for us to live is a different way.

As God's children, we are to be humble and childlike. We trust GOD to watch out for us.

Jesus gave a strong warning to those who would take advantage of the trusting, childlike believer. "See that you do not despise one of these little ones, for I say to you that their angels in heaven always look upon the face of my heavenly Father."

"Watch out that you don't treat a single one of these childlike believers arrogantly. You realize, don't you, that their personal angels are constantly in touch with my Father in heaven (The Message)?"

Who's watching out for us? God is watching out for us and has assigned angels to watch out for us. Lord Jesus, thank you for the guardian angel you have assigned to be with me as I continue my journey Home to you. Alleluia!

Sunday, October 3, 1999
Twenty-seventh Sunday in Ordinary Time
Matthew 21, 22-43
The Parable of the Tenants

Although God places the cornerstone, it may be that only the spiritually alert identify the cornerstone. After telling the parable of the tenants, Jesus said to the to the chief priests and Pharisees, "Did you never read in the scriptures:

'The stone that the builders rejected
   has become the cornerstone;
by the Lord has this been done,
   and it is wonderful in our eyes?' "

God the Father placed Jesus, his Son, as the cornerstone. Jesus, although he was the cornerstone, did not try to place himself.

It is God's place, God's responsibility to place us! God places us as stones, so to speak.

We are placed as " ... living stones ... built into a spiritual house to be a holy priesthood to offer spiritual sacrifices acceptable to God through Jesus Christ (1 Peter 2, 5)."

What about the cornerstone? How the "cornerstone" is treated reveals the nature of those around the cornerstone. The "cornerstone" is God's litmus test.

Lord Jesus, help us to remember that you are the cornerstone and that we are united with you. Alleluia!

Monday, October 4, 1999 St. Francis of Assisi
Luke 10, 25-37
The Greatest Commandment;
The Parable of the Good Samaritan

Jesus calls us to be a "neighbor." We are not to interrogate others to make sure that their beliefs about God match ours. After all, it was the Samaritan, the one considered impure, who actually carried out Jesus' teaching.

Daily life provides opportunities to put this parable into practice. Once, years ago, on the way to a class I was teaching at my church, I saw a woman standing on the street, beside her stalled car, gesturing for help.

Although I didn't want to be late, I believed that God wanted me to stop. The woman was the mother of a student at the nearby high school. Her daughter needed something brought from home and the mother's car had broken down on the way to the school. I stopped and drove her to the school. Years later, I have forgotten what I taught in the class that day, but I remember the joy of stopping to help another.

On another occasion, I was the recipient. My husband, young son, and I were in Maui for my husband to attend an international conference. A beautiful, traditionally dressed Hindu woman, came to my assistance in the coin laundry of the hotel. She smiled and said, reassuringly, "Even in paradise (Maui!), we still have to do our laundry!"

Lord Jesus, today please enlarge my heart's definition of "neighbor." Help me to respond out of love to all who cross my path today. Help me especially to love those who appear indifferent or hostile to my love. Alleluia!

Tuesday, October 5, 1999
Luke 10, 38-42
Martha and Mary

There are many opinions on the meaning of the "one thing" mentioned in today's Gospel. Jesus said, "There is need of only one thing."

The "one thing" for me is to focus on Jesus. He is my Agenda.

Lord Jesus, I rest in you. Alleluia!

Wednesday, October 6, 1999 St. Bruno
Luke 11, 1-4
The Lord's Prayer

Here comes a very hard part of a very familiar prayer:

" ...forgive us our sins, for we ourselves forgive everyone in debt to us (The New American Bible).

"Forgive us our sins, for we forgive everyone who does us wrong. ((GNT), Today's English Version)." Both of these translations assume reciprocity.

We are to forgive any one who has ever hurt us, any one who is indebted to us in any way, before we can expect God to forgive us. Only God can help us to do this, because so often our human impulse is to retaliate.

Lord Jesus, I need your forgiveness today and every day. Come into my mind, my heart, my will, my emotions, my entire being, and flood me with your power to live and to forgive. When I am tempted to dwell on the ways others have hurt me, remind me that I have already made the decision to forgive. Where there have been misunderstandings and my attempts at reconciliation have been rebuffed, help me to release the person into your loving and wise hands. Grant me your peace. Alleluia!

Thursday, October 7, 1999 Our Lady of the Rosary
Luke 11, 5-13
Further Teachings on Prayer; The Answer to Prayer

Jesus is teaching us that God knows what is best for us. If we pray amiss, thinking we know what is best for us, God will answer our prayer. The answer will be "no."

God is a wise and good Father who will not give poison to us in answer to our prayers. God hears the prayer within the prayer.

God hears the ache and the cry in our heart. It is this prayer, the true prayer of our heart, that God answers. This prayer is answered with the gift of the Holy Spirit.

Father, today, I feel so overwhelmed with several situations that don't seem to change. I wish you would wave a "Holy Spirit wand" and make all these problems just go away. I know that you are at work in these situations, but I wish you'd work faster! Today, I ask for a fresh infusion of the Holy Spirit to see these situations with your eyes and to live through them with your strength. Thank you that I can be honest with you. Thank you for your tender understanding and patience. Thank you for sending Jesus to teach me how to pray. Alleluia!

Friday, October 8, 1999
Luke 11, 15-26
Jesus and Beelzebul

Jesus had just driven out " ... a demon [that was] mute, and when the demon had gone out, the mute person spoke ... (Luke 11, 14)." This was the incident that the onlookers seized upon to impugn the authority of Jesus.

For the mute person, a whole new life beckoned. All of a sudden, the entity that had held him captive was gone. He was free! He could speak. He could live his life fully.

Lord Jesus, today, please look within my heart and remove whatever it is that is holding me captive. Free me and fill me with your Holy Spirit. Let your kingdom come and your will be done in my life. Alleluia!

Saturday, October 9, 1999 Sts. Denis and Companions,
John Leonardi
Luke 11, 27-28
True Blessedness

Interruptions. In today's Gospel, a woman interrupted Jesus. "While he was speaking, a woman from the crowd called out and said to him, 'Blessed is the womb that carried you and the breasts at which you nursed.'"

What was Jesus speaking about at that time? The previous verses tell us that he was teaching about the tactics of Satan and unclean spirits. This was very serious teaching. The woman may have appeared to be affirming and complimentary, but instead she caused an interruption, a diversion.

Jesus redirected the crowd's attention to the importance of hearing and observing the word of God. That was what it meant to be truly happy.

When we are in a time of intense concentration on God's word to us, we need to be particularly aware of interruptions. Satan is not going to roll out the red carpet for us as we draw nearer to God. The enemy of our souls knows our weaknesses and will try many tactics to divert us from doing the work we are assigned by God to complete.

Lord Jesus, help me to discerning in this matter of interruptions. Forgive me for interrupting others. Help me to know when to ignore an interruption and when to stop and attend to it. Let my focus be on you. Help me to hear your word to me today and then to follow through in active obedience. Alleluia!

Sunday, October 10, 1999
Twenty-eighth Sunday in Ordinary Time
Matthew 22, 1-14
The Parable of the Wedding Feast

The king in this story had gone to extraordinary lengths to prepare a lavish feast for his son's wedding. To be invited to this event was an honor. To ignore the invitation was beneath contempt.

God the Father gave his only Son for us. Jesus shed his precious blood on the cross to secure our eternal health and salvation. To receive Jesus is to honor the Father. To reject Jesus is to trash God's greatest gift.

Lord Jesus, you have already prepared the banquet. Today I choose to be clothed in your robe of righteousness and to feast at your table. Thank you for the supreme gift of yourself. Alleluia!

Monday, October 11, 1999
Luke 11, 29-32
The Demand for a Sign

Signs and wonders. Sometimes we are like children on the Fourth of July, looking up at the sky and pointing to fireworks. "Look at that one!" "Oh, wow!" "Beautiful!' "Awesome!"

Some of the people around Jesus became so sidetracked with "signs" that they missed the sign of the Son of Man. Jesus was right there in their midst and some of the people who saw him still "missed" him!

Jesus is in our midst! He is present in Word and Sacrament. He is present in his Body, the Church. He is present in you and me. You are a "sign." I am a "sign."

It is essential that we realize who we are in Christ. The spiritually starving around us are looking for a sign. When they look at us, do they see Jesus?

Lord Jesus, you are truly present in your Body, the Church. Let us shine forth today as signs of your presence in this world. Alleluia!

Tuesday, October 12, 1999
Luke 11, 37-41
Denunciation of the Pharisees and Scholars of the Law

Jesus rebuked the Pharisees for being obsessed with ritual cleansing, yet allowing their lives to be filled with evil. It is very easy to make excuses for ourselves and to refuse to examine our own inner lives.

Throughout our Christian pilgrimage, the Lord draws us aside periodically for times of healthy introspection. Preferably with the guidance of a spiritual director, we examine our "inner" lives so that we may live in healthier way.

This is what the Pharisees refused to do. It was easier to become fixated with cleaning "the outside of the cup and dish," and ignoring the inner spiritual bacteria. The resulting infection led to stubborn, self-inflicted blindness and hardened hearts.

Jesus invites us to "give alms." He said, "... as to what is within, give alms, and behold everything will be clean for you (Luke 11, 41, <u>The New American Bible</u>)." "Turn both your pockets and your hearts inside out and give generously to the poor; then your lives will be clean, not just your dishes and your hands (Luke 11, 41, <u>The Message</u>)."

Holy Spirit, please show me what it means today for me to "give alms."

"Create in me a clean heart, O God;
    and renew a right spirit within me. (Psalm 51, 10, K.J.V.)."

"Behold, thou desirest truth in the inward parts:
    and in the hidden part thou shall make me to know wisdom.
                    (Psalm 51, 6, K.J.V.)."

Alleluia!

Wednesday, October 13, 1999
Luke 11, 42-46
Denunciation of the Pharisees and the Scholars of the Law

The Pharisees were being "penny wise and pound foolish." They meticulously tithed the earthly, yet ignored the eternal. "You pay no attention to judgment and to love for God."

The Pharisees enjoyed the perks of the present, such as "the seats of honor in the synagogues and the greetings in the marketplaces." They were intent on guarding these status symbols. They were carriers of spiritual death.

Jesus said, "Seek first the kingdom [of God] and his righteousness and all these things will be given to you besides (Matthew 6, 33)." In other words, we are to seek the eternal over the earthly.

Lord Jesus, help me to see what is truly important in my life today and to be a wise steward of both earthly and eternal treasures. Most of all, Lord, help me to be a carrier of life to those I meet today. Alleluia!

Thursday, October 14, 1999 St. Calliustus I
Luke 11, 47-54
Denunciation of the Pharisees and Scholars of the Law

Jesus was speaking the truth to the legal scholars, as well as to the Pharisees. They were not amused. More significantly, they refused to receive the truth.

When Jesus speaks a hard truth to us, sometimes through another person, we can react with rage, either suppressed of expressed, or we can swallow our stupid pride and respond with repentance. The angels rejoice when we repent!

Earlier in Luke's Gospel, we saw Jesus speaking to the repentant woman who wept at his feet and anointed his feet with costly ointment from her alabaster flask. "Your sins are forgiven." "Your faith has saved you; go in peace (Luke 7, 48, 50)."

This tender scene is in stark contrast to the scene in today's Gospel. The religious leaders stubbornly refused to receive the truth about themselves.

They turned on Jesus with hostility and hatred. In their hearts, they had already murdered Jesus, even as their ancestors outwardly murdered the prophets of old.

Lord Jesus, this is an exhausting Gospel. Salvation history flashes before us as we remember the fate of the prophets. Help us receive your word to us today and not to "murder" your messengers. Alleluia!

Friday, October 15, 1999 St. Teresa of Avila
Luke 12, 1-7
The Leaven of the Pharisees; Courage under Persecution

"Do not be afraid." In spite of the clamoring crowd, Jesus concentrated his attention initially on his disciples. He cautioned them about the attitude they needed to maintain in the midst of the Pharisees.

"Watch yourselves carefully so you don't get contaminated with Pharisee yeast, Pharisee phoniness. You can't keep your true self hidden forever; before long you'll be exposed. You can't hide behind a religious mask forever; sooner or later the mask will slip and your true face will be known. You can't whisper one thing in private and preach the opposite in public; the day's coming when those whispers will be repeated all over town. I'm speaking to you as dear friends. Don't be bluffed into silence or insincerity by the threats of religious bullies (Luke 12, 2-7) The Message)."

Lord Jesus, as you told your first disciples, you are telling us today , "Do not be afraid." You know the most minute detail of our lives and you are in complete control. Alleluia!

280

Saturday, October 16, 1999 Sts. Hedwig and Mary Alacoque
Luke 12, 8-12
Courage under Persecution; Sayings about the Holy Spirit

Jesus, my Good Shepherd, will lead me from where I am today all the way home to the Father in heaven. Jesus will even tell the angels that I belong to him. I am secure.

With this security I can put all my trust in Jesus. He knows my fears, my weaknesses, my sorrows, and all my doubts. He knows and he forgives.

When I am in situations that are beyond me, he sends his Holy Spirit to tell me what to say. I do not have defend myself.

Dear Lord Jesus, thank you that you are Son of Man as well as Son of God. You understand me and forgive me and lead me into new freedom. Thank you for the Holy Spirit who continually instructs me and gives me the wisdom and strength I need for today. Thank you for keeping me safe. Alleluia!

Sunday, October 17, 1999
Twenty-ninth Sunday in Ordinary Time
Matthew 22, 15-21
Paying Taxes to the Emperor

It was after hearing Jesus' parable of the wedding feast about many being invited, but few being actually chosen, that "the Pharisees went off and plotted how they might entrap him in speech."

The Pharisees sent not only their own disciples in Phariseeism, but also the Herodians. This was a real "set-up!"

Jesus, "knowing their malice," did not fall into their trap. According to Proverbs 28, 10 K.J.V., "Whoso causeth the righteous to go astray in an evil way, he shall fall himself into his own pit....." Although the Pharisees tried, they could not trap or seduce Jesus into a compromising statement.

Jesus was practicing what he had preached to his disciples. He was as shrewd as a serpent and as simple as a dove (Matthew 10, 16).

Jesus was not afraid of the Pharisees. He knew that the Holy Spirit would teach him what to say (Luke 12, 12).

"Do not worry about how you are to speak or what you are to say. You will be given at that moment what you are to say. For it will not be you who speak, but the Spirit of your Father speaking through you (Matthew 10, 19-20)."

Jesus answered the Pharisees in a way that was disarmingly simple. He advised them to "... repay to Caesar what belongs to Caesar what belongs to Caesar and to God what belongs to God (Matthew 22, 21)."

We may feel trapped in certain situations. We may fear the malice of others. Jesus will show us how to face these fears. The key is to trust that the Holy Spirit lives in us and will speak through us.

Lord Jesus, help me today to cast off the rags of fear and to put on the garment of praise, "a glorious mantle (Isaiah 61, 3)." Alleluia!

Monday, October 18, 1999 St. Luke
Luke 10, 1-9
The Mission of the Seventy-two

Jesus sent the seventy-two into the human harvest field with the injunction, "Go on your way; behold, I am sending you like lambs among wolves."

Jesus did not first send them to wolf school to learn to think like wolves and to act like wolves. They were not wolves.

They were lambs, his lambs, and he was their Good Shepherd. He was teaching them not only to be aware of the wolves, but also to do God's work God's way.

Upon entering a house, they were to speak, "Peace to this household." If they were welcomed in a particular town, they were to accept hospitality, cure the sick, and proclaim, "The kingdom of God is at hand for you."

Lord Jesus, we cannot love like lambs if we live like wolves. Today, send us out to live this Gospel, to speak peace wherever you send us, to accept your provision offered through others, to be instruments of your healing, and to proclaim your reign. Alleluia!

Tuesday, October 19, 1999
Sts. John de Brebeuf, Isaac Jogues and Companions
Luke 12, 35-38
Vigilant and Faithful Servants

Be prepared for joy! So often when life is difficult for a prolonged period of time, we are braced for suffering.

We've been through so much that we begin to expect even more suffering. Jesus wants us to know that this life is not all suffering. There is joy awaiting us!

In today's Gospel, Jesus told his disciples to "be like servants who await their master's return from a wedding, ready to open immediately when he comes and knocks." The master in the parable, brimming with joy after his wedding, was returning! Having instructed his servants be prepared for his return and to keep their lamps lighted, he arrived and began to wait on them.

Lord Jesus, help me to prepare for joy by staying vigilant today. Alleluia!

Wednesday, October 20, 1999 St. Paul of the Cross
Luke 12, 39-48
Vigilant and Faithful Servants

"Much will be required of the person entrusted with much, and still more will be demanded of the person entrusted with more." It is faithfulness to the known will of God that matters.

Jesus knows our human limitations. We cannot be all things to all people. We are to be faithful in doing God's will, not knowing when our time of accountability will arrive.

Lord Jesus, I give myself to you today to do your will as I understand it. Help me to be patient with myself, knowing that you are supplying the strength I need. Alleluia!

Thursday, October 21, 1999
Luke 12, 49-53
Jesus: A Cause of Division

At the presentation of the infant Jesus in the temple of Jerusalem, Simeon said to Mary, "Behold, this child is destined for the fall and rise of many in Israel, and to be a sign that will be contradicted (and you yourself a sword will pierce) so that the thoughts of many hearts may be revealed (Luke 2, 34-35)."

In today's Gospel, we see this prophecy catching up with Jesus. It was only a matter of time and circumstance.

Jesus did not come to this earth to preach pablum. He came to shake, rattle, and roll heads! If you're a "peace at any price" person, Jesus is going to make you very hot under the collar.

"There is a baptism with which I must be baptized, and how great is my anguish until it is accomplished! Do you think I have come to establish peace on the earth? No, I tell you, but rather division."

This is not a gentle Jesus, meek and mild. This is a firebrand, a holy bolt of lightening shot straight from the arrow of the Father in heaven.

Jesus announced, "I've come to change everything, turn everything rightside up -- how I long for it to be finished! Do you think I came to smooth things over and make everything nice? Not so. I've come to disrupt and confront (Luke 12, 49-51, The Message)."

Lord Jesus, you are currently "turning everything rightside up" in my life. You are disrupting my safe little routines and confronting my fears. Thank you that when you are finished, my life will be "rightside up." Alleluia!

Friday, October 22, 1999
Luke 12, 54-59
Signs of the Times; Settlement with an Opponent

Jesus is telling us to be savvy, to be shrewd. We are to make an accurate assessment of the time we're living in, act accordingly, and live in disciplined freedom.

We don't want to spend time and energy being dragged around and dragged down by an "opponent." "Agreeing" with an adversary does not necessarily mean that we play the doormat or that the "adversary " is right and we are wrong.

It means that we keep ourselves free of the whole entanglement and proceed to God's next assignment. If we keep trying to fix a situation that God wants us out of, we are ensnared, frustrated, and ultimately disabled.

Lord Jesus, help me to break free from willful ignorance and from cages of my own making. You have opened the door of the cage and invite me to fly into freedom Alleluia!

Saturday, October 23, 1999 St. John of Capistrano
Luke 13, 1-9
A Call to Repentance; The Parable of the Barren Fig Tree

This fig tree was getting one last chance! Planted in the orchard with the other fig trees, this particular tree was not yielding fruit. No explanation was given..

The owner of the orchard was out of patience and was ready to instruct the gardener to chop it down. The gardener "interceded" for the fig tree and said, "Sir, leave it for this year also, and I shall cultivate the ground around it and fertilize it; it may bear fruit in the future. If not you can cut it down."

The parable ended with a double note. The gardener was going to lavish extra special tender, loving care on the tree for another year. There was the possibility, but not the guarantee, of growth.

Lord Jesus, sometimes I feel like that fig tree. I'm planted in your orchard, but I don't seem to be producing much fruit. Maybe my idea of fruit is not the same as yours. Thank you for the "gardeners" in my life who pray for me and intercede on my behalf. Help me to cooperate with you and to produce the fruit you are looking for in my life. Alleluia!

Sunday, October 24, 1999 Thirtieth Sunday in Ordinary Time
Matthew 22, 34-40
The Greatest Commandment

Jesus was speaking to the Pharisees in particular, in this passage. They were testing him with a loaded question, again trying to trip him up in his theology. Fat chance.

One particular Pharisee, a legal scholar, asked, "Teacher, which commandment in the law is the greatest?" Jesus answered, "You shall love the Lord, your God, with all your heart, with all your soul, and with all your mind. This is the greatest and the first commandment. The second is like it: You shall love your neighbor as yourself."

Jesus himself was the answer! He himself was the ultimate communication and demonstration of God's love.

God's life and love shone through Jesus. His life was one of perfect balance. He loved God, loved himself, and loved others.

Jesus leads us gently to come to know ourselves and to be able to love ourselves. If we cannot accept and love ourselves, we cannot accept and love God or others.

We may need a refresher course in the love of God. We need the "answers" to God-questions to blossom from our heart knowledge, as well as our head knowledge, of God.

Lord Jesus, today as I feast on your Word and feast at your Table, touch and heal and refresh my entire being. Shine through me. Alleluia!

Monday, October 25, 1999
Luke 13, 10-17
Cure of a Crippled Woman on the Sabbath

We see yet another person in the synagogue who has been tormented by an evil spirit. Do you remember the time when Jesus was in the synagogue in Capernaum on a Sabbath and liberated the man who had "the spirit of an unclean demon (Luke 4, 31-37)?" Jesus was there, the person in need was there, and it was time for freedom!

God's timing in our lives is something I absolutely do not understand. I do know that Jesus is Lord.

He is Lord of the Sabbath. He is Head of the Church, and what he says goes. Period.

In today's Gospel, the time had arrived for this woman, this "daughter of Abraham." Eighteen years of being crippled and held back were wiped out in one instant!

"Woman, you are set free of your infirmity." At the touch of Jesus, she stood up straight and tall and "glorified God" then and there in the synagogue.

Lord Jesus, thank you for your perfect timing. Help me not to chafe, but to cherish the time and the space I'm in today. Thank you for setting me free in your time. Alleluia!

Tuesday, October 26, 1999
Luke 13, 18-21
The Parable of the Mustard Seed; The Parable of the Yeast

In the kingdom of God, anything is possible! It's God's kingdom. God rules.

The tiny mustard seed grows to be a tree which shelters many birds. A bit of gray yeast transforms flour into a fragrant loaf of bread to nourish the hungry.

The man in the Gospel planted the seed in the ground. The woman in the Gospel mixed the yeast in the flour.

They did their part and waited. Transformation was God's part.

Lord Jesus, let my life today be in balance. There is a time for purposeful work and there is a time for tranquil rest. There is my part and there is your part. Thank you that you are here with me transforming my prayers, my work, and my rest into your perfect purpose. Alleluia!

Wednesday, October 27, 1999
Luke 13, 22-30
The Narrow Door; Salvation and Rejection

Jesus lived out this message of single-hearted concentration on God's agenda. He taught as he traveled through town after town, village after village, "making his way to Jerusalem," where his destiny lay.

He taught us to "strive to enter through the narrow gate ..." "Put your mind on your life with God. The way to life - to God! - is vigorous and requires your total attention (Luke 13, 24, The Message)."

Jesus warned against false familiarity. To some who assumed they knew him, he said, "Depart from me, all you evildoers!"

Jesus also startles us with what Eugene Peterson calls "the Great Reversal: the last in line put at the head of the line; and the so-called first ending up last (Luke 13, 30; The Message)."

Lord Jesus, you were single-hearted in your concentration on doing the will of your heavenly Father. Help me to walk closely with you today to "Jerusalem " where my destiny lies. Alleluia!

Thursday, October 28, 1999 Sts. Simon and Jude
Luke 6, 12-16
The Mission of the Twelve

Jesus spent the night in prayer. In the morning, he summoned his disciples. From the group of disciples, Jesus chose Twelve. He called them apostles.

The disciples were first of all called to spend time with Jesus and to learn from him. Only then were they sent out on their mission as apostles.

We are called first of all to be with Jesus, to spend time with him, and to continue learning from him. This foundation is essential.

If this foundation is not firmly in place, we will foolishly try, in our own strength, to serve God. When the inevitable storms shake the house of our soul, the pretty pictures may fall off the walls, the crystal may shatter, but the foundation will remain firm and fixed.

We are always disciples, always learning from Jesus. Jesus loves us far too much to send us out as apostles on a mission unless we have first spent time in his school of discipleship.

This was, in part, the tragedy of the life of Judas. He never fully grasped what it meant to trust and to follow Jesus as a disciple. Disappointed that following Jesus was not what he had expected, he betrayed his Lord. There are still Judases today.

Lord Jesus, you chose fallible human beings to be with you, to learn from you, and to be messengers of the Gospel. Today, I need to be immersed in your presence and in your love. There are remedial courses I need to take in your school of discipleship. Thank you that you use me in spite of myself. Thank you for your continued, unquenchable love and trust in me in spite of my fears. Let me open my workbook and learn the lessons you have marked out for me today. Alleluia!

Friday, October 29, 1999
Luke 14, 1-6
Healing of the Man with Dropsy on the Sabbath

Jesus was having a meal on the Sabbath at the home of an important Pharisee. The people were watching Jesus like a hawk.

Like ducks on a June bug, they were ready to pounce! Right in front of Jesus was a man with dropsy. Let's see what Jesus does.

Both the man with physical dropsy and the Pharisees with spiritual dropsy needed healing. Dropsy is a medical condition involving fluid retention and abnormal swelling.

Jesus healed the man with the physical dropsy and sent him on his way. Wonderful!

The Pharisees? Another matter. Their hearts, not their joints, were swollen with the pride of self-righteousness.

Jesus is standing before us today. Do we want healing? Do we want freedom? Are we humble enough to ask for help?

Lord Jesus, you are the Physician. That much I know. What I don't know is the diagnosis, much less the prognosis, for what ails me today. I yield to the work of your Holy Spirit in my life. Please heal me. Alleluia!

Saturday, October 30, 1999
Luke 14, 1; 7-11
Healing of the Man with Dropsy on the Sabbath;
Conduct of Invited Guests and Hosts

Jesus is telling us not to choose for ourselves. When we try to choose, whether it's a place at a banquet or our life's vocation, we may choose amiss.

What we choose may indeed be God's choice, planted within the deepest recesses of our being. It is for God, however, to train us and to bring our vocation to blossom and to full fruition.

"What I'm saying is, If you walk around with your nose in the air, you're going to end up flat on your face. But if you consent to be simply yourself, you will become more than yourself (Luke 14, 11, The Message)."

It is not for the pupil to place the gold star in the workbook. That is the prerogative of the teacher.

Lord Jesus, help me to live simply before you this day. Let me find my joy and my fulfillment in my relationship with you. Alleluia!

289

Sunday, October 31, 1999 Thirty-First Sunday in Ordinary Time
Matthew 23, 1-12
Denunciation of the Scribes and the Pharisees

A warning and a promise! Jesus says that when we attempt to exalt ourselves we will be humbled, but if we humble ourselves we will be exalted (Matthew 23, 12; Luke 14, 11; Luke 18, 14).

The warning applies to all of us! Jesus clearly says, "whoever."

The promise also applies to all of us! Jesus again says, "whoever."

We cannot give up on ourselves. We cannot give up on others.

We cannot point the finger and wish "they" would stop exalting themselves. We must also love ourselves and realize that we are "they."

We have done the same thing. Whenever we have cherished hatred for others, even if our discernment of their behavior was valid, we have fallen into the same trap of self-exaltation. We have indulged in pride and have set ourselves above others.

Lord Jesus Christ, Son of God, have mercy on me, a sinner. Help me today to forgive, to accept forgiveness, and leave my feelings with you. Alleluia!

November 1, 1999 All Saints
Matthew 5, 1-12a
The Sermon on the Mount; The Beatitudes

The ones who are "blessed" and "happy" start out with a realization that they are "poor in spirit." Jesus says that "theirs is the kingdom of heaven."

In this kingdom there is room for only one ruler. This ruler is God. If we try to be God, we will not only miss knowing the true God, but we will also be miserable.

The others who are promised the kingdom of God are the ones who are "persecuted for the sake of righteousness." Their lives manifest a closeness to God that provokes hatred and rejection. They are a threat to the phonies. So what! What can they lose when Jesus promises them the kingdom of heaven?

In the spectrum between poverty of spirit and persecution for righteousness, there are many gifts. There is the joy of comfort in the midst of mourning. Those who know their own limitations and are forced to trust God "inherit the land." Those starved for God will be satisfied. Those who are tender in their treatment of others will be treated tenderly by God. The "clean of heart" will "see God." Those who work for peace will be called God's children.

Lord Jesus, thank you that there are signs of the kingdom of heaven all around me today. Thank you that I can be in "heaven" this very day. Alleluia!

Tuesday, November 2, 1999 All Souls
Matthew 11, 25-30
The Praise of the Father; The Gentle Mastery of Christ

Sometimes life is just too much! We have our own personal illnesses, battles, and struggles. We are concerned about the afflictions of those near and dear, but feel powerless to help them.

There is too much noise! There always seems to be construction in the neighborhoods. The roads are congested with stressed-out drivers. Newspaper headlines scream earthquakes, wars, plane crashes, cruelty, etc. It's just too much.

Jesus offers, not an escape, but an invitation to live in this world in another way. He says, "Come to me, all you who labor and are burdened, and I will give you rest. Take my yoke upon you and learn from me, for I am meek and humble of heart; and you will find rest for yourselves. For my yoke is easy, and my burden light."

Lord Jesus, I have been carrying burdens you never intended for me to carry. These are burdens of worry, resentment, fear and despair. I am so tired. I come to you. I want to learn from you. Teach me how to live this one day with only the yoke and with only the burden you assign to me. I would like to experience your easy yoke and your light burden. Alleluia!

Wednesday, November 3, 1999 St. Martin de Porres
Luke 14, 25-33
Sayings on Discipleship

"Go figure." This is a current slang expression, often used to emphasize how obvious something is to the speaker.

Jesus is speaking to the crowds who want to be in on the action. In his own way. he says, "Go figure."

291

He challenges them to "go figure" and to see if they have what it takes to follow him. "Simply put, if you're not willing to take what is dearest to you, whether plans or people, and kiss it goodbye, you can't be my disciple (Luke 14, 33, <u>The Message</u>)."

Jesus refers to our cross. "Whoever does not carry his own cross and come after me cannot be my disciple."

It is necessary not only to carry our own cross, but also to embrace our cross. Why?

"Go figure." After we "die" on our cross, we are free to live our "resurrection."

Do you really want to be a disciple? "Go figure."

Lord Jesus, right now with all these difficulties in my life, I really feel tempted to opt for whatever is easiest. Still, I agree with a friend who laughingly says of herself, "I'm a mess, but I say 'yes!' " Today, I say "yes" to you, Lord. Thank you for putting me back together and inviting me to continue this arduous, yet exhilarating road of discipleship. Alleluia!

Thursday, November 4, 1999 St. Charles Borromeo
Luke 15, 1-10
The Parable of the Lost Sheep; The Parable of the Lost Coin

Those who knew they needed Jesus were the ones who drew near to him to listen attentively. The Pharisees and scribes, who thought they had no need of Jesus, were the ones who complained about him.

Since I am guilty of a lot of complaining, I knew I had do some quick repenting as I read this Gospel. The Pharisees and scribes specialized in complaining about Jesus. "This man welcomes sinners and eats with them." My complaining, on the other hand, was all-inclusive.

When I complain, I am very unhappy, not only with the objects of my complaints, but with myself. I complain about my complaining.

Lord Jesus, like the tax collectors and sinners, I definitely know I need you. Please forgive me for all my complaining and underlying lack of trust. Forgive my pride. Thank you for the privilege of drawing near to you and listening attentively to you. Thank you that you are the Good Shepherd who searches for the lost sheep. Thank you for not leaving me out in the desert of my complaints. I choose to walk in the joy and freedom you have given me and to be patient with myself as well as with others. Alleluia!

Friday, November 5, 1999
Luke 16, 1-8
The Parable of the Dishonest Steward

"Streetwise people are smarter in this regard than law-abiding citizens. They are on constant alert, looking for angles, surviving by their wits. I want you to be smart in the same way - but for what is right - using every adversity to stimulate you to creative survival, to concentrate your attention on the bare essentials, so you'll live, really live, and not complacently just get by on good behavior (Luke 16, 8 The Message)."

This is a time in my life when I need to use current difficulties "for creative survival" and to concentrate my time and energy on the essentials of my relationship with God. With my left foot in a surgical shoe, my left arm in a splint, and my right arm in a brace, I'm limited in mobility. No long walks or lap swimming for awhile.

Lord Jesus, help me to be a good steward of this time and not to fuss and chafe impatiently against these restrictions. Help me to be creative and to turn this time to a time of adventure with you. Alleluia!

Saturday, November 6, 1999
Luke 16, 9-15
Application of the Parable; A Saying Against the Pharisees

Jesus said, "The person who is trustworthy in very small matters is also trustworthy in great ones; and the person who is dishonest in very small matters is also dishonest in great ones." Jesus was speaking to his disciples, but the Pharisees also "heard all these things and sneered at him."

Wherever we go and whatever we say, we will have a mixed audience. This is true whether our "audience" consists of those at the dinner table with us or those who pack an auditorium to hear us speak. Some will accept our words and others will sneer.

We are not here on this earth to please others or to please ourselves, but to please God. What greater honor and responsibility is there than to serve the living God?

What God asks me to do may seem strange or trivial. However, having yielded myself to God, I strive to stay in the center of God's will by obeying the whispers of the Holy Spirit.

Lord Jesus, I want to be worthy of your trust in me. Today, I need healing and strengthening of my soul and spirit, as well as my body.

293

Thank you for the joy of serving you by trusting that this is not wasted time. Alleluia!

Sunday, November 7, 1999
Thirty-Second Sunday in Ordinary Time
Matthew 25, 1-13
The Parable of the Ten Virgins

We tend to become drowsy and to "fall asleep" as we wait and wait and wait for the Lord's answer to a particular prayer. We believe that the Lord is hears our prayer, but we've given up any real expectancy that he'll ever show up with an answer, at least with the answer we want.

Sometimes we become so focused or fixated on the problem that we actually lose sight of the Lord. There needs to be an adjustment in our praying,

It is the Lord who not only has the answer, but who also IS the answer! The answer to our prayer is already here because Jesus is already here. We're the ones who have to grow into the answer by staying prepared.

A friend told me of praying for her brother who has suffered from years from a chronic illness. Hope is still alive in his sister and in others who are interceding for him. As she continues to pray for her brother, the Lord is touching her own life in new ways. She went to a Healing Mass specifically to pray for her brother. Surprise! During Mass, she experienced an unexpected healing of her own. A little growth that had been on her face disappeared.

"Therefore, stay awake, for you know neither the day nor the hour." Lord Jesus, help me to stay focused on you and upon my relationship with you. Help me not to become drowsy, but to receive the energy of the Holy Spirit to stay awake and to stay prepared. Alleluia!

Monday, November 8, 1999
Luke 17, 1-6
Temptation to Sin; Saying of Faith

Millstones, mustard seeds, and mulberry trees! They're all in today's Gospel. What in the world do they have to do with us?

Millstones. I remember a recent occasion in which I knowingly made a selfish choice and then tried to rationalize it away. Lord, have mercy. Knowing my own constant need for God's forgiveness and mercy,

I remind myself that God requires me to forgive those who sin against me.

Mustard seeds. Mustard seeds are tiny, but powerful. My faith may be small, but if it is placed in the hands of the Lord of the universe, nothing is impossible!

Mulberry trees? Although I don't usually go around telling trees to jump into the sea, perhaps it's time to begin to step out and to speak out with new boldness. Alleluia!

Tuesday, November 9, 1999 Dedication of the Lateran Basilica
John 2, 13-22
Cleansing of the Temple

Temple! I can't seem to escape that word.

It has been a part of my life since childhood. From fifth grade through high school, I lived in Temple, Texas.

In Malachi, the last book of the Hebrew scriptures, we read "Behold, I will send my messenger, and he shall prepare the way before me: and the LORD, whom ye seek, shall suddenly come to his temple" (Malachi 3, 1 K.J.V.)

In today's Gospel, Jesus is outraged at the desecration of the Temple in Jerusalem. The Temple was intended to be "a house of prayer" (Matthew 21, 13, Mark 11, 17; Luke 19, 5), but the merchants and money-changers had defiled it by turning it into a mere marketplace.

Jesus referred to his own body as a temple. St. Paul referred to our bodies also as God's temple. "Do you not know that you are the temple of God, and that the spirit of God dwells in you? If anyone destroys God's temple, God will destroy that person; for the temple of God, which you are, is holy (1 Corinthians 3, 16-17)."

"Do you not know that your body is a temple of the holy Spirit within you, whom you have from God, and that you are not your own? For you have been purchased at a price. Therefore, glorify God in your body (1Corinthians 6, 19-20)."

In the heavenly Jerusalem, there will be no temple. That is because " ... its temple is the Lord God almighty and the Lamb (Revelation 21, 22)."

Lord Jesus, please come to me today and cleanse the temple of my life. Cleanse me from all which defiles my temple. Alleluia!

Wednesday, November 10, 1999 St. Leo the Great
Luke 17, 11-19
The Cleansing of Ten Lepers

Do what God tells you to do. As you do it, sooner or later, there will be a manifestation of the result of your trust and obedience.

That's what happened with Jesus and the lepers. They were not immediately cleansed. It was as they obeyed Jesus and "as they were going" to the priests that they were healed.

Who was the leper who realized he had been healed and then returned to thank Jesus? He was a Samaritan, a despised, "low-life" Samaritan, an alien, an "outsider."

Again and again it was the needy one, the one who was looked down on, the one who was considered unfit or inferior, who not only received healing from Jesus, but also returned to thank Jesus.

Begin to observe this in your own life. Sometimes the ones you knock yourself out for are oblivious to your efforts, while others are touchingly grateful for the least little favor.

At a recent high school reunion, I was perplexed when a woman came up to me and thanked me for having invited her to a slumber party. Slumber party? Then I remembered! Although I was painfully shy in high school, I decided to be brave and to invite several girls over for a slumber party. For whatever reason, this particular classmate had remembered that I had invited her.

We need to be wildly extravagant and generous with God's love flowing through us. Who cares whether we are thanked or not!

Our marmalade cat, Francis, is a border guard. He patrols the hedge to make sure other cats don't invade "his" turf.

We need to be border guards of another sort. We need to observe carefully the borders of our lives. Have we written someone off? It was while Jesus was passing along the border of Galilee and Samaria that he cleansed the leper. As we follow Jesus today, let us to reach out to those on the borders.

Lord Jesus, help me to love and to reach out to the "leper" within my own heart and to any other "lepers" you bring across my path today. Alleluia!

Thursday, November 11, 1999 St. Martin of Tours
Luke 17, 20-25
The Coming of the Kingdom of God;
The Day of the Son of Man

Some years ago, an irritatingly trite saying became popular. "Wherever you go, there you are." This means, of course, that you can't get away from yourself.

Wherever Jesus is present, there HE is and there is the kingdom of God. Jesus came to earth to do the will of his Father in heaven. When he is invited to reign in a particular situation, the kingdom of God is present in that situation.

Not everyone wants Jesus. Not everyone wants the kingdom of God. Jesus knew this. He knew he would "... suffer greatly and be rejected ..."

Lord Jesus, come into my life in a new way today and set up shop. Set up housekeeping. Set up your kingdom. I've tried to reign in the kingdom of my life and it doesn't work. Your kingdom come, your will be done in my life today and every day. Alleluia!

Friday, November 12, 1999 St. Josaphat
Luke 17, 26-37
The Day of the Son of Man

"As it was in the days of Noah, so it will be in the days of the Son of Man ..." Ho hum. Same old, same old. Blah.

Life as usual "... up to the day that Noah entered the ark, and the flood came and destroyed them all." All except Noah and his family.

Then there was Lot! Again, it seemed that life was going on as usual, but "on the day when Lot left Sodom, fire and brimstone rained from the sky to destroy them all."

Jesus has our attention now! "So it will be on the day the Son of Man is revealed." It will be sudden! When it comes, it will be too late to prepare.

Lord Jesus, what is it in my life you want me to do to prepare for your coming? Thank you for sending the Holy Spirit to teach me what I am personally to be doing in preparation for "that day." Alleluia!

Saturday, November 13, 1999 St. Frances X. Cabrini
Luke 18, 1-8
The Parable of the Persistent Widow

"But when the Son of Man comes, will he find faith on the earth?" This is the end of the parable sometimes called the parable of the unjust judge and sometimes called the parable of the persistent widow. The last sentence is sometimes ignored or omitted in our thinking and praying about the parable.

"But when the Son of Man comes, will he find faith on the earth?" For many years, I concentrated my attention on the dynamic between the persistent woman, her opponent, and the corrupt judge.

This judge "... neither feared God nor respected any human being." The poor woman seemed so alone as she pursued justice.

Over the years, my focus changed as I studied the parable. The woman's plight, serious as it was, would ultimately be resolved. God was just and God would have the final word in her case.

God is the only true judge. "Will not God then secure the rights of his chosen ones who call out to him day and night? Will he be slow to answer them? I tell you, he will see to it that justice is done for them speedily."

What is "speedy" for God may seem to take forever with us. Still, the lingering question remains. "But when the Son of Man comes, will he find faith on the earth?"

That is the real question for me! Can I be content to live now, resting in the knowledge that God has heard my cries? The answer is already held in the heart of God and in the hands of God.

Can I hold out and continue to trust God until the answer is made manifest? When Jesus comes, will he find faith in me?

Lord Jesus, I love you and trust you and rejoice in your presence. Thank you for the gifts of patience, persistence, and perseverance as I wait. Alleluia!

Sunday, November 14, 1999
Thirty-third Sunday in Ordinary Time
Matthew 25, 14-30
The Parable of the Talents

It was "out of fear" that the servant with one talent (a unit of money) buried it. The master, not accepting fear as an excuse, rebuked the servant, calling him "wicked" and "lazy."

The master took the single talent away from the lazy servant and gave it to the servant who already had ten talents. "And throw this useless servant into the darkness outside, where there will be wailing and grinding of teeth."

This is sometimes called the parable of the three servants. The two servants who were given five talents and two talents "immediately" used them These two servants, having been "faithful in small matters" were applauded and were rewarded with "great responsibilities." They were invited to share their master's joy.

This is a story about risk, trust, and obedience. Jesus wants us to risk losing resources and reputation in order to obey him.

Lord Jesus, help me not to play it safe and to be overly concerned with looking out for myself. I belong to you and YOU are looking out for me. Thank you for freeing me to serve you with boldness and joy. Alleluia!

Monday, November 15, 1999 St. Albert the Great
Luke 18, 35-43
The Healing of the Blind Beggar

In the three synoptic Gospels (Matthew, Mark , and Luke), the account of the healing of the blind beggar follows closely after Jesus' third prediction of his suffering and death in Jerusalem. The disciples still do not comprehend what Jesus is trying to tell them. They are as spiritually blind as the beggar is physically blind.

Jericho! God seems to like to do the impossible in Jericho.

When ancient Jericho was under siege, God told Joshua, "I have delivered Jericho and its king into your power (Joshua 6, 2)." God's method, as usual, was most unusual!

The soldiers were told to encircle the city and to march around it for six consecutive days. Seven priests were to carry ram's horns ahead of the ark of the covenant. On the seventh day, seven priests were to march around the city seven times and blow horns. All the people were to shout. The city walls would then collapse (Joshua 6, 3-5). The walls of Jericho indeed fell as the people carried out this strange command.

In today's Gospel, Jesus did not shout or blow a ram's horn. Instead, he asked the beggar a question.

"What do you want me to do for you?" Then Jesus gave a command, "Have sight ..." Jesus stated the reason for the man's healing. "Your faith has saved you."

In ancient Jericho, the walls came down as the people trusted God and obeyed God's unusual command. In the Jericho of Jesus' day, a blind beggar was healed because he trusted God, threw himself on the mercy of the Son of God, and articulated his need.

Is there a Jericho in your life? Is there a place or a situation in which all seems hopeless? Call out to Jesus.

Jesus will grant sight and insight. At the appointed time, the walls will come down.

Lord Jesus, you knew how to pace the disciples according to their level of comprehension. You kept telling them that you would suffer and die, but they just didn't get it. You were patient and kept showing that you were in charge. You did the "impossible" by restoring sight to a blind beggar in Jericho. You slowly and carefully built up your followers' trust in you. Eventually they understood that you were Lord. Eventually we will understand that you are Lord. Teach us how to speak to the Jericho walls in our lives, the walls of fear and doubt, and see them come down. Alleluia!

Tuesday, November 16, 1999
St. Margaret of Scotland, St. Gertrude
Luke 19, 1-10
Zacchaeus the Tax Collector

Zacchaeus knew when to run ahead and when to stand his ground. He took the initiative in running ahead and finding a way to see Jesus.

Climbing a sycamore tree was very ingenious. Zacchaeus sacrificed his "dignity" and his reputation because seeing Jesus was of greater importance. He did not complain because the crowd got in his way. He was creative and found another way!

Jesus noticed Zacchaeus. " 'Zacchaeus, come down quickly, for today I must stay at your house.' And he came down quickly and received him with joy."

Others complained about Jesus going to "the house of a sinner." Nevertheless, Zacchaeus stood his ground.

Zacchaeus "stood there" and spoke directly to Jesus. "Behold, half of my possessions, Lord, I shall give to the poor, and if I have extorted anything from anyone, I shall repay it four times over."

Jesus rejoiced over Zacchaeus! "Today salvation has come to this house because this man too is a descendant of Abraham. For the Son of Man has come to seek and to save what was lost."

Lord Jesus, sometime I get so weary and become dispirited and listless. I cease to expect miracles in my life. Today, please help me to see you in a new way. Help me to be like Zacchaeus and do what is necessary to "see" you. Show me what is my equivalent of climbing a sycamore tree. Alleluia!

Wednesday, November 17, 1999 St. Elizabeth of Hungary
Luke 19, 11-28
The Parable of the Ten Gold Coins

Jesus told this parable to challenge the expectations of his disciples. Because Jesus was approaching Jerusalem, where his destiny lay, the disciples falsely assumed "that the kingdom of God would appear there immediately." Jesus had to correct that notion at once.

The parable of the coins illustrates the importance of living for God in the "here and now." It reminds us of the importance of how we spend our resources in this life. How we live in the "here and now" affects how we will live in the "then and there."

The parable also reminds us not to be too concerned with "enemies" who could thwart the reign of God in our lives. They are God's problem, not ours.

The parable ends with the words, "Now as for those enemies of mine who did not want me as their king, bring them here and slay them before me." They really are not our enemies, but God's enemies. We are not to be diverted by their tactics.

Lord Jesus, help me to live in a more focused way today. Help me to use the gifts you have given me and not to be concerned with matters of timing or of opposition. These matters are your concern. Alleluia!

Thursday, November 18, 1999
Dedication of the Churches of Peter and Paul;
St. Rose Philippine Duchesne
Luke 19, 45-48
The Lament for Jerusalem

Hemmed in! Encircled!

Jesus wept over Jerusalem because he knew that a time was coming when Jerusalem would be encircled and hemmed in by enemies. Jerusalem would be destroyed for failing to recognize the time of the visitation of Christ.

Hemmed in! Encircled!

The psalmist describes another way of being hemmed in and encircled:

"Behind me and before, you hem me in
    and rest your hand upon me
(Psalm 139, 5, The New American Bible, 1970 edition)."

"Behind and before you encircle me
    and rest your hand upon me
(Psalm 139, 5, The New American Bible, 1991 edition)."

Lord Jesus, I want to be encircled by you alone and to be hemmed in by you alone. Help me to recognize the time of your visitation in my life and to know what makes for peace in my life. Alleluia!

Friday, November 19, 1999
Luke 19, 45-48
The Cleansing of the Temple

One of my relatives in Texas is a Methodist minister. He is a beloved pastor, a poet, and a rope-jumper!

Recently he said that he had always thought that we worshipped only one God. That being the case, he asked, what about the "howling multitude" within our very selves? I knew what he meant.

In today's Gospel, we read of Jesus confronting the merchants and money changers in the Temple area, in the court of the Gentiles. He told them, "My house shall be a house of prayer, but you have made it a den of thieves."

There is a "howling multitude" and a "den of thieves" within me even as I worship the one true God. Although modern psychology tells us to accept our dark side and to embrace our "shadow," we also have to make a daily decision. Will the inner "howling multitude" rule and reign in our lives or will God rule and reign?

Lord Jesus, I acknowledge the "howling multitude" and the "den of thieves" within my heart. Still, you are greater than my heart. "God is greater than our hearts and knows everything (1 John 3, 20)." Cleanse my heart today. "Create in me a clean heart, O God; and renew a right spirit within me. (Psalm 51, 10, K.J.V.)." Alleluia!

Saturday, November 20, 1999
Luke 20, 27-40
The Question about the Resurrection

To God, all people are alive! Today's Gospel is a Gospel of life.

The Sadducees, the elite priestly party from Jerusalem, did not believe in the resurrection of the dead. As the old joke goes, that is why they were "sad, you see!"

Jesus listened to their hypothetical question, also known as a trap, and went to the heart of the matter. The heart of the matter was life.

Jesus redirected their thinking from improbable earthly scenarios to heavenly realities. The heavenly reality is that, to God, "all are alive."

Jesus met the Sadducees on their own turf. Since they accepted only the teaching of the first five books of the Hebrew scriptures, Jesus limited his response to the passage about Moses and the burning bush. "That the dead will rise even Moses made known in the passage about the bush, when he called 'Lord' the God of Abraham, the God of Isaac, and the God of Jacob; and he is not the God of the dead, but of the living, for to him all are alive (Luke 20, 37, 38)."

Lord Jesus, today please lift from me undue concerns about this earthly life and remind me that I will live with you forever and ever. Alleluia!

Sunday, November 21, 1999 Christ the King
Matthew 25, 31-46
The Judgment of the Nations

Jesus said to the righteous, "... whatever you did for the least of these brothers of mine, you did for me." He gave examples, such as feeding the hungry and thirsty, clothing the naked, caring for the sick, and visiting prisoners, within the term "whatever."

I can't turn on and off the attitude of seeing and hearing Christ in each person around me. I can't stuff an offering in the poor box at church one minute and then slam the phone down on a pesky phone solicitor later that same day. That's no way to treat others for whom Christ died. At least I can try to be courteous.

I can't pray piously while driving in the solitude of my car and then think vicious thoughts about the rude driver in the next lane. That's no way to think about others for whom Christ died.

Lord Jesus, transform my whole attitude to others and let my actions express your love and your concern for them. Alleluia!

Monday, November 22, 1999 St. Cecilia
Luke 21, 1-4
The Poor Widow's Contribution

Jesus, observing people giving money into the Temple treasury, said that the wealthy people "all made offerings from their surplus wealth," but that the poor widow, "from her poverty, has offered her whole livelihood."

Jesus looks deeply into our hearts and into our lives. What do we offer God and how do we make our offering?

Do we offer God our entire lives? Do we ask God to stay out of certain areas of our lives?

Once, after flying to an ecumenical conference in another area, I took a walk in the woods surrounding the conference center. There was an outdoor chapel, with an altar and a few benches nearby.

As I approached the chapel, I was startled to see one of the women from the conference lying on the altar! Having spoken with her earlier, I knew that she was experiencing a crisis in her life. Clearly, she had placed herself, literally, on the altar offering her entire being to God.

Lord Jesus, thank you for you patience with me as I grow in my ability to trust you and to offer myself to you. Alleluia!

Tuesday, November 23, 1999
St. Clement I, St. Columban, and Bl. Miguel Agustin Pro
Luke 21, 5-11
The Destruction of the Temple Foretold; The Signs of the End

"All this that you see here -- the days will come when there will not be left a stone upon another stone that will not be thrown down." Jesus was reminding the disciples not to become so fixated on the temporal.

The reference in today's Gospel was to the Temple in Jerusalem. Jesus said that the magnificent Temple was not indestructible and was not permanent.

Jesus also warned against being deceived by imposters. There will be many who come in his name spouting "messages" that are not from God. Jesus said, "Do not follow them!" He also said, "... do not be terrified."

Lord Jesus, as we look upon so much destruction and confusion around us, help us to remember your words, "...do not be terrified." Our final destiny is not here, but in the heavenly Jerusalem. Alleluia!

Wednesday, November 24, 1999
St. Andrew Dung-Lac and Companions
Luke 21, 12-19
The Coming Persecution

"It will lead to your giving testimony." Jesus warns his followers that they will be persecuted because they bear his name. This will be a unique opportunity to give testimony to the Lord.

Everything in our lives leads to our giving testimony. We are testifying with our words, our silences, and our actions about our relationship with Jesus.

Jesus tells his followers, "Remember, you are not to prepare your defense beforehand, for I myself shall give you a wisdom in speaking that all your adversaries will be powerless to resist or refute." When we give testimony, we may not be eloquent or polished. That doesn't matter. What matters is that we speak from our heart what Jesus wants us to speak.

The great promise is that "by your perseverance you will secure your lives." When we resist the temptation to compromise the truth, we receive our very lives. Regardless of what awaits us in this passing world, we are safe forever with Jesus.

Lord Jesus, help me to give testimony to you today. Alleluia!

Thursday, November 25, 1999 Thanksgiving Day
Luke 21, 20-28
The Great Tribulation; The Coming of the Son of Man

At Jesus' Ascension, "... he was lifted up, and a cloud took him from their sight (Acts 1, 9)." Naturally, those on the ground were staring up into the sky. They were told, "This Jesus who has been taken up from you into heaven will return in the same way as you have seen him going into heaven (Acts 1, 11)."

Today's Gospel tells us about our Lord's return to earth. Jesus, Son of Man and Son of God, will return "... in a cloud with power and great glory (Luke 21, 27)."

We are to live, not in fear, but in joyful anticipation! When frightening events are multiplying around us, we are to remember the words of Jesus. "But when these signs begin to happen, stand erect and raise your heads because your redemption is at hand."

Lord Jesus, help me to look beyond the clouds of today and see you coming in glory. Alleluia!

Friday, November 26, 1999
Luke 21, 29-33
The Lesson of the Fig Tree

Jesus said, "Heaven and earth will pass away, but my words will not pass away." I'm reminded of God's words spoken through the prophet Isaiah,

> "My word is like the snow and
>   the rain
> that come down from the sky
>   to water the earth.
> They make the crops grow
>   and provide seed for planting
>   and food to eat.
> So also shall be the word that I speak --
> it will not fail to do what I

306

plan for it;
   it will do everything I send it to do
(Isaiah 55, 10-11 (GNT), Today's English Version)."

Jesus himself is the living Word. "In the beginning was the Word, and the Word was with God, and the Word was God (John 1, 1 K.J.V.)."

Lord Jesus, instead of becoming distracted over the many symbolic and literal interpretations of the "fig tree" lesson, help me to concentrate on listening to you, the living Word, and obeying your word to me today. Alleluia!

Saturday, November 27, 1999
Luke 21, 34-36
Exhortation to be Vigilant

Jesus said, "Beware that your hearts do not become drowsy ..." Jesus is always looking into our hearts.

Sometimes we are outwardly doing all the "right" things, but within the secret recesses of our heart, we have become dull, listless, dispirited, and perhaps even despairing. Jesus knows all about this condition.

No one will escape from the "day" mentioned in the Gospel. "For that day will assault everyone who lives on the face of the earth."

Lord Jesus, I lift up my heart to you. You see what needs to be healed, changed, forgiven, and renewed within my heart so that I may be vigilant and stand before you on "that day." Help me to cooperate with the corrective work of the Holy Spirit in my heart. Alleluia!

Sunday, November 28, 1999 First Sunday of Advent, Year B
Mark 13, 33-37
Need for Watchfulness

Watch. "Be watchful! Be alert! Your do not know when the time will come."

Jesus is coming! Jesus placed us "in charge, each with his work" when he left earth to return to his Father in heaven. Jesus will return to earth one day and expects to find us doing the specific task entrusted to us.

Begin today! If there is something you believe the Lord wants you to do, take the first step in doing it. Let the Lord work out the details.

Some years ago, I felt called to a particular task which involved a bit of memorization. It seemed so unlikely that I would ever have a "use" for it. I'm sorry to say that I did it in a puzzled, halfhearted way.

Then, suddenly, I was called upon in a situation in ministry to have this information on my lips as well as in my heart. With a certain amount of chagrin, I had to refer to the printed page. It did work out, but I had neglected my task. My unbelief got in the way of my obedience to the Lord's word to memorize.

Dear Lord Jesus, forgive me. Help me this day and every day to trust you and to do everything you call me to do whether I understand it or not. Help me to be ready next time. Alleluia!

Monday, November 29, 1999 Advent Weekday
Matthew 8, 5-11
The Healing of a Centurion's Servant

The servant of a military officer, a centurion, was "paralyzed" and "suffering dreadfully." Sometimes those for whom we pray are "paralyzed" or immobilized in their situations or mind sets. They are "suffering dreadfully" and yet are unable to find help for themselves.

When we go to Jesus on their behalf, we are the catalyst to release God's power on their behalf. No situation, no illness, no dilemma is beyond the ability of Jesus to heal.

Lord Jesus, help me not to despair as I pray for one who is "paralyzed" and is "suffering dreadfully." You are still the Healer. Lord Jesus, "only say the word ..." Alleluia!

Tuesday, November 30, 1999 St. Andrew
Matthew 4, 18-22
The Call of the First Disciples

Andrew and Peter, brothers and fishermen, were casting their nets into the Sea of Galilee when Jesus saw them and invited them to follow him. John and James, also brothers and fishermen, were mending their nets when Jesus saw them and called them to follow him.

Two sets of brothers. Four very different personality types. Casting nets. Mending nets. Jesus knew what he was doing when he called them.

As followers of Jesus, we're still casting nets and mending nets. Jesus takes us where we are and leads us to where he wants us to be in his Body on earth, the Church.

We cast our lives, our nets, out into the world and ask Jesus to use us to bring people to him. We mend nets when we care for ourselves and offer ourselves as instruments of reconciliation within the Church.

Lord Jesus, as I begin my Advent retreat, please mend me and cast me out again in the sea of your choosing. Alleluia!

Wednesday, December 1, 1999 Advent Weekday
Matthew 15, 29-37
The Healing of Many People; The Feeding of the Four Thousand

"Moving on from there Jesus walked by the Sea of Galilee, went up on the mountain, and sat down there. Great crowds came to him, having with them the lame, the blind, the deformed, the mute, and many others."

Moving on. Jesus had just come from the region of Tyre and Sidon, to which he had withdrawn after another clash with the Pharisees.

In the Tyre and Sidon area, he honored the faith of a Canaanite woman by healing her daughter. It was now time to move on. He traveled from Tyre and Sidon.

Moving on. Withdrawing. Climbing mountains. Walking by the sea. Jesus moved around, that's for sure.

Wherever he went, people with needs sought him. He healed them. He fed them miraculously, as in today's Gospel, and then he moved on. At the conclusion of today's Gospel we read that "... he got into the boat and came to the district of Magadan."

The Father in heaven was guiding and directing Jesus during every step of his mission to earth. Over and over, especially in John's Gospel, this is made very clear. "I came down from heaven not to do my own will but the will of the one who sent me. (John 6, 38)."

As we proceed through life, we are not moving on our own. We may feel that we are moving about aimlessly, but that is not true.

As we follow Jesus, we "will not walk in darkness, but will have the light of life (John 8, 12)." The Holy Spirit is living in us and guiding us. The quiet times, the seemingly meaningless times, the times of uncertainty, and the tragic times are all being used by God.

Lord Jesus, thank you for guiding me through this day in your own way and for your own purposes. Alleluia!

Thursday, December 2, 1999 Advent Weekday
Matthew 7, 21, 24-27
The True Disciple; The Two Foundations

I remember the lines from the 1920 poem, "A Few Figs from Thistles," by Edna St. Vincent Millay,

"Safe upon the solid rock the ugly houses
    stand:
 Come and see my shining palace built upon
    the sand!"

These words are beautiful, yet simultaneously wistful and defiant.

The "shining palace" does indeed await the followers of Christ. It is called the New Jerusalem. "It gleamed with the splendor of God. Its radiance was like that of a precious stone, like jasper, clear as crystal (Revelation 21, 11)."

Meanwhile, back in this world, we would do well to heed the words of Jesus and to build the "house" of our lives on solid rock. We do this by listening to and acting on his words.

Why bother listening to homilies, tapes, compact discs, and conference speakers and never putting our knowledge into practice? Jesus said, "Everyone who listens to these words of mine but does not act on them will be like a fool who built his house on sand (Matthew 7, 26)." Jesus also warned, "Not everyone who says to me, 'Lord, Lord,' will enter the kingdom of heaven, but only the one who does the will of my Father in heaven (Matthew 7, 21)."

Lord Jesus, help to believe your word to me today and to act on your word. Alleluia!

Friday, December 3, 1999 St. Francis Xavier
Matthew 9, 27-31
The Healing of the Blind Man

As the Gospel begins, we see Jesus leaving the house of a synagogue official. Although the official's young daughter had already died, he still came to Jesus for help.

Jesus followed him home, got rid of the noisy crowd of mourners, and then life happened! When Jesus took her hand, the young girl arose. Life!

310

As Jesus left this house, two blind men pursued him, addressing him as "Son of David," their way of acknowledging him as Messiah. They cried out for mercy.

Jesus asked them, "Do you believe that I can do this?" He knew that the plea for mercy was a plea for compassion and healing. At their "yes," he touched their eyes and said, "Let it be done for you according to your faith."

Lord Jesus, have mercy on me. Open my eyes to see as you see. Alleluia!

Saturday, December 4, 1999 St. John of Damascus
Matthew 9, 35-10:1, 6-8
The Compassion of Jesus; The Mission of the Twelve;
The Commissioning of the Twelve

"Raise the dead." Jesus sent out his twelve disciples with a message to proclaim, "The kingdom of heaven is at hand." The disciples were further instructed, "Cure the sick, raise the dead, cleanse lepers, drive out demons."

Some time ago, a friend was praying for me and believed the Lord was saying to her, "I will bring Janis back to life." I had survived a crushing, devastating experience. As a result, I learned a lot about lambs, wolves, shepherds and hirelings. Although I was physically alive, inside I seemed "dead." Something within me seem to have died.

Jesus looked with compassion on the people around him and "healed their bruised and hurt lives (Matthew 9, 36, The Message)." He then instructed his disciples to continue his work of bringing life. "He gave them power to tenderly care for the bruised and hurt lives (Matthew 10, 1 The Message)."

On this first Saturday in Advent, let us be open to being sent out into the harvest field. There are many who are in need of healing, resurrection, forgiveness, and liberation.

Come, Lord Jesus. Heal us, raise us to new life, forgive us and free us to go into the fields of harvest. Alleluia!

Sunday, December 5, 1999 Second Sunday of Advent
Mark 1, 1-8
The Preaching of John the Baptist

"John the Baptist was in the desert, proclaiming a baptism of repentance for the forgiveness of sins. All Judea and all the people of Jerusalem made their way to him, and as they were baptised by him in the river Jordan they confessed their sins (Mark 1, 4, 5 The New Jerusalem Bible)."

This is amazing! All the people in Judea and Jerusalem confessed their sins in John's presence and all were baptized. ALL! There must have been an extraordinary quality about John for all these people to come to him, a stranger in the desert, and to confess their sins in his presence.

God had carefully prepared him for his ministry. John's ministry was to prepare God's people to meet Jesus and to offer water baptism, "a baptism of repentance for the forgiveness of sins." Jesus would be the one to baptize with the Holy Spirit and with fire.

People may not come up to you every day to confess their sins and to ask to be baptized. Or, do they?

Every day you hear people saying all kinds of things in your presence. Every day you have an opportunity to help prepare people to meet Jesus for themselves.

You have the privilege of interceding for each person who crosses your path. You have the opportunity to speak the words which will carry them one step closer to Jesus.

You may be the only "Bible" they ever read. You may be the only "Jesus" they ever meet.

Lord Jesus, you choose each of us to prepare your way for those in our midst. We may not be in the desert wearing camel's hair clothing and eating locusts and wild honey. We may live in the city, in the country, by the ocean, or in the suburbs. We may wear business suits, flowered frocks, or faded jeans. We may be sustained by a double mocha latte rather than by a locust. Lord Jesus, you don't judge us by our exterior. You look deeply into our hearts. Then you send us people who need you. Thank you for trusting us. Alleluia!

312

Monday, December 6, 1999 St. Nicholas
Luke 5, 17-26
The Healing of a Paralytic

As Jesus was teaching, "... the power of the Lord was with him for healing." The Holy Spirit was clearly directing and orchestrating the agenda of Jesus. All the Pharisees and legal experts, the big cheeses of the religious establishment, were there that day.

Someone else, however, was also there. The paralytic man was there. Since he could not even get there on his own, his resourceful friends had brought him. Unable to get through the crowd, they had to find another way, through the roof!

As Jesus was teaching, "... the power of the Lord was with him for healing." Jesus took note of the man right under his nose. He stopped teaching. Acknowledging the gutsy faith of the paralytic's friends, he spoke to the man himself, "As for you, your sins are forgiven." It was clear that "... the power of the Lord was with him for healing."

The Pharisees and teachers had just seen a live, on-site demonstration of the power of Jesus and the relationship of Jesus with God the Father. Instead of rejoicing at the awesome power of Jesus to forgive sins, they believed that Jesus was speaking blasphemies.

"Who but God alone can forgive sins?" was the question the Pharisees and the teachers were asking. Jesus addressed them, " 'But that you may know that the Son of Man has authority on earth to forgive sins' -- he said to the man who was paralyzed, 'I say to you, rise, pick up your stretcher, and go home.' "

Lord Jesus, I am bold to ask you that your power for healing be with me today. Alleluia!

Tuesday, December 7, 1999 St Ambrose
Matthew 18, 12-14
The Parable of the Lost Sheep

Jesus said, "... it is not the will of your heavenly Father that one of these little ones be lost." He also said, "See that you do not despise one of these little ones, for I say to you that their angels in heaven always look upon the face of my heavenly Father (Matthew 18, 10)."

Whom do you consider a "little one" in your life? Is there anyone you consider insignificant? Someone in your family who is considered an embarrassment? Someone you would never dream of consulting? Someone you consider inferior?

We may consider such a person a "little one," not worthy of our respect, time or attention. Our Father in heaven sees this person in a different way. It is not the will of our Father that a single of these "little ones" be lost.

Lord Jesus, you continually search for those who stray. Thank you that when I stray and wander off into despair or frustration, you search for me, find me, and rejoice over me. Alleluia!

Wednesday, December 8, 1999 The Immaculate Conception
Luke 1, 26-38
Announcement of the Birth of Jesus

Mary was greeted by the angel Gabriel as "favored one." She was told, "Do not be afraid, Mary, for you have found favor with God."

God clearly favored Mary. Indeed, God specifically selected Mary for this unique vocation.

Through the messenger Gabriel, God gently reassured this young Jewish teenager that the Holy Spirit would be the explanation of her motherhood. Mary was given further reassurance that her older relative, Elizabeth, had also experienced a divine intervention in her life.

Have you ever considered the fact that God clearly favors you for the vocation to which he is calling you? Perhaps you have only recently understood the nature of your vocation.

Perhaps you are already walking in the fullness of your vocation. Mary's vocation was "impossible." Perhaps the vocation to which God is calling you is "impossible." Be encouraged, for "... nothing will be impossible for God."

Lord Jesus, thank you for being the explanation of "impossible" vocations. Alleluia!

Thursday, December 9, 1999 Advent Weekday
Matthew 11, 11-15
Jesus' Testimony to John

The kingdom of heaven is where the action is! "All the prophets and the law prophesied up to the time of John." John the Baptist did indeed go before Jesus "in the spirit and power of Elijah (Luke 1, 17)."

According to Jesus, "... if you are willing to accept it, he (John the Baptist) is Elijah, the one who is to come."

What about that puzzling statement, "from the days of John the Baptist until now, the kingdom of heaven suffers violence, and the violent are taking it by force?" What in the world does that mean? Flannery O'Connor even wrote a novel called The Violent Bear It Away.

There are some who want the kingdom without acknowledging the total authority of the King. They want to be in on the action, but they are operating only in the limited realm of the human, not in the spacious realm of the spirit. They try to "take the Kingdom" by force.

It is necessary first of all to surrender to the King. The King will make sure we are included in the action of the kingdom.

Lord Jesus, purify our hearts for kingdom living. Alleluia!

Friday, December 10, 1999 Advent Weekday
Matthew 11, 16-19
Jesus' Testimony to John

A kingdom (kingdom of God!) mind set is the minimum requirement for entering into today's Gospel, which is a continuation of Jesus' description of the vocation of John the Baptist. It is essential to remember that "all the people who listened, including the tax collectors, and who were baptized with the baptism of John, acknowledged the righteousness of God; but the Pharisees and scholars of the law, who were not baptized by him, rejected the plan of God for themselves (Luke 7, 29-30)."

There are some people you not only can't please, but with whom it is very difficult to communicate. They are determined to hold onto their preconceived notions, even when confronted by the truth.

It is a waste of time to try to explain or to defend your beliefs to them. Back off. Wait. Remember the words of Jesus, that "wisdom is vindicated by her works."

Lord Jesus, you compared your generation to contrary children in the marketplace. They were peevish and ungrateful no matter what choices were offered to them. They criticized John for his asceticism and they criticized you for your open enjoyment of life. Help me to have a kingdom mind set, to enjoy this life to the full, and to fulfill your will for my life. Alleluia!

315

Saturday, December 11, 1999 St. Damasus I
Matthew 17, 10-13
The Coming of Elijah

Jesus continued to speak of the vocation of John the Baptist. "Elijah will indeed come and restore all things; but I tell you that Elijah has already come, and they did not recognize him but did to him whatever they pleased."

Restoration. Recognition.

We cry to God to "restore" us. In addition, we need to pray for eyes, ears, and hearts to "recognize" God's instruments of restoration.

Some of God's prophets, those who speak forth God's messages, are not readily recognized. Nor are their messages usually well-received.

Lord Jesus, I need restoration. I have grown weary of watching and waiting. As you strengthen me to continue waiting, please open my eyes, ears, and heart to recognize any prophets you may send across my path today. Alleluia!

Sunday, December 12, 1999 Third Sunday in Advent
John 1, 6-8, 19-28
Prologue; John the Baptist's Testimony to Himself

"Who are you?" "What are you ...?" "Who are you?" The hostile priests and Levites had traveled from Jerusalem to question, indeed to grill, John the Baptist.

John knew very clearly who he was and who he was not. He knew how to respond to these guardians of the faith, some of whom were jealous, insecure, and threatened.

"John answered them, 'I baptize with water, but there is one among you whom you do not recognize ...'" John testified to himself as "the voice crying out in the desert" with the mandate to "make straight the way of the Lord."

"There is one among you whom you do not recognize." As we continue our Advent journey, let us pray to recognize who we are!

We are indeed the "children of God" if we have accepted Jesus and "believe in his name (John 1, 12)." Our acceptance of Jesus is active! It is a "getting hold of" kind of acceptance, not merely a passive acknowledgement of the existence of Jesus.

316

Lord Jesus, help me to recognize your presence in my life and to recognize myself as a child of God. Alleluia!

Monday, December 13, 1999 St. Lucy
Matthew 21, 23-27
The Authority of Jesus Questioned

What right do you have to be here? Who do you think you are?

Satan delights in saving his choice attack when we are exactly where we should be and when we are doing exactly what God has called us to do. Satan loves to speak through those who should be speaking for God, but who are, instead, the enemies of God.

Jesus was in "the sacred enclosure of the temple (Matthew 21, 23 The Amplified Bible)." He had every right to be there.

Remember how Satan tested and tempted Jesus in the desert? He tempted Jesus to question his identity. "If you are the Son of God, command that these stones become loaves of bread (Matthew 4, 3)." "If you are the Son of God, throw yourself down (Matthew 4, 6)."

If. If. If.

Satan tempted Jesus to doubt his identity. In today's Gospel, the religious authorities, zealous and jealous guardians of what they perceived to be "their" faith and "their" power, challenged Jesus by questioning his authority.

Jesus had an answer for Satan and he had an answer for the chief priests. He countered Satan's deviously quoted Scripture with correctly quoted Scripture.

Jesus countered the chief priests' deviously posed questions with appropriately posed questions. In the first case, "... the devil left him, and behold, angels came and ministered to him (Matthew 4, 11)." In the second case, the chief priests admitted, "We do not know."

Jesus had the answer because he was a straight arrow shot directly from God. He knew who he was.

What right do you have to be here? Who do you think you are?

Remember who you are! You are God's child. You are here on this earth on God's assignment.

317

Lord Jesus, thank you reassuring me of my identity today. Alleluia!

Tuesday, December 14, 1999 St. John of the Cross
Matthew 21, 28-32
The Parable of the Two Sons

This parable portrays the tragedy as well as the glory of free will. The prostitutes and the tax-collectors were ripe for the picking. When they heard the message of John the Baptist, they believed both the message and the messenger.

The message was one which called them to repentance. The messenger, John the Baptist, as clothed in righteousness.

The chief priests and elders, on the other hand, were not ripe for the picking. They were not only green with envy over the ministry of Jesus, but they were also shriveled in spirit.

They had lived a lie for so long that they refused truth even when Truth was standing before them. They had refused to believe John and now they refused to believe Jesus.

Lord Jesus, no wonder you wept over Jerusalem. "Jerusalem, Jerusalem, you who kill the prophets and stone those sent to you, how many times I yearned to gather your children together, as a hen gathers her young under her wings, but you were unwilling (Matthew 23, 37)." Help me to be willing to do the work you have asked of me today. Alleluia!

Wednesday, December 15, 1999 Advent Weekday
Luke 7, 18-23
The Messengers from John the Baptist

John the Baptist was in prison, no doubt wondering if he had correctly heard from God . After all, he had fulfilled his mission and was then tossed into prison!

John told two of his followers to go to Jesus and inquire, "Are you the one who is to come, or should we look for another?" Wouldn't you have asked the same question?

Jesus did not rebuke John or his disciples for needing reassurance. Jesus was in the midst of ministry when this question was posed.

John's disciples carefully watched Jesus in action. "At that time he cured many of their diseases, sufferings, and evil spirits; he also granted sight to many who were blind." Jesus then told John's followers to return. "Go and tell John what you have seen and heard: the blind regain their sight, the lame walk, lepers are cleansed, the deaf hear, the dead are raised, the poor have the good news proclaimed to them."

Then there was the clincher as Jesus added "... blessed is the one who takes no offense at me." In other words, Jesus was saying that he was going to fulfill his ministry in a certain way.

We may not understand his way, but we will be happier if we accept and embrace his way. This is another way of saying to yield to God's plan for our lives.

When we wonder if we're really hearing from God, we will be given the answer. We're not to be shaken by the package in which the answer is enclosed.

Lord Jesus, thank you for your reassurance today. Alleluia!

Thursday, December 16, 1999 Advent Weekday
Luke 7, 24-30
Jesus' Testimony to John

Only you, because of your free will, can thwart God's plans and purposes for your life. Other people, no matter how much they try, cannot do that forever.

If you continue to cooperate with God, there may be setbacks and there may be delays, but eventually you and God will win! God is in the delays. God is in the detours. It will all be worth the wait.

The Pharisees and the legal scholars, alas, rejected God's redemptive plan for them. They refused to acknowledge their sins, to repent, and to be baptized.

God did not haul them off by remote control and dunk them in the Jordan River for baptism. He let them alone. He allowed them to refuse his plan of redemption.

When we accept God's plan for our lives, we are not told immediately what it will involve. All we know is that even though we may be "the least in the kingdom," we are still greater than the mighty John the Baptist! Once in the kingdom, the King will lead us and guide us to fulfill our vocation.

Lord Jesus, thank you that your will for my life will be fulfilled as I continue to trust and obey you. Alleluia!

Friday, December 17, 1999 Late Advent Weekday
Matthew 1, 1-17
The Genealogy of Jesus

The writer of this Gospel had a purpose in drawing up this particular genealogy of Jesus. The purpose was to emphasize that Jesus was in the line of King David. Jesus was the kingly Messiah!

Every person in this genealogy was used of God to prepare us for the coming of our Savior. In spite of their flaws and imperfections, these were the human instruments in God's divine plan.

When we tell others about our family, we may be tempted to stress the "important" people and leave out the ones who seem to be an embarrassment. There are no "black sheep" to God. Each person is a beloved lamb sought out by the Good Shepherd.

Lord Jesus, help me to see myself and my family tree with your eyes of compassion. Alleluia!

Saturday, December 18, 1999 Late Advent Weekday
Matthew 1, 18-24
The Birth of Jesus

Joseph had a choice. Did he marry a Jewish teenager, pregnant out of wedlock, or did he quietly dump her and "get on with his life?"

The teenage girl was Mary, his beloved, his betrothed, his promised wife. Mary was now bearing in her womb Jesus, the Son of God.

How often do we play it safe, serve our own self-interest, cut others our of our lives and then tell those we've wounded and betrayed. "Well, sorry it didn't work out. Just get on with your life."

Thank God Joseph did not do that! Thank God Joseph listened to the messenger of God and to the message of God.

God is God, but even God depends on human beings to accomplish his purpose. What if ... ?

What if Mary had refused to become the mother of Jesus? What if Joseph had refused to become the husband of Mary?

320

What if ... ? Because of God's wisdom and sovereignty, there will always be a way. God will find someone who says "yes" to an impossible vocation.

If you are following God, God will make a way for you to fulfill the vocation to which you are called. If others choose to cast you aside and then tell you to get on with your life, that's between them and God.

What about you? Keep trusting God. God's vision for you will come to birth. The "pregnancy" may be long, the "labor" may be painful, and the "birth" may be difficult, but God is faithful and has not forgotten you. The vocation to which God has called you will be fulfilled at the right time.

Lord Jesus, strengthen us to wait. Alleluia!

Sunday, December 19, 1999 Fourth Sunday in Advent
Luke 1, 26-38
Announcement of the Birth of Jesus

Mary gave herself over to the work of the Holy Trinity in her life. God the Father sent the angelic messenger, Gabriel, to announce the conception and the birth of God the Son. This "impossibility" would be accomplished through the work of God the Holy Spirit. Mary's task was simply to yield and to cooperate.

We are called to Mary's Trinitarian trust. She is our example in trusting God when everything within us and when everyone around us shouts, "Impossible!"

Through a young girl, Mary, " ... the Word was made flesh, and dwelt among us, (and we beheld his glory, the glory as of the only begotten of the Father,) full of grace and truth (John 1, 14 K.J.V.)." Jesus! Son of God. Son of Mary.

God has a "word" to speak through your life. Say "yes" today and experience for yourself that "nothing will be impossible for God."

Lord Jesus, "yes." Alleluia!

Monday, December 20, 1999 Late Advent Weekday
Luke 1, 26-38
Announcement of the Birth of Jesus

Today's Good News, the Gospel, begins, not with Santa Claus, but with an angel! The angel Gabriel is coming to the town of Nazareth.

The angel, Gabriel, is coming to make an announcement! Gabriel does not say, "Mary, I've looked over your resume. I know how politically correct you are. I know you wear designer clothes. I know you build homes for the homeless during your vacations. Therefore, because you of your personality type and your genetically correct blood type, you have been chosen for this particular career, called Messiah's Mom.

No. The angel simply greets Mary, a Jewish teenager, with the reassuring words, " 'Rejoice, you who enjoy God's favour! The Lord is with you. 'Mary, do not be afraid; you have won God's favour (Luke 1, 28, 30, The New Jerusalem Bible).' "

The angel speaks words of reassurance before making the announcement of the birth of Jesus and Mary's role in this birth. To the bewildered young girl, the angel bestows reassurance that "nothing will be impossible for God."

On this day, late in Advent, we rejoice because God is watching over us and has already sent us a Savior, Jesus, to free us to live out our lives in joy and peace. Alleluia!

Tuesday, December 21, 1999 St. Peter Canisius
Luke 1, 39-45
Mary Visits Elizabeth

Today's Gospel begins with Mary's journey to visit Elizabeth. The Gospel ends with Elizabeth's words of encouragement to Mary. "Blessed are you who believed that what was spoken to you by the Lord would be fulfilled."

In reaching out to Elizabeth, Mary received words of encouragement for herself. "Blessed are you who believed that what was spoken to you by the Lord would be fulfilled."

When God speaks to us to do or to be the "impossible," he does not leave us stranded. He gives hints, whispers, and intimations of what we are to do to cooperate with his plan. If we don't listen to his whispers, he shouts.

There may be stretches of silence between his words of encouragement. This a time for us to spin and sow in silence. God is at work and we are at work as we trust. At times, our "work" is to rest. "Blessed are you who believed that what was spoken to you by the Lord would be fulfilled." Alleluia!

322

Wednesday, December 22, 1999 Late Advent Weekday
Luke 1, 46-56
The Canticle of Mary

Mary gave herself -- body, soul (intellect, will, emotions), and spirit -- to God. She had already said "yes" to bearing in her womb the Son of the Most High. She had received Elizabeth's initial greeting, "Most blessed are you among women, and blessed is the fruit of your womb (Luke 1, 42)." Elizabeth offered additional words of encouragement. "Blessed are you who believed that what was spoken to you by the Lord would be fulfilled."

This was a time of rejoicing! "And Mary said, My soul doth magnify the Lord, and my spirit hath rejoiced in God my Saviour (Luke 1, 46, 47, K.J.V.)."

Mary was reaping the immediate first fruits of her act of total surrender to the Lord. She praised God! Without knowing all that lay ahead, Mary praised God:

"The Mighty One has done great things for me, and holy is
his name."

When we say "yes" to God, God brings our entire being (body, soul, and spirit) into proper alignment. This alignment takes place over the course of our lifetime.

As St. Paul prayed, "May the God of peace himself make you perfectly holy and may you entirely, spirit, soul, and body, be preserved blameless for the coming of our Lord Jesus Christ. The one who calls you is faithful, and he will also accomplish it (1 Thessalonians 5, 23-24)." Alleluia!

Thursday, December 23, 1999 St. John of Kanty
Luke 1, 57-66
The Birth of John

"For surely the hand of the Lord was with him [John the Baptist]." All were asking, "What, then, will this child be?"

Today's Gospel shows how God intricately engineered the circumstances leading to the birth of John the Baptist and how God was in complete control of the timing. The Gospel begins with the words, "When the time arrived for Elizabeth to have her child, she gave birth to a son." Elizabeth had waited many years for this moment.

There was the day of birth and then there was "the eighth day," the day of John's circumcision. The eighth day of the child's life was the appointed time for this ceremony.

Then there was the situation with the baby's father, the priest, Zechariah. He had been unable to speak because he did not believe the prophecy of the angel Gabriel about John's miraculous birth.

Zechariah had now seen the fulfillment of the prophecy. The baby was here! Still, Zechariah could not speak. It was eight days after John's birth, when Zechariah wrote on a tablet, "John is his name," that "immediately his mouth was opened, his tongue freed, and he spoke blessing God."

No wonder the neighbors and relatives were all asking, " 'What, then, will this child be?' For surely the hand of the Lord was with him."

The hand of the Lord is with you today. You may have waited and waited, trusted and trusted, and still you see no fulfillment. Remember the words of another who waited and waited -- Elizabeth, the aged mother of John the Baptist. Elizabeth exulted, "So has the Lord done for me at a time when he has seen fit to take away my disgrace before others (Luke 1, 25)."

Six months later, Elizabeth spoke to Mary, "Blessed are you who believed that what was spoken to you by the Lord would be fulfilled." God is with you as with Elizabeth, Zechariah, John the Baptist, and Mary. Wait. The Lord is surely with you. Alleluia!

Friday, December 24, 1999 Late Advent Weekday
Luke 1, 67-79
The Canticle of Zechariah

At last Zechariah could speak! As the angel Gabriel had prophesied, Zechariah was unable to speak until the birth of his son. A soon as Zechariah wrote the words, "John is his name, " he was able to speak. "Immediately his mouth was opened, his tongue freed, and he spoke blessing God (Luke 1, 63-64)."

The result? "Then fear came upon all their neighbors, and all these matters were discussed throughout the hill country of Judea. All who heard these things took them to heart, saying, 'What, then, will this child be?' For surely the hand of the Lord was with him (Luke 1, 65-66)."

In today's Gospel, praise flowed from the heart and mouth of Zechariah. Over nine months of silence! He had had plenty of time to ponder God's promise and to prepare what he would say after John's birth.

What an incredible spiritual exercise if, within the context of our daily lives, we could live as silently as possible for a specific period of time. No unnecessary chatting. Silence, as we contemplate God's promise to us. Alleluia!

Saturday, December 25, 1999 The Nativity of the Lord
John 1, 1-18
Prologue

The Word. Life. The light. Jesus!

Jesus. Jesus is the Word spoken by the Father. "All things came into being through him, and without him not one thing came into being. What has come into being though him was life, and the life was the light of all people. The light shines in the darkness, and the darkness did not overcome it (John 1, 3-5 N.R.S.V.)."

Jesus. "He came to what was his own, and his own people did not accept him. But to all who received him. who believed in his name, he gave power to become children of God, to those who believe in his name ... (John 1, 11-12 N.R.S.V.)."

Jesus. The Word spoken by the Father. "And the Word was made flesh, and dwelt among us, (and we beheld his glory, the glory as of the only begotten of the Father,) full of grace and truth (John 1, 14 K.J.V.)."

Jesus. When we live for Jesus, we step into all that he is. He is the Word. God then speaks through our lives.

Life. We live in God. God's life flows in us and through us.

The light. The light of Christ in us shines to those around us who dwell in darkness.

Lord Jesus Christ, thank you for coming into our world. You are the Word. Your life is our light. Shine on us today. Alleluia!

Sunday, December 26, 1999 The Holy Family
Luke 2, 22-40
The Presentation in the Temple; The Return to Nazareth

Mary and Joseph presented the infant Jesus "to the Lord." Then they returned to Nazareth to resume their daily lives.

325

Presentation. Return. This morning, as I was pondering this familiar passage, the words "presentation" and "return" stayed with me.

Mary and Joseph did not stay in the Temple and keep presenting Jesus over and over. They carefully fulfilled their obligation and then they returned home.

How often do I remain in the "presentation" part of the Gospel? Over and over I "present" the Lord with a particular prayer. Over and over I "give" it to the Lord.

Today, I realize that it's time to "return." It's time to return to my own "Nazareth" and simply live my life. I've presented my concern to the Lord. It's a done deal. He will take care of it.

Lord Jesus, thank you for the freedom to trust you and to know that you are working in my life. Alleluia!

Monday, December 27, 1999 St. John
John 20, 2-8
The Empty Tomb

What's going on here? Although we just celebrated the birth of Jesus, today's Gospel features Mary Magdalene, Peter, and John running to and from the empty tomb of the resurrected Christ.

This is the day the Church celebrates the life of St. John, apostle and evangelist. The Gospel does not name John, but simply refers to him as "the other disciple whom Jesus loved."

The Gospel, strange as it seems at Christmastide, does remind us of the road which lies ahead for Jesus. I have an unusual card which illustrates today's Gospel. The card is black and white, except for a bit of red and green holly. There is an angel in the foreground simultaneously blowing two trumpets, one red and one green. In the background, at the end of the road is a Cross. Beyond the Cross are the clouds.

Lord Jesus, thank you for walking this road ahead of us and leading us to our own Cross and resurrection. Alleluia!

Tuesday, December 28, 1999 The Holy Innocents
Matthew 2, 13-18
The Flight to Egypt; The Massacre of the Infants

Joseph's mind and heart were finely tuned to hear the voice of God. This particular message, urging Joseph to take Mary and Jesus and to flee to Egypt, was delivered to Joseph in a dream by the angel of the Lord.

That is far out! Why can't God just tell us what to do in a plain, simple way?

Listen, God is telling us what to do in a plain, simple way. Do we hear God's message? Do we recognize God's messenger?

So often we have amorphous, floaty ideas of how God should speak to us. Then we go to the other extreme and try to "make" God speak in a certain way.

Heavenly Father, you saved the life of your infant Son Jesus, by sending your message to Joseph via Angel Express! Fortunately, Joseph listened to your message and obeyed. Jesus was safely removed from the scene of the massacre of the innocent little boys. Help us to grow and to mature in our own ability to hear your voice in our lives. Thank you for filling us with the Holy Spirit and giving us the gift of discernment to recognize your voice. Alleluia!

Wednesday, December 29, 1999 St. Thomas Becket
Luke 2, 22-35
The Presentation in the Temple

The Spirit. The sign. The sword. All are part of today's Gospel.

The Spirit. The Holy Spirit was at work arranging all the circumstances for the presentation of the infant Jesus in the Temple in Jerusalem. The Holy Spirit was upon Simeon. The Holy Spirit had revealed to Simeon that the he would live to see the promised Messiah. Simeon "came in the Spirit into the Temple ..."

The sign and the sword. Simeon praised God for being allowed to live to see Jesus. Then Simeon addressed Mary. "Behold, this child is destined for the fall and the rise of many in Israel, and to be a sign that will be contradicted (and you yourself a sword will pierce) so that the thoughts of many hearts may be revealed."

Mary would be caught up in issues and dynamics with far greater ramifications than she realized. She herself would suffer greatly as Jesus, her son, lived out his vocation as a sign of contradiction.

The Spirit. The sign. The sword. Today's Gospel gives a glimpse of the glory and the grief which were to follow in the lives of Jesus, Mary, and Joseph.

The Spirit, the sign and the sword are all present in our lives today as we follow Jesus. The Holy Spirit dwells within us and guides us to complete our vocation. The more we resemble Jesus, the more the world will see us as a sign of contradiction and will attempt to silence us with the sword of its judgment.

The Spirit. The sign. The sword. Lord Jesus, thank you for inviting us to participate in these mysteries. Alleluia!

Thursday, December 30, 1999
Luke 2, 36-40
The Presentation in the Temple; The Return to Nazareth

The elderly Anna and the infant Jesus were both free and were both bound by the confines of time and place. Anna stayed in the Temple enclosure. Within the confines of the Temple, she fulfilled her prophetic vocation.

Joseph and Mary returned to Galilee, to their town of Nazareth, taking the infant Jesus with them. Within the confines of Nazareth, Jesus "grew and became strong, filled with wisdom, and the favor of God was upon him."

The Temple enclosure. The town of Nazareth. It was within these respective confines that both Anna and Jesus flourished.

Sometimes we chafe and say, "Why do I have to be here? I wish I could be somewhere else."

Indeed, God may at some time take us "somewhere else." For today, however, let us seek to do God's will where we are.

Let us accept ourselves and our circumstances. God is our enclosure. We are enclosed in God and God chooses to be enclosed in us. We are safe in God's loving embrace to flourish and to become strong and wise. Alleluia!

Friday, December 31, 1999 St. Sylvester I
John 1, 1-1
Prologue

The beginning! John's Gospel begins with the beautiful prologue which tells us that Jesus was there in the beginning with God the Father. Jesus came into our world bringing life, light, grace, and truth.

There is a card by the artist Mary Englebreit of a little girl wearing one of those sandwich board signs. This sign, instead of saying, "The End is Near!" says, "The Beginning is Near!"

Today a new beginning is near for you and for me. We have light, life, grace and truth within us as baptized Christians. Do we access these gifts?

What is our deepest need? Since "grace and truth came through Jesus Christ," all we need to do is to tap into this treasure house within us!

We don't have to wring our hands and phone all our friends to pray for us. Prayer is wonderful, but we can tap into the treasures of light, life, grace and truth, for ourselves. Jesus, our greatest treasure, has given us the Holy Spirit to live within us.

Rejoice! The beginning is near! We are beginning a brand-new level in our relationship with Jesus. He is filling us with his life, his light, his grace, and his truth. Alleluia!

Saturday, January 1, 2000 Mary, Mother of God
Luke 2, 16-21
The Visit of the Shepherds

The angel of the Lord appeared to the shepherds in the fields with a startling, yet joyful, message. "For today in the city of David a savior has been born for you who is Messiah and Lord. And this will be a sign for you: you will find an infant wrapped in swaddling clothes and lying in a manger."

The shepherds took this message and literally ran with it! Today's Gospel tells us that they "went in haste and found Mary and Joseph and the infant lying in the manger."

The shepherds then made known the message that had been told them about this child. All who heard this news marveled.

329

Having fulfilled their mission, the shepherds returned to their fields and to their flocks. They returned to their "day jobs." which, for shepherds, included keeping watch at night also. They returned, " … glorifying and praising God for all that they had heard and seen, just as it had been told to them."

There is a role for each of us to play in this life. We may wonder what it is. We may know what it is, but the time has yet come for its fulfillment. We continue to pray and trust and wait in joyful expectation.

We have do to our part and be ready. As Shakespeare said, "If it be now, 'tis not to come; if it be not to come, it will be now; if it be not now, yet it will come: the readiness is all (<u>Hamlet</u>, V, ii, 232)."

When the right time comes, remember the shepherds. Take the message and run with it. It is your turn at last! Alleluia!

Sunday, January 2, 2000 Epiphany
Matthew 2, 1-12
The Visit of the Magi

The magi were looking for Jesus and I was looking for a tiny scrap of paper which I had misplaced. The magi rejoiced when they saw the star and found the child. After dashing around the house and searching diligently, I too rejoiced at finding this little paper!

Several weeks ago at Mass, the third Sunday in Advent, 1999, to be precise, there were baskets near the doors of the church. The priest who was presiding at this liturgy had thoughtfully placed copies of a poem which he had quoted in his homily.

This is the poem which was quoted on an Iranian Christmas card:

"If, as with Herod,
   we fill our lives with things;
      and again with things;
   if we consider ourselves
      so important
   that we must fill every
      moment
      of our lives
      with action,
   when will we have the time
      to make the long, slow
      journey
   across the burning desert

330

as did the Magi?
or sit and watch the stars
    as did the shepherds?
or brood over the coming
    of the child -- as did Mary?

For each of us
    there is a desert to travel
A star to discover
    And a being within ourselves
    to bring to life."

Herod could not stop the plan of God. He could not prevent the magi from fulfilling their mission, nor could he could manipulate the magi to fulfill his own evil plan.

It was God who was guiding each person in this drama to fulfill a specific role. Mary, Joseph, the shepherds, and the magi listened to God and accepted God's invitation.

There is a "being within ourselves" crying out for God. There is a desert in our lives which sooner or later we all have to travel.

Lord Jesus, I feel discouraged at the length of time I've been in the "desert." Will I ever get out? Will the "being" within me ever be born? Thank you for helping me to find this poem today. Thank you for sending your Holy Spirit to guide me across this desert into a new discovery. Alleluia!

Monday, January 3, 2000
Matthew 4, 12-17; 23-25
The Beginning of the Galilean Ministry;
Ministering to a Great Multitude

The prophet Isaiah referred to "the people who sit in darkness" in the land of Zebulun and Naphtali. Jesus left Nazareth and moved to Capernaum by the sea to be with these very people.

"The land of Zabulon, and the land of Nephthalim [Napthali], by the way of the sea, beyond Jordan, Galilee of the Gentiles; The people which sat in darkness saw great light; and to them which sat in the region and shadow of death light is sprung up (Matthew 4, 15-16, K.J.V.)

Light had arisen for the people in darkness because Jesus was there! Jesus had moved into their midst.

331

With Jesus there, nothing was impossible. He cured "all who were sick with various diseases and racked with pain, those who were possessed, lunatics, and paralytics ..." He stressed repentance. Repent. Re-think. Think again.

When we "sit in darkness," we become paralytics of a sort. After a while in a "dark" situation, we become so accustomed to the darkness that we forget the light. Our situation seems intolerable. We become accustomed to the darkness.

Then Jesus arrives and everything changes! Jesus is light! Jesus brings light, hope, and healing to us in our darkness. His presence makes all the difference.

Very gently, Jesus takes us from the darkness to the light. He knows how to proceed with us and his timing is very deliberate. An immediate transition from darkness to bright light might be too traumatic for some. For others, it's just the remedy that's needed. Jesus knows. Alleluia!

Tuesday, January 4, 2000
Mark 6, 34 - 44
The Feeding of the Five Thousand

The people who came to Jesus had made a special effort to be there. They somehow knew where the "deserted place" was, the place where Jesus and his disciples had gone. From the nearby towns they came on foot and managed to get there before Jesus!

Jesus knew they were serious. "When he disembarked and saw the vast crowd, his heart was moved with pity for them, for they were like sheep without a shepherd; and he began to teach them many things."

God lamented, through the prophet Hosea, "My people perish for want of knowledge (Hosea 4, 6)." This was an indictment against the priests for not properly fulfilling their high calling.

In today's Gospel, Jesus, filled with compassion for the weary multitude who had gone out their way to find him, "began to teach them many things." The miracle of the multiplied loaves and fish was secondary to the ministry of teaching.

What does Jesus want to teach us today? Are we willing to go out of our way to spend time listening to Jesus?

Lord Jesus, you have the words to feed my spirit today. You have the words to sustain me on this journey. Help me today to learn to listen to you. "I will hear what the LORD God will speak; for he will speak peace unto his people …. (Psalm 85, 8, K.J.V.)." Alleluia!

Wednesday, January 5, 2000
Mark 6, 45-52
The Walking on the Water

Jesus insisted that his disciples get into the boat without him. As was his habit, he sought a time and place for solitude and for prayer.

No one can minister effectively without time alone with God. Even this time with God loses its balm if it is overstuffed with particular prayers. Pray this prayer, do this, do that, blah, blah, blah. The whole thing can degenerate into a obsessive-compulsive exercise in legalism. This is not what the Lord wants!

Silence. Stillness. This is not self-indulgence. This is sanity.

In my days of busy hospital ministry, I learned to find ways to take mini-retreats. Walking from one unit of the hospital to another, I might climb an extra flight of stairs and step onto the roof terrace for a moment of solitude. Another time I might sit for a moment in a breezy passageway between two buildings or slip into a tiny chapel which was hardly bigger than a closet.

Yes, Jesus cared about his disciples. Yes, he deliberately watched the wind toss them about while he stayed on shore. Yes, he went to them in their distress and reassured them. "Take courage, it is I, do not be afraid."

In our efforts to "minister" to people, sometimes we exhaust ourselves and keep others from maturing. There may be pride lurking under what we call "ministry." The best thing we can do for ourselves and for others is to take care of ourselves first. This is true humility. Alleluia!

Thursday, January 6, 2000 Blessed Andre Bessette
Luke 4, 14-22
The Beginning of the Galilean Ministry

"Jesus returned to Galilee in the power of the Spirit, and news of him spread throughout the whole region." Jesus had recently experienced a powerful encounter with the Holy Spirit.

"After Jesus was baptized, he came up from the water and behold, the heavens were opened [for him], and he saw the spirit of God descending like a dove [and] coming upon him. And a voice came from the heavens, saying, 'This is my beloved Son, with whom I am well-pleased (Matthew 3, 16-17).' "

"Filled with the holy Spirit, Jesus returned from the Jordan and was led by the Spirit into the desert for forty days to be tempted by the devil (Luke 4, 1-2a)." Repeatedly, Jesus countered the devil's temptations by saying, "It is written." Jesus knew the Hebrew Scriptures and knew which part to quote to frustrate, foil, and defeat the devil's machinations.

Jesus returned "in the power of the Spirit" to Galilee, to his own town of Nazareth. During his temptation in the desert, he had experienced the power of speaking aloud the written word of God.

It was now time to proclaim Scripture in his home town synagogue. "The Spirit of the Lord is upon me, because he hath anointed me to preach the gospel to the poor; he hath sent me to heal the broken-hearted, to preach deliverance to the captives, and recovering of sight to the blind, to set at liberty them that are bruised, To preach the acceptable year of the Lord (Luke 4, 18-19 K.J.V.)."

Jesus then announced to the startled congregation, "Today this scripture passage is fulfilled in your hearing." Jesus himself was the fulfillment of this prophecy!

Jesus knew his Father in heaven, he knew the Scriptures, and he knew his own identity. His commission to minister came directly from his Father.

Our commission to minister was given to us at our baptism. We are filled with the Holy Spirit, the same Holy Spirit who empowered Jesus. Let us step out today, trusting in the power of the Holy Spirit to work in us and through us. The Holy Spirit works wonderfully! Alleluia!

Friday, January 7, 2000 St. Raymond of Penyafort
Luke 5, 12-16
The Cleansing of a Leper

In an instant, Jesus accomplished what would have been a complicated eight day process of purification. This process for the cleansing of a leper is described in detail in Leviticus 14, 2-32.

Jesus still required the man he had cleansed to go to the priest and offer what Moses had prescribed. There needed to be legal "proof" of the man's healing in order for him to be accepted again in his community

334

When Jesus performs a "miracle" in our life, the miracle is not only for us. It is for those around us, also, to see God's mighty power. Alleluia!

Saturday, January 8, 2000
John 3, 22-30
Final Witness of the Baptist

Boundaries. We hear this word a lot today. It usually refers to relationships.

John the Baptist was keenly aware of the boundaries of his own life and work. He was firmly rooted in the reality of his mission. He knew he was not the Messiah. His role was to prepare the way for Jesus, the Messiah, God's Anointed One.

Jesus was the Bridegroom sent from heaven to win for himself a holy Bride, the Church. John was the "best man," the one who was there to stand by Jesus, the Bridegroom. John himself proclaimed, "... this joy of mine has been made complete. He [Jesus] must increase; I must decrease."

We have boundaries in our own lives which we must respect. In our thought lives, we need to stay within the boundaries of trust in God and obedience to God. If we push out of this safety zone, we enter a war zone of fear and torment.

Lord Jesus, let our joy be made complete as we live and love within the safe boundaries which you, in your wisdom, have designated for us. Alleluia!

Sunday, January 9, 2000 Baptism of the Lord
Mark 1, 7-11
The Preaching of John the Baptist; The Baptism of Jesus

All ministry that is true ministry requires knowing one's identity. Only this kind of ministry transforms lives.

Jesus was firmly and deeply rooted and grounded in his identity as the Son of God. As he came up from the waters of baptism, "... he saw the heavens being torn open and the Spirit, like a dove, descending upon him. And a voice came from the heavens, 'You are my beloved Son; with you I am well pleased.' "

God has a specific plan and purpose for our lives. Accepting Jesus also means accepting ourselves as God's beloved children. It is then a matter of cooperating with the Holy Spirit to direct us.

Come Holy Spirit. Rekindle within us the knowledge of our true identity. Help us to be firmly rooted and grounded in your love for us and your favor upon us. Alleluia!

Monday, January 10, 2000
Mark 1, 14-20
The Beginning of the Galilean Ministry;
The Call of the First Disciples

"After John had been arrested, Jesus came to Galilee proclaiming the gospel of God: 'This is the time of fulfillment. The kingdom of God is at hand. Repent, and believe in the gospel.' "

Jesus said, "This is the time." John had been faithful to fulfill his mission to prepare the way for Jesus. He had been unjustly arrested and tossed into prison by the paranoid King Herod.

This was not an easy time, but it was "the" time. Time for Jesus to begin his public ministry of describing and living the Good News of just how close God really was. "Repent, and believe in the gospel." Think again and trust in the good news of what God is really like. "This is the time."

For Peter, Andrew, James, and John, it was also "the" time. Time to decide. Jesus was inviting them to go with him on another kind of fishing expedition.

In this time of Jubilee, Jesus is inviting us to accompany him. It may not be easy, but it is "the" time. Alleluia!

Tuesday, January 11, 2000
Mark 1, 21-28
The Cure of a Demoniac

The man with the unclean spirit was right there in the synagogue in Capernaum when Jesus entered. He was in the right place at the right time for being liberated by Jesus.

Jesus taught with authority and he spoke with authority. He did not bother to argue with the unclean spirit, but merely spoke the word of command. "Quiet! Come out of him!" The man who had been tormented by the foul entity was set free.

Jesus not only taught the word, he himself was the Word. "In the beginning was the Word, and the Word was with God, and the Word was God (John 1, 1 K.J.V.)."

His life lined up with his message. The people were already "astonished at his teaching, for he taught them as one having authority and not as the scribes."

After Jesus commanded the unclean spirit to leave the man, "all were amazed." "What is this? A new teaching with authority."

Lord Jesus, speak your word of authority to whatever it is within us today that needs to depart. Alleluia!

Wednesday, January 12, 2000
Mark 1, 29-39
The Cure of Peter's Mother-in-Law; Other Healings;
Jesus Leaves Capernaum

Where did Jesus live? His "home" was found in the will of his Father. He said over and over that he had not come to this earth to do his own will, but the will of his Father (John 6, 38). Jesus taught with authority, healed with authority, and drove out demons with authority, because he was acting in the authority given to him by his Father.

In today's Gospel, we see Jesus at the end of a long day in which he had taught in the synagogue, freed a man in the synagogue who had been tormented by an unclean spirit, and healed Peter's mother-in-law. In the evening, there was still work to do.

That same evening, the people of Capernaum "brought to him all who were ill or possessed by demons. The whole town was gathered at the door. He cured many who were sick with various diseases, and he drove out many demons, not permitting them to speak because they knew him."

It was time now to leave Capernaum. "Rising very early before dawn, he left and went off to a deserted place, where he prayed." This was his time to spend concentrated time "at home" with his Father. After his followers "pursued" him even to this place of private prayer, he said, "Let us go on to the nearby villages that I may preach there also. For this purpose have I come."

Wherever Jesus went, from village to village, from synagogue to synagogue, he was "at home." Being in his Father's will was his home. Doing the will of his Father was his food (John 4, 34).

337

Come, Holy Spirit, lead me as you led Jesus, to be in the center of the Father's will today, to be "at home." Alleluia!

Thursday, January 13, 2000 St. Hilary
Mark 1, 40-45
The Cleansing of a Leper

Jesus short-circuited "the process." We hear so much about "process" that we may forget that Jesus is far above all human notions of "process." He knew who he was and he knew what his vocation was.

Jesus did not come to abolish the Law, but to fulfill the Law. He touched the leper and the leper was instantly cleansed.

Still, Jesus told the man to go through the ceremonial process. As Jesus said, "that will be proof for them." The man himself did not need proof. Jesus did not need proof. The proof of the cleansing was for others, "for them."

Sometimes God requires us to go through something, not for ourselves, and not even for God, but for others, "for them." We are the proof of God's pudding.

Lord Jesus, help us to be patient with ourselves and to be patient with you when you ask us to go through something "for them." Alleluia!

Friday, January 14, 2000
Mark 2, 1-12
The Healing of a Paralytic

The four men carried their paralyzed friend to Jesus. Perhaps they had "carried" him emotionally, financially, and physically for a long time. Perhaps they were truly at their wit's end with their own resources of hard work and hard prayer dwindling.

"Unable to get near Jesus because of the crowd, they opened up the roof above him. After they had broken through, they let down the mat on which the paralytic was lying. When Jesus saw their faith, he said to the paralytic, 'Child, your sins are forgiven.' "

That was the real "miracle," the real breakthrough. Jesus then said to the paralytic, "I say to you, rise, pick up your mat, and go home."

Sometimes we reach a point at which we are unable to "carry" a person any longer. We are desperate for a breakthrough. We don't have to break through a roof to get to Jesus.

338

Jesus is already here with us. We do need to give the person we're "carrying" to Jesus and let Jesus take over from there. Jesus knows how to break through to the person's real need, whether it is forgiveness of sins, physical healing, or some other form of healing. Jesus knows.

Lord Jesus, I have been "carrying" someone in prayer for so long. This person truly seems "paralyzed" and unable to move. I relinquish this person to you. I trust you to "break through" and to bring healing. Alleluia!

Saturday, January 15, 2000
Mark 2, 13-17
The Call of Levi

It was by the sea of Galilee that Jesus saw Simon (Peter) and his brother, Andrew. He also saw James and his brother John. Jesus said, "Come after me and I will make you fishers of men (Mark 1, 17)."

In today's Gospel, "once again he went out along the sea." This time, he saw Levi, and said to him, "Follow me."

We know about Peter's human failings. We know that James and John were hotheads. Even Jesus called them "sons of thunder (Mark 3, 17)."

Levi (Matthew) was a tax collector. The tax collectors were considered the low life, the scum of the earth.

Why on earth was Jesus calling these characters to follow him? What did he see in them?

"Those who are well do not need a physician, but the sick do. I did not come to call the righteous but sinners."

Jesus walks beside us in another sea. In the waters of baptism, he calls us. "Follow me."

Jesus knows all about us. Maybe we're like Peter, always clumsy and blundering. Maybe we're like James and John, struggling with hot tempers. Maybe we're like Levi, an outcast. Jesus knows and Jesus calls us. "Follow me."

Lord Jesus, we still need you as our physician. We can't diagnose our illness, much less heal ourselves. Come today as our wise and compassionate physician and heal us. Let us follow you with joy. Alleluia!

339

Sunday, January 16, 2000 Second Sunday in Ordinary Time
John 1, 35-42
The First Disciples

Andrew was initially a disciple of John the Baptist. When John the Baptist saw Jesus and referred to Jesus as the Lamb of God, Andrew, of course, began to follow Jesus. John was simply God's instrument to point to Jesus.

Andrew then went to his brother and declared, "We have found the Messiah." Andrew took his brother to Jesus. Jesus took one look at Andrew's brother and said, "You are Simon ... you will be called Cephas (which is translated Peter).

Everyone had a role here, a crucial part to play. John the Baptist succeeded in directing his followers to Jesus. Andrew somehow knew that his brother should meet Jesus. Jesus took over from there.

Is there someone we need to take to Jesus today in prayer? Let us present this person to Jesus. Jesus will take over from there. Alleluia!

Monday, January 17, 2000 St. Anthony
Mark 2, 18-22
The Question about Fasting

The question in today's Gospel about fasting is really a question about timing. As the author of Ecclesiastes tells us, "There is an appointed time for everything ..." and God "has made everything appropriate to its time ... (Ecclesiastes 3, 1, 11a)."

Timing. It was not appropriate for the disciples of Jesus to fast while Jesus was with them during his earthly ministry.

Jesus was talking about what was proper and fitting for a particular time and situation. "No one cuts up a fine silk scarf to patch up old work clothes; you want fabrics that match. And you don't put your wine in cracked bottles (Mark 2, 21-22 The Message)."

There is "an appointed time" for everything God has planned for our lives. Our part is to cooperate with God and not to try to push or to change God's timetable. God is in charge and is arranging everything in our life to be fitting and appropriate at the correct time. Alleluia!

Tuesday, January 18, 2000
Mark 2, 23-28
The Disciples and the Sabbath

The Sabbath is God's gift to us. Jesus is in charge of the Sabbath. Jesus is Lord of the Sabbath.

In the South, where I grew up, there were strict "blue laws" about what could and could not be open on Sunday. Ray's, a convenience store, was open if you needed food. Mr. Marshall, or one of the other pharmacists, was "on call" if you needed an emergency prescription. Otherwise, the town was closed up, "tighter than Jack's hat box," as Lydia, my grandmother, would say.

Today we see people streaming into the shopping malls on the Sabbath. Once I saw a long line of teenagers waiting on Sunday morning for the opening of a popular music store. They were not lined up to get into the nearby churches which all had open doors.

Come Holy Spirit and free us to enjoy each Sabbath rest in our lives. Teach us how to rest and to play and to be recreated. Alleluia!

Wednesday, January 19, 2000
Mark 3, 1-6
The Man with a Withered Hand

Anger and grief. Jesus was able to experience both emotions at the same time.

Jesus was furious with the Pharisees for putting their rules and regulations above human suffering. At the same time, he was "grieved at their hardness of heart."

Neither emotion deterred Jesus from healing the man with the withered hand. Disregarding the hostility of the Pharisees, he said to the man, " 'Stretch out your hand' He stretched it out and his hand was restored."

Jesus was not afraid of the Pharisees. He saw right through their sham, their pretense, and their misuse of authority. Jesus ministered directly to those in need, regardless of any threat of retaliation.

Lord Jesus, when we are experiencing strong emotions, please send your Holy Spirit to direct these emotions to appropriate action. Help us to do your will regardless of the outcome. Alleluia!

Thursday, January 20, 2000
Mark 3, 7-12
The Mercy of Jesus

Jesus needed to get away during times of particular stress in his earthly ministry. In today's Gospel, "Jesus withdrew toward the sea ..." Huge crowds pursued him, seeking healing.

Huge crowds probably do not pursue us on a daily basis! Still, we need to get away. Even a tiny "retreat" refreshes us. God is our "shelter" and our "hiding place" as Psalm 32, 7 reminds us.

Lord Jesus, today, "Keep me as the apple of the eye; hide me under the shadow of thy wings ... (Psalm 17, 8, K.J.V.)." You are my retreat house. Alleluia!

Friday, January 21, 2000 St. Agnes
Mark 3, 13-19
The Mission of the Twelve

The first call is the call to transformation. Jesus called the twelve apostles first of all to "be with him."

Being with Jesus, observing him, learning to trust him and obeying him are all part of discipleship. It is necessary to be a good disciple, a good learner, before becoming an apostle and being sent out on a mission.

Ambassadors to other countries must first study and learn the language and culture of the country to which they are being sent. They must be careful at all times to represent their own country.

Our own country, our true country, is the kingdom of heaven. As the Father sent Jesus to our world, so Jesus sends us to this same world.

Before we can represent Jesus, we must know him. Getting to know Jesus requires spending time with him.

We spend time with Jesus in prayer. We immerse ourselves in the Gospels and learn how Jesus deals with people and situations. We turn to Jesus with every concern, knowing that he loves us and cares about every single detail of our lives. We are "with him."

Lord Jesus, transform us as we are with you. Send us out to represent you as you truly are. Alleluia!

Saturday, January 22, 2000 St. Vincent
Mark 3, 20-21
Blaspheming of the Scribes

"He came home." "Home," at this moment, was approximately the space between a rock and a hard place. Although this "home" was the home of one of his disciples, Jesus could not rest and relax.

The crowd made it "impossible for them even to eat." To make this crazy scene even worse, Jesus' relatives "set out to seize him, for they said, 'He is out of his mind.'"

That's it! That's the Gospel, the "Good News" for today.

Two verses. A scene of seeming chaos.

It gets worse before it gets better. I sneaked a look at Monday's Gospel, which continues on in Mark.

Back to the uncomfortable reality of today's Gospel. "He came home."

Trying to come to terms with this Gospel, I read my reflection for the Gospel for January 12. "Jesus' home was in the will of his Father." Challenging though the situation was, Jesus was in the center of God's will. He was "home."

Lord Jesus, when we can't "escape," help us to realize that we're already "home." "Now the Lord is the Spirit, and where the Spirit of the Lord is, there is freedom (2 Corinthians 3, 17)." You are here and we are free. You are here and we are "home." Alleluia!

Sunday, January 23, 2000 Third Sunday in Ordinary Time
Mark 1, 14-20
The Beginning of the Galilee Ministry;
The Call of the First Disciples

Mark has been called the "go" Gospel, or the "straightaway" Gospel. Jesus is on the move and the time is now!

John the Baptist had completed his time of active ministry of preparing the way for Jesus. Now it's Jesus' time.

In the Galilee, Jesus proclaimed, "This is the time of fulfillment. The kingdom of God is at hand. Repent, and believe in the gospel."

Your "time" is getting closer and closer. You have prepared, you have waited, you have repented, you have worked, and you have believed. It is difficult, but essential for you to stay steadfast and remain in a state of readiness. Jesus knows your "time." At the right time, he will look at you and say, "Now." Alleluia!

Monday, January 24, 2000 St. Francis de Sales
Mark 3, 22-30
Blasphemy of the Scribes; Jesus and Beelzebul

Jesus was really up against it. His relatives thought he was crazy (Mark 3, 21) and the scribes from Jerusalem thought he was demon-possessed. Jesus knew better than to try to reason with them.

Instead, Jesus "confronted their slander with a story: 'Does it make sense to send a devil to catch a devil, to use Satan to get rid of Satan (Mark 3, 23, The Message)?' " He gave the illustration of the divided kingdom doomed to failure.

Jesus then confronted the scribes directly. "Listen to this carefully. I'm warning you. There's nothing done or said that can't be forgiven. But if you persist in your slanders against God's Holy Spirit, you are repudiating the very One who forgives, sawing off the branch on which you're sitting, severing by your own perversity all connection with the One who forgives (Mark 3, 28-29, The Message)."

Thank you, Lord Jesus, that you are our defender. It is up to you to confront those who slander us . Alleluia!

Tuesday, January 25, 2000 Conversion of Paul
Mark 16, 15-18
The Commissioning of the Eleven

The risen Jesus appeared to the eleven and said, "Go into the whole world and proclaim the gospel to every creature. Whoever believes and is baptized will be saved; whoever does not believe will be condemned."

As baptized Christians, we proclaim the Gospel every day by what we say and how we live. Our responsibility is that of proclamation.

We cannot "make" anyone believe. That is the responsibility of the Holy Spirit.

Jesus said that certain "signs" would accompany believers. There is a saying that Christians do not follow signs, but that signs follow Christians.

The signs that Jesus said would accompany us are part of the discipleship package. They are there, if necessary, for our proclamation of the Gospel.

Lord Jesus, thank you for calling us and equipping us with all we need to proclaim the Good News. "For we do not preach ourselves, but Jesus Christ as Lord, and ourselves as your slaves for the sake of Jesus (2 Corinthians 4, 5)." Alleluia!

Wednesday, January 26, 2000 Sts. Timothy and Titus
Mark 4, 1-20
The Parable of the Sower; The Purpose of the Parables

If a Nobel laureate physicist was scheduled to lecture, the auditorium would probably be packed! People would come for all sorts of reasons.

Students and professors from the nearby university would be there. Locals might show up just to see a famous person. Perhaps even small children would be there.

If the physicist had only one lecture to give in this particular place, what would the content be? There would be people with all sorts of reasons for attending and with varying levels of abilities to understand the lecture.

Jesus also had a mixed audience that day by the Sea of Galilee. Because of the huge crowd, he sat in the boat as he spoke.

Jesus spoke about the sower and the seed and about the different kinds of soil. The people would receive his message according to their level of receptivity and commitment.

When we go into the world today, we ARE the message. We are the "... letter, known and read by all, shown to be a letter of Christ ... written not in ink but by the Spirit of the living God, not on tablets of stone but on tablets that are hearts of flesh (2 Corinthians 3, 2-3)."

Come Holy Spirit. Take the "letter" of our lives and speak whatever message is needed by the one who "reads" it. Alleluia!

Thursday, January 27, 2000 St. Angela Merici
Mark 4, 21-25
Parable of the Lamp

A lamp fulfills its purpose when it shines! It was not made to be hidden away. The lamp would not be fulfilling its purpose and the people in its vicinity would remain in darkness.

"For there is nothing hidden except to be made visible; nothing is secret except to come to light." The lamp is not called to be popular, but to be faithful. It is called to shine, shine, shine!

What the light of the lamp reveals is a message to those nearby. They have two choices.

They can be thankful for what the light has revealed or they can try to destroy the lamp which shed the light. Either way, the lamp has fulfilled its purpose.

Lord Jesus, shine through us today and let our lives reveal your light to everyone around us. Alleluia!

Friday, January 28, 2000 St. Thomas Aquinas
Mark 4, 26-34
Seed Grows of Itself; The Mustard Seed

Trusting and timing. Trusting is our part. Timing is God's part.

We sow the seed and trust that God is at work in the seed. We do not go to the field or garden and dig up the seed to monitor its progress.

"Of its own accord the land yields fruit, first the blade, then the ear, and then the full grain in the ear. And when the grain is ripe, he wields the sickle at once, for the harvest has come."

The mustard seed appears tiny and insignificant. "But once it is sown, it springs up and becomes the largest of plants ... so that the birds of the sky can dwell in its shade."

Holy Spirit, direct me this day how and where to sow. Take my prayers and action of this day and bring forth a harvest for your glory. Alleluia!

Saturday, January 29, 2000
Mark 4, 35-41
The Calming of a Storm at Sea

The storm at sea occurred "on that day, as evening drew on ..." This was the same day in which Jesus had been teaching the crowds by telling parables.

Jesus privately explained the purpose of the parables to his followers. Then he proceeded to tell more parables about the kingdom of God. This was the "classroom instruction."

The storm at sea occurred on this same evening. Instead of another parable about the kingdom of God, there was a surprise "field trip" on the sea.

Terrified in the midst of the storm, the disciples were convinced that they are perishing. Jesus was right there with them in the boat, but he was asleep!

When the disciples awakened him, he calmed the sea with three words. " 'Quiet. Be still!' The wind ceased and there was great calm."

Jesus knows when to take us out of the classroom and out for a field trip, not only to learn, but also to experience his power. Alleluia!

Sunday, January 30, 2000 Fourth Sunday in Ordinary Time
Mark 1, 21-28
The Cure of a Demoniac

Jesus came to set the captives free. When he walked on earth, he set the captives free, even on the Sabbath and even in the synagogue.

How many of us today need to be set free? We believe in Jesus and we try to trust him. Yet, something seems amiss. Something is holding us captive.

We've prayed. We've asked others to pray. We may received the sacrament of reconciliation and powerful words of absolution. We've forgiven those who have injured us. We have received Holy Communion. All these are powerful ways in which God reaches us and heals us.

Today, as we pray the prayer we call the Lord's Prayer, let us pray fervently that our Father will truly "deliver us from evil" and believe it! Let us receive our Lord in Holy Communion and let us live this day rejoicing. We will not be deceived by our fragile feelings, but will embrace the reality of the presence of Christ in our lives. Alleluia!

Monday, January 31, 2000 St. John Bosco
Mark 5, 1-20
The Healing of the Gerasene Demoniac

Jesus had just calmed the storm at sea. Now he was confronted with another kind of storm. A man from Gerasene, buffeted and tormented by demons, lived among the tombs.

The man who lived among the tombs had no support group. No step program of any number. No half way house. Death and destruction seemed to reign as the man howled and cut himself with stones.

In yesterday's Gospel, Jesus spoke directly to the evil entity inhabiting a man in the synagogue. "Quiet! Come out of him (Mark 1, 25)!"

In today's Gospel, Jesus also spoke directly to the evil entity within the tormented man. "Unclean spirit, come out of the man!" Jesus then asked, " What is your name? " The answer was, " Legion is my name. There are many of us."

Although this was an extremely serious situation, Jesus was still the One with ultimate power. He allowed the unclean spirits to enter two thousand swine. These crazy pigs then "rushed down a steep bank into the sea, where they were drowned."

The newly liberated man was now clothed and calm. You would think that the witnesses would rejoice.

Not so! They begged Jesus to leave. This kind of power was too much for them. So Jesus left, after first instructing the man to tell his family what had happened.

Lord Jesus, you are amazing! You can do anything. Help me never to give up, no matter how long I've dwelt among the tombs. Come and speak your word of command to any darkness within me. Set me free to witness to your awesome love and power. Alleluia!

Tuesday, February 1, 2000
Mark 5, 21-43
Jairus' Daughter and the Woman with a Hemorrhage

Jesus reaches out to two women in "impossible" circumstances. The woman with the hemorrhage had been ill for twelve years and had tried traditional medicine without success. Not only had she sought out the help of the medical profession for twelve years, but she had also "suffered greatly at the hands of many doctors and had spent all that she had. Yet she was not helped but only grew worse."

Amazingly, she still nurtured a tiny flicker of hope. Wisely, she placed this hope in Jesus and was not disappointed. One moment in the presence of Jesus accomplished what twelve years of medical care had failed to accomplish. She was instantly healed! Jesus spoke gently to her. "Daughter, your faith has saved you. Go in peace and be cured of your affliction."

Then there was the twelve year old girl who was dying. It took courage for Jairus, her father, to go to Jesus for help. Jairus was a synagogue official and his colleagues were certainly not cottoning to Jesus. Perhaps Jairus thought, "Who cares! With my child about to die, I'll try anything."

For Jesus, nothing was impossible. Some may have thought that if Jesus hadn't been stopped by that woman in the crowd, then he could have gotten to Jairus' house earlier and healed the young girl.

If. If. If.

It's never too late with Jesus. Even when Jairus was told that his daughter had died, Jesus pressed on.

"Disregarding the message that was reported, Jesus said to the synagogue official, 'Do not be afraid; just have faith.' " Taking only the girl's parents and Peter, James and John, he went to her, took her hand, and spoke to her, " '*Talitha koum*,' which means 'Little girl, I say to you, arise!' "

Too late? Impossible? Not with Jesus. Alleluia!

Wednesday, February 2, 2000 Presentation of the Lord
Luke 2, 22-40
The Presentation in the Temple; The Return to Nazareth

Timing. Timing. Timing.

349

The eternal God of time orchestrated each part of the presentation of the infant Jesus in the Temple. This is a fascinating Gospel, brimming over with encouragement for those who seek to live for God's glory.

Every person in the Temple was there by divine appointment. They were in God's place at God's time.

The forty days of purification were now completed. It was time to consecrate the infant Jesus to God.

Simeon had been waiting a long time for this moment. The Holy Spirit was upon him and had revealed to him that he would live to see the promised Messiah.

Now! Now was the moment.

Simeon "… came by the Spirit into the temple: and when the parents brought in the child Jesus, to do for him after the custom of the law, Then took he him up in his arms, and blessed God, and said, Lord, now lettest thou thy servant depart in peace, according to thy word: for mine eyes have seen thy salvation, Which thou hast prepared before the face of all people; A light to lighten the Gentiles and the glory of thy people Israel (Luke 2, 27-32, K.J.V.)."

Simeon also spoke of the agony awaiting Mary, the mother of Jesus. Her role in salvation history would be fraught with grief as well as glory.

A prophet, Anna, experienced in the ways of prayer and fasting, had also been strategically placed for this moment. "And coming forward at that very time, she gave thanks to God and spoke about the child to all who were awaiting the redemption of Jerusalem."

Back home in Nazareth, Mary and Joseph continued faithfully in their vocation of raising Jesus. "The child grew and became strong, filled with wisdom; and the favor of God was upon him."

Lord Jesus, when we feel blah and think our lives are going nowhere, help us to remember that you are truly present and active. You are steadily preparing us in order to present us for your own purposes. Alleluia!

Thursday, February 3, 2000 St. Blase, St. Ansgar
Mark 6, 7-13
The Mission of the Twelve

Two by two. Equally yoked. Yoked to Jesus.

The Twelve went out in twos. Have you ever wondered who was Judas' ministry partner?

As Christians, we are in a both/and situation, not simply an either/or situation. We experience a certain amount of solitude which is vital for nurturing our relationship with Jesus. We also have ministry relationships, which require working closely with others.

Before sending the Twelve on their mission, Jesus told them, "Whatever place does not welcome you or listen to you, leave there and shake the dust off your feet in testimony against them." Strong words!

Jesus was silent at this time about the internal relationships within the Twelve. According to John 6, 64, Jesus knew from the beginning who would betray him. Yet he continued to allow Judas to remain in ministry. Why?

Lord Jesus, sometimes we feel unequally yoked in ministry. It may not be a "Judas" situation. It may be simply a personality clash. Or, more seriously, it may be a matter of feeling manipulated or suffocated. It may be a matter of jealousy or of thwarted ambition thinly disguised as "ministry." Or it may indeed be a "Judas" situation. Thank you for your presence with us. Thank you for your guidance in our ministry relationships. Alleluia!

Friday, February 4, 2000
Mark 6, 14-29
Herod's Opinion of Jesus; The Death of John the Baptist

Prophets are scary people to be around. It's even scarier to be a prophet.

Prophets report to God and have to be willing to be misunderstood. They are easy targets for those who do not place a high priority on following God.

"Herodias harbored a grudge against him [John the Baptist] and wanted to kill him but was unable to do so. Herod [her husband] feared John, knowing him to be a righteous and holy man, and kept him in custody." A tragic series of actions followed, all birthed out of fear and frustration.

Herod would have done well to fear God rather than the wrath of his wife and the scorn of his dinner guests. He feared John the Baptist because John fearlessly followed God and because John was not a game player. John spoke the truth, a dangerous thing to do when dealing with bullies and tyrants.

Herodius' daughter was even dragged into this vendetta. With her mother's coaching, she was used as a pawn to procure the goal of Herodius' hatred, namely the severed head of the holy prophet.

Lord Jesus, we still have prophets amongst us. We still silence them because their holy lives are a constant reproach to our own duplicity. Reorient our lives to revolve around you, so that we will know you, love you, follow you, and welcome your word. Alleluia!

Saturday, February 5, 2000 St. Agatha
Mark 6, 30-34
The Return of the Twelve

Rest. <u>Webster's Seventh New Collegiate Dictionary</u> definition of "rest" is "to be free from anxiety or disturbance." Another is "to remain based or founded." "Peace of mind or spirit." "A rhythmic silence in music." "Renewed vigor." "To remain confident." Rest means so much more than a mere cessation of activity.

The disciples were all wound up and eager to tell Jesus all about their mission. Jesus wisely told them, "Come away by yourselves to a deserted place and rest a while."

Perhaps we haven't been off on an exciting mission. The day in and day out routine of work still takes a toll.

When we travel the road of worry, fear and anxiety, there is a price to pay. The "toll gate" waits for us all.

Jesus doesn't want us to get to the point where we are so depleted that we no longer see any point in living. He came to give us life! "A thief comes only to steal and slaughter and destroy; I came so that they might have life and have it more abundantly (John 10, 10)."

Lord Jesus, I need to learn to rest. Thank you for helping me. Alleluia!

352

Sunday, February 6, 2000 Fifth Sunday in Ordinary Time
Mark 1, 29-39
The Cure of Peter's Mother-in-Law; Other Healings;
Jesus Leaves Capernaum

Jesus knows the best way to bring healing. In the case of Simon Peter's mother-in-law, Jesus "approached, grasped her hand, and helped her up. Then the fever left her and she waited on them."

Jesus heals us, but often asks us for an act of cooperation. He told the man with the withered hand to stand up before everyone in the synagogue (Mark 3, 3).

Lord Jesus, help me to listen for your directions today and to cooperate with you as you continue to heal me. Alleluia!

Monday, February 7, 2000
Mark 6, 53-56
The Healings at Gennesaret

The marketplace. On Saturday mornings in our town, from May through November, there is a lively Farmer's Market, complete with musicians! Banjos are strummed, songs are sung, and one time a flutist performed.

At this particular market, there is a pie lady with coffee and doughnuts as well as her famous Cornish pasties and apricot pies. There are fragrant bunches of fresh herbs, Chinese long beans, dense local honey, "designer bread," fresh fish from the coast, and a profusion of bright flowers.

The marketplace. "Whatever villages or towns or countryside he [Jesus] entered, they laid the sick in the marketplace and begged him that they might touch only the tassel on his cloak; and as many as touched it were healed."

The marketplace. Not just the Saturday morning Farmer's Market. The marketplace is just outside your door. The sick are there. They may mask their sickness with determined smiles. They may appear hostile. They may have fallen into despair. They are there.

Lord Jesus, we too are in need of your healing touch. Help us to touch you in prayer today. Let your love and healing flow through us to others in the marketplace. Alleluia!

Tuesday, February 8, 2000 St. Jerome Emiliani
Mark 7, 1-13
The Traditions of the Elders

Jesus confronted the religious leaders with the truth about themselves. "You disregard God's commandment, but cling to human tradition." He had just quoted the Isaiah prophecy:

'This people honors me with their lips,
    but their hearts are far from me.
In vain do they worship me,
    teaching as doctrines human precepts.'

Jesus continued, " 'You disregard God's commandments but cling to human tradition.' He went on to say, 'How well you have set aside the commandment of God in order to uphold your tradition!' "

The last condemnation was the worst. "You nullify the word of God in favor of your tradition that you have handed on."

Jesus said, "If you remain in my word, you will truly be my disciples, and you will know the truth, and the truth will set you free (John 8, 31-32)."

Come Holy Spirit and help us to remain in Jesus' word. Lord Jesus, help us to be open to knowing the truth about ourselves. Heavenly Father, free us to serve you as you really are and as you want us to serve you. Alleluia!

Wednesday, February 9, 2000
Mark 7, 14-23
The Tradition of the Elders

What happens to us from the "outside" cannot permanently damage us. What injures us is our reaction.

To be free and to be healed, we must give God an offering. We offer to him the tragedy, the injustice, the betrayal, or whatever it was.

We cannot not take it within ourselves. Our poor frail humanity cannot bear it.

Lord Jesus, we offer it all to you. Take it and transform it. Let us experience a freedom and lightness today knowing that this is no longer ours to carry. Thank you that the final word is yours to speak. Alleluia!

Thursday, February 10, 2000 St. Scholastica
Mark 7, 24-30
The Syrophoenician Woman's Faith

"For a day in thy courts is better than a thousand. I had rather be a doorkeeper in the house of my God, than to dwell in the tents of wickedness (Psalm 84, 10, K.J.V)." This psalm is the prayer of a pilgrim to Jerusalem.

The woman in today's Gospel was a pilgrim of sorts. As a Greek woman living in Israel, she was considered an alien, an outsider.

Still, she was a pilgrim. She was on a pilgrimage, a journey to Jesus.

Jesus was the one who could help her. Jesus was the one who could liberate her daughter.

She had to persist! She had to stand up, even to Jesus! "Lord, even the dogs under the tables eat the children's scraps."

Jesus was impressed at this rare combination of unpretentious humility and feisty faith. "For saying this, you may go. The demon has gone out of your daughter."

Lord Jesus, I come to you today as a pilgrim. You are the goal of my pilgrimage and you are my companion on this journey Home. I know I need adjustments and balance in my life. Thank you that you are skillfully leading me through the remainder of my pilgrimage. Alleluia!

Friday, February 11, 2000 Our Lady of Lourdes
Mark 7, 31-37
The Healing of a Deaf Man

I recall hearing a British Scripture expositor refer to this passage. Referring to the part when Jesus put his finger in the man's ear and spits, the esteemed teacher commented, "That's not exactly Mayo Clinic!"

Although this is not a Gospel reflection on the properties of saliva, it is to be noted that even today, saliva is still of interest to the medical profession. For example, there are differing opinions about whether saliva or blood analysis yields more accurate information about the functioning of the adrenal glands.

"*Ephphatha!*" Be opened! Jesus spoke the word and the deaf man could hear. His speech impediment was gone and he could speak clearly.

Please don't spit on people today and claim their healing! Still, use what you have -- your love, your prayers, and your acts of compassion -- and God will open their hearts. Alleluia!

Saturday, February 12, 2000
Mark 8, 1-10
The Feeding of the Four Thousand

Jesus said, "My heart is moved with pity for the crowd, because they have been with me now for three days and have nothing to eat. If I send them away hungry to their homes, they will collapse on the way, and some of them have come a great distance."

You know the rest of the Gospel. Jesus asked his disciples how many loaves they had. He then took what they had, gave thanks, broke the loaves, then gave them back to the disciples to distribute to the crowd. The fish also were blessed and distributed.

Someone once asked me whether or not the fish was raw. I don't know! Maybe it was raw and then was cooked over coals. Maybe it had been dried. These culinary speculations are amusing, but tangential. The point is that all the people ate and were satisfied.

There are people in our lives today who are spiritually starving. If we send them away hungry, they may "collapse." Let us simply offer what we have to Jesus. He will bless what we give him and return it to us to give to the hungry ones we see today. No one will go home hungry. Alleluia!

Sunday, February 13, 2000 Sixth Sunday in Ordinary Time
Mark 1, 40-45
The Cleansing of a Leper

A person suffering from leprosy also suffered humiliation, rejection, and ostracism. First, the leper was required to go to the priest for verification of the disease. Then, if it truly was leprosy, the leper was in quarantine. The leper was required to cry out, "Unclean, unclean!" and was forced to "dwell apart ... outside the camp (Leviticus 13, 44)."

This particular leper somehow summoned the courage to go to Jesus, kneel before him, and beg for healing. "If you wish, you can make me clean."

"Moved with pity," Jesus "stretched out his hand, touched him, and said to him. 'I do will it. Be made clean.' " In order for the leper to be reinstated into the community, it was necessary for a priest to validate the healing. Jesus instructed the man to comply with this rule.

Sometimes when we've suffered rejection and humiliation, it's easy to stay on the outside of life. We may be even be afraid to approach Jesus in prayer. What if Jesus refuses us?

Let's stomp on those "what ifs" and approach our loving Savior with confidence! Jesus will heal us and set us free beyond our wildest imaginings. Jesus knows how we've been hurt and also knows the exact timing and method of healing that is best for us.

Lord Jesus, I trust in you for healing and restoration. Alleluia!

Monday, February 14, 2000 Sts Cyril and Methodius
Mark 8, 11-13
The Demand for a Sign

Malice was running rampant as the Pharisees questioned Jesus. They were not seeking to understand Jesus or his teaching. They were intent on discrediting both Jesus and his message.

Jesus left them and went to the other shore. He "... sighed from the depth of his spirit ..." He had no intention of playing their game.

We need to learn from Jesus that there is a time to accommodate hostile questioners and there is a time to terminate the interrogation. We are unable to please everyone and we are unable to fulfill our own ministry if we are constantly having to justify ourselves.

Lord Jesus, you knew when to stay and when to walk away. Thank you for showing us your will in situations in which we feel frustrated and pressured. Alleluia!

Tuesday, February 15, 2000
Mark 8, 14-21
The Leaven of the Pharisees

In the previous passage, the Pharisees had been questioning Jesus with hostile intent, trying to trap him. Jesus had had it and decided to leave. He got into his boat and "went off to the other shore (Mark 8, 13)."

Now his own disciples became a source of annoyance to him. They just didn't get it!

Jesus had been trying to warn them about the malice of the Pharisees and all the disciples could do was to fuss about bread. They just didn't get it.!

Jesus was attempting, without much success, to direct the disciples' attention to a higher level. "Watch out, guard against the leaven of the Pharisees and the leaven of Herod."

Bread is fed by yeast. The Pharisees were fed by malice.

These leaders seemed to thrive on attempts to harass and discredit Jesus. Still, Jesus was in control.

Lord Jesus, you knew what it was like to feel not only annoyed, but also dismayed. In our time on earth, help us to lift the eyes of our hearts to you and to see with your perspective. You said, "Heaven and earth will pass away, but my words will not pass away (Matthew 24, 35)." Help us to be still and to remember that you are in charge, no matter how frustrating our circumstances. Alleluia!

Wednesday, February 16, 2000
Mark 8, 22-26
The Blind Man of Bethsaida

Jesus took the blind man by the hand and led him outside the village. He knew when to heal in private and when to heal in public.

Others would eventually know of this healing, but this was not the right time. This was the time for a private encounter between Jesus and the blind man.

This was a gradual healing. At first, there was just a little improvement. The man could see a bit, but not distinctly. At the second touch from Jesus, he could see clearly.

I believe in instantaneous healings. I believe also in the mercy of God in opening our eyes gradually to situations which require tender, loving care and serious discernment. Perhaps the truth, given too soon, would overwhelm us.

After the man was able to see clearly, Jesus told him to go home and not to return to the village. The newly healed man needed time alone, away from the usual round of life, to assimilate this amazing change in his life.

Jesus is gentle with us as he opens our eyes. All will become clear at the right time. Alleluia!

Thursday, February 17, 2000
Seven Founders of the Order of Servites
Mark 8, 27-33
Peter's Confession about Jesus;
The First Prediction of the Passion

"It is necessary that the Son of Man proceed to an ordeal of suffering ... (Mark 8, 31, The Message)." These were Jesus' startling words which came swiftly upon Peter's declaration that Jesus was the Christ.

When Peter tried to reproach Jesus, "... Jesus confronted Peter. 'Peter, get out of my way! Satan, get lost! You have no idea how God works (Mark 8, 32-33, The Message).' "

God's ways are not our ways. God's Son was not born in a palace, but in a smelly stable. God's Son did not vanquish his enemies in the religious establishment. Instead, he humbly "submitted to an ordeal of suffering" which involved torture and murder.

God's ways are still not our ways. We still do not see clearly. We still think God should do things a certain way -- our way!

"For my thoughts are not your thoughts, neither are your ways my ways, saith the LORD. For as the heavens are higher than the earth, so are my ways higher than your ways, and my thoughts than your thoughts (Isaiah 55, 8-9, K.J.V.)."

Lord Jesus, we know who you are. You are the crucified and risen Lord. Today, help us to rest our weary minds and hearts again in the sure knowledge that you, as Lord, are truly in control. Thank you that the time will come when we see you "face to face (1 Corinthians 13, 12)." Help us to stop trying to figure everything out, but to rest in you and to trust in you. Alleluia!

Friday, February 18, 2000
Mark 8, 34-9, 1
The Condition of Discipleship

Mere belief is not discipleship. The demons believe and they are not disciples.

Jesus said, "You believe that God is one. You do well. Even the demons believe that and tremble (James 2, 19)."

359

Discipleship is something else. Beginning with some level of belief, faith, and trust, discipleship leads to being conformed to the image of Christ (cf. Romans 8, 29). What lies in between is called our life as Christians.

We cannot jump from A to Z, from alpha to omega. Only God can do that. " 'I am the Alpha and the Omega,' says the Lord God, 'the one who is and who was and who is to come, the almighty (Revelation 1, 8).' "

We progress step by step. Sometimes we leap. Sometimes we lag.

Jesus said, "Whoever wishes to come after me must deny himself, take up his cross, and follow me." Note the personal pronoun. It's a personal cross.

His cross. Her cross. Your cross. My cross. <u>Webster's Seventh New Collegiate Dictionary</u> defines "cross" as "an affliction that tries one's virtue, steadfastness, or patience."

There are twists and turns along this road of discipleship. I may take a detour and start trying to be a disciple on my own by trying to imitate other disciples. I may try to pray a certain way or do this or not do that. I may stop focusing on Jesus and start focusing on myself and my problems. That is not discipleship. That is unhealthy self-absorption.

Jesus wants me first of all to spend time with him, to get to know him as he really is. Then I will follow him, not only because I believe in him, but also because I trust him. Then, whatever is my "cross" in this life will be just right for me.

Lord Jesus, sometimes we do certain things, thinking we are following you. Flood us anew with a realization of your love for us and your complete acceptance of us. Today, let us rest in your love, bask in your love, and be strengthened for the next step of this exciting road of discipleship. Alleluia!

Saturday, February 19, 2000
Mark 9, 2-13
The Transfiguration of Jesus; The Coming of Elijah

The disciples experienced a glimpse into glory! Moses and Elijah were on the mountain with Jesus, who was transfigured before them. They heard the voice of God, saying, " 'This is my beloved Son. Listen to him.' "

As they came down the mountain, Jesus "charged them not to relate what they had seen to anyone, except when the Son of Man had risen from the dead." Although the disciples did not understand what resurrection meant, they still "kept the matter to themselves."

Sometimes Jesus takes us away with himself. We see him in a new way and we see ourselves in a new way. In an instant, old misconceptions about Jesus and what he asks of us can be swept away.

At that moment we are very fragile and very vulnerable. This is not a time to talk with others. This is a time to continue in the presence of the Lord as he heals us, restores us, and sometimes gently redirects our path.

The Father tells us as he told the first disciples, "This is my beloved Son. Listen to him." Alleluia!

Sunday, February 20, 2000 Seventh Sunday in Ordinary Time
Mark 2, 1-12
The Healing of a Paralytic

"Child." In this Gospel, in The New Jerusalem Bible, Jesus addressed the paralyzed man as "My child, " and then said, "your sins are forgiven."

"Child." It has been very fashionable for some time to speak of the "inner child." In her pioneering healing ministry, Agnes Sanford noted that it was sometimes the "little child" still living within the adult who was wounded and in need of healing.

In some editions of Alice In Wonderland, Lewis Carroll added, "An Easter Greeting to Every Child Who Loves Alice." The letter begins, "Dear Child" and touches the heart of each "child" who reads it.

When Jesus addressed the paralyzed man as "My child," he was speaking to him in a very personal way. It was important for this grown man to be thus addressed and to be assured that his sins were forgiven.

It was after this that Jesus added, "I say to you, rise, pick up your mat, and go home." The wording is even stronger in The New Jerusalem Bible: "I order you: get up, pick up your stretcher, and go off home." Jesus was making it clear to those who accused him of blasphemy that he did indeed have the power, not only to heal, but that he had the even greater authority to forgive sins.

Jesus is speaking to you today. He sees your suffering. He sees your courage. He is speaking to you tenderly. "My child, your sins are

361

forgiven." He is inviting you to "rise" to a fresh new life of freedom. Alleluia!

Monday, February 21, 2000 St. Peter Damian
Mark 9, 14-29
The Healing of a Boy with a Demon

"If you can!" This expression of amazement comes from Jesus.

The father of the son "possessed by a mute spirit" has just described the horrors of his son's affliction. The father has to watch helplessly as the mute spirit literally seizes control of the boy who then "foams at the mouth, grinds his teeth, and becomes rigid."

Since the son has had this affliction since childhood, the father has probably come close to despair. He sees a glimmer of hope when he asks the disciples to help him. His fragile hope is dashed when the disciples are unable to cast out the spirit.

Now, his son is face to face with Jesus! Upon seeing Jesus, "the spirit immediately threw the boy into convulsions."

The father pleads with Jesus, saying, "It has often thrown him into fire and into water to kill him. But if you can do anything, have compassion on us and help us."

"If you can!" Jesus assures the father, "Everything is possible to the one who has faith."

Jesus then speaks directly to the unclean spirit tormenting the son. "Mute and deaf spirit, I command you: come out of him and never enter him again!"

The deliverance was so complete that the son lay as one dead. Many bystanders, looking only on the external evidence, said, "He is dead."

Not so! Jesus "took him by the hand, raised him, and he stood up."

In your seemingly hopeless situation, Jesus is there, in spite of what you think. To your wavering doubts and fears, Jesus is looking at you and saying, "Everything is possible to the one who has faith!" Even if you feel lifeless, Jesus is taking your hand at this moment, raising you, and helping you to begin a new life. Alleluia!

Tuesday, February 22, 2000 The Chair of Peter
Matthew 16, 13-19
Peter's Confession about Jesus

To skirt the question of Peter's primacy, some point to the Greek translations of Matthew 16, 18 to contrast the words for "Peter" (Petros) and "this rock" (petra). This method avoids acknowledging the true language spoken by Jesus.

Jesus did not speak Greek. Jesus, a Jew, spoke Aramaic. The Aramaic words for "Peter" and "this rock" are, respectively, "Kepa, " and "kepa."

Peter received from God the Father the revelation of who Jesus really was. Jesus was indeed the Messiah, the Son of the Living God.

After Peter articulated Jesus' identity, Jesus articulated Peter's identity and Peter's vocation. "Blessed are you, Simon son of Jonah. For flesh and blood has not revealed this to you, but my heavenly Father. And so I say to you, you are Peter, and upon this rock I will build my church, and the gates of the netherworld shall not prevail against it. I will give you the keys of the kingdom of heaven. Whatever you bind on earth shall be bound in heaven; and whatever you loose on earth shall be loosed in heaven."

Lord Jesus, as we pray for unity in the Church, help us to remember that your word on the matter of authority in the Church has already been spoken. Let your word be received and obeyed. Alleluia!

Wednesday, February 23, 2000 St. Polycarp
Mark 9, 38-40
Another Exorcist

The "not invented here" syndrome was in evidence in first century Palestine. There is a striking example of this attitude in today's Gospel.

The disciples had a complaint to voice to Jesus. "Teacher, we saw someone driving out demons in your name, and we tried to prevent him because he does not follow us."

Jesus confronted this rigid attitude of exclusivity. Smugly assured of Jesus' approval, the disciples complained about this person who was using Jesus' name to drive out demons.

Jesus was not about to allow his disciples to get away with this attitude. "Do not prevent him. There is no one who performs a mighty deed in my name who can at the same time speak ill of me. For whoever is not against us is for us."

Who knows! Perhaps this lonely follower was destined to become a committed disciple. He was ministering in the only way he knew at the time, which was to speak the mighty name of Jesus to drive out demons. More power to him!

Lord Jesus, thank you that our security is in belonging to you. Within the shelter of this security, help us to do "mighty deeds" in your name. Alleluia!

Thursday, February 24, 2000
Mark 9, 41-50
Another Exorcist; Temptations to Sin

"Anyone who gives you a cup of water to drink because you belong to Christ, amen, I say to you, will surely not lose his reward." "Keep salt in yourselves and you will have peace with one another."

Today's Gospel begins with water and ends with salt. As followers of Jesus we are to be salt.

Authentic discipleship creates a thirst in others for Jesus. Jesus said, "You are the salt of the earth (Matthew 5, 13)."

So many problems arise in the Church, the Body of Christ, because we personally do not have enough "salt." When we don't have the salt we need, we may become envious of salt-filled disciples.

What is preventing us from following Jesus with our whole heart? Jesus tells us to get rid of whatever causes us to sin.

Jesus issues a terrible warning for those who cause others to sin. "Whoever causes one of these little ones who believe [in me] to sin, it would be better for him if a great millstone were put around his neck and he were thrown into the sea."

Jesus said, "Whoever believes in me, as scripture says,

'Rivers of living water will flow from
    within him.'

He said this in reference to the Spirit that those who came to believe in him were to receive (John 7, 38-39)."

When we maintain a healthy "salt" level in our lives, we will also have this "living water" to offer to thirsty seekers after God. When our own "salt" level is healthy, we will not try to snatch the saltshaker, or quench the Spirit, in the life of another Christian. There is plenty of salt and water for all.

Come Holy Spirit. Illumine our minds and hearts. Teach us how to receive and how to maintain the correct balance of spiritual salt and water in our lives. Alleluia!

Friday, February 25, 2000
Mark 10, 1-12
Marriage and Divorce

Jesus said, "... from the beginning of creation, 'God made them male and female. For this reason a man shall leave his father and mother [and be joined to his wife] and the two shall become one flesh.' So they are no longer two but one flesh. Therefore what God has joined together, no human being must separate."

God's plan was that the two would become one. The prerequisite is that the man leave his father and mother and be joined to his wife. Then, "... in marriage he becomes one flesh with a woman - no longer two individuals, but forming a new unity (Mark 10, 8 The Message)."

As Christians, we are "married" to the Lord. "For thy Maker is thine husband; the LORD of hosts is his name; and thy Redeemer the Holy One of Israel; The God of the whole earth shall he be called (Isaiah 54, 5 K.J.V.)."

Jesus, Son of God, our Bridegroom, "left "his Father in heaven to become one with us. Jesus, Son of Man, "left" his mother Mary's home in Nazareth, to fulfill his ministry and to become one with us. No one can destroy our union with Jesus.

Lord Jesus, please send the Holy Spirit to us to deepen our awareness of you as our Lover and Spouse. Let us be one with you in attitude and approach to others today. Alleluia!

Saturday, February 26, 2000
Mark 10, 13-16
Blessing of the Children

"And people were bringing children to him that he might touch them ..." For many years, I met with other mothers to pray for our children.

These "children" are now young adults. In prayer, we continue to bring them to Jesus and ask Jesus to touch them. We trust Jesus to embrace them and bless them.

Lord Jesus, thank your for the privilege of bringing our children to you, confident that you welcome them. Thank you for your hand on their lives. Alleluia!

Sunday, February 27, 2000 Eighth Sunday in Ordinary Time
Mark 2, 18-22
The Question about Fasting

Timing. With Jesus, it's always a question of timing.

Wedding guests obviously don't fast with the bridegroom in their midst. That's the time to celebrate!

A piece of fresh, new, cloth, which is not preshrunk, is not used to patch an old garment. It just won't work. The fabrics don't "mix."

Fresh, robust, new wine does not belong in old wineskins. The wineskins will burst.

God is constantly refreshing us, transforming us, and preparing us for what is ahead. The ministries in which we served at one time may not be where God wants us right now.

If we try to rejoice when others are mourning and fasting, it just won't work. If we try to pour our energies into tired, old ministries that no longer have God's fresh anointing, we will become discouraged and disheartened.

Lord Jesus, I choose this day to follow you into the new vineyards where you are planting me. Help me not to look back. Alleluia!

Monday, February 28, 2000
Mark 10, 17-27
The Rich Man

Life on two levels. Life in two kingdoms.

Jesus said, "How hard it is for those who have wealth to enter the kingdom of God!" Why would he say that?

Even though the disciples were astonished at these words, Jesus continued his discourse, addressing his disciples as "children."

"Children, how hard it is to enter the kingdom of God! It is easier for a camel to pass through [the] eye of [a] needle than for one who is rich to enter the kingdom of God."

The disciples now became "exceedingly astonished." They asked Jesus, "Then who can be saved?"

Jesus assured them, "For human beings it is impossible, but not for God. All things are possible for God."

Two levels. Two kingdoms.

The kingdom of God and the kingdom of self. The humility of the childlike who acknowledge God's sovereignty or the arrogance of some of the rich who are deluded into thinking that they are in control.

Jesus said, "... unless you turn and become like children, you will not enter the kingdom of heaven (Matthew 18, 3)." In today's Gospel, Jesus addressed his disciples as "children," an indication of their status.

The rich man was not truly rich. He still lacked the "one thing" needed to "inherit eternal life." He lacked childlike trust. "You are lacking in one thing. Go, sell what you have, and give to [the] poor and you will have treasures in heaven; then come, follow me."

Lord Jesus, today, help me to trust you with the trust of a child. As I live now in this world, help me to remember that there is another world, another kingdom where your will is always done. Alleluia!

Tuesday, February 29, 2000
Mark 10, 28-31
The Rich Man

Jesus said, "... many that are first will be last, and [the] last will be first." Human beings can push and shove and compete and jockey for power all they want, to no avail.

It is ultimately God who places people in power. God is the One who "casts down," "raises up again," "humbles" and "exalts (1 Samuel 2, 6)."

We are not pawns on a chessboard. We were created with free will and we exercise free will each moment of our lives.

We cannot, however, choose our position. That is God's call. We can only choose or refuse fidelity to the revealed will of God for our lives.

The rich man chose to clutch his coins rather than to cling to Christ. The disciples chose to deny themselves in order to dedicate themselves to Jesus.

Jesus promised them a hundred fold repayment "in the present age" along with the inevitable persecution attached to true discipleship, and "eternal life in ages to come." But many that are first will be last, and [the] last first."

Lord Jesus, help me to lay aside all concern or curiosity about this "first "and "last" business. Let me simply offer myself to you and trust you. Alleluia!

Wednesday, March 1, 2000
Mark 10, 32-45
The Third Prediction of the Passion;
Ambition of James and John

Jesus and his followers were "on the way, going to Jerusalem, and Jesus went ahead of them." Jesus told them, for the third time, of his approaching suffering, death, and resurrection.

The disciples were still unwilling or unable to accept these words of Jesus. So far, they had known Jesus as a teacher and a wonder worker. Jesus seemed invincible! How could he suffer?

James and John seemed to brush aside any talk of suffering and rush to the glory part. "Grant that in your glory we may sit one at your right and the other at your left."

Jesus basically told them that they were crazy. "You do not know what you are asking."

Jesus asked if they really thought they could drink the cup of suffering which he would drink, The other disciples, hearing about the audacity of John and James, were indignant.

Jesus acknowledged the power structure of the day in which "the Gentiles Lord it over" others and "the great ones make their authority over them felt." He then redirected their attention to the dynamic operative in the kingdom of God.

"But it shall not be so among you. Rather, whoever wishes to be great among you will be your servant; whoever wishes to be first among you will be the slave of all. For the Son of Man did not come to be served but to serve to give his life as a ransom for many."

Lord Jesus, thank you that you are with us as we travel to our own "Jerusalem" and to our own appointment with destiny. Thank you that you know what is ahead for us and that you are already there. You are with us as we drink our cup of suffering and you will be with us when we share your glory. Lord Jesus, help us to be content today where we are. Alleluia!

Thursday, March 2, 2000
Mark 10, 46-52
The Blind Bartimaeus

Jesus was leaving the Jericho scene. Mark records that Jesus and his followers "came to Jericho," and in the next sentence, that they were "leaving Jericho."

It was as Jesus was leaving Jericho that the encounter with Bartimaeus, a blind man, took place. Significant encounters sometimes occur upon leaving a place.

Bartimaeus persisted in crying out to Jesus, even when others were trying to silence him. In fact, "... he kept calling out all the more, 'Son of David, have pity on me.' " Jesus was right there and Jesus could change his life!

Why, then, should Bartimaeus be quiet? What did he have to lose? "He threw aside his cloak, sprang up, and came to Jesus."

His need seemed obvious, Still, Jesus required Bartimaeus to articulate it.

"What do you want me to do for you?" The blind man answered, " 'My teacher, let me see again.' Jesus said to him, "Go; your faith has made you well.' Immediately he regained his sight and followed him on the way (Mark 10, 51-52, N.R.S.V.)."

Jesus is here with me today in the Person of the Holy Spirit. He is not coming to my "Jericho" and leaving without changing my life. What do I want Jesus to do for me?

Lord Jesus, there are so many things I can't "see" or understand. What I want you do for me today is to help me to trust you. Everything else will fall into place, Alleluia!

Friday, March 3, 2000
Mark 11, 11-26
The Entry into Jerusalem; Jesus Curses a Fig Tree;
Cleansing of the Temple; The Withered Fig Tree

Jesus did not speak a word of life to the fig tree, to put it mildly! It has been said that the fig tree represented the nation of Israel -- all "leaves" (outer image) and no "fruit" (belief in Jesus). At any rate, this fig tree was a goner!

The Temple was next on Jesus' hit list. The Temple was definitely not fulfilling its purpose of being a house of prayer. Instead, it had become a noisy, congested shopping mall.

The chief priests and the scribes were getting hot under the collar. Jesus had just made a triumphal entry into Jerusalem to shouts of "Hosanna." He was right there in their midst. Feeling frightened, angry and threatened, they wanted him out of the way, preferably permanently.

Meanwhile, back at the fig tree ... The disciples observed the fig tree which had withered to its very roots. Jesus chose this moment to emphasize the power of the spoken word.

Jesus instructed his followers, "Have faith in God. Amen, I say to you, whoever says to this mountain, 'Be lifted up and thrown into the sea,' and does not doubt in his heart but believes that what he says will happen, it shall be done for him. Therefore I tell you, all that you ask for in prayer, believe that you will receive it and it shall be yours. When you stand to pray, forgive anyone against whom you have a grievance, so that your heavenly Father may in turn forgive your transgressions."

We speak life or death to ourselves and to others with our tongue. If we forgive others, which is not synonymous with condoning their actions, we choose life for ourselves. If we refuse to forgive and to release others to God, we may as well as wither like the fig tree.

Lord Jesus, today I choose to live life to the full. I speak to the "mountain" of grievances within my heart, and choose to forgive and to release all who have injured me. Let me experience a joyful light heart today. Alleluia!

Saturday, March 4, 2000 St. Casimir
Mark 11, 27-33
The Authority of Jesus Questioned

Jesus was the one with true authority in this encounter with the chief priests, scribes, and elders. Instead of falling at his feet and worshipping him as Son of God, these leaders taunted him with a trap question.

We may not be so blatant as to try to trap Jesus, but still we resist his authority in subtle ways. The Holy Spirit may gently, or not so gently, lay it upon our heart to call someone or to forgive someone.

We don't want to hear this message, so we brush it off or rationalize it. We think, "Maybe I didn't really hear from God."

At the root of our resistance is fear. What would happen if we really trusted and obeyed the Lord in everything?

Underneath the root of fear is the ancient enemy, pride. We are afraid because we don't want to lose the illusion of being in control of our lives.

Lord Jesus, I yield anew to your authority in my life. Heal old wounds from the past. You know me and love me and want to lead me into a deeper level of trust in you. Heal me and hold me. Alleluia!

Sunday, March 5, 2000 Ninth Sunday in Ordinary Time
Mark 2, 23-3, 6
The Disciples and the Sabbath; A Man with a Withered Hand

The Sabbath is God's gift of life. It is intended for renewal. It is not a burden, but a joy!

Jesus is Lord of the Sabbath. What he says goes.

Jesus longed to release the Pharisees from their distorted, fussy religiosity about the Sabbath. The Sabbath was made for our benefit! Jesus is in charge of every day, including the Sabbath.

Jesus wants us to enjoy the gift of life! In the synagogue, he reached out to the man with a withered hand and restored him.

The Pharisees seemed to be focused on death. Sometimes, they brought death of spirit to others.

In contrast, Jesus focused on life. Jesus brought life to others! He brought life of body, soul (mind, will, emotions), and spirit.

Lord Jesus, thank you for liberating us to enjoy life. Alleluia!

Monday, March 6, 2000
Mark 12, 1-12
Parable of the Tenants

This is a "fill in the blanks" parable. The vineyard is said to stand for Israel. The religious leaders are the tenants who were meant to care for the vineyard. God is the true owner of the vineyard.

God sent special servants (prophets) to the vineyard. The unworthy tenants did not want to listen to the message of these prophets, so they killed them, Finally, God's very own Son was sent to the vineyard.

We have been referred to as God's vineyard (1 Corinthians 3, 9). Let's "fill in" the vineyard.

God has planted a hedge of protection around the vineyard of our lives. God has installed a watchtower over the vineyards of our lives to spy out any threat to us. Although our lives are challenging, we are safe and protected in God's care.

What about the winepress? To become pure wine, we have to submit to the winepress.

We are pressed to produce fragrant and fresh new wine. This is our destiny and our joy

Does it hurt to be in the winepress? Of course. It destroys whatever there is in us which is not of God.

What about Jesus? The cross was his ultimate winepress. From his cross came our life. From our time in the winepress will come a purified life poured out for others. Alleluia!

Tuesday, March 7, 2000 Shrove Tuesday
Mark 12, 13-17
Paying Taxes to the Emperor

David, after being delivered from the devices of his enemies, wrote of God's ways

"Toward the faithful you are faithful;
   to the honest you are honest;
toward the sincere, sincere;
   but to the perverse you are devious (Psalm 18, 26-27)."

Jesus knew how to deal with the hostile Pharisees who were trying to trick him, "to ensnare him in his speech." They had carefully placed a snare before him and waited to see what he would say.

Surprise! Jesus refused to be trapped. The Pharisees were trapped in their own evil scheme.

Jesus was disarmingly honest and simple as he dealt with them. He wasn't there to dance to their tune. He was there on his Father's business. If they didn't like it, tough!

He countered their question about paying taxes to Caesar with another question. "Why are you testing me? Bring me a denarius to look at …. Whose image and inscription is this?"

Of course they had to answer, "Caesar's." Jesus told them, "Repay to Caesar what belongs to Caesar and to God what belongs to God." Bingo.

Lord Jesus, you calmly trusted in your Father's provision of wisdom. Let me live this day in calmness and trust that you will give me what I need to live in this world. Alleluia!

Wednesday, March 8, 2000 Ash Wednesday
Matthew 6, 1-6, 16-18
Teaching about Almsgiving; Teaching about Prayer;
Teaching about Fasting

Your Father sees. Your Father knows. Your Father will repay you.

Sometimes we wonder. Does God see? Does God know? Does God even care?

Yes! Jesus assures us that our merciful deeds, our prayers, and our fasting are known to God and will be repaid by God.

Jesus takes it for granted that we give alms, pray, and fast. "When you give alms …" "When you pray …" "When you fast …"

It's not a matter of "if" or "when," but "how." We fast for the purposes of our Father in heaven, not for the approval of people on earth.

Father, thank you for this springtime, this wonderful time of Lent. Draw us into your presence by the power of the Holy Spirit as we gaze on Jesus, your Son.

Thursday, March 9, 2000 St. Frances of Rome
Luke 9, 22-25
The First Prediction of the Passion;
The Conditions of Discipleship

Suffer. Be rejected by the elders, the chief priests, and the scribes. Be killed. Be raised on the third day.

That's the assignment for Jesus. That's what Jesus is telling his disciples is going to happen to him.

Jesus then warned that following him meant radical denial of self. Following him meant a daily carrying of one's own cross. He challenged those who would follow him to question the value of getting everything this world has to offer if it meant losing one's true self.

You will lose yourself, your true self, if you try to watch out for yourself. You will save yourself, your true self, if you embrace your "cross," your assignment, and follow Jesus every day.

Friday, March 10, 2000 Lenten Weekday
Matthew 9, 14-15
The Question about Fasting

This is a "sandwich" Gospel, even though is about fasting. It is sandwiched between Jesus' requirement of mercy, rather than not sacrifice, and his teaching about mending a garment and filling wineskins. Fasting is matter of motivation and appropriate timing.

What do I live on? Are my words sweet or bitter? Would I want to eat my own words? Do I feed on fear, anger, negativity, bitterness, or despair?

Lord Jesus, with your spiritual stethoscope, examine my heart this Lent. Show me how and when to fast.

Saturday, March 11, 2000 Lenten Weekday
Luke 5, 27-32
The Call of Levi

Jesus looked intently at a certain tax collector and then spoke to him. "Follow me."

Levi was considered an outcast, but Jesus knew Levi's heart. Jesus reached out to him with the words, "Follow me."

Not only did Levi follow Jesus, but he also threw a big party for Jesus! Levi even had the boldness to invite others who were considered outcasts.

The Pharisees, not known for their compassion, complained about this to Jesus' disciples." Why do you eat and drink with tax collectors and sinners?"

Jesus answered, "Those who are healthy do not need a physician, but the sick do. I have not come to call the righteous to repentance but sinners."

If you are sick in spirit, you need a physician right away. You don't have to fight your HMO to get to a specialist. You don't have to wait for the next available operator. You don't have to be told that your call will be answered in the order in which it was received.

Jesus is your specialist and he's right here. He's God, so he already knows your diagnosis. He knows right now what's the matter with you and how to heal you. He is looking intently at you with love and understanding. Follow him.

Sunday, March 12, 2000 First Sunday in Lent
Mark 1, 12-15
The Temptation of Jesus;
The Beginning of the Galilee Ministry

For Jesus, the time in the desert, a time of trial, temptation, beasts and angels, led to a new beginning. This was a necessary time before the beginning of his public ministry.

In our churches this Lent, we see the desert or wilderness motif displayed in various ways. There is a starkness around the altar. Instead of flowers, there may be briars, rocks, cacti, or other reminders that this is a time of austerity. It is also a time of confrontation.

Jesus confronted the vicious power of Satan. The same Holy Spirit who drove him into this wilderness experience enabled him to endure until the time of testing was over.

The same Holy Spirit may also drive us to confront various personal issues which we would prefer to ignore. The same Holy Spirit who sustained Jesus will also sustain us as we confront these "beasts." God will send messengers, "angels," to us.

This time in the "desert" will not go on forever, thank God. After the wilderness, there was a new beginning for Jesus. He began his ministry in the lovely Galilee. The Holy Spirit is preparing us, also, for a new beginning.

Monday, March 13, 2000 Lenten Weekday
Matthew 25, 31-46
The Judgment of the Nations

"When the Son of Man comes in his glory, and all the angels with him, he will sit upon his glorious throne, and all the nations will be assembled before him." Jesus, the Lamb of God, the gentle Shepherd, the suffering Servant, will be the Judge.

If we could live this day seeing Jesus in his glory surrounded by all the angels, how would we live? Could we forget ourselves long enough to serve the suffering ones around us?

Recently, a homeless man was found dead in a busy downtown, near a restaurant. His body was hastily covered so the diners would not see a dead man right outside the window of the restaurant. How distasteful, to be faced with reality, in that wealthy town.

Lord Jesus, have mercy on us. Deliver us from our addiction to ourselves. Help us to treat every person we encounter today with the same respect that we would give to you.

Tuesday, March 14, 2000 Lenten Weekday
Matthew 6, 7-15
The Lord's Prayer

"Your Father knows what you need before you ask him." The prayer that Jesus teaches us to pray is actually a pattern to create a new life for ourselves and for those around us.

A pattern for a garment is just that -- a pattern. It is not the finished garment. It is only a means to an end.

The "end" in this prayer pattern is the will of God being accomplished in all its fullness. God does not press a button and force us to participate in the carrying out of his will.

We participate by learning to live as God calls us to live. We learn to acknowledge God as Father and to trust him with our lives.

We embrace God's plan for our lives because God's plan is perfect. God's plan, sometimes called the will of God, brings us the joy and fulfillment for which we hunger and thirst.

We trust God to give us "our daily bread" and to forgive us. Our part is to forgive those who have sinned against us. We trust God to take care of us, emotionally as well as materially.

We don't have to continue to carry around the heavy burden of the sins of others. We forgive them and release them into God's hands. God gives us freedom!

Heavenly Father, you know all about me. I trust you today to do what is best for me. Thank you for helping me to grow in my ability to rest in you and to trust you.

Wednesday, March 15, 2000 Lenten Weekday
Luke 11, 29-32
The Demand for a Sign

"Just as Jonah became a sign to the Ninevites, so will the Son of Man be to this generation." The Ninevites were the inhabitants of Ninevah, a huge city. They were quick to believe Jonah when he predicted destruction. Their king called a fast. Even the animals fasted!

The king ordered the people to convert and to cry out to God for mercy. God, seeing that the Ninevites had truly repented and converted, did not destroy their city after all. Jonah was the initially disobedient, reluctant, instrument sent by God to save Ninevah.

Jesus was Son of God and Son of Man. He was the obedient, willing instrument sent from God to proclaim the Good News, the Gospel of God to save us.

"This is the time of fulfillment. The kingdom of God is at hand. Repent, and believe in the gospel (Mark 1, 15)."

Someone greater than the reluctant prophet Jonah is here. Jesus is here!

Someone greater than the wise King Solomon is here. Jesus is here!

"In times past, God spoke in partial and various ways to our ancestors, through the prophets; in these last days, he spoke to us through a son, whom he made heir of all things and through whom he created the universe ... (Hebrews 1, 1-2)."

The ultimate Sign is here. Jesus is here!

Thursday, March 16, 2000 Lenten Weekday
Matthew 7, 7-12
The Answer to Prayers; The Golden Rule

The answer is "yes." The answer is always "yes " to the prayer within the prayer, to the deepest longing in our hearts.

Jesus instructed us, "Ask and it will be given to you; seek and you will find; knock and the door will be opened to you." Your heavenly Father will give "good things to those who ask him."

Jesus also told us, "Do unto others whatever you would have them do to you." How can we cheer others on as they try to fulfill the call of God on their lives?

Lord Jesus, thank you for sending "good things" in answer to my prayers. Help me also to be to others what I would like others to be to me.

Friday, March 17, 2000 St. Patrick
Matthew 5, 20-26
Teaching about the Law; Teaching about Anger

Jesus is always looking into our hearts. Murder is the outer act which begins with the smoldering anger within our hearts.

When we are unable to deal with our own anger, sometimes the judgment to which we are delivered is the judgment of our own bodies. We cannot sustain rage forever. It tears away at our physical, mental, emotional, and spiritual resources.

"Settle with your opponent quickly ..." "Be reconciled ..." Perhaps we've tried this and it didn't seem to work. Offering forgiveness is our part. Offering forgiveness is within our control.

Reconciliation, however, is not within our control. The other person, exercising free will, may choose to remain stubborn and inflexible.

What then? Even then, the anger within our hearts needs to be released to God. When we have done our part, we are free!

Lord Jesus, this is easier said than done. I give you all my emotions, anger included. Please take this gift of myself to your altar and transform me.

Saturday, March 18, 2000 St. Cyril of Jerusalem
Matthew 5, 43-48
Love of Enemies

Jesus said, "... love your enemies, and pray for those who persecute you, that you may be children of your heavenly Father, for he makes the sun to rise on the bad and the good, and causes rain to fall on the just and the unjust." He added, "So be perfect, just as your heavenly Father is perfect."

How impossible, and yet Jesus told us to do it! What are we up against?

The dictionary defines "enemy" as "one that seeks the injury, overthrow, or failure of an opponent." There is "antagonism showing itself in hatred or destructive attitude or action."

The Latin word for "enemy" is "inimicus," from "in" (not) and "amicus" (friend). An enemy is not our friend.

"Friend." This word comes from the Old English word "freon" (to love) and "freo" (free). Often, an "enemy" not only does not love us, but also does not want us to be free.

The synonym "foe" refers to "one who shows hostility or ill will." An enemy seeks to injure us in some way or to overthrow us. An enemy seeks our failure.

What does the dictionary say about the word "persecute?" Again, there is the intent to annoy or to injure.

What about the word "perfect?" There are many shades of meaning of this word. To be "perfect" means to be "sound," "complete," and "mature."

Pondering these definitions helps us to translate the Gospel imperative into daily life. We are to "love" our enemies and to show concern for their well-being. As a priest once advised, "Pray for their happiness."

Lord Jesus, what you're after in this Gospel is to bring us to maturity. This is a maturity so profound that we are enabled to see other people as our heavenly Father sees them. We receive the grace to treat them as our heavenly Father treats them. You know we can't do this on our own. Perhaps we don't even want to try. Thank you that the Holy Spirit lives within us to help us and to change us!

Sunday, March 19, 2000 Second Sunday in Lent
Mark 9, 2-10
The Transfiguration of Jesus

For three terrified disciples, this was the mountain top experience of all mountaintop experiences. Peter, James, and John saw Jesus transfigured before their very eyes. Elijah and Moses also appeared with Jesus on the mountain.

"Then a cloud came, casting a shadow over them; then from the cloud came a voice, 'This is my beloved Son. Listen to him.' Suddenly, looking around, they no longer saw anyone but Jesus alone with them."

We are living in such a stressful times. Some people seem always in a hurry and unwilling to defer to others, whether it's on the highway, the lab, the committee meeting or even at the health club, where the object is to relax as well as to exercise.

I was thinking and praying about this one day while I was lap swimming . The answer I sought was in today's Gospel.

In a stressful situation, if I can remember, I try to think of a "cloud" over all the people involved. Jesus is present. The Father is present. I try to listen to the voice of the Holy Spirit before speaking. This takes practice.

Ultimately, all the earthly situations we are currently so concerned about will cease. We will see Jesus as he truly is!

We may as well practice now. We don't have to go to a mountain top. Jesus is already with us. "Listen to him."

Monday, March 20, 2000 Lenten Weekday
Luke 2, 41-51
The Boy Jesus in the Temple

"How can this be ...?" Mary asked the angel Gabriel this question at the time of the Annunciation of the birth of Jesus.

At the time of the presentation of the infant Jesus in the Temple in Jerusalem, Simeon told Mary that Jesus would be a sign of contradiction and that Mary herself "a sword will pierce."

In today's Gospel, we read about Jesus at age twelve. No longer a child, he was beginning to take his place as a young Jewish man. The teachers in Jerusalem were "astounded at his understanding."

Jesus understood a great deal. He understood that he was now a young man who needed to be about his Father's business.

Mary and Joseph, however, did not see it that way. All they knew was that Jesus was missing and that they were frantic!

Jesus went back to Nazareth with his family as an obedient son. The time would come when he would no longer live with Mary and Joseph, but that time had not yet arrived.

Jesus waited. He worked. He trusted. He obeyed Mary and Joseph. Mary, his mother, "kept all these things in her heart."

Lord Jesus, in the midst of family matters which we do not understand, help us to trust you. Thank you that your will is being accomplished in us and in our family members.

Tuesday, March 21, 2000 Lenten Weekday
Matthew 23, 1-12
Denunciation of the Scribes and Pharisees

Jesus said, "The greatest among you must be your servant." Choosing to exalt oneself leads to being humbled, but willingly humbling oneself leads to being exalted.

The scribes and Pharisees just did not believe this. They were always promoting themselves and making sure that they were noticed.

Tragically, these leaders, even though they were religious leaders, were frauds. They hated Jesus for exposing them. Bullies, also known as cowards, never like to be exposed.

"They love to sit at the head table at church dinners, basking in the most prominent positions, preening in the radiance of public flattery, receiving honorary degrees, and getting called 'Doctor' and "Reverend (Matthew 23, 6-7, The Message).' " Jesus does not want us to be that way.

Jesus wants us to be simple and authentic, to be ourselves and to trust him with our lives. Serving is our business. Exalting is God's business.

Wednesday, March 22, 2000 Lenten Weekday
Matthew 20, 17-28
The Third Prediction of the Passion;
The Request of James and John

The clash with the chief priests was inevitable. Jesus, the most humble of all servants, was determined to go through whatever was necessary to pay the price for our redemption.

Jesus paid the ransom to set us free from the bondage of sin. He himself was the ransom. He himself was the sacrificial Lamb of God.

This clash with the authorities was inevitable. The chief priests and scribes had already condemned Jesus to death. They were merely waiting to make it official.

The mockery of a trial and the torture of the crucifixion would follow. The leaders could not and would not see Jesus as the fulfillment of prophecy. They could only see him as a threat to their power.

The clash with the disciples was also inevitable. Some of the disciples seemed eager to cash in on Jesus.

The disciples had seen his power. They loved him and followed him, true, but they also wanted to get in on the goodies of the future kingdom.

Jesus knew all about these clashes between the earthly and the heavenly. He knew he would die, but he also knew he would be raised on the third day.

Lord Jesus, there are sometimes clashes between the way in which you call us to serve you, the way in which others tell us to serve you, and the way which we think we should serve you. You alone are Lord! Empower us to serve you as you have called us to serve you, trusting in our own resurrection as well as in yours.

Thursday, March 23, 2000 St. Turibius de Mongrovejo
Luke 16, 19-31
The Parable of the Rich Man and Lazarus

The God who tests and probes the human heart will eventually set things right. It may seem that the rich get richer and the poor, such as Lazarus, get poorer, but it will not always be so.

We are living in springtime, in Lent, a time of grace. We are invited to ask the Holy Spirit to search our hearts and to show us how to live in the light of eternity.

Friday, March 24, 2000 Lenten Weekday
Matthew 21, 33-43, 45-46
The Parable of the Tenants

Jesus told the parable of the tenants and then asked, "Did you never read in the scriptures:

'The stone that the builders rejected
    has become the cornerstone;
by the LORD this has been done,
    and it is wonderful in our eyes?' "

The scribes and Pharisees knew that the parable was aimed at them and that Jesus was also aiming the quotation (from Psalm 118, 22) at them. Instead of accepting this rebuke, they dug in their heels and hated him even more.

Cornerstones have a hard time. They may look just like the other stones, but they are not.

God has selected cornerstones for a specific place. They are foundational for the whole structure.

Lord Jesus, thank you for being our cornerstone.

Saturday, March 25, 2000 The Annunciation of the Lord
Luke 1, 26-38
Announcement of the Birth of Jesus

Timing and trust. Angels and anxiety. Miracles and mothers. This Gospel has them all!

Timing. For Elizabeth, it was the six month of her pregnancy. For Mary, it was the beginning of the greatest adventure of her life. God's timing is unique and perfect for each of our lives.

Trust. "Behold, I am the handmaid of the Lord. May it be done to me according to your word." We can trust God. God is for us. God loves us.

Angels. God sent an angel, Gabriel, as the messenger to announce the birth of Jesus. God may send an "angel" or a special messenger into our lives today.

Anxiety. Mary was "greatly troubled at what was said and pondered what sort of greeting this might be." God knows our human frame and understands our need for reassurance.

Miracles. "Behold, you will conceive in your womb and bear a son, and you shall name him Jesus." God wants to do something extraordinary in our lives!

Mothers. The young virgin Mary asked, "How can this be, since I have no relations with a man?" The angel (messenger) answered. "The holy Spirit ..." The Holy Spirit will bring to birth the dreams or visions God has planted within us, as we continue to trust.

Heavenly Father, we trust you. Your timing is perfect. Thank you for the angels you send us, messengers who speak your word to us. We give you our anxiety. You are a God of miracles. Nothing is impossible for you. Thank you for choosing Mary to be the mother of Jesus our Lord. Her vocation was "impossible" and yet you fulfilled your word to her. Thank you that you will fulfill your word to us.

Sunday, March 26, 2000 Third Sunday in Lent
John 4, 5-42
The Samaritan Woman

Jesus told his disciples, "My food is to do the will of the one who sent me and to finish his work." Jesus, traveling from Judea to the Galilee, passed through Samaria.

It was here in Samaria that he met a woman at Jacob's well. "Jesus, tired from his journey, sat down there at the well. It was about noon."

Even though he was tired, he was still about his Father's business. His conversation with an "outsider," a woman, a despised Samaritan, transformed her life.

She was changed from an outcast to a woman on a mission! This extraordinary conversation covered everything from spiritual thirst, personal relationships, and Jewish worship, to the identity of the Messiah.

Are you tired? Are you tired physically, spiritually, emotionally, or mentally?

Jesus can refresh you with living water. Even in your weariness, as you await an infilling of the Water of Life, you can still do the will of the Father. You can still trust Jesus during this time of waiting. You can still speak to others in such a way that their lives will be changed. Your own thirst won't last forever. Jesus is here to refresh you.

Monday, March 27, 2000 Lenten Weekday
Luke 4, 24-30
The Rejection at Nazareth

Jesus is not playing church politics. He is speaking the truth and upsetting the apple cart!

The people in the synagogue turned on Jesus with fury. From speaking " highly of him" and being "amazed at the gracious words that came from his mouth" (Luke 4, 22), they became "filled with fury." "They rose up, drove him out of town, and led him to the brow of the hill on which their town had been built, to hurl him down headlong." Not exactly an affirmation of his prophetic ministry!

His prophetic ministry! Ah, therein lies the rub. They most definitely did not want anyone around who had a prophetic ministry, even if that someone was the Son of God.

Jesus knew this. "Amen, I say to you, no prophet is accepted in his own native place." When Jesus reminded the people in the synagogue about the prophetic ministries of Elijah and Elisha, they became unglued with rage.

Why? Why were they so mad? Jesus simply told the truth about the ministries of Elijah and Elisha.

The prophet Elijah did not minister to the widows in Israel, but rather to a poor widow in Zarephath in Sidon. The prophet Elisha ministered to another "foreigner," a Syrian leper named Naaman. Naaman did what Elisha said and was healed of leprosy!

Today's Gospel begins and ends with Jesus being in complete control. At the beginning of the Gospel, Jesus accepted the fact that a prophet was not accepted on home turf. At the end of the Gospel, surviving an attempt on his life, he calmly "passed through the midst of them and went away."

A true prophet speaks forth the word of God. In a litmus test, the paper turns red if dipped into an acid solution and blue if dipped into an alkaline solution. The litmus is merely the lichen-based coloring matter used as an indicator. How one responds to a true prophet of God is another kind of litmus test.

A prophet, according to the dictionary, is "one gifted with more than ordinary spiritual and moral insight." This definition certainly applies to Jesus and to his committed followers.

Lord Jesus, help us to live for you and to speak boldly for you. Help us not to take it personally if we are not accepted and affirmed on our earthly pilgrimage. Especially during this Lenten season, help us to be concerned only with pleasing you.

Tuesday, March 28, 2000 Lenten Weekday
Matthew 18, 21-35
The Parable of the Unforgiving Servant

A new mind-set. A new frame of reference. A new way of viewing those who have injured us. This is what Jesus is trying to teach us in this parable.

We don't have to secure justice or vengeance or even vindication for ourselves. That's all in the hands of our heavenly Father. We don't have to go out and make a house arrest or file a defamation of character lawsuit or even a class action suit.

Yes, yes, yes. What "they" did was wrong. Yes, there will be a time of reckoning.

But, no, it's not up to us to make it happen. In fact, it won't happen as long as we're trying to take matters into our own hands.

God knows. God is in charge.

God calls us, not to a mind-set of retaliation, but to a heart-set of forgiveness. Only the Holy Spirit can effect this connection of mind and heart. It happens when we truly realize that we ourselves have been forgiven.

We are unable to treat others as God requires if we persist in wanting to secure "justice" for ourselves. That's putting the cart before the horse.

Heavenly Father, change my mind and my heart. Forgive me and help me to realize the exhilaration of being forgiven. Thank you for the amazing power of the sacrament of reconciliation. Thank you for freedom.

Wednesday, March 29, 2000 Lenten Weekday
Matthew 5, 17-19
Teaching about the Law

Regarding the Law of Moses and the teaching of all the prophets, Jesus said, "I have not come to do away with them, but to make their teachings come true (Matthew 5, 17, <u>Good News Bible</u> (GNT))." Jesus came "not to abolish, but to fulfill."

In our own lives, sometime we still secretly fear that God wants to take from us. God's love for us, revealed in Christ's passion, death, and resurrection, is so overwhelming that the word "subtraction" is probably not even in the divine dictionary. With God, it's always giving, giving, and more giving.

Why stumble around on our crutches when we can abandon them and run with wild and joyful abandon in the meadows of God's amazing love and abundance? God gives us everything to enjoy.

During this Lent, let us focus not so much on subtraction or "giving up" as in gazing on this amazing God who gave and gave and gave so that we could live and live and live.

Thursday, March 30, 2000 Lenten Weekday
Luke 11, 14-23
Jesus and Beelzebul

The silent person could not speak as long as the "demon" of muteness was within. After Jesus had driven out this controlling entity, "the person spoke and the crowds were amazed."

You may say that that was then and this is now. However, Jesus has not changed. Our human condition has not changed.

We still need Jesus or one of his followers to set us free from whatever is hindering us or silencing us. Then we are free indeed!

It can work the other way. Once, at Mass, an obviously disturbed person kept talking and interrupting. Inaudibly I said, "Be silent, in Jesus' name." The talking ceased.

Do you have anything within you that hinders you? I do.

Lord Jesus, please speak to this entity, whatever it is, and tell it to go away. Let this day bring freedom and rejoicing!

Friday, March 31, 2000 Lenten Weekday
Mark 12, 28-34
The Greatest Commandment

The initials "W.W.J.D." have become very popular. They stand for "What would Jesus do?"

After reading today's Gospel, we might ask, "How would Jesus love?" Jesus makes it very simple and very severe.

"You shall love the Lord your God with all your heart, with all your soul, and with all your strength." "You shall love your neighbor as yourself."

Saturday, April 1, 2000 Lenten Weekday
Luke 18, 9-14
The Parable of the Pharisee and the Tax Collector

In this parable, the Pharisee stood by himself and congratulated himself that he was not like other people. He "posed," as The Message has it.

"Meanwhile, the tax man, slumped in the shadows, his face in his hands, not daring to look up, said, 'God, give mercy. Forgive me, a sinner.' Jesus commented, 'This tax man, not the other, went home made right with God. If you walk around with your nose in the air, you're going to end up flat on your face, but if you're content to be simply yourself, you will become more than yourself (The Message)."

To be right with God we have to come to a point of being honest with ourselves and being honest with God. How can we ask God for something, such as forgiveness, if we don't think we need it?

A person dying of thirst knows what is necessary for life to continue -- water! The tax collector, knowing that receiving God's mercy was imperative in his life, was desperate enough to beg, "O, God, be merciful to me a sinner."

388

In God's strange economy, the tax collector was the person to be exalted. Jesus said that exalting oneself leads to being humbled and that humbling oneself leads to being exalted.

Lord Jesus, sometimes I am afraid to face myself. Thank you for knowing me and loving me. You know what others do not know. You know what I am not yet ready to know. Thank you for sheltering me with your mercy.

Sunday, April 2, 2000 Fourth Sunday in Lent
John 9, 1- 41
The Man Born Blind

The blind man, who now saw clearly, was thrown out of the synagogue for his trust in Jesus and for his testimony to Jesus. Jesus quickly dismissed the notion that the blindness was due to sin. "Neither he nor his parents sinned; it is so that the works of God might be made visible through him."

This healing brought wholeness to the blind man, but caused division among the Pharisees. Some tried to discredit Jesus, while others asked, "How can a sinful man do such signs?"

The man's parents were bound by fear of the synagogue leaders. Their standing with the synagogue seemed to mean more to them than their standing with their own son.

The clincher came when the man who received his sight believed in Jesus, the Son of Man, and worshipped him. The synagogue leaders "threw him out." Jesus said, "I came into this world for judgment, so that those who do not see might see, and those who do see might become blind."

When Jesus opens your eyes, don't expect congratulations. Be prepared for misunderstanding, opposition and possibly division.

Monday, April 3, 2000 Lenten Weekday
John 4, 43-54
Return to Galilee; Second Sign at Cana

No matter how difficult the situation is, when Jesus speaks, the situation can instantly change. The word of Jesus has power!

This Gospel portrays a lonely Jesus. He is surrounded by people eager to see him do something miraculous. They seem driven by curiosity.

389

In Cana of Galilee, Jesus had turned the water into excellent wine for the enjoyment of the wedding guests. The signs he performed in Jerusalem during the feast of the Passover must have been stupendous. It was because of these signs that "the Galileans welcomed him" back to their region.

Returning to Cana, Jesus was approached by a royal official whose son was critically ill in Capernaum. Jesus did not offer immediate encouragement. "Unless you people see signs and wonders, you will not believe."

The official persisted and again asked Jesus to come to heal his son. It was at one o'clock in the afternoon when Jesus said to the official, "You may go; your son will live, " that the fever left the son. The official and "his whole household came to believe."

Lord Jesus, I know that you are powerful and that your word is powerful. Help me to seek you, not for your signs and wonders, but for you yourself. Draw me into the pavilion of your presence and let me rest and be restored.

Tuesday, April 4, 2000 St. Isidore
John 5, 1-3; 5-16
Cure on a Sabbath

Jesus is a confronter! He went to the pool of Bethesda and saw the man who had been ill for thirty-eight years. Although Jesus was aware of this lengthy illness, he still asked the man, "Do you want to be well?"

Ignoring the man's fixation on being healed a certain way, Jesus surprised him with a new approach. "Rise, take up your mat, and walk." The man was instantly healed and walked!

At the time of the healing, Jesus did not address the reason for the man's illness. He did that somewhat later.

Jesus sought out the man in the temple area. "Look, you are well; do not sin any more, so that nothing worse may happen to you."

Not all sicknesses are connected to sin, but some are. It's clear that this man's sickness, in some measure, was a result of sin. Jesus first healed this man physically and then, later, at the right time, confronted him about his sin.

390

Lord Jesus, is there something in my life that you want to confront today? During this Lent, help me to take the time to be still and to listen to you. Help me not to be afraid of what you might say. Thank you that your purpose in confrontation is healing.

Wednesday, April 5, 2000 St. Vincent Ferrer
John 5, 17-30
Cure on a Sabbath; The Work of the Son

Resurrection and judgment are tied together in this Gospel. Jesus ties them together.

Resurrection. "Do not be amazed at this, because the hour is coming in which all who are in the tombs will hear his voice and will come out ..." The Greek root of the word "resurrection" is "anastasis," which means, according to <u>Strong's Exhaustive Concordance</u>, "a standing up again."

Judgment. Jesus will make this decision, this judgment. "Nor does the Father judge anyone, but he has given all judgment to his Son, so that all may honor the Son just as they honor the Father. Whoever does not honor the Son does not honor the Father who sent him." All who are in the tomb will indeed come out, "... those who have done good deeds to the resurrection of life, but those who have done wicked deeds to the resurrection of condemnation."

Jesus! The Father gave Jesus "power to exercise judgment, because he is the Son of Man." Jesus knows, from first-hand experience, what it is to be human. He knows how hard it is.

Lord Jesus, I feel dead sometimes. Thank you that you can "resurrect" me even in this life. I look at you and I stand up again.

Thursday, April 6, 2000 Lenten Weekday
John 5, 31-47
Witnesses to Jesus; Unbelief of Jesus' Hearers

Jesus ultimately had to give up trying to convince his critics of his identity. He cited the testimony of his heavenly Father, the testimony of John the Baptist, the testimony of the works his Father had authorized him to accomplish, and of course, the testimony of sacred scriptures.

Enough already! How can Jesus give up? Even Jesus, the Son of God and Son of Man, could not and would not violate the free will expressed in the flinty hostility of his critics.

We know, of course, that Jesus did not really give up. He continued his ministry. He continued doing the work that his Father had given him to do.

Jesus knew that it was not ultimately up to him to convince people. "But there is another who testifies on my behalf, and I know that the testimony he gives on my behalf is true."

How much energy do we spend trying to convince those who will not believe? There is Another who testifies on our behalf.

Friday, April 7, 2000 St. John Baptist de la Salle
John 7, 1-2, 10, 25-30
The Feast of the Tabernacles; The First Dialogue

Have you ever tried and tried, without success, to thread a needle? The eye of the needle just seems to elude your best your efforts. It's very frustrating. The thread has to go through the eye of the needle in a very precise way at a very precise time.

Jesus is being threaded through the eye of a needle. The Father in heaven is not one bit frustrated. He is in complete control of the times and events in the life of his Son.

Jesus does not try to squeeze himself through the eye of the needle. He yields to his Father and allows his Father to guide him.

The opponents of Jesus could rage and fume all they wanted. They could do nothing because "his hour had not yet come."

We are being threaded through the eye of a needle this Lent. The Father is taking us from where we are and squeezing us, if we are willing to cooperate, through the eye of a needle. On the other side of the needle's eye is a "place" where we've never been before in our life with God. It is a place of deeper maturity and a place where we will fulfill our destiny.

It hurts to be compressed as we go through the eye of the needle. If we resist we will become scruffy and ragged. If we submit to the threading, we will be woven into a bright new tapestry.

Saturday, April 8, 2000 Lenten Weekday
John 7, 40-53
Discussions about the Origins of the Messiah

Jesus was clearly marching to the beat of another Drummer.

He was listening to his heavenly Father and speaking and acting through the power of the Holy Spirit. The whole dynamic of the Holy Trinity was in action.

"What was happening before?" and "What is happening after?" are key questions to ask in Gospel reflection." Before" today's Gospel, Jesus had just spoken of the power of the Holy Spirit (John 7, 37-39).

It was "after" hearing these words that the division spoken of in today's Gospel occurred. After the discussions about the origins of the Messiah, everyone went home, except Jesus. He went to the Mount of Olives until early the next morning.

There are at least two ways to live the life of faith. The first way is to listen to Jesus and respond to the Holy Spirit.

The other way is to nitpick and bicker with others about points of misunderstanding or disagreement. The choice is ours.

Some of the people in the crowd heard Jesus and said, "This is truly the Prophet." Others in the crowd said, "The Messiah will not come from Galilee, will he? Did not scripture say that the Messiah will be of David's family and come from Bethlehem, the village where David lived?"

Jesus, of course, was born in Bethlehem. He grew up in the Galilee area, in Nazareth, but he was born in Bethlehem.

The fact is, the Pharisees were so stubborn that nothing could convince them. When Nicodemus, one of their own, tried to appeal to their own law, they turned on him.

Lord Jesus, when we are in discussions which involve disagreement about you, give us the grace to listen to you and to trust you. You always have the final word because you are the final Word.

Sunday, April 9, 2000 Fifth Sunday in Lent
John 11, 1- 45
The Raising of Lazarus

Jesus was clearly in charge of life and death. At his command, "Lazarus, come out!" the dead man emerged from the tomb,

Jesus, however, still chose to involve others in this amazing drama. The requirement to be in on the action was to respond in trust and obedience to his word.

393

When told of the sickness of Lazarus, Jesus declared, "This illness is not to end in death, but is for the glory of God, that the Son of God may be glorified through it." With those words fresh in the minds and hearts of his hearers, Jesus still waited for two days. Lazarus died.

After all hope seemed gone, Jesus addressed his disciples. "Let us go back to Judea." He told his disciples bluntly, "Lazarus has died. And I am glad for you that I was not there, that you may believe."

Now came the really hard part. Jesus had to face Lazarus' sisters, Martha and Mary!

Because Jesus didn't show up in time, their brother was dead. Martha, with her tough trust, still affirmed her belief in the power of God working through Jesus. She told her friend, Jesus, "[But] even now I know that whatever you ask of God, God will give you." Jesus promised her, "Your brother will rise."

Acknowledging, yet correcting Martha's belief in her brother's future resurrection, Jesus redirected her attention to the present moment. "I am the resurrection and the life; whoever believes in me, even if he dies, will live, and everyone who lives and believes in me will never die. Do you believe this?"

Martha, with great faith, answered that she did believe. "Yes, Lord, I have come to believe that you are the Messiah, the Son of God, the one who is coming into the world." Present tense.

Now, Jesus had to face the sensitive, weeping Mary, falling at his feet. "When Jesus saw her weeping and the Jews who had come with her weeping, he became perturbed and deeply troubled, and said, 'Where have you laid him?' " Then Jesus himself wept.

At the burial cave, however, Jesus gave a simple order. "Take away the stone." Responding to the objections of practical Martha, Jesus said, "Did I not tell you that if you believe you will see the glory of God?"

After the stone was removed, Jesus proceeded to the next step. He prayed.

Note carefully how Jesus prayed. He began with thanksgiving, even in the face of death.

"Father, I thank you for hearing me. I know that you always hear me; but because of the crowd here I have said this, that they may believe that you sent me." A powerfully simple prayer.

With all the preparatory work completed, Jesus then spoke directly to Lazarus. "Lazarus, come out!"

Jesus made it clear that there was important work for the bystanders to do. "Untie him and let him go."

Yes, Jesus raised Lazarus. Yes, he spoke to a dead man and the dead man became alive again. Yet even Jesus did not act in a vacuum. He chose to involve others.

Do we presume to clutch a ministry tightly? It is not ours to clutch. We belong to Jesus. The ministry currently entrusted to us also belongs to Jesus. Sometimes a ministry has to "die " before this is realized.

Monday, April 10, 2000 Lenten Weekday
John 8, 1-11
A Woman Caught in Adultery

This was another attempt on the part of the scribes and Pharisees to trap Jesus. The woman was simply a convenient pawn to them.

Jesus refused to be trapped. After writing on the ground, he looked up and faced the woman's accusers. "Let the one among you who is without sin be the first to throw a stone at her." Again, he wrote on the ground until all had left.

Jesus then said to the woman, "Woman, where are they? Has no one condemned you?' "

The woman, whose life had been spared, answered, "No one, sir." Jesus, in his mercy, responded, "Neither do I condemn you. Go, [and] from now on do not sin any more."

This is a case of mercy triumphing over judgment. Jesus neither denied the woman's sin nor excused it. He transcended her sin with his own verdict. "Go, [and] from now on do not sin any more."

"For the judgment is merciless to one who has not shown mercy; mercy triumphs over judgment (James 2, 13)." This is a wake-up call for me, when I get into a critical, condemning mode. I need to back off, remember how merciful God has been to me, and then extend that same mercy to others.

It was for this woman's sins, as well as for all of our sins, that Jesus shed his precious blood on the cross. He is the Lamb of God who not only forgives our sins, but also takes them away.

395

That may be hard for us to understand. When Jesus forgives us, he literally takes our sins away. There are consequences of our sins, but the sins themselves are gone. The merciful God may even remove the consequences.

> "If you, LORD, mark our sins,
>   LORD, who can stand?
> But with you is forgiveness
>   and so you are revered (Psalm 130, 3-4)."

Tuesday, April 11, 2000 St. Stanislaus
John 8, 21-30
Jesus, the Father's Ambassador

Jesus was not here on earth on an ego trip. He was here on a Father trip. Everything he did was part of the Father's assignment for him, especially his death on the cross.

"When you lift up the Son of Man, then you will realize that I AM, and that I do nothing on my own, but I say only what the Father taught me. The one who sent me is with me. He has not left me alone, because I always do what is pleasing to him."

What is our frame of reference? For Jesus, the frame of reference was his relationship with his Father.

Wednesday, April 12, 2000 Lenten Weekday
John 8, 31-42
Jesus and Abraham

The people to whom Jesus spoke in today's Gospel seemed to be hermetically sealed, in some respects. They had come to believe in Jesus and yet they were sealed against the claims of Jesus. They were therefore sealed against the truth.

Jesus was and is the Truth! He said, "I am the way and the truth and the life (John 14, 6a)."

The frame of reference for his hearers was Abraham. "We are descendants of Abraham and have never been enslaved to anyone. How can you say, 'You will become free?' "

Jesus graciously accommodated himself to their frame of reference and yet they still refused to believe that they were enslaved to sin. They refused to face the truth about themselves.

"Abraham believed God, and it was credited to him as righteousness (Romans 4, 3)." The Mosaic law did not come before the promises made to Abraham.

The Mosaic law came long after, some four hundred years later (Galatians 3, 17). Still, the people in today's Gospel were trying to live the law without having truly grasped the promise.

Do we do that? We try so hard to please God. So many prayers. So much church going. So many efforts. That's all well and good, but what are we missing?

Sometimes we are refusing to face the truth about ourselves, that we were enslaved to sin and Jesus set us free. We are already free and yet we don't realize it. We don't live like it.

We keep trying to earn something that we already have. Jesus said, "If you remain in my word, you will truly be my disciples, and you will know the truth, and the truth will set you free."

Lord Jesus, thank you for setting me free from my sins. Thank you for setting me free to live for you today.

Thursday, April 13, 2000 St. Martin I
John 8, 51-59
Jesus and Abraham

Just who do you think you are? "Who do you make yourself out to be?"

That's what it came down to. Those questioning Jesus were not really looking for truth. They were looking for blood!

Jesus knew who he was! He was not searching for his identity. He knew who he was. He knew where he came from. He knew his vocation, He knew his final destiny.

His interrogators couldn't stomach this kind of vocational certainty. Nowadays, someone like Jesus would be sent off for therapy to explore his inner whatever.

Vocational confidence baffles and infuriates those who do not know God and who do not know themselves. Jesus knew who he was and whose he was.

So do we. "Beloved, we are God's children now; what we shall be has not yet been revealed. We do know that when it is revealed we shall be like him, for we shall see him as he is (I John 3, 2)."

Friday, April 14, 2000
John 10, 31-42
Feast of the Dedication

Jesus had just said, "The Father and I are one (John 10:30)." This astonishing statement follows the Good Shepherd passage in John's Gospel.

Jesus made it clear that the reason the Jewish authorities did not believe was because they were not among his own flock. "My sheep hear my voice; I know them, and they follow me (John 10:27)."

The religious authorities tried to stone Jesus to death because they could not grasp the concept of the incarnation. Their minds were tilting and their hearts were closed.

How could this carpenter from Nazareth be one with the heavenly Father? "You, a man, are making yourself God." That was the gist of their accusation.

What do we do when God acts in ways we don't understand? Do we shoot the messenger?

Lord Jesus, you were secure in your identity and your vocation. Help us to rest in your love for us and continue to minister as you lead us.

Saturday, April 15, 2000 Lenten Weekday
John 11, 45-57
Session of the Sanhedrin; The Last Passover

Jesus was always a sign of contradiction and a cause of division. After he raised Lazarus from the dead, many came to believe in him. Some, however, went to the Pharisees to report this latest deed.

The rubber had hit the road. "So the chief priests and the Pharisees convened the Sanhedrin and said, 'What are we going to do? This man is performing many signs. If we leave him alone, all will believe in him, and the Romans will come and take away our land and our nation.'"

Caiaphus, the high priest, had the perfect solution. "You know nothing, nor do you consider that it is better for you that one man should

398

die instead of the people, so that the whole nation may not perish." Jesus had just been elected as scapegoat!

Jesus, who performed signs, was himself the Sign! As Son of God, he was the greatest Sign of God.

The Prince of Peace was inevitably a cause of division because the proud, the haughty, and the politically motivated never want God. They only want their own power. They worship their power and will do anything to protect their power.

Lord Jesus, help us to walk closely with you, hand in hand, as we prepare for Holy Week. Help us to face the "Sanhedrins" in our own lives, knowing that we, who have shared your suffering, will also share in the joy and triumph of your resurrection.

Sunday, April 16, 2000 Passion Sunday
Mark 14, 1-15, 47
The Conspiracy against Jesus; The Anointing at Bethany;
The Betrayal by Judas; Preparation for the Passover;
The Betrayer; The Lord's Supper; Peter's Denial Foretold;
The Agony in the Garden; The Betrayal and Arrest of Jesus;
Jesus Before the Sanhedrin; Peter's Denial of Jesus;
Jesus Before Pilate; The Sentence of Death;
Mockery by the Soldiers; The Way of the Cross;
The Crucifixion; The Death of Jesus; The Burial of Jesus

Of all the events which sweep before us in today's Gospel, only one remains today. Only one is continued day after day.

The conspiracy of the high priests and scribes to kill Jesus is over. The beautiful anointing of Jesus at Bethany is over. The tragic betrayal by Judas is over. The preparation for that unique Passover is over. Jesus' prediction of woe to his betrayer have been spoken. Peter has been told that even he would deny his Lord. The time in which Jesus agonized in prayer in the Garden of Gethsemane is over. The brutal arrest of Jesus, complete with swords and clubs, is over. The mockery of the shabby, night trial of the Sanhedrin (the chief priests, scribes and elders) is over. The pitiable denial by Peter is over. Jesus' time of standing before the pathetic puppet, Pilate, is over. The sentence of death is over. The violent, savage scourging is over. The sneering mockery of the soldiers is over. Jesus has walked the way of his cross; this walk is over. The crucifixion is over. Jesus' death on the cross is over. The burial of Jesus is over.

All these events, so necessary for our salvation, are over. What remains?

The Lord's Supper remains. Jesus took bread, blessed it, broke it, gave it to his disciples, and said, "Take it; this is my body." "Then he took a cup, gave thanks, and gave it to them, and they all drank from it. He said to them, 'This is my blood of the covenant which will be shed for many (Mark 14, 21-24)."

We continue to proclaim the mysterious truth of our faith. "When we eat this bread and drink this cup, we proclaim your death, Lord Jesus, until you come in glory (Acclamation C from the Liturgy of the Eucharist)."

Monday, April 17, 2000 Monday in Holy Week
John 12, 1-11
The Anointing at Bethany

This dinner party at Bethany was a celebration sandwiched between two death and life experiences. The dinner occurred shortly after Jesus raised Lazarus from the dead and shortly before Jesus himself would suffer, die, and be raised from the dead.

In this dinner given for Jesus, we don't remember the menu. We don't even know what was served.

What we do remember is the worship, the costly, extravagant, fragrant worship. "Mary took a liter of costly perfumed oil made from genuine aromatic nard and anointed the feet of Jesus and dried them with her hair; the house was filled with the fragrance of the oil."

All through our lives, we are going to be in in-between situations. It is fitting that we continue to celebrate and to worship. The fragrance of our love and worship honors Jesus and refreshes others. There will be resurrection!

Tuesday, April 18, 2000 Tuesday in Holy Week
John 13, 21-33, 36-38
Announcement of Judas' Betrayal;
The New Commandment; Peter's Denial Foretold

In between betrayal and denial, there is glory! Jesus said, "Now is the Son of Man glorified, and God is glorified in him."

As The New Jerusalem Bible notes, "The Passion has already begun, since Judas has just gone out to do Satan's work: Jesus speaks of his victory as already won." One of the definitions of "glory," according to the dictionary, is "to shed radiance or splendor on." This is what God the Father was doing, as he bestowed praise and honor on his Son.

Yes, there was still the arrest, the mockery of a trial, the cruel scourging, and the crucifixion ahead. This was a moment, however, to see beyond that and to rejoice.

"For the sake of the joy that lay before him he [Jesus] endured the cross, despising its shame, and has taken his seat at the right hand of the throne of God. Consider how he endured such opposition from sinners, in order that you may not grow weary and lose heart (Hebrews 12, 2b, 3)."

Wednesday, April 19, 2000 Wednesday in Holy Week
Matthew 26, 14-25
The Betrayal of Judas; Preparation for the Passover

Have you ever had a Judas in your life? Someone you deeply trusted, someone you broke bread with, who then turned on you and betrayed you out of self-interest? That person chose self over you.

Jesus was keenly aware that his "hour," his "appointed time" was drawing near. At the feast of the Passover he told the Twelve, "Amen, I say to you, one of you will betray me."

Jesus knew he was to suffer and die. Still, he said, "The Son of Man indeed goes, as it is written of him, but woe to that man by whom the Son of Man is betrayed. It would be better for that man if he had never been born."

Lord Jesus, as we offer forgiveness to the "Judas" in our lives, we also ask forgiveness for the times we have betrayed you. In the holy days ahead, let us spend time in your presence. You are our Paschal Lamb who was sacrificed for us. "Therefore, let us celebrate the feast, not with the old yeast of malice and wickedness, but with the unleavened bread of sincerity and trust (1 Corinthians 5, 8)." Let us gaze on you. "All of us, gazing with unveiled face on the glory of the Lord, are being transformed into the same image from glory to glory, as from the Lord, as from the Lord who is the Spirit (2 Corinthians 3, 18)."

Thursday, April 20, 2000 Passover, Holy Thursday
John 13, 1-15
The Washing of the Disciples' Feet

Judas was a tool of the devil. "The devil had already induced Judas, son of Simon the Iscariot, to hand him [Jesus] over."

Jesus knew that "his hour had come to pass from this world to the Father." In the past, Jesus had said that "his hour" had not yet come. Now, however, was the time, the appointed "hour."

Today is Passover. We remember that the Lord provided a sacrificial lamb. God's people feasted on the lamb and then they put the blood of the lamb on their doorposts. Seeing the blood, God would "pass over" the Israelites and spare them from destruction as he struck the land of Egypt with this last plague.

Jesus is our Passover Lamb. When God saw the blood of this Lamb, he "passed over" judging our sins. Our sins were judged and destroyed on the Cross.

Now Jesus invites us to follow him in laying down our lives. We don't necessarily have to wash dirty feet and we don't have to be nailed to a cross. We simply offer ourselves to be used as God directs.

Tragically, Judas was a tool of the devil. Let us be tools in the hands of our God to serve one another in humility.

Friday, April 21, 2000 Good Friday
John 18, 1-19, 42
Jesus Arrested; Peter's First Denial;
The Inquiry before Annas; Peter Denies Jesus Again;
The Trial before Pilate; The Crucifixion of Jesus;
The Blood and Water; The Burial of Jesus

John's Gospel portrays our Lord as sovereign God clothed in human flesh. Jesus, knowing that his earthly mission was soon to be consummated, calls himself, "I AM." That is the divine name, the name of majesty and authority.

When interrogated by Annas, the high priest, about his disciples and his doctrine, Jesus was undeterred. "I have spoken publicly to the world. I have always taught in a synagogue or in the temple area where all the Jews gather, and in secret I have said nothing." When struck in the face, Jesus remained in control and replied, "If I have spoken wrongly, testify to the wrong; but if I have spoken rightly, why do you strike me?"

To Pilate's question, "What have you done?" Jesus responded with a reference to his sovereignty. "My kingdom does not belong to this world. If my kingdom did belong to this world, my attendants [would] be fighting to keep me from being handed over to the Jews. But, as it is, my kingdom is not here."

To Pilate's persistent questioning, "Then you are a king?" Jesus answered, 'You say I am a king. For this I was born and for this I came into the world, to testify to the truth. Everyone who belongs to the truth listens to my voice.' "

Pilate began to be very uneasy, as all cowards do when faced with someone of unshakable integrity. He asked Jesus, "Where are you from?" Jesus remained silent.

Pilate must have been baffled. "Do you not know that I have the power to release you and I have power to crucify you?" Jesus knew that Pilate in himself had no power. "You would have no power over me if it had not been given you from above. For this reason the one who handed me over to you has the greater sin."

John's Gospel portrays Jesus carrying his own cross to Calvary. He willingly lays down his life.

From the cross, Jesus made provision for his mother. "When Jesus saw his mother and the disciple whom he loved, he said to his mother, 'Woman, behold your son.' Then he said to the disciple, 'Behold your mother.' "

"After this, aware that everything was now finished, in order that the scripture might be fulfilled, Jesus said, 'I thirst.' There was a vessel filled with common wine. So they put a sponge soaked in wine on a sprig of hyssop and put it up to his mouth. When Jesus had taken the wine, he said, 'It is finished.' And bowing his head, he handed over the spirit."

Lord Jesus, they crucified you but they did not break your determination to carry out your Father's will. You were given temporarily into the hands of evil ones so that the power of the Evil One over us could be broken forever. You are Lord!

Saturday, April 22, 2000 Holy Saturday;
Mark 16, 1-8
The Resurrection of Jesus

Darkness. Silence. Waiting.

On this day of all days we wait. We know that the crucified Lord has already been gloriously raised. Still, we wait.

We often live our lives in the space of Holy Saturday. We are continually experiencing death and resurrection in different aspects of our lives. Between the death and resurrection is our personal Holy Saturday, our time of waiting and trusting.

Mary Magdalene and the other women eagerly sought the Lord. "Very early when the sun had risen, on the first day of the week, they came to the tomb. They were saying to one another, 'Who will roll back the stone for us from the entrance to the tomb?' "

The women were startled to see that the stone had already been rolled back. God's messenger, a young man in white, told them, "Do not be amazed! You seek Jesus of Nazareth, the crucified. He has been raised; he is not here. Behold, the place where they laid him."

The women were quickly given a mission. "But go and tell his disciples and Peter, 'He is going before you to Galilee; there you will see him, as he told you.' "

Their grief was turned to amazement and their amazement was directed to mission. They were to "go and tell."

As we patiently and joyfully wait within the confines of our own Holy Saturday, we are certain of two things. First, this time of waiting will come to an end. There will be resurrection! Second, we will be given a new assignment to "go and tell." Alleluia!

Sunday, April 23, 2000 Easter Sunday
John 20, 1-9
The Empty Tomb

Lord Jesus, sometimes our lives do not declare that you have risen from the dead. We believe and yet we are not shining with Easter joy.

Let us trust even though we do not fully understand. Let us run, like Mary Magdalene, and tell others what we do know. You will lead us, as you led Peter and John and all your followers into fuller understanding.

Lord Jesus, we place all our trust in you. Let your Easter triumph shine forth in our lives. Alleluia!

Monday, April 24, 2000 Easter Monday
Matthew 28, 8-15
The Resurrection of Jesus; The Report of the Guard

Life and truth reigned in the midst of death and falsehood. The lying continued even in the face of the resurrection. The chief priests and elders, who had never accepted Jesus, lied about him, plotted his death, mocked him in his agony on the cross, now bribed the soldiers to lie. Jesus was still a threat to them.

Jesus, however, could not be silenced. The crucified Lord was now the risen Lord!

Jesus broke the death barrier. He continues today to be "the way and the truth and the life (John 14, 6)."

The women at the tomb were "fearful yet overjoyed" as they hurried to tell the disciples. The empty tomb was simultaneously a mystery and a joy to them because they were living in the reality of life and truth.

The risen Jesus met the women and greeted them. "Do not be afraid. Go tell my brothers to go to Galilee, and there they will see me."

Lord Jesus, we rejoice in you and we exult in you! Thank you that you won! You won over the powers of evil and death. Let us walk today in the joy and the power of this new life of truth that you have won for us. Alleluia!

Tuesday, April 25, 2000 Easter Tuesday
John 20, 11-18
The Appearance to Mary of Magdala

Mary Magdalene was overwhelmed with love, grief, confusion, and exhaustion. With her whole heart, she loved Jesus, this man who had changed her life, who had liberated her from seven demons (Mark 16, 9).

In her wild grief, she was determined to be near him, even if he was in a tomb. The tomb was empty. She was confused as she wept, wondering where he had been taken. She was exhausted, having kept vigil at the cross with the other women.

"Mary!" The risen Christ spoke her name.

In an instant, everything changed! Jesus was alive! He was right there with her. "She turned and said to him in Hebrew, 'Rabbouni,' which means 'Teacher.' "

Jesus gave her a mission. "Stop holding on to me, for I have not yet ascended to the Father. But go to my brothers and tell them, 'I am going to my Father and your Father, to my God and your God.' " "Mary

405

of Magdala went and announced to the disciples, 'I have seen the Lord,' and what he told her."

In our love, our grief, our confusion, and our exhaustion, Jesus speaks to us. He knows us by name and speaks our name. He reassures us of his presence with us and then he gives us a new assignment. Alleluia!

Wednesday, April 26, 2000 Easter Wednesday
Luke 24, 13-38
The Appearance on the Road to Emmaus

A retired clergy friend, not given to mystical experiences, told of an experience many years ago when she was studying in a Protestant seminary. She was in a seminar, with other students, seated around a large conference table. It seemed to be just another class, but it was not. My friend was startled to "see" JESUS sitting at the conference table with the seminarians listening to their discussion. The others did not seem to see him, but she did. The experience, brief though it was, was of critical importance in her vocation.

Two followers of Jesus, Cleopas and another person, did not expect to see Jesus himself on the road to Emmaus. They were bewildered over the events that led up to his crucifixion." Jesus himself drew near and walked with them, but their eyes were prevented from recognizing him."

On this walk, Jesus broke open the scriptures for his followers. In the village, the three stopped for a meal. "And it happened that, while he was with them at table, he took bread, said the blessing, broke it and gave it to them. With that their eyes were opened and they recognized him, but he vanished from their sight. Then they said to one another, 'Were not our hearts burning [within us] while he spoke and opened the scriptures to us?' "

Lord Jesus, thank you for your presence with us today. Help us be open to your surprise ways of speaking to us. Alleluia!

Thursday, April 27, 2000 Easter Thursday
Luke 24, 35-48
The Appearance on the Road to Emmaus;
The Appearance to the Disciples in Jerusalem

Jesus made himself known to two of his followers in the breaking of bread. This took place after Jesus, while on the way to Emmaus, "interpreted to them what referred to him in all the scriptures (Luke 24, 27)."

Jesus, if he chose, could suddenly appear as a celestial Superman, but that is not usually the way he manifests his presence and his identity. His usual way is to lead us gently from our present understanding of him into the next step of a deeper understanding.

This step is tailor-made for us. Jesus knows exactly what we need in order to advance on the road of discipleship.

In Jerusalem, Jesus stood in the midst of the debating disciples and said simply, "Peace be with you." "But they were startled and terrified and thought they were seeing a ghost."

Jesus reassured them by inviting them to touch him. "Touch me and see, because a ghost does not have flesh and bones as you can see I have."

Jesus did not ridicule them. He reassured them. He even ate a piece of fish in their presence.

Again, Jesus referred to the scriptures. "He said to them, 'These are my words that I spoke to you while I was still with you, that everything written about me in the law of Moses and in the prophets and psalms must be fulfilled.' Then he opened their minds to understand the scriptures."

Lord Jesus, thank you that you are present with us today. Help us to meet you in the scriptures and in the breaking of the bread. Alleluia!

Friday, April 28, 2000 Easter Friday
John 21, 1-14
The Appearance to the Seven Disciples

Peter! Peter jumped into the water yet again, wanting to be where Jesus was.

Once, when the disciples were in the boat on the stormy sea, Jesus came to them, walking on the water. Peter alone ventured out of the safety of the boat and into the uncertainty of the sea (Matthew 14, 22-33).

In today's Gospel, it was again Peter who left the safety of the boat and plunged into the sea to swim ashore to the risen Jesus, waiting on the shore. It was Peter who dragged the huge catch of one hundred fifty-three fish ashore.

The encounter of Jesus and Peter (John 21, 15-23) is not part of today's Gospel, and yet today's Gospel is a necessary prelude to this meeting. We see the predisposition of Peter's heart and we see Jesus' tender preparation for the dialogue that was to come.

Jesus invited the disciples to a seaside breakfast. After their futile night time fishing expedition, they saw Jesus on the shore, but did not recognize him. After the miraculous catch of fish, "they realized it was the Lord."

Lord Jesus, help me today to jump into your arms of love by trusting you. Thank you that you will not let me drown. Alleluia!

Saturday, April 29, 2000 Easter Saturday
Mark 16, 9-15
The Appearance to Mary Magdalene;
The Appearance to the Disciples;
The Commissioning of the Eleven

This is a terse, compacted Gospel. Mark's Gospel has been called the "go" Gospel or the "straightaway" Gospel. Mark doesn't mince or waste words.

We are told that Jesus appeared to his eleven disciples and "rebuked them for their unbelief and hardness of heart because they had not believed those who saw him after he had been raised."

Still, Jesus sent the disciples out into the world. "Go into the whole world and proclaim the gospel to every creature." Regardless of the state of our puzzled minds and anxious hearts, we too are to carry out this command.

Lord Jesus, thank you that you triumphed over death. You are alive! You won! You love us and long for us to share your life and your love with the "whole world." You don't wait for perfection in us. You send us out today, as we are, to "proclaim the gospel." Alleluia!

Sunday, April 30, 2000 Second Sunday of Easter
Divine Mercy Sunday
John 20, 19-31
Appearance to the Disciples; Thomas; Conclusion

After his resurrection, "Jesus did many other signs in the presence of his disciples, which are not written in this book. But these are written so that you may come to believe that Jesus is the Messiah, the Son of

408

God, and that through believing you may have life in his name (John 20, 30-31 N.R.S.V.).

God has already given us what we need to believe. Jesus graciously complied with Thomas' need to see the nail marks and to put his hand into the side of his Lord. Still, Jesus said that those who have not seen and yet believe are happy and blessed.

Through our belief and our trust in the risen Jesus, we have "life in his name." We have his Easter peace, his "shalom." With this peace and with the power of the Holy Spirit, we have all we need to fulfill our vocation. Alleluia!

[Apparently, with the time between the original writing, entering the text into the computer, and then resuming the writing, I wrote reflections for the first week in Easter twice! I will just leave them as they are.]

Monday, April 21, 2003 Easter Monday
Matthew 28, 8-15
The Resurrection of Jesus; The Report of the Guard

Are we attuned to Life and Truth or to death and deception? Both mind-sets are illustrated in today's Gospel.

Mary Magdalene and the other Mary (Matthew 28, 1) sought Jesus even when he was in the tomb. The risen Jesus met them and gave them a mission.

The chief priests and elders, on the other hand, in refusing Life and Truth, lost their Way. Jesus himself was the Way, the Truth and the Life (John 14, 6).

In the face of the resurrection, they pathetically clung to their lies and bribed the soldiers of the guard to lie. In the face of Life and Truth they clung to death and deception.

Lord Jesus, you broke through the tomb with radiant truth. You yourself are Truth! Today, let my life reflect Life and Truth. Alleluia!

Tuesday, April 22, 2003 Easter Tuesday
John 20, 11-18
The Appearance to Mary of Magdala

What do you DO when you are depressed or even when you are in despair? You know how you "feel," but what action do you take?

Mary Magdalene was in deep despair by the tomb of Jesus. What could seem a more definitive "no" than a tomb?

Death reigned. Jesus was dead and gone. Really?

However, she did not run away. She remained outside the tomb even after Peter and the other disciple went home. She stayed.

Although she was weeping, she was also trying to peer into the tomb. It was then that she saw God's messengers, the two angels in white. The angels were in the place where Jesus had been lying.

It was as she answered the question of the angels, God's messengers, that she saw Jesus! Never mind that she thought he was the gardener.

Jesus spoke to her and asked her why she was in tears. He asked her to tell him whom she was seeking.

Mary just didn't comprehend. Then Jesus spoke again. "Mary!

Hearing her name as only Jesus could say it, Mary turned to the risen Jesus. "Rabbouni!" "Teacher!"

She attempted to hold onto him. Jesus wisely gave her a mission. Something new to do! He commissioned Mary to go and tell. Mary Magdalene has been called "the apostle to the apostles."

Mary went, as Jesus told her, to his brothers. She proclaimed to them her experience of the risen Lord.

Mary, although initially very much in depression and despair, still acted. She took one step after another. Her obedience and her actions led her to the risen Christ.

Lord Jesus, even when I'm feeling "down," you still have something for me to do. Help me to keep on doing the next thing you tell me to do. Thank you that you are with me always. Alleluia!

Wednesday, April 23, 2003 Easter Wednesday
Luke 24, 13-35
The Appearance on the Road to Emmaus

Be ready! You don't know when Jesus will show up.

For that matter, you don't know when one of the followers of Jesus will show up.

Usually an early riser, I'd slept later than usual on Good Friday, just last week. I was in the kitchen making coffee when the phone rang.

Surprise! It was a delightfully unexpected call from a clergy friend in another area, We had been in ministry together in the Clinical Pastoral Education program many years ago.

That phone call changed my entire outlook on Good Friday. I was in an anticipatory frame of mind and heart all day.

Jesus surprised two of his followers on the road to Emmaus. He was right there with them, but they did not recognize him. He prepared them by leading them through the Hebrew scriptures which referred to him.

It was at table as he took, blessed, and broke the bread that the eyes of their understanding were opened and they recognized the risen Lord.

He vanished from their physical sight. Still, they rejoiced.

Lord Jesus, thank you that you are always with me in the Person of the Holy Spirit. Today, let me anticipate you and be open to your appearance in my life. Alleluia!

Thursday, April 24, 2003 Easter Thursday
Luke 24, 35-48
The Appearance to the Disciples in Jerusalem

Yesterday's Gospel concluded with two excited, energized disciples who had encountered Jesus on the road to Emmaus, sharing their stories back in Jerusalem. As they spoke, surprise! There was Jesus again, right there with them.

Truly, wherever two or three have assembled in the name of Jesus, he is right there with them. (Matthew 18, 20) This is true whether or not

411

the two or three or however many "feel" his presence. He is there and his power is available.

This time, Jesus, understanding the fright of the disciples, spoke words of peace and reassurance to them. As with his friends on the Emmaus road, he referred to the Hebrew scriptures and to the prophecies which he had fulfilled. He promised his dazed disciples that he would send the Holy Spirit to empower them.

Lord Jesus, thank you that you are always present when we gather in your name. Sharpen our awareness of your presence and your power amongst us. Alleluia!

Friday, April 25, 2003 Easter Friday
John 21, 1-14
The Appearance to the Seven Disciples

How will Jesus reveal himself to you today? Over the last few days, we've watched as he revealed himself, through Scripture and the breaking of the bread, to his initially perplexed friends on the Emmaus road and then again to his frightened friends in Jerusalem.

In today's Gospel, Jesus reveals himself a third time. This time it is to seven of his disciples. The seven had been out on a fruitless fishing expedition. When they returned at dawn, Jesus was on the shore!

Aware of their lack of success, Jesus advised them to cast their net from the boat's right side. What was there to lose?

The beloved disciple recognized Jesus first and then told Peter. Peter, being Peter, plunged right back into the water, while the others remained in the boat!

Sound familiar? In Matthew's Gospel, it was Peter alone who jumped out of the boat to go to Jesus on the water (Matthew 14, 22-33). It was also Peter who dragged the heavy net, laden with fish, to the shore.

The disciples now understood that the Risen Lord was with them. Again, Jesus took bread and gave it to them.

Lord Jesus, you knew exactly how and when to appear to your friends. My nets seem empty, but I know you will show up at the right time and tell me how and where to fish today. More than "fish," I long for you to reveal yourself to me. Alleluia!

Saturday, April 26, 2003 Easter Saturday
Mark 16, 9-15
The Appearance to Mary Magdalene;
The Appearance to the Two Disciples;
The Commissioning of the Eleven

What are you waiting for before you tell your world about your Risen Lord? You are ready! You don't have to be perfect and you don't have to understand everything.

Mary Magdalene fulfilled Jesus' mandate to go and tell his disciples. She has been called "the apostle to the apostles."

The two on the Emmaus road told the Eleven of their encounter with the Lord. How could they not tell?

Jesus himself appeared to the Eleven and reproved them for not truly believing the report of the others. Still, he commissioned them to preach the Gospel to all.

We are responsible for proclaiming the Gospel. We may ask for an increase of boldness and confidence, but we are still called to proclaim Jesus by our lives and in our words.

Lord Jesus, forgive us for evading and avoiding doing what you have commissioned us to do. Fill us afresh with your Holy Spirit to live and to speak for your glory. Alleluia!

Sunday, April 27, 2003 Second Sunday of Easter
Divine Mercy Sunday
John 20, 19-31
Appearance to the Disciples; Thomas

Jesus said it! JESUS said the most startling "f" word. "FORGIVE!"

On the Cross, Jesus prayed that his Father in heaven would forgive those who had put him to death. Now, after the Resurrection, Jesus had something to teach his disciples about forgiveness.

The poor, frightened disciples were cringing behind locked doors on the evening of the Resurrection. No problem for Jesus.

Jesus simply walked right in the room. Doors? What doors?

After speaking peace to his followers, Jesus showed them his wounded side and his hands. As they marveled and rejoiced, Jesus again

413

spoke words of peace. Jesus then simply breathed on his disciples and told them to receive the Holy Spirit.

Jesus immediately began to speak of forgiveness. He gave to his disciples the privilege and the responsibility of forgiving sins.

Jesus, as you recall, tied the Father's forgiveness of our sins to our willingness to forgive others (Matthew 6, 14-15 and Mark 11, 25). Every time we pray the Lord's Prayer, we pray this way.

Lord Jesus, you went out of your way to show all your disciples, including Thomas, your love and your understanding. You knew that the gift of the Holy Spirit would be necessary, not only for the proclamation of the Gospel, but also for the forgiveness of sins. If for no other reason than our own need to have our sins forgiven, we choose, as an act of the will, to forgive others. Thank you for your peace, joy, and, most of all, for the gift of the Holy Spirit. Alleluia!

Monday, April 28, 2003 St. Peter Chanel
John 3, 1-8
Nicodemus

Another kind of birth is the prerequisite for seeing and entering the kingdom of God. This kingdom is the realm where the will of God is perfectly accomplished.

Nicodemus, a Pharisee and probably one of the seventy-one members of the elite Sanhedrin, could not shift his earthbound thinking. As a religious insider, he may have thought he had the ways of God all figured out. Surprise!

At one his huge crusades, a well-known contemporary evangelist told a true story of a Christian woman on a train. Noticing a fellow commuter, she struck up a conversation and asked if he was a Christian. The man replied, complacently, by stating his status in the church. The woman politely countered, "I did not ask that. I asked if you were a CHRISTIAN."

The shaken man of high position returned home and began to think and to pray. He knelt and asked Jesus to forgive his sins and to come into his heart in a decisive way. Jesus heard and answered that prayer in the affirmative.

Alleluia!

Tuesday, April 29, 2003 St. Catherine of Siena
John 3, 7-15
Nicodemus

Incarnation! The mysterious blending of flesh and spirit. God becoming a human being. Born from above.

Poor Nicodemus. The teacher. The expert. The scholar. What does he know? What does he really know? Who does he really know?

Jesus, the Messiah, the Son of Man and Son of God stands before him. Nicodemus just doesn't get it. He is in spiritual nursery school.

The Holy Spirit breathes. The Holy Spirit whispers. The Holy Spirit reigns.

Jesus, who came down from heaven, will be lifted high on a Cross. Death for Jesus. Life for us.

Then, Jesus, infused with the Holy Spirit, is lifted again to heaven. Home.

Who can understand? The Holy Spirit is our gentle Teacher.

Lord Jesus, how can we aspire to the heavenly when we gasp at the temporal? We fly into your heart and rest in you as you reveal the mysteries of the kingdom. Alleluia!

Wednesday, April 30, 2003 St. Pius V
John 3, 16-21
Nicodemus

God loved, so God gave. It is impossible to love without giving.

God loved us so much that Jesus came to live among us, to love us, to comfort us, to confront us, and to die for us.

Why? Why would Jesus do that?

God wants us to live with him forever. With our sins, with all that separates us from a holy God, that would not be possible.

The solution? Jesus, the Son of God, took all our sins into himself. Then he died on the Cross. Our sins were in Jesus, and when he died, our sins "died."

Jesus made it possible for us to be free! Do we really believe that?

St. Paul knew first-hand about having his own sins forgiven. He helps us to understand this mind-boggling truth. He wrote, " I have been crucified with Christ; it is no longer I who live, but it is Christ who lives in me. And the life I now live in the flesh I live by faith in the Son of God, who loved me and gave himself for me" (Galatians 2, 20, N.R.S.V.).

It is possible to know this truth and still not to enjoy it. Jesus has made it possible for us to live!

We are now free to pursue the specific way God's love is to be worked out in our lives. How do we love? How do we give?

Lord Jesus, help us not to waste time and energy in condemning ourselves or others. Show us how to live truth and speak truth today. Thank you for your life, your eternal life, flowing through us today. Alleluia!

Thursday, May 1, 2003 St. Joseph the Worker
John 3, 31-36
The One from Heaven

Jesus came from heaven to earth, via the Blessed Virgin Mary. God sent Jesus to us. Jesus spoke and lived God's words.

In the preceding days, we have read in John's Gospel about God's love. God's love always involves giving.

Today's Gospel emphasizes God's love of Jesus. God has given everything to his Son.

Lord Jesus, you came into this world as a tiny, helpless infant in a poor family, and yet you have all the riches of heaven at your disposal. Help us not to be frightened when we pray. Help us to be confident that you, our wise, older Brother, will take us by the hand and lead us through our time on this earth to our loving Father in heaven. Alleluia!

Friday, May 2, 2003 St. Athanasius
John 6, 1-15
Multiplication of the Loaves

Jesus told his followers to gather all the fragments of the loaves so that nothing would be wasted. Although the multiplication of the loaves is recorded in all four Gospels, only John's Gospel records this specific instruction to gather the fragments.

416

Jesus instructed the disciples to gather the leftover fragments. They collected twelve wicker baskets of fragments. Twelve disciples. Twelve baskets.

What is in your basket of leftover fragments? What is in my basket of leftover fragments? Lost hopes? Forgotten dreams? Fears that never go away? Can these be offered to Jesus?

Jesus desires a total offering of our lives. Forget reality television. This is reality discipleship.

Lord Jesus, thank you for transforming us even at this moment. Thank you for the miracle awaiting us as we offer back to you the leftover fragments of our lives. Alleluia!

Saturday, May 3, 2003 Sts. Philip and James
John 14, 6-14
Last Supper Discourse

Jesus did not say he was "a" way. He said he was THE way.

Jesus was responding to a question from Thomas. Thomas was asking about the way to the Father's house.

Thomas was the disciple who later required tangible proof of Jesus' resurrection. Jesus did not ridicule Thomas. For Thomas, it was necessary to see the risen Lord for himself, seeing his nail-pierced hands and touching his side.

Nor did Jesus ridicule Thomas at the Last Supper for his question about knowing the way to the place Jesus would prepare for him. Jesus knew how to respond to the deepest concerns in Thomas' heart.

Jesus assured Thomas and assures us that he himself IS the way to the Father. Earlier in John's Gospel (John 1, 1-18), Jesus referred to himself, not only as the Good Shepherd but also as the actual gate to the sheepfold.

Philip must have been from Missouri (the "show me" state), because, along with Thomas, he also wanted to be shown! Philip asked Jesus to show him the Father

Jesus assured Philip that his request had already been granted. The words spoken by Jesus and the works performed by Jesus originated and emanated from the heart of God.

Amazing! Also amazing that Jesus promised his followers that they would do even greater works than the one he, in his limited mission to earth, would accomplish.

Lord Jesus, thank you that you yourself ARE the way to the Father in heaven. You said that if we ask anything in your name, you will do it. How you answer and when you answer may be beyond our current comprehension. Thank you that you will answer. Alleluia!

Sunday, May 4, 2003 Third Sunday of Easter
Luke 24, 35-48
The Appearance to the Disciples in Jerusalem

Jesus will come and enter into your words. JESUS!

As you speak of your experience of Jesus, Jesus himself is with you. It was as the two excited followers of Jesus who had walked with him on the road to Emmaus were telling their story to the disciples in Jerusalem that Jesus appeared!

We may think we are all alone and that we are awkward as we tell others of Jesus, but that is not so. Jesus is present. Did he not tell us that when two or three are gathered in his name he is right there with them (Matthew 18, 20)?

So what if our words are not accepted? So what? We have fulfilled our mission to go and tell.

Jesus will take up where we left off. He will tell the ones we were speaking to what they need to hear.

As Jesus interpreted the prophetic passages in the Law of Moses, the prophets, and the psalms to the disciples, he will interpret your words to the ones who hear your testimony. He will make sure they hear what they need to hear, not necessarily what you think they need to hear. He is Lord! He is in charge.

Lord Jesus, thank you for your presence with us and power within us as we bear witness to you. Alleluia!

Monday, May 5, 2003
John 6, 22-29
The Bread of Life Discourse

Jesus sees through and walks through closed hearts and minds as well as through closed and locked doors. The crowd had asked one question.

Jesus, knowing their intent, answered the real question. His answer exposed their motive.

The words of Jesus are words are spirit and life (John 6, 63). Jesus himself IS the Word. Jesus himself is Life.

Jesus admonished the crowd, so intent on signs, wonders, and physical food, not to labor so intently for temporary, perishable, edible food.

Then the crowd naively asked how to do the works of God. Jesus again referred to himself. To do God's work, it was first necessary to believe in God's Son, the true and living Bread of Life.

Lord Jesus, you alone see and understand our motives. As you directed the questioning of the crowd in today's Gospel, so direct us into our true work of trusting and believing in you. Revive hope when we have grown weary and discouraged. Alleluia!

Tuesday, May 6, 2003
John 6, 30-35
The Bread of Life Discourse

The people in the crowd seemed to think that Jesus was up for an interview! They showed curiosity, but not necessarily reverence as they questioned him.

They asked Jesus what he could do. They reminded Jesus what Moses had done in providing manna in the wilderness.

Jesus immediately corrected them. It was not Moses, but God, who had provided the miraculous manna from heaven to their ancestors.

God gave his Son Jesus as the living and true Bread. Jesus told the curiosity seekers that he himself was the Bread of Life. He told them that it was necessary to come to him and to put their trust in him in order never to hunger or thirst.

Lord Jesus, I hunger and thirst for you. I come to you, adore you, worship you, and ask you for a deeper understanding than I've ever had of you as the true Bread and sustenance of my life. Alleluia!

Wednesday, May 7, 2003
John 6, 35-40
The Bread of Life Discourse

Seeing is not necessarily believing. The crowds saw Jesus. They saw him perform miracles. They heard him speak of the kingdom.

However, we are the ones Jesus called happy and blessed! We are the ones who believe and trust Jesus without having seen (John 20, 29).

Jesus assured his listeners that he would not reject anyone who came to him. His business was not to condemn the world, but rather to rescue the world (John 3, 17). His mission was search and rescue!

It is the will of God that Jesus not lose anything given to him, but rather to raise it. God's will is eternal life for all who believe in and trust Jesus. Jesus will raise us on the last day.

Lord Jesus, sometimes it is hard to trust you, not because we do not believe in you, but because life is so hard. We have been wounded by life and have become suspicious. We come to you today and ask for strength to live the life entrusted to us, knowing that we are secure. You will never reject us and you will raise us to new life. Alleluia!

Thursday, May 8, 2003
John 6, 44-51
The Bread of Life Discourse

God is the One who draws us to Jesus. It is Jesus who will raise us to new life. Jesus assures us that EVERYONE who listens to God and learns from God will indeed come to him, to Jesus, the Son.

God, as initiator, is not exclusive. According to Isaiah 54, 13, God will teach all. According to Jeremiah 31, 34, all people will know God.

Jesus referred to himself as bread from heaven, living bread. The manna consumed in the wilderness had an expiration date on it. It was only temporary.

Jesus, however, is forever! Because Jesus lives forever and we trust in him, we live forever also.

Lord Jesus, thank you for giving us yourself as the living and true Bread. Alleluia!

Friday, May 9, 2003
John 6, 52-59
The Bread of Life Discourse

Hey, there's trouble in Dodge City! Actually, the trouble is in the synagogue in Capernaum.

Jesus spoke the truth in church and a big fight erupted. So what else is new? Instead of praying and asking God's view of the situation, the synagogue leaders started a big fuss amongst themselves.

Same old story. Feeling threatened? Don't understand the message? Attack the messenger! That's what they did.

Jesus had used a rather down to earth expression for eating his body. It is a verb that connotes chomping, or, as some say, "chowing" down. This was not a prim, pious, eyes modestly cast down, way of speaking.

EAT! Jesus said that it was necessary to eat his body and to drink his blood in order to have life, real life.

Lord Jesus, thank you for giving us your very self. You want us to dive right in and feast upon you. We are starving. We are sick and tired of being sick and tired. We are fed up with church games, church fights, and church politics. We need YOU! I pray this day for all who believe in you and trust in you to receive you, to receive your precious Body and your precious Blood. Thank you for this foretaste of the heavenly Banquet, the Supper of the true Lamb of God. Alleluia!

Saturday, May 10, 2003 Bl. Damien de Veuster
John 6, 60-69
The Words of Eternal Life

Today's Gospel is all about the Word and the words. Jesus himself is the Word who became flesh and took up residence amongst us (John 1, 14).

Descriptive references about words from the Psalms and from Isaiah are distilled into a particularly pure and potent form in today's Gospel. At least, as my friend Bee would say, "This is my OPINION."

The outstanding example which first came to my mind is from one of the Servant Songs in Isaiah. The Servant tells of being given an instructed tongue with which to energize the exhausted with the mere speaking of a timely word (Isaiah 50, 4).

We know the power of a single word. A word, whether written or spoken, may cast us down into a gloomy pit or lift us up into realms of hope and glory.

The words Jesus speaks are words of LIFE! We may not understand his words right away. That is not the time to run away from Jesus as some of his early disciples did. That is the time to press in like Peter. Peter knew that Jesus had the words of everlasting life.

Lord Jesus, your words were a source of puzzlement to surface seekers. You do not want us to stay on the surface, but to enter your Sacred Heart where you will breathe new life and spirit into our weary souls and speak the word we need to hear. Alleluia!

Sunday, May 11, 2003 Fourth Sunday in Easter
John 10, 11-18
The Good Shepherd

Jesus, the God-Shepherd, is the Good Shepherd, our model and example of sacrificing oneself for the sheep. Shepherds and flock both need to stay close to Jesus.

Shepherds grow weary and may be tempted to serve as mere hirelings. Perhaps once they were full of zeal and on fire with love and devotion to serve God and the Church.

Time, betrayal, loneliness, misunderstanding, politics, lack of appreciation, etc. etc. may have ground them down into mere hirelings. They go through the motions, but their hearts are dead.

Jesus offers his life for the sheep because he is in constant communication and in complete accord with his Father. Not only does he know the sheep, but he also knows his Father and the Father knows him.

Jesus does not lay down his life and leave it there. He knows when to lay down his life and when to take it up again. There is concentrated wisdom tucked into this precept.

Lord Jesus, thank you for all your shepherds. Come to the rescue of your weary, depleted, demoralized shepherds. Refresh your shepherds so that they may refresh your flock. Alleluia!

Monday, May 12, 2003 Sts. Nereus and Achilleus, St. Pancras
John 10, 1-10
The Good Shepherd

Life! Abundant life. That is why Jesus, as the Good Shepherd, came to give us.

Not just scraping by spiritually, emotionally, or in any other way, but joyfully living the abundant life. Jesus is not talking about the half empty or half full glass. This is overflow! Spilling over.

Are we living that way or are we cringing and cowering our way through this life? Are we whining about the hirelings and wolves we have encountered or are we trusting our Good Shepherd to watch out for us?

Jesus, the Good Shepherd, is himself the gate to the sheepfold. He is not "a" gate. He is THE gate (John 10, 7, 9).

Lord Jesus, thank you that you are the gate for the sheep. Thank you that you rescue us from the robbers. Thank you for the green pastures you have prepared for us. Alleluia!

Tuesday, May 13, 2003
John 10, 22-30
Feast of the Dedication

Jesus had some very straightforward words for the religious leaders of his day. Jesus, the Good Shepherd, bluntly told them that they were not his sheep. He told them that they did not believe because they were not his sheep.

The sheep belonging to Jesus hear his voice. He knows them intimately and they trust him and follow him.

The official religious leaders were so against Jesus that they refused to hear his voice and to believe. They asked questions, but refused Jesus, the answer to their questions, who was standing right there before them.

Lord Jesus, thank you for your loving protection of your flock. You keep us safe from the hirelings and the wolves. We cannot perish because no one can take us away from you. Alleluia!

423

Wednesday, May 14, 2003 St. Matthias
John 15, 9-17
The Vine and the Branches

Jesus wants to hang out with us! In today's Gospel, he calls us his friends, not his servants.

You can tell your trusted, spiritually mature friends things you'd never dream of telling mere acquaintances. You can speak in a natural way with your real friends and not have to fret about their misunderstanding.

You run for the phone to share happy news with your friends. Life is not supposed to be all tears and travail, is it?

I think Jesus must be frustrated and lonely sometimes. He wants to be our friend and yet we're too busy. Too busy to hang out with him. We may acknowledge his presence in the morning, pray for direction during the day, and scream when we have problems. That's all OK, but is that all friends do?

The times I've stayed in silence in the presence of God have been more productive than all my frantic efforts to "serve" God. Alone, in God's presence, God has the chance to speak. Action and service flow naturally from time in God's presence.

Jesus is King of Kings and Lord of Lords. We are to obey his commands. The command in today's Gospel is the command to love.

Lord Jesus, thank you for laying down your life for us in the way you lived on this earth and in the way you died on the Cross. Help us to experience your joy today by relinquishing our own agendas into your hands. Help us to love others as you direct us to love them. Alleluia!

Thursday, May 15, 2003
John 13, 16-20
The Washing of the Disciples' Feet

This passage is all about how we treat others. Jesus, the Master and Teacher, has just humbled himself and washed his disciples' dirty, smelly feet.

This was a crucial learning station in the discipleship training of the Twelve. They were to take the example of Jesus and begin to put practical service of others into practice.

Jesus told his disciples that whoever welcomed his messenger was really welcoming him. Whoever welcomed Jesus was in reality welcoming God the Father who had sent Jesus.

Lord Jesus, knowing the one who would betray you, you still stooped down to wash his feet and the feet of all your first disciples. Today, let us be especially aware of how we respond to each person you send to us. There is a reason each person crosses our path. Let us respond according to your plan. Alleluia!

Friday, May 16, 2003
John 14, 1-6
Last Supper Discourses

Jesus has a place for us. He as gone ahead of us to make sure our place is all prepared. This place is awaiting us in our Father's house.

Jesus told us how to get there. We go to the Father's house by way of Jesus. Jesus IS the way. Only through Jesus do we go to the Father.

Jesus spoke truth because he WAS truth. Jesus told us of the life we could live because he who WAS life, gave his life for us.

Therefore, we can live this day with untroubled hearts. Jesus is leading us each day.

Lord Jesus, forgive me when I wake up and fret and worry about the day ahead. You are gently leading me closer to the place you have for me. Alleluia!

Saturday, May 17, 2003
John 14, 7-14
Last Supper Discourses

Just one more thing. One more sign. One more book. One more set of teaching messages. One more seminar. One more way of praying. One more. And then I'll know. And then ....

Philip wanted one more piece of evidence about Jesus. He asked Jesus to show the Father to the disciples. Then, said Philip, that would suffice.

Jesus! It's all about Jesus. It's all about the Father. It's all about Jesus doing the works of the Father. It's all about our doing even mightier works than Jesus!

We already have all we need. Jesus made it so simple. We are to love God with all that is within us and then love others, including ourselves (Matthew 22, 37-40). That's it.

Lord Jesus, you haven given us all we need. You invite us to ask in your name, with the purpose of the Father being honored and glorified in you. Thank you for the Holy Spirit who comes to aid us in truly believing that all this is true. Alleluia!

Sunday, May 18, 2003 Fifth Sunday in Easter
John 15, 1-8
The Vine and the Branches

Jesus again invites us, indeed dares us to ask and to expect an affirmative answer. What's the catch?

The catch is the condition of discipleship. It's not really a catch.

What is it, really? It's a relationship.

The branch does not bargain with the vine. Jesus is the vine. The branch depends on the vine for its nourishment and sustenance. Broken from the vine, the branch perishes,

Broken off from Jesus, the true vine, we are branches that go through life collecting grapes and trying to glue them on our lives. It is pathetic, but it happens. It happens when we decide we can live without Jesus, the vine, and then find ourselves cut off from all of life.

Lord Jesus, thank you that the glory and honor of the Father will be evident as we relate to you as a branch relates to the vine. Alleluia!

Monday, May 19, 2003
John 14, 21-26
The Advocate

Jesus, linking love with obedience, is preparing his disciples for the coming of the Holy Spirit. The Holy Spirit will continue to teach and to guide his followers after Jesus returns to his Father in heaven.

Jesus is stating that loving him means keeping his commandments. Jesus tells us that we are to love one another (John 15, 16).

Loving Jesus and keeping his commandments leads to greater revelation. The Father, the Son, and the Holy Spirit delight to come and to dwell with us.

426

Lord Jesus, thank you for continuing to teach us through the Holy Spirit sent from the Father. Thank you for continuing to teach us to trust you and to know that obedience to you is for our benefit. Alleluia!

Tuesday, May 20, 2003 St. Bernadine of Siena
John 14, 27-31
The Advocate

Peace. Soundness. Wholeness. A gift from the Anointed One, the Messiah.

Jesus' peace is not like the world's peace. The world's peace is fragmented and momentary at best. It can vanish in a flash.

Jesus places his peace at the core of our being. It is deeply within us, whatever the turbulence on the surface of our lives. We have the privilege of drawing upon this peace.

The SHALOM plaque (written in the Hebrew) I brought back from Jerusalem in 1985 occasionally broke if I slammed the door. My patient husband glued back and reassembled it a number of times. I felt mortified, but also comforted that God forgives hasty tempers!

The SHALOM Jesus gives is permanent. We may try to break it or even walk away from it, but it is still there. It is Jesus' gift to us. He wants us to accept it and to walk in it.

Jesus tells us to have brave hearts, not frightened hearts. He is going away only to return. Our permanent home will be with him.

Lord Jesus, thank you for your peace, your permanent gift to us. Let us live, breathe and walk in your peace today. Alleluia!

Wednesday, May 21, 2003
John 15, 1-8
The Vine and the Branches

Abiding IS action! For all us hyperactive types, abiding IS doing something.

We've heard the expressions, "Don't just stand there. DO something," "You can't go anywhere in a parked car," and so on. The other extreme, the extreme of passivity, is equally unacceptable. You know the types. They won't budge without an angelic visitation.

ABIDE! All outer action, all service, is to flow from our relationship with Jesus.

In a time of quiet, the Lord has a chance to speak. Perhaps we are directed to a certain action to take. Perhaps, we are to bask in his presence without an agenda

Complaining is my enemy. Silence is my friend.

Complaining exhausts me and drains my energy. Silence energizes me and leads me to Jesus even in the busiest of circumstances.

Lord Jesus, today is a bright shiny new day. Thank you for forgiving the mistakes of my yesterdays. Help me to abide quietly in you today. Thank you that you will direct me into fruitful discipleship. Alleluia!

Thursday, May 22, 2003
John 15, 9-11
The Vine and the Branches

We are totally secure in the love of Jesus. He tells us that he loves us just as the Father loves him.

Keeping the commandments of Jesus indicates that we are trusting him and staying close to him. He is the vine and we are the branches. Our joy as branches is complete as we remain united to Jesus, the vine, our source of life.

One of the literal meanings of the word "complete" is "crammed." Jesus wants us to be filled up and crammed with joy!

Lord Jesus, thank you for loving us and calling us to be deeply united with you. Alleluia!

Friday, May 23, 2003
John 15, 12-17
The Vine and the Branches

For the last several days, we've learned of the Gospel imperative of abiding in Jesus, the vine, and obeying his commands. Today's Gospel begins and ends with his command to love one another, to act in love for the benefit of one another, indeed to put aside our own agenda in order to serve others.

The human cry is to protest and to seek to protect and defend oneself first. Then, maybe if there's anything left over, we can throw a crumb of compassion to others.

Jesus has another way. He instructs us to love one another. Trusting Jesus, our vine and our source of life, we are free, as branches, to grow, to blossom, and to bear fruit.

Lord Jesus, thank you for pouring your life into us and refreshing us as we offer ourselves to be used as you wish. Alleluia!

Saturday, May 24, 2003 St. Bede, St. Gregory VII,
St. Mary Magdalene de Pazzi
John 15, 18-21
The World's Hatred

We want it both ways, don't we? As disciples, we yearn to follow Jesus. As branches, it is crucial that we remain united to Jesus, the vine.

However, we do live in this world. If we are insecure in our relationship with Jesus, we may seek and crave the approval of the world.

We want to feel at home in our own skin, but the way to go about it is to be at home in the heart of God. That is our place of rest, strength, and security.

If God the Father sent his beloved Son into this world and the world rejected him, can we expect an easy time? If the religious leaders despised Jesus and arranged for his execution, can we expect the approval of institutions?

As disciples of Jesus, we are marching to the tune of a different drummer. We do not have to go out of our way to provoke hatred. The world will be puzzled by our discipleship. Unfortunately, even other Christians may also be puzzled, if not hostile.

If we refuse to compromise our faith, we will indeed be a sign of contradiction. So be it.

Lord Jesus, following you makes it all up to us. You are our vine. You are our source. You are the prize. Strengthen us to keep our eyes on you. Alleluia!

Sunday, May 25, 2003 Sixth Sunday in Easter
John 15, 9-17
The Vine and the Branches

Joy! Our union with Jesus brings joy to him. Our union with Jesus brings our joy to maturity and produces fruit that will endure.

We abide or remain in the love of Jesus as we continue to lay down our lives for our friends. Jesus calls himself our friend.

As we choose service to others over slavery to self, we are loving and obeying Jesus. We don't have so anxious about ourselves. Jesus, our friend, the friend who died for us, is watching out for us.

Lord Jesus, thank you for calling us friends. Thank you for telling us all that you heard from the Father. Thank you for sending us out to love others as you love us. Thank you for your joy in us. Alleluia!

Monday, May 26, 2003 St. Philip Neri
John 15, 26- 16, 4
The World's Hatred; Jesus' Departure;
Coming of the Advocate

Jesus warns his disciples that following him will be arduous. It will not be all about marching down the aisle, gloriously vested, in a candlelight processional. It will not be all about Sunday School picnics.

Jesus is giving advance warning to the disciples so that they will not crumple when the going gets tough. It will get very tough indeed.

Jesus warns his followers that faith in him will provoke the religious leaders to expel them from the synagogues. These leaders, in spite of their positions, do not truly know either Jesus or his Father. They are deluded and truly think they are serving God by getting rid of the followers of Christ.

The Holy Spirit, the Advocate, however, will testify to Jesus. The disciples of Jesus will also testify.

Someone recently asked me how I defined success. Fidelity to God and to God's purpose for my life was my answer.

Lord Jesus, thank you for the gift of the Holy Spirit to strengthen us to testify to you. Alleluia!

Tuesday, May 27, 2003 St. Augustine of Canterbury
John 16, 5-11
Jesus' Departure; Coming of the Advocate

The Holy Spirit. The Holy Spirit. The Holy Spirit.

It is the Holy Spirit, the Advocate, who has the vocation of convicting, convincing, and confuting others.

We may rant and rave. We may preach and pray. We may weep and wail But we cannot convict others. That is simply not our assignment.

Jesus assures us, however, that he will indeed send the Holy Spirit, the Advocate, to be with us. When we are in situations we are powerless to change, we may call upon our Advocate, the Holy Spirit, to intervene.

Lord Jesus, thank you for the gift of the Holy Spirit to be with us and to be our Advocate. You returned to your Father in heaven and you are preparing a place for us where we will be with you forever. Help us not to waste time and energy here on earth trying to do what only the Holy Spirit can do. We release the people and the situations we are powerless to change to you, to your Father, and to our holy Advocate. Alleluia!

Wednesday, May 28, 2003
John 16, 12-15
Jesus' Departure; Coming of the Advocate

Sometimes we awake mulling over a problem that seems insoluble. We brood and go round and round with it in our minds, to no avail. It's easy to lose heart and to lose hope, when there just doesn't appear to be any solution.

Jesus promised to send the Holy Spirit to guide us. The Holy Spirit is our advisor and navigator through this life. He is the Holy Spirit of truth and it is to truth that he guides us.

Truth can seem frightening. We have to face ourselves and face situations in a whole new way. Jesus, however, promised us that it was the truth that would set us free (John 8, 32)!

The Holy Spirit is intimately related to Jesus and brings glory to Jesus. The Holy Spirit, who comes to live in us, knows exactly what to say to us and precisely how to guide us.

Jesus knows what we need and what we can bear at any given moment. Jesus has everything the Father has and it is from this treasury of truth and wisdom that the Holy Spirit guides us.

Lord Jesus, thank you for your mercy and compassion. You know what we need. You know how and when to confront us when we need to change. Thank you for the gift of the Holy Spirit to lead us through this day. Alleluia!

Thursday, May 29, 2003 Ascension Thursday
John 16, 16-20
Jesus' Departure; Coming of the Advocate

As a follower of Jesus, if you think you're swimming against the current, welcome! You are in just the right place at the right time.

Jesus warns and comforts his disciples about time and tears. They will not see him for a time and then they will see him again. They will weep while the world exults. However, the grief of Jesus' followers will be turned into joy!

Lord Jesus, thank you for teaching us that following you means a complete change of the way in which we perceive the flow of time and tears. Let us rest in your love today and trust you. Alleluia!

Friday, May 30, 2003
John 16, 20-23
Jesus' Departure; Coming of the Advocate

JOY! Today's Gospel is all about joy. Even though there will be tears and grief when it seems to the disciples that Jesus is gone forever, there is joy on the horizon.

Jesus promises his followers that he will see them again. No one will be able to take away their joy.

The pain of labor in childbirth does not last forever. It leads to new life and joy.

Lord Jesus, thank you for giving us your name to speak when we come before our Father in prayer. Help us to pray confidently and joyfully whatever bold, radical, and imaginative prayers which are placed in our hearts by the Holy Spirit. Let us trust that the answer will be for our good and for your glory. Since you rose from the dead and ascended to heaven, anything is possible! Alleluia!

Saturday, May 31, 2003 The Visitation of Mary to Elizabeth
Luke 1, 39-56
Mary Visits Elizabeth; The Canticle of Mary

Have you just about given up? Have you given up on God?

Have you given up on ever seeing God's promises fulfilled in your life? You watch while others are blessed and you wonder. You may feel cast aside and that nothing will ever work out for you.

In today's Gospel, two women burst upon the scene to confront and to confound our weariness, despair, and cynicism. One is young. One is old.

The older one, Elizabeth, had waited and waited for years for a child. When it seemed too late, God burst on the scene. God sent the angel Gabriel, no less, to tell Elizabeth's husband, the priest Zechariah, that Elizabeth would indeed bear a son. (Luke 1, 1-25) This child would be John the Baptist, who would announce the coming of the Messiah. It was not too late. God was right on time!

Some months later, the angel Gabriel also appeared with an announcement to a young virgin, Mary of Nazareth. Mary would also bear a son. Through the power of the Holy Spirit, Mary would bear the Son of God.

The visit of Mary to Elizabeth was a time of wonder, joy, and fulfillment. John the Baptist leapt in Elizabeth's womb as Mary, bearing the Christ-child, entered the home.

Time. It was time for the fulfillment of God's word to Zechariah (Luke 1, 20). It was time for the anguish that Elizabeth had suffered for years to be taken away (Luke 1, 25)!

Mary's song glorified the Lord. God can do anything! God can cast down the haughty ones. God can lift up the little ones. It is all about God and God's power and mercy.

Lord Jesus, thank you for your mother Mary. Thank you for coming to us through this remarkable young woman. Father, thank you for the miracle of the birth of John the Baptist, that you came to Elizabeth and brought to her the fulfillment of her hopes, even though it seemed impossible. Thank you, mighty Holy Spirit, for making what we call impossible happen before our very eyes. Alleluia!

433

Sunday, June 1, 2003
(the date in some provinces for the transfer of
the Solemnity of the Ascension of the Lord)
Mark 16, 15-20
The Commissioning of the Eleven; The Ascension of Jesus

The risen Jesus appeared to Mary Magdalene. She was called "the apostle to the apostles."

Later, he appeared to two disciples on the Emmaus road. The eleven disciples, however, found it difficult to believe the reports of those who claimed to have seen the resurrected Lord.

Nevertheless, Jesus entrusted to these eleven disciples the mission of preaching the Gospel. He told them to go all over the entire world and to proclaim the Good News. He told them of various signs that would accompany the proclamation of the Gospel.

As soon as he had spoken these words of mission to his disciples, Jesus was taken to be with God the Father. Mission accomplished!

Even though the eleven were still struggling to understand these amazing events, still they obeyed Jesus and proceeded forth with the understanding they did have. As they told others of Jesus, Jesus was with them and underscored their words with confirming signs.

So with us. We still do not have full understanding, do we? Still, Jesus entrusts us with the mission to live and to preach the Gospel. He is with us.

Lord Jesus, thank you for the confidence you have in us, even when we may not have much confidence in our abilities as evangelists. Thank you for being with us and authenticating our words with your power. Alleluia!

Monday, June 2, 2003 Sts. Marcellinus and Peter
John 16, 29-33
Jesus' Departure; Coming of the Advocate

The Father was the North Star, the pole star, for Jesus throughout his ministry. Jesus continually deferred to his Father and referred to his Father. During his brief, earthly ministry, Jesus spoke and acted only as the Father directed. They were in perfect accord.

The time had come for Jesus to suffer, to die, and to return to his Father. His disciples seemed slow to grasp who Jesus really was. Jesus, knowing that his suffering and death were approaching, attempted to prepare his disciples.

They seemed to have an "aha" moment, a moment when they indeed grasped who Jesus was. However, they did not yet understand themselves. They did not yet comprehend their own frailty.

Jesus understood. He knew that he would be left without human support. However, he would not be alone. His Father was with him, even during the time when he seemed abandoned.

Lord Jesus, thank you for your love and your patience with us as we seek to understand you and to understand ourselves. Thank you for reminding us that our peace is in our relationship with you, not in our relationship with this world. Thank you for conquering the world. Thank you for the gift of the Holy Spirit to infuse us with courage. Alleluia!

Tuesday, June 3, 2003 St. Charles Lwanga and Companions
John 17, 1-11
The Prayer of Jesus

This is the prayer, the high priestly prayer, Jesus prayed before his suffering and death. He prayed earnestly for his disciples.

Throughout the Gospels, we've often read about the "hour" or the "time." Sometimes Jesus would not take certain actions because it was not yet the "hour."

This time, however, was indeed the "hour." Jesus, seeking the glory and honor of his Father, acknowledged the authority the Father had bestowed upon him. The Father had given to Jesus authority over all.

It was the Father who had given Jesus his disciples. They belonged to the Father and the Father had given them to Jesus. They now appear to understand that Jesus was sent by God the Father. It was quite a journey of understanding for these first disciples.

Jesus, knowing that he would fulfill his mission and return to his Father, prayed for the unity of his disciples. He desired profound unity amongst his followers. He prayed that they would be one just as he and the Father in heaven are one.

Lord Jesus, thank you for interceding for your disciples when the time, the "hour" had arrived. Be glorified and honored in us today as we seek unity with other Christians. Alleluia!

Wednesday, June 4, 2003
John 17, 11-19
The Prayer of Jesus

As a follower of Jesus, do you ever feel you just don't belong here in this world? Do you sense that you just don't fit in?

Well, that's good! That's an answer to prayer!

You aren't meant to belong here and neither am I. Our time on this earth is an assignment, not our final destination or our final destiny.

Jesus, in his high priestly prayer, openly said to his Father that his followers did not belong to this world. He knew that the world would hate them. They just didn't fit in and they wouldn't play the game.

Jesus did not pray for his followers to be removed from the world. He prayed that his Father would consecrate them in the truth. The word of God is truth.

Living the truth is how we live in this passing world. Just as God the Father sent his Son Jesus into the world, so Jesus sends us into the world.

Jesus prayed that his followers be kept and protected in his name. He prayed for the unity of his followers.

Lord Jesus, thank you for praying for your early disciples and for us. You knew it would be hard for us here on earth. You knew that if we really and truly followed you, the world would hate us. You want us to be bearers of truth in a world that seems to thrive on lies. Thank you for consecrating us for this vocation. Alleluia!

Thursday, June 5, 2003 St. Boniface
John 17, 20-26
The Prayer of Jesus

This is where we come in! Jesus specifically prayed, not only for his first disciples, but also for us.

We are the ones who are blessed to believe, without having seen, because we believe the words of the eyewitnesses, the disciples, who were soon to become apostles. We are called the Father's gift to Jesus.

Sometimes, I wish I could just go and be with Jesus. Jesus also wants us to be with him. He told us he was going to prepare a place for us for this very purpose, so that we could be with him (John 14, 1-3).

Meanwhile, back in this world, there's work to do! What work?

Jesus said that our work was to believe in him (John 6, 29). All other activities flow from our relationship with Jesus.

The believing and the trusting come first. Jesus wants us to be so close to the Father, so close to him, and so close to other believers that the world may believe.

Believe what? Believe that the Father sent Jesus to the earth. Believe that the Father loved us just as he loved Jesus.

This is our mission! Our love for one another, flowing out of our common commitment to the Lord Jesus, is what will draw the world to believe.

Lord Jesus, we are caught up into the holy of holies in these verses. We are caught up into the very mystery of the Holy Trinity. Even though we do not fully comprehend, we worship you and confess you as Lord. Thank you for the gift of the Holy Spirit to enable us to reach out in love to our sister and brother believers in order to fulfill your mission for us on this earth. Alleluia!

Friday, June 6, 2003 St. Norbert
John 21, 15-19
Jesus and Peter

Love, lambs, life and death. Peter was a rough fisherman. Jesus was God in the flesh.

Yes, there are different Greek verbs for "love" used in this passage. No, this is not going to be difficult to understand.

Basically, it's like this. Although Peter just didn't get it, the guy was sold out to Jesus. Jesus decided to use him in the Church. It wasn't going to be easy. Peter would not be in control of his vocation. Jesus would be in control.

Jesus did not go into details. He just told Peter to feed the sheep and the lambs and to follow him, These were not Peter's lambs. They belonged to Jesus.

437

Lord Jesus, you are the Good Shepherd. Thank you for choosing Peter to feed your flock. Alleluia!

Saturday, June 7, 2003
John 21, 20-25
The Beloved Disciple

The mystic and the mechanic may seem at odds, at opposite ends of the spectrum. The mystic is contemplative and is comfortable with silence. The mechanic (in a generic, not a literal sense) always has to be buzzing around doing something.

Peter. Peter, the fisherman, was an "in your face," upfront sort of guy. Peter was audacious and asked Jesus the most extraordinary questions.

John. John was a fisherman, too. John, however, seemed more of a mystic, a contemplative, even though he had a temper. He wanted to be in Jesus' presence.

There is room in the Church for all personality types. The problem occurs when people with a particular vocation try to force others into that same vocation.

Jesus had said certain things to Peter about Peter's future. Peter unwisely asked Jesus about John. Jesus basically told Peter to mind his own business.

Your business, my business, is to follow Jesus as Jesus leads us. As Jesus leads us, not necessarily as others would try to lead us.

Lord Jesus, thank you for the freedom to follow you. Alleluia!

Sunday, June 8, 2003 Pentecost Sunday
John 15, 26-27; 16, 12-15
The World's Hatred; Jesus' Departure;
Coming of the Advocate

The Holy Spirit is our wise Teacher, who always leads us to the next lesson. For the early disciples, the Holy Spirit took up where Jesus left off. Jesus had more that he could have imparted to the disciples, but he knew that this was not the right time.

Jesus referred to the Holy Spirit as the Advocate and as the Spirit of truth. The Holy Spirit would testify of Jesus. The disciples would also be empowered to testify of Jesus.

438

Lord Jesus, thank you for knowing what we can bear at any given moment. Thank you, Father, for sending us the Holy Spirit. Come Holy Spirit. Alleluia!

Monday, June 9, 2003 St. Ephrem
Matthew 5, 1-12
The Sermon on the Mount; The Beatitudes

Well, I initially typed this in as the Sermon on the "Mound!" Perhaps baseball fans can find some applications from this Gospel.

What does the world teach? You feel good if you get your own way. You feel great if you climb and claw your way to the top.

Jesus confronts the world's facile lies and its darkness with his own frightening truth and dazzling light. What does Jesus say?

Jesus says you are blessed or truly happy if you know are in spiritual poverty. You will have the whole kingdom of God within which to run and to frolic.

Jesus says if you are grieving a loss, you have a unique gift to anticipate. You will be deeply and tenderly comforted by the God of the universe. This is the God who created you, knows you intimately, and loves you.

Jesus says that if you have a realistic assessment of yourself and if you are gentle and courageous, you have an inheritance waiting for you. You will inherit the kingdom of God. You will live God's way.

Jesus says that if you seek and crave for righteousness, your hunger will not go on forever. You will know the satisfaction only God can give you.

Jesus says that if you make allowances for others and don't stomp on them, even if you think they deserve it, you are making a wise investment. You are going to receive a huge dividend of compassion, understanding, and mercy when you yourself need it.

Jesus says that if you are of a pure and undivided heart, you will see what the perverse and polluted never see. You will see God.

Jesus says that if you bring peace and concord into this contentious world, you will have a new title. You will be one of God' s own children.

Jesus says that if you are trying to do what's right and you are vilified and even persecuted, you have every reason to rejoice! You are living in the tradition of God's holy prophets Look what happened to them for speaking God's truth! God is holding a great reward for you in heaven.

Lord Jesus, thank you for giving us a whole new way to view ourselves, our circumstances, and the world around us. Alleluia!

Tuesday, June 10, 2003
Matthew 5, 13-16
The Similes of Salt and Light

If you are a follower of Jesus, you are salt and you are light. Right now! Jesus says so. You are salt and light regardless of your feelings.

When God sprinkles the saltiness of your life into the thirsty world around you, the whole dynamic changes. You are there! Others will be thirsty for Jesus because you are there. You are salt.

When God shines the brightness of your life into the world around you, the whole dynamic changes. You are there! Others will long for the light of Christ which is shining through you. You are light.

You are there for others. In spite of your limitations and failures, others will see God at work in you and will glorify God.

Lord Jesus, thank you for calling us salt and light. Let us live out this calling and glorify you. Alleluia!

Wednesday, June 11, 2003 St. Barnabas
Matthew 10, 7-13
The Commissioning of the Twelve

Jesus instructed his disciples to begin their mission work close at home. Starting close at home is always a good idea.

Why import what isn't working right here? It's easier, sometimes, to puff out with pride and charge into a foreign mission field rather than to live the Gospel under one's own roof and within one's usual sphere of influence.

We are uncomfortably aware that the people around us know all our foibles and failings and therefore we may lack confidence. Still, we are to follow the Lord.

Jesus told his followers to proclaim the immediacy of the kingdom! What does that mean? What is the kingdom?

Get ready! You will see the will of God in action. Through flawed and fallible human beings, God is going to demonstrate his will.

What does this mean? It means that the sick will be made whole. The dead will experience life again. The lepers, the outcasts, will be sparkling clean and welcome again. Demons will be evicted.

The followers of Jesus are to live simply. God is with them. God is providing for their needs as they proclaim the kingdom.

It is important to offer the gift of peace to each place we enter. This peace is alive and real. If the gift of peace is not received, it is still present and will return to us.

Lord Jesus, thank you for showing us your plan for ministry. Thank you for equipping us, imperfect as we are, to carry out your plan. Keep us alert today to proclaim your kingdom at home and everywhere we go. Alleluia!

Thursday, June 12, 2003
Matthew 5, 20-26
Teaching about the Law; Teaching about Anger

The kingdom of God, the realm in which God's will is done, is not so much out there, but is in here, within us and among us. The psalmist wrote of God's law hidden deep within the heart. The psalmist valued God's law as an antidote to sin (Psalm 119, 11).

God's law, in the deepest sense, terrifies us when we have glimpses into our tattered hearts and impure motives. As we cry out for God's mercy, God shines the light of his purity and holiness into our hearts and begins to cleanse us and transform us.

Lord Jesus, search our hearts today. Show us how to settle with our opponent, even when our opponent is hidden deeply within. Let the wars within and the wars without come to an end. May your kingdom come in us. Thank you for shedding your blood to cleanse us and to free us to live a new life of wholeness. Alleluia!

441

Friday, June 13, 2003 St. Anthony of Padua
Matthew 5, 27-32
Teaching about Adultery; Teaching about Divorce

Jesus is compelling his listeners to examine their hearts and not to use legal machinations to justify selfish behavior. He is taking the Law to a level impossible to keep without the help of the Holy Spirit.

Whatever we do outwardly began in our hearts. Following God involves total surrender of our thought life as well as our outer actions.

Lord Jesus, show us today what needs to be cut off in our thinking. Create in us an overwhelming desire to please you in all our thoughts as well in our words and our actions. We pray to be filled with the Holy Spirit to think and to live according to God's plan for us. Alleluia!

Saturday, June 14, 2003
Matthew 5, 33-37
Teaching about Oaths

Jesus is probing even more deeply into the hearts of his hearers. He knows and understands what is in the human heart (John 2, 24-25).

This is not a passage about jury duty! This is a passage which challenges us to be honest. We have to be honest with ourselves and honest with others. Ostentatious speech and wordiness are discouraged in favor of plain speech.

Lord Jesus, cleanse our hearts and simplify our speech. Alleluia!

Sunday, June 15, 2003 The Most Holy Trinity
Matthew 28, 16-20
The Commissioning of the Disciples

A mixture of worship and doubt! That is what the first disciples were experiencing after the crucifixion and even after the resurrection of Jesus.

Jesus did not send them off for a few years of theological reflection followed by a long retreat. He reminded them, in case they didn't already know it, that he had been given all power on earth and in heaven! Jesus knew their condition and he still chose to send them out into the world.

Jesus sent them into the world to baptize in the name of the Father, the Son, and the Holy Spirit. They were instructed to make disciples and to teach these new disciples what Jesus had taught them. Jesus promised to be with them on their mission.

Lord Jesus, how we have embroidered and complicated your commission. Simplify us and strengthen us to go out into the world today to love you and to serve others in joyful trust that you are with us. Alleluia!

Monday, June 16, 2003
Matthew 5, 38-42
Teaching about Retaliation

Limitations versus liberality. Brutality versus benevolence. Law versus love. The Lex Talionis, which limited the parameters of retaliation, was superseded by Jesus. Jesus, the radical rabbi, said not to retaliate at all!

Gee whiz, we whine. Who is going to watch out for us? Does God want us to be wimps or what?

Jesus was preparing his hearers for a whole new way of living and loving. Give. Give. Give.

God is so rich and has bestowed boundless riches of all kinds on us. No matter what our financial or spiritual bank accounts, we can afford to give.

God is our reference point. We don't have to worry about standing up for ourselves as we did in former times. God is currently giving to us and we can afford to give out of this bounty. We cannot out give God (Luke 6, 38).

Lord Jesus, help us to know that, when we've been hurt or taken advantage of, you are still there, still looking out for us. Thank you for giving us wisdom and discernment to know how to respond. With eyes and hearts wide open, help us to give to others the love, understanding, and forgiveness you have freely given us. Alleluia!

Tuesday, June 17, 2003
Matthew 5, 43-48
Love of Enemies

Jesus is not advocating naivete when he commands his listeners to love their enemies. He is simply continuing the teaching of the Hebrew Scriptures. The people of God were not allowed to hold hatred in their hearts or to hold onto grudges (Leviticus 19, 17-18).

What's new, then? Jesus is calling us to an active love for those who are clearly not our friends. He is calling us to an active intercession for those who injure us.

The rationale is that God the Father allows his sunshine and rain to benefit all, regardless of their conduct. We are simply to imitate God in this matter.

Lord Jesus, when we are treated unjustly, let us trust the Holy Spirit to show us how to respond out of the Father's wealth of compassion. Transform our hearts so that we may love those who do not care to be our friends. Show us how to pray for those who injure us. Thank you for the compassion and mercy which have been freely showered upon us. Alleluia!

Wednesday, June 18, 2003
Matthew 6, 1-6, 16-18
Teaching about Almsgiving; Teaching about Prayer;
Teaching about Fasting

It's all about you and the Father. Either you believe your Father in heaven knows you and is lovingly watching over you and everything that concerns you, or you don't.

If you believe this with your head, but not with your heart, you will try to perform, to do, and to outdo. You will be restless and exhausted.

Almsgiving, I remember years ago a very holy, brilliant physicist who would ignore the collection plate at church because he gave in secret. Another physicist, as a teenager, tithed the earnings from his summer job, quietly depositing a curious assortment of bills in a tiny chapel. An engineer went into a little country church during the week and placed a secret offering in an envelope on the pulpit. C. S. Lewis quietly gave away about two thirds of his income. An elderly childless couple lived very simply and willed all to a ministry that sends Bibles all over the world. There are many ways to give.

However you give and whatever you give, give it first to the Father. He will make it up to you. He will reward you.

Prayer. Don't compose preachy prayers and spout them off either alone or in prayer groups. Pray from your heart to your all-loving Abba in heaven, who knows what you need. If you did not have an earthly father who was worthy of your trust, forgive him, even if he has died. You will be healed. Ask God to help you. You are assured that your heavenly Father is worthy of your trust. He will reward you.

Fasting. Jesus tells us not to appear melancholy about it. That's the way the scribes and Pharisees, the ones he constantly called hypocrites, looked when they fasted They received receipts, not rewards. Your Father knows that you are fasting and why you are fasting. He will reward you.

Lord Jesus, thank you for the gift of the Holy Spirit to teach us how to give, pray, and fast, in order to glorify our Father in heaven. Alleluia!

Thursday, June 19, 2003 St. Romuald
Matthew 6, 7-15
The Lord's Prayer

God, whose very name is holy, is in heaven. We are still on earth.

In heaven, the will of God is already in effect. It is already being done. We are to pray that God's will is also done on earth. God's kingdom will come on this earth when God's will is done on earth.

We ask God to give us the sustenance we need for this day. This is the bread we need to fulfill our part in the coming of the kingdom on earth.

We ask God to release us from the debts we owe him because of our sins. We ask that God forgive or release us from our burdensome debts in exactly the same way that we forgive or release others.

We pray not to be subjected to the severe testing and trials that will occur before Jesus, the Messiah, returns. We pray to be delivered from the source of all evil.

Jesus then circles back to the hard issue of forgiveness. If we refuse to forgive others, our Father will not forgive us.

Lord Jesus, you have taught us the way to pray. Thank you for dying on the Cross so that all our sins are forgiven and erased. No matter how our transitory feelings may protest, we choose to forgive all who have sinned against us. As you canceled the debt we owed God, so we choose to cancel the debt others owe us. They cannot pay us, but you will repay us for the harm they caused in our lives. You will heal us and restore us. What they did is now between you and them. Let our lives hasten the coming of your kingdom. Alleluia!

Friday, June 20, 2003
Matthew 6, 19-23
Treasure in Heaven; The Light of the Body

Treasure! Where is your treasure? In the bank? With the brokers? With the company? With the university? With the church? With your family?

You are a treasure. Where are you spending yourself? Where are you allowing yourself to be spent?

Jesus said to store up for ourselves treasures in heaven. How? By offering our lives to be used as God wishes.

Light! Where is the light? The shutters are pulled down. It is dark. No one is home. The furniture may still be there, but there is no life inside, no joy, no movement, and no hope..

That is the outer equivalent of the light of the spirit being dimmed or extinguished. Jesus told us that we are the light of the world (Matthew 5, 14). We are to shine! Sometimes, though, the lamp needs help in order for the light within us to shine.

Lord Jesus, please redirect our investing strategies. Regardless of Wall Street and the market here on earth, there is a thriving market in heaven. There are riches galore! You are our heart's desire, our true treasure. Help us to spend ourselves for you. When the light within us grows weary and dim, thank you for the gift of the Holy Spirit to enliven us. Thank you that you are opening the shutters and flinging open the doors. Alleluia!

Saturday, June 21, 2003 St. Aloysius of Gonzaga
Matthew 6, 24-34
God and Money; Dependence on God

How important is the state of my finances, my food, and my clothing in the light of eternity? God owns everything and God is in control of my life.

Even when I lament and agonize over past failures, especially the failure to trust, God is still in charge and still loves me.

In an instant, we could lose everything. In an instant we could also be surprised with unbelievable wealth.

Remember the Book of Job. God is still here! God still loves us. God is still watching out for us.

So, how do we live? Jesus says to seek God's kingdom and God's righteousness first of all. This is top priority.

This is the search of a spiritual bloodhound. It means actively welcoming God's sovereignty over our lives.

Over and over, Jesus says not to worry about our temporal needs. He reassures us that our Father in heaven knows what we really need.

Lord Jesus, I still need help in this matter of worrying. I'm an all-inclusive worrier. Forgive me ways in which I have not been a wise steward. Forgive me for the sin of unbelief. Thank you for taking my hand and leading me gently in a new walk of trust. Alleluia!

Sunday, June 22, 2003 The Most Holy Body and Blood of Christ
Mark 14, 12-14, 22-26
Preparations for the Passover; The Lord's Supper

From hearty Gospel hymns extolling the power of the Blood of Jesus through mild to major discomfort with ideational feast days all the way to Corpus Christi processionals! There is a wide spectrum of scholarship and devotions throughout the Body of Christ on earth about the Feast of the Body and Blood of Christ, Corpus Christi.

Jesus made it very simple. He told two of his disciples exactly where to go in Jerusalem to prepare for the Passover. The disciples obeyed and found that the arrangements for the room had already been made. This was the first day of the Feast of Unleavened Bread. This was the day the sacrificial Passover lamb was offered in the Temple.

That evening, while Jesus and his twelve disciples were eating the unleavened bread associated with the Passover, Jesus took a piece of the bread. He blessed the bread, broke the bread, and gave it to his followers. He did not say that it was a piece of bread. Jesus said, "This is my body."

Jesus took the cup filled with wine and offered thanks to God. All the disciples drank from this cup. Jesus said, "This is my blood." He referred to the new covenant. Jesus himself would become the lamb of sacrifice. His blood would be shed once and for all for our sins to be forgiven. He himself would not take wine until the new wine of God's kingdom.

Lord Jesus, thank you for being our Lamb. Thank you for offering yourself to the Father for the forgiveness of our sins. Thank you for the celebration through the centuries of your precious Body and Blood. You are here. You are present. You live within us. Alleluia!

Monday, June 23, 2003
Matthew 7, 1-5
Judging Others

We may listen to the words and observe the behavior of others, but we are not competent to see into their hearts and to discern their motives. Only God can do that.

Therefore, we are not qualified to be judge and jury. That is not part of our job description.

We are to love others, in the sense of longing for God's best for them. We are to pray God's blessing upon them. God will do what only God can do in their lives.

The same measuring tape we use to measure or to evaluate others will be the same one God uses to evaluate us. For selfish reasons, if for no other, it is to our advantage to offer mercy. Who knows what others are going through? Who knows how they are tormented? Only God knows.

Lord Jesus, thank you for the compassion, mercy, and forgiveness you have showered upon us. Help us today to begin new habits of gentleness and generosity with others. Alleluia!

Tuesday, June 24, 2003 The Birth of John the Baptist
Luke 1, 57-66, 80
The Birth of John the Baptist; The Canticle of Zechariah

In the desert. In the wilderness. John was hidden away until the time God chose to manifest him to Israel. God knew when John was ready. God knew when Israel needed to hear John's message.

Timing had always played a crucial factor in John's life. His own mother, Elizabeth, had waited and waited for a child. She waited in hope, she waited with fading hope, and she waited, possibly, with hope that had died.

God chose to step in when it all seemed impossible. Elizabeth was just too old to have a child. It was out of the question. Really?

John's elderly father, priest though he was, manifested unbelief when told by the angel Gabriel, no less, that he and Elizabeth would have a son. Because of his unbelief, Zechariah was silenced by God for at least nine months.

Zechariah's first words came eight days after John's birth. After writing on a tablet that the child's name was John, confirming what Elizabeth had already spoken, at last Zechariah was free to speak. He began to praise God!

When God makes a promise, that promise will be fulfilled. The timing may seem incomprehensible, but God knows what he is doing. It is necessary to be formed in the wilderness, in the desert, for God's purposes. In the desert, one grows strong. In the desert, one learns to trust God.

Heavenly Father, thank you for preparing John the Baptist in the wilderness for his mission of preparing the way for Jesus. Thank you for sending the Holy Spirit to strengthen us as we wait in the wilderness for your purposes to be fulfilled in us and through us. Alleluia!

Wednesday, June 25, 2003
Matthew 7, 15-20
False Prophets

Regardless of their titles, true servants in the Body of Christ on earth lay down their lives for others. Regardless of their titles, wolves are on the prowl to exploit and to destroy.

Jesus counsels caution and discernment because wolves may not be easy to detect. Cleverly camouflaged, they are like chameleons, changing with the current political climate.

Jesus states that prophets, those claiming to speak forth God's word, will be known by their fruit. A good fruit test is found in the letter to the Galatians. The fruit of the Holy Spirit is " ...love, joy, peace, longsuffering, gentleness, goodness, faith, Meekness, temperance ...." (Galatians 5, 22-23, K.J.V.). Do those claiming to speak for God have this kind of fruit manifested in their lives?

Lord Jesus, you said that good trees bear good fruit and that bad trees bear bad fruit. Thank you for grafting us into the tree of life, to your Cross, that we may die to our selfish agendas and live out your mandate of love and service. Alleluia!

449

Thursday, June 26, 2003
Matthew 7, 21-29
The True Disciple; The Two Foundations

In Psalm 24, David wrote that cleanliness of life and purity of heart were prerequisites for being in God's presence. We do not go in moral filth into the presence of an all-holy God.

Jesus is telling his followers that only true disciples will enter the kingdom of heaven. They are the ones who do the will of the Father in heaven.

Those who presume to use the name of Jesus, even in ministries of prophecy and deliverance, but who are not living as true disciples, will be told by Jesus himself to depart. He called them doers of evil. He said he did not even know them!

Listening to the words of Jesus and acting upon those words are two different things. The one who listens and puts into practice what is heard is wise. This person is on solid ground. When the storms of life come, the wise person is affected, but not destroyed. The one who merely listens to the words of Jesus in a casual way and ignores these words, is foolish and will not withstand the storms of life.

Jesus spoke with authority. He was the sinless Son of God. He was living and speaking in obedience to the will of his Father in heaven.

Lord Jesus, show us specifically what we need to put into practice as your disciples. Thank you that we may come to you and receive forgiveness and cleansing. Thank you for the gift of the Holy Spirit to teach us how to carry out the Father's will in our lives. Alleluia!

Friday, June 27, 2003 The Most Sacred Heart of Jesus
John 19, 31-37
The Blood and the Water

These verses show us, with terrifying reality, that Jesus died a horrible death on the Cross. The Lamb of God shed his blood for us and for our salvation. Although he had already died, the soldiers cruelly pierced his side from which flowed blood and water.

Lord Jesus, we are silent in the face of mysteries we will never comprehend during our brief time on this earth. Thank you for coming to this earth, living amongst us and showing us what God the Father is really like. Thank you for suffering unspeakable agonies in the Garden of Gethsemane. Thank you for your willingness to suffer misunderstanding, rejection, condemnation, and torture at the hands of the religious leaders. Thank you for your triumphant death. As you proclaimed from the Cross, you finished the work God gave you to do! Thank you for your glorious resurrection and return, mission accomplished, home to heaven, where you await us. Show us today how to love you and to thank you by allowing our lives to be poured out for others. Thank you that will return to earth in dazzling glory! Alleluia!

Saturday, June 28, 2003 The Immaculate Heart of Mary
Luke 2, 41-51
The Boy Jesus in the Temple

Jesus, Son of God though he was, was not yet ready to be released into public ministry. It seemed that he was in the right place that particular Passover, when he was twelve years old. He was in Jerusalem, in the Temple. He was doing the right things. He was listening to the teachers and asking very perspicacious questions. Jesus, fully human adolescent that he was, believed that it was time to be about the business of his heavenly Father.

Not quite yet! The natural concerns of Joseph and Mary were evident. Jesus had scared them silly. Where in the world was he?!

The Father in heaven knew the time frame. This was Nazareth time for Jesus, Mary, and Joseph. Time for Jesus to go home to Nazareth and to continue growing in wisdom as well as in years.

The twelve year old Jesus, Son of God and son of Mary, returned to Nazareth. He continued living in obedience to Mary and Joseph. His mother reflected deeply upon these matters.

Lord Jesus, you know all about how hard it is to wait. Thank you for the gift of the Holy Spirit to purify us, to fine-tune us, and to prepare us in a most meticulous way for the work you have called us to do, the ministry which originated in the heart of the Father. Alleluia!

Sunday, June 29, 2003 Sts. Peter and Paul
Matthew 16, 13-19
Peter's Confession about Jesus

The revelation that Jesus was the Messiah, the Son of God, was given to Peter directly from God the Father. Jesus immediately stated Peter's identity and Peter's vocation.

451

Peter had previously been known as Simon, the fisherman (Mark 1, 16, Matthew 4, 18, Luke 5, 1-11). Jesus had a new name for this fisherman. Simon, the son of Jonah, would be called Peter.

Peter ("Kepa" in the Aramaic spoken by Jesus) was the rock ("kepa") on which Jesus chose to build his Church, his community. Jesus gave Peter specific authority in the Church.

Jesus gave to Peter alone the keys to the kingdom of heaven. Instead of flippant jokes about St. Peter at the gate, we need to reflect deeply on Peter's authority.

Jesus gave to Peter, and later to all the apostles (Matthew 18, 18) the power to bind and to loose, to open and to close. Peter alone was given the keys.

Lord Jesus, while others called you a prophet, Peter called you the Christ, the Son of the living God. Thank you for building your Church upon this rock. Thank you that the gates of hell will not prevail against your Church. Alleluia!

Monday, June 30, 2003 First Martyrs of the Church of Rome
Matthew 8, 18-22
The Would-be Followers of Jesus

Psalm 84 celebrates the joys of being in God's presence. Just as the sparrow has a little home and the swallow has a nest for her young, so the psalmist's true home is by the altars of God.

Jesus, referring to this psalm, is cautioning those who would follow him that they may be stripped of external comforts. They may also have to shed themselves of self-imposed obligations. Jesus himself had no permanent address on this earth.

Jesus lived in the presence of God the Father. His sustenance was to do the will of his Father (John 4, 34).

If we are to follow Jesus, we are also to live in God's presence in a focused, purposeful way. We are not here to follow and to fulfill our own agendas. We are here for a limited time on earth to fulfill God's purpose.

Lord Jesus, sometimes I have charged around here and there thinking I'm serving you. Today, as I prepare for an Eight Day silent retreat, help me to learn to still my thoughts as well as my actions. Thank you for the guidance of the Holy Spirit to teach me how I am to follow you today. Alleluia!

Tuesday, July 1, 2003 Bl. Junipero Serra
Matthew 8, 23-29
The Calming of the Storm at Sea

The turbulence on the sea ceased at the word of Jesus. Although Jesus was in the boat with the disciples in the midst of the storm, the winds still blew and the waves still crashed into and covered the boat until Jesus spoke the word.

Jesus was with his disciples in the boat and he was sleeping! Fast asleep. Storm? Waves? No problem. When Jesus spoke the word, the storm ceased.

Lord Jesus, you rebuked the raging elements, but you did not rebuke your terrified disciples. You did ask why they were so afraid. You did refer to their small faith. Thank you for your loving understanding of us when our faith seems powerless and tiny. Thank you for your presence with us in the storm. Thank you for manifesting your power and authority to us in the midst of the storm. Thank you for your perfect wisdom and timing in stopping the storm. Alleluia!

Wednesday, July 2, 2003
Matthew 8, 28-34
The Healing of the Gadarene Demoniac

When Jesus, having just stilled the storm on the Sea of Galilee, arrived on the other shore, he was confronted with another storm. Two demoniacs met him! They emerged from the tombs, where they lived.

The storm on the Sea of Galilee was a storm without, a storm on the outside. The storm in the demoniacs was a storm within, within the shattered spirits and psyches of these suffering ones.

The demoniacs were so filled with death that they assumed even Jesus had come to torment them. They lived in the tombs and were blinded by the light and love shining forth from Jesus.

They spoke, begging Jesus not to torment them. Yet, they were not really the ones speaking. It was actually the unclean spirits residing in them who spoke. Needing some place to go, a new place of residence, the terrible spirits beseeched Jesus to send them into the nearby pigs. The pigs then rushed to the sea where they drowned. This was too much for the people of the town!

Lord Jesus, how amazing that the whole town wanted you to leave. Why couldn't they rejoice in the new life you gave to the poor, tormented

453

tomb dwellers? Please come to us today. Revive us and free us from any tombs, or places of death, we have been inhabiting. Thank you for new life and freedom. Alleluia!

Thursday, July 3, 2003 St. Thomas
John 20, 24-29
Thomas

Jesus said we are actually happy and blessed if we have not seen him and yet we believe. Thomas, who did not see Jesus until a week after the other disciples, insisted on seeing Jesus' for himself. He needed to see that it was indeed Jesus, the crucified and resurrected Jesus.

Sometimes, even if we see, we still do not believe. Life has so wounded us, so traumatized us, that even when Jesus manifests himself to us in various ways, we are not able to recognize his presence.

When this is the case, all we can do is to persist gently in trusting the Lord. He IS real and he IS with us. One day we will see.

Lord Jesus, thank you that you knew the best way to manifest yourself to Thomas. You knew what Thomas needed. Thank you for manifesting yourself to us in the way that is best for us. Thank you for your love, your understanding, and your gentleness. Alleluia!

Friday, July 4, 2003 St. Elizabeth of Portugal
Matthew 9, 9-11
The Call of Matthew

Jesus is passionately concerned with how we treat others. He is the wise physician who longs to heal us all and to make us whole. When we are truly whole, we will long to love others as Jesus has loved us.

Jesus called a tax collector, Matthew, to follow him. Other tax collectors and so-called sinners tagged along with Matthew, not only for dinner but also to check out this Jesus person.

That was fine with Jesus, but not fine with the religious leaders. They again practiced their indirect method of attacking Jesus. They asked Jesus' disciples why Jesus would eat with tax collectors and with others who were considered sinners.

Jesus, of course, heard the leaders and answered them directly. He told the religious leaders that he had come specifically to call sinners.

The sinners were the ones humble enough to know they needed help. Jesus challenged the learned Pharisees to learn that he desired mercy.

Lord Jesus, we are always in need of your forgiveness, healing, and love. Please come to us today and heal us and set us free from whatever holds us back from truly knowing, loving, and serving you in others. Alleluia!

Saturday, July 5, 2003 St. Anthony Mary Zaccaria
Matthew 9, 14-17
The Question about Fasting

Wherever Jesus is, there is life and joy! His life cannot be contained in the old constraints. His life bursts forth and pours out in abundance.

Jesus did not say that fasting was wrong. In fact, he taught his disciples how to fast. (Matthew 6, 16-18) and assumed that they would fast.

Not now, though. Not while he walked the earth with them. That was not the appropriate time to fast, but to rejoice!

Patching the old with the new never works. Pouring robust new wines into tired old wineskins will burst the skins. They cannot handle the explosion of that exuberant newness.

Going through the same old formulaic prayers does not always work. The prayers are fine. That's not the point.

However, when Jesus pours forth new life into us, our old, often self-imposed formulas will burst! They may have been what we needed at one time, but not now.

Lord Jesus, thank you for pouring new life into me today. Thank you for a fresh infilling of the Holy Spirit. Alleluia!

Sunday, July 6, 2003
Fourteenth Sunday in Ordinary Time
Mark 6, 1-6
The Rejection at Nazareth

Who IS this person called Jesus?! How on earth can he say and do such things?

He's just Jesus the village carpenter, isn't he? His mother is Mary, isn't she? His other relatives are right here in Nazareth, aren't they? So, who IS he?

The people in the synagogue in Nazareth were baffled. They could not understand Jesus. Therefore, they did not want to try to understand. It is so much easier to reject someone we do not understand.

Jesus understood. He understood that a true prophet is not honored close to home.

The old saying that familiarity breeds contempt comes to mind. We see people at the grocery store, at work, or at church, or at the monastery, and we think we know them. They're nothing great, we think.

Jesus, Son of God though he was, did, in one sense, have his hands tied. Jesus would not violate human free will.

If people did not want to believe, so be it. It just meant he was unwelcome do the work in them that he was capable of doing there.

They were the ones who were the losers. The lost the opportunity to see Jesus in action on their behalf.

Lord Jesus, when we feel our hands are tied, when we feel boxed in, help us to remember how you felt during your time on this earth. You went through so much misunderstanding and rejection. Help us to look to you and to keep on doing what you call us to do. Alleluia!

Monday, July 7, 2003
Matthew 9, 18-26
The Official's Daughter and the Woman with the Hemorrhage

The touch of Jesus heals. Sometimes, as in the case of Jairus' daughter, Jesus goes directly to the person. Other times, as in the case of the woman with the bleeding problem, the afflicted person takes the initiative and reaches out to Jesus.

Jesus is present! Jesus is willing to heal and longs to heal.

We cannot limit his power to our time frame or to our methodology. He may wait until it seems too late, as in the case of the twelve year old girl who had died.

Those who scoffed and thought it was too late because the young girl had died were proven wrong. She arose when Jesus came to her, took her hand, and spoke to her.

Lord Jesus, thank you that it is never too late with you. No matter how prolonged or hopeless the situation has seemed, when you arrive on the scene, life happens. Alleluia!

Tuesday, July 8, 2003
Matthew 9, 32-38
The Healing of the Mute Person; The Compassion of Jesus

When Jesus drove out the demons, the mute person was then free to speak. How terrible to be in the grip of an entity that stifles and silences. How glorious to be freed to be the person God created you to be!

The crowds were stunned by this deed. The Pharisees, full of sour grapes, thought that Jesus drove out demons by demonic power. How idiotic!

Jesus kept on. He continued his ministry of teaching, preaching, and healing.

Matthew's Gospel tells us that Jesus healed every kind of sickness. That should give us hope if we think what ails us is considered beyond cure.

When Jesus saw all the crowds of people, he was filled with tender, true compassion, not merely clinical compassion. The people surrounding him were like poor abandoned sheep, without a gentle shepherd to care for them. Jesus instructed his disciples to pray for workers to go out into the spiritual harvest field.

Lord Jesus, drive out whatever hinders us from speaking and living the message you created us to proclaim. Nothing is beyond your power to reach, to heal, and to transform. Send strong, gentle, and wise shepherds to tend your flock and to bring lost lambs to you, the Good Shepherd. Alleluia!

Wednesday, July 9, 2003
Matthew 10, 1-7
The Mission of the Twelve; The Commissioning of the Twelve

Stay close to home with your ministry. If it isn't working there, why export it?

Jesus gave his disciples authority to drive out evil spirits and to heal every illness. He sent them out.

Out, yes. Far away, no. He sent them close to home. Israel.

There were little lost sheep right there in Israel. Jesus instructed his followers to announce that the kingdom was right there.

Right where we are, we are to proclaim the heavenly kingdom. As baptized Christians, we are to witness to the risen Lord Jesus. Close to home or far away, we are to fulfill the Lord's commands and to leave the results with him.

Lord Jesus, thank you for equipping us to minister in your name. Show us today who needs attention in our immediate surroundings. Show us how to feed the little lambs at home, regardless of their age. Alleluia!

Thursday, July 10, 2003
Matthew 10, 7-15
The Commissioning of the Twelve

Jesus gave his disciples everything they needed to fulfill his commission. They did not have to work up anything on their own steam. They simply had to obey Jesus.

They were to cure those who were sick, raise the dead, cleanse those afflicted with leprosy, and drive out demons. Since Jesus said to do these things, he stood behind them and gave them the necessary authority.

They were to travel light and not get all upset if they were not always well-received. If the peace they offered was rejected, it would simply return to them. No big deal. Too bad for the places that rejected them.

Lord Jesus, help us to do what you tell us to do, even if it seems impossible. If you said to do it, you will make a way for it to be done. Help us to shake off the dust of discouragement and to follow you into the light. Alleluia!

Friday, July 11, 2003 St. Benedict
Matthew 10, 16-23
Coming Persecutions

Stay shrewd and simple. Keep your eyes open. You will pay a price if you truly follow Jesus

Suffering does not necessarily mean being thrown to the lions. It may mean encountering wolves in sheep's clothing.

No one wants to think about this. It's so much easier to play it safe, to play Church.

We can't "play" Church. We ARE Church! We are the Body of Christ on this earth. If Jesus, the Head of the Church, suffered, so will we.

What does Jesus, the supreme realist, say? He tells us not to be concerned about trying to defend ourselves. The Holy Spirit, who lives within us, will tell us what to say. Awesome! The Spirit of the heavenly Father will actually speak through us.

Jesus warned his disciples about betrayal by family members. He said that everyone would hate them because of his name.

Is there any bright light in this passage? Jesus said that endurance to the end would bring salvation.

We get to practice, in little ways, what Jesus teaches in this Gospel. In everyday life, there are opportunities to persist and to ask Jesus to help us to endure.

Lord Jesus, this is a scary Gospel. And yet, it is Good News, because you are with us. You are holding us close in your arms, close to your heart, as we live for you in this world. Alleluia!

Saturday, July 12, 2003
Matthew 10, 24-33
Coming Persecutions; Courage under Persecution

Three times in today's Gospel, Jesus instructs his followers not to be afraid. They are about to experience a terrifying ride in the God-lane. Their experience can help us when we are in various frightening situations.

459

Do not be afraid. Don't be afraid to speak up and to speak out for Jesus. There will be no secrets. It will all come out into the open. Speak what Jesus tells you to speak.

Do not be afraid. Don't be afraid for your physical safety. Your body might be killed, but you, the real you, will be alive and well. Don't be afraid of mere mortals. Be in awe of God. Only God has sovereignty over your body and soul. You are safe in God's care.

Do not be afraid. Your Father, who knows about the destiny of the little sparrows, knows every single detail about you, even how many hairs are on your head. You are of infinite value to your Creator.

If we publicly acknowledge Jesus, Jesus promises to acknowledge us before his Father in heaven. If we deny Jesus, he will deny us before his Father.

Lord Jesus, thank you for telling your followers three times not to be afraid. Thank you for your love which cleanses us, restores us, and gives us the courage to live and to die and to live again for you. Alleluia!

Sunday, July 13, 2003 Fifteenth Sunday in Ordinary Time
Mark 6, 7-13
The Mission of the Twelve

Jesus told the disciples to travel light! Because they carried his authority to do their mission, little else was needed. Tunic, sandals, and a walking stick. That's about it.

They were instructed to accept hospitality, but not to get bent out of shape if they were not always welcomed. They were simply to shake the dust off their feet and travel on to their next assignment.

The disciples, thus prepared, set off on their great adventure! They told the people to repent, to turn away from sin. They expelled demons. They anointed the sick with oil and the sick were healed.

Lord Jesus, show us how to travel light today. Forgive us and free us of any excess baggage. Alleluia!

Monday, July 14, 2003 Bl. Kateri Tekakwitha
Matthew 10, 34-11, 1
Jesus: A Cause of Division;
The Conditions of Discipleship; Rewards

Truly following Jesus will eventually cause division. Those who prefer self or others to Jesus cannot be disciples. They may be admirers of Jesus, but, by their own choice, they cannot be true disciples.

Receiving those who live and speak the words of Jesus is the same as receiving Jesus. Receiving Jesus is the same as receiving the Father in heaven.

Lord Jesus, help us to die to our own agendas of how to live. Raise us to the life of discipleship you have ordained for us. Alleluia!

Tuesday, July 15, 2003 St. Bonaventure
Matthew 11, 20-24
Reproaches to the Unrepentant Towns

Same Jesus. Same mighty deeds. Different places. Different responses.

Jesus reproached the towns of Chorazim and Bethsaida. Although he had done mighty deeds there, the residents were still unresponsive.

Tyre and Sidon, on the other hand, wicked though they were, had responded favorably to Jesus and to his message. You never know.

A separate reproach, or lament, was reserved for Capernaum. Jesus had lived in Capernaum after leaving Nazareth. He had healed the centurion's servant and Peter's mother-in-law there. Condemning Capernaum for its pride, Jesus prophesied its doom. He said Sodom's fate looked good compared to what was in store for Capernaum.

Lord Jesus, you were in anguish over the places where you had poured yourself out in ministry. Strengthen us today to continue to trust you as we offer ourselves for the purposes of the heavenly Father. Alleluia!

Wednesday, July 16, 2003 Our Lady of Mount Carmel
Matthew 11, 25-27
The Praise of the Father

Jesus pauses for a praise break! After lamenting over the unrepentant lake towns, he praises his Father. This is a pause that refreshes both Jesus and his listeners.

Jesus knows that the simple, the childlike, and the unsophisticated ones are the ones humble enough to receive instruction on the eternal mysteries of God's kingdom. The ones who think they already know it all are more difficult to reach. They exclude themselves by refusing to learn from Jesus, who is privy to all the resources of his Abba, his Father in heaven.

Lord Jesus, you experienced joy as you praised your Father!. Thank you for illustrating for us what the Father is really like. Reveal to us today aspects of the Father that we may know in our busy brains, but have yet to experience in our wounded hearts. Alleluia!

Thursday, July 17, 2003
Matthew 11, 28-30
The Gentle Mastery of Christ

After my Eight Day retreat, which ended a week ago, I have experienced a new lightness of spirit. Very unexpected and very appreciated.

Without intending to, somehow over the years, I had started bearing burdens which proved too heavy for me. There is a subtle line between reaching out to others and bearing burdens God never intended for us to carry.

Do you feel heavy in spirit or weighted down emotionally? I pray for you to experience a release.

Lord Jesus, you invite us to come to you when we are burdened. You promise to give us rest. Show us how to take your yoke, not one of our own making, upon us. We want to learn from you today. Thank you for your gentleness. Our burden is light because you are in charge and you are with us. Alleluia!

Friday, July 18, 2003 St. Camillus de Lellis
Matthew 12, 1-8
Picking Grain on the Sabbath

Higher and higher! Jesus offers two examples of the application of a higher law in order to serve a higher purpose.

Jesus takes his disciples and the ever-vigilant Pharisees higher still. He refers to himself as Lord! He himself is Lord and ruler even of the Sabbath. He is Lord. He is greater than the temple and greater than its sacrifices. He is Lord.

Jesus made it clear (Matthew 5, 17) that he did not come to eradicate the Law, but rather to fulfill it in the highest way. This way is the way of mercy.

Lord Jesus, you are here with us now. Thank you for the countless mercies you have extended to us. Show us how to offer your mercy to each person we encounter today. Alleluia!

Saturday, July 19, 2003
Matthew 12, 14-21
The Man with a Withered Hand; The Chosen Servant

Within the synagogue, Jesus had just healed a man with a paralyzed hand. The infuriated Pharisees wanted to kill him.

Jesus left. Many people followed him and he healed them all, cautioning them to keep quiet about the healings.

This part of Matthew's Gospel includes the beautiful quote from Isaiah 42 about the beloved Servant of the Lord. This is Jesus!

This is the gentle and merciful Jesus who understands suffering. This is the strong and mighty Jesus who leads us to victory. Justice will triumph because Jesus will triumph!

Lord Jesus, you bring new life and new hope to withered hopes and paralyzed dreams. Your ways are ways of gentleness, yet you are the strong and mighty victorious Lord of all. Alleluia!

Sunday, July 20, 2003 Sixteenth Sunday in Ordinary Time
Mark 6, 30-34
The Return of the Twelve; The Feeding of the Five Thousand

With all that Jesus and the twelve disciples had been going through, they needed time out! A break! A respite. An oasis of peace.

What had been happening? Jesus had recently experienced rejection in his hometown synagogue of Nazareth. He had also been meticulously training his disciples and then sent them out on a mission. He had experienced deep grief at the murder of John the Baptist. Now his disciples were excitedly returning from their great adventure in ministry!

Jesus had poured himself into caring for the twelve. They had seen for themselves the power of God at work as they carried out their ministry.

Jesus knew it was time for them to have a rest. Just as he had given specific instructions to the twelve about their ministry to others, so he now gave them specific instructions about caring for themselves.

Rest! Jesus knew from experience that periods of intense ministry require periods of intentional rest and relaxation.

People followed Jesus everywhere! Although he and the twelve did get away in a boat at least for a little while, they were pursued by a crowd. The tender heart of Jesus, the Good Shepherd, was moved with compassion for the multitude and he began to teach them.

At least the disciples had the time with Jesus in the boat. It is the time with Jesus that counts. It is the time with Jesus that renews and refreshes us.

Lord Jesus, people in need will always be here. There will always be demands on our time and resources. Loving Shepherd, show us how to care for ourselves. Help us to remember that YOU are our first priority Time alone with you is our greatest need. You are our spa. You are our retreat. You are our Beloved. Time alone with you is the deep well out of which we are able to offer you to others. Alleluia!

464

Monday, July 21, 2003 St. Lawrence of Brindisi
Matthew 12, 38-42
The Demand for a Sign

The form of address and the subsequent request did not match.
They were incongruent, at the least. The Pharisees and the scribes, the
very ones who were considered to be the teachers and spiritual leaders,
addressed Jesus as one addressed a respected teacher. To address and to
respect someone as a teacher implies that you listen with respect to the
words of that person. The learned scribes and Pharisees of Jesus' day did
not do this. Continually, they attempted to discredit both Jesus and his
message.

To request a sign is a serious matter. It may come from a sincere
desire to know. It may come from an insecure person seeking endless
reassurance or confirmation. It may arise from a superstitious mind and
heart. It may come from an arrogant, supercilious person who does not
really want to know and would not respect the teacher even if a sign was
forthcoming.

Jesus knew all this. He saw right through his opponents. He told
them that it was those who were unfaithful to God who sought signs.

Jesus reminded the scribes and the Pharisees that the wicked
inhabitants of Ninevah had repented at the preaching of the prophet,
Jonah. The only sign Jesus promised to give to his critics was Jonah's
sign. Just as Jonah was in the darkness of a huge fish for three days and
nights, so Jesus, the Son of Man, would be in the darkness of the tomb
for three days and nights.

At the time of judgment, the Queen of the south (Sheba) will
condemn the generation of the time of Jesus' earthly ministry. She will
condemn it for not believing in Jesus. She had traveled from a great
distance to drink in the wisdom of Solomon. Here, right before the
scribes and the Pharisees, was someone greater than Solomon. Here was
Jesus!

Lord Jesus, you are the Sign. Teach us to follow you in humility
and obedience. Alleluia!

Tuesday, July 22, 2003 St. Mary Magdalene
John 20, 1-2; 11-18
The Empty Tomb; The Appearance to Mary Magdalene

The first run. The second run.

465

We can only run with what we have experienced. It was the same with Mary Magdalene, after the death of Jesus.

The first run! Jesus had been crucified and buried. In the darkness before dawn, Mary Magdalene had come to the tomb. It was still dark, true, but the stone was no longer there. With even that bit of knowledge, she ran to Peter and the other disciple, to tell them that Jesus had been taken away.

She had earlier experienced the power of Jesus to deliver and to heal. She had been set free by Jesus. She had been among the women who accompanied Jesus and his twelve disciples on some of their travels (Luke 8, 1-2). She had stood close to the Cross of Jesus (John 19, 25).

The second run! This time the weeping Mary remained by the tomb. Where else could she go? This time, however, she encountered the risen Lord Jesus! She recognized him when he spoke her name. "Mary!"

Jesus then instructed Mary to return to his disciples, whom he called his brothers, and to tell them that he would be returning to his Father. Mary Magdalene had the joyful mission of proclaiming the risen Christ! She has been called the "apostle to the apostles."

Both the first and the second runs are part of the discipleship package. In between, there are many times of apparent darkness and death. We may seem stuck standing by tombs of various sorts.

Lord Jesus, sometimes it seems we are camped outside tombs. No signs of life, as far as we can tell. You don't seem present. We don't seem to be going anywhere in life. Thank you that you are always with us. Thank you for preparing us in our times of darkness for a new ministry of light and life. Thank you for preparing our hearts and our feet to run again. Alleluia!

Wednesday, July 23, 2003 St. Bridget of Sweden
Matthew 13, 1-9
The Parable of the Sower

Jesus, wise teacher that he is, knows the hearts and minds of his listeners. He knows exactly how to speak to each person. In yesterday's Gospel, Mary Magdalene recognized the risen Lord Jesus when he spoke her name.

In today's Gospel, Jesus is speaking to a large crowd. There were many people with many needs and many motives. Some would

466

be humbly receptive to Jesus. Others would be mere curiosity seekers. Others would be there to test him or to discredit him.

How was Jesus to approach them? How would he prepare their minds and hearts to comprehend the mysteries of the Kingdom of God? With a story! A simple story about a sower.

How they responded to the story would determine the next level of their relationship with Jesus. Would they pray for understanding and so advance to further understanding? Or would they thoughtlessly listen to the story and then shrug it off?

Lord Jesus, help us today to cooperate with you to receive the word you are sowing within our minds and hearts. Alleluia!

Thursday, July 23, 2003 St. Bridget
Matthew 13, 10-17
The Purpose of the Parables

We may not like Jesus' explanation of the purpose of the parables, but there it is, complete with a quotation from Isaiah! The parables are intended to send the message in such a way that some will not understand.

Unfair? The Isaiah passage implies that the people themselves have chosen to close their eyes and to choose ignorance. Unfair? Only God knows.

Jesus, as teacher, is definitely challenging, not spoon-feeding, his listeners. Receptivity and commitment are required from those who listen.

Clearly, the disciples are receptive to Jesus and to his teaching. He rewards them with more and more insights.

Clearly, the disciples are committed to Jesus. They are following him and learning to put his teachings into practice for themselves.

The crowds, on the other hand, seem to want to gawk and to collect miracles. Jesus cares for them tenderly. He heals them and feeds them. Do they really want him, though, or only the miracles? Do they want the gift without the giver?

What is their level of receptivity to the teaching of Jesus? What is their level of commitment? Again, only God knows. We do know that Jesus himself stated that he would not reject anyone who came to him (John 6, 37).

Lord Jesus, help us to be willing to dig a little deeper when you say something that we do not initially understand. Help us to persevere, to persist, and to press in to you for whatever you are trying to tell us. Thank you for the gift of the Holy Spirit to teach us. Alleluia!

Friday, July 25, 2003 St. James
Matthew 20, 20-28
The Request of James and John

Two kingdoms. Two ways.

God's kingdom. Our kingdom.

God's way. Our way.

They wage war against one another. Can they be reconciled? Can they be meshed or fused?

You cannot truly live in God's kingdom and expect the perks and privileges of this world. That's our problem, isn't it?

We call ourselves Christians, yet we continue to want our own way plus whatever this passing world has to offer. No.

Jesus has another way. It is the way of the Cross. It is the way of servanthood and suffering. It is the way that leads to life.

The other way, the way of seeking power, honor and fame, leads to stagnation of spirit. Serving self stifles our true self.

James and John made their request for power through their mother. This startling request came immediately after Jesus had predicted, for the third time, that he would suffer, die, and only then be raised. The disciples just didn't get it. Not yet. They were not ready.

Lord Jesus, we still struggle for what we think will make us happy and fulfilled in this life. You came to serve, to suffer, and to show us another way. Purify our hearts to seek you and to follow you in the way that leads to true life. Alleluia!

Saturday, July 26, 2003 Sts. Joachim and Anne
Matthew 13, 24-30
The Parable of the Weeds among the Wheat

Wait and let God decide what's what. I believe that is the purpose of this parable Jesus told about the weeds planted amongst the good wheat.

468

This kind of weed was not just a nuisance. It was actually a poisonous weed, deliberately planted in the midst of wheat.

In the parable, while the landowner was asleep and unsuspecting, "his" enemy, not just any old enemy, but his enemy, slipped in, sowed his poison, and slipped out. No one knew until the weeds started to grow.

No one knew? God knew.

Unlike the landowner's servants in Jesus' parable, God was just going to wait. The servants were quite willing to get right in there in the field and pull up the weeds. No.

In the Body of Christ on this earth, the Church, there has always been the tragedy of those who slip in and sow poison. Reputations are ruined. Ministries are put on the shelf.

It seems God does not see. It seems that God does not care. However, God does see. God cares. God waits. The poisonous weeds will be destroyed in God's time.

Lord Jesus, teach us to wait patiently. Even if we want to charge in and fight the wrongs we see, that is not always your way. You told us to love our enemies. This includes the ones who plant poisonous weeds. You are sovereign. You know things about the weeds and the wheat that we do not know. You know the time and the method for gathering the wheat and burning the weeds. Alleluia!

Sunday, July 27, 2003 Seventeenth Sunday in Ordinary Time
John 6, 1-15
Multiplication of the Loaves

There are always catalysts in the Body of Christ. They are the unassuming ones who think little of themselves. They always point to God. Catalysts initiate life-giving reactions, while remaining inconspicuous.

Perhaps Andrew was such a catalyst. Andrew, initially a follower of John the Baptist, heeded John's words pointing to Jesus as the Lamb of God.

Andrew then began to follow Jesus. Recognizing Jesus as the Messiah, Andrew sought out Peter, his brother, and took him to Jesus (John 1, 35-42). The rest, as they say, is history.

In today's Gospel, it was Andrew who told Jesus about the lad with the loaves of barley bread and the two fish. Although Andrew wondered how far that would go, he did take the initiative to tell Jesus. It was from these loaves and fish that Jesus fed the large crowd. The focus was on Jesus!

Lord Jesus, thank you listening to Andrew and then taking the loaves into your hands to offer thanks to God and to distribute to the people. Thank you for taking our lives into your hands to bless and to use as you wish to feed others. Alleluia!

Monday, July 28, 2003
Matthew 13, 31-35
The Parable of the Mustard Seed; The Parable of the Yeast;
The Use of Parables

Because of the human component, the Kingdom of Heaven takes time to be made visible, God could speak the word and the Kingdom would instantly materialize, but that is not usually God's way. Because God chooses to work through us, that usually means working slowly.

A man takes a mustard seed, plants it, and waits. Only in time does the seed become a flourishing tree where birds fly to perch on its branches.

A woman takes yeast and kneads it into the flour. Only in time are the baked loaves ready to offer to others.

In both parables, or stories, human labor is blessed by God, and, in time, the results are seen by all. God is there in the time of waiting as well in the time of working

Jesus fulfilled Psalm 78, 2 as he continued to tell stories, or parables, as he spoke to the crowds. The listeners would have to do their part, to expend some effort, to draw forth God's purpose for them in the telling of the story.

Lord Jesus, thank you that you are with us as we work and as we wait. Alleluia!

470

Tuesday, July 29, 2003 St. Martha
John 11, 19-27
The Raising of Lazarus

In the midst of death, we are in life. In John's Gospel, the time is drawing closer and closer for Jesus' suffering and death. Still, wherever Jesus is, there is life.

Good News for Martha! Even though Lazarus, her brother, was dead and buried, Martha sprang into action when she heard Jesus was on the way.

Taking the initiative to meet Jesus on his way to Bethany, the grieving Martha reproached him for not being there earlier. Still, she knew that Jesus had complete authority, even in hopeless situations. She affirmed her conviction that here before her was Jesus, the Son of God, the Messiah.

Lord Jesus, we are in the midst of life, because you are in our midst. Alleluia!

Wednesday, July 30, 2003 St. Peter Chrysologus
Matthew 13, 44-46
More Parables

Treasure hidden in a field! An exquisite pearl sought out by a merchant. Jesus is teaching the crowds about the value of the kingdom of heaven.

In the first of this set of parables, someone finds buried treasure and then sells everything in order to buy the whole field to acquire the treasure. The joy of possessing the treasure is worth everything.

In the second of the parables, the merchant is actively seeking precious jewels. Finding the perfect pearl, the merchant then sells everything in order to purchase this pearl.

There is a sense of finality in both parables. Everything was given for the kingdom of heaven.

Lord Jesus, you are the treasure! You delight to be sought after and to be found. The joy of being in your presence and serving you is worth everything. Alleluia!

Thursday, July 31, 2003 St. Ignatius of Loyola
Matthew 13, 47-53
More Parables; Treasures Old and New

The time for parable telling is drawing to a close. Jesus is preparing to conclude this particular time of teaching the large group by the sea.

The last parable in this section involves a comparison of the kingdom of heaven with a large net flung out into the sea. The fishermen and the angels all have assignments to fulfill.

The fishermen, of course, are the ones who throw their nets out into the sea and then sort through all the fish. They place the good fish in buckets. The other fish, presumably unsuitable for consumption, are discarded.

Jesus compares this sorting activity to the task of the angels when it is time for this age to come to an end. At that time, the angels will distinguish between the holy ones and the evil ones, between those considered righteous and those considered unrighteous. The latter will be hurled into a fiery furnace where they will cry out and gnash their teeth.

Jesus, the teller of this parable, asks the people if they understand. Amazingly, they say they do!

Jesus then tells them that those who have been carefully instructed in the kingdom of heaven will have the discernment to be able to draw out both the old and the new teachings. Jesus gives the comparison of the head of the house knowing what to bring forth from the storehouse. Having completed the telling of this powerful parable, Jesus leaves.

Lord Jesus, help us to understand and to accept our particular role in your kingdom. Even if we are baffled, lead us to be faithful to your call as we understand it. We pray to be filled with the Holy Spirit and for wise teachers to guide us. Help us to know when our work is complete in a particular place and when to move on, as you direct, to a new assignment. Alleluia!

Friday, August 1, 2003 St. Alphonsus Liguori
Matthew 13, 54-58
The Rejection at Nazareth

The Word spoke the word! In the majestic prologue to John's Gospel, Jesus was called the Word. Jesus, the Word, was with God from the very beginning and indeed was God (John 1, 1).

In today's Gospel, Jesus comes to Nazareth, to his hometown synagogue. Having just come from teaching the crowds by the sea, he was now teaching a much smaller group of people.

The people in the synagogue were not strangers. They knew Jesus, but, apparently were so entrenched in their mind-sets and heart-sets that they failed to recognize Jesus, the Word of God speaking God's word to them. They thought they knew him, but they knew him not.

Jesus understood. He knew his Hebrew scriptures. He knew the plight and the fate of prophets, those who truly speak forth God's words. Because of the people's unbelief, Jesus did not perform mighty works in that place.

Lord Jesus, you are the Word made flesh. You came to your own people and were rejected. Give us renewed trust in you and courage to speak your words. Let us joyfully live in your light and truth, regardless of how we are perceived and received in this world. Alleluia!

Saturday, August 2, 2003
St. Eusebius of Vercelli, St. Peter Julian Eymard
Matthew 14, 1-12
Herod's Opinion of Jesus; The Death of John the Baptist

Herod is one of the most pathetic people in the Gospels. Maintaining his image and guarding his political power were the ruling passions of his life.

Clash! There was bound to be a clash when Herod encountered John the Baptist. John's ruling passion was boldly speaking forth God's word. John was a true prophet.

Prophets and unscrupulous politicians usually do not get along. Mixing truth and lies? No!

John the Baptist spoke the truth about Herod's marriage. This marriage to the wife of one of Herod's half-brothers was strictly prohibited (Leviticus 18, 16).

King Herod, although he personally desired to kill John the Baptist, did not yet proceed with his plan. Why not?

Herod was afraid of what the people would think. The people truly believed that John the Baptist was a prophet sent from God.

473

Delighted and distracted by the dance of his wife Herodius' daughter, Herod rashly promised the girl that he would give her whatever she wanted. Herodius prompted her daughter to ask for the severed head of John the Baptist.

This turn of events disturbed Herod, but not enough to spare the prophet's life. Because he did not wish to lose face with his guests, he complied with the request. John was murdered.

Lord Jesus, it's the same today. Those who speak the truth often suffer at the hands of those who driven by their need to save face and to guard power. Thank you for the gift of the Holy Spirit to speak your words with wisdom and power, regardless of the consequences. Alleluia!

Sunday, August 3, 2003 Eighteenth Sunday in Ordinary Time
John 6, 24-35
The Bread of Life Discourse

Let us raise our eyes higher and look to Jesus. Temporary manna will not last. It will not satisfy. Only Jesus, the Bread of Life, will sustain us forever.

The sign seekers wanted temporal security. We all do.

They tested Jesus. We all do.

They asked what Jesus could do. We all do.

What does Jesus say? He tells us that our true vocation is to believe in him.

Lord Jesus, you came from heaven and you are the Bread of Life. Pull us out of this quagmire of earthly concerns in which we become stuck from time to time. Teach us to trust you and free us to follow you wherever you lead us. Alleluia!

Monday, August 4, 2003 St. John Vianney
Matthew 14, 13-21
The Return of the Twelve; The Feeding of the Five Thousand

Grief. An attempt at solitude. A return to caring for others. A miracle.

Jesus, having just been informed of the tragic death of John the Baptist, departed. He took a boat, intending to find a quiet place for solitude and reflection.

However, even before he disembarked, there they were. So many people! His heart was touched with compassion and he reached out to the sick and cured them.

When the disciples saw the problem of the late hour and the lack of food, they turned to Jesus. Jesus turned the situation around. Instead of getting rid of the people, he simply told his disciples to feed them.

Whatever is brought to Jesus is always enough. Jesus took the five loaves of bread which were given to him. Always in communication with his Father, Jesus acknowledged his Father's presence, prayed a blessing on the bread, broke the bread, and then gave the bread to the disciples to give to the people.

When Jesus blesses what is brought to him, there is always more than enough. In this case, there were twelve baskets of bread remaining after the crowd had been fed.

Lord Jesus, you set aside your grief and your need to be alone in order to feed the little ones. Sometimes we feel so depleted we may think that we have nothing left to give. We give you our very selves to take, to bless, and to give to others. Energize us, empower us, and use us as you see fit to feed your people. Thank you for even giving us surplus energy, so that our baskets overflow. Alleluia!

Tuesday, August 5, 2003
Dedication of the Basilica of St. Mary in Rome
Matthew 14, 22-36
The Walking on the Water; The Healings at Gennesaret

Touch Jesus. You will walk on water.

Touch Jesus. You will be made whole.

Peter risked drowning in a storm on the sea in order to get to Jesus. At least he got out of the boat!

At the invitation of Jesus, Peter began to walk on the water. As soon as he was distracted by the fierce wind and started to sink, he cried out to Jesus

Jesus, of course, reached out and grasped Peter's hand. Those safely tucked up in the boat marveled and acknowledged that Jesus was indeed the Son of God. Peter, however, had actually touched Jesus and knew Jesus in a whole new way.

The sick people of Gennesaret flocked to Jesus, hoping merely to touch the tassel of his cloak. Simply touching his garment brought healing.

Lord Jesus, breathe fresh courage into us today. You do care about us and you are with us. Peter reached out to you. The people in Gennesaret reached out to you. You had compassion on them. We reach out to you today in prayer, in our longing to live the this Gospel, in receiving you in Holy Communions, and in serving others. Thank you for making us whole. Alleluia!

Wednesday, August 6, 2003 Transfiguration of the Lord
Mark 9, 2-10
The Transfiguration of Jesus

The curtain is drawn aside for a brief moment. Light from heaven suffuses the scene.

Flash! There is fulfillment. There is understanding. There is the promise of complete and final fulfillment.

For Peter, James, and John, on the mountain with Jesus, this was such a moment. Jesus, the rabbi, Jesus, their friend, Jesus the Messiah, Jesus, the Son of Man, was brilliantly revealed as Son of God!

Jesus, the Word made flesh, summed up in his brief earthly life the totality of what God gave through Moses in the Law and what God gave Elijah through prophecy. JESUS!

God the Father spoke from the overshadowing, luminous cloud, confirming the identity of Jesus. Jesus is God's own Son, God's own beloved Son. The Father instructs the dazed disciples to listen attentatively to his Son.

Jesus and his three disciples came down from the mountain. What happened on the mountain was not going to be assimilated immediately. Jesus cautioned Peter, James, and John not to tell about this experience until he, as Son of Man, had risen from the dead.

Lord Jesus, you have risen from the dead! Your disciples have told us of your glorious transfiguration on the mountain. As we toil in the valley, remind us of this glimpse of glory and the eternal glory awaiting us. Alleluia!

Thursday, August 7, 2003
St. Sixtus II and Companions, St. Cajetan
Matthew 16, 13, 13-23
Peter's Confession about Jesus

Flesh and blood may illustrate, but not illuminate. Flesh and blood, human power, did not reveal to Simon Peter the true identity of Jesus, the rabbi. That was the work of God the Father in heaven.

Our lives may be used of God to illustrate Jesus. Only God the Father, however, illuminates who Jesus really is.

Painters may illustrate the waves of the ocean. Their work is very beautiful and may give us, if we have never seen the ocean, an impression of what the ocean is like.

Standing before the majestic ocean -- seeing the waves roll in and out, smelling the salt air, hearing the waves crash upon the beach, watching the sea birds both whirling in the sky and skating along the shore, and contemplating the sky at sunrise and sunset -- is another matter. Now we know what the ocean is really like. We are in its presence. We are there.

Lord Jesus, we are in your presence this very moment. You are here. Reveal to us more and more who you really are and what you are really like. We think we know you and we do, up to a point. You are infinite in beauty. You are majestic in holiness. Heavenly Father, thank you for sending the Holy Spirit to reveal Jesus to us today and every day, until we stand before him face to face. Alleluia!

Friday, August 8, 2003 St. Dominic
Matthew 16, 24-28
The Conditions of Discipleship

"You're hard to work for." Startled, I heard the Holy Spirit gently whisper these words to me as I was fussing over a trifle, trying to make something just so. Yes, working for myself, trying to please myself, is a burden.

Jesus is easier to follow, really, than our own stubborn self-will. We, who are so hard on ourselves, are usually hard on others.

How do we follow Jesus? He gives us three requirements of discipleship in today's Gospel.

477

We are to deny ourselves. This is more than giving up a chocolate malt. This is saying scat to our inner self and to our idiotic desire to be in control. We're not in control. God is. God is in the driver's seat.

Jesus requires that we take up our cross. Whatever suffering results as a consequence of our following Jesus is our cross. Anyway, that is my own belief about my own cross. There is always a price to be paid if we truly follow Jesus.

Follow Jesus! This is the third condition of discipleship He is leading in the dance of our lives.

Clutching our ideas of how things ought to be or should be is not the way to be a disciple. Jesus breathes freshness and delight into our discipleship.

When Jesus, as Son of Man, comes with the angels in the shining glory of his Father, he will give to us according to our actions. We are charged to follow Jesus and let Jesus indicate how we are to serve him.

Lord Jesus, thank you for the times of silence, for the times of speaking, for the times of waiting, for the times of working, as we follow you. Alleluia!

Saturday, August 9, 2003
Matthew 17, 14-20
The Healing of a Boy with a Demon

Two scenarios, with various issues, as they say, are being played out in today's Gospel. We see both the humanity and the divinity of Jesus in a startling way.

The father of the afflicted boy is suffering anguish. In deep humility, he comes to Jesus and kneels before him. He had not gone directly to Jesus in the beginning. Perhaps, because of his humility, he had initially approached Jesus' disciples for help for his son. Since they had not been able to help, he had then gone to Jesus.

Jesus was thoroughly exasperated with his disciples! He had carefully trained them and they had seen his mighty works. Three of them had even seen his glorious transfiguration on the mountain. Still, their faith level was faltering and lacking.

As for the afflicted boy, Jesus healed him! The boy was set free to live a new life.

478

Now back to those disciples! Jesus told them in no uncertain terms that their faith was too little. With even the tiniest bit of true faith, nothing would be impossible.

Lord Jesus, you were so tender with the ailing lad and his father, yet so irritated with your obtuse disciples. Have mercy on us, Lord. We, too, need your healing. We too need to grow in our level of trust and belief that you can do absolutely anything. Nothing is impossible with you. Alleluia!

Sunday, August 10, 2003 Nineteenth Sunday in Ordinary Time
John 6, 41-51
The Bread of Life Discourse

How would you react if a man in your town starting saying that he was the bread that had come down from heaven? What if he called God his Father? What if he referred to his own flesh as bread?

Jesus said that no one could come to him unless drawn by the Father in heaven. Jesus then referred to prophecies of Isaiah and Jeremiah.

The prophets had promised that God would teach all his people (Isaiah 54, 13) and that they would truly know their God (Jeremiah 31, 33-34). Jesus came to flesh out and to fulfill what the prophets had anticipated. Jesus was indeed the long expected One, and yet he was not recognized or acknowledged by all his people.

Jesus specifically said that every person who listened to God and learned from God would come to him, to Jesus (John 6, 45). Jesus is forever!

The manna given in the desert was for temporary sustenance. Jesus is the true and living Bread that sustains us for this life and forever. Jesus is forever.

Lord Jesus, thank you for coming from heaven to earth to teach us and to show us what God is really like. We are starved from trying to stuff ourselves with the stuff of this world. Thank you for giving us your very self as the true staff of life, as true and living Bread. Alleluia!

Monday, August 11, 2003 St. Clare
Matthew 17, 22-27
The Second Prediction of the Passion;
Payment of the Temple Tax

Death and taxes. Jesus is in charge of both.

Death. As Son of Man, Jesus naturally shrinks from the suffering awaiting him at the hands of the evil ones who will betray him, torture him, and kill him. He knowingly submits to this mysterious suffering to secure our salvation. He knows he will be raised on the third day.

Taxes. A temporal concern. This was a once a year tax to maintain the temple. The temple tax collectors approached Peter to ask if Jesus paid the temple tax. Peter answered yes. The Son of God paying taxes to the church? Imagine!

Jesus has a most creative way to come up with the tax money. He instructs Peter to go to the sea, catch a fish, and open its mouth. The temple tax, enough for the two of them, will be there in the mouth of the fish. Money received from a fish's mouth is not the IRS' usual method of collecting taxes! The coin Peter found was twice the amount of the temple tax, enough for both Peter and Jesus.

Lord Jesus, thank you for being Lord of life, death, and taxes. Today, show us how to accept and to survive the suffering which accompanies our decision to follow you. Help us to trust your provision for all our temporal matters, taxes and all. Suffering, death, and taxes are not forever. You are forever! Life is forever. Joy with you in heaven is forever. Alleluia!

Tuesday, August 12, 2003
Matthew 18, 1-5, 10, 12-14
The Greatest in the Kingdom; The Parable of the Lost Sheep

Healthy and happy children do not have hidden agendas. Perhaps that is why Jesus said that whoever is as humble as a child will be greatest in the kingdom.

Indeed, Jesus says that unless his disciples become like children, they will not even enter the kingdom! Receiving such a child is considered equivalent to receiving Jesus.

Despising such a little one is forbidden. Even at this moment, their angels are gazing upon the heavenly Father.

A good shepherd leaves the safely grazing ninety-nine sheep in search of the one stray. Just so, it is not the heavenly Father's desire that even one of the little ones is lost.

Lord Jesus, forgive us when we, even in the silence of our hearts, look down on or make unloving judgments of others. They are your cherished little ones, of infinite value in your eyes. Touch and soften our cold, cynical, wounded hearts to look with love and compassion on all who cross our paths today, especially your little lost ones. Alleluia!

Wednesday, August 13, 2003 Sts. Pontian and Hippolytus
Matthew 18, 15-20
A Brother Who Sins

Confrontation 101! Class is in session. Jesus teaches how to handle conflict with another believer, another disciple.

First, you are to confront the person directly, just the two of you. Most of us don't do this. We tell others instead.

Second, Jesus says that if private, direct confrontation is ineffective, try again. This time, take one or two other witnesses with you.

Third, submit the matter to the local church if the first two forms of confrontation do not bring resolution. If the person in question refuses to listen to the assembly, that person is to be treated as a Gentile or a tax collector. People in those categories were not respected. They were considered pagans and outsiders.

Outsiders. And yet, Jesus reached out to them. Matthew, called by Jesus to be a disciple, was a tax collector. The Samaritan woman at the well was despised by some as a half-breed and yet Jesus considered her worthy of his time and concern (John 4).

Jesus promised to be in the midst of two or three believers who drew together to pray in his name. He promised that his Father in heaven would the grant the request for which they prayed.

Lord Jesus, we shrink from confrontation, and yet you instructed us how to do our part. Give us the courage to confront according to this pattern and to leave the results with you. Thank you for your promised presence as we pray with one another. Alleluia!

Thursday, August 14, 2003 St. Maximilian Kolbe
Matthew 18, 21-19, 1
The Parable of the Unforgiving Servant

Jesus takes Peter's question about how many times it is necessary to forgive and answers with a parable. The answer is basically forever!

No matter what we are required to forgive in others, it is still relatively little compared to what God has had to forgive in us. No matter how much we think someone owes us, it is still peanuts compared to what we owe God.

Jesus shed his blood and died on the Cross for our sins to secure our salvation and our eternal bliss. Anything, anything, anything, no matter how horrible, we have had to forgive in others is unworthy of comparison to what God has done for us in sending Jesus, the pure Lamb of God, to die for us.

This parable is especially difficult if we think we are not particularly in need of forgiveness. If that is the case, we are the very ones most in need of forgiveness. We are the very ones who need to cry out to God for the grace to ask for forgiveness and for the grace to forgive all who have injured us.

Fr. Maximilian Kolbe did not deserve to die in a concentration camp in World War II. He gave his life so another man, a married man with a family, could live.

Lord Jesus, thank you, I think, for this tough parable. I need to be confronted with the truth about myself and the requirement to forgive. Thank you for the gift of the Holy Spirit to work in my heart to show me my own need of forgiveness. Thank you for your mercy. Alleluia!

Friday, August 15, 2003 The Assumption of Mary
Luke 1, 39-56
Mary Visits Elizabeth; The Canticle of Mary

Vocation. Completion. Assumption. This is Mary's day of days!

Vocation. Mary fulfilled the call of God on her life. She said yes to an impossible vocation. A virgin mother! Virgin mother of the Son of the Most High God. The Holy Spirit was in charge of Mary's vocation and the impossible became reality. The Word of God was clothed in flesh and came to live amongst us as Jesus, Son of God and son of Mary.

Completion. The impossible vocation did not preclude the earthly, the mundane, and the ordinary. Mary was practical in her practice of the presence of God. She, the young teenage girl, hurried off to visit the older Elizabeth, pregnant with John the Baptist. Mary praised God. What could be more practical than praising God? She knew it was the Mighty God who had done the impossible for her. She deemed herself a lowly handmaid in the hands of an amazing God.

Mary suffered, as all true disciples suffer, in completing her vocation. Her heart was pierced as she watched the unfolding of her Son's life. She pondered. She knew grief.

Assumption. Mary's day of days. This was the time for Mary to be summoned to God. Her impossible vocation was successfully completed.

Lord Jesus, thank you the example of Mary, your mother. She is our role model, our example, in trusting the heavenly Father with our vocation. Come Holy Spirit and fill us with new life and promise. Alleluia!

Saturday, August 16, 2003 St. Stephen of Hungary
Matthew 19, 13-15
Blessing of the Children

Impartation of blessings. Love. Healing. Power.

Probably that's why the children were brought to Jesus. The ones who brought them knew that the touch of Jesus would bring healing. The prayer of Jesus would impart power.

The disciples still did not understand the significance of children. Children with their trusting, loving, wholehearted belief were themselves outward, visible signs of a powerful inward, spiritual grace. God was at work in them, regardless of their age. Children were important to God!

We may ask Jesus to restore our own childlike trust and belief. If our childhood memories are not happy ones, we may ask Jesus to heal us.

If the world has ground us down, we may come to Jesus and ask him to touch us and to restore us. We may ask Jesus to pray for us to be filled anew with fresh zeal and power.

Lord Jesus, you said the kingdom of heaven belonged to those who were willing to be as humble as little children. Restore to us the lost qualities of trust and hope. Thank you for the gift of the Holy Spirit to energize us to do your will today. Alleluia!

Sunday, August 17, 2003 Twentieth Sunday in Ordinary Time
John 6, 51-58
The Bread of Life Discourse

Jesus is real! The food he gives us is real. He said his flesh was real food and his blood was real drink. Body. Blood. Soul. Divinity.

His hearers in the synagogue disputed and fussed about his choice of words. Even today, some Christians try to spiritualize his words away. Nevertheless, Jesus spoke the truth.

Lord Jesus, thank you for the gift of the Holy Spirit to help us to understand your words. You are speaking of life. Your Father in heaven is alive. You have life because of your Father. You are the Bread of Life. You are the true Bread from heaven. Thank you that we will live forever as we feast upon you, your Body and your Blood. Alleluia!

Monday, August 18, 2003 St. Jane Frances de Chantal
Matthew 19, 16-22
The Rich Young Man

Life! Jesus is telling this particular man what to do in order to experience the fullness of life.

There are certain decrees which apply to all of us. That is why Jesus refers to keeping the commandments.

This man specifically asked Jesus what good he must do. He was already keeping the commandments, but he knew that something was lacking.

Jesus told this particular man to sell his earthly possessions in order to have heavenly treasures. The man did not want that answer, so he went away.

Lord Jesus, thank you for the gift of the Holy Spirit to zero in on whatever is holding us back from living life to the full. You are our treasure. Regardless of our bank account or our earthly possessions, you are all we really need. Forgive us for presuming that we know what we need. Forgive us for clutching tightly to what we think will make us happy. Free our weary hearts of all that keeps us from loving and serving you. Alleluia!

Tuesday, August 19, 2003 St. John Eudes
Matthew 19, 23-30
The Rich Young Man

We don't give to God. Not really. Everything already belongs to God.

We don't give up anything. Not really. Everything already belongs to God.

Jesus knows how difficult it is for those with an abundance of earthly riches to come into the heavenly kingdom They may tend to seek security in the things of this world.

It is not impossible, however, for the wealthy to sell out to God. It is a matter of yielding to God's loving plan..

Peter often seemed to pipe up to ask what others might be thinking. Peter reminded Jesus that the disciples had relinquished all. He flat out asked what they would get out of their investment. That's Peter!

Jesus was not one bit perturbed by this kind of direct and honest question. He knows us inside out. He knows what we think about and what frightens us. Jesus assured the disciples that when he comes in glory, they too will share in his rule.

Everyone who has sacrificed for Jesus in this world will be lavishly rewarded by Jesus. We are free to live boldly for Jesus!

Lord Jesus, forgive us when we are stingy stewards. Help us to be wise in managing the resources you have put temporarily into our hands. Each day, show us how to give to others, knowing that it is all from you. Alleluia!

Wednesday, August 20, 2003 St. Bernard
Matthew 20, 1-16
The Workers in the Vineyard

Dawn. Nine o'clock in the morning. High noon. Working in the heat of the sun in the vineyard. Five o'clock in the late afternoon. Heat. Dust. Sweat.

The last workers, who worked the least time, were the first to be paid. Not only were they paid, but they were also paid just the same amount as the workers who were out there all day in the heat of the sun.

This parable drives the equality police crazy. Equal rights? Equal pay for equal work? Out the window!

This is a parable about the kingdom of heaven. Heaven. The realm where God's will is done. We can't take our notions about how things should be done in the kingdom of earth and transpose them into this new realm.

God knows perfectly well the work we have done and will not let us go unrewarded (Hebrews 6, 10). Still, God is God. God is Sovereign. God owns all.

Lord Jesus, please give us the heart transplant we need in order to rejoice! Help us to rejoice that those who enter the vineyard at the very last moment and labor a short time will enjoy the benefits of the kingdom. We are all in need of your mercy and grace. Thank you for the privilege of serving in the vineyard for whatever time you give us. Thank you that we will rejoice with you and all the holy angels and saints for all eternity. Alleluia!

Thursday, August 21, 2003 St. Pius X
Matthew 22, 1-14
The Parable of the Wedding Feast

Sometimes I have a tendency to be so eager about something that I run ahead of God's timing. Last month, truly thinking the Open House at a nearby monastery was on the 28th from 2:00 pm - 4:00 pm, we arrived early. No cars were there. Strange, I thought. Well, we'll just go into the beautiful chapel and wait a bit. After a period of time, it was clear that no one was coming to an Open House that day. Returning home, I checked the invitation. Yes, it was from 2:00 pm - 4:00 pm. However it was on September 28th, not on July 28th!

While reading today's Gospel, I wanted to jump ahead to the beautiful Marriage Feast of the Lamb. It's not quite time for this particular event, but it still plays a part in my personal musing on the Gospel.

Jesus was continuing to speak to the chief priests and the Pharisees. Of course, they perceived that his previous parable, the one about the wicked tenants in the vineyard, was aimed at them (Matthew 21, 33-46). Even so, Jesus relentlessly kept at it. He kept speaking to them in parables in order for them to see themselves in the story and repent.

Jesus was describing in story form what the kingdom of heaven is like. The parable of the wedding feast may be seen as a most glorious

486

enticement to come one day to the ultimate wedding feast, the Wedding Feast, the Supper, of the Lamb (Revelation 19, 9).

Jesus is the Son of the great King. Jesus is the Messiah. Jesus is the holy, sinless Lamb of God. The Father in heaven, the King of all, will throw the party of parties, the feast of feasts, the ultimate celebration of eternity.

Do the chief priests and the Pharisees, religious leaders of the day, care? Apparently not. They refused the invitation by refusing Jesus. They insulted the messengers of the great King.

This is not a feast to attend wearing dirty rags. Jesus, the Son of God, the Lamb of God, died on the Cross, to provide suitable wedding garments for each of us who accepts the invitation. This garment is the vestment of salvation (Isaiah 61, 10).

The price for this dazzling white robe of righteousness was purchased by the Blood of Jesus, the Son, the Lamb of God. That is what it cost the Father in heaven to invite each of us to the wedding feast.

Lord Jesus, your Father has opened his heart to invite all to the Feast. You have given us a beautiful garment to wear to this feast. Let all earthly, petty, temporal concerns fade away as we contemplate you. You will come again in glory! You came so quietly the first time, as a tiny Baby. You will return as the conquering King! Let us continue to say yes to every invitation you give us, until at last we feast with you in the heavenly Jerusalem. Alleluia!

Friday, August 22, 2003 The Queenship of Mary
Matthew 22, 34-40
The Greatest Commandment

The Pharisees were at it again, trying to discredit Jesus. Although Jesus had just triumphed in his encounter with the Sadducees, the Pharisees were still eager to have a go at trapping him with their own clever queries. Their designated scholar asked Jesus which commandment was the greatest.

Lord Jesus, you turned the tables on your interrogators with your serene simplicity. You told your questioners to love God totally and to love and to care for others. We are to love others as ourselves. Purify our hearts and heal us. Thank you for the gift of the Holy Spirit to strengthen us to keep these commandments. Alleluia!

Saturday, August 23, 2003 St. Rose of Lima
Matthew 23, 1-12
Denunciation of the Scribes and Pharisees

Opposites do not always attract. They may clash and spark. This
was true in the case of Jesus and his encounters with the Pharisees and
scribes.

Jesus instructs both the crowd and his disciples to follow the
teaching expounded by these leaders. What Jesus is warning against is
following their personal examples. Some of them were quite swollen
with pride and enjoyed flaunting the perks of their office.

If you want to see an opposite life style, go to Matthew 6. Jesus tells
us how to live simply before God and others. He tells us how to pray, to
fast, and to give.

Lord Jesus, you are our Teacher. You have taught us to humble
ourselves and not to attempt to exalt ourselves. We have complete
freedom to be all you have called us to be. Alleluia!

Sunday, August 24, 2003 Twenty-first Sunday of Ordinary Time
John 6, 60-69
The Words of Eternal Life

Following Jesus was becoming difficult for his disciples Even in
our time, not everyone is willing to stick it out, to admit that some things
are very difficult to understand, and to pray in humility for clarity.

The disciples are struggling with Jesus' claim to be the Bread of
Life. What on earth does that mean? Jesus tells them that life comes from
the Spirit, not from mere human effort.

Jesus also refers to his Ascension to heaven. If his followers
are grappling with the Bread of Life teaching, how will they deal with
actually seeing the Ascension of the Risen Lord Jesus Christ?

Many of Jesus' disciples, not just a few, but many, simply could
not take this teaching about the Bread of Life. They crawled back to their
comfort zone. They returned to whatever they were doing before they
began following this puzzling rabbi, Jesus of Nazareth. Moving in the
Spirit was becoming too heavy for them.

Jesus asked the Twelve if they were inclined to bail out, also. Peter
understood that there was no other place to go, because with Jesus, there

was eternity. The words of Jesus were eternal. Peter spoke for the Twelve in affirming Jesus' true identity.

Lord Jesus, we come to you because your Father has drawn us to you. When we do not understand what you are saying to us, help us not to run away, but to stay close to you and to pray for the illumination of the Holy Spirit. Alleluia!

> Monday, August 25, 2003 St. Louis, St. Joseph Calasanz
> Matthew 23, 13-22
> Denunciation of the Scribes and the Pharisees

The scribes and the Pharisees still didn't get it! Sometimes, we just don't get it either.

Jesus had already stated what was the most important commandment. Love God with your whole heart. Then love others unselfishly (Matthew 22, 34-40).

Every other commandment depends on these two. If these two great commandments are attended to, all the other matters of faith will fall into place.

These particular religious leaders seemed so preoccupied with their own baggage that they could not see into the heart of the matter. They could not discern what truly mattered in this life. They could not see God, even though God, in the Person of Jesus, was standing right before them.

They could not see into their own hearts, because their hearts were so encrusted with deception and hypocrisy. They were terribly threatened by the reality of the kingdom of heaven. They refused the kingdom for themselves and attempted to prevent others from entering this kingdom where the glorious will of God was supreme.

Good golly, Miss Molly, what's the Messiah to do?! Jesus was fed up. No wonder he pronounced the ominous "woe" word so many times.

Lord Jesus, thank you for teaching us what is truly important. Thank you for your mercy as you lead us through this rocky, earthly pilgrimage safely into your arms. Alleluia!

Tuesday, August 26, 2003
Matthew 23, 23-26
Denunciation of the Scribes and Pharisees

I saw a funny drawing in a little booklet about depression and other mood disorders. The booklet was written by a physician who was one of the speakers at a recent conference I attended of the Association of Christian Therapists. The physician spoke of very serious matters, yet his robust sense of humor helped his audience to look within, without being terrified.

The drawing showed a real macho type guy, arms akimbo, who was glaring and saying, "I'm fine!" He was not going to admit that maybe, just maybe, he was not fine. Certainly he was not going to admit to being depressed. No, indeed.

The scribes and the Pharisees thought that they were just fine too. Jesus locked horns with them because of their arrogant, pathetic, and willful denial.

The poor in spirit, the little forgotten ones, knew that they were sinners in need of a Savior. The scribes and Pharisees, on the other hand, seemed to believe that they had already arrived and that they were just fine.

It's amusing to consider the meticulous tithing of even the little garden herbs of mint, dill, and cumin. They are so light, especially the feathery dill.

The heavy matters, Jesus said, are those involving faithfulness, judgment, and mercy. Jesus called the religious leaders blind for not being able to attend to the heavy matters, the really important matters, without neglecting the lighter matters of herb tithing.

Jesus offers a fascinating image about carefully cleansing the outside of a cup which is filled with filth. Yet that is what we do when we put on a happy face when we are harboring rage and hatred within the secret recesses of our hearts.

The sacrament of reconciliation is a marvelous opportunity for cleansing. We meet Jesus in this sacrament in a very special way. We meet ourselves too, if we are as honest as we know how to be. The priest pronounces God's forgiveness and we are set free! We are clean.

Lord Jesus, thank you for your love and your understanding even when we deceive ourselves into thinking we are just fine when we are not. Lead us gently to see ourselves as you see us and then lead us to the Cross where we are made whole. Alleluia!

Wednesday, August 27, 2003 St. Monica
Matthew 23, 27-32
Denunciation of the Scribes and Pharisees

The unrelenting promises of woe continue. Jesus has stopped telling parables. He is now speaking directly and with righteous fury to the religious leaders.

They look so good on the outside -- clean and sparkling like white tombs freshly washed -- but they are full of filth and decay on the inside. They are evil doers with angelic exteriors.

These particular religious leaders exuded a lot of pious hogwash by building ostentatious memorials to the holy prophets of old Those prophets were martyred for their fidelity to God.

The ancestors of these leaders had killed the prophets. The current generation of leaders continued doing the very same thing.

Lord Jesus, as we read these last two indictments, help us to continue to be aware of the same tendencies to hypocrisy and lawlessness within our own hearts. Forgive us and cleanse us. Thank you for the gift of the Holy Spirit to teach us to honor you and honor those who speak your word to us today. Alleluia!

Thursday, August 28, 2003 St. Augustine
Matthew 24, 42-51
The Unknown Day and Hour;
The Faithful or the Unfaithful Servants

Fear is not meant to be the ruler in my life. God rules and overrules. It is not for me to try to figure out this or that, but rather to be faithful to fulfill what is possible for me to fulfill within the parameters of my life.

Lord Jesus, you know exactly how and when to manifest your presence. You are always with us and yet our awareness of your presence pierces us more deeply at certain times. As we continue faithfully in our daily assignments, help us to trust you and not to give in to fear. Thank you that you will come in glory with the holy angels. Alleluia!

491

Friday, August 29, 2003 Martyrdom of John the Baptist
Mark 6, 17-29
The Death of John the Baptist

Ultimate allegiance. To whom is it given?

King Herod gave ultimate allegiance to his own ego. He violated his conscience in order to keep an impulsive, stupid oath. This man was tormented. This man was king.

John the Baptist, on the other hand, gave his ultimate allegiance to God. When he saw Herod violating one of God's laws, he spoke out and told the king bluntly that what he was doing was wrong.

Herodius gave ultimate allegiance to herself and to her desire for revenge. She seized the opportune moment, using her own child to carry out a murder.

The daughter of Herodius, it appeared, gave ultimate allegiance to her mother. She voiced what she knew was her mother's desire, even thought she knew this would cost the life of an innocent man.

The executioner, of course, gave ultimate allegiance to King Herod. That was his job. There is no record of his disputing the king's wicked order.

Lord Jesus, we say our ultimate allegiance is to you. However, we desire to have our own way and to look good, just like Herodius and Herod. Sometimes, we carry out the wishes of others, knowing that they are wrong. Within the context of our everyday lives, show us how to give you true, undivided, uncompromised allegiance in our thoughts, words, and deeds. Alleluia!

Saturday, August 30, 2003
Matthew 25, 14-30
The Parable of the Talents

Jesus is calling us to daring resourcefulness and fidelity. He calls us to be bold and to trust him as we faithfully live our vocation.

Sometimes we become so consumed with what we perceive to be our failures that we stop daring to live boldly for Jesus. That attitude won't cut the mustard in kingdom living.

Jesus tells us what the kingdom of heaven is like. It is a realm where generosity and courage are joyfully rewarded and where stinginess and cowardice are considered contemptible.

Lord Jesus, everything I have is from you. Help me not to hoard any resource, but to invest myself in you and live bravely for you. Alleluia!

Sunday, August 31, 2003 Twenty-second Sunday Ordinary Time
Mark 7, 1-8, 14-15, 21-23
The Tradition of the Elders

Hypocrites. Play actors. Jesus called the Pharisees and the scribes, educated though they were, hypocrites. He called them hypocrites for making mere human traditions as important as God's commandments.

Jesus quoted from Isaiah 29, 13. Centuries before, Isaiah lamented that God's people had taken to observing the mere externals of worship. They were not truly worshipping God with all their hearts. They were merely going through the motions.

Jesus then turned his attention to the crowd and told the people about what was truly clean and unclean. The Pharisees had just criticized some of Jesus' disciples for eating without having properly washed their hands.

Jesus, while not promoting poor hygiene, told the people that what was truly unclean came from within the human heart. The evil thoughts which lead to evil actions are what really makes someone unclean.

Lord Jesus, cleanse and purify our hearts so we may worship you in purity and power. Alleluia!

Monday, September 1, 2003
Luke 4, 16-30
The Rejection at Nazareth

Jesus was grounded! He was grounded in his identity and in his mission. He knew who he was.

In the wilderness, he had endured and triumphed over the assaults of the devil. Filled with the Holy Spirit, he began his ministry in the Galilee.

It was a good thing Jesus knew who he was, because the testing which began in the desert would continue throughout his sojourn on earth. There would always be people who acclaimed him. There would

493

always be people who scoffed at him. There would always be people striving to silence him.

In today's Gospel, Jesus is speaking in the synagogue at Nazareth, the village in the Galilee where he had grown up in the home of Mary and Joseph. Jesus proclaimed the passage from Isaiah 61, 1-2, sat down, and announced, "This day is this scripture fulfilled in your ears (Luke 4, 21 K.J.V.)."

Jesus himself was the fulfillment of this passage in Isaiah! God's Spirit was upon him. He was anointed by God to free the captives and bring joyful news to the poor and oppressed.

All acclaimed him, in spite of their puzzlement about his confidence. Wasn't he just the son of Joseph, the village carpenter?

Jesus, in turn, referred to the past. The distant past. The past history of the people of God.

Jesus reminded the people in the synagogue that prophets do not fare well in their native place. True prophets are intent on fulfilling God's mission. The prophets Elijah and Elisha were sent to minister to so-called outsiders.

The people in the synagogue did not like that at all! They became furious and tried to throw this upstart off the cliff. Jesus calmly walked away.

Lord Jesus, you knew who you were. You were deeply rooted and grounded in your identity as God's beloved Son. You knew, from the words spoken at your baptism, that your Father was pleased with you. Help us to remember, whether we meet with acclaim or disdain in this passing world, that you are with us and that we are securely grounded in our identity as God's children. Let us resolutely focus on living for you and completing the mission entrusted to us. Alleluia!

Tuesday, September 2, 2003
Luke 4, 31-37
The Cure of the Demoniac

Instead of brooding over his rejection in the synagogue at Nazareth, Jesus proceeded to Capernaum, another town in the Galilee. Another adventure in another synagogue awaited him.

In the synagogue at Nazareth, Jesus proclaimed the word of God. First, he was acclaimed by all and then he was defamed by all.

In the synagogue at Capernaum, Jesus proclaimed the word by speaking directly to the evil entity inhabiting a human being. Interestingly enough, the evil spirit knew exactly who Jesus was, God's Holy One!

Jesus ordered the evil spirit to come out of the man. When the man who had been tormented by this evil occupier was set free, all the people in the synagogue were flabbergasted at the power of Jesus' word!

Lord Jesus, thank you for the continuing power of your word. Speak to us today the words we need to hear. Deliver us from all evil and free us to speak your word and to do your will. Alleluia!

Wednesday, September 3, 2003 St. Gregory the Great
Luke 4, 38-44
The Cure of Peter's Mother-in-Law; Other Healings;
Jesus Leaves Capernaum

Jesus went from the synagogue in Capernaum to Peter's house. After leaving Peter's house, he sought a place of solitude.

In the synagogue in Capernaum, he had liberated a man tormented by a demon. Leaving the synagogue, he continued to Peter's home, where Peter's mother-in-law was feverish and ill. The presence of Jesus and the word of Jesus healed her.

At twilight, a huge healing service apparently took place at Peter's home. So many people. So many diseases. Jesus had time and attention for each person. He personally laid his hands on each person. Each person was made whole.

Wherever Jesus went, it seemed, the demons tagged along. The demons knew who he was, even if the religious elite did not. The demons were terrified in the presence of the Son of God. They knew he was the Messiah.

As the sun rose the next morning, Jesus left for a time of solitude. Of course, the crowds sought him out and strove to keep him close at hand. It was time, however, to leave that place.

Jesus knew his purpose and stayed focused on that purpose. His purpose was to proclaim the Gospel, the Good News of God's kingdom. He continued preaching in the synagogues.

Lord Jesus, thank you for having time for each person who needs you. When we become overextended, gently call us to stay focused on you. Our purpose is to follow you. Guide us through our times of visible ministry and also our times of seclusion and restorative silence. Alleluia!

> Thursday, September 4, 2003
> Luke 5, 1-11
> The Call of Simon the Fisherman

Simon Peter's reply to Jesus' instruction to go out into the deeper waters and catch fish reminds me another person's reply to Jesus. When the centurion's son was very ill, Jesus offered to go to the home. The centurion, however, knew the power of the word of Jesus. He knew that if Jesus simply spoke the word, his son would be healed. And so it happened (Luke 7, 7; Matthew 8, 8).

In today's Gospel, Simon Peter, the fisherman, definitely knew the power of Jesus' words. He was very discouraged after having fished all night with no results. Still, he heard the command of Jesus and acted upon it, with weary, perhaps skeptical obedience.

The results were overwhelming! The boats nearly sank under the weight of all the fish.

Seeing Jesus' power, Peter, the exhausted fisherman then saw himself as he truly was, in all his sinfulness. He begged Jesus to away.

Jesus, however, could see more. Jesus could see Peter the apostle, to whom he would entrust the keys of the kingdom (Matthew 16, 18-19).

Jesus spoke to Peter again, telling him not to be afraid. Then Jesus spoke to Peter about his future vocation as a fisher of people.

Lord Jesus, you are so patient with us as we struggle with all our weaknesses and all our fears. Thank you for speaking to us words of hope for our future. Alleluia!

> Friday, September 5, 2003
> Luke 5, 33-39
> The Question about Fasting

Disciples. Disciples. Disciples. The disciples of John the Baptist. The disciples of the Pharisees. The disciples of Jesus.

The Pharisees were criticizing Jesus because his disciples were different. While the disciples of John the Baptist and their own disciples were fasting and praying, Jesus' disciples were having a great time eating and drinking.

Jesus, knowing both the value of fasting and the necessity of prayer, asked the Pharisees about wedding etiquette. Wedding guests would not be expected to fast at the wedding banquet. They would be expected to rejoice and to celebrate!

Nor would it be appropriate to remove cloth from a new garment and use it to patch a frayed, shabby old garment. They would not match.

Likewise, pouring new wine into old wineskins would ruin them. There must be new containers for fresh, new wine.

Lord Jesus, pour your fresh, new wine of joy into us today. If our spiritual and emotional wineskins have grown too old for such joy, heal us and renew us. If we are trying to patch our spiritual life with tired old ways that are no longer life-giving, come and show us how to live for you at this particular time in our lives. If we are mourning and fasting when we should be rejoicing, heal us and free us to love you, love ourselves, love others, and then to dance at the banquet! Alleluia!

Saturday, September 6, 2003
Luke 6, 1-5
Debates about the Sabbath

Jesus, Son of Man, was greater than the Sabbath. Jesus referred to himself as Son of Man, not as Son of God, when he reiterated to the Pharisees that he was lord of the Sabbath.

Jesus is Lord of every day! He is God and Man. He is Son of God and Son of Mary.

Meeting human need is allowed on every day, the Sabbath included. That is why Jesus saw no problem with his hungry disciples picking and munching wheat grains on the Sabbath.

Lord Jesus, you are greater than the great King David who also fed his hungry followers from the bread of the Presence, reserved for the priests. You are greater than all human rules and regulations. You are Lord of all days and all destinies. Alleluia!

Sunday, September 7, 2003
Twenty-third Sunday in Ordinary Time
Mark 7, 31-37
The Healing of the Deaf Man

Jesus took a route that seemed a little indirect. He was in the area of Tyre when he decided to go north to Sidon and then to another area by the Sea of Galilee. This is where he was presented with a man with a serious handicap. The afflicted man could neither hear nor speak.

Jesus showed great sensitivity as he led the man away from all the curious onlookers to pray for him. Jesus, touching the man's ears and his tongue, acknowledged his heavenly Father's presence and power by gazing upward. He was doing the will of his Father as he took some of his own saliva (considered at that time to be imbued with healing qualities) and put it on the tongue of the mute man. The man's passageways of hearing and speech were opened as Jesus cried out and spoke the word of healing. The man who had been imprisoned in a world of silence could now hear and speak!

Lord Jesus, thank you that sometimes you take what seems to us an indirect route to find what are the passageways of our hearts and lives that have been closed. You know why we seemed closed down, mute and unable to hear your gentle words of hope. Speak "Ephphatha" to our crushed spirits. Let us hear you and shout your praise with our lips and our lives. Alleluia!

Monday, September 8, 2003 The Birth of Mary
Matthew 1, 1-16; 18-23
The Genealogy of Jesus; The Birth of Jesus

Many years ago at a conference, I stopped at the tape table. Among the people working at the table was a young woman with dark hair gently pulled back from her head. She had a serene manner and vivid, sparkling dark eyes. Instantaneously I thought to myself, "I wonder if this is how Mary looked."

Mary was a real person. The men and women listed in the genealogy in today's Gospel were real people with all sorts of flaws and hang-ups. Real people just like us.

Out of this unlikely group of real people emerged Joseph, who became the husband of Mary. Mary, the young virgin, became the earthly mother of the divine, royal Messiah. Jesus was the Son of God. Jesus was the son of Mary.

It was simple, yet seemed impossible. Joseph, a truly good and righteous man, was not buying this Holy Spirit explanation of the conception of Mary's baby. Joseph loved Mary and was in a real dilemma. Since they were legally betrothed, he did not want to see her stoned to death for her presumed infidelity.

God chose to communicate to Joseph in a dream that Mary was indeed carrying a son conceived by the power of the Holy Spirit. The angel of the Lord instructed Joseph to name the child Jesus, a Hebrew name which signifies the saving power of God.

Jesus would save us from our sins. Prophecy was about to be fulfilled! A virgin would bear a son. The son would be named Emmanuel (Isaiah 7, 14). Mary was that virgin! Jesus was that son!

Lord Jesus, wonder of wonders! Thank you for coming to us through an earthly mother as well as from Almighty God. You were not delivered by a stork. You were not dropped from heaven by a holy helicopter. You spent nine months in the womb of your mother, just as we did. You were born. You grew up in a family. You lived among us and you died for us. You saved us from our sins and you are with us at this very moment. Alleluia!

Tuesday, September 9, 2003 St. Peter Claver
Luke 6, 12-19
The Mission of the Twelve; Ministering to a Great Multitude

From many disciples, Jesus chose twelve to be apostles. Jesus, Son of God though he was, spent the night alone in prayer on a mountain before making this decision which would change history. This selection of the apostles would change history because Jesus would change history through them. Others would also be called apostles, sent out on God's mission.

Coming down from the mountain, the so-called real world was waiting. Crowds of followers and people from all over that area had gathered to hear Jesus and to be healed. God's power surged forth from Jesus and all were healed.

Lord Jesus, you were Son of Man as well as Son of God. You knew the necessity of spending concentrated time in your Father's presence. Help us to invest time, time, and more time in prayer. Redirect our prayer lives as you see fit. If we are talking too much, quiet us and still us. If we are afraid of you or afraid to ask, encourage us. You know how you want us to pray at this time. Your choice of apostles changed the world. Our choices affect all with whom we come in contact and all for whom we pray. Thank you for all the gifts of the Holy Spirit. Use us today to speak your word and to bring your healing to all you bring across our path. Alleluia!

Wednesday, September 10, 2003
Luke 6, 20-26
Sermon on the Plain

Now and then. Jesus is telling us how to view our lives.

Now. Right now! If we know we don't know it all, we're fortunate. That means God's kingdom is our kingdom

Now. If we're weeping right now, we will laugh! Jesus promises it.

Now. If we suffer because of our trust in Jesus, we will jump for joy. That means we're hanging out with the right people. The Hebrew prophets also suffered for speaking and living God's word.

Now. The rich who think they don't need God now are already receiving all they're going to get.

Then. The sated will be starving.

Then. Those laughing with scorn will weep and mourn.

Now. If your good reputation is based on compromising your faith in Christ, that is a tragedy. The false prophets also enjoyed respect based on their faithlessness.

How we are living now? How we will live then in the real world? The real kingdom is God's kingdom

Lord Jesus, in the midst of our struggles to serve you faithfully in this life, help us not to become so discouraged that we lose sight of the joy that is ours right now, in this present time, and then in the dazzling expanse of all eternity. Alleluia!

Thursday, September 11, 2003
Luke 6, 27-38
Love of Enemies; Judging Others

The words of a king, David, and the words of a friend, Hilda, sounded in my heart this morning as I read this Gospel. In Psalm 37, King David counsels trusting God and doing good to others. Hilda once gave me a short, powerful prayer. The prayer is "Bless them. Heal me."

Jesus presents various examples of injustice and then tells us what our response is to be. It is necessary to be filled with the Holy Spirit even to desire to respond in this way of love. It is necessary to be controlled by the Holy Spirit in order to respond in love.

Trust the Lord and do good . We have to believe and to trust that God is fully aware of all injustice and that he is in charge. Trust is the attitude of our heart.

Do good. Our response is to continue to do good, no matter what other may choose to do. Doing good is the concrete expression of our trust in God. Trust is the attitude of our heart. Doing good is the action of our will.

God does not expect us to be docile doormats. Instead, we are to be the strong ones who take the initiative to carry out the Gospel imperative, trusting in God's justice and mercy. We are taking the initiative to be loving and mature when we respond in a way the world cannot understand. We are not standing still, absorbing abuse. We are rising on our spiritual tiptoes, knowing God will triumph with mercy and justice.

Lord Jesus, our trust in the heavenly Father is challenged in this radical Gospel. We need to be filled to overflowing with the Holy Spirit in order to love, bless, pray for, and forgive those who injure us. Thank you that you promise us that as we give and forgive, we will be showered with your gifts. Alleluia!

Friday, September 12, 2003
Luke 6, 39-42
Judging Others

We just don't know what is going on beneath the surface. There are sometimes land mines waiting to erupt both within us and within others.

Years ago, I was extremely irritated by someone whom I rashly judged to be a plastic Christian. She always seemed to have a plastic smile and plastic answers to everything. I was polite to her, but privately thought, "WHY can't she just be real?!"

Then one day, in a small group setting, she erupted in a tearful fury over something that had been seething within her family for years. All of a sudden, she was real. Instead of being plastic, she was, in reality, struggling bravely with a chronically distressing situation over which she had little control. I began to see her in a different way, as a real person I could relate to, respect, and wholeheartedly admire.

501

What about me? What about you? Sometimes, when I've been vulnerable, it has established a rapport with others. Other times, I have been criticized for revealing personal weaknesses. What does it matter, really?

Really, it's what Jesus has to say about us that truly matters. He tells us that if we are blind to ourselves, we are unfit to direct someone else who is blind. Jesus is our teacher in these matters. We have to be willing to acknowledge the mess in the rooms of our own lives before charging in to tell others how to clean up theirs.

Lord Jesus, it's just easier sometimes to tell others how to live than to come to you, our teacher, and to ask you how you want us to live. Thank you for your patience and gentleness as you help us to look into the mirror of our lives. Thank you for transforming us. Alleluia!

Saturday, September 13, 2003 St. John Chrysostom
Luke 6, 43-49
A Tree Known by Its Fruit; The Two Foundations

Tag patrol! Sometimes if we dress hastily, the tag, or label, sticks out behind our collar. All the world knows now what brand we're wearing. Some kind soul may be our tag patrol and inform us gently of this sartorial oversight.

Tag patrol! What is in our heart also sticks out, just as a brand label. What is in our heart eventually comes out of our mouth. Joy, bitterness, hope, anger, despair, love, etc. etc. It's in there somewhere and it will eventually surface. Just as a tree produces a certain kind of fruit, our hidden lives, our inner motives will produce fruit for all to see.

Jesus tells us it's a waste of time to bother to call him our Lord if we ignore his commands. To be truly wise is not only to listen to Jesus, but also to act upon his instructions for living our lives. When the storms of life come, the house of our lives will not be shaken.

Lord Jesus, you are the solid foundation of our lives. Purify our hearts so that our words and lives produce good fruit. Alleluia!

Sunday, September 14, 2003 Exaltation of the Holy Cross
John 3, 13-17
Nicodemus

The Teacher is teaching the teacher. The first part of this chapter tells us that Nicodemus, Pharisee, a leader, a teacher, came surreptitiously to Jesus by night.

Nicodemus' name means that he is triumphant over his people. He is coming to the One who will triumph by being lifted high on a Cross. Jesus, Son of God and Son of Man, teaches the esteemed Nicodemus the very basics.

How often do we think we know it all, or know a lot, when, in fact, we are in the spiritual equivalent of nursery school? We may have advanced degrees in theology, but we don't know God, not really.

We may continue to hide behind scholarship or we may come to Jesus. We may come to Jesus, who came from heaven. We may come to Jesus to learn what God is really like. Jesus came among us, lived among us, and is still with us in the Person of the Holy Spirit. He was lifted high on a Cross of death so that we might see him and live.

God the Father cared for us so much that he relinquished his beloved only Son to come to earth on a rescue mission. God's love found ultimate expression in sending Jesus, not to condemn us, but to rescue us and to make us whole.

Lord Jesus, we trust in you and enter life, life that is forever. You were lifted high on the Cross. Thank you for lifting us into true life. Alleluia!

Monday, September 15, 2003 Our Lady of Sorrows
John 19, 25-27
The Crucifixion of Jesus

Standing. Mary was standing as Jesus suffered and died on the Cross. The sword of sorrows prophesied by Simeon was piercing her heart (Luke 2, 35). Still, Mary stood.

Jesus was standing. In the spirit, he was standing as his body was lifted on the Cross. He would triumph. The Holy Cross would triumph. The Holy Cross would be exalted.

Daily, Marianists and others around the world pray the "Three O' Clock Prayer." We acknowledge that our sins are the cause of Jesus' death. We pray that the apostle John, who stood by the Cross with Mary, will be our example in honoring Mary.

Lord Jesus, you instructed John to look upon Mary, your mother, as his mother also. Thank you for Mary's example of strength in the midst of sorrow as she stood by your Cross. Thank you for her tenacity in staying with you, standing by you throughout your life on this earth, and standing with you as you suffered and died. Thank you for your glorious resurrection and for the manifestation of the triumph of your will as we stand for you and with you in our life. Alleluia!

Tuesday, September 16, 2003 Sts. Cornelius and Cyprian
Luke 7, 11-17
Raising the Widow's Son

Life happens! Jesus saw through the crowd to the woman overcome with grief. He was filled with compassion for her and yearned to reach out to her. She had already carried so much grief. First, her husband had died. Now, her only son had died.

Jesus interrupted the funeral procession and turned it into a celebration! Life! He ordered the dead man to get up. The young man sat up and began to speak.

Life in the midst of death. Hope in the midst of a deadening despair. Jesus is here. Jesus brings life!

Lord Jesus, thank you for bringing life into situations where death seems to reign. If we have ceased to hope, speak words of life to us. Fill us today with a buoyant expectancy and hope. Fill us with your life. Alleluia!

Wednesday, September 17, 2003 St. Robert Bellarmine
Luke 7, 31-35
Jesus' Testimony to John

Live for God and place the results in God's hands. That is my assignment. That is your assignment.

If John the Baptist and Jesus were criticized and condemned no matter what they did, how on earth can we expect to be understood, much less affirmed? Jesus and John the Baptist lived for the glory of God and so do we.

The people in our day are as fickle as the people were when Jesus and John the Baptist walked on this earth. We offer them the love of God, but it is not our task to change them or to try to make them understand us.

Lord Jesus, you illustrated the meaning of wisdom by the way you lived among us on this earth. Thank you for the gift of the Holy Spirit to fill us with wisdom, perspective, and joy as we abandon ourselves to you and live for your glory. Alleluia!

Thursday, September 18, 2003
Luke 7, 36-50
The Parable of the Sinful Woman

In the home of Simon, a Pharisee, a sinful woman bravely made a beeline for Jesus. She showed great contrition and great courage. These two qualities often go together.

It takes no courage to hug a false sense of self-righteousness to oneself. This is what Simon the Pharisee did when he silently condemned Jesus for allowing the woman to minister to him.

The weeping woman offered to Jesus the ministry that Simon the Pharisee had neglected to offer. This was the kissing of one's guest in welcome, the washing of the guest's dusty, sandal-clad feet, and anointing the guest's head with oil.

The woman ministered to Jesus in a unique way. She kissed the feet of Jesus. She washed his feet with her tears. She anointed his feet with a fragrant ointment.

Everything she was and everything she did in her love for Jesus was unacceptable to the Pharisee. Her offering, however, was most acceptable to the Lord Jesus.

Jesus gratefully received the loving, courageous acts of service and the gratitude she offered him. He knew of her contrition for her sins and her deep sorrow.

Simon, on the other hand, seemed to have little, if any, contrition for his sins. Jesus reminded him that the person who has been forgiven a great deal loves greatly and is generous in expressing that love. The one who seems self-satisfied may show little or no gratitude. It is easier to focus on the sins of others than to invite God to look within oneself.

Lord Jesus, you have forgiven us over and over. Thank you for the example of this woman's courage in coming to you. You received her in gentleness and accepted her acts of service. Help us to serve you today by rejoicing in the forgiveness you have so freely given to us. Help us to be gentle and generous in how we perceive others, how we speak of them, and in how we treat them. Thank you for your love and your mercy. Alleluia!

Friday, September 19, 2003 St. Januaris
Luke 8, 1-3
Galilean Women Follow Jesus

The women following Jesus expressed their gratitude in a tangible way. Jesus had healed them and freed them from their afflictions! Out of their own resources, the women contributed to Jesus and the twelve.

Three women are named in today's Gospel. They are Mary Magdalene, Johanna, and Susanna. Many others also followed Jesus.

Lord Jesus, you reached out to women, healed them, and freed them to follow you and to minister to you. Free all who love you to follow you and to serve you according to your perfect will. Alleluia!

Saturday, September 20, 2003 Sts. Andrew Kim Taegon,
Paul Chong Hasang and Companions
Luke 8, 4-15
The Parable of the Sower; The Purpose of the Parables;
The Parable of the Sower Explained

This past summer, I planted a little Peter Pan squash plant behind the garage where there is a lot of sunshine. The soil was rocky and dry, but I persisted in watering the squash. Beautiful yellow blossoms appeared on this rather pathetic little plant and even tiny squashes. The plant was trying! Then the little squashes would mysteriously disappear. Perhaps the friendly squirrel visitors were enjoying them!

I learned that even water and sun are not enough if the soil is poor and if the squashes are not allowed to grow to maturity. It was frustrating to keep watering only to have the soil dry out so quickly.

Jesus used these homey illustrations of seeds and soils when he addressed the crowds. To the disciples, those committed to following him, he explained the true meaning. They were the ones entrusted to become apostles, to be sent out on mission.

Lord Jesus, please come to us today and loosen the soil of our souls and spirits. If we have been too shallow to allow your word to take root, help us to put our relationship with you first in our lives. If we have become hard and cynical, soften us. If we have watered the weeds of worry and tended the thorns of temporal distractions, refocus our exhausted, agitated souls on you and not on our distressing circumstances. When we have flitted away from you and sought diversion and distraction in this passing world, gently bring us back to you, our source, our spa of peace. Help us to run to you and to yield to you. Strengthen us to believe your word to us and to bear fruit for you. Alleluia!

Sunday, September 21, 2003
Twenty-fifth Sunday in Ordinary Time
Mark 9, 30-37
The Second Prediction of the Passion;
The Greatest in the Kingdom

Suffering and greatness are linked in this Gospel. Jesus addressed both topics. For the second time, Jesus told his disciples that he would be betrayed and killed. He spoke of his resurrection after three days. The disciples did not yet comprehend his prediction.

Instead of grappling with the frightening words of Jesus, the disciples distracted themselves with speculation about who among them was the greatest. Then they were embarrassed when Jesus confronted them.

Jesus patiently taught them about true greatness. In God's kingdom, the first shall be last. The leader will serve all. Jesus placed his arms around a child and explained that receiving such a child was equivalent to receiving him. Furthermore, receiving Jesus was just the same as receiving God the Father, who had sent Jesus.

Lord Jesus, we do the same thing as your disciples. We don't want to think about suffering. It's easier to distract ourselves with pointless speculations. Help us to learn to trust you with the simple confidence of a little child and then to serve others as you direct. Alleluia!

Monday, September 22, 2003
Luke 8, 16-18
The Parable of the Lamp

In times of sickness or discouragement, it often seems that we have very little light. Life seems to drain us of strength and to strip us of joy and hope.

Jesus, the light of the world (John 8, 12), also told us that we are the light of the world (Matthew 5, 14). The light of Christ within us is not meant to be concealed. We may think that the light is burning rather dimly, but it is still there!

Eventually, the hidden things will come to light. Mysteries will become known and understood. If we will accept and act upon what God has revealed to us, more understanding will be given.

Lord Jesus, fill us anew with your bright light and with a robust hope. Alleluia!

Tuesday, September 23, 2003
Luke 8, 19-21
Jesus and His Family

Jesus told parables about the meaning of the kingdom of God. He was in the midst of the teaching aspect of his ministry when he was interrupted by a message that his mother and his brothers were outside trying to see him. They had been unable to get through the crowd.

Jesus used this incident to give his definition of his family. Jesus told the people who had been listening to his teaching that his family consisted of those who heard the word of God and responded in obedience.

Lord Jesus, sometimes it seems that we cannot push through whatever is crowding our lives to get to you. Thank you for telling us that we are your family if hear God's word and respond in active obedience. Speak your word to us today and show us how to put that word into action. Thank you for the gift of the Holy Spirit to enable us to do the will of the Father. Alleluia!

Wednesday, September 24, 2003
Luke 9, 1-6
The Mission of the Twelve

Jesus gave the twelve disciples everything they needed to fulfill their mission. He told them what they were to do and also instructed them to travel light!

What did they need? They needed God's power! Jesus gave his disciples authority and power over all the evil spirits and all the illnesses that were hurting the people. The disciples themselves, acting on behalf of Jesus, would liberate the suffering ones.

Armed with this power and with the authority to act, they were to travel light and to stay in one place until it was time to leave. Not only were they not to take food, money, or extra clothing, they were also to travel light emotionally.

Jesus did not want them carrying around excess baggage of any kind. He instructed them what to do if they were not welcome. They were simply to shake the dust from their feet and to continue to travel.

Then they would be free to minister in a new place without the smelly dirt of the old place clinging to them.

Lord Jesus, you are the ultimate travel agent! You know exactly how we are to travel through this life. Thank you for providing us with all we need to do your will. Help us today to travel light and to trust you anew. Alleluia!

Thursday, September 25, 2003
Luke 9, 7-0
Herod's Opinion of Jesus

An olive-on-a-toothpick pericope! A little appetizer for Herod in this slice of Gospel. Will Herod take the appetizer, the reports of Jesus, and actually come to know Jesus for himself? Or will he continue to play politics and stay in darkness?

Free will at work. Very scary. Very promising.

Herod was intrigued and puzzled by the person of Jesus. He couldn't figure out who Jesus really was. Having been responsible for the execution of John the Baptist, Herod was perplexed. Who was Jesus? Today's Gospel ends with the statement that Herod continued to try to see Jesus.

Herod had been afraid of the prophet John the Baptist because of the prophet's holiness. John had demonstrated prophetic zeal to speak God's word without compromise. That usually terrifies politically correct cowards.

How much more terrified would Herod have been of Jesus himself? Herod chose to remain in his comfort zone of curiosity. He preferred to continue his delusion that he was the one in control. He did not intend to venture into the realms of knowledge and commitment.

Lord Jesus, it's easy for us to criticize Herod, and yet we are sometimes indolent curiosity seekers in matters of faith. We may be dazzled and attracted by miracles, but afraid of true, costly discipleship. When we are perplexed, remind us that you are with us. We don't have to settle for an appetizer. We may come to you and know you in Scripture and in all the sacraments. Thank you for your promise to be with us when we gather in your name (Matthew 18, 20). Alleluia!

Friday, September 26, 2003 Sts. Cosmos and Damian
Luke 9, 18-22
Peter's Confession about Jesus

This is a compact version of Peter's statement of belief about Jesus. We are probably more familiar with the longer passage in Matthew's Gospel (Matthew 16, 13-20).

Peter was first to respond to Jesus' question. After spending time in solitude and in prayer, Jesus asked his disciples how his identity was being perceived by the crowds who had been witnessing his miracles. The most recent miracle had been the feeding of the five thousand.

Peter responded by stating that Jesus was the Messiah. God's Messiah. God's Anointed One. Jesus cautioned all the disciples to keep silent about this.

Lord Jesus, you are the Messiah! You will come again, not as the helpless babe in Bethlehem or as the humble, suffering servant of God who was rejected and crucified by his very own people. You will come as the dazzling King, the royal Messiah. We long for the time when you come back in all your glory to establish your kingdom on earth. We yearn for the time when God's wonderful will is carried out on earth as it is in heaven. The time will come when all will acknowledge you and all will worship you as you deserve to be worshipped. Let us yield anew to you and to your sovereignty in our lives. Alleluia!

Saturday, September 27, 2003 St. Vincent de Paul
Luke 9, 43-45
The Second Prediction of the Passion

The power of God flowing through Jesus amazed the onlookers. Jesus had just healed a tormented boy who had been subject to convulsions. Jesus expelled the demon and healed the boy.

Immediately, Jesus turned to his disciples and commanded them to heed the words he was about to say. He told them that he, Jesus, would be given into human hands.

The startled disciples did not know what in the world Jesus meant. They not only could not understand, but they were also too frightened to ask Jesus what he meant.

Lord Jesus, even in the midst of the temporary acclaim of the crowd, you were aware that the clock was ticking. The time would indeed come when you would be betrayed into the hands of those who would mock you, ridicule you before a kangaroo court, scourge and crucify you. You knew this was part of the package. You knew resurrection would follow, but only after acute agony and apparent defeat. Help us to keep our hearts and our minds strictly focused on you as we live in this land mine of our earthly existence. Thank you that we will see you soon and live with you forever. Alleluia!

Sunday, September 28, 2003
Twenty-sixth Sunday in Ordinary Time
Mark 9, 38-43, 45, 47-48
Another Exorcism; Temptations to Sin

Jesus cautioned his disciples against a particular form of exclusivity. He commanded them not to try to stop another person from ministering in his name, even if that person was not part of their particular group. Honoring the name of Jesus the Christ was what mattered.

Jesus strictly warned of the dire consequences awaiting those who cause others, deemed insignificant or of little stature, to stumble or to sin. Being thrown into the sea with a giant stone hung around one's neck would be preferable to the consequences of hurting one of God's little ones.

Jesus then addressed the matter of causes of sin. Whatever the cause, Jesus said to excise it. Nothing is worth hanging onto if it prevents us from entering God's kingdom.

Lord Jesus, you emphasize the supremacy of following you regardless of recognition and regardless of obstacles. Let us rejoice when we see others following you and serving you. Let us rejoice and not feel threatened by their particular ministry. Give us the grace to offer to you and to relinquish to you whatever appears to be obstacles to our full surrender to you and to your amazing and glorious will for us. Alleluia!

Monday, September 29, 2003
Sts. Michael, Gabriel, and Raphael, Archangels
John 1, 47-51
The First Disciples

How are titles related to perception and to mission? A variety of titles flowed back and forth in this conversation between Nathanael and Jesus.

Jesus observed the approach of Nathanael, noting that Nathanael was an Israelite of deep integrity. Nathanael wondered how on earth

511

Jesus had such perception. After all, Jesus had only noticed that Nathanael was under a fig tree!

Nathanael initially called Jesus a teacher or rabbi. Then he proceeded to acknowledge that Jesus was Son of God and King of Israel. That's quite a progression of titles.

Jesus told Nathanael to hold his horses, metaphorically speaking, and not to base his belief solely on Jesus' powers of perception. Greater things were in store!

Jesus then referred to himself as Son of Man. That was the title he chose for himself as he told Nathanael of the glories to come. Nathanael would see Jesus, the Son of Man, in the sky with the holy angels.

Lord Jesus, you are truly our rabbi, our teacher. You are truly Son of God and King of Israel. Yet, with great humility, you chose to refer to yourself as Son of Man. Thank you that one day, with Nathanael and all the saints, we will see you with the glorious angels. Strengthen us to fulfill our mission of bearing witness to you during our time on earth. Alleluia!

Tuesday, September 30, 2003 St. Jerome
Luke 9, 51-56
Departure for Jerusalem; Samaritan Inhospitality

Flint and fire! They are both referred to in today's Gospel.

Flint! Jesus knew that this particular time in his ministry was complete. It was time to begin the journey to Jerusalem. Jesus set his face "like a flint" (Isaiah 50, 7, K.J.V.) to Jerusalem. The completion of his ministry of suffering, death, and resurrection could be accomplished only in Jerusalem (Luke 13, 33).

Fire! Because his destination was Jerusalem, the inhabitants of a village in Samaria refused to welcome him. The disciples, James and John, who had been called sons of thunder (Mark 3, 17) grew hotly indignant over this treatment.

Turning to Jesus, they asked if he would like them to summon heavenly fire on the Samaritans! Jesus, perhaps with a weary smile, reproved them and continued the journey.

Lord Jesus, nothing deterred you from fulfilling your mission. Instead of brooding over rejection, you steadily continued your journey to Jerusalem. Please forgive us for the times we have halted our own journey in order to camp in valleys of despair, rejection, futility, etc. Thank you for your presence with us and your power within us as we continue our way to our own Jerusalem. Alleluia!

> Wednesday, October 1, 2003 St. Therese of the Child Jesus
> Luke 9, 57-62
> The Would-be Followers of Jesus

Follow Jesus and leave the results with Jesus. We cannot truly be disciples if we are glancing this way and that. We cannot feed upon and crave human approval and also follow Jesus with freedom and abandon. He wants us to follow him freely, completely, and without reservation.

Lord Jesus, it is especially difficult to follow you when we don't exactly know where you are leading us! We know we are to follow you in your footsteps. We will experience what you experienced. We will know suffering, rejection, and misunderstanding. We will also know the joy of your presence. Thank you that we are in the Home stretch where you will receive us, where we will live with you and with all the angels and the saints forever and ever. Alleluia!

> Thursday, October 2, 2003 Guardian Angels
> Matthew 18, 1-5, 10
> The Greatest in the Kingdom

Jesus turned the tables on the disciples by telling them to turn and to change! He turned the table on their question.

They had asked him who would be greatest in the kingdom of heaven. Jesus cautioned them to be more concerned about ENTERING the kingdom of heaven.

Turn. Jesus told the disciples to make a turn, a change, in their lives. Referring to a child in their midst, Jesus instructed his ambitious, yet misguided, followers that total, childlike dependence on God was required to enter the kingdom.

Greatness? Simple, childlike, unassuming believers who are truly dependent on God will be greatest in God's kingdom.

Welcoming such followers is equivalent to welcoming Jesus himself. Looking down on such believers is ill-advised. Their angels are beholding the Father in heaven. These believers may not have earthly connections, but they have powerful, heavenly connections.

Lord Jesus, no matter how old we are, we are still to turn and to acknowledge our complete dependence on you. You know us completely. Forgive us if we are afraid to acknowledge our total dependence upon you. Let us rejoice in your love and in the protection of guardian angels. Alleluia!

Friday, October 3, 2003
Luke 10, 13-16
Reproaches to the Unrepentant Towns

I would rather have Jesus look at me and say, as he said to the Canaanite woman, "O woman, great is thy faith!" (Matthew 15, 21-28) than to have him look at me and pronounce the woe he pronounced on these towns. The Canaanite woman was considered an outsider, a nobody, and yet she persisted in asking Jesus to heal her daughter. Jesus did so, even though his primary mission was to his own people.

Several towns, on the other hand, received the pronouncement of woe from Jesus. Especially Capernaum. How Jesus must have grieved over Capernaum. Chorazin, Bethsaida, and Capernaum had all witnessed the powerful acts of Jesus and yet still they did not come to repentance.

The Canaanite woman, on the other hand, recognizing that she was an outsider, nevertheless lay siege to the compassionate heart of Jesus. Astounded at her belief and courage, Jesus granted her request and healed her daughter.

Jesus told his disciples that those who listen to them are, in reality, listening to him! Likewise, rejecting the disciples of Jesus is equated with rejecting Jesus.

Lord Jesus, we want you to exclaim with delight over our trust in you. Thank you for your trust in us as you send us out to serve you today. Alleluia!

Saturday, October 4, 2003 St. Francis of Assisi
Luke 10, 17-24
Return of the Seventy-two

Flush with joy and exuberance, the seventy-two disciples, sent out two by two (Luke 10, 1) returned to Jesus! They had been commissioned to travel light, to bring peace, and to proclaim the kingdom of God as they healed the sick (Luke 10, 4-9).

514

Now they were returning to Jesus, full of exultation. Now they knew for themselves the power of the name of Jesus. Now they knew for themselves that even evil is subject to the mighty name of Jesus.

Jesus acknowledged that the evil spirits were indeed subject to his disciples. However, he cautioned his followers not to base their joy on their ministry. Their joy was to be based on Jesus himself. Their joy was to be based on the fact that their names were recorded in heaven.

Lord Jesus, thank you for the privilege of serving others in your strong and mighty name. What matters, however, when our ministry here on earth is over? What matters except our relationship with you? What matters except that our citizenship is registered in heaven and that we are heading Home? Alleluia!

Sunday, October 5, 2003
Twenty-seventh Sunday in Ordinary Time
Mark 10, 2-16
Marriage and Divorce; Blessing of the Children

Union is of primary importance to Jesus. When the Pharisees asked him about the legality of divorce, Jesus responded with a question of his own. He asked about Moses' teaching on the matter. Moses' teaching was a provisional teaching. Jesus then led his questioners back to God's original and perfect plan for marriage. Two people were to become truly one. Having become truly one, they were not to be separated.

Likewise, Jesus stood his ground in the matter of children. People flocked to Jesus and beseeched him to bless their children. The misguided disciples tried to keep the children away from Jesus. Jesus was very displeased with this exclusion. He wanted the children to come freely to him. He knew that they belonged in God's kingdom.

Lord Jesus, thank you that you yearn for us to be one with you. You prayed that your followers would be one just as you and the Father are one (John 17, 21). Thank you for filling us with your Holy Spirit and for setting all our relationships in your perfect order. Alleluia!

Monday, October 6, 2003 Blessed Marie-Rose Durocher
Luke 10, 25-27
The Parable of the Good Samaritan

The despised Samaritan, the one considered an outsider and an outcast by the so-called true believers, was the true neighbor, the one who manifested God's love. The religious elite, on the other hand, did not want to get their hands dirty.

515

God often surprises us! The very ones we thought were so close to God may disappoint us greatly. God seems to allow this to happen sometimes. Then God surprises us with unexpected consolation through unexpected sources.

Lord Jesus, thank you that you are our neighbor, dwelling near us and indeed dwelling within us, showering us with mercy. Thank you for allowing us to be vessels of mercy. Thank you for pouring out your compassion to flow through our lives today. Alleluia!

Tuesday, October 7, 2003 Our Lady of the Rosary
Luke 10, 38-42
Martha and Mary

One thing. The essential. The primary. David the psalmist knew that it was in God's presence that we find joy in all its fullness (Psalm 16, 11).

Mary of Bethany was experiencing this fullness of joy as she sat at the feet of Jesus. Learning from him, yes, but more significantly, simply being in his presence.

Jesus chose his disciples first of all to be with him, simply to be with him, and only later to go forth in ministry (Mark 3, 14-15). Experiencing the presence of the Lord is crucial if we are to serve others as Jesus would have us serve. We need to experience our deep need for forgiveness and then God's healing, cleansing love.

Guarding our time in the Lord's presence is the one thing that is of primary importance. Without this time, even ministry may devolve into a routine, a chore, a bore, perhaps. Life and health and growth and service flow from our time with the Lord.

Lord Jesus, forgive me when I substitute serving you for time spent in silence alone with you. It is easier to run around trying to do things for you than it is to be in your presence without an agenda. In your presence, I am confronted with a deeper sense of my need for you. In your presence, I am faced with my need of forgiveness. Thank you for the refreshment and renewal you have for me as I bask in your presence and then go forth, as you direct, to serve others. Alleluia!

Wednesday, October 8, 2003
Luke 11, 1-4
The Lord's Prayer

The Our Father in Luke's Gospel is very terse, tight, and compact. We blink and re-read it, being more accustomed to the slightly longer, more familiar form in Matthew's Gospel (Matthew 6, 9-15).

The words of the prayer are not cozy and comfortable. They are stern and demanding. The prayer is interactive. Something is required of us. We are not merely to recite this prayer.

We are to acknowledge the holiness of God. We are to reverence the majestic name of God.

We are to pray for God's kingdom to be realized. This will not happen as we wait in idleness. God has work for us to do. I have an assignment. You have an assignment.

We are to pray for daily sustenance. We are to acknowledge our dependence on God.

We are required to forgive each person who has wronged us, each person to whom we may be harboring a grudge, each person who owes us something. We are to forgive others in order for our Father to forgive our own sins. Forgiveness is free, but it is not automatic.

We are to pray to be spared from the severe trials predicted before the Messiah comes to earth as the great, conquering King. This can be a time of great temptation. We do not know the time, but Jesus commands us to pray in advance.

Lord Jesus, we can no longer glibly rattle off this prayer without pondering its requirements. Each petition requires something from us. We are to live in the balance of trusting God and doing our part. You knew this would not be a simple prayer. Thank you for the power of the Holy Spirit to teach us today how to live this prayer more deeply. Alleluia!

Thursday, October 9, 2003 St. Denis and Companions,
St. John Leonardi
Luke 11, 5-13
Further Teachings on Prayer; The Answer to Prayer

The Father in heaven, eager to bestow the great gift of the Holy Spirit, still delights in our plucky persistence! Jesus instructed the disciples to persist in prayer, to ask, to seek, and to knock. He promised that the door would open, the seeker would find, and that the one who asked would indeed receive.

Lord Jesus, increase our trust and expectancy that the Father indeed gives good gifts beyond our imagining to those who dare to ask and to believe. Alleluia!

Friday, October 10, 2003
Luke 11, 15-26
Jesus and Beelzebul; The Return of the Unclean Spirit

It was by the power of God that Jesus drove demonic spirits out of people. They were set free to live their lives without the internal harassment they had endured. Jesus set them free!

Lord Jesus, thank you for continuing to liberate the captives. Forgive us and let us continually forgive and continually release those who sin against us. We pray to be filled completely with the Holy Spirit so that there is no room for evil to enter in and to take up residence within us. Thank you for the power of the Holy Spirit to keep the house of our soul swept clean. Alleluia!

Saturday, October 11, 2003
Luke 11, 27-28
True Blessedness

You and I have specific ideas of what constitutes the state of being happy or blessed. We may think in terms of this, that, or whatever.

Jesus knows the sure-fire way to be happy in this world. The truly happy people are the ones who listen to the word of God and then live the word of God.

Lord Jesus, we think we know what it takes to make us happy. Yes, we have deep joy, but we want to be happy, too! Show us what word we need to apply in our lives today. Let us experience the exhilaration and delight of knowing that we have entered into a new realm of discipleship. Alleluia!

Sunday, October 12, 2003
Twenty-eighty Sunday in Ordinary Time
Mark 10, 17-30
The Rich Man

There is no such thing as sacrificing to God. God is debtor to no one.

It is sad that this rich man was so poor. He was very poor in understanding. He did not understand that the one thing Jesus required him to relinquish was only a prerequisite for him to come into true wealth. The poor rich man had no concept of how God rewards obedience.

Peter, of course it had to be Peter, spoke up! Peter always spoke up. Thank God that Peter often voiced what others may have been wondering. Peter voiced the practical concern of what was in it for those who offered their lives completely for God's service.

Jesus did not rebuke Peter for asking this honest question. Jesus assured Peter and the rest of us that we will be lavishly repaid for whatever we offer for the sake of Jesus and for the sake of the Gospel.

With God everything is gloriously possible! God knows how to reward those who offer their all. Rewards in this life! Eternal life in the age which is ahead! However, Jesus, the realist, noted that persecution was also part of the discipleship package.

Lord Jesus, you are our teacher and we are your disciples. Thank you for giving us the broad picture of what it means to follow you with all our heart. Whatever it is that stands in the way of our complete surrender to you, we offer to you today in trust. Your know us inside out. You know how much we truly want to follow you, in spite of our fears and our foibles. Take us by the hand today, smile on us, and lead us into the next step of our discipleship. Alleluia!

Monday, October 13, 2003
Luke 11, 29-32
The Demand for a Sign

Signs. Signs. Signs.

Jesus condemned the seekers after signs. He said that it is an evil generation that chases after signs. The demand for signs is never satisfied. Jesus himself is the greatest sign!

Signs often tell us to stop. On neighborhood streets, we usually keep driving until we see the red stop sign. It is a stop sign, not a pause sign. Ignoring the sign could cause a collision.

God sometimes allows stop signs in the midst of our lives. Perhaps we are traveling in the fast lane of our lives and then there appears a big stop sign. An illness, a problem, or a clear mandate of one kind or another to stop!

Time to ponder. Time to pray. Time to realign our will with the will of God.

Long ago, the wicked people of Ninevah changed their minds. They repented because of the sign of the reluctant prophet, Jonah. Jonah, eventually, after a detour, obeyed God and preached repentance to the people of Ninevah. Jesus, Son of God and Son of Man, is far greater than Jonah.

A famous queen once traveled a great distance to listen to and to learn from the wise King Solomon. Jesus is far wiser than Solomon.

Lord Jesus, thank you for being the great sign, the sign telling us to stop. While we are stopped and still, speak to us. Show us if there is new direction you want us to take in our lives. Tell us how to be signs in our own generation pointing to you. Alleluia!

Tuesday, October 14, 2003 St. Callistus I
Luke 11, 37-41
Denunciation of the Pharisees and the Scholars of the Law

Give from within. YOU are the gift. Give from within and then you will become truly clean.

Jesus was speaking to the religious leaders who were so concerned with appearances and so preoccupied with the exterior. They were very careful to wash their cups and their dishes. Jesus was asking them and indeed challenging them to look within their hearts.

Jesus always looks within. It is from within that true almsgiving arises. We give ourselves first to God who gave himself first to us.

Dazzling in holiness, God is yet very gentle with us. The Holy Spirit helps us to look within. Within our hearts, we will become aware of hidden motives, hidden hurts, and hidden agendas. Offering our heart in its entirety delights God! God delights to receive the gift of ourselves.

God will begin a process to transform us with our cooperation. God delights to give us to feed the starving world.

Lord Jesus, cleanse me from within. Purify me. Thank you for your constant forgiveness. Thank you for showing me today how to give from within. Alleluia!

Wednesday, October 15, 2003 St. Teresa of Avila
Luke 11, 42-46
Denunciation of the Pharisees and Scholars of the Law

Is it easier to pay tithes or to pay attention? Jesus went after the Pharisees because, although they dutifully gave their tithes on even the tiniest of garden herbs, they did not pay attention to God's requirements for justice and love.

The Pharisees gave tithes, but they did not give love. Jesus said to give both.

Jesus also roundly condemned the legal scholars for their failure to love. They had no problem with imposing heavy burdens, rules of all sorts, on the people, with no intention of helping them to carry those burdens.

We falter under the burden of our sins. Jesus, Son of God, Word made flesh, stepped into our world most humbly and carried our burden. He carried our burden of sin all the way to the Cross and he died. When Jesus died, we died. Our burden fell off and we were free. This is what we celebrate in baptism. When Jesus died, we died (Romans 6, 4-6). Really! Now we are free to live for God as part of God's family

Lord Jesus, help us to offer not merely tithes but also the totality of ourselves to love you and to love others. Alleluia!

Thursday, October 16, 2003 St. Hedwig,
St. Mary Margaret Alacoque, St. Marguerite d'Youville
Luke 11, 47-54
Denunciation of the Pharisees and the Scholars of the Law

Speak God's truth and you will probably suffer. That's what happened to the prophets of the Hebrew scriptures. That's what happened to the apostles of Jesus. That's what happens today.

Jesus welcomed sinners because they knew they were sinners. They knew they were in need of a Savior.

Jesus denounced the Pharisees and the legal scholars because of their deliberate deception. They deceived themselves about their own righteousness and they thought they deceived others. They did not deceive Jesus. He saw through them and confronted them.

Naturally this did not endear Jesus to these leaders. Frauds hate being exposed. They are bent on maintaining their image and their perks.

Lord Jesus, thank you for your mercy when we acknowledge our need of you. You always speak the truth, because you are the Truth. Forgive us when we deceive ourselves and drift away from you. Thank you for sending the Holy Spirit to convict us, to confront us, and to bring us to repentance and to restoration. Alleluia!

Friday, October 17, 2003 St. Ignatius of Antioch
Luke 12, 1-7
The Leaven of the Pharisees; Courage under Persecution

Fears fade in the knowledge of the all-consuming presence and power of God! We are not stumbling in darkness, silently fearful that even God does not notice what we are going through.

Jesus assures us that our loving God notices. The same God who notes the fall of a little sparrow in the garden notes the most minute detail of our lives.

There will come a time for revelation. The present darkness will be torn by the dazzling light of Christ.

Lord Jesus, you counseled your disciples to be aware of the hypocrisy of the Pharisees. You did not, however, counsel your followers to be afraid of the Pharisees or of anyone else. Thank you for reminding us that our eternal destiny is in God's strong and loving hands. Thank you for assuring us and reassuring us of God's keen awareness and God's mighty power. Alleluia!

Saturday, October 18, 2003 St. Luke
Luke 10, 1-9
The Mission of the Seventy-two

For YOU! The kingdom is right here for you.

Right now. It's not some place, some thing somewhere else for some other person or some other people. It's for YOU! The kingdom of God. A whole new realm.

Jesus told the seventy-two missioners to tell of this kingdom in the places where they were welcomed. Traveling light, with the realistic mind-set of being lambs in the midst of wolves, each pair of disciples was to speak peace first of all and then to bring healing to the sick.

For you! The kingdom is for you. It is very near. It is right here. Jesus is here.

Lord Jesus, we continue to pray for workers willing to go into the harvest field of those starving for you. First, let us understand with our hearts that the kingdom is for us. Let your kingdom truly come in our lives. Let your glorious will truly be done in our lives. Thank you for sending us into the harvest fields to live for you. Alleluia!

Sunday, October 19, 2003
Twenty-ninth Sunday in Ordinary Time
Mark 10, 35-45
Ambition of James and John

Are you willing to be dissolved for God's purposes? That's basically how Jesus responded to the preposterous request of James and John. They thought it would be nifty to be close to Jesus when he reigned as King, as the conquering Messiah.

Jesus told them that, first of all, that was none of their business. God alone designates places and positions of honor.

Even Jesus, Son though he was, would not be propelled into a fast-forward mode from controversial rabbi to reigning king. He would serve others, suffer for others, and die in the place of others.

The accumulated sins of the centuries would be heaped upon Jesus. He would carry all our sins to the Cross. He would assimilate all our sins within his very being. The sinless One would drink the poison of our sins and the sins of all humanity. He would die. Who could bear this? Only Jesus.

Unless the grain of wheat falls into the prepared ground and dies, it does not fulfill its destiny. If it consents to die, there will be a great harvest (John 12, 24).

Do you remember those little colored tablets that fizzed in a glass of water? The tablet was not meant to stay in tablet form. It had to be immersed in a glass of water to become a flavored drink.

Are you willing to be dissolved for the purposes of Christ? Are you willing for your own plans and dreams to be dissolved for the purposes of Christ?

Lord Jesus, forgive us when we, like James and John, foolishly seek recognition. Take us as we are and let us be incorporated into you and into your divine purpose for our lives. Alleluia!

Monday, October 20, 2003 St. Paul of the Cross
Luke 12, 13-21
Saying against Greed; Parable of the Rich Fool

God or greed? What we feed grows. What we starve dies.

When we feed and nourish our relationship with God, God becomes of greater and greater importance in our lives. Everything else falls into place. When we fuss and fret about temporal possessions and concerns, they begin to possess us and we become impoverished in God's sight.

Lord Jesus, without your smile, without your blessing, nothing we possess on this earth is of any value. No possession, no position, no title, no relationship, nothing. Thank you for setting us free to follow you and to be truly wise and truly wealthy in your eyes. Alleluia!

Tuesday, October 21, 2003
Luke 12, 35-38
Vigilant and Faithful Servants

Dressed and ready to go! No more lounging about in cosy pajamas, metaphorically speaking. Jesus does note want us to be dozing off when he returns. He wants us to be alert and ready.

Sometimes our homework in "Waiting for God 101" is even harder than that in "Trusting God 101." We wait and wait and wonder when God will ever come into our situation. When will our breakthrough come? We may give up and decide just to forgot it all and go to sleep. Some of us live our lives in a state of dull listlessness.

Jesus is coming! He is here with us now, yes, but he is also coming back to this earth to reign. Jesus, Son of Man, will return as King of kings!

We are called to be ready to greet Jesus when he comes in glory. These are not just words we sing. Jesus is truly coming. We do not know when he will suddenly appear.

524

What is it I need to do today to be ready for Jesus? It is crucial that I pray for the grace to forgive from my heart all who have sinned against me in order that my own sins are forgiven. It is crucial that I do my part to be faithful to the vocation to which I am called.

Lord Jesus, restore lost hopes and replace listlessness with new life and with vibrant expectation. Thank you that you are coming soon. Alleluia!

Wednesday, October 22, 2003
Luke 12, 39-48
Vigilant and Faithful Servants

Abuse of authority always brings the judgment of God. When those entrusted with positions of privilege and leadership forgot that they are stewards acting on behalf of another, they are in for a rude surprise. Not only do they face the wrath of God, they are also reclassified as unfaithful,

No one knows the exact time when Jesus will return. Jesus cautions us to be in a state of constant readiness. Greater responsibilities require greater accountability. Fidelity to one's assigned task is what is required.

Lord Jesus, thank you for reminding us that we are here for your purposes, not our own. Thank you for forgiving us, healing us, redeeming us, and restoring us. Strengthen us this day to serve others with humility and to continue to be faithful to do the work you have set before us. Gladden our hearts with the certain knowledge that you are with us and that you will return for us and take us to live with you forever. Alleluia!

Thursday, October 23, 2003 St. John of Capistrano
Luke 12, 49-53
Jesus: A Cause of Division

I'm reading an old novel in which the heroine has just been told that she has only a year to live. Having always yielded meekly to the wishes and the dictates of others, she had no real life of her own. No longer! She decides to start to live. She decides to start to speak up for herself and to speak out the truth. All around her are astonished and horrified.

Jesus knew he would soon suffer and die. Unlike the heroine in the old novel, Jesus had always spoken up and spoken out. People either welcomed him or resisted him. He brought light because he was Light (John 8, 12). Light always exposes darkness. Darkness may lead to repentance or to resistance. Division may be a result, because not all welcome the light.

Lord Jesus, let us live boldly for you while we still have the opportunity. Alleluia!

Friday, October 24, 2003 St. Anthony Mary Claret
Luke 12, 54-59
Signs of the Times; Settlement with an Opponent

Once when I was away for a couple of days, Christopher, who was a teenager at the time, had a surprise call that his godfather was in town and on the way to Terry's office. Then they would come to our home. Christopher called Terry at the office, asking, rather breathlessly, "Can you stall him a while?" A few minutes to straighten up the house a bit!

Jesus tells us to be savvy about the time and the times we are living in. What is the season? What time is it on God's clock? What do we need to do to be ready for the return of Jesus? Whom do we need to forgive and to reconcile with, if possible? We only have to do our part. That is all God expects.

Lord Jesus, you don't want us to be in a panic and to be rushing around, but you do want us to persist in getting the house of our soul ready for you. Show us today one step to take in cleaning this house. Alleluia!

Saturday, October 25, 2003
Luke 13, 1-9
A Call to Repentance; The Parable of the Barren Fig Tree

Repent! Think again about your life. Reconsider.

Do not make unwarranted assumptions about the misfortunes of others. Look at yourself. Look to God. Repent now.

Lord Jesus, it's easy to look at the misfortunes of others and to wonder. Instead, you tell us, through history and parable, to look at ourselves. Thank you for your patience with us. Purify our hearts and let us bear fruit for you. Alleluia!

Sunday, October 26, 2003 Thirtieth Sunday in Ordinary Time
Mark 10, 46-52
The Blind Bartimaus

Two invitations. Three responses We have no idea how long Bartimaus, a blind man, had sat in his darkness, living as a beggar by the Jericho roadside.

However, when Jesus arrived on the scene, things changed and changed quickly! No more darkness. No more begging. No more sitting on the sidelines of life. Jesus was here!

Knowing that Jesus was near, Bartimaus cried out for help. Although initially many told him to shut up, Bartimaus cried out even more. What did he have to lose?

Jesus stopped his journey and told the people to call Bartimaus. Calling him, they gave him two commands. They told him to have courage and to get up because Jesus himself was now calling for him.

Not only did Bartimaus get up, he jumped up and sprang to his feet. He had called to Jesus and now Jesus was calling for him!

The people who had tried to silence him now encouraged him. Before running to Jesus, Bartimaus flung off his cloak, as though to be free of any encumbrance as he sped to Jesus.

Now he was before Jesus. This was his moment. Jesus required that Bartimaus himself to articulate his need. It may have seemed obvious, but still Jesus asked Bartimaus what he wanted.

Bartimaus addressed Jesus with respect. He addressed him as Master and told Jesus he wanted to see.

Jesus granted this request and directed Bartimaus to go. Bartimaus' bold belief and trust in Jesus had been effective in saving him and making him whole.

Lord Jesus, sometimes we sit in darkness on the sidelines of life, begging for scraps. We don't have to live this way. We are your brothers and sisters. You are here! You are calling us. Help us to throw off every impediment, to take fresh courage, leap to our feet, and tell you what we need. Heal us and return us to life. Alleluia!

Monday, October 27, 2003
Luke 13, 10-17
Cure of a Crippled Woman on the Sabbath

This was her day, her dancing day, her dancing with delight day! She had been held hostage by an unnamed spirit for eighteen years. Long enough. Too long.

Jesus saw her! Jesus called to her. That special Sabbath day, Jesus announced to her and to all in the synagogue that she was now free from this terrible, crippling condition. Jesus laid his hands on her.

The woman was free at last. She stood up straight and strong. She glorified God! Wouldn't you?

Lord Jesus, you chose the time and the place to set this woman free, this woman you called a daughter of Abraham. Free! You did not make her wait a moment longer. In the synagogue. on the Sabbath. How appropriate. Set us free today. Let us stand up straight and tall. Let us sing and dance and glorify God today. Alleluia!

Tuesday, October 28, 2003 Sts. Simon and Jude
Luke 6, 12-19
The Mission of the Twelve; Ministering to a Great Multitude

Power, suffused with holiness and love, flowed from Jesus. Jesus drew this power from his relationship with God the Father, his Abba, his heavenly Dad.

Even Jesus, Son though he was, did not presume, without intense prayer, to select the Twelve who would be apostles. He prayed all night on the mountain before announcing his decision.

An assignment was waiting when Jesus and the Twelve came down from the mountain. People! So many people! There were other disciples of Jesus there. There were people from Jerusalem and from all over Judea. There were even those who came from the seaside, from Tyre and Sidon.

All these people wanted to be close to Jesus and to touch him. They wanted to hear him speak. They wanted to see him heal. Jesus healed all of them, even those who suffered torment because of unclean spirits. God's power flowed through Jesus to heal them all. No case was beyond the power and the love of God to reach and to heal. There were no cases deemed too difficult or impossible.

Lord Jesus, show us today how to put first things first. The temptation is always present to do God's work without God's power. Burnout and ineffective ministry are the inevitable results. You were the Son of God and yet you did not presume to act without intentionally immersing yourself in God's presence and spending yourself in prayer seeking God's will. Balance our prayer life, Lord. Let your life and love flow within us making us strong and clean. Thank you for continually making us aware of the priority of our relationship with you. Thank you that our ministry will flow naturally from our time in prayer. Alleluia!

Wednesday, October 29, 2003
Luke 13, 22-30
The Narrow Door; Salvation and Rejection

Jesus, a Jew, was warning his Jewish listeners not to bank on their ethnic heritage when it came to matters of salvation and entrance into the kingdom of God. As he had previously taught, rejection of Jesus was equivalent to rejection of God the Father. God the Father had sent Jesus, the Son, into this world (Luke 10, 16).

The patriarchs, the prophets, and even the so-called outsiders, the Gentiles, who trust in Jesus, will feast at God's table in the coming kingdom. Jesus was endeavoring to warn his listeners before it was too late and the door was shut.

Lord Jesus, when the ones you choose do not choose to choose you, you choose to choose others who do accept you and the free gift of salvation you offer to all. Let us choose you today and allow you to put us on the spiritual diet that will allow us to enter the narrow gate. Alleluia!

Thursday, October 30, 2003
Luke 13, 31-35
Herod's Desire to Kill Jesus; Lament over Jerusalem

Jesus knew what it was like not only to be unwelcome, but also to be told that his death was actually desired. The Pharisees, unfriendly at best, told him to go away. They had plotted against him themselves (Mark 3, 6, Luke 6, 11, Luke 11, 53-54, etc.). This time, however, they told Jesus that Herod wanted to kill him.

Jesus refused to be deterred from completing his ministry. His ministry would culminate in the triumph of the Cross in Jerusalem.

Jesus referred to Herod as a fox, not the most politically correct characterization. Then, with calm confidence, Jesus continued his own ministry.

Jesus would continue to speak out, to heal people, and to cast out demons until the very end of his ministry on earth. He knew he would die in Jerusalem. A true prophet dies in Jerusalem (Luke 13, 33).

Jesus lamented over Jerusalem. He longed to gather her children to himself as a mother hen protectively gathers her little ones under her wings. The people, his own people, refused.

Lord Jesus, in spite of the hostility of others and the grief in your own heart, you steadily continued your assignment. When we are tempted by opposition or by desolation to give up, help us to remember that we are walking in your footsteps. Strengthen us to complete the work that has been assigned to us. Alleluia!

Friday, October 31, 2003
Luke 14, 1-6
Healing of the Man with Dropsy on the Sabbath

Silent opposition. Active ministry.

At the Sabbath meal in the home of a Pharisee, the people were carefully scrutinizing Jesus to see if he would heal a man with an obvious ailment. Jesus responded to their silent hostility and opposition by asking them a legal question about the Sabbath. After healing the man, he asked them another question which they were unwilling to answer.

Lord Jesus, you continued your ministry in the midst of spoken or unspoken challenges. Strengthen us to do the work you have entrusted to us. Let us live to please you and rejoice in you. Alleluia!

Saturday, November 1, 2003 All Saints Day
Matthew 5, 1-12
The Sermon on the Mount; The Beatitudes

The kingdom of heaven! Comfort. The land. Satisfaction. Mercy. Seeing God. Identity as God's children. The kingdom of heaven. A great reward in heaven.

Sometimes we get so mired in the sorrows of this passing world that we forget the rewards awaiting us. There are rewards both here on earth (Psalm 27, 13) as well as in heaven for those who seek God and find their treasure in God.

Lord Jesus, when we know how poor we are without you, thank you for giving us the kingdom of heaven. When we are mourning, thank you for your comfort. When we are able to have a realistic and humble opinion of ourselves, thank you for giving us an inheritance. When we offer mercy to others, thank you for the mercy awaiting us. When we desire purity of heart, thank you for showing us God. When we seek to bring peace, thank you that we are called God's children. When we suffer injustice and actual persecution for following you, thank you that the kingdom is ours. When we are insulted and slandered because of our trust in you, thank you for reminding us of the faithful prophets of old. Let us rejoice and remember the great reward you have for us. Alleluia!

Sunday, November 2, 2003 All Souls Day
John 6, 37-40
The Bread of Life Discourse

This is an extraordinary, compact, intense exposition of the relationship between Jesus and the Father. Our relationship with Jesus and our relationship with the Father is intimately bound up with the relationship of Jesus, Son of God, with his Father, his Abba, in heaven. Deep comfort may be drawn from these few verses.

Jesus assures us that he will never reject anyone who comes to him. He came from heaven for the very purpose of doing God's will on earth.

We need not fear the will of God, but rejoice in it! God's will is clear.

God desires that his beloved Son, Jesus, raise all who believe in him. What could be more wonderful?

Lord Jesus, thank you that you will raise us on the last day. Until that day, thank you for your arms outstretched to welcome us. Thank you that we may live joyfully for you in this present time, knowing that our future for all eternity is safe and secure. Alleluia!

Monday, November 3, 2003 St. Martin de Porres
Luke 14, 12-14
Conduct of Invited Guests

As soon as I read this passage, I was reminded of a poem by Christine Rodgers. This poem refers to offering oneself as hospitality. Gracious as it is to offer tea and cakes, are we willing to offer our very selves?

Jesus, having instructed the guests at the wedding banquet how to conduct themselves, now turned his attention to the host. Jesus said

531

not merely to invite one's neighbors and relatives. That would imply easy reciprocity.

Instead, Jesus instructed the host to invite the very ones who could not offer hospitality in return. Jesus said to reach out and to invite the ones who were poor, the crippled, the lame, and the blind. Jesus assured the host that hospitality to those considered least of the least would be repaid at the time of the resurrection of the righteous.

We tend to offer ourselves only to those who we think will understand us and affirm us. We feel safe with them. We seek their acceptance and approval. Why?

Offering ourselves to others involves a risk, as we step outside our comfort zone. Others may be rich in material possessions, but too poor in spiritual wealth to understand us, much less to affirm us. They may have strong bodies, but be too crippled in spirit to hold us up when we need help. They may wear designer shoes, but be too lame to jog along beside us in our spiritual journey. They may be too spiritually blind to see themselves, much less us.

Lord Jesus, you offered your very self to us. You are with us as we offer ourselves as hospitality to the blind, the lame, the crippled, and the poor. You are with us and that is all that matters. No matter how our hospitality is received, you will repay us. Alleluia!

Tuesday, November 4, 2003 St. Charles Borromeo
Luke 14, 15-24
The Parable of the Great Feast

God is always inviting us to feast in his presence. We continually find excuses to avoid this invitation. Maybe we're too busy with work. Maybe we plead family responsibilities. Maybe we're too busy serving God to enjoy simply basking in God's presence.

What is your excuse? What is mine?

Sometimes I avoid spending time in God's presence in silence because I have to face myself. However, as we learn to spend time consciously and comfortably in God's presence without an agenda, we are preparing for the joys of living in God's presence for all eternity.

The blind, the lame, the poor, and the crippled were all invited to the feast. Even those out in the hedgerows and highways, considered outsiders by some, were summoned to the banquet. Tragically, those first invited made foolish excuses.

Lord Jesus, forgive me for making excuses to avoid spending time in your presence, whether it is in your Eucharistic presence, your presence in the reading of Scripture, your presence when two or three or more are gathered together in your name, or simply celebrating your presence within me. Forgive me for running and wanting to avoid you. Heal me and renew me and refresh me as I come now to feast in your presence. Alleluia!

Wednesday, November 5, 2003
Luke 14, 25-33
Sayings on Discipleship

Jesus says that if we do not carry our own cross, we cannot truly be his disciples. We may be admirers of Christ, but we are not yet true disciples.

We cannot carry another's cross or live another's vocation. We can only daily embrace both the call and the cross in our own life.

We may periodically call out to others to strengthen us and to pray for us, but that is all they can do. They cannot carry our cross. They cannot live out God's purpose for us.

Do we really want to be disciples? Jesus said to count the cost.

Jesus is in the driver's seat of our lives when we are true disciples. We do not plan the journey. When we are true disciples, Jesus is the one in charge of our destination and our destiny.

Lord Jesus, forgive me when I yield to a shallow and naïve view of discipleship. Forgive me when I try to follow you on my own terms. Forgive me for seeking the approval of others more than I seek your approval. Forgive me for running too much to others for the comfort only you can give. I offer my life to you anew. Fulfill your purpose in me and through me. Alleluia!

Thursday, November 6, 2003
Luke 15, 1-10
The Parable of the Lost Sheep; The Parable of the Lost Coin

The tax collectors and the sinners were eagerly flocking to Jesus. They knew that he was their Shepherd. They knew that he was their Savior.

Not so with the Pharisees and the scribes, the religious leaders, who were fussing and complaining as usual. That is why Jesus directed these two parables to them.

The wording in the parable of the lost sheep is very intimate and very personal. The shepherd does not hesitate to search diligently for the lost sheep, his own sheep. He does not drag the lost back to the fold. He joyfully places this beloved lamb on his own shoulders and invites others to celebrate with him!

The woman who had ten coins and lost one was not content until she had searched all over her house and found the lost coin. As with the shepherd, the woman invited others to share her delight and her joy at recovering her lost coin.

Lord Jesus, even the angels in heaven rejoice when one sinner repents. You are our Good Shepherd and you have a tender, personal regard for each ram, ewe, and lamb in your fold. Thank you that your love and care for us is not just routine or professional, but passionately personal. You are not just a CEO, intent on cultivating image and counting units. You are our Shepherd. You are our Savior. Alleluia!

Friday, November 7, 2003
Luke 16, 1-8
The Parable of the Dishonest Steward;
Application of the Parable

Jesus told this parable, not to the crowds, but to his disciples. He had previously addressed the scribes and the Pharisees in the parables of the lost sheep, the lost coin, and the lost son.

The steward in this parable was deemed unfaithful because he had foolishly wasted the riches entrusted to his management. Afterwards, he scrambled to insure his personal financial future by cheating his employer. Jesus commented that the people who live only for temporal rewards seem to be more astute in their business dealings than the ones who are presumably living for God.

Lord Jesus, you desire that we become wise stewards of all you have entrusted into our care. Nothing is really ours. It is all yours and we are all yours! Teach us how to live now in such a way that we will not fear to give you an account of our stewardship. Forgive us for past misuse of time and resources. Please send your Holy Spirit to enlighten us and to teach us how to live. Let us be wise and faithful stewards, trusting in your provision. Alleluia!

Saturday, November 8, 2003
Luke 16, 9-15
Application of the Parable

We are counseled in Proverbs 4, 23 to guard our hearts with strict vigilance. It is from the heart that the very springs of life flow!

Jesus did not need a high-tech ultrasonic device to see into the human heart. He keenly discerned all human motives.

This parable, addressed to his disciples, is not very easy to understand. Jesus seems to be advising his disciples to be smart about how money is used, but not to trust in it.

The Pharisees, who really loved money and prestige, mocked Jesus. Jesus was right, though. It is not possible to live for money and to live for God at the same time. Jesus expects us to use money wisely, but to love and to serve God alone.

How worthy of trust are we? If we cannot be trusted with money, a mere exchange medium of this temporary world, how on earth can God trust us with heavenly wealth? Faithfulness in caring for what has been entrusted to us is what God is requiring of us.

Lord Jesus, help us to be found worthy of your trust. Help us to manage wisely the money you give us and to remember that you are our true source. Help us to use wisely the spiritual gifts and treasures you have given us. Thank you that your resources are bountiful and infinite. Alleluia!

Sunday, November 9, 2003
Dedication of the Lateran Basilica in Rome
John 2, 13-22
Cleansing of the Temple

The cleansing of the temple in Jerusalem is recounted in all four Gospels. This was an explosive event!

Jesus exploded into holy wrath over the perversion of the purpose of the temple. In Matthew 21, 13, Jesus quoted Isaiah 5, 7, in which the temple is called a house of prayer for all people.

The temple was also a place of healing. Jesus healed the blind and lame in the temple (Matthew 21, 14).

Jesus referred to another temple, also. Jesus knew he would die and be raised in three days. The temple of his body would die. This temple would be raised to life in three days.

Lord Jesus, you look with grief whenever your temple is used for wrong purposes and when your people suffer. Purify us, purify our places of prayer, and prepare us for worship in the new Jerusalem, the heavenly Jerusalem. Alleluia!

Monday, November 10, 2003 St. Leo the Great
Luke 17, 1-6
Temptations to Sin; Sayings of Faith

Jesus thrice exhorts his disciples to keep watch on themselves! It's so much easier to search for what's wrong with someone else than to ask God to search and to examine our own hearts.

First, Jesus warns his committed followers of the dire consequences awaiting those who lead others astray. Keep watch on yourself!

Second, Jesus counsels confrontation if a fellow Christian wrongs you. Jesus also commands forgiveness. Keep watch on yourself!

Third, Jesus redirects the request for more faith into a recognition of the faith that is already present. Use this faith boldly. Keep watch on yourself!

Lord Jesus, you won't let us squirm away from your demands for mature discipleship. Today, let our eagle eye, used for spotting the faults of others, be turned instead, to you. As we look to you, show us what there is within our own hearts that needs to be purified, forgiven, and strengthened. Alleluia!

Tuesday, November 11, 2003 St. Martin of Tours
Luke 17, 7-10
Attitude of a Servant

Jesus himself came as a servant. He said that he was among us as one who serves (Luke 22, 27). With a towel tied round his waist, he knelt to wash the feet of his disciples (John 13, 3-5).

Jesus is instructing his disciples about their attitude. They are there to serve.

Jesus is speaking of the attitude of the heart, not merely the action of the hands. It is possible to serve with the hands and still harbor haughtiness in the heart.

Lord Jesus, we pray today for the attitude of a servant. Let us be so secure in your love that we gladly serve others, knowing we are serving you. Alleluia!

Wednesday, November 12, 2003 St. Josaphat
Luke 17, 11-19
The Cleansing of the Ten Lepers

It was as the lepers continued on the road that they were cleansed. Jesus did not tell them to stand still and to wait until they felt healed or looked healed.

He told them to go! He told them to go to the priests to verify their healing and to be received back into their community. It was only as they were going that they were healed.

Sadly, nine of the ten did not even bother to return to give thanks. Only the outcast, the despised Samaritan, fell at Jesus' feet to express his gratitude. Jesus told him that his trust and faith had made him well. Jesus told him to stand on his feet and go.

Lord Jesus, it's hard to keep moving when it seems our lives are standing still and that nothing is happening. Something is happening, though. You are with us and you are always beckoning us to follow you. Help us to keep moving in the direction you have indicated to us and to trust that your plan for us will indeed be fulfilled. Alleluia!

Thursday, November 13, 2003 St. Frances Cabrini
Luke 17, 20-25
The Coming of the Kingdom; The Day of the Son of Man

The Coming of the kingdom is all about the coming of the King! Jesus, Son of Man, will come in glorious light.

Jesus told the Pharisees that it was not possible to observe the arrival of this kingdom. Jesus was referring to a different kind of kingdom, a kingdom within, a kingdom in their very midst.

Jesus instructed his disciples not to run after those who presumed to know all about the coming of the King. When Jesus comes as King, it will be like lightening!

537

Lord Jesus, let your kingdom come in our lives. Let your will be done in our lives. Let us live in joyful expectation of your reign. Alleluia!

Friday, November 14, 2003
Luke 17, 26-37
The Day of the Son of Man

Do not panic, but do prepare. Jesus told his disciples that when he comes in glory, it may seem to be in ordinary times.

It was in an ordinary time that the flood came! It was in an ordinary time that God decided to rain and brimstone on Sodom.

Noah listened to God, prepared for the flood, and was safe. Lot left the city of Sodom just in time and was safe.

Don't look back. Remember Lot's wife!

Our real life is with God. Our life is on God's terms.

Lord Jesus, help us not to clutch the things of this life. Help us not to clutch our plans or our agendas. You are in charge. You are our goal. You will come for us at the right time. Help us to stay joyfully prepared for you. Alleluia!

Saturday, November 15, 2003 St. Albert the Great
Luke 18, 1-8
The Parable of the Persistent Widow

Jesus told this parable, sometimes called the parable of the unjust judge, to his disciples. He wanted them to be confident and to persist in prayer.

When an answer is a long time coming, we may become weary and listless in soul and spirit. We may even begin to fear that God has simply forgotten. We may harbor fears that God apparently does not care.

God does care, but God's timing is not ours. What is speedy to God seems like aeons to us.

Even the judge in the parable, who cared neither for God nor for human rights, eventually yielded to the widow's demands for justice. How much more will our loving God make sure that justice is secured for us?

Lord Jesus, when you come, I want you to find me in faith and in trust, not in despondency or in bitterness. I rejoice in you! Thank you for bringing restoration and renewal. Alleluia!

Sunday, November 16, 2003
Thirty-third Sunday in Ordinary Time
Mark 13, 24-32
The Coming of the Son of Man; The Lesson of the Fig Tree;
Need for Watchfulness

Jesus had been telling his disciples about the coming Roman destruction of the Temple in Jerusalem and the persecutions the believers at that time would suffer. Then he referred to the time after that particular tribulation. He referred to a time when the sun and moon would be dark and when stars would fall from the sky.

Jesus, Son of Man, will come in glory! The angels will gather his elect wherever they are..

As if to emphasize that this really will happen, Jesus told his followers that earth and heaven will pass away, but that his words will never pass away. Only the Father knows exactly when this will happen. Jesus himself does not know. The angels do not know. Human beings certainly do not know. As we observe a fig tree sending forth new leaves and knowing that summer is approaching, we may observe general seasons in history. Still, we do not know the exact day or hour when Jesus will come.

Lord Jesus, our finite human senses begin to tilt, tilt, tilt when we read these awesome words. You are the Word made flesh. You are eternal. The words you speak are eternal. Thank you for sending the Holy Spirit to strengthen us and to instruct us how to live each day in trust and in readiness to meet you when you come for us. Alleluia!

Monday, November 17, 2003 St. Elizabeth of Hungary
Luke 18, 35-43
The Healing of the Blind Beggar

The poor man was blind and could not see Jesus approaching. He could only hear the crowd.

Using what he had, his sense of hearing, his sense of need, and his courage, he concentrated these resources by repeatedly calling out to Jesus as Son of David. He used what he had to get what he needed and wanted.

Jesus did indeed stop. He asked the man what he wanted, even though it seemed obvious. To regain his sight! Jesus simply told the man to see. The man saw and immediately gave glory to God.

Lord Jesus, sometimes we forget to use what resources we already have. We become so intent on lamenting our limitations that we forget to forge ahead with what we do have. Show us today what resource we have been neglecting. Thank you for giving us fresh insight. Alleluia!

Tuesday, November 18, 2003 St Rose Philippine Duchesne
Luke 19, 1-10
Zacchaeus the Tax Collector

What is lost in my life? Jesus is here to seek and to save whatever is lost.

Zacchaeus, short in stature, had probably learned well the ways of compensation. He was rich. He was a tax collector. The chief tax collector!

Instead of lamenting his shortness of stature, he knew what to do when Jesus came to town, to Jericho. He did not even try to compete with the crowd for a view of Jesus. He knew he wouldn't be able to see over the heads of all the other people.

Ingeniously, he ran on ahead of the crowd and scrambled up a sycamore tree. He was more than willing to scrap his pride in order to see Jesus!

Jesus must have been delighted with this resourcefulness. Jesus responded by looking up into the tree and inviting himself to Zacchaeus' house. When others criticized Jesus for going to the home of a sinner, Zacchaeus stood his ground. He promised Jesus to give away half of all that he had and to restore fourfold whatever he had extorted from others before he had encountered Jesus.

Jesus announced to Zacchaeus that salvation had come to his house! Jesus, Son of Man, had come to save. He referred to Zacchaeus, not as a sinner, but as a descendant of Abraham.

Lord Jesus, you know what is lost in my life. Thank you for seeking me, saving me, and restoring me. Alleluia!

Wednesday, November 19, 2003
Luke 19, 11-28
The Parable of the Ten Gold Coins

Jesus is Lord whether or not he is acknowledged as such. One day he will be acknowledged and served as King. He told this parable of the coins in the presence of those who had gathered in Zacchaeus' house in Jericho.

Jesus was preparing to enter Jerusalem. It was time to address erroneous expectations of the kingdom of God.

The kingdom of God is the realm in which God's will is carried out. In this parable, Jesus described the fate of two groups. One group consisted of committed servants of the future king. The other group consisted of those opposed to the future king.

The ten servants in the parable were each entrusted with a gold coin and instructed to use this coin wisely until the king returned. The king eventually returned and required an accounting.

The servant who increased his one coin to ten was congratulated as a good servant and rewarded with ten cities to govern. His fidelity in money matters was merely practice for greater responsibility in the king's service.

The servant who produced five coins was likewise awarded five cities over which to govern. Alas, the servant who did not produce an increase had even his hidden coin taken away from him and given to the industrious servant who had ten.

What happened to those who had opposed the new king? They were sentenced to death.

Lord Jesus, show us today how to use wisely the resources you have given us. If we have grown fearful or lazy, show us how to take risks! You are our King and we long for you to delight in how we have used our time and all our other resources on this earth. Alleluia!

Thursday, November 20, 2003
Luke 19, 41-44
The Lament over Jerusalem

Jerusalem! The place where God's true prophets often suffer martyrdom. It was impossible that Jesus could die anywhere else

541

(Luke 13, 33). Yet, Jesus wept not for himself, but for Jerusalem, the city which killed the prophets sent from God (Luke 13, 34).

Jesus wept because Jerusalem did not know what would have brought true peace. Jesus knew of the enemies who would surround the city and bring destruction.

Yet, the great tragedy was that Jerusalem did not recognize the time of Jesus' visitation. Jesus was there and Jerusalem did not recognize him for who he was.

It is a great tragedy when any follower of Jesus does not recognize the time of Jesus' visitation. We may not recognize the prophets sent to us by God. We may not recognize situations and circumstances in which it is God who is visiting us. We may have stiff and rigid expectations and do not realize that is God whispering to us or shouting urgently to us. Jacob awoke from a dream and suddenly realized that God had been there (Genesis 28, 16).

Lord Jesus, for the remainder of my life, let me not miss any of your visitations. Let me recognize you and welcome you and continue to follow you. Forgive me for the times when I did not know it was you. Let your purpose be accomplished in each of your visitations. Alleluia!

Friday, November 21, 2003
Presentation of the Blessed Virgin Mary
Luke 19, 45-48
The Cleansing of the Temple

St. Paul reminds us that we are God's temple and that the Spirit of the living God actually lives within us (1 Corinthians 3, 16) . We belong to God. We do not belong to ourselves (1 Corinthians 6, 19).

Jesus was fierce about protecting the temple in Jerusalem from misuse. The temple was meant to be a place of prayer. Its purpose was being thwarted by those who cared primarily for commerce.

The priests and other religious leaders, those who should have been the most zealous in protecting the temple, appeared to be preoccupied with protecting their own power. Jesus represented a serious threat to them. The people were listening to Jesus because he taught with authority (Matthew 7, 28-29).

I wonder if there are too many competitors within the temple of our lives? Are there too many conflicting claims on our time and our resources? Are we being ruled by our own agendas, the agendas of others, or by Jesus?

Lord Jesus, we will soon celebrate the last Sunday before Advent. We will acclaim you as Christ the King! Forgive us for the times when we have tried to rule in the temple of our lives. Cleanse the temple of our hearts and lives so that we may truly welcome you as King. Alleluia!

Saturday, November 22, 2003 St. Cecilia
Luke 20, 27-40
The Question about the Resurrection

Jesus lived truth and taught truth by his parables. Those who opposed him, the Sadducees in this case, sought to preserve their own beliefs, even though these beliefs were not true.

The Sadducees denied the resurrection, even though their own belief system, with its adherence to the law of Moses, supported the concept of resurrection. After all, at the burning bush, God told Moses, "I am the God of your father, the God of Abraham., the God of Isaac, and the God of Jacob" (Exodus 3, 6 N.R.S.V.).

Jesus told the Sadducees that in the resurrection, people will not marry as they do on earth. They will be fully alive, however. God is the God of the living.

In the age to come, the resurrected ones will be like angels. They will not be angels. They will be like angels because they will not die. They are God's children and they are alive.

Lord Jesus, thank you for living and dying, so that we may live with you here on earth and live with you forever in the age to come. Alleluia!

Sunday, November 23, 2003 Christ the King
John 18, 33-37
The Trial before Pilate

Jesus was summoned into Pilate's presence in the praetorium, the Roman governor's residence in Jerusalem. Devout Jews would not have gone there willingly at the time of Passover. They would have been considered defiled and therefore unfit to partake of the Passover.

However, Jesus himself was the Passover! He was the Passover Lamb of God soon to be slain.

543

Jesus had come from heaven to earth, born of the Virgin Mary, to a ministry involving misunderstanding, rejection, betrayal, indescribable agony in the garden, vicious scourging, the Cross, the tomb, resurrection, and then a glorious ascension back home to heaven. Mission accomplished!

In this Gospel passage, however, he was before Pilate in the praetorium. Pilate, the compromiser, Pilate the coward, quizzed Jesus about whether or not Jesus was King of the Jews. How could Jesus be a king if his own people had rejected him and wanted to kill him?

Jesus was born to testify to the truth. He testified to the truth by his life and death. His kingdom was not like the kingdoms of this world. Those who belong to the truth are eager to listen to Jesus.

Lord Jesus, you are our Savior and our King. Let us listen attentively to your words of truth. Let us understand the truth about who you really are and who we really are. Thank you that we do not need to be afraid of the truth. The truth sets us free. Free us to serve you as our gentle Lord and triumphant King. Lord Jesus, come in glory! Alleluia!

Monday, November 24, 2003
St. Andrew Dung-Lac and Companions
Luke 21, 1- 4
The Poor Widow's Contribution

Years ago, I heard someone comment that Jesus did not commend this woman for her action of giving all she had. I felt puzzlement and sorrow over this comment.

Jesus, I believe, was deeply moved by the poor widow's implicit trust in God. She had so little and yet she gave all to God.

How did her story continue? I believe God must have repaid her in ways not recorded in this Gospel. God is debtor to no one. It is impossible to outgive God.

This overflowing generosity is illustrated when Jesus fed the multitude from one small lunch of five barley loaves and two fish (Matthew 14, 13-21; Mark 6, 30-44; Luke 9, 10-17; John 6, 1-14). John's Gospel records that the lunch was that of a boy in the crowd who was willing to give what he had. From so little, Jesus fed thousands. Baskets and baskets of food were leftover!

Lord Jesus, if we are poor, lonely, or insignificant in the eyes of others, we may still be rich in joy. Thank you for the joy you give us as we offer to you all that we have and all that we are. Alleluia!

Tuesday, November 25, 2003
Luke 21, 5-11
The Destruction of the Temple Foretold;
The Signs of the End

It is possible to spend endless hours in research, study, and speculation about the end times. Jesus concisely condensed two aspects.

First, Jesus said that the temple is Jerusalem would be destroyed. In 70 A.D., Rome did indeed destroy this rebuilt temple. So don't set so much store on the beauty or the cost of any temporary temporal temple.

Second, there will be an end to the way life is currently lived. This is necessary before Jesus comes in glory. Jesus warns against deception. Be cautious about what you believe, but do not be frightened. Be aware, but not afraid.

Lord Jesus, people have lived and died, having spent much of their lives speculating about these subjects. I don't want to live that way. The world is in such upheaval with terror on all sides. Help me not to be consumed by terrible possibilities, but to continue to trust you and to pray for your will to be done on this earth as it is in heaven. Alleluia!

Wednesday, November 26, 2003
Luke 21, 12-19
The Coming Persecution

Jesus instructed his followers how to conduct themselves in times of persecution and betrayal. True followers of Jesus have always suffered some form of betrayal and persecution, subtle or severe, throughout the centuries.

According to St. Paul, all who truly desire to live a godly life in Christ will be persecuted (2 Timothy 3, 12). This is the Christian's opportunity to bear witness to the Gospel by giving testimony.

Jesus, the supreme realist, warned that his followers would be hated and betrayed even by friends and relatives. "I have said this to you, so that in me you may have peace. In the world you face persecution. But take courage; I have conquered the world" (John 16, 33 N.R.S.V.). Although some would be killed, no eternal harm would ever come to his followers.

545

Lord Jesus, we yearn to be in control and yet we are not. It seems that evil is in control, and yet it is not. You said not to bother about defending ourselves. You will supply all the wisdom that is necessary when the time comes to speak. Strengthen us today to persevere and to follow you. You are the Lord. You are in control. Alleluia!

Thursday, November 27, 2003 Thanksgiving Day U.S.A.
Luke 17, 11-19
The Cleansing of Ten Lepers

Jesus did not jet to Jerusalem, although that is where his destiny awaited him. He was Son of God, yet he still had to travel on the roads available at the time.

Samaria was in a special category. It could be a place where he would be welcomed, as in the account of the woman at the well (John 4, 4-42) or it could be a place where he would not be received well at all (Luke 9, 51-55). That's just the way it is with journeys!

On his way to Jerusalem, Jesus continued to minister to people. Some expressed gratitude and others did not bother. The Samaritan leper, wonderfully cleansed and healed by Jesus, returned to Jesus to express his thanks. Not so with the other nine lepers, who had also been healed. They did not go back to Jesus to express gratitude.

Lord Jesus, thank you for your presence with us as we continue our journey to you. You are our companion and you are our destination. Thank you for the times you have healed us, especially the times when we did not realize how sick we really were. Thank you for cleansing us from sin and setting us free to serve you and to serve others. Alleluia!

Friday, November 28, 2003
Luke 21, 29-33
The Lesson of the Fig Tree

California tree sitters were recently in the news. A definite clash, a definite difference of opinion about whether the trees would be saved or sacrificed.

Jesus is speaking of the fig tree and all trees in today's Gospel. The hand of God is always seen, whether the leaves are falling and branches are barren or whether there are pale green buds and fragrant blossoms signaling summer.

Just as Jesus ascended into the clouds, he will return to earth in clouds of glory (Acts 1, 11, Matthew 24, 30, Matthew 26, 64, Mark 13, 26,

Luke 21, 27). Signs in the celestial bodies will precede his return as King. The time will come when we will see God's kingdom in its fullness.

When? I don't know. There are shelves and shelves of books in theological libraries and in bookstores about this subject.

Jesus does say that it will happen. Jesus does say that, although earth and heaven will become history, his words will remain.

Lord Jesus, we do know that you will come again in glory. In our own lives, reawaken this hope in us. Show us how to live this short life in the way we are called to live it. Let your will be done completely in us as we joyfully wait for your kingdom to come in all its fullness. Alleluia!

Saturday, November 29, 2003
Luke 21, 34-36
Exhortation to be Vigilant

Jesus said to be careful that our hearts do not become weary and listless from either dissipation or despair. The concerns of this life can become so overwhelming that we seek escape in various ways and become professional worrywarts. Substitutes for God can paralyze our hearts.

Jesus did not say to be vigilant over our minds, but over our hearts. When we have been deeply hurt or disappointed in life, we may put our minds and wills on autopilot while our hearts become numb with grief that seems to go on forever.

King David understood this kind of grief as he wailed, "How long wilt thou forget me, O LORD? for ever? how long wilt thou hide thy face from me? How long shall I take counsel in my soul, having sorrow in my heart daily? how long shall my enemy be exalted over me (Psalm 13, 1-2 K.J.V.)?"

When the day of the Lord comes, when Jesus comes in glory, it will be in a way that seizes each person on earth. Jesus does not want us to be surprised in a fearful way.

Jesus wants us to keep watch. He wants us to pray for strength to withstand all the trouble of this life and to stand in confidence before him.

Lord Jesus, heal us and restore us to a state of glad anticipation. Help us to forgive others, to forgive ourselves, and to focus the energies of our hearts, as well as the energies of our minds and our wills, on you. Come in glory, Lord Jesus! Alleluia!

> Sunday, November 30, 2003 First Sunday of Advent - Year C
> Luke 21, 25-28, 34-46
> The Coming of the Son of Man; Exhortation to be Vigilant

Jesus came silently the first time. A poor, humble birth in Bethlehem. No room for this Child in the inn.

He will return as the triumphant King, the royal Messiah. He will return in dazzling glory!

The unprepared may literally be scared to death. After all, the sun, moon, stars, and waves of the ocean will all be in tumult!

Everyone will see Jesus, as Son of Man, come in the glory clouds. The Infant born in Bethlehem has come back to reign.

Do we really believe that or do we settle for the weary substitutes of self-indulgence? Jesus cautions us against letting our hearts become lethargic.

The day of the Lord will seize every single person on earth. We pray to be prepared.

Lord Jesus, sometimes we just get tired of it all. Tired of waiting. Tired. We believe, yet we behave as though we don't believe. We say "someday" and go on about our lives as though you will never come. Teach us this Advent how to offer every moment of our lives and every secret place of our hearts to you. Strengthen us and brighten the eyes of our hearts as we work and as we wait in joyful hope for your coming in glory. Alleluia!

> Monday, December 1, 2003 Advent Weekday
> Matthew 8, 5-11
> The Healing of a Centurion's Servant

Jesus was the Word (John 1, 1). He lived God's word and spoke God's word, so that we could be forgiven, freed, and made whole.

The Gentile centurion in Capernaum knew the power of the spoken word. With great humility and with great trust, he told Jesus that he was not worthy for Jesus to come to his home. Instead, he said that if Jesus merely spoke the word of power, the paralyzed servant at home would be healed! The servant was indeed healed (Matthew 8, 13).

Jesus was flabbergasted by this demonstration of bold faith. Jesus saw in the Gentile centurion a quality of faith that he had not yet seen among his own people in Israel.

Lord Jesus, you are the Word made flesh who came to dwell among us. You are still with us in the Person of the Holy Spirit. You will return in glory as King, as the royal Messiah. Speak the word we need to hear today and let us speak and live that word with courage and with renewed faith in you. Alleluia!

Tuesday, December 2, 2003 Advent Weekday
Luke 10, 21-24
Praise of the Father

Jesus listened thoughtfully to the exuberant report of seventy-two of his followers who had just returned from their mission. They were rejoicing because they had proven for themselves the power of the mighty name of Jesus. They knew now that even the demons are subject to the name of Jesus (Luke 10, 18).

Jesus also rejoiced. Jesus, however, rejoiced in the Holy Spirit!

He praised his Father for revealing deep truths to these humble believers and hiding these truths from those who were considered the religious experts, those who may have thought they already knew it all.

God the Father is gracious. God gives all to Jesus. Jesus is the only one who truly knows the Father and accurately portrays and reveals the heavenly Father.

Lord Jesus, thank you for revealing your Father to us. He is just like you! Help us to relax in our Father's love today. Alleluia!

Wednesday, December 3, 2003 St. Francis Xavier
Matthew 15, 29-37
The Healing of Many People; The Feeding of the Four Thousand

Jesus kept moving and miracles kept happening wherever he was. From city to sea to mountain he moved. Jesus did not wander around aimlessly. He moved purposefully, God's will to reveal.

Impossible cases were brought to Jesus. The blind, the crippled, the mute, and the deaf. They were not cases to Jesus and they were not impossible. They were his little ones. He would not let them suffer any longer. He healed them.

The crowd was not a crowd to Jesus. They were hungry people, starving for God. Jesus fed them spiritually with his presence, his compassion, and his words. He fed them physically with loaves and fish. After thanking God, Jesus broke the bread and fed all.

Lord Jesus, you are still moving among us to heal us and to feed us. Let us look to you and be whole. Alleluia!

Thursday, December 4, 2003 St. John of Damascus
Matthew 7, 21, 24-27
The True Disciple; The Two Foundations

It is unwise to throw around the name of Jesus. We are here to know, love, and to follow the Lord on the Lord's terms, not our own. Merely mouthing words to justify ourselves is an insult to the power and holiness of Almighty God.

True wisdom is evident when we begin to live the Lord's words. The Lord is gentle and tender. He knows how weak and fallible we are. He wants us to trust him by acting on his words. Our love and our trust are to be lived out in obedience.

Lord Jesus, forgive us when we try to serve you in a superficial way or on our own terms. In this time of Advent, let us nestle into your strong embrace and learn to rest in you while the storms of life rage around us. Alleluia!

Friday, December 5, 2003 Advent Weekday
Matthew 9, 27-31
The Healing of Two Blind Men

The two blind men were persistent! They not only followed Jesus at a distance on the road, calling out to him, but they also approached him directly. They were not content to cry out from afar. They confronted Jesus directly and personally. They expressed their belief that Jesus could heal them. Jesus did indeed restore their sight.

How often do I call out to Jesus from a distance? How often do I ask others to pray for me? Am I afraid to go directly to Jesus and ask him to heal me? Am I afraid he will be silent? Am I afraid he won't heal me? Have I given up?

Lord Jesus, thank you for the ways in which we may come to you and the ways in which you come to us. Thank you for the sacrament of reconciliation. Thank you for the anointing of the sick. Thank you for giving us your Body and Blood in the Holy Eucharist. Thank you for speaking to us in the sacred Scriptures. Thank you that you are present when two or three gather together in your name. Thank you that you will never leave us. In this time of weariness, waiting, and illness, I come to you. I ask you to heal me in all the ways I need healing. Breathe fresh life into me and let me see. Alleluia!

Saturday, December 6, 2003 St. Nicholas
Matthew 9, 35 - 10, 1, 6-8
The Compassion of Jesus; The Mission of the Twelve

We see an extension of compassion in today's Gospel. The compassionate Jesus, the one who preached the Gospel and healed every ailment, was still limited, for a time, to his earthly body.

Jesus extended his ministry by sending out the twelve to do the same work he himself was doing. He equipped the twelve with authority, his own authority. The twelve were instructed by Jesus to expel evil spirits and to heal every illness.

Jesus told them that their ministry at that time was to be limited to the little lost sheep of Israel. They were to announce to Israel that the kingdom of heaven was at hand! Right then and there!

They were commissioned to heal the sick, to raise the dead, to make the lepers clean again, and to cast out demons. They were to give themselves freely to this work, the very work of Jesus. They were his extension, his way of reaching out and stretching forth his ministry.

Lord Jesus, thank you for working through human beings to extend your ministry. Thank you for working through your first disciples, flawed though they were. Thank you for working through us, flawed though we are, to go everywhere in the world and proclaim the Gospel. Alleluia!

Sunday, December 7, 2003 Second Sunday of Advent
Luke 3, 1-6
The Preaching of John the Baptist

Today's Gospel does not plunge us immediately into the familiar words from the prophet Isaiah about the fiery prophet, John, without giving us an exhaustive history. It was only at a certain time and in a certain place that John appeared.

It was the fifteenth year of the reign of the Emperor Tiberius, and when Herod was Galilee's ruler, and when his brother Philip was ruling in Iturea, and when Lysanius was ruling in Abilene, and, during the time of the high priesthood of Annas and Caiphas. Everything and everyone was in place.

NOW! Now was the time for God to take his bow and shoot forth this arrow of a prophet.

Now was the time for John! Now was the time to do the work he had been chosen from the womb to do, to prepare the way of the Lord (Luke 1, 17). John was filled with the Holy Spirit even in the womb (Luke 1, 15). John, as a little one in the womb of his mother, Elizabeth, leaped for joy, when the Virgin Mary, bearing the Christ in her womb, came to visit.

Now was the time and this was the place for John to proclaim a baptism for the forgiveness of sins. Here, at last, was the one prophesied by Isaiah, the one crying in the wilderness to make a way for the Lord.

Time and place. John did not choose his vocation. God chose him. God decided the time and God decided the place. Even before his conception, John had been selected for this vocation.

Lord Jesus, thank you for calling us to live at this particular time and in this particular place. It may not be an easy time. It may not be a comfortable place. You are in charge. You are coming as our King. Show us how to accept, with humility and gratitude, both our current assignment and also the assignments you have in store for us in the future. Alleluia!

Monday, December 8, 2003 The Immaculate Conception
Luke 1, 26-38
The Announcement of the Birth of Jesus

God is very particular about time and about place. God carefully selected the time of the Annunciation, the sixth month of John the Baptist's life in the womb of Elizabeth, his aged mother. God also carefully selected the place, a town in the Galilee called Nazareth.

God carefully selected the young Virgin Mary, the woman for this unique vocation. The angel Gabriel was selected to announce to Mary that her plans for her life were about to be interrupted for a higher purpose, God's purpose.

Mary was betrothed to Joseph. This was a very serious commitment, a binding commitment to fidelity.

Mary's fidelity to Joseph was not questioned by God or by Gabriel. Gabriel reassured Mary and told her not be frightened. The angel then assured Mary that the Holy Spirit would be the reason and the power behind her motherhood.

Jesus, her baby, was truly the Son of God, the Most High God. Nothing is impossible when God is involved!

Lord Jesus, thank you for coming to us as a little child, born most humbly. You were Mary's baby and God's own Son. Wonder of wonders! You are our brother and our King. Thank you for coming into this world as an vulnerable infant. Thank you that you will return to reign. Alleluia!

Tuesday, December 9, 2003 St. Juan Diego
Matthew 18, 12-14
The Parable of the Lost Sheep

God's family is not complete until YOU are home safe and sound. God's family is not complete without you!

God's family is not complete with even one person missing. Jesus, the Good Shepherd, is not content until the lost sheep is found and brought back to songs of rejoicing.

People with their agendas and their issues may exclude, vote out, or cast out. Not so with God. God's heart yearns over us and calls us home.

Lord Jesus, let us remember this parable when we are inclined to think we don't count. We count with you. Alleluia!

Wednesday, December 10, 2003 Advent Weekday
Matthew 11, 28-30
The Gentle Mastery of Christ

This morning I feel like Rip van Winkle, having awakened after a long, long time Yesterday I had a medical procedure with sedation. A lot of sedation. I slept and slept.

That's not quite what Jesus had in mind in today's Gospel. The kind of rest Jesus gives is not the kind that blots out consciousness. The rest Jesus gives is a rest that accompanies life.

We are all weary and overburdened some of the time. However, this is not the way we are meant to live on a daily basis.

Jesus offers three invitations, accompanied by wonderful promises. If we respond in trust and obedience, our lives will change. We will experience true rest.

Jesus tells us that if we are laboring and are burdened from trying to live for God in a heavy, legalistic way, to come to him. He invites us to take his yoke and to learn from him.

When we are yoked with Jesus, we do only the work Jesus assigns to us. Jesus himself only did the work assigned to him by his heavenly Father.

Lord Jesus, let us experience for ourselves today that your assignments for us are just exactly suited to us. Let us experience the rest you promised. Thank you for giving us the strength to do what you have called us to do. Free us to live as you intended. Alleluia!

Thursday, December 11, 2003 Advent Weekday
Matthew 11, 11-15
Jesus' Testimony to John

Jesus honored John the Baptist in a profound way. He even went so far as to say that, up until that time, there had been no one greater than John.

And yet, John's mission was to prepare the people of that time to enter the kingdom of heaven. Once in the kingdom, the least was considered greater than John.

God's economy. God's methods. God's instruments.

We wonder. We marvel.

Violence? Taking the kingdom of heaven by violence? Could it be that one must do violence to one's own preconceived ideas of what the Messiah would be like or what the kingdom of heaven would be like in order to enter the kingdom? Could it be?

We do know that we must enter the kingdom simply and humbly, as a little child (Matthew 18, 2- 4; Luke 18, 16-17). The mindset of humility does violence to any preconceived ideas, both ours and others, of what the kingdom is like.

There is no room for promoting our agenda. It is God's agenda that we seek. It is God we seek to glorify.

Later, St. Paul would have something to say about what the kingdom was and what the kingdom was not. "For the kingdom of God is not food and drink but righteousness and peace and joy in the Holy Spirit" (Romans 14, 17, N.R.S.V.).

Jesus also said that, for the ones willing to be receptive, John the Baptist was Elijah. The prophet Elijah was the one who would come before the day of the LORD (Malachi 4, 5).

Lord Jesus, there is much we do not understand. Thank you for the ministry of John the Baptist and for his zeal and courage in bearing witness to you. Thank you for the wonder of being brought into your kingdom. Let us remember that your kingdom is our true home. Alleluia!

Friday, December 12, 2003 Our Lady of Guadalupe
Luke 1, 39-47
Mary Visits Elizabeth

Mary was very young in years but very wise in the ways of God. She had already given her consent to the mysterious working out of the will of God in her life (Luke 1, 38). Her attitude, although, puzzled, was also positive.

She speedily set out to visit Elizabeth, her elderly relative. Elizabeth was another woman with aseemingly impossible vocation. Elizabeth, after all the years, tears, and prayers, was finally going to be a mother! She would be the mother of John the Baptist, the prophet who would prepare the way for Jesus.

Elizabeth wisely reminded the young Mary that Mary would be very blessed and happy by believing that what the Lord had promised would come true. The Lord had promised Mary that she would be the mother of the Son of the Most High God. God's promise would be fulfilled.

Elizabeth acknowledged and rejoiced in Mary's identity and in Mary's vocation. Mary was called blessed among all women because she was the mother of the Lord.

How do we wait? Do we whine as we wait? Do we wring our hands and despair of God's promise ever coming true? Do we wonder if we really heard from God? Do we rejoice in God and trust that whatever God truly promised will be fulfilled?

Lord Jesus, thank you for Mary's example. She is our model for discipleship. She shows us how we are to wait. She put her trust in you and then reached out to another. Help us to trust you with our hearts and to reach out to encourage someone today who may be growing weary in the waiting. Alleluia!

Saturday, December 13, 2003 St. Lucy
Matthew 17, 10-13
The Coming of Elijah

God is always surprising us and challenging us. We seem to learn slowly and painfully that we are to serve God rather than our expectations of how we think things should be.

The disciples were quizzing Jesus about the expectation that Elijah was to come before the Messiah. Jesus surprised them by saying that John the Baptist had already fulfilled the mission of Elijah! John had been misunderstood, mistreated, and eventually murdered. Jesus himself would also suffer in order to fulfill his own mission.

Lord Jesus, we cannot fit you into our limited mold. You work in ways far too mysterious for us to grasp. Help us to relinquish any preconceived ideas we may be clinging to that are not in accord with our freedom to follow you. Alleluia!

Sunday, December 14, 2003 Third Sunday of Advent
Luke 3, 10-18
The Preaching of John the Baptist

Everyone around John was clamoring to have John tell them what they should do to express their repentance. The crowds were asking him. The tax collectors were asking him. The soldiers were asking him.

John's response was so simple. He told the crowds to share their food and clothing. He told the tax collectors not to collect more than the appropriate amount of taxes. He told the soldiers not to engage in extortion or false accusations and to be content with their salaries. No big deal.

However, the people were so moved by this fiery preacher of righteousness that they all wondered if he could be the Messiah. John put that question to rest once and for all.

John made it clear that his baptism was one of water. Jesus, the Messiah, the One to come, would be the one to baptize with the Holy Spirit and indeed with fire. John could preach with such power because he knew who he was and who he was not. He had the freedom to minister within certain boundaries.

Lord Jesus, you are the one who baptizes us with the Holy Spirit and with fire. Immerse us today in your Holy Spirit. Fill us anew with the Holy Spirit. Let the fire of the Holy Spirit remove any chaff that may be clinging to the wheat in our lives. Prepare us to meet you when you come again in glory. Alleluia!

Monday, December 15, 2003 Advent Weekday
Matthew 21, 23-27
The Authority of Jesus Questioned

What is truly motivating me? What is the driving force in my life? What is my motive in any given conversation or situation?

After the vigorous cleansing of the Temple in Jerusalem and the subsequent healing of the lame and the blind (Matthew 21, 12-17), Jesus went to Bethany and then returned. The chief priests and the elders confronted him in the temple area. This upstart rabbi was upsetting their apple cart again and they were getting really hot under the collar!

By asking Jesus a loaded question, they revealed more about themselves and their motives than they realized. Trying to trap Jesus, they asked him about the source of his authority.

Jesus responded by asking them the source of John's baptism. Aha! However they responded, they would be neatly skewered.

Lord Jesus, you understood the motives in the hearts of those who questioned your authority. Purify my own heart this Advent. Let me see the motives struggling for expression and resolution in my heart. I give you my heart for repair and restoration. Free me to live for your glory. Alleluia!

Tuesday, December 16, 2003 Advent Weekday
Matthew 21, 28-32
The Parable of the Two Sons

Jesus continued to address the religious leaders, the elders and the chief priests in this very direct, pointed parable. Jesus hinged the order of entrance into the kingdom of heaven on one's treatment of John the Baptist.

John was rather like a litmus test, a prophet straight from God, sent to prepare the way for the Son of God. How he was received would reveal the hearts of his hearers.

557

The tax collectors and the prostitutes, scorned and despised as they were, knew very well their need of God. Knowing their need of repentance, they believed the message of John the Baptist.

The chief priests and the elders, on the other hand, could not see their need for God. They were satisfied and content with their own righteousness. They refused to believe John, righteous though he was. They did not want to lose face by admitting that they had been wrong about him. That is how much maintaining their image and guarding their power meant to them. Therefore, Jesus told them that the prostitutes and tax collectors would precede them into the kingdom.

Lord Jesus, help us to be like the first son in the parable. In spite of his initial reluctance, he did indeed fulfill the will of his father and went to work in the vineyard. If you are trying to speak to us through an unlikely person and if we are resisting, open our hearts and our minds. Help us to receive, in humility, the message you are sending us. Strengthen us to go and do the work you have given us to do as we wait for your return. Alleluia!

Wednesday, December 17, 2003 Late Advent Weekday
Matthew 1, 1-17
The Genealogy of Jesus

Hope abounds in this genealogy! Hope abounds in my genealogy and in yours.

Redemption abounds in this genealogy. Redemption abounds in my genealogy and in yours.

Matthew began the genealogy of Jesus with Abraham. Abraham knew all about hope and about redemption. Abraham believed God (Romans 4, 3). Abraham knew that God could bring life even to the dead (Romans 4, 17). He knew the amazing creative power of God (Romans 4, 17). He believed God's promises (Romans 4, 20). The fourth chapter of Paul's letter to the Romans abounds with the vibrancy of the patriarch Abraham's extraordinary trust in God.

Matthew did not blushingly gloss over certain characters in the family tree of Jesus. These were real people who were identified and acknowledged. God always delights in taking tragedy and turning it into triumph.

One example was the story of Ruth. Ruth, the grieving young widow, eventually married Boaz. They became the grandparents of King David.

558

These are not dull names to gloss over with a bored sigh. These are real people with a real history, a history God would redeem.

Lord Jesus, thank you for coming to us from God and also from a very human family tree. Thank you for coming as our redeemer to take us into your family. Thank you for giving us hope to persevere in our life of faith and trust, irrespective of either our family tree or our own past. Thank you that you will come as our King. Alleluia!

Thursday, December 18, 2003 Late Advent Weekday
Matthew 1, 18-24
The Birth of Jesus

Joseph's resolution was interrupted by an angel, no less. Joseph, a man of deep integrity, was struggling to understand how Mary, his betrothed, could be pregnant because of the Holy Spirit. Joseph was attempting to the right thing in an incomprehensible situation.

Even when we think we are doing the right thing, God may interrupt our intentions and our plans. God's ways are so far above our ways and God's thoughts are so far above our thoughts (Isaiah 55, 9).

The angel told Joseph in a dream not to be afraid, but to take Mary into his home. The angel confirmed what Mary had already told him. This child, to be named Jesus, was indeed conceived by the power of the Holy Spirit. Jesus, the Son of God, was coming to be born amongst us, to live with us, and to save us from our sins.

Lord Jesus, we try so hard to do the right thing and we think we know what is right. Still, you are the Lord and you know the path on which you are leading us. You know how to redirect our path when you know that is for your glory and for our good. Thank you for interrupting our intentions with your higher intentions as you prepare us for your coming as King. Alleluia!

Friday, December 19, 2003 Late Advent Weekday
Luke 1, 5-25
The Announcement of the Birth of John the Baptist

This announcement came during a time of intense prayer. The entire assembly was praying outside the sanctuary.

Inside the sanctuary, the aged priest, Zechariah, was also praying. This was the hour of the fragrant incense offering at the altar.

Long ago David had prayed, "Let my prayer be set forth before thee as incense; and the lifting up of my hands as the evening sacrifice (Psalm 141, 2, K.J.V.)." The book of the Revelation also linked incense and prayer (Revelation 8, 3-4).

It was at that particular time of prayer at the altar that the angel Gabriel appeared to the terrified old priest with amazing news. Impossible news! After all these years of prayer, a son was to be born to the elderly Elizabeth, also of priestly lineage.

Perhaps the elderly priest, righteous though he was, had fallen into silent despair of his prayers ever being answered in the way he had hoped. The angel assured Zechariah that his prayers had indeed been heard. The angel promised him that he would experience joy and gladness! It was not too late. He would be a father, after all!

Gabriel outlined the future of the child to be born. This child, to be named John, would be filled with the Holy Spirit while still in the womb of Elizabeth. John would experience the power of the mighty prophet Elijah and would prepare the people for the coming of Jesus, the Lord.

Elizabeth stayed in seclusion for five months. She gave God all the glory for this glorious answer to prayer and for removing the disgrace she had suffered for so long.

Lord Jesus, help us to persevere in prayer and in joyful expectation as we wait for you. Let us not fall into apathy or unbelief. Thank you that you are with us as we wait for the fulfillment of your promise to us. Thank you that you will come at the right time. Alleluia!

Saturday, December 20, 2003 Late Advent Weekday
Luke 1, 26-38
Announcement of the Birth of Jesus

The Holy Spirit brought forth the conception of Jesus in the womb of Mary, a young virgin. The Holy Spirit would guide and empower Jesus throughout his ministry on earth. The Holy Spirit would raise the crucified, dead, and buried Jesus to life. Nothing is impossible when the Holy Spirit is involved!

Lord Jesus, as we wait for your coming in glory, fill us afresh with the Holy Spirit to live our lives fully with power and with gladness. Alleluia!

Sunday, December 21, 2003 Fourth Sunday of Advent
Luke 1, 39-45
Mary Visits Elizabeth

Jesus, in Mary's womb, was hidden from Elizabeth's sight. Yet, when Mary came to visit her, Elizabeth was filled with the Holy Spirit. She was amazed and honored that this blessed one among women, the mother of her Lord, would come to visit her. John the Baptist, the little one in her womb, leapt for joy!

Lord Jesus, when we are aware of your presence, we are joyful in spite of our difficult circumstances. Even when you are hidden from our sight, we know you are present. Teach us to rejoice as we wait for your shining presence when you come again in all your glory. Alleluia!

Monday, December 22, 2003 Late Advent Weekday
Luke 1, 46-56
The Canticle of Mary

Mary had already given herself wholly and completely for the Lord's purpose when she told the angel Gabriel that she was the Lord's servant. This amazing young woman gave herself to the Lord in deep humility in spite of her initial, normal apprehension.

In the song we call the Magnificat, Mary referred to her soul and to her spirit. With her soul (intellect, will, emotions), she proclaimed the Lord's greatness. With her spirit, she rejoiced in the saving power of God.

The writer to the Hebrews described the word of God as sharper than a sword, even to the dividing of spirit and soul (Hebrews 4, 12). St. Paul prayed for the Thessalonians to be made complete in spirit, soul, and body (1 Thessalonians 5, 25).

Mary, the bearer of the Word made flesh, is our example in giving ourselves completely, body, soul, and spirit to God. Because she was so yielded to God, she was free to exult with strength and with confidence in God's power and God's mercy.

Lord Jesus, as we wait for your coming in glory, we offer ourselves to you. We give you our entire selves, body, intellect, will, emotions, and spirit. Thank you for fulfilling your mysterious purposes in us and through us. Alleluia!

Tuesday, December 23, 2003 Late Advent Weekday
Luke 1, 57-66
The Birth of John

Sometimes it seems as if we are always pregnant, but that the birth never comes. We may grow larger and larger and even think we are having labor pains, only to find out that it's not time yet for the birth. Sometimes the waiting seems to be just too much. We may feel that the life, the dream, or the vision within us has died.

Elizabeth had waited a long, long time to have this baby who was destined to prepare the way of the Lord. Her biological clock had stopped ticking.

God's clock, however, had not stopped ticking. God was in charge. Nothing would be impossible. Elizabeth would have this baby on God's timetable.

When God's time arrived, Elizabeth gave birth. John the Baptist was here. Jesus was on the way. God's time had come!

What are you waiting for that seems too big? Nothing is too big for God.

Lord Jesus, forgive us for sinking into doubt about your promise. Help us to live fully this day in joyful expectation that you will come. Your time is perfect. Your timing is perfect. Alleluia!

Wednesday, December 24, 2003 Late Advent Weekday
Luke 1, 67-79
The Canticle of Zechariah

How tragic to be set free and not to know it! Why stay behind prison bars if the gates have been flung open and we are free to rejoice and to begin a new life?

Zechariah, in a prison of silence for nine months, was now free to speak again! After John's birth, he was released to proclaim God's word in a powerful new way.

Before John's conception, Zechariah had voiced doubts, his own doubts. Now, with the birth of the promised infant, he voiced joy and hope.

Zechariah was filled with the Holy Spirit and began to prophesy. He referred to prophets in times past. He even addressed his infant son as a prophet. John would be the one to prepare the way of the Lord.

John would be God's voice to tell the people of salvation, to tell them that they could be free to live a new life! This would be accomplished through the total remission and forgiveness of their sins.

This was all because of God's mercy. Jesus was to come and to shine on all in darkness. He would live and die and rise again so that we might be whole, that we might be free to live in his light.

Lord Jesus, thank you for coming to shine on us, in us, and through us. Thank you for all the prophets who have spoken forth the word of God. You are the Word made flesh. You are with us and we are truly free. Alleluia!

Thursday, December 25, 2003 The Nativity of the Lord
John 1, 1-18
The Prologue

Jesus! He was there at the very beginning (Genesis 1, 1). He was the Word. He was with God. He truly was God. Jesus was the Word through whom God the Father spoke the universe.

When John the Baptist testified to the light, he was bearing witness to Jesus. Jesus was the light, the true light.

Jesus came first to his very own. Israel!

His own people did not receive him. However, those who did accept him were given power, tremendous power, the power of the Holy Spirit. They were given the power to become God's own children and the power to grow up. They received power to become like their big brother, Jesus.

What God did through Moses was wondrous indeed. The Law came through Moses.

What God did through Jesus, his Son, was of far greater magnitude. What God did through Jesus, was far more wondrous. Through Jesus, born of the Virgin Mary, came grace and truth.

Lord Jesus, thank you for coming to us humbly as a little one in Mary's womb. You came from the shining presence of God to be the light in our darkness. Shine on us today. Alleluia!

563

Friday, December 26, 2003 St. Stephen
Matthew 10, 17-22
Coming Persecutions

The babe in Bethlehem would grow up and suffer rejection and death. In today's Gospel, Jesus warned his disciples to be very cautious about people.

Jesus warned his followers that they would be handed over to various authorities. Jesus' followers would be betrayed, betrayed by those they had trusted, even betrayed by family members.

Jesus reassured his followers that his Father would give the Holy Spirit to them so that they would know what to say in such extraordinary times. They would be in these situations because of their trust in the Lord. They were not there to save their own skin or to protect their own reputations.

Lord Jesus, you told your followers that they would be hated by all. You said that the ones who endured would be saved. As we put away the ribbons and the wrapping paper of Christmas, help us to put away any unrealistic expectations of what it may cost us to serve you. Strengthen us to continue to serve you without expecting human affirmation. Alleluia!

Saturday, December 27, 2003 St. John
John 20, 2-8
The Empty Tomb

Running and stopping. Waiting. Looking. Believing.

The Gospel begins with Mary of Magdala running from the tomb where Jesus had been buried. She ran to give the news of the empty tomb to the disciples.

Peter and John both ran to the tomb, but John, although he arrived first, stopped. It was Peter who was first to enter the tomb. Then John, who had been waiting, also entered, saw the burial cloths, and believed.

There are times in our Christian journey when we seem to be running, to be skipping, to be racing, and to be consciously on the way. Then we stop. We stop of our own volition or we are stopped. Life stops us. Even God seems to stop us.

We wait, and as we wait, we look. We look at God and look for God. We look within ourselves. We look at others. Perhaps we will look and see and believe. Perhaps we look and are even more puzzled than ever. Belief will eventually follow.

Lord Jesus, thank you for your guiding presence in our running, our stopping, our waiting, our looking, and our believing. Alleluia!

Sunday, December 28, 2003
Holy Family of Jesus, Mary, and Joseph
Luke 2, 41-52
The Boy Jesus in the Temple

Timing. Days. Years. Age. Wisdom.

It was probably about five days that Joseph and Mary were separated from Jesus, who was twelve years old. They had traveled with their group for about a day before realizing that he was not with the others after all. It took another day to return to Jerusalem. Mary and Joseph searched for another three days in Jerusalem before finding him in the Temple.

The time had just not yet come for Jesus to begin his earthly ministry in a formal way. He still had days and years ahead. He progressed in both age and in wisdom.

When the infant Jesus was taken from his presentation in the Temple in Jerusalem to his home in the village of Nazareth, he had to grow in wisdom and strength as well as in age. Twelve years later, he still had growing up to do. He continued his growth both in age and in wisdom.

Lord Jesus, we think we know when to be about our Father's business. We don't. Even you had to return to Nazareth for more growth in age and wisdom. Help us not to chafe at the waiting and the training, but to cherish our time in our Nazareth. Alleluia!

Monday, December 29, 2003 St. Thomas Becket
Luke 2, 22-35
The Presentation in the Temple

Simeon was already waiting. When Joseph and Mary brought the infant Jesus into the temple in Jerusalem, Simeon was there, specifically waiting for them. They were expected!

How did Simeon know that he was to be there at just that time? The Holy Spirit. The same Holy Spirit who had been the explanation for Jesus' conception in the womb of a virgin, was the explanation for Simeon's presence at this significant time of dedication and presentation.

This was a holy time. This was a time when God's word was spoken and God's name proclaimed.

The aged Simeon was very sensitive to the ways of the Holy Spirit. The Holy Spirit was upon him and told him that he would live to see the Messiah! The Christ. The Anointed One. Jesus.

In the power of the Holy Spirit, Simeon came into the temple on that particular day. He welcomed Mary and Joseph and took the holy infant into his old arms. He held the One who was light for the Gentiles and the glory of Israel. Jesus! Simeon voiced words of intense gratitude and fulfillment to God.

Now! Now Simeon could depart this life in peace. He had lived to see what God had promised. He had lived to see the coming of Jesus, the Messiah, into the world. How long he had waited for this moment.

Simeon, after blessing Mary and Joseph, singled Mary out for an additional prophetic word. He spoke mysterious and terrifying words about the future of her child and about her own future.

Jesus was to be a sign of contradiction. The hidden thoughts of many hearts would be revealed through the Word made flesh.

Mary? A sword would pierce her heart.

Lord Jesus, this was the moment of moments for Simeon. He had longed for you, waited for you, and prayed to see you. At long last, he finally saw you for himself and held you in his arms in the temple in Jerusalem. When we are tempted to give up on your promises and are advised by others to get on with our lives, let us remember your word to us. Let us pray, wait, and be prepared for your coming. Alleluia!

Tuesday, December 30, 2003
Luke 2, 36-40
The Presentation in the Temple

Anna's life was an intensely rich life of worshipping God with prayer and fasting. Her life was literally lived out in the area of the temple in Jerusalem. Night and day she was there, enclosed with God for God's purposes.

At the time of the presentation of the infant Jesus in the temple, Anna was a very old woman, a widow of many years. However, she was still strong and vibrant in her faith and in her trust in God. As a prophet, she had learned to listen and to hear from God. She was trusted to speak forth God's words.

Anna appeared on the scene in the temple at precisely God's moment. As a prophet, she spoke forth God's words to all who were longing for Jerusalem's redemption.

The infant Jesus was then taken by Joseph and Mary to Nazareth. The favor and blessing of God were upon him as he grew in strength and wisdom, as well as in years.

Lord Jesus, we know that your Father was watching over you carefully both in the temple in Jerusalem and in your home in Nazareth. Certain people were brought into your life at certain times and for certain reasons. Let us be quietly content today to believe that the times, the seasons, the people, and the places in our lives are also being divinely orchestrated. Thank you for even factoring our sins and failures into your plan for us. Thank you for your mercy and forgiveness. Help us continue to grow in both strength and wisdom as we wait for the continued unfolding of your purpose in our lives. Alleluia!

Wednesday, December 31, 2003 St. Sylvester I
John 1, 1-18
The Prologue

The beautiful prologue to St. John's Gospel! A prologue is an introduction or a preface to the real action. The prologue is very important because it sets the scene.

There is a wonderful story, a true story, told about the future Pope John Paul I. On a country road, a woman and her son were frantically trying to catch a ride to the church. Their car had broken down and they were in a great hurry. The driver of a passing car obligingly stopped and gave them a lift. The woman expressed concern about getting to the church on time. She was to sing in the choir for the Bishop's Mass. Her young son was to serve at the altar. The driver assured her that they would not be late.

Surprise! At the church, the woman, now in the choir, glanced at the processional. The kind man, Albino Luciani, who had given her a ride to the church was the Bishop! Later, he became the Bishop of Rome.

Jesus, the Good Shepherd, was not always recognized, either. Jesus was in the world, the world which had come into being through him. Yet the world did not recognize him.

However, some did recognize him. They believed in him and accepted him. They were empowered to become God's own children. Amazing.

Lord Jesus, you are light! You still shine in the darkness. You made God the Father known to us. Thank you for the example of John the Baptist who faithfully bore witness to you. Help us to recognize your presence. Fill us with your light and let those still in darkness recognize your life and your light within us. Alleluia!

Thursday, January 1, 2004 Blessed Virgin Mary,
The Mother of God
Luke 2, 16-21
The Visit of the Shepherds;
The Circumcision and Naming of Jesus

Once, a boy who had been in a street gang, began to seek help from an inner city mission. A woman whose brother was one of the priests in the mission, offered hospitality to this boy and to other former gang members. Academic and vocational skills are still taught and lives are still transformed in this mission.

Once, the boy said to this particular priest, "Everyone around here has a life. You have a life. You are a priest. Your sister has a life. She is a teacher. Everyone has a life. I don't have a life."

Well, he did have a life. He had an identity as God's child and his vocation was in process. In spite of all he had suffered, he did have a life.

Everyone in today's Gospel had a life. Each had an identity. Each had a specific role to play.

It was to shepherds in the fields that the angel entrusted the news of the birth of the Son of God. The shepherds hastened to Bethlehem and found Mary, the child's mother, the strong and steadfast Joseph and the Infant in the manger. The shepherds relayed the message entrusted to them. They proclaimed Jesus as Savior, Messiah, and Lord.

Mary, the Virgin Mother, the active contemplative, cherished these words about Jesus. The shepherds' words were stored for safekeeping in her heart.

The shepherds had fulfilled this particular mission and returned to their flocks. They were filled with praise!

Jesus, after his circumcision, was officially named. Jesus! This had been the name that the angel Gabriel gave him even before his conception in Mary's womb.

Lord Jesus, thank you for coming amongst us as a little one in the womb of Mary and as a newborn in the manger. Your identity was secure. You were Son of God! You were the Word made flesh in the womb of your Virgin Mother. Your vocation would become known to all. You had a life! Help us to know that we have a life. We are your brothers and sisters. God is our Abba, our Father. Mary is our Blessed Mother. We are here on earth with a mission. Even though we may not fully understand it, help us to rejoice in your birth and to be content with your presence in our midst. Alleluia!

Friday, January 2, 2004 Sts. Basil and Gregory Nazianzen
John 1, 19-28
John the Baptist's Testimony to Himself

Who are you? What are you? Why are you doing what you are doing? John the Baptist was pummeled with pointed questions from the priests and Levites from Jerusalem and also from the Pharisees.

John was in Bethany at the time, baptizing people in the Jordan River. He assured his questioners that he knew both his identity and his vocation. He was not the Messiah. He did not even claim to be a special prophet.

John was the prophesied voice in the wilderness. He was called to make ready the way of the Lord Jesus. It was Jesus, among them as the unrecognized Messiah, whom he served.

Lord Jesus, in this new year, thank you for helping us to live comfortably in our identity as God's sons and daughters and to pursue courageously our vocation to follow you. Alleluia!

Saturday, January 3, 2004
John 1, 29-34
John the Baptist's Testimony to Jesus

In yesterday's Gospel, John testified to himself and to his role. He was not the Messiah. He was the one who administered water baptism to prepare the people for the ministry of Jesus.

John now directed the people to Jesus, the Lamb of God. Jesus was the one who would baptize with the Holy Spirit. Jesus was the one on whom the Holy Spirit would descend and remain.

Jesus was the Lamb who would be slain. Jesus was the one who would take away the world's sin. Jesus was the Son of God.

All three Persons of the Holy Trinity were recognized, named, and honored in this Gospel. God the Father. Jesus, the Son of God. The powerful Holy Spirit.

Lord Jesus, thank you that you are the Lamb of God . Thank you for not only forgiving our sins, but also for taking away our sins. Thank you for filling us with the Holy Spirit so that we may be about our Father's business today. Alleluia!

Sunday, January 4, 2004 Epiphany of the Lord
Matthew 2, 1-12
The Visit of the Magi

At ordinations in the Roman Catholic Church, the candidates prostrate themselves as the gathered community prays and invokes the intercession of the saints. Pray for us. Pray for us. Pray for us.

The wise men, or magi, were on a journey in which they would prostrate themselves before the infant Christ. Observing a rising star, they began their journey by traveling to Jerusalem to inquire about the new king.

Of course that did not settle well with the earthly king, Herod. Truly, and for good cause, Herod was troubled. The chief priests had informed him that the Messiah would be born in Bethlehem.

The magi then traveled to Bethlehem. Guided by the star, they stopped at the place where the new king was staying with Mary and Joseph. As soon as the magi saw the infant king, they joyfully prostrated themselves before him. They worshipped their divine king and gave him beautiful and costly gifts. Gold. Frankincense. Myrrh.

Lord Jesus, we worship you as our true King. We joyfully abandon ourselves to you and offer ourselves for your service and for the service of your people. We lay our lives at your feet. We offer to you whatever we hold most dear. You are our King. Alleluia!

Monday, January 5, 2004 St. John Neumann
Matthew 4, 12-17; 23-25
The Beginning of the Galilean Ministry;
Ministry to a Great Multitude

Jesus moved from Nazareth to live by the sea in Capernaum. He had endured severe testing in the wilderness and had triumphed over the temptations of the devil (Matthew 4, 1-11). John the Baptist had been arrested. It was time to move.

It was in Capernaum and throughout the synagogues of the Galilee that Jesus began to proclaim the kingdom of heaven. He illuminated the kingdom.

What was this kingdom like? What is it like when God reigns?

Jesus showed us. Health! In God's kingdom, people are healthy.

Jesus cured every kind of sickness. Pain? Paralysis? Possession? No problem. Jesus healed every kind of ailment.

Lord Jesus, move into our lives and illumine our lives. Where we have sat in darkness, shine your light. Thank you for healing us and shining through us. Alleluia!

Tuesday, January 6, 2004 Blessed Andre Bessette
Mark 6, 34-44
The Feeding of the Five Thousand

Jesus graciously took what he was given and looked to heaven. Then he blessed the five loaves, broke them, and gave them to his disciples to give to the people.

This was not a mechanical miracle. The tender shepherd heart of Jesus was touched as he looked at the people. They were so much like lost, forlorn sheep. He gave them the gentle and wise teaching they needed. He gave them the food they needed for sustenance.

Lord Jesus, you are the same shepherd who fed your lambs on the green grass of Galilee. At times, we may be like the bewildered, forlorn sheep of that day. At other times, we may be like the disciples who wondered about the supply of food. We may believe that we don't have enough to offer you. Today, we offer you what we do have. We offer ourselves for your service. Thank you for the miracle of love you will perform in us and through us today. Alleluia!

Wednesday, January 7, 2004 St. Raymond Penafort
Mark 6, 45-52
The Walking on the Water

Jesus! Truly God. Truly human.

Jesus needed a break. He needed space. He needed solitude. He had spent a significant time teaching the multitude and then feeding them from the five loaves and two fish.

He directed his disciples to go ahead of him in the boat to the other side of the Sea of Galilee. He withdrew to the mountain for solitude and prayer.

The disciples' boat was being rocked in more ways than one. The boat was tossed about by the gusts of wind on the sea. Sometime, between three and six in the morning, Jesus, having observed his disciples' dilemma, went to them to reassure them.

The poor guys! They were already battling the wind and the waves. Then they saw someone walking on the water headed straight for them!

Jesus reassured them by reminding them of who he was. He told them to have courage and not be afraid. As soon as he entered their boat, the wild wind ceased. Although, the disciples were comforted, they still did not understand many things about Jesus.

Lord Jesus, Thank you that we are not really out there alone in the storms of life. You understand where we are. You are watching over us and you are with us. Alleluia!

Thursday, January 8, 2004
Luke 4, 14-22
The Beginning of the Galilean Ministry
The Rejection at Nazareth

The Holy Spirit. The Holy Spirit. The Holy Spirit.

Jesus, after his baptism, was filled with the Holy Spirit and then led by the Holy Spirit into the wilderness for a time of testing (Luke 4, 1-2). When he returned to Galilee, he was filled with the power of the Holy Spirit.

Filled. Led. Empowered.

All seemed to be going well for him at that time. He read from Isaiah one particular Sabbath in the synagogue in Nazareth. He read the beautiful passage about the Holy Spirit, the Spirit of the Lord (Isaiah 61, 1-2).

The Holy Spirit was upon Jesus. The Holy Spirit anointed Jesus to proclaim the amazingly good news of God's favor. After Jesus had finished reading from the scroll, he announced that this prophecy had just been fulfilled.

Lord Jesus, the Holy Spirit was clearly working in you and through you throughout your earthly ministry. The Holy Spirit would lead you from the praise of all through the rejection of all. The Holy Spirit would lead you through all your suffering, your death, burial, and resurrection, all the way back home to your loving Father in heaven. Send the Holy Spirit to strengthen us today for the fulfilling of the Father's plan for our lives. Alleluia!

Friday, January 9, 2004
Luke 5, 12-16
The Cleansing of a Leper

Love. Law. Teaching. Solitude. Balance.

Jesus' love and compassion for the leper was expressed by healing the man. To the leper's hesitancy about Jesus' willingness to heal, Jesus responded that of course he would heal him!

Jesus showed his respect for the law of Moses by directing the man to go to the priest to have the healing verified. After the verification, the one cleansed from leprosy would be required to make an offering (Leviticus 14).

Jesus continued to minister to the crowds. They gathered to listen to his teaching and to seek healing.

Solitude. After these times of active ministry, Jesus knew he needed solitude. He withdrew to pray.

Lord Jesus, you showed by your words and deeds that you did not come to destroy the Law of Moses. You came to fulfill the Law. Your life was in balance. You ministered to others and you took time to pray and to be alone. If you needed this balance during your time on earth, how much more do we need balance in our own lives. Help us to stop pushing ourselves into a state of depletion and then have the nerve to call it ministry. Please bring the stability and symmetry for which we yearn. Provide for us the times and the places where we may rest and be restored. Alleluia!

> Saturday, January 10, 2004
> John 3, 22-20
> Final Witness of John the Baptist

John was joyful! He knew who he was and who he was not. He was not the Messiah. He had specifically been assigned the mission of preparing the way for Jesus, the Anointed One, the Messiah.

This single vision empowered John to step firmly and decisively through the controversies surrounding his ministry and the ministry of Jesus. His ministry was to refer people to Jesus, the Lamb of God.

John exhibited no jealousy about Jesus because he knew that Jesus was the Messiah, the Bridegroom. John's privilege was to be the best man and to rejoice in Jesus.

Lord Jesus, we waste so much time and energy trying to be someone we are not. Show us who we really are. Help us to rejoice in who you are and in who we are. Alleluia!

> Sunday, January 11, 2004 The Baptism of the Lord
> Luke 3, 15-16, 21-22
> The Preaching of John the Baptist; The Baptism of Jesus

Identity and vocation. John the Baptist knew who he was and who he was not. His identity was safe and secure. He knew he was not the Messiah.

John knew his vocation. He was sent to preach, to baptize, and to prepare the people for Jesus, the Christ, the Anointed One, the Messiah.

The heavenly Father proclaimed the identity of Jesus at his baptism. Jesus was God's own Son, his beloved. Jesus' identity was safe and secure.

As John indicated, it was Jesus who would baptize with the Holy Spirit and with purifying and refining fire. The Holy Spirit descended upon Jesus at his baptism to confirm his vocation.

Lord Jesus, after your water baptism, while you were praying, heaven did indeed open! Your Father spoke, confirming your identity as his beloved Son. Your Father was so pleased with you, so proud of you. The Holy Spirit, in actual physical form, like a dove, rested upon you.

Thank you that we are also God's beloved children. Our identity is safe and secure. Thank you that the Holy Spirit will give us the power to fulfill our vocation to follow you. Alleluia!

> Monday, January 12, 2004
> Mark 1, 14-20
> The Beginning of the Galilean Ministry;
> The Call of the First Disciples

Fishermen or fishers of men? What a difference a little preposition makes.

Andrew and his brother Simon (Peter) and James and his brother John relinquished their nets to go on another fishing expedition. Fishing with Jesus was going to be the fishing trip of their lives.

Lord Jesus, thank you for the early apostles and their successors who were fishers of souls to bring us into your kingdom. Alleluia!

> Tuesday, January 13, 2004 St. Hilary
> Mark 1, 21-28
> The Cure of a Demoniac

The man in the synagogue had what a friend of mine calls "company." Unwelcome company. He was not himself. However dreadful it seems, evil, unclean entities of some sort had taken up residency within him.

Jesus did not suggest digging around in the man's past to try and figure out the how or the why of the man's condition. Neither did he ask the man to confess his sins. Jesus, with strong authority, simply commanded the vile entity to get out! The man was then free!

Lord Jesus, if we have uninvited, unwelcome company, speak the word and set us free. Alleluia!

> Wednesday, January 14, 2004
> Mark 1, 29-39
> The Cure of Simon's Mother-in-Law; Jesus Leaves Capernaum

Jesus did not have to advertise his ministry. He simply lived before God and ministry happened. Jesus lived immersed in God's presence.

In today's Gospel, Jesus left the synagogue where he had just cast a demon out of a man. James and John accompanied Jesus to the home of Simon (Peter) and his brother Andrew. Since Peter's mother-in-law was feverish and ill, Jesus simply took her hand and helped her get up. She was well!

Later that same evening, the people in Capernaum flocked to Peter's house. Jesus healed many people and cast out many demons. Quite a day.

Even so, before dawn, Jesus left to seek silence, solitude, and time in the presence of God. Although he always lived in God's presence, he needed specific times alone with his Abba.

Peter and others searched for him and found him. Jesus invited them to go with him to other villages in the Galilee where he continued to preach and to cast evil spirits out of people.

Lord Jesus, you consistently immersed yourself consciously in the presence of your Father. You did not have to seek out opportunities to minister. People came to you out of their need. Let us know that our greatest need is to spend time consciously in your presence. As we get to know you, we will begin to reflect your love and your power. You will bring to us opportunities to serve. Alleluia!

Thursday, January 15, 2004
Mark 1, 40-45
The Cleansing of a Leper

Clean. Strong. Whole. Restored.

When Jesus, in his compassion, touched the leper kneeling before him, he did more than effect a skin-deep cure. He made it possible for the man to be restored to his community after the priest had confirmed the cure.

Leprosy of the soul (the mind, will, and emotions) is also tragic, as is leprosy of the spirit. It is possible to endure sickness, "... but a wounded spirit -- who can bear? (Proverbs 18, 14b)" When life has wounded and crushed us, we may have interior leprosy even when our skin is radiant and healthy.

No condition of body, soul, or spirit is beyond the Lord's reach. Jesus can touch our innermost secret wounds and bring us to wholeness.

Lord Jesus, thank you that you are healing the wounds we may have tried to hide from you, from others, and even from ourselves. You know the true origin of our wounds. You are restoring us by making us clean and whole. Alleluia!

Friday, January 16, 2004
Mark 2, 1-12
The Healing of a Paralytic

Nothing is impossible when Jesus is involved! Nothing baffles Jesus. He can forgive sins. He can restore life and mobility of body, soul, and spirit.

The ingenious friends of the paralytic were not about to be blocked. Too many people to get to Jesus? No problem. They found a creative solution! Somehow they carried their friend on his mat up to the roof and then let him down through an opening they had made.

Jesus was deeply affected by this kind of sturdy faith with its implicit trust that he could and would heal. Jesus started with the greatest healing. He gently told the man that his sins were forgiven. Then, in the presence of the skeptical scribes and all the onlookers, he told the man to get up, collect his mat, and to go on home. The forgiven paralytic was now walking around. Amazing!

Lord Jesus, we bring to you any seemingly intractable, impossible condition in our lives or in the lives of those for whom we pray. We release our faith and trust to know that you will speak the word to forgive us, to heal us and to reactivate us. Alleluia!

Saturday, January 17, 2004
Mark 2, 13-17
The Calling of Levi

Jesus came specifically to call sinners. They knew they were sick! Jesus is the physician who knows what truly ails us and knows how to help us.

We must not criticize those we consider sinners. That was the problem with the scribes and the Pharisees. They could not rejoice that Jesus was calling those whom they considered inferior to be his first followers.

Lord Jesus, thank you for calling Levi (Matthew) to follow you. You were glad to be at his house, at his table, to share conversation as well as food. Matthew and his friends were comfortable with you. Come into the house of our bodies, souls and spirits and examine our diet. What have we been feeding on? Have we been eating the bread of bitterness? Have we been consuming fear and anxiety? Thank you for calling us to be with you. Thank you for feeding us in Word and sacrament. In your presence, we will begin to find the peace and the healing we need. Alleluia!

Sunday, January 18, 2004 Second Sunday in Ordinary Time
John 2, 1-12
The Wedding at Cana

The third day. A reference to the third day (after Jesus' encounter with Nathanael and Philip) precedes the account of Jesus' first miracle in the village of Cana of Galilee.

At the wedding in Cana, Jesus transformed six large stone jars of water, intended for purification rites, into wine! Each jar held around twenty of thirty gallons of water. After this miracle, this first sign, the disciples of Jesus believed in him. An understatement!

The third day. In the first account of creation, it was on the third day that God collected the water and referred to it as the sea. The earth began to bring forth vegetation. Fruit trees blossomed and bore fruit continually from their seeds (Genesis 1, 9-13).

The third day. It was on the third day that the anxious Mary and Joseph found the twelve year old Jesus in the temple in Jerusalem (Luke 2, 41-52).

The third day. It was on the third day that Jesus, after his crucifixion, arose, triumphant over death (Mark 8, 31). The supreme sign.

Lord Jesus, thank you for this first sign, on the third day. Sometimes our lives seem like the still, motionless water cramped into stone jars. Thank you for your perfect timing to transform us, to give us new life whenever our third day arrives. Help us to trust, as Mary, that you will work your will in us and through us. Alleluia!

Monday, January 19, 2004
Mark 2, 18-22
The Question about Fasting

Joy! Jesus is about joy!

In yesterday's Gospel, we read of the extravagant, yet quiet, transformation of simple water into exquisite wine. Jesus is neither miserly nor miserable.

578

Some people, poor dears, just could not understand why Jesus' disciples were not fasting. After all, the disciples of the Pharisees and even the disciples of John the Baptist were fasting.

Some people only understand the following of certain rules. They are not yet able to understand joy. They truly think that pleasing God is only about keeping rules and regulations.

Jesus made it clear that he had not come to destroy the Law, but rather to fulfill the Law, to bring it to completion (Matthew 5, 17-20). Jesus came so that we could have life in abundance (John 10, 10)! Life includes joy!

Jesus offered two simple examples of what he was trying to convey. One example was about attempting to patch an old garment with new cloth. The second was of trying to pour fresh new wine into weary old wineskins. These ways just do not work.

Jesus was not instructing people not to fast. He assumed that his disciples would give alms, pray, and fast (Matthew 6, 1-16). During his brief time on earth, however, it was not the appropriate time to fast. It was the time to celebrate! Jesus was the Bridegroom.

Lord Jesus, we still don't get it. We still try to pour old ways into the new. It still does not work. Maybe we have grown exhausted trying to serve you in tired old ways. Fill us anew with your Holy Spirit. Breathe new life into us. Let us find joy in experiencing your love. Everything else will follow. Alleluia!

Tuesday, January 20, 2004 Sts. Fabian and Sebastian
Mark 2, 23-38
The Disciples and the Sabbath

The hungry disciples made a path through the fields of grain. As they walked along, they picked some of the grains to eat. The ever-vigilant Pharisees had a holy fit and asked Jesus how he could allow his followers to do what was considered unlawful on the Sabbath. Jesus reminded the Pharisees that David and his hungry men were given permission by the priest to eat the bread which was considered holy (1 Samuel 21, 2-7).

Jesus is Lord! Jesus is Lord of the Sabbath and Lord of our lives.

We commit idolatry when we try to deify human made rules. These rules, good though they may be, are not Lord. Jesus is Lord!

Our fears, phobias, and worries are not Lord. Our sins and failures and unfulfilled, inarticulate longings are not Lord. Jesus is Lord.

Lord Jesus, thank you that your authority is supreme. You have the authority to forgive our sins, to feed us with the Bread of Heaven, and to teach us to live joyfully in Sabbath rest. Alleluia!

Wednesday, January 21, 2004 St. Agnes
Mark 3, 1-6
A Man with a Withered Hand

The Pharisees were watching Jesus like a hawk. Jesus, however, responded with the power of a dove. Jesus, filled with the Holy Spirit, responded to the need of the person before him, instead of caving in to the criticism of the Pharisees. He looked upon the Pharisees with a mixture of anger and grief.

Here was a suffering person in the synagogue on the Sabbath. The Pharisees cared more about appearance and power than they did about people. Jesus put people first, especially the sick, the sinful, and the suffering. He loved them and he had come expressly for them. They knew they needed him.

Jesus healed the man with the withered hand, even though it was the Sabbath. Jesus was Lord of the Sabbath, remember?

Lord Jesus, we need you and you are here to heal. You responded with a holy blend of anger and grief to the hard hearts of the Pharisees of your day because their surface spirituality was so pathetic and so injurious to the people in their care. Help us to remember that we are living before you and before the angels and the saints. Help us to love you and serve you by responding to the needs of those before us. Alleluia!

Thursday, January 22, 2004 St. Vincent
Mark 3, 7-12
The Mercy of Jesus

Bounty and boundaries. The mercy, power, and compassion of Jesus flowed bountifully to all the people. He was almost overwhelmed by the multitudes thronging to him for healing.

Jesus knowing that balance and boundaries were crucial for his own survival, withdrew to the seashore, where his disciples kept a boat in readiness for him. He cared so deeply and yet his mercy and compassion had to extend to himself.

580

Lord Jesus, when you walked this earth, you were pursued by the multitudes. Even the unclean spirits were in awe of you. You were God and all-powerful. You were human and vulnerable. In whatever way we are called to serve you, show us how to extend mercy to ourselves as well as to others. Alleluia!

Friday, January 23, 2004
Mark 3, 13-19
The Mission of the Twelve

To be with Jesus. That was the first privilege of the twelve. Before being sent forth in public ministry, they were called to be with Jesus.

To be with Jesus is our greatest privilege. Immersed in his presence, we will be formed, transformed, and conformed into his image and likeness (Romans 8, 29). Everything else will follow.

To be with Jesus is our greatest need. Jesus knows all about us and longs for us to be with him and to spend time alone with him without an agenda.

Jesus knew all about Peter and the others he had chosen to be apostles. He knew about John and James, those sons of thunder! What fiery tempers they must have had. Jesus still called them. Jesus even called Judas.

Lord Jesus, thank you for the high calling and privilege of being with you. Before we venture forth on a mission for you, let us first learn how to be quiet and still in your presence. Let us learn to discern your voice. Thank you for sending us on the mission you have chosen for us. Thank you for the times when we fulfill your will without fully understanding it. Let us carry your strength and your peace with us into the world. Alleluia!

Saturday, January 24, 2004 St. Francis de Sales
Mark 3, 20-21
Blasphemy of the Scribes

It is always easier to reject and to accuse than to try to understand. Understanding requires honesty and humility.

This is a very jarring, short account of the insistent crowds pressing around Jesus, disrupting even the ability of Jesus and the others to have a meal. To add to the confusion, some of Jesus' relatives questioned his sanity!

We have to draw back, sometimes, and really consider our motives? What is driving us? Need for security? Need for endless affirmation?

Forget it. Ponder the words of Scottish poet, William Dunbar, who advised, "… please thy Maker and be merry.…"

Lord Jesus, you had to live with a fixed determination to do your Father's will, regardless of what anyone thought of you. Help us not to be so dependent on human approval. Let us learn to please you and to be merry. Alleluia!

Sunday, January 25, 2003 Third Sunday in Ordinary Time
Luke 1, 1-4; 4, 14-21
The Prologue; The Beginning of the Galilean Ministry;
The Rejection at Nazareth

Luke carefully acknowledged previous writings about the life of Jesus. He then offered his own meticulous account of our Lord's years on earth.

Jesus was to experience both human praise and human rejection as he fulfilled ancient prophecies. The ones truly sent by God always experience some form of rejection by the world, the church, or both. They are not living for the applause of others. They are living for God, for God's purposes, and for God's glory.

Still, rejection is not pleasant, especially among those we expect to understand us. Jesus experienced praise as he taught on one particular Sabbath in the synagogue in Nazareth. In the very near future, his quiet confidence in his vocation would prove a bit too much for the folks in this synagogue.

Nazareth. Hometown. Nazareth, where everyone knew Jesus.

How in the world could Jesus, supposedly the carpenter's son, get up right there in the synagogue, their synagogue, and say that the Isaiah prophecy (Isaiah 61, 1-2) he had just read was now fulfilled in their hearing. Fulfilled? Now?

What on earth was Jesus talking about? You can almost see the eyes popping and the necks being scratched in perplexity. Jesus? What on earth?

What would you think if, on Sunday, the lector read the assigned Scripture, sat down, and then announced that an ancient prophecy had just been fulfilled?! Would you thank God or would you think the person was just nuts?

Yet Jesus, the Christ, was filled with the Holy Spirit and anointed to bring Good News to the poor. God the Father had sent Jesus to inform the captives that they were now free! The captives were free and the blind would see!

Lord Jesus, you came to minister in Galilee after your time of testing and temptation in the wilderness. You were filled with the Holy Spirit. You were flowing in God's plan and purpose for your life. Deliver us from any notion that following you will be easy. Steel us and strengthen us to follow you to the end when we will see you face to face! Alleluia!

Monday, January 26, 2004 Sts. Timothy and Titus
Mark 3, 22-30
Blasphemy of the Scribes; Jesus and Beelzebul

At first I thought the heading was "blasting" of the scribes! I write these reflections in early morning with a cup of coffee and my writing is a little scribbly. It is sometimes a challenge to decipher my own writing when I type the reflection later in the morning.

In a way, Jesus did blast the scribes. The scribes, the ones who were supposed to be the great legal scholars, did not show a high degree of spiritual intelligence when they ascribed the works of Jesus to the prince of the demons. They even said Jesus was possessed. Jesus had to confront them.

Confronting his accusers in parables, Jesus asked how Satan could drive out Satan. Double duh. An internally divided kingdom cannot stand. A divided family cannot stand. Certainly a divided Satan could not stand.

Then Jesus confronted the scholars directly. He told them that God will forgive all sins and all. blasphemies. However, blasphemy against the Holy Spirit of God will never be forgiven. It is an eternal sin. If we are sensitive enough to worry that we have committed this sin, it is unlikely that we have.

Lord Jesus, the Holy Spirit was the explanation of all your mighty works. Thank you that you are strong and that you are guarding us. No one can break in and steal us from you. We are safe with you. Alleluia!

583

Tuesday, January 27, 2004 St. Angela Merici
Mark 3, 31-35
Jesus and His Family

There is an ache, a yearning in the human heart for family, for a place to belong and to be accepted and welcomed. There is a legitimate need for protection, security, and the freedom to give and to receive love.

The mother and brothers of Jesus arrived on the scene at a time when Jesus was engaged in speaking to a large group of people. They were sitting all around him, listening to the words of life he offered them. Jesus was not going to be distracted even by his mother and his brothers.

Jesus used this interruption to offer his definition of family. The one who does God's will is the sister, the brother, and the mother of Jesus. Jesus simultaneously contracted and expanded our concept of family.

Lord Jesus, thank you for being our brother. Thank you for giving us a place in your family where we are safe and loved. Thank you for increasing in us the desire to know and to do God's will. Thank you for all our brothers and sisters in your family. Thank you for a glimpse in this life of the family reunion awaiting us in heaven, where God's will is always done. Alleluia!

Wednesday, January 28, 2004 St. Thomas Aquinas
Mark 4, 1-20
The Parable of the Sower

In the past, the condition of the soil and the predisposition of the hearer of the word have been my primary concerns in reflecting on this Gospel. Today is different.

In the present, I am more interested in the sower. We all are sowers in one way or another. What kind of words am I sowing? Am I more concerned with what I sow or with the response to the words sown?

In the future, I long to sow healthy thoughts that will lead to life-giving words. I want to sow life-giving words that will lead to transformation in my life and in the lives of those for whom I pray.

Lord Jesus, thank you for the parable of the sower. Help me to say and to sow today the words you give me. Thank you for the time of harvest. Alleluia!

Thursday, January 29, 2004
Mark 4, 21-25
Parable of the Lamp

Even more! The way we measure will be measured back to us, and even more.

The lamp will not be forever frustrated in fulfilling its purpose. One day, it will be placed on a lampstand. The lamp is meant to be filled with light. It is meant to shine! God knows what will be brought to light through our lives.

Lord Jesus, this seems a mysterious Gospel, yet a Gospel shining with promise. With whatever understanding we possess, let us listen carefully to you and receive even more understanding. Let your presence within us shine forth from us. Pour your words and your light into us even more. Alleluia!

Friday, January 30, 2004
Mark 4, 26-34
Seed Grows of Itself; The Mustard Seed

The kingdom of God is so amazing that Jesus told picturesque parables about it. Little glimpses of understanding began to flash into the minds and hearts of the multitudes who listened to him. To his own committed disciples, Jesus taught with more precision and in greater depth.

The mustard seed simply needed to be sown. Although tiny and seemingly insignificant, it grew to be strong and quite large, a shelter of shade for the birds of the air.

Sow and sleep. Making the seed grow is not within my power. I can only sow the seed and go about my life. God does the rest. I may as well learn to trust God with the sown seed.

Lord Jesus, help me simply and quietly to do the work of sowing and then trust you to bring a golden harvest. Alleluia!

Saturday, January 31, 2004 St. John Bosco
Mark 4, 35-41
The Calming of a Storm at Sea

As he was? Other boats?

These two little phrases puzzled me and sent me to other translations and then to an interlinear new testament. Hopefully, my seminary professor of New Testament Greek won't read this, since I did not immediately go to the original Greek!

What happened, perhaps, was that Jesus was already in the boat. The disciples just got in and off they went across the Sea of Galilee.

We don't know about the other boats mentioned in the Gospel, but we do know about the boat of Jesus and his disciples. Although the storm raged and the water sloshed over and into the boat, Jesus was sound asleep!

The disciples were scared out of their wits. They even wondered if Jesus cared about them. How could he just sleep? To make sure he was aware of the storm, they awakened him.

Jesus simply spoke to the wind and it ceased raging. Calm. Perfect calm. Perhaps an eerie calm. Jesus asked his disciples why they had been so afraid.

Lord Jesus, I am not getting into a boat and then asking you to come along for the ride. You are already in the boat of my life. You are there and you are in charge. Thank you that your authority is greater than the storms. Alleluia!

Sunday, February 1, 2004 Fourth Sunday of Ordinary Time
Luke 4, 21-30
The Rejection at Nazareth

Jesus passed through praise and condemnation with equal grace. He knew who he was. He did not need to play politics. He was secure in his Father's love. He was on earth on his Father's mission of redemption.

His words brought praise and his words brought condemnation. His words were gracious. He spoke of the fulfillment of the beautiful passage from Isaiah. His word cut to the quick.

Jesus referred to the great prophets Elijah and Elisha. Elijah, the prophet who would call down fire from heaven (1 Kings 18), was previously sent on a mercy mission to a poor widow, not in Israel, but in Sidon (1 Kings 17). Elisha, the prophet who succeeded Elijah, was God's instrument in the healing a leper, not in Israel, but in Syria (2 Kings 5).

Lord Jesus, the people in the synagogue received your words into their ears, but not into their hearts. You did not need to prove yourself.

586

You were the prophet who not only spoke God's word, but indeed you were God's Word! You did not need to heal yourself. You were the Physician sent to heal others. You knew that true prophets are not welcome on their native turf. Thank you for leading us in peace, power, and purpose as we pass through this world on your mission. Alleluia!

Monday, February 2, 2004 The Presentation of the Lord
Luke 2, 2-40
The Presentation in the Temple; The Return to Nazareth

Jesus to Jerusalem! How many times in his life would he go to Jerusalem?

This was probably the first time. Jesus was carried as a forty day old infant to be dedicated to God in the Temple. Mary and Joseph were too poor to offer a lamb for a sacrifice, so they offered two young doves.

Simeon, the aged Simeon, was waiting for Jesus in the Temple in Jerusalem. Simeon reverently held the infant Messiah in his arms and prayed in thanksgiving for being allowed to see the Savior.

Anna, the aged prophet Anna, was also in the Temple in Jerusalem. She also thanked God and spoke of the Child who would redeem Jerusalem.

Jesus was then carried as an infant to the Galilee, to the town of Nazareth. With God's favor upon him, Jesus grew in wisdom and in strength as well as in years.

Lord Jesus, you would eventually return to Jerusalem to suffer and to die as the sacrificial Lamb of God. You said that it was impossible for a prophet to be killed anywhere but Jerusalem. (Luke 13, 33). As you were dedicated to God in Jerusalem, we dedicate ourselves to you on this day, Candlemas, to shine as your lights in this dark world. We long for your return in glory and for the radiant manifestation of the new Jerusalem. Alleluia!

Tuesday, February 3, 2004 St. Blasé, St. Ansgar
Mark 5, 21-43
Jairus's Daughter and the Woman with a Hemorrhage

Fear-based or faith-based? How do we live?

Someone said that fear activates Satan and that faith activates God. All I know is that fear paralyzes and that faith energizes.

Jesus told the twelve year old girl who had died to get up, to arise! He told the dead son of the widow of Nain to get up, to arise (Luke 7, 11-17).

Some high and holy, perhaps desperate, kind of faith energized the woman who touched Jesus' cloak She pushed through her fear and reached Jesus. She had gone to earthly physicians for twelve long years and they had been unable to help her. She touched Jesus and was healed in an instant! He told her that her trust in him had healed her.

Some high and holy, perhaps desperate, kind of faith also energized Jairus, a synagogue official, to push through the crowd and come to Jesus. Surely, he experienced fear and yet his love for his daughter and his trust in Jesus were greater than the fear.

Once, at the Pelican Inn at Muir Beach, I read the inscription over the fireplace. "Fear knocked at the door. Faith answered. No one was there." My version would be, "Fear knocked at the door. Faith answered the door anyway. Jesus was there!"

Lord Jesus, thank you for your love and your mercy for those of us who have lived so long with fear. Please fill us with renewed confidence that will energize us to take the next step in trusting you. Alleluia!

Wednesday, February 4, 2004
Mark 6, 1-6
The Rejection at Nazareth; The Mission of the Twelve

Jesus left Nazareth. He continued his mission and his ministry elsewhere.

The people in Nazareth presumed that they knew all about Jesus. To them, he was merely a member of the village carpenter's family. What could be so great about that?

Then, one Sabbath in the synagogue, they were marveling at his wise teaching. The next moment they were huffy and offended. They rejected him.

Jesus knew that a prophet is honored and esteemed except by his own kith and kin. He left Nazareth, after compassionately healing several sick people.

Lord Jesus, you left Nazareth, but your mission was not stopped, only expanded. Thank you for giving us the strength to remain and to bloom where we are planted. Thank you also for the times when we are root-bound and you mercifully transplant us to a larger place. Alleluia!

Thursday, February 5, 2004 St. Agatha
Mark 6, 7-13
The Mission of the Twelve

First the summons. Then the sending. Then the authority for ministry. Then the specific instructions for the particular mission. It all goes together. It's a package deal!

First of all Jesus called and summoned the Twelve to himself. I was reminded of the poem, "The Call," by George Herbert, which begins, "Come, my Way, my Truth, my Life."

Jesus then sent the Twelve out in pairs. He gave them authority to drive out unclean spirits. He gave them instructions for the journey regarding food, clothes, and money. They were to accept hospitality, but not to remain where they were unwelcome. They were told not only to leave, but also to shake the very dust off their feet.

So off they went! They had responded to the call to be with Jesus. Then they learned from him. They observed how he lived, how he prayed, and how he ministered to people.

Then, and only then, Jesus sent them out, armed with his authority and instructed in his ways. They proclaimed repentance. They cast out evil spirits. They anointed sick people with oil and many were healed.

Lord Jesus, when I start to feel weary and depleted, help me to remember that I need to return to you, my first love, and to spend time in your presence and continue to learn from you. Thank you that you are in charge of my life and my vocation. Alleluia!

Friday, February 6, 2004 St. Paul Miki and Companions
Mark 6, 14-19
Herod's Opinion of Jesus; The Death of John the Baptist

A life lived for God never dies. There is a power in holiness that transcends death. John the Baptist exemplifies this truth.

Herod, the king, was a tormented man. He knew what was right and refused to do it. He knew that John the Baptist was a holy man, a man who lived for God and who spoke the truth.

Herod cared more for the opinions of others, in this case, the guests at his birthday party. His logic was perversely and tragically flawed and twisted. Did he really believe that it was right to authorize the murder of an innocent person in order to save face?

Herods are still here. Herodiuses are still here. They live for image and power. They nurture grudges and eagerly look for ways to retaliate if they feel threatened or thwarted. None of us is exempt from these temptations.

Those who live for God are still here, also. They are not perfect. They have sins, flaws and failures, but they know what to do with them. They take them to Jesus to receive forgiveness and healing. Then they continue on the path of holiness. The writer to the Hebrews referred to the holiness without which we will not see the Lord (Hebrews 12, 14).

Lord Jesus, thank you for living for the praise and the purpose of your Father in heaven. Help us to live this day for you, for your praise and for your purpose. Thank you for the example of the holy prophet, John the Baptist. Thank you for the power in holiness that transcends death Alleluia!

Saturday, February 7, 2004
Mark 6, 30-34
The Mission of the Twelve; The Feeding of the Five Thousand

Some retreats are shorter than others! What matters is not the duration or the location of the retreat, but the presence of Jesus.

The Twelve were excitedly telling Jesus all about their mission. Jesus wisely recommended that they take some time away, in a quiet place, to rest. The atmosphere around them was so hectic and frantic with the crowds of people that there was not even a chance to eat.

So Jesus and the Twelve took a boat across the lake with the intention of going away to a quiet place for awhile. Alas, the eager crowds saw them embark and managed to arrive at the place of retreat before Jesus and the Twelve.

When Jesus left the boat and saw the multitude waiting for him, he felt deep compassion for them. They were like poor, hungry lost sheep in need of a shepherd.

What about the Twelve? Well, they did have the time with Jesus in the boat. The trip across the lake was their retreat.

Lord Jesus, thank you for your presence with us and within us. You are our refuge. Thank you that each day with you has spaces for silence. Thank you that each day with you brings us opportunities for reaching out to your lambs and your sheep. Alleluia!

Sunday, February 8, 2004 Fifth Sunday of Ordinary Time
Luke 5, 1-11
The Call of Simon the Fisherman

The fear that seized Simon (later to be called Peter) was the fear that seizes all of us when we have a God-given glimpse into who Jesus is and who we are. Simon, seeing the miraculous, inexplicable catch of fish, fell before Jesus and begged him to depart.

At that moment all Simon could see was his own sinfulness. He was overwhelmed, defenseless in the presence of such love and such power.

The best antidote to pride is a sense of one's own sinfulness in the presence of God's purity and holiness. This cannot be worked up or manufactured. It is a gift, an aweful gift.

We may pray for the grace to see what God wants us to see about ourselves and then pray for the grace to repent. The Holy Spirit is with us to help us in our prayers.

Jesus, the gentle Lord, told the fisherman not to be afraid. From then on, Simon Peter would be catching people.

Lord Jesus, you stepped from the lakeside into Simon's boat. Simon, skeptical, yet obedient, lowered his nets because of your word. From empty nets to nets bursting with flashing fish! Poor Peter. You spoke gently to him. You speak gently to us. You are calling us to get up, to receive the forgiveness you offer, to forsake our fears, and to follow you. Alleluia!

Monday, February 9, 2004
Mark 6, 53-56
The Healings at Gennesaret

Jesus had barely stepped out of the boat on the shore of the lake before people rushed to him for healing. As he traveled through the countryside and the villages, the sick were brought to him. Merely touching the edge of his mantle, his cloak, brought healing.

591

Lord Jesus, we don't have to rush around looking for you. You are right here with us. The Holy Spirit lives within us. We may not know what is wrong with us. We may not be able to articulate what kind of healing we need. You know. We reach out to you at this moment. Thank you for making us strong and whole. Alleluia!

Tuesday, February 10, 2004 St. Scholastica
Mark 7, 1-13
The Tradition of the Elders

Jesus hated to see people hurt by so-called religion. He hated to see the religious leaders bully people. He knew what it was to experience a combination of anger and grief at the hardness of heart of some of the leaders (Mark 3, 1-6).

The shepherd heart of Jesus was outraged by abuse of power. The power to serve and to lead had been distorted into ways in which the leaders could flaunt themselves and justify their own rules. They were deluded and were corrupt to the core. They served themselves, not God.

Nothing new. Centuries before, Isaiah had referred to this evil. Isaiah had referred to routine ritual and to lip service devoid of heart service (Isaiah 29, 13). Nothing new.

Lord Jesus, you are the Good Shepherd, the Chief Shepherd, and the Head of the Church. Help us to worship you with all our hearts. Heal our hearts when they have been wounded, bruised, or crushed. Alleluia!

Wednesday, February 11, 2004 Our Lady of Lourdes
Mark 7, 14-23
The Tradition of the Elders

Within or without? Outside or inside? Jesus said that whatever enters from the outside cannot hurt or defile a person. It is that which comes from within that causes harm.

Years later, the writer to the Hebrews warned against allowing a bitter root from within to spring up. If it springs up and grows, trouble may result and many may be defiled (Hebrews 12, 15).

It is the inner thought life that concerns Jesus. From the secret recesses of the human heart, unhealthy and evil thoughts may arise which may result in harmful actions.

King David had learned this long ago. He prayed that God would create a pure and clean heart within him (Psalm 51, 12). He also prayed that God would search, probe, and examine his heart and then lead him in the right way (Psalm 139, 23-24).

Lord Jesus, when I have strong reactions to other people or to events, it is my own heart revealing itself. When I react in hurt or anger, please look within the depths of my heart and forgive me and heal me. Help me to look to you and ask for your help before responding to others. Thank you for your love, wisdom, and patience as you continue to transform me into your image. Alleluia!

Thursday, February 12, 2004
Mark 7, 24-30
The Syrophoenician Woman's Faith

Mark's telling of this story is clipped and cursory. Yes, the woman was culturally considered an outsider, a Gentile. No, Jesus did not let the fact that she was not Jewish stop him from healing her suffering daughter.

Matthew's telling of the same story adds the commendation of the compassionate Jesus. Not only did Jesus heal the daughter, but he also commended the mother for her confidence and trust in him. He called her a woman of great faith (Matthew 15, 28).

Lord Jesus, when we feel like unwelcome outsiders, help us to remember that you are with us, you love us, and you will act on our behalf. Alleluia!

Friday, February 13, 2004
Mark 7, 31-37
The Healing of a Deaf Man

Through a circuitous journey, Jesus arrived at last in the area around the Sea of Galilee which was within the borders of the ten cities. It was there that the man in an inner prison of silence was freed both to hear and to speak. Who knows his interior life before Jesus took him aside and prayed for him?

Jesus not only prayed for him, looking up to heaven, but he also agonized in prayer for him. Jesus must have known the years of silent frustration the man had endured. When Jesus commanded the man's ears to open, the silent man was free at last! At last he could hear others! At last, he himself had a voice. He was allowed to speak. Jesus had given him a voice.

Lord Jesus, it seems a long, slow, circuitous path to be able truly to hear others and truly to be allowed to speak the words you have given us to speak. Thank you for giving us courage, patience, and hope as we wait for our ears to be opened and for our tongue to be released. We will praise you all the more. Alleluia!

Saturday, February 14, 2004 Sts. Cyril and Methodius
Mark 8, 1-10
The Feeding of the Four Thousand

Jesus knows how far we can travel and how much we can endure without losing our strength. He is here to sustain us and to energize us to continue the journey.

The crowd had been drinking in Jesus' teaching for three days and were now heading home. Deeply moved by their devotion and concerned for their temporal as well as spiritual needs, Jesus, the compassionate Shepherd, was eager to feed them.

Jesus asked his disciples what they had on hand. Taking the seven loaves, Jesus offered a prayer of thanksgiving, broke the bread, and gave it back to his disciples. The disciples had the joyful privilege of distributing the bread. A few fish were also distributed. Everyone had plenty and still there were seven baskets of leftovers! Jesus immediately dismissed the people and got into the boat with his disciples.

Lord Jesus, you know when we are about to lose strength on our journey. You know when our patience is worn thin and when our inner resources seem depleted. Thank you for coming in creative ways to revive us, refresh us, and send us on our journey. Alleluia!

Sunday, February 15, 2004 Sixth Sunday of Ordinary Time
Luke 6, 17; 20-26
Ministering to a Great Multitude

The crowd on the plain had come to hear Jesus teach and to be healed. He healed all of them! They received what they had desired.

It was to his disciples, however, that Jesus addressed this discourse rife with hard words. His words would not be the words chosen by prosperity preachers and feel-good life coaches and therapists. This was Discipleship 101, the lifelong, continuing education class for committed followers of Christ.

Jesus told his disciples to take the long view of this life, with all its ups and downs, joys and sorrows, honors and rejections. A disciple is continually learning to look at life as Jesus looks at life.

How did Jesus tell his disciples to look at life? You're happy if you're poor, hungry, weeping, hated, excluded, insulted, and denounced?

What on earth?! No, it's not about earth. It's about living in the kingdom.

Jump up and down and be exuberant with joy! You're hanging out with the right crowd, the communion of saints.

Remember Jeremiah and all his suffering. True prophets always have a hard time of it on this earth. The reward waiting for you will be worth the price of true discipleship.

The ones on earth who were doing so well were also given hard words, words of woe, by Jesus. They had no heavenly reward to look forward to, since they had lived for earthly rewards. Remember, the false prophets were treated well.

Lord Jesus, we are tilting with all these hard words. How soft we have become. We want to consider ourselves disciples, yet we pout and complain if we are not understood on this little planet. Help us to have a proper assessment of the things of this life and to live bravely for you. You are with us every step of the way. Alleluia!

Monday, February 16, 2004
Mark 8, 11-13
The Demand for a Sign

Jesus was fully human. Sometimes he got frustrated and fed up with people and situations, just as we do. From the depths of his spirit, he sighed in wordless grief and asked why.

Why were the hostile religious leaders, the Pharisees, so intent on arguing with him and testing him? Why were they so intent on seeking a sign which would supposedly prove his identity? They twisted everything he said and did.

He was God in their midst. They saw him, but did not recognize him.

Jesus left. He got into a boat and left.

Lord Jesus, we want to draw near to you and bring you joy by our trust in you. Forgive us when we fearfully ask for signs or proofs. Forgive us when we argue with you, even silently in our spirits. You are the Lord. We are here on this earth for your purposes. You know what you are doing in our lives. Thank you that you will never leave us or forsake us. Alleluia!

Tuesday, February 17, 2004 Seven Founders of the Servite Order
Mark 8, 14-21
The Leaven of the Pharisees

Poor Jesus! He was back in the boat with his disciples after a particularly exasperating exchange with the Pharisees.

A little breather, maybe? No way.

Jesus had the Pharisees and Herod's crowd in mind when he cautioned his followers to be on guard against leaven. Leaven has the ability to permeate.

The disciples, dismayed because there was only one loaf of bread in the boat, thought that Jesus was talking about physical bread, the kind we eat. No.

Jesus, remarkably patient, reminded his followers that they had recently witnessed two amazing multiplications. When the five loaves were broken for at least five thousand people, there were baskets, wicker baskets, twelve wicker baskets of leftover bread!

When Jesus broke seven loaves of bread to feed at least four thousand people, there was still bread left, seven baskets. After witnessing these events, the disciples still did not understand.

Lord Jesus, have mercy on us. We still don't understand either. Thank you for your incredible tenderness and patience with us as you continue to show us how trustworthy you truly are. Alleluia!

Wednesday, February 18, 2004
Mark 8, 22-26
The Blind Man of Bethsaida

A very gentle healing. Jesus took the hand of the blind man and led him outside the village of Bethsaida.

This healing was gradual. Laying his hands on the man, Jesus inquired if he was able to see anything at all. The man answered that he could see more than before, but not clearly. People were still indistinct to him. To him, people looked like walking trees!

It was the second touch of Jesus that brought clarity. Now he could see!

If we have been in darkness for a very long time, it is possible that instantaneous, complete clarity would be too great a shock. Perhaps we need a gradual healing.

Lord Jesus, thank you that you know the best way to heal us. You don't want us to stay in the dark. You don't want us to see people as walking trees forever, though. You take us by the hand, touch us again, and lead us gently into clarity and truth. Alleluia!

Thursday, February 19, 2004
Mark 8, 27-33
Peter's Confession about Jesus;
The First Prediction of the Passion

Fullness of identity. Fullness of vocation.

Peter had it right about Jesus' identity. Jesus truly was the Messiah, the Christ, the Anointed One.

However, Peter did not understand the fullness of Jesus' vocation. The vocation of Jesus as Redeemer would encompass terrible rejection and suffering at the hands of the religious leaders, the chief priests, the elders, and the scribes. They would sit in judgment on him and condemn him. Jesus would be killed, but would rise again after three days.

Peter wasn't much into the suffering part. The glory, yes. The suffering, no.

Jesus was not about to be detoured from his vocation. He had already sternly set his face as flint to his destiny in Jerusalem. Our redemption was dependent upon his willingness to endure the Cross.

Lord Jesus, you were both Messiah and Suffering Servant. Help us to learn to think as you think about identity and vocation. We rejoice in our identity as God's children. We pray for the grace to be faithful to our vocation to follow you. Alleluia!

Friday, February 20, 2004
Mark 8, 34- 9, 1
The Conditions of Discipleship

When Jesus comes in glory with the holy angels, I want him to be happy with the way I have lived. That is my goal.

Lord Jesus, help me to offer myself completely for your service. Help me to put myself completely into your hands and let your purpose be worked out and completed in my life. Alleluia!

Saturday, February 21, 2004 St. Peter Damian
Mark 9, 2-13
The Transfiguration of Jesus; The Coming of Elijah

Transfiguration of Jesus. Light!

Mountain. Peter, James, and John.

Light from heaven. Jesus shining!

Cloud. God's voice from the cloud. Moses. Elijah. Suffering in the forecast. Rising from the dead.

Lord Jesus, we gaze upon you and listen to you. Transfigure us. Let your light shine around us, through us, and into our dark world. All honor and glory and praise to you, Lord Jesus Christ. Alleluia!

Sunday, February 22, 2004 Seventh Sunday of Ordinary Time
Luke 6, 27-38
Love of Enemies; Judging Others

Pray for their happiness. Pray for their happiness?! They said and did all that and you want me to pray for their happiness?

Years ago I was at a healing service where you stand in a line from one side of the church to the other. A number of priests were assisting at the service. When it was your turn, a priest would ask what you wanted healing for. I mentioned a trauma that was still affecting my life. The priest said to pray for the happiness of the people involved. He anointed me with oil and prayed.

The priest was right. When I think of those people, I still try to pray for their happiness. Injured and wounded people tend to injure and wound others. I don't want to perpetuate the cycle.

Jesus said to love our enemies, those who do not wish us well. We are to bless them and to speak well of them. We are to pray for them and even to do good to them, expecting nothing in return.

After all, that is how our Father in heaven treats us. God is gentle and merciful. He knows why we do the things we do. We simply draw from God's infinite storehouse of mercy and then pass that mercy on to others.

Only God is the judge. Only God can judge. Only God looks deeply into the human heart and sees the why behind the what, the motive behind the deed. Only God knows. Only God has the final word. At the right time, God will bring justice.

If we stop judging and condemning others, God will not judge or condemn us. If and only if we forgive others will we be forgiven.

If we give forgiveness, God will overwhelm us with gifts. Gifts that cannot be measured or even described. God will reward us as no one else is able to reward us.

Lord Jesus, you know we cannot do any of this on our own. Thank you for the Holy Spirit who fills us to overflowing and empowers us to forgive as you have instructed us. Thank you that we are children of the Most High God. Alleluia!

Monday, February 23, 2004 St. Polycarp
Mark 9, 14-29
The Healing of a Boy with a Demon

It was in the presence of Jesus that the vile spirit within the afflicted boy manifested itself and became enraged. Truly a case of the symptoms getting worse right before the healing.

Jesus! The name of Jesus. The presence of Jesus. The person of Jesus. How do others respond? How do we respond?

Jesus' disciples were still learning not only the theory but also the practice of ministry. They had tried, unsuccessfully in this difficult case, to help the boy.

The crowds pressed in on Jesus wherever he went. The ones who needed healing longed for him. They knew Jesus would help them.

Demons, on the other hand, erupted when he arrived. They knew Jesus would expel them. He would evict them from the people in whom they had taken up residence. The lease was up and they were out!

Lord Jesus, let our response to your presence be one of adoration, honesty, and trust. Let us be honest and acknowledge that we are still growing in faith. We are still in need of a greater trust. Help us not to be intimidated by the frightening things we see in ourselves and in others. You are here with us. You will expel what needs expelling You will heal and comfort us. As we are being healed, thank you for trusting us to serve others. Alleluia!

Tuesday, February 24, 2004
Mark 9, 30-37
The Second Prediction of the Passion;
The Greatest in the Kingdom

The film "The Passion of the Christ" is to be released tomorrow, Ash Wednesday. It is said to be ruthlessly realistic in portraying the violence of the scourging and the crucifixion of our Lord.

The historical Passion of Christ involved so much more than the physical suffering of the last hours of Our Lord's life. The suffering he encountered throughout his life and especially in the Garden of Gethsemane is forever beyond our comprehension. This cannot be filmed or fathomed.

Jesus, traveling through Galilee with his disciples, attempted a second time to prepare them for what was approaching. He told them plainly that he would be betrayed, killed, and would rise again. They did not understand.

Instead of asking Jesus what he meant, the disciples began to play power games. Who would be the greatest among them? Jesus gently confronted this line of reasoning by taking a child into their midst. With the child secure in his arms, Jesus told the disciples that to receive a powerless one, such as a child, was just like welcoming or receiving him. Receiving Jesus was equivalent to welcoming the Father.

Lord Jesus, we can never comprehend your Passion, your suffering in spirit, soul, and body, on our behalf. Help us this Lent to put aside all striving for earthly recognition or understanding. You understand us. You recognize us as your own. We are secure in your arms. Let us reach out to those who seem have no importance in this world. They are important to you. Help us to love you by serving them for your sake. Alleluia!

Wednesday, February 25, 2004 Ash Wednesday
Matthew 6, 1-6, 16-18
Teaching about Almsgiving; Teaching about Prayer;
Teaching about Fasting

Lord Jesus, this Lent, show us how to enter into the inner room of our spirits. You are there already and you desire to commune with us. Teach us to give in various, secret and creative ways this Lent and to know that our Father smiles upon us and will repay us. Teach us to pray in private, knowing that the Holy Spirit will guide our prayers and that the Father will repay us. Help us to fast, knowing that our Father will more than make up to us any sacrifice we are asked to make. Let us meet you this Lent.

Thursday, February 26, 2004 Thursday after Ash Wednesday
Luke 9, 22-25
The First Prediction of the Passion,
The Conditions of Discipleship

Designer discipleship? Just because we can never suffer as Jesus suffered does not mean that we will not suffer. If we are true disciples, if we are truly learning from Jesus and following Jesus, we will suffer.

St. Paul wrote that all who desired to live a truly godly life in Christ would suffer persecution (2 Timothy 3, 12). St. Peter wrote of Christ's suffering on our behalf, showing us how to entrust ourselves to God when we suffer (1 Peter 2, 21-23).

We are to deny our ways of how we think our discipleship should look. We are disciples, not designers. Jesus has his own design for our discipleship. Our cross has been weighed and designed specifically for us. No one else can carry it for us.

Lord Jesus, we look to you this day and entrust ourselves to your design for our lives. Thank you for the specific purpose, tailored exactly to size, to which you are calling us. Thank you that we will save our lives by losing our lives in your service.

Friday, February 27, 2004 Friday after Ash Wednesday
Matthew 9, 14-15
The Question about Fasting

Once, in graduate school days, we had visitors who made sure we knew they were fasting. Until midnight, that is. At midnight, they broke their fast with relish! That's fine, but Jesus cares more about our obedience and our motives. Jesus prefers that our fasting be a private matter.

Lord Jesus, help us to fast this Lent as you direct. Thank you for the guidelines clearly given by the Church regarding our Lenten discipline on Ash Wednesday, Good Friday, and all Fridays, Open us to a deeper understanding of this ancient practice of fasting. Thank you that our time of fasting will end and that we will one day enjoy the Wedding Supper of the Lamb. Lord Jesus, you are our Bridegroom. You are the Lamb of God. Thank you for your sacrifice for us.

Saturday, February 28, 2004 Saturday after Ash Wednesday
Luke 5, 27-32
The Call of Levi

Levi had been on the job, sitting in his tax office as usual. He looked up to see Jesus!

At the invitation to follow Jesus, Levi, who would be called Matthew, got up and followed Jesus. He didn't just sit there. He looked up, arose, and followed the Lord.

We follow in the way Jesus directs. We need to be actively watching and listening for his directions. He came to call us to follow him. He knew we needed him. He has a specific task for us to do for him.

Lord Jesus, you came to call sinners to repentance, to a whole new life of health and purpose. You are the wise and loving physician of our spirit, soul, and body. Help us to look to you, listen to you, get up out of our weary old ways, and follow you!

Sunday, February 29, 2004 First Sunday of Lent
Luke 4, 1-13
The Temptation of Jesus

Jesus did not wander into the desert, the wilderness, on his own. He did not stumble into this time of sustained temptation.

The Holy Spirit guided him, led him, and directed him into the wilderness. Jesus was prepared. He was filled with the Holy Spirit.

At his baptism, the heavens had opened! God the Father had spoken in a most definitive way. The identity of Jesus was confirmed. He was God's own beloved Son. God was so pleased with his Son. The Holy Spirit, in the form of a dove, rested on Jesus.

Jesus was prepared for this time of testing in the wilderness. He knew who he was. He was God's own beloved Son. He was filled with the power of the Holy Spirit.

Jesus knew the Word of God, the Sacred Scriptures. He could counter each temptation the devil threw at him by quoting Scripture. These were temptations to doubt or to question his personal identity, to misuse his power, and to be diverted from his mission by false promises of earthly power. Jesus was ready.

Lord Jesus, let us immerse ourselves this Lent with the knowledge of who we are, who we really are. Let the waters of our baptism continue to flow. We are God's children. You are our elder Brother, You came to save us and to show us how to live during our time on earth. Let us remember that the Holy Spirit lives in us and will energize us to face and to overcome our trials. Help us to remember that our Father in heaven loves us.

Monday, March 1, 2004 Lenten Weekday
Matthew 25, 31-46
The Judgment of the Nations

Jesus the King will ask not what we believed, but rather what we did with what we believed. Belief, however, is very important.

Belief is foundational. Jesus even said that our very work was to believe (John 6, 29)! He knew that appropriate action would flow from our trust and belief in him, that he was truly sent from God.

Contradictory? No. What we do with our lives illustrates what we believe.

Do we believe that we are nothing and that we don't count? We won't do anything. We will not be able to live effectively for God.

Do we really and truly believe that we are God's children? Do we believe God loves us and sent Jesus to live and to die for us, to redeem us (John 3, 16)? Do we know we are deeply secure in God's love for us? We are free to live!

Do we believe? Do we act?

Faith, without works of mercy, is meaningless (James 2, 20). Do you believe and do nothing to live out your belief? Our father in the faith, Abraham, showed forth faith that was lived out in action (James 2, 21-23).

603

Lord Jesus, this Lent, please readjust our beliefs about you and about ourselves. Heal us and show us how to live out our beliefs.

Tuesday, March 2, 2004 Lenten Weekday
Matthew 6, 7-15
Teaching about Prayer; The Lord's Prayer

Seeking to honor and to glorify God. Simplicity before God. Honesty before God. Alone in God's presence. Trusting in God's provision. Longing for God's kingdom to be made manifest here on earth. Delivered and rescued from every form of evil.

Lord Jesus, thank you for teaching us how to come to our loving Father in prayer. Thank you for giving us the desire and the grace to release others from our judgment. We may safely trust our wise Father to right all wrongs. Thank you for giving us the grace to forgive and to release all who have hurt us. Thank you for walking beside us this Lent.

Wednesday, March 3, 2004 Lenten Weekday
Luke 11, 29-32
The Demand for a Sign

No more hoops! No more so-called process.

Jesus knew who he was. He knew where he had come from and where he was going. He had nothing to prove.

Jesus recognized that no sign would ever convince or satisfy. If people had stubbornly and obstinately determined in their hearts to refuse to believe he was the Christ, the Messiah, the Anointed One, the One sent from God, nothing he could ever do would convince them or satisfy them.

Jesus himself was the sign and still is the sign. A far greater sign than the reluctant prophet Jonah was to the people of Nineveh.

After all, the people of Nineveh fasted, prayed, and repented at the preaching of Jonah. Jesus was greater than Jonah. The people of Nineveh would condemn those who did not believe in Jesus.

The great queen of the south who marveled at the wisdom of King Solomon would condemn Jesus' generation (Matthew 12, 42, Luke 11, 31). In an age when travel was arduous, she had traveled a great distance to hear for herself the wisdom possessed by Solomon. Jesus was far greater than Solomon. She will condemn those who did not believe in Jesus, whose wisdom exceeded that of Solomon.

Lord Jesus, you refused to jump through theological or ecclesiastical hoops to prove your identity. Thank you that we are secure in your love for us. Let us no longer jump through hoops to try and prove our identity. We are God's children! We are your sisters and brothers. The Holy Spirit lives in us.

Thursday, March 4, 2004 Lenten Weekday
Matthew 7, 7-12
The Answer to Prayers; The Golden Rule

God filters our prayers and gives us the very best answers! We ask according to the light we have, knowing that God, who is Light, sees everything and knows everything about our prayers. We seek God, the Answer within the answer. We knock, knowing that God will open the door that is right for us. We are instructed to treat others the way we would like to be treated ourselves.

Lord Jesus, thank you that we may fling ourselves and all our concerns into your hands and into your heart, knowing that you love us and will do whatever is the absolute best. Focus our energy today on reaching out and serving others.

Friday, March 5, 2004 Lenten Weekday
Matthew 5, 20-26
Teaching about the Law; Teaching about Anger

Jesus knows that our words are rooted in our hearts (Matthew 12, 34). He knows that if anger and resentment are seething within our hearts, sooner or later they will erupt in our words..

Unless! Unless we take these wild emotions, often rooted in our response to injustice, and give them to Jesus, we will be controlled by them. Do we want to live that way?

The Lord himself is our righteousness and he will secure our justice (Jeremiah 23, 5; 33, 16). The scribes and the Pharisees carefully observed outward forms of righteousness, but that was not enough. It was superficial.

Jesus wants us to act out of his righteousness, the righteousness with which he has clothed and vested us (Isaiah 61, 10). Then our actions will flow from a cleansed and renewed heart. Out of this healed heart, we may reach out in strength and humility to all, especially to those who have grievances against us.

Lord Jesus, you know how frustrated we feel when we are angry. Thank you that you are in control. You will give us the aid we need to respond wisely. Thank you that no weapon devised against us will succeed and that you are in charge of our vindication (Isaiah 54, 17). Thank you that we may rest in you and live the life you have called us to live.

Saturday, March 6, 2004 Lenten Weekday
Matthew 5, 43-48
Love of Enemies

My love goes where God directs. God is in charge of my life.

God directs my love to my friends and also to those who may not consider themselves my friends, those who do not wish me well. They are not to be excluded from my love. They are to be welcomed into the circle of my love.

Lord Jesus, throw the pebble of defensiveness and resentment out of my life. Let it make an ever-widening circle and spiral of acceptance and love all around me. While I was far from you and not following you, you died for me ((Romans 5, 8). Let me live for you and love all.

Sunday, March 7, 2004 Second Sunday of Lent
Luke 9, 28-36
The Transfiguration of Jesus

The startling change, the transfiguration came as Jesus was praying. White! Dazzling! Light!

Peter, James, and John had dozed off during this prayer retreat on the mountain. They were awake now! They saw the glorified Lord Jesus talking with Moses and Elijah about his destiny in Jerusalem.

A cloud. A shadow. Entering into the cloud, Peter, James and John became quite frightened. What was happening? From within the cloud came the voice of God the Father. God told them that Jesus was his chosen, his own Son. They were instructed to listen to Jesus.

Silence. Alone with Jesus on the mountain again.

Lord Jesus, thank you that we are transfigured as we spend time in your presence. We are transfigured as we pray. We are in your presence and you are transfiguring us (1 Corinthians 3, 18). Still us today to listen to your voice. In your time, you will speak of our destiny in our Jerusalem.

Monday, March 8, 2004 Lenten Weekday
Luke 6, 36-38
Love of Enemies; Judging Others

What a privilege to be invited to be like our Father in heaven, to be merciful and compassionate to all! Our Father is not stingy and calculating. Our Father, who gave Jesus for us and for our salvation, pours out mercy and compassion upon us every single day.

We are to live out of this richness of mercy. We are simply to draw from the wealth of all the mercy we have been given, more than we can imagine, and then freely share it with those in need. If we are tempted to make harsh judgments of others, we dip instead into our vast reservoir of mercy and give them some of that same mercy God gave to us when we needed it.

If we have been condemning others, even in the silence of our hearts, we will learn to begin to give and to forgive. We will give mercy, as God gave mercy to us.

God did not condemn us. We have no authority to condemn others. As we give and forgive, God will astonish us with unimaginable gifts.

Lord Jesus, we are so rich, so wealthy, with the mercy and compassion freely given to us. Help us this day to live and to speak out this awareness of our wealth and freely give mercy to others.

Tuesday, March 9, 2004 Lenten Weekday
Matthew 23, 1-12
Denunciation of the Scribes and Pharisees

Jesus acknowledged that the scribes and the Pharisees were competent teachers of the Mosaic law. He was not questioning their academic qualifications.

Rather, Jesus was denouncing the way they lived and the way they tried to control the way others lived. They were devoted to preserving their image as leaders. They appeared to care more for titles and other perks of office than for serving God and God's people in simplicity and in humility.

Lord Jesus, let us become so secure in our relationship with you that we will be free to be ourselves. We will then be free to serve others in strength and in humility.

Wednesday, March 10, 2004 Lenten Weekday
Matthew 20, 17-28
The Third Prediction of the Passion;
The Request of James and John

Suffering in fulfilling God's will. Jockeying for position. The two were tragically juxtaposed both then and now, within our personal lives and within the life of the community of the faithful.

We will suffer, if we are truly living for God and serving others. We will also know the joy and peace which this world cannot bestow. Positions of honor, however, are not our concern.

Lord Jesus, help us to stay especially close to you in our thoughts, our words, and our actions this Lent. Show us what is truly important as we continue our journey to our own Jerusalem.

Thursday, March 11, 2004 Lenten Weekday
Luke 16, 19-31
The Parable of the Rich Man and Lazarus

Jesus told this parable to illustrate that what we do in this life matters and will affect us when we leave this life. Injustices suffered in this life will be addressed and made right.

The rich man knowingly and deliberately lived extravagantly, day after day. Poor Lazarus was at his gate, in his face, so to speak, day after day, in all his misery. When Lazarus died, he was taken by the angels to Abraham. Only after the rich man himself died, did he give a thought to Lazarus. Even then, he was concerned only for himself and his relatives.

How we treat others matters. Ignoring the poor is ignoring Jesus in our midst. Jesus is present in the very least (Matthew 25, 45).

Lord Jesus, forgive us for the times when we have been too busy, too indifferent, or too hard of heart to express compassion. Let us acknowledge all who cross our path today and treat them with respect and compassion.

Friday, March 12, 2004 Lenten Weekday
Matthew 21, 33-43, 45-46
The Parable of the Tenants

The tenants had everything needed to produce a good harvest. The vineyard, with winepress and watchtower, was safely hedged around. The owner of the vineyard had every right to anticipate a successful harvest.

608

Instead, at the time of the grape harvest, the time of vintage, the vineyard had become a place of chaos and struggle. The landowner's personal representatives were treated outrageously by the tenants, the ones who had merely been granted temporary stewardship of the vineyard. Clearly these tenants did not accept the authority of the landowner's designated representatives, his servants. Tragically, the tenants killed even the son of the landowner. What to do?

Jesus, telling this parable to the chief priests and the Pharisees, zeroed in for the application. He quoted from the Psalms and from Isaiah about the rejected stone becoming the very cornerstone (Psalm 118, 22), one that was precious, one that had been tested (Isaiah 28, 16).

Jesus told the furious Pharisees and the chief priests that the kingdom of God would be taken from them and given to those who would produce fruit, fruit worthy of the kingdom.

Lord Jesus, you are the very cornerstone of our lives. Send us today into the vineyard to serve you. You have given us all that is needed to produce a harvest.

Saturday, March 13, 2004 Lenten Weekday
Luke 15, 1-3; 11-32
The Parable of the Lost Sheep; The Parable of the Lost Son

Have you ever seen anyone completely uninhibited in expressing joy? There is an incredible abandon that is wonderful to behold.

Once, when I was in the seminary, I was startled to observe one of the professors greet someone and then fall on the floor, whooping with delight! Apparently, someone presumed gone forever, had returned unexpectedly. It was quite a sight.

More recently, we sent a piñata as a birthday gift to our little niece in another state. As her mother reported, when little Abigail opened the box, she squealed with joy and carried the burro piñata all around the house.

The father in the parable in today's Gospel is wild with joy at the return of his long-lost younger son. The father had sadly concluded his son was dead and gone. He had waited and watched for his son for so long.

Now, his son was back home! The father, in his wild relief and exuberance, lavished his son with honors. A ring. New clothing. New sandals. A feast! How sad that the older brother would not join in the rejoicing.

Jesus, speaking to the closed-hearted scribes and Pharisees, was trying to illustrate just how great is the joy in heaven when the lost are found. All heaven rejoices (Luke 15, 7, 10)!

Lord Jesus, help us to be like our Father in heaven. Help us to rejoice and reach out to all, especially to those in most need of your unconditional love.

Sunday, March 14, 2004 Third Sunday of Lent
Luke 13, 1-9
A Call to Repentance; The Parable of the Barren Fig Tree

Is your repentance current? Is it up to date? Is mine?

We renew our magazine subscriptions to keep them current. We even pay to renew our subscriptions.

Jesus paid the price for our salvation. We don't pay the price. Jesus already paid for us. We receive this priceless gift and then pray for the grace to live it out all our lives.

John the Baptist told the religious leaders, the Pharisees and the Sadducees, to show forth fruit as evidence of their repentance. Repentance? The Pharisees were dedicated to strictly keeping the Law and all the many rules and regulations. The Sadducees were held in high esteem as the priestly elite. Yet John the Baptist, preparing the way for the Lord Jesus, the Christ, the Messiah, told these leaders to repent.

As the fig tree in the orchard was granted a little more time in which to produce figs, so God is patient with us. We are continually invited to repent. United with Jesus, we are called and commissioned to bear fruit (John 15, 5).

Lord Jesus, thank you that you invite us to come to you, repent of all our sins, receive your forgiveness, and bear fruit.

Monday, March 15, 2004 Lenten Weekday
Luke 4, 24-30
The Rejection at Nazareth

Jesus was not surprised at his treatment in the synagogue. He emphasized that no prophet is ever welcome on home turf. The prophet lives and speaks for God. There is no way to be popular if one is truly longing to live this way.

When the Israelites were pestering God for a human king so that they would be like the other nations, the prophet Samuel was very troubled. God assured Samuel that the people were not rejecting him so much as they were rejecting God's sovereignty (1 Samuel 8, 6-8). In other words, Samuel was told not to take it so personally.

Later, the prophets Elijah and Elisha ministered to the Gentiles , who were considered by some to be outsiders. Elijah exercised a powerful ministry in Sidon (1 Kings 17). His successor, Elisha, ministered healing to a Syrian military commander, Naaman
(2 Kings 5).

The people in the synagogue were so infuriated at Jesus' references to these prophets and to God's concern for outsiders that they tried to push Jesus off a cliff. Rejection.

Lord Jesus, thank you for enduring so much hostility and so much rejection all throughout your earthly ministry. You were truly God and truly human. You were filled with love and compassion for all and yet you were hated and despised. You suffered in countless ways longer before Gethsemane and Calvary. Help us today to keep our eyes on you and speak forth your words, knowing that we are secure in your love.

Tuesday, March 16, 2004 Lenten Weekday
Matthew 18, 21-35
The Parable of the Unforgiving Servant

This parable about forgiveness is really more about God and about me than it is about anyone who sins against me. It is a tight parable, without a lot of wiggle room.

God. Who is God? Is God big?

Is God big enough to erase, to cancel, to wipe out, to obliterate my sins, the things I've thought, said, and done that make me cringe inside and curl my toes when I remember them? Is God big enough to strike these offences from my record?

When I acknowledge and confess my sins, God forgives my sins and cleanses me (1 John 1, 8-10). Amazingly, God also forgets all about my sins (Hebrews 8, 12)!

As far as God is concerned, my sins are gone. The prophet Micah said that God casts our sins into the depths of the sea (Micah 7, 19).

God can do that! God is big enough to do that. I am FREE!

Do I really believe all this? Do I really trust God to settle the score when I have been wronged? Since it is God's business to avenge me, I am not to try to take matters into my own hands (Hebrews 12, 19).

Especially in the sacrament of reconciliation, I experience assurance of God's forgiveness. I am absolved. I am free. God is healing me in very deep ways. As St. James said, we are to confess our sins to one another and we are to pray for one another in order that we may be healed (James 4, 16).

I am so free and full of joy that I am strong (Nehemiah 8, 10). I am strong enough to be generous. I draw from the huge, limitless deposit, the gigantic, limitless reservoir of God's love and forgiveness and offer this same love and forgiveness to others, the same love and forgiveness that was freely bestowed upon me.

Lord Jesus, thank you, thank you for the freedom in which you want us to live, in which you have made it possible for us to live. You suffered. You died. You paid the price. We can't pay the price. It has already been paid. You paid it. Let us be generous today to release anyone we have held captive in the prison of our resentment. We are free today and so are they. Praise to you, Lord Jesus Christ.

Wednesday, March 17, 2004 Lenten Weekday, St. Patrick
Matthew 5, 17-19
Teaching about the Law

Already. Not yet. Here and now. Still to come. A rough sketch. The completed masterpiece.

In the hallway at home, we have little night lights. They are useful for the night time only. In the morning, I turn them off, because their purpose has been fulfilled. Day has come. All is bright.

Lord Jesus, you came not to destroy the teaching of Moses, but to bring it to glorious fulfillment, to illumine its deepest meaning. Fill us with your light so that we may shine in this dark world and then take us with you to that realm where all is bright.

Thursday, March 18, 2004 Lenten Weekday, St. Cyril
Luke 11, 14-23
Jesus and Beelzebul

Jesus steadfastly continued to do the will and the work of his heavenly Father in spite of the constant static which came from those who refused to believe in him. They were determined to impugn his motives and to attribute his power to the prince of demons, rather than to God.

Jesus knew that the kingdom of God was in their very midst because he was doing God's will. He knew that whoever was not actively with him was against him.

Lord Jesus, help us to continue to follow you even if we are irritated with static of all sorts in our own lives, sometimes static of our own making, static of weariness and static of unbelief. Strengthen us to do your will. You are the source of our strength and the silencer of all static.

Friday, March 19, 2004 Feast of St. Joseph
Matthew 1, 16, 18-21, 24
The Genealogy of Jesus; The Birth of Jesus

Jesus, Mary, and Joseph. Each person in the Holy Family was there by God's design and God's intention. Each had a specific role to fulfill in salvation history.

It was in a dream that Joseph was told his part. The angel of the Lord came to in a dream. The angel addressed Joseph as a descendant of David, reminding him of his royal ancestry. Knowing how troubled Joseph was because of Mary's seemingly inexplicable pregnancy, the angel reassured Joseph that the Holy Spirit was the explanation for the conception of Mary's baby. Joseph was told not to be afraid to take Mary into his home. Joseph would have the honor of naming Jesus.

Mary, the blessed, a young virgin, was chosen to bear the Savior of the world, Jesus. However, she was still dependent on Joseph's obedience to God.

Jesus, Son of God, would be dependent on Joseph also. Joseph would name him Jesus, the One who would save from sin. Joseph would provide a home for the Child.

Lord Jesus, thank you for coming so humbly into our world, the world you created, the world so desperate for you. We are in awe of the trust and obedience of Joseph, the man you called Abba when you were a little child. Help us to trust you, do our part, and continue to believe that God's promise to us will come to pass.

Saturday, March 20, 2004 Lenten Weekday
Luke 18, 9-14
The Parable of the Pharisee and the Tax Collector

The Pharisee fasted and tithed, which was fine, but they did not comprehend who Jesus was. They did not understand themselves very well, either. They thought they were not like other people, the sinners, the ones whose conduct offended God.

The tax collector, on the other hand, could not even lift his eyes. He smote his breast and prayed for God's mercy. He knew who he was, a sinner.

Jesus was telling this parable to those who relied on themselves to be right with God. Jesus had a surprise for the Pharisees! Jesus said that it was the tax collector, who had humbled himself before God and cried out for mercy, who went home justified and truly right with God.

Jesus said that trying to elevate or promote oneself leads inevitably to being humbled. On the other hand, being unpretentious, humbling oneself, and realistically recognizing one's own sinfulness, leads to promotion and elevation.

Lord Jesus Christ, you were Son of God and yet humbled yourself to come into this world as a helpless infant. You, the sinless One, suffered and died for us so that we could truly live for you. Have mercy on us.

Sunday, March 21, 2004 Fourth Sunday of Lent
Luke 15, 1-3; 11-32
The Parable of the Lost Sheep; The Parable of the Lost Son

The sinners who knew they were sinners drew near to Jesus. They knew they needed him. The sinners who refused to recognize their offenses were critical of Jesus' willingness to associate with the ones they considered insignificant outcasts

Jesus told several parables to those who complaining about his compassion. One parable was about a lost sheep and another was about a lost coin. In today's Gospel, we read the parable Jesus told about a lost son.

Lost children. We see their faces on milk cartons, in the newspaper, and on television. Their parents are desperately searching for them, hoping against hope for their safe return. Can you imagine one of these frantic parents observing their lost child of whatever age coming home and the parents not welcoming them?

It is true that the adult son in this parable left of his own accord, but the loving heart of the father was still bursting with joy at his son's return. The father did not start a tirade. He started a party! He wanted everyone, including his conscientious older son, to celebrate.

Lord Jesus, we just don't get it. We may still think that our acceptance and our worth is based on our good works. Let us grasp, in the depths of our hearts, that our heavenly Father's love for us is so overwhelming, so overpowering, that nothing we could ever do would stop our Father from loving us, forgiving us , and welcoming us home.

Monday, March 22, 2004 Lenten Weekday
John 4, 43-54
Return to Galilee; Second Sign at Cana

The distance from Cana to Capernaum was about fifteen miles. Between the two towns, the royal official, whose son was desperately ill, traveled with only the word of Jesus to sustain him. The word of Jesus was all he needed.

The official had truly believed the word of Jesus in Cana as he hastened home to his son in Capernaum. Before he arrived, he was told the wonderful news. His son had begun to get well! His fever was gone.

When did this happen? It happened in Cana, at exactly the time Jesus had said that the official's son would live.

Lord Jesus, thank you for your presence with us today as we travel from our own Cana to our own Capernaum. We believe that your word to us will be fulfilled. Just as all the the official's family believed in you, let all those around us believe in you as they see us continue to travel and to trust in the strength of your word.

Tuesday, March 23, 2004 Lenten Weekday
John 5, 1-16
Cure on a Sabbath

Sometimes, even when the cage door is opened, the bird does not fly out. The poor little birdie has become so accustomed to a confined existence that free flight does not seem to be a possibility.

Sometimes, when people are sick for a long time and there does not seem to be a cure, hope dies or at least becomes paralyzed. A change in thinking needs to occur!

In today's Gospel, Jesus began by asking the man who had been paralyzed for thirty-eight years if he would like to get well. Jesus was opening the door of the man's mind to the real possibility of healing. The man seemed stuck in thinking that his healing could occur in only one way, the way he had seen it happen for others at the Pool of Bethesda by the Sheep Gate.

Surprise! Jesus had another way. Jesus simply spoke to the man. Jesus told the man who had been paralyzed for thirty-eight years to arise, to get up, to start walking, and to carry his mat with him. The man was instantaneously healed! He walked.

Lord Jesus, thank you for finding us and speaking to us the word that reawakens hope. You are the Good Shepherd who reaches out in mercy and in power to your sheep. Thank you for forgiving us, healing us, and directing us to arise and to walk!

Wednesday, March 24, 2004 Lenten Weekday
John 5, 17-30
Cure on a Sabbath; The Work of the Son

What is the Father like? Look and see. Look and see what is Jesus doing. Look and see. Pray for the grace to believe.

Jesus heals. Jesus gives life! Jesus is Judge of all. God the Father gave Jesus the Son that authority. Jesus lived and moved within the framework of love and power given to him by his Father, his Abba in heaven.

The time will come when all who have left this life will hear the voice of Jesus. Jesus will assess their lives and assign them to one of two resurrections, the resurrection of life for those who did good in this life or the resurrection of condemnation for the ones who did evil in this life.

Because Jesus knows firsthand what this life is like, he knows how to judge. He know exactly what we go through in this life. The person who believes God, who sent Jesus, will not come into judgment, but has already passed out of spiritual death into true life.

Lord Jesus, your motives were completely pure and completely focused. You came to do the will of God, your Father in heaven. Purify us and our motives so that we may honor you and be trusted more and more to do the work you have assigned for us to do. Remind us that our true work is to believe. All else will follow.

Thursday, March 25, 2004 Annunciation of the Lord
Luke 1, 26-38
Announcement of the Birth of Jesus

From God to Galilee via Gabriel! The angel Gabriel made quite a celestial journey to give God's message to a teenager in Nazareth.

Gabriel knew how to deliver God's message to the young Mary. He began by assuring Mary, the young virgin betrothed to Joseph that the Lord was with her. She was told not to be afraid.

God was very, very pleased with Mary. She was highly favored among all the women in the world. Mary would bear Jesus, the Son of the Most High God. Jesus would be the ruler of a kingdom that would never end, unlike the passing kingdoms of this earth

Gabriel then proceeded from announcing the message to revealing the method. Mary had asked an honest question. How could this be? How could a virgin bear a child?

Gabriel had the answer. The Holy Spirit! With God, anything is possible!

Mary gave her response. She referred to herself as the Lord's servant, the Lord's handmaiden. Mary, puzzled though she was, yielded to the extraordinary work of God.

God is speaking to us every day. The angel Gabriel may or may not appear to us, but God is still speaking to us in countless ways.

Lord Jesus. when we think nothing is happening in our lives or that God is silent, we are simply wrong. Please open our hearts, weary of spiritual winter, and raise the level of our expectancy to hear and to respond with trust in this springtime, this Lent.

Friday, March 26, 2004 Lenten Weekday
John 7, 1-2, 10, 25-30
Feast of Tabernacles; The First Dialogue

Jesus, who came from the presence of God, his Father, his Abba in heaven, knew what God was really like. Jesus did not come to earth on his own initiative. His Father sent him.

We may say we know what God is like, but do we? We may say we trust God, but do our lives illustrate our trust?

In the midst of all the angry controversies and disputes about Jesus' identity, Jesus remained steadfast. He knew that his Father, his Abba, was both sheltering him from the strife surrounding him and strengthening him to continue his ministry.

King David had long ago referred to this shelter (Psalm 27, 5). Jesus could not be touched. His time, his hour of destiny, had not yet come.

Lord Jesus, we want to know your Father as you knew him. We long to trust him as you trusted him in the midst of your suffering. You suffered all your life. You endured so much misunderstanding and so much unbelief. You were God veiled in flesh and yet not all recognized you. Thank you for the time when we shall all recognize you for who you are and we shall all kneel before you (Philippians 2, 10). We kneel before you now and thank you and love you.

Saturday, March 27, 2004 Lenten Weekday
John 7, 40-53
Discussion of the Origin of the Messiah

Do we ever condemn someone without truly listening and seeking to understand the truth behind the accusations? Of course we do, sometimes by our unholy silence. That is one way reputations are ruined, lives are devastated, and vocations seem to be temporarily derailed.

That was the question Nicodemus, a Pharisee himself, asked his fellow Pharisees. He asked if the law judged people without giving them a hearing to discern the truth (John 7, 50-51).

The Pharisees were so agitated that all they could do was to ask was if Nicodemus was from Galilee! The Pharisees were fixated on the belief that a real prophet did not, could not, ever come from Galilee.

Jesus did not originate from Galilee. He had lived and ministered there, but he did not originate from Galilee

Jesus originated from God. He was there in the beginning with God (John 1, 1). He was born in Bethlehem From tiny Bethlehem came the One who would rule Israel (Micah 5, 1-2). From Bethlehem came the One to shepherd God's flock (Micah 5, 3).

The crowd was in an uproar over whether or not Jesus was the Messiah. Naturally, they were divided. Jesus, as the aged prophet Simeon had predicted, would be a sign of contradiction (Luke 2, 34).

Lord Jesus, you came from God and knew that you would soon return to God. You did not have to defend yourself or justify yourself. Help us to remember that we too come from God and are intended to live a life doing the good that God has assigned us to do (Ephesians 2, 10). Help us not to be overly concerned with how we are perceived in this world. You are our Savior. You are with us.

Sunday, March 28, 2004 Fifth Sunday of Lent
John 8, 1-11
A Woman Caught in Adultery

After the heated arguments about the origins of the Messiah, everyone went home. Jesus, however, went to the Mount of Olives and returned the next morning to face the the fracas in the temple.

As usual, the people flocked to him. The Pharisees and the scribes were right there, too, loaded with their verbal ammunition, seeking to discredit him,

Would Jesus consent to the stoning of the woman caught in adultery? Death by stoning was the fate of an unfaithful woman who had been betrothed in marriage (Deuteronomy 22, 23-24).

Joseph was deeply troubled by the knowledge of Mary's pregnancy. If she was deemed unfaithful, she would be stoned to death. The angel of the Lord came to Joseph to reassure him that Mary was pregnant because of the Holy Spirit (Matthew 1, 18-20). Mary would bear Jesus, the Savior (Matthew 1, 21).

Jesus did not rise to the bait and contest the Law, as the Pharisees had hoped. If he had, they would have had ammunition against him.

Instead, Jesus turned the table on his interrogators. He liked to do that. He did it a lot. It irritated them no end. Jesus told the scribes and the Pharisees that the one among them who was sinless should be the one to start throwing the stones at the accused woman. As he was writing in the dirt, they began to leave. The oldest ones left first. Jesus told the woman to leave and not to sin again.

Lord Jesus, the longer we live, the more we know we need you to be our Savior. We need your mercy and your forgiveness. Help us to remember this Lent that you took upon yourself all of our sins of thought, word, and deed.

Monday, March 29, 2004 Lenten Weekday
John 8, 12-20
The Light of the World

Jesus is the Light! Jesus is our Light. Soon, at the Easter Vigil, the words, "The Light of Christ!" will ring forth as the Exultet is chanted.

When we follow Jesus, we have his light with us and within us. We may not understand our circumstances. Others may not understand us, but Jesus understands and lightens our way Home.

Lord Jesus, you were not alone during your time on earth. Your Father was with you. We are not alone. You are with us. You do not judge by external standards and appearances. You see into the depths of our hearts. Let your light within us grow brighter and brighter. Let us shine for you.

Tuesday, March 30, 2004 Lenten Weekday
John 8, 21-30
Jesus, the Father's Ambassador

Where was Jesus going? Back to his Father. Those who refused to believe could not follow him there.

However, Jesus told those who believed in him and followed him that they would go to the place where he was going, to the Father, where Jesus himself would prepare a place for them (John 14, 1-3). The Father's house is very roomy!

Those who refuse to believe in Jesus will die in their sins. That is what Jesus is saying in today's Gospel. Those who do believe in Jesus and place their trust in him have their sins forgiven. God even forgets their sins (Hebrews 8, 12). Amazing! God can do anything.

Jesus promised that he would never reject anyone who came to him (John 6, 39). God's will is that no one would be lost, but instead would come to repentance (2 Peter 3, 9).

We may come to Jesus with all our doubts, fears, and sins, and give them all to him. He knows how to sort everything out. He knows how to fit the puzzling pieces of our lives together in the very best way.

It was frustrating for Jesus to try and communicate with those who had closed their minds and their hearts to his love and to his message. They were bent on remaining on the earthly level of understanding. Jesus was endeavoring to bring them to the heavenly level, but they refused.

Lord Jesus, when we don't understand, let us still stay very close to you. Let us not run away in anger or in unbelief, but trust you, especially in these last days of Lent.

Wednesday, March 31, 2004 Lenten Weekday
John 8, 31-42
Jesus and Abraham

How much room does Jesus and his teaching, his word, have in my life? Is Jesus one option among many? Is Jesus my life? Is his word the definitive word in my life?

God's word was definitive for Abraham. Abraham believed God, trusted God, and lived according to God's word.

Jesus was closely tied to his Father with cords of love. He came to us from the Father's presence and spoke to us the words his Father gave him. He acted as the Father directed. He was not a puppet. He was a Son.

Because Jesus is the Son of God, he has the authority to set us free. He also has the power to set us free. He longs for us to allow him to set us free.

Lord Jesus, you came to set us free. We were in bondage to sin and could not free ourselves. Speak the truth to us about ourselves. Let us realize anew our need for true freedom, freedom to know you as you are, and to follow you.

Thursday, April 1, 2004 Lenten Weekday
John 8, 51-59
Jesus and Abraham

Well, this is getting worse and worse. Two different wavelengths. Two different ways of perceiving reality.

Actually, it's getting better and better, because the lines are being drawn. Truth is being illustrated as Jesus speaks.

Jesus was perceived in many ways as he walked this earth. Carpenter. Rabbi. Prophet. Son of Man. Carpenter. The Christ, the Messiah, the Anointed One. Son of God. The Good Shepherd. The Lamb of God. The True Vine. The Bread from heaven. Etc., etc., etc. Yes. Yes. Yes to all the above.

Jesus was God in human form. God veiled in flesh, but still God. Of course he preceded the great patriarch Abraham. Jesus, as Son of God, knew what God was really like, because his Dad, his Abba, his Father was God.

And yet, what was happening as Jesus spoke of life and death, of truth and lies? The encounter between Jesus and his questioners began with their doubt-packed questions and ended with their attempt to stone Jesus.

As Jesus was hidden from their physical eyes, he was also apparently hidden from their spiritual eyes, the eyes of their understanding. One moment he was there in their midst. The next moment he was gone. The hidden Jesus had passed through their midst.

Lord Jesus, you are the Eternal One, the great I AM. Since our desire is to keep your word and to follow you, we will never see death. We will take our last breath on this earth and our next breath in your presence. During these last days in Lent, draw us into a deeper heart understanding of who you really are and who we really are in relation to you.

Friday, April 2, 2004 Lenten Weekday
John 10, 31-42
Feast of the Dedication

The beginning. The call to ministry. Rejection. Opposition. Refuge. Solace. Silence. Solitude. Reflection. Recollection.

Jesus had suffered so much from his opponents. They were determined to discredit him. Nothing he said and nothing he did convinced them that he was God's Son. They were enraged and intent upon removing him.

Jesus left. He went across the Jordan River to the place where his forerunner, John the Baptist had begun to baptize people for repentance. This was a time of deep reflection for Jesus.

If Jesus, the Son of God, did not violate people's free will and try to force belief, neither can we. We can live for God, in spite of our human flaws and failings, but we cannot make others believe. That is the work of the Holy Spirit.

Lord Jesus, you were so patient with those who opposed you. They had witnessed the mighty works you performed and yet they refused to believe in your relationship to your Father. Help us to know that you are with us, just as you knew that the Father was with you.

Saturday, April 3, 2004 Lenten Weekday
John 11, 45-56
Session of the Sanhedrin

To the desert. That is where Jesus withdrew one last time. This is where Jesus entered into seclusion with his disciples.

After Jesus had raised Lazarus from the dead, the Sanhedrin was getting desperate. They had to get rid of Jesus.

The Lamb of God would die for all. God's purpose would be fulfilled.

Lord Jesus, with Holy Week approaching, let us follow you into the desert. Clarify our thoughts. Purify our hearts. Simplify our words. Direct our deeds.

Sunday, April 4, 2004 Palm Sunday of the Lord's Passion
Luke 22, 14-23-56
The Passion Narrative

The Last Supper. On the Resurrection side of the Cross, we continue to do what Jesus did at the Last Supper. This was the Last Supper before the culmination of his last suffering on earth.

Jesus took bread. Jesus took the cup. He was broken for us. He was poured out for us.

Lord Jesus, Lamb of God, your sacrifice is beyond our comprehension. You came to your own and you were rejected, tortured, and crucified. You absorbed into your very being all our sick and sinful thoughts, words, and deeds. You did this for everyone! Help us to receive you tenderly and offer you our love as we continue to receive your most precious Body and Blood.

Monday, April 5, 2004 Monday of Holy Week
John 12, 1-11
The Anointing at Bethany

Fragrance! The intense fragrance from the anointing oil filled the air in the house of Lazarus. This house was now a place of great rejoicing!

The weeping was over. Jesus had raised Lazarus from the dead. Lazarus had been in the tomb for days, but at the word of Jesus, he walked out of the tomb.

A dinner party was in progress. Martha served the food. Mary lovingly anointed the feet of Jesus. There is no record of the words, if any, spoken by Mary as she anointed the feet of Jesus.

The dinner was also one of calm anticipation of the death of Jesus. Jesus candidly referred to the anointing oil and its purpose.

Although the fragrance of the costly perfumed oil currently filled the house in Bethany, it was intended for the burial of Jesus. Jesus, the one who raised Lazarus from the dead, was soon to die.

Several dynamics were being played out at this dinner. Judas tried to interfere with Mary's anointing of Jesus. Curious crowds arrived, hoping to see the newly raised Lazarus. They had heard the story and now wanted to see for themselves. Whether or not they were able to see Lazarus, they probably were aware of the sweet fragrance.

Fragrance! The fragrant anointing oil wafted over the home.

Our lives are to be a sweet fragrance to others. A fragrance that tells of our love for the Lord who sacrificed his life for us.

Lord Jesus, let us anoint you today with our love, our trust, and our obedience. Let our lives be fragrant with your presence.

Tuesday, April 6, 2004 Tuesday of Holy Week
John 13, 21-33; 36-38
Announcement of Judas' Betrayal; The New Commandment;
Peter's Denial Predicted

Relationships. Emotions. Glory.

Jesus experienced anguish, knowing he would be betrayed by the crafty Judas. Jesus also knew he would be denied by the stouthearted Peter.

Glory? What a poignant time to speak of glory. Jesus the Son would be glorified and God the Father would be glorified in his Son.

Love. Jesus instructed his disciples to love one another as he had loved them. This kind of sacrificial, selfless love, which would startle and astonish the world, would be the sign of authentic discipleship.

Lord Jesus, you love us even when we betray you and deny you. Teach us to love as you loved. Be glorified in us.

Wednesday, April 7, 2004 Wednesday of Holy Week
Matthew 26, 14-25
The Betrayal by Judas; Preparations for the Passover;
The Betrayer

It was an inside job. Judas, one of the twelve disciples, one who had been with Jesus, was the betrayer. Greed, disappointment, frustrated ambition? Who knows all the motives in the mind and heart of Judas?

It was an inside job. Inside each of us is a betrayer of Jesus. We betray Jesus by our lack of trust. We betray Jesus when we fail to love him by keeping his commandments (John 14, 15). Jesus was our Passover Lamb sacrificed for all our sins and for all our betrayals of his love.

Lord Jesus, thank you for forgiving us when we do not live up to the high calling of our discipleship. Let us begin afresh today to obey you as Lord.

Thursday, April 8, 2004 Holy Thursday
John 13, 1-15
The Washing of the Disciples' Feet

Jesus, Head of the Church, stooped to wash the feet of his disciples. He is our example. He shows us how to relate to others in his Body on earth, the Church.

Jesus washed the feet of his betrayer. His love knew no limits.

Lord Jesus, behold your poor Body, your Church, on this earth. We have wandered off from you. We have pursued private ambition and called it ministry. On this Holy Thursday, let us look to you and remember that you washed the filthy feet of your disciples. Wash the filth from our minds, our hearts, our mouths, and our hands. Let us come to you to be washed clean again. Let us drink of the living water of the Holy Spirit. Let us receive you in Holy Communion and then live in holy communion with our brothers and sisters.

Friday, April 9, 2004 Good Friday
John 18, 1-19, 42
The Passion of our Lord Jesus

Gardens. Adam and Eve in the garden of Eden. Jesus in the garden of Gethsemane. Jesus and his disciples in a garden across from the

Valley of Kidron. A garden with a new tomb in which the body of the Crucified was buried.

Sin surfaced in Eden. Jesus took our sins entirely into himself when he agonized in prayer in Gethsemane.

When Jesus died on the Cross, we died. Our sins died. We don't need to remember them or to hang onto them. They are gone. They went into Jesus. He took them. They are gone. Believe.

The garden with the new tomb was the place to watch. Jesus walked out of that tomb.

We will walk out of our tomb. We will walk out of the tomb of sins, destroyed hopes, grief, old wounds, staleness, and despair.

Jesus died for us to walk in the freedom of forgiveness, new hopes, joy, health, freshness, and bright expectation. One day we will walk into his presence, see him as he truly is, and live with him in the heavenly mansions forever.

Lord Jesus, we stay in silence with you today as we remember the price you paid in the Garden of Gethsemane and on the Cross for us. We stay close to you as we remember your time in the garden tomb.

Saturday, April 10, 2004 Holy Saturday, Easter Vigil
Luke 24, 1-12
The Resurrection of Jesus

Preparation for burial. Prepare the spices, but you may not need them.

As the women were thinking of death, Jesus surprised them with life! The tomb was empty. The spices were not needed.

We think we know what is happening. We prepare as seems wise. It was customary to anoint the dead with spices.

Jesus, however, did not need anointing for burial. He had been there, done that, and was already out of that tomb. Alleluia! The sorrowing women were looking for a living person among the dead.

Mary Magdalene, Johanna, and another Mary, whose son was James, and others tried to tell the startling news of the empty tomb to the apostles. The apostles did not believe them.

Later, however, Peter went to the tomb and saw the burial cloths, but not see Jesus. He went back in puzzled amazement

Lord Jesus, we prepare for death but not for Life. We fall into doubt and unbelief. We don't believe when Life is staring us in the face. Let us look into your shining face and prepare for Life. Alleluia!

Sunday, April 11, 2004 The Resurrection of the Lord
John 20, 1-9
The Empty Tomb

Still looking. Where is Jesus?

Mary Magdalene knew that Jesus was no longer in the garden tomb, but she did not know where he was.

Peter and another disciple ran to the tomb. They entered the tomb, Peter first. Still no Jesus. The linen burial cloths were there, but Jesus was gone. The disciple who reached the tomb ahead of Peter did believe.

Jesus had tried his best to tell his disciples that he would suffer, die, and rise again. They had seen him suffer. They had seen him die on the Cross. They had not seen him since. Rise from the dead? What was Jesus talking about? What did he mean?

Lord Jesus, your early followers did not understand the Scriptures. It had been prophesied that you would suffer, die, and rise again. When it had actually happened, your disciples could not understand at first. Help us to know in the depths of our hearts that you are alive and that you are with us. Alleluia!

Monday, April 12, 2004 Easter Monday
Matthew 28, 8-15
The Resurrection of Jesus; The Report of the Guard

I cannot choose the place where I find Jesus. Mary Magdalene and another Mary looked for the crucified body of Jesus at the tomb. He was not there. God's messenger, an angel, met them where they were, at the tomb, and then directed them to Galilee where the risen Jesus was going.

As they hurried to Galilee, Jesus, the risen Jesus, met them on the way! They did not have to go to Galilee. Jesus himself was their destination, and Jesus was with them.

Jesus greeted them and gave them a mission. First, he told them not to be afraid. Only then did he tell them to proceed to Galilee and give the good news to his disciples.

The chief priests and the elders, who had refused to believe the claims of Jesus, now refused to believe the reports that Jesus was resurrected from the dead. They responded with lies and bribery in order to protect themselves.

Lord Jesus, open my heart to meet you today in the place of your choosing. Alleluia!

Tuesday, April 13, 2004 Easter Tuesday
John 20, 11-18
The Appearance to Mary of Magdala

Once, in the rack of a church pew, I saw a prayer request card. It read. "I think we should pray for ____." It appeared that a child that had scribbled in "God." Pray for God?

Mary Magdalene not only wanted to pray to God, she also wanted to hold God, the Son of God, the crucified, dead, and buried Jesus. In her grief and exhaustion, as she lingered by the tomb, she wanted to hold the body of the Crucified.

Jesus revealed himself to her by speaking her name, Mary, as no one else had ever spoken her name. Jesus was not in a tomb. He was alive. She was conversing with the Risen Lord Jesus Christ.

Lord Jesus, help us not to cling to death when you are standing beside us offering us Life. Alleluia!

Wednesday, April 14, 2004 Easter Wednesday
Luke 24, 13-35
The Appearance on the Road to Emmaus

I was reminded of the true story a retired clergy friend told me years ago. When she was in the seminary, she saw Jesus! While the seminarians were seated around a conference table, engaged in theological reflection, she glanced up and briefly saw Jesus.

In today's Gospel, Jesus' followers on the way to Emmaus actually saw him and talked with him for quite a while before they recognized him. When he took bread, blessed it, broke it, and gave it to them, they recognized him! Then he was gone from their sight.

Jesus promises to be with us always. He will come again in glory. Until then, he is still truly present with us. He is the fulfillment of our heart's longing. Our hearts will burn within us as we recognize his presence more and more.

Lord Jesus, we are on a journey, not to Emmaus, but to you. You are with us, you teach us, you feed us, and you are our destination. Alleluia!

Thursday, April 15, 2004 Easter Thursday
Luke 24, 35-48
The Appearance on the Road to Emmaus;
The Appearance to the Disciples in Jerusalem

Rest. Wait.

Jesus is alive! He has triumphed over the Cross and the tomb.

Wait. Rest.

Walking to Emmaus, Jesus conversed with two of his followers. He interpreted to them the Hebrew scriptures which referred to him.

In Jerusalem, Jesus again opened the minds of his disciples to understand, truly to understand the scriptures. He told them again of the predictions of his suffering and his rising from the dead on the third day.

Jesus showed them that he was really alive. He ate a bit of fish and honey from a honeycomb. He told them of the future proclamation of repentance and forgiveness of sins which would go out to all, beginning in Jerusalem.

Not yet, though. Wait.

The disciples, the witnesses, were told to wait in Jerusalem until Jesus sent the Father's promise to them, the Holy Spirit. They were told, literally, to sit.

Wait. In God's time, they would be vested with power from above. For now, however, they were to wait.

Lord Jesus, we want to charge out and save the world. We can't. You have already done that. When we truly see you, when we truly know you as the Anointed One who suffered, died and rose again, we want to tell everyone. Yet you told even your early followers to wait and to rest

629

until they were clothed with the Holy Spirit. Help us today to be still, to rest, and to wait. You know when we are ready. Alleluia!

Friday, April 16, 2004 Easter Friday
John 21, 1-14
The Appearance to the Seven Disciples

This is a Gospel of revelation and preparation. This is a Gospel which sets a scene.

Earlier in John's Gospel, there is the scene of Jesus coming to his fearful disciples hiding behind locked doors. Jesus walked right in, spoke peace to his followers, and breathed the Holy Spirit into them.

He gave them the authority to forgive sins. He showed Thomas his wounded hands and side, because that seemed to be what Thomas needed in order to believe in the resurrection (John 20, 19-29).

In today's Gospel, seven disciples, Thomas included, have had no success in their fishing expedition. Jesus, for all practical purposes, was merely a stranger on the seashore offering advice about fishing.

The disciples did not know at first who he was, The beloved disciple was the first to recognize Jesus. Then Peter jumped right in to swim to the shore to be with Jesus!

Jesus had already prepared breakfast for the disciples, a breakfast of bread and grilled fish. This was the third time he had revealed himself to the disciples since he rose from the dead.

Jesus was also preparing for a serious conversation with Peter. Jesus was about to speak to Peter about Peter's future vocation.

Lord Jesus, you reached out in loving concern to your disciples who had failed in their efforts to catch fish. You gave them wise counsel. You graciously prepared breakfast for them. Thank you that you are with us today. You are with us when we seem to fail in our efforts to serve you by serving others. Reveal yourself to us. Let us recognize you. Lead us to a deep heart knowledge of you. Prepare us for the work you have prepared for us to do. Let us glorify you with our trust. Alleluia!

Saturday, April 17, 2004 Easter Saturday
Mark 16, 9-15
The Appearance to Mary Magdalene;
The Appearance to Two Disciples;
The Commissioning of the Eleven

Mark's Gospel is known for being terse. Today's reading is no exception.

Mary Magdalene saw the risen Jesus. She told the disciples. They didn't believe her.

The two on the road also saw the risen Jesus. They told the disciples. The disciples didn't believe them, either.

Finally, Jesus appeared to the eleven disciples. He reproached them for not believing and also for their hardness of heart. Even so, he sent them out to proclaim the Gospel everywhere.

Lord Jesus, sometimes we make excuses for not believing. Maybe we have tried to believe and have been disappointed. Maybe we have become cynical and we cannot believe anything anymore because we have been hurt too many times. Come to us today, Lord Jesus. You are alive. You have risen from the dead. Death has no power over you. Come to us. Forgive us for our weary excuses. Lead us gently to a new life of belief and trust in you. Send us out to proclaim the Good News. You are alive. Alleluia!

Sunday, April 18, 2004 Second Sunday of Easter;
Divine Mercy Sunday
John 20, 19-31
Appearance to the Disciples; Thomas; Conclusion

Holy C.P.R.! Jesus breathed life, breathed the Holy Spirit into his disciples.

Jesus was alive. The disciples were alive. He breathed the Holy Spirit into them. He told them to receive the Holy Spirit.

He conferred on them the amazing power to forgive sins. Only God could do that! Now, Jesus was telling his disciples that they too could forgive sins.

Jesus was alive, but the disciples weren't acting like it. They were huddled behind locked doors. Maybe the people who killed Jesus would come and kill them too.

Locked doors? No problem.

Jesus walked right through and was there in their midst. He spoke peace to his poor, frightened followers.

Jesus showed Thomas, who needed visual proof, his hands and his side. He told Thomas to believe and Thomas did. He really did. He called Jesus "God."

Wouldn't it be fun to know the other things Jesus did during this time? There is enough recorded here, however, for us to believe.

Jesus is the Messiah. Jesus is God's own Son. Let us believe and have life.

Lord Jesus, you breathed the Holy Spirit into your disciples. You breathed the Holy Spirit into their hearts. You told them to receive the Holy Spirit. Lord Jesus, breathe on us today. We believe, but we still need new life. Breathe new life, new hope, and new expectancy into us. Alleluia!

Monday, April 19, 2004
John 3, 1-8
Nicodemus

A teacher came to the Teacher. Quietly. At night. Nicodemus was a leader in his community, a Pharisee, an esteemed teacher.

Nicodemus realized that Jesus was not an ordinary teacher or rabbi. He recognized and acknowledged that Jesus was a teacher sent from God.

We are all in need of continuing education. We need to be instructed in the depths of our spirits about the Holy Spirit.

We tend to go on mind trips, but Jesus wants to lead us into fresh, uncharted territory. This is a journey into the terrain of the Holy Spirit! Our journey is one of body, soul (intellect, will, emotions) and spirit.

Lord Jesus, let us remember this Easter that we are born from above, born of the Spirit. Thank you for inviting us into a new space of freedom, the freedom to follow the Holy Spirit. Alleluia!

Tuesday, April 20, 2004
John 3, 7-15
Nicodemus

Lifted up! Yes, lifted up, but lifted high upon a Cross to continue to suffer and to die.

Jesus was exalted. He was exalted on the Cross. He triumphed.

Just as the Israelites in the wilderness gazed on the bronze serpent to be healed, we may gaze upon the Crucified Christ and be healed. His death brings us life and health.

The serpent in the desert was lifted high by Moses. Our sins lifted Jesus on the Cross. We may look upon Jesus, believe in Jesus, and have life that is eternal.

The Israelites had grown weary of their desert journey to freedom. They became impatient and began to complain. They complained against Moses and even against God

God did not like that at all. He judged them by sending serpents to bite them! Only then did they realize that they had sinned grievously by complaining. They were not trusting God to get them to the Promised Land.

Lord Jesus, forgive us for complaining on our journey. Forgive us for not trusting you. Nicodemus was also grasping after understanding of the spiritual realm. You told Nicodemus, the teacher, that you would be lifted on the Cross. You would pay the price for our sins. You made it possible for us to be at peace with God. Let us not complain about our journey, but gaze on you, praise you for triumphing over death, and let us be healed. Alleluia!

Wednesday, April 21, 2004 St. Anselm
John 3, 16-21
Nicodemus

Light is the verdict! Love is the messenger and the message.

God the Father, out of great love and concern for us, sent his only Son to us. He gave us his Son.

Jesus was and is the Light of the world. Light shines forth to reveal and to pierce the darkness.

We see! We see Jesus. We see ourselves. Light heals us of our spiritual blindness.

Living the truth we have will bring us more and more into the light. More and more light will be given to us. David, the psalmist, wrote that God will even make our vindication shine, just like the light (Psalm 37, 6)!

Lord Jesus, let us not run from the light, but run to the light. You are Light! You are Truth. You are the Way to the Father. Let us live the truth we have as we trust you for more light. Alleluia!

Thursday, April 22, 2004
John 3, 31-36
The One from Heaven

Frame of reference. Heaven? Earth?

Origin. Heaven? Earth?

Jesus came from heaven, from God the Father. He spoke God's word. God the Father gave everything over to Jesus, his beloved Son. The one who trusts in Jesus has life that is eternal.

Lord Jesus, reframe our reference. Alleluia!

Friday, April 23, 2004 St. George, St. Adalbert
John 6, 1-15
Multiplication of the Loaves

Stretching! Jesus, perhaps with a twinkle in his eye, asked Philip, with all seriousness, where they could find bread to feed the multitude. A crowd was pursuing Jesus, because of the signs he performed. Jesus had healed the sick, so people were increasingly drawn to him at this time before Passover.

Jesus already had a plan to feed the crowd. He questioned Philip only in order to enlarge Philip's trust and expectancy.

Philip was dubious. He was looking at the situation financially. It would take half a year's income to purchase only a little bit of food for that crowd. Jesus wanted to Philip to look to him and not to the obvious means, money.

You know the story. Jesus took the food that was available, the boy's lunch of five loaves of barley bread and two fish. He offered thanks to God and offered the food to the people. There were twelve baskets of leftovers from one person's lunch.

Jesus had known how he would feed the people. He knew something else.

Jesus knew the people's intention. They knew a good thing when they saw it. They would have tried to make him their bread king. That was not the purpose of his mission.

Jesus left them and retreated to the mountain. Passover was approaching.

Lord Jesus, you are the Bread of Life. You are our Passover Lamb. You know how to stretch our trust in you. You know how to rekindle a sense of expectancy within us when we have grown weary and listless. When we look too much to the passing things of this world and wonder how we will cope, you know what to do. We look to you today. This is Eastertide! You have risen from the dead! Anything is possible. Breathe new life and expectancy into us today as you gently stretch us and expand our capacity for joy and for wonder. Alleluia!

Saturday, April 24, 2004 St. Fidelis
John 6, 16-21
Walking on the Water

Jesus gets us to our destination, but he may do so in a curious way and in his mysterious time. Jesus knows the best way to get us there.

The disciples' destination, in today's Gospel, was the town of Capernaum, on the other side of the sea. They had rowed out about three or so miles when the winds started to blow wildly. Then they saw someone out there, walking on the water. This mysterious person was walking towards the boat!

The disciples' fears subsided when they learned the identity of the night-time walker on the stormy waves. Jesus! It was Jesus. All was well. All of a sudden, they were in Capernaum.

Lord Jesus, we get frightened on this stormy passage through life. Thank you for your presence with us, even when we do not initially recognize you. You are the Risen Lord. All is well. You will get us there. Alleluia!

Sunday, April 25, 2004 Third Sunday of Easter
John 21, 1-19
The Appearance to the Seven Disciples; Jesus and Peter

Jesus' appearance to the seven disciples was the Gospel reading on Easter Friday. Jesus had just prepared a fresh seaside breakfast for his discouraged disciples. They had been out that night, fishing without success, until Jesus told them to cast their net to the boat's right side. An abundance of fish filled the net!

Peter. It was now time, after breakfast, for Jesus to talk with Peter. The impetuous Peter loved the Lord Jesus, but he was still growing in his understanding of what it would mean to love Jesus sacrificially and to follow him.

Three times, Peter had denied even knowing Jesus. Three times, Peter, with his limited understanding of the meaning of love, affirmed his love for Jesus.

Jesus, three times, charged Peter to tend his flock, his lambs and his sheep. The flock belonged to Jesus. Peter was entrusted with the care of Jesus' flock.

Jesus also told Peter that Peter would die a difficult death in order to glorify God. Peter was then charged to follow Jesus.

Lord Jesus, you truly choose the weak. Over a period of time and training, you make them strong. They witness to you by their life and their death. Remind us today that we are called to love you by loving your people. We are called to follow you, our Good Shepherd, wherever you lead us. Alleluia!

Monday, April 26, 2004
John 6, 22-29
The Bread of Life Discourse

Motives. Motives. Motives.

Jesus knew the crowd was intent on searching for him because he had fed them in a miraculous way. Jesus did indeed feed them with physical food, bread, but he did not want them to stay fixated on the physical, the temporal.

Jesus told the people not to labor so arduously, to strive so diligently, for mere perishable food. He wanted them to seek the eternal.

What were they to do, they asked. How could they do God's work?

Believe! Jesus said that God's work for them was to believe in him, in Jesus, the One sent from God.

Lord Jesus, we so much want to do something, to be busy, busy, busy. Purify our hearts and our motives. Let us learn to be still and to listen to you. Let us truly trust you. Everything else will follow. Alleluia!

Tuesday, April 27, 2004
John 6, 30-35
The Bread of Life Discourse

Jesus came to his own and was not received (John 1, 11). The poignant words from the Prologue to John's Gospel ring through the earthly life of the Messiah.

Signs. The people kept demanding more and more signs, even after Jesus had multiplied the loaves.

Jesus himself is the Sign! Jesus is the true life, the true and living Bread. He came from heaven. Because he did not come as the conquering King, the people did not recognize him.

Long ago, God gave his people manna to eat. The manna was a temporary provision. The manna sustained them during their time in the wilderness. Moses was their temporary human leader.

The Bread of Life, Jesus, is forever and ever. Eternal life. Life everlasting. The hungry coming to Jesus will no longer be hungry. The thirsty coming to Jesus will no longer thirst. Jesus is enough.

Lord Jesus, you continue to come to us. Let us be attuned to you. Let us recognize you. Let us receive you with trust. Let us comfort you with our love and our obedience. Alleluia!

Wednesday, April 28, 2004 St. Peter Chanel, St. Louis Montfort
John 6, 35-40
The Bread of Life Discourse

After his resurrection, Jesus told Thomas, who insisted on seeing before believing, that the ones who believed without seeing would be happy and blessed (John 21, 29). In today's Gospel, Jesus reproved his listeners for seeing him and still not believing.

Jesus continued patiently to teach the people about the nature of God and the will of God. Jesus came from heaven to accomplish the will of God. Eternal life is God's will. It is not God's desire that any should be eternally lost, but rather that all come to repentance (2 Peter 3, 9).

Jesus reassures us that he will not reject anyone who comes to him (John 6, 37). He will raise us on the last day. It is God's will that all who believe in Jesus have eternal life.

Lord Jesus, we do believe. We believe in you, but we have difficulty believing in ourselves. We may become discouraged and wonder if we're truly believing in you or truly following you. Thank you for believing in us. Thank you that we may come to you in our sorrow and weariness as well in our joy and our strength. You are the same Lord who loves us and leads us Home. You will raise us to new life here and now as well as then and there. Alleluia!

Thursday, April 29, 2004 St. Catherine of Siena
John 6, 44-51
The Bread of Life Discourse

The Father! It is the Father who draws us to Jesus.

Indeed, Jesus said that everyone who had learned from God the Father would come to God the Son. Jesus emphasized that all would be taught by God. This was made clear by prophets of old (Isaiah 54, 13; Jeremiah 31, 33-34).

God desires that no one be lost, but that all come to Jesus, believe in Jesus, enter into eternal life, and be raised on the last day (John 6, 39-40). How could a loving Father wish other than to give the gift of eternal life, as well as the gift of temporal life, to his children?

Jesus is the true and living Bread from heaven. Partaking of Jesus means that we will live forever. Jesus came from heaven. He has seen God the Father.

Jesus is our Bread. Jesus is our very life.

Lord Jesus, thank you for coming to earth and giving your very life to us. Thank you for telling us over and over that the it is because of the Father's beckoning that we have come to you. Thank you for sending the Holy Spirit to continue to enlighten us. Alleluia!

Friday, April 30, 2004 St. Pius V
John 6, 52-59
The Bread of Life Discourse

To live, we need Jesus! Jesus is our food and drink. He is the food for our journey.

The Father sent Jesus to us. Jesus drew his own nourishment from his Father. He spoke and acted only as the Father directed. His food, his sustenance, was to accomplish his Father's purpose (John 4, 34). He knew that we do not live by bread alone, but on every word from God the Father (Matthew 4, 4).

Lord Jesus, thank you for feeding us with yourself. You are the Word made flesh. You continue to give us your true Body and your precious Blood. Transform us more and more into your image as we yield to you, in humility and trust, and partake of you. Alleluia!

Saturday, May 1, 2004 St. Joseph the Worker
Matthew 13, 54-58
The Rejection at Nazareth

Surprise. Suspicion. Jealousy. Offense. Hostility. Rejection.

Assuming they already knew all about Jesus and his family, the people in Jesus' hometown synagogue in Nazareth were at first surprised and then suspicious. They could not comprehend how on earth Jesus could have all this wisdom and do all these powerful works.

Jealousy is a close runner-up to suspicion. Why should Jesus have all this wisdom and power? Why should Jesus, of all people, be so gifted? They began to be offended. Hostility was brewing.

Rejection. Jesus was not like everyone else. They wanted to get rid of him!

Jesus knew. Jesus understood. A prophet, one who truly speaks forth God's words, is honored, but not always on the prophet's home turf.

Lord Jesus, let us be so secure in your love for us that we boldly live our vocation regardless of the response of others. Alleluia!

Sunday, May 2, 2004 Fourth Sunday of Easter
John 10, 27-30
Feast of the Dedication

Lord Jesus, thank you that you are our Lamb-Shepherd. You are
the Lamb of God. Your Blood has cleansed us. You are our Shepherd.
You guide us. You lead us. We are safe. Your Father has given us to you.
We are safe in your care. We will never perish. We will live with you
forever. Alleluia!

Monday, May 3, 2004 Sts. Philip and James
John 14, 6-14
Last Supper Discourses

If you look on a map, you may find many ways to reach your
destination. You usually have several choices about getting there.

The Father is our destination. Jesus is the Way to the Father. He
and the Father are one.

We do not choose our own way to the Father. Jesus is the Way.
Jesus is the Truth. Jesus is the Life. No one reaches the Father except by
way of Jesus. The Gospel map is very clear about this.

Amazingly, Jesus told his disciples that they would do, not only
the works that he was doing, but also even greater works! Why? Because
Jesus was returning to the Father.

How do we begin to do these works? Our motive must be the
Father's glory. Our motive is to see the Father glorified in Jesus, his Son.
We make our request in the powerful name of Jesus.

Lord Jesus, purify our hearts that we may pray confidently about
what will bring the greatest glory to God the Father. Thank you for the
great adventure before us as we learn what it means to ask in your name.
Alleluia!

Tuesday, May 4, 2004
John 10, 22-30
Feast of the Dedication

The Feast of the Dedication of the Temple in Jerusalem. Hanukkah.
Lights!

This was a great celebration in cold December. The people of
God were remembering the time in 164 B.C. when the once desecrated

Temple was re-consecrated by the brave Maccabees. The altar was also rededicated to God.

It was during this wintertime festival that Jesus was walking on the warmer east side of the Temple area, Solomon's Portico. He was having a rather difficult time with the religious leaders. Jesus was no stranger to strained relationships and confrontations with the authorities who guarded the faith.

Earlier, Jesus had referred to himself as the Good Shepherd These leaders surrounded Jesus, ready to pounce on him like a duck on a June bug.

The authorities demanded to know if Jesus was really and truly the Messiah. Jesus told them plainly that they did not believe, although he had performed mighty works in the name of God his Father. They did not believe because they were not his sheep. They did not belong to him.

Naturally! The ones who were Jesus' sheep heard his voice, believed in him, and followed him. It only stood to reason that refusal to believe in Jesus would make it very hard to hear his voice.

Jesus spoke the truth. He was not concerned with being politically correct. He was here to do his Father's will. The works he did in his Father's name testified to him that he and his Father were indeed one.

Lord Jesus, in the midst of the Hanukkah lights, you spoke words of light and life. Thank you that you are still our Good Shepherd leading us into more and more light as we follow you and lay our lives on the altar for your service. Alleluia!

Wednesday, May 5, 2004
John 12, 44-50
Recapitulation

Jesus shines forth with all that is within the Father! Jesus speaks what the Father inspires him to speak. Believing in Jesus is equivalent to believing in God the Father who sent him.

Lord Jesus, we don't have to remain in darkness. You are here. You are Light. You are the Word made flesh. You speak words of light to us. You speak to us words of life everlasting. Let your light fill us today. Let your light heal us. Let your light shine through us to those in darkness. Alleluia!

Thursday, May 6, 2004
John 13, 16-20
The Washing of the Disciples' Feet

Understanding is one thing. Happiness, however, results only when that understanding is put into practice.

Knowing that Jesus calls us to serve others is one thing. Living out this knowledge results in being blessed.

Reluctant tolerance is one thing. Service from the heart is something else.

Lord Jesus, let us receive you by receiving, with deep respect, each person placed in our lives today. Alleluia!

Friday, May 7, 2004
John 14, 1-6
Last Supper Discourses

Roomy and spacious is our Father's house! How comforting that Jesus, our older Brother has gone ahead to prepare a place there just for us.

Thomas was quizzing Jesus about all this. Thomas verbalized the question that others were perhaps silently asking.

Thomas asked Jesus how to know the way to the Father. Jesus answered that he himself was the way to the Father. Jesus was the truth. Jesus was the life. Thomas was speaking to the incarnate answer to his own question.

Lord Jesus, you are still the way to our Father in heaven. You are still the truth. You are still the life. Thank you for going ahead of us. Help us this day to take fresh courage and continue to follow you. You know where you are taking us. Thank you for sending the Holy Spirit to be with us on the journey. Thank you for waiting for us in our Father's house. Alleluia!

Saturday, May 8, 2004
John 14, 7-14
Last Supper Discourses

When people look at you, do they see Jesus? You are still you, but do others also see Jesus acting through you? Do they hear Jesus speaking through you?

God the Father spoke through Jesus. God the Father worked through Jesus. The agenda of Jesus was to do the will of his Father.

Jesus said that if his followers trusted in him, they would do works even greater than his works. Prayer in the name of Jesus means something! It is not just an act of liturgical courtesy.

Prayer in the name of Jesus is an explosive power to release the Father's glory! Jesus can do anything asked in his name.

Lord Jesus, sometimes we tend either to ignore these promises or to use them ignorantly. Thank you for sending your Holy Spirit to instruct us how to pray in your name according to your will. Alleluia!

Sunday, May 9, 2004 Fifth Sunday of Easter
John 13, 31-33, 34-35
The New Commandment

Jesus, with open eyes, open mind, and open heart, loved his disciples. He continued to love them in spite of their failings. He kept leading them closer and closer to himself. He kept revealing himself and his mission to them. Jesus knew all about them and yet he did not give up on them.

Jesus told his followers to love each other as he had loved them. This is a sturdy love, a sacrificial love, a love that confronts and challenges, as well as a love that comforts. This love was to be the sign, the indication, that they were indeed disciples of Jesus.

Lord Jesus, be glorified in us today. Let us take seriously and joyfully your commission to love others as you have loved us. Alleluia!

Monday, May 10, 2004 Blessed Damien Joseph of Molokai
John 14, 21- 26
The Advocate

Talk is cheap. A relationship with Jesus is costly. True discipleship is even more costly.

Authentic discipleship will involve giving ourselves, in simple, trusting obedience, into the hands of our Lord Jesus Christ. It may cost more than we think. It may cost our comfort, our convenience, our time, our money, our reputation, or our security. It may cost our life.

Following Jesus and obeying Jesus ushers us into a reciprocal love relationship with God the Father and God the Holy Spirit. The Holy Trinity dwells within us.

How can that be? We become involved, intimately involved, in the life of God. We begin to experience God in ways undreamed of before, when we were content with mere mental assent to the tenets of the faith.

We who were on a head trip are now on a new journey of the heart as well as of the intellect. Jesus promises to send us the Holy Spirit to teach us and to guide us on this journey.

Lord Jesus, intensify our focus on what is truly important in this life. Thank you for manifesting yourself to us as we follow you. Thank you for your gentleness and compassion as we struggle with ourselves, with others, and even with you. Thank you for the presence of the Holy Spirit to be within us and to strengthen us. Alleluia!

Tuesday, May 11, 2004
John 14, 27-31
The Advocate

Peace. Shalom!

Jesus told his followers not to allow their hearts to become agitated or afraid. He was going back to his Father. He wanted his disciples to love him enough to rejoice with him. He was completing his mission here on earth.

Peace! Shalom. What is that breaks our peace?

When I was in Jerusalem in 1985, I bought a small plaque with the word "shalom," written in Hebrew. It was periodically off and on the front door. The times it was off reflected the times I had slammed the door when I was less than peaceful. My husband peacefully glued the little plaque back together.

What breaks your shalom, your Easter peace? What disturbs or agitates or frightens you?

Lord Jesus, forgive us and heal us. We need you in order to live in this world where there is so little peace. Calm our restless, frightened, and agitated hearts. Thank you for completing your Father's mission. Thank you for sending the Holy Spirit to strengthen us to arise and to complete the mission for which the Father sent us to this earth. Alleluia!

Wednesday, May 12, 2004
Sts. Nereus and Achillus, St. Pancras
John 15, 1-8
The Vine and the Branches

The branch has two destinies. The branch which is bearing fruit will be carefully trimmed and cleansed of superfluous matter in order to increase its ability to bear even more fruit.

The branch bearing no fruit at all will be removed and destroyed. It is not fulfilling its purpose.

Jesus is the vine. God the Father is the vinedresser. God is in charge of the pruning of the branches. We are the branches. If we stay united with Jesus, the vine, we will bear fruit and God will be glorified.

Jesus said that we were already cleansed and pruned because of his word. When Jesus speaks to us and we listen and obey, we are being pruned for new growth and new fruitfulness.

Lord Jesus, thank you that you are the true vine and we are your branches. Let us yield to the Father's love and wisdom as we are being pruned. Let us rejoice that we will bear even more fruit. Remind us that the fruit makes the pruning worth it. Alleluia!

Thursday, May 13, 2004
John 15, 9-11
The Vine and the Branches

Our joy will be complete as we seek to live out these words of Jesus. His joy was to do the will of his Father!

Jesus loves us just as his Father loved him. We are caught up into the intimate dynamics of the Holy Trinity as we remain in the love of Jesus.

Lord Jesus, we were created for joy, not for misery or despair. Free us to love as you love. Free us to forgive others generously and freely, as you generously and freely forgive us. Let your joy flow through us to heal us and to energize us to love others as you love us. Alleluia!

Friday, May 14, 2004 St. Matthias
John 15, 9-17
The Vine and the Branches

Jesus' commandment is that we love one another as he loves us. This is a sacrificial, not a superficial, love.

This is not a weak love. This is not a doormat kind of love. This is a strong love, a love with open eyes as well as open heart. This is a love which may confront the beloved.

Jesus called his disciple his friends, not his slaves. Slaves may be kept in the dark and may not know what is really happening. Jesus did not keep his disciples in the dark. He let them in on everything he himself had heard from his Father!

Jesus took the initiative in choosing his disciples. They freely responded to his call and to his choice.

Lord Jesus, you continue to call us and to choose us to bear fruit for you. Heal us and cleanse us of false ideas about love. Strengthen us to stand firm as we live counter to our culture by laying down our lives for our friends. Alleluia!

Saturday, May 15, 2004 St. Isidore
John 15, 18-21
The World's Hatred

These are hard words. Who wants to be hated?

We all seek security, acceptance, and approval. However, if we are going to follow Jesus, the affirmation we yearn for is certainly not going to come to us from the world.

The world hated Jesus. If we follow Jesus, the world will hate us. We don't belong to the world. We belong to Jesus. Jesus warned that persecution would arise because those who live for this world do not truly know the One who sent him.

Lord Jesus, let us learn to find our security in you. We are living in this world, but it is not our true home. Help us to be brave and to trust in you as we continue our journey to the heavenly Jerusalem. Alleluia!

Sunday, May 16, 2004 Sixth Sunday of Easter
John 14, 23-29
The Advocate

The peace that Jesus gives us is not like the frail, temporary peace of the world, which is dependent on circumstances and the free will of fallible human beings. The peace of Jesus offers is the strength to live above our circumstances.

The Father, in his mercy, sends us the Holy Spirit to remind us of Jesus' teaching. The Holy Spirit dwells within us, comes along beside us, and is our Advocate, who offers us wise counsel.

Lord Jesus, when our hearts are small and frightened, it is difficult to comprehend the powerful gift of your peace. Enlarge our hearts to take in this amazing peace. Thank you for the Holy Spirit's guidance as we continue to learn to love others as you have loved us. Alleluia!

Monday, May 17, 2004
John 15, 26 - 16, 4
The World's Hatred

Jesus told his disciples about the power of the Holy Spirit before he told them about the unholy power of those who were not his followers. Jesus himself would send the Holy Spirit from the Father to his disciples. The Holy Spirit would testify on Jesus' behalf.

Because the disciples would soon testify to Jesus, they would not be popular. Jesus warned them to expect to be ejected from the synagogues.

Tragic. The synagogue, where God's word was proclaimed. The synagogue, a place of prayer. How tragic that the truth would not be welcome there.

Jesus told his disciples to expect more than rejection from the synagogues. They could also be killed. Their murderers would even believe that by killing the disciples they were worshipping God!

Why? Why? Why?

Jesus said that these atrocities would occur because those committing them did not know either Jesus or his Father. Tragic.

Lord Jesus, thank you for sending the Holy Spirit to enable your followers to testify to you. Thank you for the power of the Holy Spirit, the Advocate, to bear witness to you. Alleluia!

Tuesday, May 18, 2004 St. John I
John 16, 5-11
Jesus' Departure; Coming of the Advocate

Are we trying to do the work that only the Holy Spirit, the Advocate, can do? It is the work of the Holy Spirit to convict and to convince others.

Jesus told his sorrowful disciples that it was actually to their advantage that he return to his Father in heaven. He would then send the Holy Spirit to do the work of convicting and convincing in matters involving sin, righteousness, and condemnation.

Lord Jesus, thank you for sending the Holy Spirit to do the work of convicting and convincing. Thank you for sending the Holy Spirit to fill us and to strengthen us to follow you. Alleluia!

Wednesday, May 19, 2004
John 16, 12-15
Jesus' Departure; Coming of the Advocate

How wonderful is the wisdom of the Holy Spirit! The Holy Spirit knows how to take what we need from the teaching of Jesus and to translate it into our minds, our hearts, and our lives. The Holy Spirit knows what we need.

Lord Jesus, thank you that the Holy Spirit guides us into all truth. Thank you that the Holy Spirit always glorifies you. Help us to grow increasingly sensitive and responsive to the ways the Holy Spirit communicates to us. Alleluia!

Thursday, May 20, 2004 The Ascension of the Lord
Luke 24, 46-53
The Appearance to the Disciples in Jerusalem; The Ascension

Triumph! Jesus, the Christ, the Anointed One, the Messiah, was born on this earth, lived among us, suffered, died for us, and rose from the dead.

Jesus would soon send the Holy Spirit to give power to his disciples. Beginning in Jerusalem, they would proclaim repentance in the powerful name of Jesus. Tremendous news! Forgiveness of sins! Release to the captives who thought they could never have a new life.

Jesus paid the price for our sins. Our account is wiped clean. We are free to live a new life of wholeness.

Lord Jesus, bless us as you blessed your first disciples on that triumphant day. Born in Bethlehem, you ascended in Bethany back to your Father. Mission accomplished! Help us to walk in the strength and joy you died for us to enjoy. Let us not brood over the past, but rise with you into a transformed life here and now on this earth as we joyfully await your return. Alleluia!

Friday, May 21, 2004 St. Christopher Magellanes
and Companions
John 16, 20-23
Jesus' Departure;
Coming of the Advocate

When we see Jesus, we will not question him. In the presence of the Risen Christ, what is there to ask?

We may question and fret and fume about all sorts of things on this earth. We may say we have a few things, or many things, to ask Jesus about when at last we see him in his glory. I don't think so. Our grief will have turned to joy everlasting when we see him.

Lord Jesus, you directed your disciples' distress over your departure into another channel, the channel of prayer. Whatever we ask the Father in your name will be given to us. We ask today to see you and to see our lives in a fresh way. We lift our hearts to you in praise and adoration. Alleluia!

Saturday, May 22, 2004 St. Rita of Cascia
John 16, 23-28
Jesus' Departure; Coming of the Advocate

Ask! Jesus told his disciples to ask. He told them to ask, so that they could receive. He instructed them to ask so that they might have joy, complete joy.

We are not supposed to crawl around this life and call it humility. That is not humility.

Jesus has so much to give us, but we are told to ask! Why doesn't he just give us everything automatically? I don't know why. I do know that he told us to ask!

The Father loves us so much. He loves us because we love Jesus. Loving Jesus is not just an emotion.

Loving Jesus means that we are seeking to follow him and to keep his commandment to love one another. We are seeking to love one another in the same sacrificial way in which he loved us.

Lord Jesus, remove our faithless fears and give us joyful boldness to ask according to your wonderful will. Let us know complete joy as we ask and receive in your name. Alleluia!

Sunday, May 23, 2004 Seventh Sunday of Easter
John 17, 20-26
The Prayer of Jesus

The Father loved Jesus even before the world was created! Even then there was the mysterious dynamic of love within the Persons of the Holy Trinity. Love flowed between Father, Son, and Holy Spirit.

Amazingly, Jesus is in us and the Father is in Jesus. We are all tightly knit together, caught up in this divine love.

The glory the Father bestowed upon his beloved Son may be shared with others. Jesus actually gave this glory to his disciples.

Jesus knew what the Father was really like and sought to impart this knowledge of the heart to his followers. The same love is flowing from the Father to the Son to the disciples and to all the succeeding followers of Jesus.

We are in this happy company, this blessed family. Jesus is praying for us and about us at this moment.

Lord Jesus, thank you for including us as you prayed for your first followers Help us truly to believe that the Father loves us just as he loved you. Thank you for longing for our presence with you in heaven. At last, we will see you in all your glory. Let us continue to learn to love other Christians in such a way that the world will see you and will know the Father sent you. Alleluia!

Monday, May 24, 2004
John 16, 29-33
Jesus' Departure; Coming of the Advocate

Jesus knows everything! Jesus truly came from God.

It was not necessary to question Jesus. Finally, the disciples were getting it. Finally, they were perceiving that Jesus really did know everything.

Jesus also knew that his disciples would soon desert him when the going got tough. Jesus knew that, even though his friends left him, he was not alone. His Father was with him.

Peace. Jesus knew that his disciples' peace was found in their relationship with him.

Jesus instructed his disciples to be courageous, in the midst of the inevitable persecution awaiting them. Jesus had overcome the world. He was the conqueror. He was the victor!

Lord Jesus, thank you that you know everything. You know everything about us and still you call us to follow you through the mazes and land mines of this world. Thank you for reminding us that you have indeed won the victory. Alleluia!

Tuesday, May 25, 2004
John 17, 1-17
The Prayer of Jesus

Jesus looked up to pray! He looked up and began to talk to his Father about his concerns for his disciples.

Jesus knew that all was under the control of God, his Father. His frame of reference was God.

The time had come for Jesus to return to his Father in heaven. He looked up to his Father and prayed for his disciples. He prayed for their protection and for them to know the unity amongst themselves which he experienced with his Father.

Lord Jesus, when we pray, remind us to look up, to raise our hearts to heaven. Help us not to look so much at seemingly insoluble circumstances, but instead to look up! Reframe our reference and enlarge our vision. Be glorified in us and in our union with all who name your name. Alleluia!

Wednesday, May 26, 2004 St. Philip Neri
John 17, 11-19
The Prayer of Jesus

Protection, divine protection, but not escape. Jesus prayed that his Father would keep his disciples from the power of evil, the power of the devil.

While he was with them, Jesus had carefully guided them, guarded them, and given them God's word. They were hated and would continue to be hated, just as Jesus was hated.

Why? The disciples did not buy into the world's ways. They were living counter to their culture. They were following Jesus and living in a different way.

Into this realistic picture, Jesus injected a vibrant note of joy. Joy!

Joy! Jesus longed for his disciples to share his joy, the joy that comes from abandoning oneself to God and to God's purposes for one's life. This is the sacred elixir enjoyed by those serving God in the midst of a world that does not love God.

Lord Jesus, you carefully guarded and protected your followers up to the time of your return to heaven. Thank you for praying for the Father to continue to protect us. Thank you for petitioning the Father to consecrate us, to set us apart in the truth and for the truth. Let us learn to live in the truth of God's word and so experience your joy in the midst of this world. Alleluia!

Thursday, May 27, 2004
John 17, 20-26
The Prayer of Jesus

Jesus prayed for us as well as for his first disciples. We are the ones who have believed through the teaching of the early disciples and apostles.

Jesus gave us his glory! This glory was given that we might know the same unity with other Christians that Jesus had with his Father.

Glory, love, unity, and knowledge of the heart. They are all intermingled in this prayer, often called the high priestly prayer of Jesus.

The world did not recognize that the Father had sent Jesus. Jesus knew that the Father had sent him. The disciples came to realize that

Jesus was sent to make God's name alive. Jesus was truly God with skin on, incarnate. Jesus was the Word made flesh.

God's splendor shone in and through Jesus. What Jesus prayed is almost too wondrous for us to grasp. Jesus prayed for his disciples and for us that this glory, this splendor, would shine in and through us!

Lord Jesus, awaken us to the significance of your prayer for us. You want to live and breathe, speak and act through us! You want us to be of one heart with other Christians as we continue our journey to you, where at last we will see you in all your glory. Alleluia!

Friday, May 28, 2004
John 21, 15-19
Jesus and Peter

Jesus knew that Peter's formation was not over, not by any means. Peter still did not fully comprehend the questions Jesus was asking him. However, the promised Holy Spirit would soon come to Peter and to the other disciples. The Holy Spirit would continue to teach and to remind Peter of the words of Jesus.

At this post-resurrection meeting, Jesus returned to addressing Peter as Simon, his old name, and reminded the fisherman of his earthly father, John or Jonas. Earlier, after Simon's declaration of the true identity of Jesus -- the Messiah, the Son of God -- Jesus had given him a new name, Peter, and a new vocation (Matthew 16, 16-19).

After Peter had three times professed his love, a love still growing, a love still in process, Jesus again charged Peter with feeding and shepherding the sheep and the lambs. The lambs and sheep belonged to Jesus.

Jesus, however, appointed Peter the fisherman to be their earthly shepherd. Jesus then gently told Peter that the future would not be easy. Peter would not be in charge of his life.

Lord Jesus, thank you for occasionally reminding us of where we came from before you renamed us and gave us the vocation of following you. Clarify and enlarge our understanding of our vocation to follow where you lead. Thank you for the Holy Spirit's illumination of your words. Alleluia!

Saturday, May 29, 2004
John 21, 2-25
The Beloved Disciple

Peter followed Jesus and died a martyr's death. John followed Jesus and probably died in exile.

What concern of that is yours? What concern of that is mine? You and I will follow Jesus in the way Jesus directs!

Lord Jesus, thank you for sending the Holy Spirit to empower us to be faithful in bearing witness to you. Alleluia!

Sunday, May 30, 2004 Pentecost Sunday
John 20, 19-23
Appearance to the Disciples

Locked doors. Are you locked in or locked out?

The disciples thought that by locking the doors, they would be safe from the religious authorities. Jesus walked right through those doors!

Twice, Jesus spoke peace, shalom, to his disciples. He breathed on them and instructed them to receive the Holy Spirit. Jesus was sending his disciples forth as his Father had sent him forth into the world.

Immediately after instructing his disciples to welcome the powerful Holy Spirit into their lives, he brought up the subject of forgiveness of sins. Jesus granted his disciples the authority to forgive sins. No more locked doors.

Lord Jesus, no doors remain locked when you are present. Walk into any room of our hearts where we have been hiding out of fear. Speak your peace to us and let us experience the power of the Holy Spirit to live for you and to offer your forgiveness to others. Let us not transfer the sins of others into ourselves by thinking that we are withholding forgiveness. Let us free ourselves and others by forgiving. Thank you unlocking doors to allow us to live out our vocation to follow you. Alleluia!

Monday, May 31, 2004
The Visitation of the Blessed Virgin Mary
Luke 1, 39-56
Mary Visits Elizabeth; The Canticle of Mary

Let's make the Magnificat our own canticle of praise! This is an especially powerful way to pray when we are feeling uncertain, perplexed, weary of waiting, or even downcast in soul and spirit. Praying this canticle is a tremendous attitude adjuster.

Soul. With our soul, or psyche (will, intellect, and emotions), we consciously choose to proclaim and to magnify God's greatness. Immediately, our focus shifts from our current circumstances to God's power and God's sovereignty over all. Our circumstances are temporary, but God is eternal. God is great. God is in charge.

Spirit. From the innermost depth of our spirit, we rejoice! We rejoice because we know it is God who saves us. We have a Savior. We are not helplessly drifting through life. We are not victims. God is directing us.

Body. Both Mary and Elizabeth were pregnant. Mary was young and pregnant. She was expecting Jesus. Elizabeth was old and pregnant. She was expecting John the Baptist. Both were pregnant with hope. The promise of God came to completion for both.

Lord Jesus, we are hungering for you today. Visit us today with your mercy. We trust you for the completion of your promises to us. As we concentrate on proclaiming you greatness, we rest in quiet hope of new life. Alleluia!

Tuesday, June 1, 2004
Mark 12, 13-17
Paying Taxes to the Emperor

The Pharisees and Herodians in today's Gospel were real word hounds. They were attempting to catch Jesus with his own words. They knew how true and pure he was in his heart and with his words.

Jesus knew that they were being very calculating and crafty in their own words. He understood the hypocrisy resident in their hearts which was manifested in their speech.

Calmly refusing to be caught in their word trap, Jesus caught them by using their own device. Words.

Jesus inquired of them whose picture was on the coin they showed him. Caeser's. Then, said Jesus, give to Caesar what belongs to him. Give to God what already belongs to God.

Lord Jesus, your opponents marveled at your wisdom. Help us today to be pure and true in our hearts and wise with our words. Alleluia!

Wednesday, June 2, 2004 Sts. Marcellinus and Peter
Mark 12, 18-27
The Question about the Resurrection

Although the Sadducees quoted from the scriptures, Jesus told them that they did not really understand either the scriptures or the power of God. Just like today.

The Sadducees began with Moses. They quoted Moses' injunctions about marriage. Jesus, therefore, stayed within their Mosaic framework and quoted Moses right back to the Sadducees!

Twice, Jesus told them that were just plain wrong. They did not really understand either the scriptures or God's power.

The Sadducees were preoccupied with matters related to death. Jesus quoted from Moses to remind them that God was all about life!

Lord Jesus, thank you for the illumination of the Holy Spirit as we read the scriptures. Let us grow in our understanding of the scriptures. Let us grow in our understanding of God's power. Alleluia!

Thursday, June 3, 2004 St. Charles Lwanga and Companions
Mark 12, 26-34
The Greatest Commandment

Who's in charge around here? What are we supposed to do? The erudite scribe was asking these questions of Jesus.

Jesus answered the scribe and answered us. The scribe, scholar of the law though he was, still asked Jesus this question.

God is in charge around here and everywhere. He is the Lord! God is One. Remember the Shema (Deuteronomy 6, 4)!

What are we to do? We are to love God with all that is within us. We are to make God our first priority. We are to love and honor God with our strength, our intellect, and all our heart. Jesus taught that this kind of love implies trusting obedience (John 14, 15).

We are to love others as ourselves. It is implicitly understood that we accept and love ourselves. How can we love others if we are at war with ourselves?

Lord Jesus, bring us into wholeness. Let us understand your love with our hearts as well as with our minds. Let us learn to accept and to love ourselves. Free us to love you by trusting you and obeying you. Free us to manifest our love for you by loving, forgiving, and serving others. Alleluia!

Friday, June 4, 2004
Mark 12, 35-37
The Question about David's Son

Jesus is the Messiah, the Son of God, not the son of David. Jesus is David's Lord, not his son.

Jesus had to know his identity as God's beloved Son before he could fulfill his vocation. He would be tried and tested. He would suffer and die. He had to know who he was and whose he was.

It also matters that we know who we are. It also matters that we know whose we are

We are secure in our relationship with our loving Father. Jesus is our Brother. The Holy Spirit is guiding us.

We are God's children. We belong to God.

God arranged it so that we would come into this world through our birth parents. We are to honor them, but we do not belong to them. We belong to God. Likewise, our children are God's gifts to us for a time, but they are not really ours. They belong to God.

Lord Jesus, you knew who you were and whose you were. Thank you that the Holy Spirit reminds us that we may be secure in the knowledge that we are God's children. We belong to God. We are filled with the power of the Holy Spirit to live the vocation to which we are called. Alleluia!

Saturday, June 5, 2004 St. Boniface
Mark 12, 38-44
Denunciation of the Scribes;
The Poor Widow's Contribution

Jesus doesn't miss a thing! He knows exactly why people do what they do. He sees the outer actions. He also sees the motives of the heart. His compassionate discernment is both sharper and gentler than we can comprehend.

Jesus certainly noticed the scribes. He warned his disciples to be on guard, to be cautious, to be wary of the scribes who loved to flaunt their vestments and to bask in the esteem in which they were held.

Others looked up to the scribes and constantly deferred to them. That was balm to the shriveled souls of these particular scribes. They prayed and they preyed. They prayed long prayers. They preyed upon widows, greedily seizing their houses. Jesus spoke of the great condemnation in store for the scribes.

On the other hand, Jesus not only noticed a poor widow, but he also commended her. She was poor, but not too poor to give. Although the rich gave their leftovers to God, she gave her all.

Lord Jesus, help us to have compassion for all and to offer compassion to all. Only you can see into the human heart. Only you are qualified to judge. Thank you for your mercy. Alleluia!

Sunday, June 6, 2004 Most Holy Trinity
John 16, 12-15
Jesus' Departure; Coming of the Advocate

The Holy Spirit guides and glorifies! The Holy Spirit guides and leads us into complete truth. The Holy Spirit always glorifies Jesus. We are caught up into the sacred, intimate mysteries of the Holy Trinity as the Holy Spirit draws from the riches of Jesus, given to him by the Father, and then gives to us.

Lord Jesus, thank you that the powerful Holy Spirit resides within us. Let us boldly and confidently pray to glorify you this very day. Alleluia!

Monday, June 7, 2004
Matthew 5, 1-12
The Sermon on the Mount

Jesus reframes our reference in these beatitudes. These are truly attitudes that will arise from the core of our being when we make a decision to live for God's glory.

We finally begin to realize that God is our point of reference, God is our audience, and God is our reward. Whatever temporal notice or acclaim the world can offer is not to be compared with the consolation offered by God.

Blessed. Happy. Nine times Jesus uses this word. He uses it to describe conditions that those who live only for this world would not describe as happy at all.

How can there be happiness in poverty or in mourning? How could the gentle, the meek, the merciful, those who long for righteousness, those with pure and clean hearts, and the peacemakers, be considered happy in this ruthless world? How could those persecuted for the sake of righteousness be happy? How could those who are reviled and insulted for their faith in Jesus be happy?

Jesus not only said that there is present happiness in these states, but he also reminded his disciples that a great reward awaits them in the future. Prophets all through the centuries have suffered persecution because they lived and spoke for God.

Lord Jesus, thank you for your presence with us as we long to experience true happiness by living these attitudes. Thank you for the gifts and the graces you are giving us at the present moment. Thank you also for the reward you reserving for us in heaven. Alleluia!

Tuesday, June 8, 2004
Matthew 5, 13- 16
The Similes of Salt and Light

In this passage on salt and light, Jesus sums up what our lives will look like and be like as we live out, in the power of the Holy Spirit, the beatitudes outlined in the Sermon on the Mount. Jesus expects our light to shine in this world!

Jesus expects that our lives will be so full of flavor that we will be the salt of the earth! We are not to live as those who plod drearily through life, believing that this life is all there is.

Lord Jesus, you called us to be the salt of the earth and the light of the world. Thank you for sending the Holy Spirit to fill us with power to live as salt and light and to glorify our Father in heaven. Thank you for placing heaven in our hearts as we continue our journey to the place you have prepared for us. Alleluia!

> Wednesday, June 9, 2004 St. Ephrem
> Matthew 5, 17-19
> Teaching about the Law

Jesus came to fulfill, to fill up, and to satisfy all the demands of the law and the prophets. He came as the glorious fulfillment of the ancient prophecies in the Hebrew scriptures.

There was no way that we, as flawed and fallible as we are, could begin to keep all the demands of the law. Jesus came to do it for us. We are now free to live in the fullness and the power of the Holy Spirit.

Far from dismissing the requirements of the law, Jesus emphasized that every tiny detail of the law had to be fulfilled. The law was not to be trivialized or despised. It was to fulfilled.

Lord Jesus, this is beyond us. You knew that there was no way we could do all this. There was no way we could save ourselves. Thank you that came as our Passover Lamb to shed your precious blood to take away our sins and to release us into a new life. Thank you that you are truly the bread of our life and the cup of our salvation. Alleluia!

> Thursday, June 10, 2004
> Matthew 5, 20-26
> Teaching about the Law; Teaching about Anger

Expansion! Jesus expands our limited concepts about discipleship. The Holy Spirit blows great gusts of truth into our astounded souls.

Jesus expects our righteousness to be even more expansive and abundant than that of the Pharisees. The Pharisees!

The Pharisees were absolutely the rule keepers of the rule keepers. They even tithed their little garden herbs. Yet Jesus says that our righteousness has to exceed theirs for us even to enter the kingdom of heaven.

Jesus expands our concepts of anger and name calling. Unrestrained anger is linked to murder. If we indulge in name calling or

660

attacking the character of another, we are inviting God to judge us and to condemn us!

Giving offerings to God? Don't even bother if you are aware that someone is upset with you.

If someone is angry with you, leave your offering right there at the altar and take the initiative in reconciliation. Be conciliatory with your legal adversaries while there is still time to avoid a jail sentence. If you go into that prison, you will pay everything.

Lord Jesus, we're mopping our brows at these words! Thank you that you promised that the Holy Spirit would fill in the blanks of our understanding and continue to teach us and guide us. Let us trust you for the grace and the strength to put your words into practice. Alleluia!

Friday, June 11, 2004 St. Barnabas
Matthew 5, 27-32
Teaching about Adultery; Teaching about Divorce

More expansion in today's Gospel! Jesus illuminates and expands the definition of adultery.

As in his teaching about murder, Jesus goes back to the heart attitude. With murder, the action erupted from unrestrained anger. With adultery, the attitude in the heart was indulged lust. Divorce? Jesus prohibited it.

Lord Jesus, we squirm and look for legal loopholes when we are confronted with your uncompromising words. Forgive us. Heal us. Fill us with the Holy Spirit to live radically for you. Fill and expand our hearts with an abundance of your love. Alleluia!

Saturday, June 12, 2004
Matthew 5, 33-37
Teaching about Oaths

In the past. In the present. Then. Now. The word of then. The word of now.

Instead of elaborate oaths involving heaven, earth, Jerusalem, or even one's own head, Jesus tells us simply to speak the truth and to speak the truth simply. Yes means yes. No means no. Embroidering on this simplicity comes from evil, the evil one.

Lord Jesus, let us live before you and speak only the words you give us. Alleluia!

Sunday, June 13, 2004 Body and Blood of Christ
Luke 9, 11-17
The Return of the Twelve; The Feeding of the Five Thousand

Receiving. Speaking. Healing. Taking. Praying. Blessing. Breaking. Giving. Jesus' ministry flowed in God's rhythm and in God's time, from the deserted place of refuge first with God, then with the Twelve, and then back into public ministry.

Lord Jesus, you welcomed the ones who sought you. You told them about God's kingdom. You cured those in need of healing. You took what was offered to you, the five loaves of bread and two fish. You looked up and prayed to your Abba Father. You blessed the offering before breaking the offering. You gave the transformed offering to the people. Even after the multitude was nourished, there were still twelve baskets overflowing with abundance. Thank you for welcoming us, teaching us, healing us, and then taking us, praying for us, blessing us, breaking us, and giving us to the starving around us. Alleluia!

Monday, June 14, 2004
Matthew 5, 38-42
Teaching about Retaliation

The more we are able to trust God to settle the score, the less driven we are to try to retaliate. God has another way, a better way than we could possibly dream of, to bring about our vindication. We may rest secure in this knowledge and be about the work we are called to do at this time.

Lord Jesus, help us to give to others from the amazing abundance of mercy you have given to us. Alleluia!

Tuesday, June 15, 2004
Matthew 5, 43-48
Love of Enemies

What is your true parentage? In order to live as God's children, Jesus tells us to love those who are our enemies and to pray for those who hurt us. After all, God pours the rain and shines the sun on all.

We are to bless, to speak well of, those who curse us, those who do not speak well of us. There is always something good to say about others.

662

We are to pray for those who have abused us or persecuted us. There is no reward from God if we merely love those who already love us. Anyone can do that.

Lord Jesus, you knew you were God's beloved. You were here on God's mission. You knew that God was in charge. You knew when to confront those whose deeds were evil. You endured suffering beyond our comprehension. You knew who you were, God's beloved. Thank you for sending the Holy Spirit to remind us that we are also God's beloved children. The King of the universe is our Father, our Abba, our Dad. We can afford to be generous to all as we travel to heavenly mansions. Alleluia!

Wednesday, June 16, 2004
Matthew 6, 1-6, 16-18
Teaching about Almsgiving; Teaching about Prayer;
Teaching about Fasting

Jesus says that our Father is hidden and yet sees. Our Father, our Dad, our Abba, sees us. Tenderly, he watches over us and rejoices in us as we take our baby steps in trust, as we try to offer ourselves, our prayers, and our fasting.

We may feel discouraged and unappreciated by others. So what? Our loving Father is smiling upon us.

Lord Jesus, let us learn to be real, increasingly real, as we live the rest of our time here. Let us truly know that our Abba loves us and is very patient with us. Alleluia!

Thursday, June 17, 2004
Matthew 6, 7-15
Teaching about Prayer

This is a passage we still need to read very carefully! We are very familiar with the prayer called the Our Father. The last two verses about forgiveness may be a rude shock, however. The prayer Jesus taught us is of little practical value without our willingness to practice forgiveness.

God's hands are tied, in a sense. Even the all-powerful God cannot and will not forgive us as long as we refuse to release others who have hurt us. We cannot blithely pray about daily bread if we are stingily withholding the nourishment of forgiveness it is in our power to offer others.

God's kingdom won't come and God's will won't be done on this earth if we refuse to pray God's way. God's name will not be held holy if we who are called Christians portray a mean-spirited God by the way we speak about others and by the way we treat others.

Lord Jesus, this is not an easy prayer to pray. It may be an easy prayer to say, but not to pray. Thank you that we are not left on our own. Thank you that the Holy Spirit lives within us and longs to help us to do what seems impossible on our own. Thank you for your lavish outpouring of generosity in living and dying and rising for us. Thank you for forgiving us. Father, thank you for sending the Holy Spirit to teach us the specifics of living out this prayer. Alleluia!

Friday, June 19, 2004 Sacred Heart of Jesus
Luke 15, 3-7
The Parable of the Lost Sheep

Before reading the Gospel early this morning, I was observing Francis, our elderly marmalade cat, happily rolling on the floor and enjoying his catnip treat. How much delight he has brought us over the years, just by being himself, a cat! When he is outside a bit long, I open the door and call him or go looking for him.

If we love our children, and even our pets, so much, why is it so hard sometimes to believe that God loves us rapturously and longs for us?

We may not have run away with our feet or with our minds. We may hold correct doctrine and adhere strictly to the teachings of the church, and yet feel far from God.

God is always with us, but we may feel otherwise. Why? Because if our hearts have been deeply wounded, we tend to run away emotionally. We build invisible walls around our hearts, wounded by sin and by the injustices of this life. We try desperately to keep everyone out, even God.

This parable Jesus told illustrates the shepherd heart of God. God longs for us and searches for us, longing to enfold us with tender love and forgiveness. We may run back to our God and be welcomed. The angels will rejoice!

Lord Jesus, may all who have run away return and run into your Sacred Heart. Alleluia!

Saturday, June 19, 2004
The Immaculate Heart of the Blessed Virgin Mary
Luke 2, 41-51
The Boy Jesus in the Temple

Mary was Mary. Yes, she was the Blessed Virgin Mary, the Blessed Mother of our Lord. Yes, she was specifically chosen by God for this unique vocation.

Still, she was Mary. She was a human mother.

Lost! The word strikes fear into the heart of any mother. The twelve year old Jesus was lost for days. He wasn't really lost, but Mary did not know where he was.

Mary's heart must have raced in fear as she and Joseph returned to Jerusalem, indeed, raced back to Jerusalem, as fast as they could, to look for Jesus. Where could he be?

Mary had once traveled in haste to visit her relative, Elizabeth, pregnant with John the Baptist. Now, Mary was traveling in even greater haste to find her child.

Jesus! Where was he? The twelve year old was in the temple in Jerusalem, calmly sitting with the teachers, asking them questions.

Mary must have experienced the usual combination of great relief mingled with some degree of exasperation. She was a mother! Of course, she would be anxious. Why in the world would Jesus do such a thing and cause such concern?

Jesus may have thought it was perfectly natural be in his Father's house. Mary and Joseph thought otherwise. Back to Nazareth he went.

Mary kept this incident, including the words of her child, safely in her heart. Her heart was expanding more and more with the wonder as she watched her Son grow into his vocation.

Lord Jesus, help us always to honor your mother Mary and to speak of her with respect and love. Alleluia!

Sunday, June 20, 2004
Twelfth Sunday in Ordinary Time
Luke 9, 18-24
Peter's Confession about Jesus;
The First Prediction of the Passion;
The Conditions of Discipleship

Why would Jesus be so stern with his disciples? He had asked them who the multitudes of people thought he was. Peter answered correctly. Jesus was the Christ, the Anointed One, the Messiah!

Correct. And yet, Jesus warned his disciples to keep quiet about this and not to tell anyone.

It was all about discipleship. True discipleship is not only about believing. True discipleship is a radical following of Jesus, who was destined for suffering, rejection, murder, and resurrection on the third day.

Day after day after day, a true disciple must make the decision to follow self or to follow Jesus in trust and obedience. When push comes to shove, who wins?

Do I truly desire to follow Jesus or do I just say I do? Do I want my own way or do I want his will? They may be the same or they may be different.

Do I want to save my soul by sacrificing my will to God's will? Do I believe that God's will for me is good?

Lord Jesus, you said we have to take up our cross every day and follow you if we wish to be your disciples. We place our trust in you today. You are in charge. You are Lord. Alleluia!

Monday, June 21, 2004 St. Aloysius Gonzaga
Matthew 7, 1-5
Judging Others

Twigs and logs! Same substance, but different sizes.

Jesus does not say there is anything wrong with our noting the little twigs, the failings of others. What Jesus says is that we are not even able to notice their twigs as long as there is a big log of our own which is blocking our view.

We need to deal with ourselves first. Then we may be able to help others.

Lord Jesus, you told us to stop judging others. You alone are fit to judge. You alone know all and see all. Please forgive our presumption in judging others. Please remove the log, whatever is obstructing our lives and our vision. Then, out of the extravagant grace and forgiveness that you have poured into us, let us offer mercy and compassion to others. Alleluia!

Tuesday, June 22, 2004 St. Paulinus, Sts. John Fisher
and Thomas More
Matthew 7, 6, 12-14
Pearls before Swine; The Golden Rule; The Narrow Gate

Dogs, pigs, and pearls! Sloppy or sacred?

Jesus is telling us a, in vivid, colorful ways, about how to live and how not to live. We are not to bother offering spiritual treasures in unwise ways. Our offering will be misunderstood at best, desecrated at worst. We will be attacked, indeed mauled.

How do we live, then? We are already aware that it's easier to live an aimless, sloppy life, which leads to destruction, than it is knowingly and intentionally to choose the sacred way. The golden guide is to offer to others the same wide berth of understanding for which we ourselves long.

Jesus himself is the gate to our true life (John 10, 7, 9). The sheep enter the fold through Jesus. Following the difficult, yet joyful, path of Jesus leads us to ultimate fulfillment. We will be living the life for which we were created and destined.

Lord Jesus, thank you for calling us to follow you. Your way leads to the life for which we yearn. Thank you for showing us how to live the Gospel with both prudence and zeal. Alleluia!

Wednesday, June 23, 2004
Matthew 7, 15-20
False Prophets

True or false? The litmus test is fruit.

Jesus gave instructions to beware of those who presumably speak God's words and yet whose lives do not match their words. Be on guard! Beware. Be cautious.

They may appear to speak as true prophets, but they are not. They are crafty and manipulative. They are excellent at deception. Jesus called them wolves, ravenous, voracious wolves.

Being uncomfortable or ill at ease around people who seem to be saying the right things may be the way the Holy Spirit whispers to us to beware. We don't want to be suspicious, but we do need to be discerning.

Jesus gave us a very practical way to discern the true and the false. What kind of lives are they living? What is the fruit of their lives? Good trees produce good fruit. Sometimes it takes awhile to know the quality of the fruit.

Lord Jesus, let our lives produce good fruit. Alleluia!

Thursday, June 24, 2004 Nativity of John the Baptist
Luke 1, 57-66; 80
The Birth of John the Baptist

Enter into agreement with God quickly! Then you will sing and bless God all the sooner.

God's word will come to pass. You may as well practice praising right now.

Zechariah, John's father, was a priest who had trouble believing that God's promise, that he and Elizabeth would have a son, would really be fulfilled (Luke 1, 18). It seemed too late. Because of Zechariah's unbelief, he was silenced for at least nine months (Luke 1, 19-20).

When John was born and as soon as Zechariah confirmed his wife Elizabeth's naming of the child, then and only then was he able to speak again. He burst into praise of God!

Lord Jesus, forgive our unbelief. Energize us when we are weary. We wait and wait and wonder and wonder. When? How? Your timing is perfect. Your methodology is flawless. We praise you now, right now! Alleluia!

Friday, June 25, 2004
Matthew 8, 1-4
The Cleansing of a Leper

First, the teaching. Then, the practicum. Jesus came down from the mountain where he had been teaching and was greeted with an immediate opportunity for ministry.

Amidst the crowds was a leper who approached Jesus with humility and hesitancy. He knew that Jesus, if willing, could heal him.

Jesus reached out, touched him, and immediately the man was cleansed. Jesus stayed within the parameters of Jewish teaching by directing the man to go to the priests for verification of the healing.

All day long, we are in a teaching or healing ministry in one way or another. A distressed person who calls us is in need of God's word and God's healing. As we listen and pray for wisdom in our words, God is at work. We may silently intercede all day for others and their needs. St. Francis invited us to proclaim the Gospel at all times and, if necessary, to use words.

Lord Jesus, you proclaimed the Gospel by your teaching and your healing. Let us realize that our quiet lives of trust are also proclaiming you as Lord. Alleluia!

Saturday, June 26, 2004
Matthew 8, 5-17
The Healing of a Centurion's Servant;
The Cure of Peter's Mother-in-Law

No spiritualizing away what Jesus said and what Jesus did! Jesus spoke words of truth and power. When Jesus touched people, they were healed! No spiritualizing this away.

Jesus continually, over and over, healed people in body as well as in soul and spirit. The whole person was healed.

Jesus said some serious words to the centurion. He told the centurion that as he, the centurion, believed, that was what would be done for him.

The centurion clearly believed in the power of the spoken word of Jesus. After informing Jesus of the distress of the paralytic servant in his home, he went on to say that Jesus did not have to come to his home in order for the healing to occur.

The centurion had such respect and trust in the spoken word of Jesus that, if Jesus simply spoke the word of healing, the paralytic would be healed. And that's exactly what happened!

The healing took place at the very time Jesus told the centurion to go and to know that his request had been granted. Jesus, even Jesus, marveled at the faith of this centurion, a person considered outside Israel's faith community.

In the case of Peter's mother-in-law, we don't know what Jesus actually said. What we read in the Gospel is that Jesus simply touched her hand and the fever left her. She arose and began to minister to those around her.

Lord Jesus, sometimes we spiritualize away the healings we read about in the Gospels. On the other hand, we may truly believe and still no healing is apparent. We may become discouraged. While we have breath and are still living in this world, let us confidently abandon ourselves to a new level of trust and believing, truly believing in your desire, as well as your ability, to heal body, spirit, and soul. Alleluia!

Sunday, June 27, 2004 Thirteenth Sunday in Ordinary Time
Luke 9, 51-62
Departure for Jerusalem; Samaritan Inhospitality;
The Would-be Followers of Jesus

The hostile Samaritans refused to accept Jesus in their territory because of his destination. Jerusalem! Destination and destiny are always woven together.

Jesus had work to do which could only be accomplished in Jerusalem. He set his face to continue to Jerusalem. He was determined to complete the mission entrusted to him by his Father, his Abba, in heaven.

No one would deter him. No one with poorly informed views of discipleship would be allowed to follow him. His followers were to leave the dead past behind and go forward to announce God's kingdom.

Lord Jesus, as you were fulfilling your days on earth, you showed both tender mercy and severe honesty. In mercy, you would not allow your hot-tempered, indignant disciples, John and James, to call down vengeance on those who rejected you. However, you would not accept as followers those who were not determined to follow you on your terms. Let us set our faces resolutely to our own Jerusalem where our destiny will be completed. Alleluia!

Monday, June 28, 2004
Matthew 8, 18-22
The Would-be Followers of Jesus

Follow Jesus right now! Don't try to fix things first. Things will never be fixed on this earth.

Jesus calls us to live in another realm, another kingdom, the kingdom of God. We are not in permanent residence on this earth. We are traveling through here on a pilgrimage to our real home, our true home, the heavenly Jerusalem.

Lord Jesus, I struggle with my inadequacies, longing for you to fix me and to fix everything around me, and then I will follow you. You are telling me to focus on following you. You will take care of everything else. Alleluia!

Tuesday, June 29, 2004 Sts. Peter and Paul
Matthew 16, 13-19
Peter's Confession about Jesus

Gates and keys. Heaven and hell. Jesus and Peter. The Church.

The gates of hell will not prevail against the Church, the Body of Christ, the Bride of Christ. The Church belongs to Jesus and Jesus is Lord. Jesus is Head of the Church. Jesus always wins.

Keys. Jesus gave to Peter, only to Peter, the keys!

Jesus knew the rock upon which he, the Son of God, the Messiah, was building his Church. Jesus gave to Peter the keys, the keys to heaven's kingdom.

Lord Jesus, thank you for continuing to choose the ones considered weak and making them powerful in witnessing to you. Thank you that your will is supreme. Alleluia!

Wednesday, June 30, 2004
Matthew 8, 28-34
The Healing of the Gadarene Demoniac

Jesus walked right into the devil's territory, freed the hostages who lived among the tombs, and then sent the demons away. He sent them into pigs and then the pigs rushed down the steep cliff into the sea and drowned!

Everyone in town came to Jesus and implored him to leave. Jesus always brought life to people and death to demons.

Lord Jesus, you freed the hostages who had been inhabited by evil entities. Forgive us and free us to follow you into the light with hearts singing with joy. Alleluia!

Thursday, July 1, 2004 Bl. Junipero Serra
Matthew 9, 1-8
The Healing of a Paralytic

What thoughts are swimming around in the harbor of our thoughts? What thoughts are we harboring today?

Jesus perceived the thoughts the scribes were harboring. They were harboring evil thoughts. They were harboring angry thoughts.

Jesus spoke with compassion to the paralytic. He told the paralytic to take courage and to know that Jesus had forgiven him.

At that, the scribes seethed with indignation. They thought Jesus was speaking blasphemy, since God alone had the authority to forgive sins. Who did Jesus think he was, anyway?

The friends of the paralytic, on the other hand, were energetically harboring thoughts of trust, hope, and expectation. After all, they had brought their paralyzed friend to Jesus! They fully expected Jesus to take action.

Jesus, Son of Man, told the forgiven paralytic to arise and to walk! The man stood up and went home, having experienced the great liberation of forgiveness.

Lord Jesus, thank you that we may ask and receive forgiveness. Thank you for speaking words of encouragement to us. Father, thank you for sending the light of the Holy Spirit into the harbor of our thoughts to shine truth, light, joy, and renewed hope. Alleluia!

Friday, July 2, 2004
Matthew 9, 9-13
The Call of Matthew

Jesus did not have to run around looking for ministry opportunities. People came to him! They flocked to him. They sensed his compassion.

672

Jesus lived in constant communion with his Dad, his Abba, his Father. Jesus only did what the Father asked him to do. Jesus came to show us what the Father was really like.

At the dinner with his new follower, Matthew, people who were considered outsiders came to be with Jesus. They did not observe the strict culinary laws. The Pharisees who were there were going bonkers, but Jesus expressed mercy.

Jesus knew that the strong did not need healing. The sick needed healing. The sick basked in the healing presence of Jesus. Jesus knew the nature of their sin sickness. Jesus knew how to heal them.

Lord Jesus, you called Matthew from his place of business and he followed you. He followed you into a situation of controversy. Help us to accept the fact that following you always leads to controversy. Let us remember your heart for the weak, the poor, and the sick. Let others sense your compassion flowing through us. Heal us and let your healing virtue flow through us to heal others. Alleluia!

Saturday, July 3, 2004 St. Thomas
John 20, 24-29
Thomas

Jesus, the Risen Jesus, walked through closed doors, spoke peace to his gathered disciples. Then Jesus spoke personally to Thomas. Jesus knew what Thomas needed.

Jesus knows what we need. Throughout our Christian pilgrimage, we need for Jesus to walk through doors which have been slammed in our faces or doors we ourselves have closed. We need Jesus to speak peace to us. We need Jesus to speak the words we need to hear.

Lord Jesus, walk through the closed and locked doors of our hearts. You are gentle and kind. Merciful Jesus, help us to trust you and to offer to you our hearts which have been wounded, broken, frozen, or hardened. Send your Holy Spirit to speak words of peace and new life to us. Alleluia!

Sunday, July 4, 2004 Fourteenth Sunday of Ordinary Time
Luke 10, 1-12, 17-20
The Mission of the Seventy-two; Return of the Seventy-two

Jesus redirected his followers' joy. They had returned, rejoicing and exuberant, from their mission! They had experienced for themselves the power of the name of Jesus.

Well and good! They were doing what Jesus had prepared them to do. He had warned them that they would be as lambs among wolves. They would go to the places which Jesus himself was planning to visit.

His followers would go forth proclaiming the nearness of the kingdom of God and healing the sick. They exulted in the power of the mighty name of Jesus!

Lord Jesus, you told your followers not to rejoice so much at the success of their ministry, but rather to rejoice because their names were written in heaven. Thank you that you are the triumphant Lamb of God and that our names are written in your book in heaven. Alleluia!

Monday, July 5, 2004 St. Anthony Mary Zaccaria
Matthew 9, 18-26
The Official's Daughter and the Woman with a Hemorrhage

Jesus took life as it came, not in a passive way, but in a way which expressed both his relationship with his Father and his response to human need. He lived in the present moment and was fully present to each person.

We see him in today's Gospel on his way to the home of a twelve year old girl who had just died. He was accompanied by the girl's distraught, yet faith-filled father and also by the disciples.

On the way, another person in a seemingly hopeless circumstance reached out to Jesus. Jesus patiently took the time to speak words of strong and gentle encouragement to a woman who had been ill for twelve years. She knew that if she merely touched the cloak of Jesus, she would be well, and so she was!

Jesus also knew how to deal firmly with interruption another sort, if it was hindering his ministry. The doomsayers at the home of the dead girl were definitely hindrances. He told them to go away! Then he entered the house, took the hand of the dead girl, and she rose to her feet.

Lord Jesus, let us touch you in prayer and be healed. Guide us through this day and show us how to live and to love according to your will. Alleluia!

Tuesday, July 6, 2004 St. Maria Goretti
Matthew 9, 32-38
The Healing of a Mute Person; The Compassion of Jesus

Silent weakness as well as obvious disease. Jesus is concerned about every aspect of our health of body, soul, and spirit.

Yes, Jesus cast out demons, enabling the mute to speak. Yes, Jesus cured every disease and every sickness.

Jesus did not tell the people that sickness was God's will for them. Jesus healed them! He also cared for every weakness of the weary, suffering people.

His shepherd's heart was moved with compassion for them. Limited as he was at that time to his physical body, he yearned for others to go forth all over the world to proclaim the Gospel and to heal.

Jesus told his followers that they would do the works which he had done and that they would do even greater works because he was returning to his Father (John 14, 12)!

Lord Jesus, you know our every weakness of mind, will, and emotions. You know every weakness of our bodies. You know even the silent weaknesses in our spirits. If we have grown weary and distracted, thank you for the Holy Spirit's power to energize us. Heal us and send us forth, as your Body on earth, into your harvest. Alleluia!

About the author

Janis Walker was born in Louisiana and grew up in Oklahoma and Texas. As an Episcopalian, she served in hospital ministry, parish ministry, ecumenical prayer group ministry, and retreat ministry. She is a member of the ecumenical Order of St. Luke the Physician. In 1991, she received a Master's degree in Theology from St. Patrick's Seminary. She also studied at Fuller Theological Seminary and at the Graduate Theological Union in Berkeley. Janis was received into the Roman Catholic Church in a Chrism Mass for Christian Unity on May 13, 1998, in Rossi Chapel at the Jesuit Retreat Center in Los Altos, California. She lives with her family in California, enjoys visiting a village in Vermont, and swimming in the Atlantic Ocean by the Jersey shore. Janis has a continuing interest in the ecclesial effects of the Oxford Movement and the legacy of Cardinal Newman.

A.M.D.G.

You may order additional copies of this book

from www.amazon.com, www.barnesandnoble.com,

or at your favorite independent bookstore.

Breinigsville, PA USA
22 October 2010
247655BV00008B/2/P